Mobil ★★★★★
Travel Guide®

SOUTH

ACKNOWLEDGMENTS

We gratefully acknowledge the help of our representatives for their efficient and perceptive inspections of the lodging and dining establishments listed, the establishments' proprietors for their cooperation in showing their facilities and providing information about them, and the many users of previous editions who have taken the time to share their experiences. Mobil Travel Guide is also grateful to all the talented writers who contributed entries to this book.

Front and back cover images: ©iStockPhoto.com

All maps: created by Mapping Specialists

The information contained herein is derived from a variety of third-party sources. Although every effort has been made to verify the information obtained from such sources, the publisher assumes no responsibility for inconsistencies or inaccuracies in the data or liability for any damages of any type arising from errors or omissions.

Neither the editors nor the publisher assume responsibility for the services provided by any business listed in this guide or for any loss, damage or disruption in your travel for any reason.

ISBN: 9-780841-60866-5   Manufactured in Canada

10 9 8 7 6 5 4 3 2 1

TABLE OF CONTENTS

3

SOUTH

★
★★
★★
★★
★

WRITTEN IN THE STARS

Because time is precious and the travel industry is ever-changing, having accurate, reliable travel information at your fingertips has never been more important. With this in mind, Mobil Travel Guide has provided invaluable insight to travelers through its Star Rating system for more than 50 years.

The Mobil Corporation (known as Exxon Mobil Corporation since a 1999 merger) began producing the Mobil Travel Guide books in 1958 following the introduction of the U.S.-interstate highway system in 1956. The first edition covered only five Southwestern states. Since then, our books have become the premier travel guides in North America, covering all 50 states and Canada, and beginning in 2008, international destinations such as Hong Kong and Beijing.

Today, the concept of a "five-star" experience is one that permeates the collective conciousness, but few people realize it's one that originated with Mobil. We created our star rating system to give travelers an easy-to-recognize quality scale for choosing where to stay, dine and spa. Based on an objective process, we make recommendations to our readers that we believe will enhance the quality and value of their travel experiences. Our trusted Mobil One- to Five-Star rating system is the oldest and most respected lodging and restaurant inspection and rating program in North America. Most hoteliers, restaurateurs and industry observers favorably regard the rigor of our inspection program and understand the prestige and benefits that come with receiving a Mobil Star rating.

The Mobil Travel Guide process of rating each establishment includes unannounced inspections, incognito evaluations and a review of unsolicted comments from the general public. We inspect more than 500 attributes at each property we visit, from cleanliness to the condition of the rooms and public spaces, to employee attitude and courtesy. It's a system that rewards those properties that strive for and achieve excellence each year. And the very best properties raise the bar for those that wish to compete with them.

Only facilities that meet Mobil Travel Guide's standards earn the privilege of being listed in the guide. Properties are continuously updated, and deteriorating, poorly managed establishments are removed. We wouldn't recommend that you visit a hotel, restaurant or spa that we wouldn't want to visit ourselves.

★
★
★
★
★

★★★★★The Mobil Five-Star Award indicates that a property is one of the very best in the country and consistently provides gracious and courteous service, superlative quality in its facility and a unique ambience. The lodgings and restaurants at the Mobil Five-Star level consistently continue their commitment to excellence, doing so with grace and perseverance.

★★★★The Mobil Four-Star Award honors properties for outstanding achievement in overall facility and for providing very strong service levels in all areas. These award winners provide a distinctive experience for the ever-demanding and sophisticated consumer.

★★★The Mobil Three-Star Award recognizes an excellent property that provides full services and amenities. This category ranges from exceptional hotels with limited services to elegant restaurants with a less formal atmosphere.

★★The Mobil Two-Star property is a clean and comfortable establishment that has expanded amenities or a distinctive environment. These properties are an excellent place to stay or dine.

★The Mobil One-Star property is limited in its amenities and services but provides a value experience while meeting travelers' expectations. The properties should be clean, comfortable and convenient.

We do not charge establishments for inclusion in our guides. We have no relationship with any of the businesses and attractions we list and act only as a consumer advocate. We do the investigative legwork so that you won't have to.

Restaurants and hotels—particularly small chains and stand-alone establishments—change management or even go out of business with surprising quickness. Although we make every effort to continuously update information, we recommend that you call ahead to make sure the place you've selected is still open.

STAR RATINGS

MOBIL RATED HOTELS

Whether you're looking for the ultimate in luxury or the best bang for your travel buck, we have a hotel recommendation for you. To help you pinpoint properties that meet your needs, Mobil Travel Guide classifies each lodging by type according to the following characteristics.

★★★★★The Mobil Five-Star hotel provides consistently superlative service in an exceptionally distinctive luxury environment. Attention to detail is evident throughout the hotel, resort or inn, from bed linens to staff uniforms.

★★★★The Mobil Four-Star hotel provides a luxury experience with expanded amenities in a distinctive environment. Services may include automatic turndown service, 24-hour room service and valet parking.

★★★The Mobil Three-Star hotel is well appointed, with a full-service restaurant and expanded amenities, such as a fitness center, golf course, tennis courts, 24-hour room service and optional turndown service.

★★The Mobil Two-Star hotel is considered a clean, comfortable and reliable establishment that has expanded amenities, such as a full-service restaurant.

★The Mobil One-Star lodging is a limited-service hotel, motel or inn that is considered a clean, comfortable and reliable establishment.

For every property, we also provide pricing information. The pricing categories break down as follows:

$ = Up to $150

$$ = $151-$250

$$$ = $251-$350

$$$$ = $351 and up

All prices quoted are accurate at the time of publication; however, prices cannot be guaranteed.

MOBIL RATED RESTAURANTS

Every restaurant in this book has been visited by Mobil Travel Guide's team of experts and comes highly recommended as an outstanding dining experience.

★★★★★The Mobil Five-Star restaurant offers one of few flawless dining experiences in the country. These establishments consistently provide their guests with exceptional food, superlative service, elegant décor and exquisite presentations of each detail surrounding a meal.

★★★★The Mobil Four-Star restaurant provides professional service, distinctive presentations and wonderful food.

★★★The Mobil Three-Star restaurant has good food, warm and skillful service and enjoyable décor.

★★The Mobil Two-Star restaurant serves fresh food in a clean setting with efficient service. Value is considered in this category, as is family friendliness.

★The Mobil One-Star restaurant provides a distinctive experience through culinary specialty, local flair or individual atmosphere.

Because menu prices can fluctuate, we list a pricing category rather than specific prices. The pricing categories are defined as follows, per diner, and assume that you order an appetizer or dessert, an entrée and one drink:

$ = $15 and under

$$ = $16-$35

$$$ = $36-$85

$$$$ = $86 and up

MOBIL RATED SPAS

Mobil Travel Guide's spa ratings are based on objective evaluations of hundreds of attributes. About half of these criteria assess basic expectations, such as staff courtesy, the technical proficiency and skill of the employees and whether the facility is clean and maintained properly. Several standards address issues that impact a guest's physical comfort and convenience, as well as the staff's ability to impart a sense of personalized service. Additional criteria measure the spa's ability to create a completely calming ambience.

★★★★★The Mobil Five-Star spa provides consistently superlative service in an exceptionally distinctive luxury environment with extensive amenities. The staff at a Mobil Five-Star spa provides extraordinary service beyond the traditional spa experience, allowing guests to achieve the highest level of relaxation and pampering. These spas offer an extensive array of treatments, often incorporating international themes and products. Attention to detail is evident throughout the spa, from arrival to departure.

★★★★The Mobil Four-Star spa provides a luxurious experience with expanded amenities in an elegant and serene environment. Throughout the spa facility, guests experience personalized service. Amenities might include, but are not limited to, single-sex relaxation rooms where guests wait for their treatments, plunge pools and whirlpools in both men's and women's locker rooms, and an array of treatments, including a selection of massages, body therapies, facials and a variety of salon services.

★★★The Mobil Three-Star spa is physically well appointed and has a full complement of staff.

INTRODUCTION

If you've been a reader of Mobil Travel Guides, you may have noticed a new look and style in our guidebooks. Since 1958, Mobil Travel Guide has assisted travelers in making smart decisions about where to stay and dine. Fifty-one years later, our mission has not changed: We are committed to our rigorous inspections of hotels, restaurants and, now, spas, to help you cut through all the clutter, and make easy and informed decisions on where you should spend your time and budget. Our team of anonymous inspectors are constantly on the road, sleeping in hotels, eating in restaurants and making spa appointments, evaluating hundreds of standards to determine a property's star rating.

As you read these pages, we hope you get a flavor of the places included in the guides and that you will feel even more inspired to visit and take it all in. We hope you'll experience what it's like to stay in a guest room in the hotels we've rated, taste the food in a restaurant or feel the excitement at an outdoor music venue. We understand the importance of finding the best value when you travel, and making the most of your time. That's why for more than 50 years, Mobil Travel Guide has been the most trusted name in travel.

If any aspect of your accommodation, dining, spa or sightseeing experience motivates you to comment, please contact us at Mobil Travel Guide, 200 W. Madison St., Suite 3950, Chicago, IL 60606, or send an email to info@mobiltravelguide.com Happy travels.

ALABAMA

IF YOU'VE NEVER BEEN TO ALABAMA, YOU'RE IN FOR A SURPRISE. IT IS A SCENIC, VERSATILE place marked by sophisticated cities, diverse geography and Southern charm. From postcard-perfect beaches to the gentle Appalachians, Alabama offers plenty of space for visitors to play outdoors, and its cities and towns chronicle the state's fascinating—if sometimes turbulent—history. Alabama's cultural offerings are as rich as anywhere else in the South: the state lays claim to the famed Alabama Shakespeare Festival, one of the nation's finest year-round theaters; the National Civil Rights Museum, the country's first comprehensive museum dedicated to civil-rights history; and countless art museums, musical venues and performing arts groups.

Alabama has the dubious honor of being the birthplace of both the Civil War and the civil-rights movement, separated by about 100 years. The order to fire on Fort Sumter—the first shots of the War Between the States—came in April 1861 from Confederate Gen. P.G.T. Beauregard in Montgomery. Alabama contributed between 65,000 and 100,000 troops to the South's efforts. (The white male population at the time was about 500,000.) The state did not see much fighting, and by the late 19th century, it was regaining its economic strength.

Nearly a century after the Civil War, a black seamstress named Rosa Parks refused to give up her bus seat to a white man, thereby sparking the Montgomery Bus Boycott that ignited the civil-rights movement, much of which played out on Alabama soil. Dr. Martin Luther King Jr. preached his first messages of nonviolence in a church in Montgomery, and wrote his "Letter from Birmingham Jail," explaining the importance of street demonstrations to the movement.

Alabama preserves and tells its history with candor and compassion, but its historical legacy stretches beyond these events to quieter stories that bear telling. Helen Keller was born and raised in Tuscumbia, and visitors can see the water pump where her teacher, Anne Sullivan, finally broke through Keller's dark world and taught her how to communicate despite her inability to see, speak or hear. And W.C. Handy, a.k.a. "Father of the Blues," grew up here, giving the South a powerful musical legacy.

Another of the state's important—and obvious—legacies is its link to sports. Bo Jackson, Hank Aaron, Willie Mays, Jesse Owens, Bobby Allison and many more sports icons perfected their swings, sprints and sacks in Alabama. Birmingham's Alabama Sports Hall of Fame celebrates stars from many different games, but football is king here, fueled by a healthy rivalry between Auburn University's Tigers and the University of Alabama's Crimson Tide. Certainly their annual clashes attract many visitors, but even after the season ends, the state has another unique sports draw: the Robert Trent

★ **FUN FACTS** Alabama gave us baseball legend Hank Aaron, crooner Nat "King" Cole, Supreme Court Justice Hugo Black and author Harper Lee.

Alabama's French settlers introduced Mardi Gras to the New World in 1703.

10

ALABAMA

★
★
★
★

Jones Trail, the largest golf construction project ever undertaken. The project provides 378 holes stretching over more than 100 miles of golf.

So no matter what your pleasure, chances are you'll find it in the Heart of Dixie. History, culture, gorgeous scenery and plenty of places to play—it's all here.

Information: www.touralabama.org

ALEXANDER CITY

Known as "Alex City" to the locals, this community—southeast of Birmingham, northeast of Montgomery—is the perfect spot to indulge your inner Gilligan. Lake Martin on the Tallapoosa River is one of the South's finest inland recreation areas.

Information: Chamber of Commerce, 120 Tallapoosa St., Alexander City, 256-234-3461; www.alexandercity.org

WHAT TO SEE AND DO

WIND CREEK STATE PARK

4325 Highway 128, Alexander City, 256-329-0845; www.dcnr.state.al.us

This 1,445-acre park along Lake Martin's shores offers a prime spot for swimming, boating, camping or just relaxing on the beach. Bathhouses, a marina and ramps, hiking and bicycling paths, picnic areas, concessions, improved campsites and an observation tower are all at the park. Daily.

HOTELS

★BEST WESTERN HORSESHOE INN

3146 Highway 280, Alexander City, 256-234-6311, 800-780-7234; www.bestwestern.com

90 rooms. High-speed Internet access. Complimentary continental breakfast. Bar. Outdoor pool. $

★JAMESON INN ALEXANDER CITY

4335 Highway 280, Alexander City, 256-234-7099, 800-526-3766; www.jamesoninns.com

60 rooms. Complimentary continental breakfast. Fitness center. Outdoor pool. $

RESTAURANT

★CECIL'S PUBLIC HOUSE

243 Green St., Alexander City, 256-329-0732

Set in a restored turn-of-the-century home, this local favorite offers country staples such as chicken-fried steak and an array of sandwiches. Feeling indulgent? Opt for the chicken margaux or lobster ravioli. American menu. Lunch, dinner.

ANNISTON

Built on the edge of the Appalachian foothills, Anniston was founded by Samuel Noble, an Englishman who headed the ironworks in Rome, Georgia, and Daniel Tyler, a Connecticut capitalist. They established textile mills and blast furnaces to help launch the South into the Industrial Revolution after the devastation of the Civil War. Today, residents work hard to preserve the town's past by refurbishing storefront

ALABAMA

★
★
★
★

facades and historic homes. Stop by for a little small-town Southern charm, only 90 miles from Atlanta.

Information: Convention & Visitors Bureau, 1330 Quintard Ave.,
Anniston, 256-237-3536, 800-489-1087; www.calhounchamber.com

WHAT TO SEE AND DO
ANNISTON MUSEUM OF NATIONAL HISTORY
Lagarde Park, 800 Museum Drive, Anniston, 256-237-6766; www.annistonmuseum.org
Where else can you find full-scale models of an Albertosaurus and a meteorite mere feet from Egyptian mummies and a 9-foot-tall termite mound? Located on the 185-acre John B. Lagarde Environmental Interpretative Park, the museum offers nature trails, open-air exhibits and picnic facilities.

BERMAN MUSEUM
Lagarde Park, 840 Museum Drive, Anniston, 205-237-6261; www.bermanmuseum.org
Need your James Bond fix? Check out these unique artifacts, collected by a real spy from his treks all over the world. The museum features paintings by European and American artists, historical documents, art from Asia and treasures from the American West and World War II eras, including a Royal Persian Scimitar encrusted with 1,295 rose-cut diamonds, 60 carats of rubies and a single 40-carat emerald set in three pounds of gold. September-May: Tuesday-Saturday 10 a.m.-5 p.m., Sunday 1-5 p.m.; June-August: Monday-Saturday 10 a.m.-5 p.m.

CHURCH OF ST. MICHAEL AND ALL ANGELS
1000 W. 18th Street and Cobb Avenue, Anniston, 256-237-4011; www.stmaaa.org
Celebrated for its architectural beauty and historical significance, St. Michael's boasts, among other wonders, a 95-foot bell tower and a 12-foot Carrara marble altar, imported in the late 1800s from England and Italy. Daily

COLDWATER COVERED BRIDGE
Coldwater, three miles south via Highway 431, five miles West
on Highway 78 at Oxford Lake and Civic Center
Built before 1850, this bridge is one of 13 restored covered bridges in Alabama.

HOTELS
★★AMERICA'S BEST VALUE INN-RIVERSIDE/PELL CITY
11900 Highway 78, Riverside, 205-338-3381; www.americasbestvalueinn.com
70 rooms. Restaurant. **$**

★BAYMONT INN AND SUITES
1600 Highway 21 S., Oxford, 256-835-1492, 877-229-6668;
www.baymontinns.com
129 rooms. High-speed Internet access. Complimentary continental breakfast. Outdoor pool. Pets accepted. Business center. **$**

★★★THE VICTORIA COUNTRY INN

1604 Quintard Ave., Anniston, 256-236-0503, 800-260-8781; www.thevictoria.com
Built in 1888, this beautifully restored country inn is a wonderful example of early Victorian architecture. Enjoy comfortable rooms, fine dining and a piano lounge. 60 rooms. Restaurant. $

RESTAURANTS
★BETTY'S BAR-B-Q

401 S. Quintard Ave., Anniston, 256-237-1411
American menu. Lunch, dinner. Closed Sunday. $

★★THE VICTORIA

1604 Quintard Ave., Anniston, 256-236-0503; www.thevictoria.com
American menu. Dinner. Closed Sunday. $$$

ATHENS

A short jaunt from aerospace Mecca Huntsville, Athens does not need rocket boosters to attract visitors. Its location—in the Tennessee Valley, along the Appalachian foothills—offers natural beauty, and its tree-lined streets and Greek Revival houses remind visitors of the old antebellum South.

Information: Athens-Limestone County Chamber of Commerce,
256-232-2600, 256-232-2609; www.tourathens.com

WHAT TO SEE AND DO
ATHENS STATE UNIVERSITY

13

300 N. Beaty St., Athens, 256-233-8100; www.athens.edu
Alabama's oldest institution of higher learning, Athens State University began as a women's college in 1822. Stroll across campus for a peek at its Greek Revival architecture, and then check out Founders Hall to see crystal chandeliers from the Carnegie estate and the chapel's hard-carved altar.

ALABAMA

HOTELS
★BEST WESTERN ATHENS INN

1329 Highway 72, Athens, 256-233-4030, 800-780-7234; www.bestwestern.com
88 rooms. High-speed Internet access. Complimentary continental breakfast. Outdoor pool. Pets accepted. $

★QUALITY INN

1488 Thrasher Blvd., Athens, 256-232-0000, 800-426-7866; www.qualityinn.com
56 rooms. Wireless Internet access. Complimentary continental breakfast. Outdoor pool. $

AUBURN

Home to Auburn University and its 23,000 students from across the globe, Auburn is a quintessential college town. School spirit is practically a religion here, especially during football season. The rest of the year, public parks, golf courses and a historic downtown shopping district offer plenty of fun to keep residents and visitors entertained.

Keep an eye out for the town's rich architectural history on display, including examples of Greek Revival, Victorian and early-20th-century buildings.

Information: Auburn/Opelika Convention & Visitors Bureau, 714 E. Glenn Ave., 334-887-8747, 800-321-8880, 866-880-8747; www.auburn-opelika.com

WHAT TO SEE AND DO

AUBURN UNIVERSITY
202 Mary Martin Hall, Auburn, 334-844-4000; www.auburn.edu

Alabama's first four-year institution to admit women on an equal basis with men, Auburn is a university steeped in campus traditions and lore. One example: local legend suggests that the school's famous "War Eagle" battle cry dates back to 1892—the first time Auburn and the University of Georgia met on the football field. According to the legend, a Civil War veteran brought his pet eagle to the game; all of a sudden, the eagle broke free and circled the field, just about the time Auburn began its steady push toward the end zone. A thrilled crowd began yelling "War Eagle" to cheer on its team.

CHEWACLA STATE PARK
124 Shell Toomer Parkway, Auburn, 800-252-7275; 334-887-5621; www.alapark.com

The 696-acre park offers a little something for every kind of nature enthusiast. Water lover? Rent a boat and fish in Chewacla Lake. Landlubber? Opt for a hike on the trails and a picnic. Facilities include bathhouses, a playground, concessions, campgrounds and newly renovated cabins.

JOHN B. LOVELACE MUSEUM
Donahue Drive and Stamboard Avenue, Auburn, 334-844-0764;
www.lovelacemuseum.com

This orange and blue shrine pays homage to famous Auburn University athletes, such as Bo Jackson and Charles Barkley. Interactive exhibits are also available. Monday-Friday 8 a.m.-4.30 p.m., Saturday 9 a.m.-4 p.m.

HOTELS

★★BEST WESTERN UNIVERSITY CONVENTION CENTER
1577 S. College St., Auburn, 334-821-7001, 800-282-8763; www.bestwestern.com

122 rooms. High-speed Internet access. Complimentary continental breakfast. Restaurant, bar. Fitness center. Outdoor pool. Pets accepted. $

★★★THE HOTEL AT AUBURN UNIVERSITY
241 S. College St., Auburn, 334-821-8200, 800-228-2876; www.auhcc.com

Located near the university and downtown Auburn, this hotel and conference center offers elegant Southern hospitality. 248 rooms. Wireless Internet access. Restaurant, bar. Outdoor pool. $

SPECIALTY LODGING

CRENSHAW HOUSE BED & BREAKFAST
371 N. College St., Auburn, 334-821-1131, 800-950-1131;
www.auburnalabamalodging.com

This restored Victorian house built in 1890 is on the National Register of Historic Places. Six rooms. Wireless Internet access. Complimentary continental breakfast. $

BESSEMER

Founded in 1887 and named for a scientist who invented the steel-making process, Bessemer has a long history of manufacturing iron and steel, explosives and building materials. Today, this town of about 30,000 residents is a growing suburb of Birmingham. Its downtown core is listed on the National Register of Historic Districts.

Information: Bessemer Area Chamber of Commerce, 205-425-3253, 888-423-7736; www.bessemerchamber.com

WHAT TO SEE AND DO

ALABAMA ADVENTURE THEME PARK

4599 Alabama Adventure Parkway, Bessemer, 205-481-4750; www.alabamaadventure.com

Satisfy your inner wild child with a ride on Rampage, one of the nation's oldest and fastest wooden roller coasters in the park's Magic City USA. Or cool off on the slides at Splash Beach, the adjacent water park. The summer concert series features famous Alabama natives. May-September: daily.

HALL OF HISTORY MUSEUM

1905 Alabama Ave., Bessemer, 205-426-1633; www.bessemerhallofhistory.com

Housed in a former train terminal (Southern Railway Depot), the museum tells the story of Bessemer's triumphs and trials. Tuesday-Saturday 9 a.m.-4 p.m. (closed noon-1 p.m. for lunch).

TANNEHILL IRONWORKS STATE HISTORICAL PARK

12632 Confederate Parkway, McCalla, 205-477-5711; www.tannehill.org

If you've ever wondered what life might have been like in the height of Alabama's 19th-century iron boom, visit Tannehill to find out. In addition to the park's 1,500 acres for hiking and camping, the restored pioneer cabins house artisans. From fall to spring, you can catch the blacksmith and miller hard at work. The park features bathhouses, fishing, nature trails, picnicking, concessions, camping (hookups, dump station; fee). Park daily.

HOTEL

★★DAY'S INN

1121 9th Ave. S.W., Bessemer, 205-424-9780, 800-272-6232; www.daysinn.com

156 rooms. High-speed Internet access. Restaurant, bar. Outdoor pool. Pets accepted. $

RESTAURANT

★BOB SYKES BAR-B-Q

1724 9th Ave. N., Bessemer, 205-426-1400; www.bobsykes.com

Lunch, dinner. Closed Sunday. $

BIRMINGHAM

Alabama's largest city, Birmingham has found a way to preserve its history and still give off an air of urban sophistication—a combination that appeals to visitors and residents alike. Beautiful city streets, stylish boutiques and restaurants and diverse cultural attractions make Birmingham a must-see stop on any trek through central Alabama.

★
★
★
★

DOWNTOWN BIRMINGHAM

Birmingham, home of the Civil Rights Institute, offers a powerful lesson about African-American history and culture.

Start at the **Historical Fourth Avenue Visitor Center** *(319 17th St. N., 205-328-1850)*, where you can pick up a map or take a guided tour of the historic African-American business district.

Across the street from the visitor center is the **Alabama Jazz Hall of Fame**, located within the historic Carver Theater *(1631 Fourth Ave. N., 205-254-2731)*. Exhibits cover the history of jazz and celebrate such artists as Dinah Washington, Nat King Cole, Duke Ellington and W.C. Handy, among others. The theater also hosts live performances. On the other side of the visitor center, the **Alabama Theater** *(1817 3rd Ave. N.)* has been restored to its 1920s splendor and is now a cinema.

Head west along Third Avenue one block to **La Vase** *(328 16th St. N.)*, a restaurant that serves hearty home-style soul food. After your meal, trek north up 16th Street three blocks to Kelly Ingram Park, the scene of civil-rights clashes in the 1950s and 1960s.

The Birmingham Civil Rights Institute *(520 16th St., 205-328-9696)*, across the street from the park, is the city's premier attraction. A short film introduces the city's history, and vintage footage illustrates the Jim Crow era and the development of the civil-rights movement. Exhibits emphasize Birmingham's role—positive and negative—in the civil-rights movement, and the bookshop has a good selection of African-American history and heritage titles.

Cross Sixth Avenue to reach the **16th Street Baptist Church** *(1530 6th Ave. N., 205-251-9402)*, where four girls were killed when a Ku Klux Klan member bombed the church in 1963. The rebuilt church hosts tens of thousands of visitors each year.

Founded in 1871 and named for a British industrial city, Birmingham started out as a center of steel production. The late 19th century brought disease and a nationwide financial panic that almost ruined Birmingham, but the city boomed in the early years of the 20th century. Just as Birmingham was enjoying a streak of prosperity after the end of World War I, a secret white supremacist group, the Ku Klux Klan, garnered power, leading to violence against African-American citizens that lasted for decades.

Not surprisingly, Birmingham served as the setting for many battles during the civil-rights movement, including of course, Dr. Martin Luther King Jr.'s "Letter from Birmingham Jail," written April 16, 1963. In it, King explains why the demonstrations in the streets of Birmingham and other Southern cities were crucial to the fight for civil rights for African-Americans. Several months later, on September 15, 1963, a member of the Ku Klux Klan bombed Birmingham's 16th Street Baptist Church, killing four girls. The emotional response to the bombing galvanized the movement and helped lead to the passage of the 1964 Civil Rights Act.

By the 1970s, Birmingham was booming again, and in 1979, its citizens elected the city's first black mayor, Dr. Richard Arrington Jr. Today, Birmingham is not only a rich historic area, it is also home to the University of Alabama Medical Center, which attracts patients from all over the world and beefs up the local economy.

By day, soak up Birmingham's history, and by night, swing by Five Points South, Birmingham's entertainment district, where you'll find great people-watching, fine dining and clubs to satisfy even the pickiest music aficionados.

Information: Convention & Visitors Bureau, 2200 Ninth Ave. N., 205-458-8000, 800-458-8085; www.birminghamal.org

WHAT TO SEE AND DO

ALABAMA SPORTS HALL OF FAME MUSEUM

2150 Richard Arrington Jr. Blvd. N., Birmingham, 205-323-6665; www.ashof.org

The museum celebrates sports heroes from the Heart of Dixie, including Willie Mays, Carl Lewis and Jesse Owens. See vintage equipment and uniforms, awards and photographs, and interactive kiosks and life-sized sculptures. Monday-Saturday 9 a.m.-5 p.m., Sunday 1-5 p.m.

ARLINGTON ANTEBELLUM HOME AND GARDENS

331 Cotton Ave. S.W., Birmingham, 205-780-5656; www.birminghamal.gov

Visit Birmingham's last remaining antebellum house in the Greek Revival style, built circa 1850 on a sloping hill in Elyton. The oak and magnolia trees that surround the house suggest that Rhett Butler might stroll by any minute. Tuesday-Saturday 10 a.m.-4 p.m., Sunday 1-4 p.m.

BIRMINGHAM BOTANICAL GARDENS

2612 Lane Park Road, Birmingham, 205-414-3900; www.bbgardens.org

Much more than just flowers, the botanical gardens offers tours, a garden maintained by the green thumbs at *Southern Living* magazine and a full calendar of events and classes. Don't miss the Japanese Garden, offering a bonsai collection and an authentic Japanese teahouse. And if you get hungry, there's a restaurant on the grounds. Daily, dawn-dusk.

BIRMINGHAM CIVIL RIGHTS INSTITUTE

520 16th St. N., Birmingham, 205-328-9696, 866-328-9696; www.bcri.org

Exhibits and multimedia presentations portray the struggle for civil rights in Birmingham and across the nation from the 1920s to the present. Tuesday-Saturday 10 a.m.-5 p.m., Sunday 1-5 p.m.

BIRMINGHAM-JEFFERSON CONVENTION COMPLEX

2100 Richard Arrington Jr. Blvd., Birmingham, 205-458-8400; www.bjcc.org

This complex covers seven square blocks and hosts events such as hunting expos, classic theatrical performances and sports tournaments. The center contains 220,000 square feet of exhibition space, a 3,000-seat concert hall, a 1,000-seat theater and a 18,000-seat coliseum.

BIRMINGHAM MUSEUM OF ART

2000 Eighth Ave. N., Birmingham, 205-254-2565; www.artsbma.org

Celebrated for its diverse collections, the museum is home to some 21,000 objects from almost every era of artistic production across the globe. Don't miss its collection of Asian art, including a 15th-century temple mural from China; its decorative arts, including the largest collection of Wedgwood outside of England; and the historical and contemporary work from Native American artists. Tuesday-Saturday 10 a.m.-5 p.m., Sunday noon-5 p.m.

BIRMINGHAM-SOUTHERN COLLEGE

900 Arkadelphia Road, Birmingham, 205-226-4600; www.bsc.edu

A favorite of college guides, BSC boasts a pristine 192-acre campus on wooded rolling hills. Stop to see the Robert R. Meyer Planetarium, Alabama's first. For schedule or reservations, call 205-226-4771.

BIRMINGHAM ZOO

2630 Cahaba Road, Birmingham, 205-879-0409; www.birminghamzoo.com

Where else in Alabama can you see an Indochinese tiger, a red panda and a host of sea lions within a few acres of one another? Nurture your wild side by checking out the nearly 800 animals that reside here. Daily 9 a.m.-5 p.m.; Memorial Day-Labor Day: Tuesday, Friday-Sunday 9 a.m.-7 p.m.

MCWANE/SCIENCE CENTER

200 19th St. N., Birmingham, 205-714-8300; www.mcwane.org

A natural history museum on the slopes of Red Mountain, the McWane Center offers plenty of adventure: Explore the universe at the Challenger Learning Center, catch a flick on the five-story IMAX screen or visit with sea creatures at the center's World of Water Aquarium. Don't miss the walkway carved into the face of the mountain above the expressway, where you'll see more than 150 million years of geologic history. You also can do some picnicking there. September-May: Monday-Friday 9 a.m.-5 p.m., Saturday 10 a.m.-6 p.m., Sunday noon-6 p.m.; June-August: Monday-Saturday 10 a.m.-6 p.m., Sunday noon-6 p.m.

MILES COLLEGE

5500 Myron Massey Blvd., Fairfield, 205-929-1000; www.miles.edu

Miles College boasts an extensive collection of African-American literature, exhibits of African art forms and two historic landmark buildings.

OAK MOUNTAIN STATE PARK

200 Terrace Drive, Pelham, 205-620-2520; www.alapark.com

Peavine Falls and Gorge and two lakes sit amid 9,940 acres of the state's most rugged mountains. Enthusiasts cite Oak Mountain as one of the state's best places to mountain bike. Other activities include fishing, boating (marina, ramp, rentals), hiking, backpacking, bridle trails, golf (18 holes; fee), tennis, picnicking (shelters, barbecue pits, fireplaces), concessions, camping, cabins and a demonstration farm.

RICKWOOD CAVERNS STATE PARK

370 Rickwood Park Road, Warrior, 205-647-9692; www.dcnr.state.al.us

Tour the "miracle mile," a stretch of colorful underground caverns that reveals 260-year-old limestone foundations. The 380-acre park also boasts an Olympic-sized swimming pool, hiking trails, a miniature train ride, carpet golf, a gift shop, concessions, picnic areas and camping sites. Memorial Day-Labor Day: daily; rest of September-October, March-May: weekends. Park (all year); pool (seasonal). Fee for some activities.

RUFFNER MOUNTAIN NATURE CENTER

1214-81st St. S., Birmingham, 205-833-8264; www.ruffnermountain.org

A 1,011-acre natural retreat from the bustle of Birmingham, the mountain offers 11 miles of hiking trails. Learn about the mountain's biology, geology and history at the center and then venture out to see Alabama wildlife. Tuesday-Saturday 9 a.m.-5 p.m., Sunday 1-5 p.m.

SAMFORD UNIVERSITY

800 Lakeshore Drive, Birmingham, 205-726-2011; www.samford.edu

Stroll across Samford's 172-acre campus to see brick Georgian Colonial buildings, and then duck into the Rotunda to see the Samford Murals. And don't miss the Beeson Divinity Hall Chapel's copper-clad dome with a detailed ceiling mural on the interior (tours available).

SLOSS FURNACES NATIONAL HISTORIC LANDMARK

20 32nd St. N., Birmingham, 205-324-1911; www.slossfurnaces.com

Don't let the name fool you: This industrial museum offers more than a glimpse at old furnaces. Here you'll find captivating stories about the economic and social growth of the South. But beware: Paranormal investigators have suggested that it is one of nation's most haunted places, so watch out for the ghosts of old workers. Tuesday-Friday 10 a.m.-4 p.m.

SOUTHERN MUSEUM OF FLIGHT/ALABAMA AVIATION HALL OF FAME

4343 73rd St. N., Birmingham, 205-833-8226; www.southernmuseumofflight.org

View a full-size Wright Flyer replica, try your hand at flying in two U.S. Air Force fighter jet cockpit simulators and wander through flight-related memorabilia. Tuesday-Saturday 9:30 a.m.-4:30 p.m.

UNIVERSITY OF ALABAMA AT BIRMINGHAM

1400 University Blvd., Birmingham, 205-934-4011; www.uab.edu

Known for its excellent medical and technological programs, the UAB is home to more than 18,000 students. Reynolds Historical Library in the Lister Hill Library of the Health Sciences (1700 University Blvd.) has collections of ivory anatomical manne-quins, original manuscripts, and more than 13,000 rare medical and scientific books; Alabama Museum of Health Sciences has memorabilia of Alabama doctors, surgeons and other medical practitioners as well as reproductions of turn-of-the-century doc-tors' and dentists' offices. Monday-Friday.

VULCAN

1701 Valley View Drive, Birmingham, 205-933-1409; www.visitvulcan.com

Vulcan, Roman god of fire and forge, legendary inventor of smithing and metalwork-ing, stands as a monument to the city's iron industry atop Red Mountain. Since 1939, he has held a lighted torch aloft over the city from his perch on a 124-foot pedestal. A glass-enclosed elevator takes passengers to an observation deck. Vulcan's torch shines bright red for 24 hours after a traffic fatality in the city. Park: daily.

19

ALABAMA

★
★
★
★
★

SPECIAL EVENTS

CITY STAGES

1929 Third Ave. N., Birmingham, 205-251-1272; www.citystages.org

Billed as "Birmingham's World-Class Music Festival," City Stages features approximately 160 musical performances on 11 stages. Artists include both local and nationally known musicians, such as George Clinton, Al Green and Kid Rock. Third weekend in June.

GREATER ALABAMA FALL FAIR & FESTIVAL

Alabama State Fairgrounds, 2331 Bessemer Road, Birmingham, 205-786-8100

The fall fair ushers in good old-fashioned fun with food, games, livestock demonstrations and arts and crafts. Ten days in late October-early November.

INTERNATIONAL FESTIVAL

205 20th St. N., Birmingham, 205-252-7652; www.bic-al.org

Each year, the Birmingham International Festival highlights the culture of a different country to promote education as well as business and trade relationships between Alabama and the selected country. A party early in the year kicks off a series of events to take place in the months to follow, which includes a trade expo, conferences, art exhibits, lectures and a black-tie dinner. The free educational programs bring musicians, performers and storytellers to Alabama schools. February-May.

HOTELS

★★CLARION HOTEL

5216 Messer Airport Highway, Birmingham, 205-591-7900; www.clarionhotel.com

196 rooms. Wireless Internet access. Restaurant, bar. Airport transportation available. Outdoor pool. **$**

★★COURTYARD BY MARRIOTT

500 Shades Creek Parkway, Homewood, 205-879-0400, 800-321-2211;
www.courtyard.com

140 rooms. High-speed Internet access. Restaurant, bar. **$**

★★EMBASSY SUITES

2300 Woodcrest Place, Birmingham, 205-879-7400, 800-362-2779;
www.embassy-suites.com

243 suites. Complimentary full breakfast. Restaurant, bar. Airport transportation available. **$**

★★★HAMPTON INN & SUITES BIRMINGHAM-DOWNTOWN-TUTWILER

2021 Park Place N., Birmingham, 205-322-2100, 877-999-3223;
hamptoninn.hilton.com

The rooms of this comfortable hotel are big (choose between rooms with one king-sized bed or two queens), and amenities include 32-inch TVs, DVD players and plush beds. You're also near golfing and local attractions such as the Civil Rights Institute. 149 rooms. High-speed Internet access. Complimentary full breakfast. Restaurant, bar. Airport transportation available. Fitness center. Business center. **$$$**

★HAMPTON INN BIRMINGHAM-COLONNADE

3400 Colonnade Parkway, Birmingham, 205-967-0002, 800-861-7168;
www.hamptoninn.com

133 rooms. High-speed Internet access. Complimentary continental breakfast. Fitness center. Outdoor pool, whirlpool. **$**

★★★HILTON BIRMINGHAM PERIMETER PARK

8 Perimeter Park S., Birmingham, 205-967-2700, 800-774-1500; www.hilton.com

Located in an up-and-coming business and entertainment area, this large hotel is near Birmingham's downtown cultural and corporate destinations. Among the amenities in the attractive rooms are work desks and dual phone lines. 205 rooms. Wireless Internet access. Restaurant, bar. Airport transportation available. **$**

★LA QUINTA INN

513 Cahaba Park Circle, Birmingham, 205-995-9990, 877-229-6668; www.lq.com

99 rooms. High-speed Internet access. Complimentary continental breakfast. Pets accepted. **$**

★★★MARRIOTT BIRMINGHAM

3590 Grandview Parkway, Birmingham, 205-968-3775, 800-228-9290;
www.marriott.com

A mix of cozy and contemporary furnishings gives this hotel, just off Highway 280, an inviting and comfortable feel. Friendly staff, a huge array of amenities and a location close to many business headquarters and entertainment options make the Marriott a prime option. 295 rooms. Wireless Internet access. Restaurant, bar. **$$**

★★QUALITY INN ON THE LAKE

1485 Montgomery Highway, Birmingham, 205-823-4300, 800-228-5151;
www.qualityinn.com

166 rooms. Restaurant, bar. Pets accepted. **$**

★★REDMONT HOTEL

2101 Fifth Ave., Birmingham, 205-324-2101, 800-536-2083; www.theredmont.com

114 rooms. High-speed Internet access. Restaurant, bar. Airport transportation available. **$**

★★THE RIME GARDEN INN & SUITES

5320 Beacon Drive, Birmingham, 205-951-1200, 888-828-1768; www.rimehotel.com

290 rooms. Wireless Internet access. Complimentary continental breakfast. Restaurant, bar. Airport transportation available. Business center. **$**

★★★SHERATON BIRMINGHAM

2101 Richard Arrington Jr. Blvd. N., Birmingham, 205-324-5000, 800-325-3535;
www.sheraton.com

Located in downtown Birmingham, this hotel is a short stroll on the skywalk to the convention center. Explore the zoo, the art museum and Five Points South historical district nearby. 770 rooms. Restaurant, bar. **$$**

ALABAMA

★
★
★
★

★★★THE WYNFREY HOTEL
1000 Riverchase Galleria, Birmingham, 205-987-1600, 800-996-3739;
www.wynfrey.com
The Wynfrey Hotel offers Birmingham's best lodging. Located on the edge of the city, this gracious hotel combines Southern hospitality with European panache. The rooms and suites offer comfort, style and plenty of amenities. This hotel is a favorite destination of shoppers, with special access to the city's renowned Riverchase Galleria. After a day of bargain hunting, guests retire to the Spa Japonika to recharge and relax, or enjoy a meal at one of the hotel's three restaurants. 329 rooms. Wireless Internet access. Three restaurants, bar. Airport transportation available. Outdoor pool. Spa. $$

RESTAURANTS
★GOLDEN CITY CHINESE RESTAURANT
4647 Highway 280, Birmingham, 205-991-3197
Lunch, dinner. $$

★★★HIGHLANDS
2011 11th Ave. S., Birmingham, 205-939-1400; www.highlandsbarandgrill.com
French cuisine meets Southern traditions at Highlands, one of Birmingham's premier restaurants. French menu. Dinner. Closed Sunday, Monday. $$$

★★NIKI'S WEST
233 Finley Ave. W., Birmingham, 205-252-5751; www.nikiswest.com
American menu. Lunch, dinner. Closed Sunday. $$

CLANTON
When you see its giant peach-shaped water tower, you'll know you've arrived in Clanton, Alabama's largest producer of peaches. The town also caters to fishermen along the Coosa River and its tributaries.
Information: Chamber of Commerce, 205-755-2400, 800-553-0493; www.clanton.al.us

WHAT TO SEE AND DO
CONFEDERATE MEMORIAL PARK
437 Chilton Road, 63 Marbury, 205-755-1990
Alabama's only resting place for Confederate veterans, the park comprises two cemeteries on 100 acres that once were the grounds of the Confederate Soldiers Home of Alabama. The museum contains mementos of Alabama's role in the Civil War as well as artifacts, records, documents and photographs. There's also hiking trails and picnicking (shelters) available. Daily.

CULLMAN
Col. John G. Cullmann, a German immigrant whose dream was to build a self-sustaining colony of other German refugees and immigrants, founded Cullman in the early 1870s. In 1873, five German families settled on the 5,400 square miles of land he had purchased from the Louisville & Nashville Railroad. Notice the

town's 100-foot-wide streets, a gift from Cullmann when he laid out the town. Today, Cullman is part of metropolitan Birmingham.

Information: Cullman Area Chamber of Commerce,
301 Second Ave. S.W., 256-734-0454; www.cullmanchamber.org

WHAT TO SEE AND DO

AVE MARIA GROTTO

1600 St. Bernard Drive S.E., Cullman, 256-734-4110; www.avemariagrotto.com
Brother Joseph Zoettl, a Benedictine monk, spent nearly 50 years building some 150 miniature replicas of famous churches, buildings and shrines, including the Basilica of St. Peter's, the California missions and famous buildings from Jerusalem and the Holy Land, using such materials as cement, stone, bits of jewelry and marble. The miniatures cover 4 acres of a terraced, landscaped garden. There are free picnic grounds adjacent to parking lot. April-September: daily 8 a.m.-6 p.m.; October-March: daily 8 a.m.-5 p.m.

CLARKSON COVERED BRIDGE

Highway 278 W., Cullman, 256-734-3369; www.cullmancountyparks.com
One of the largest covered bridges in Alabama, the truss-styled Clarkson is 270 feet long and 50 feet high. The site of Civil War Battle of Hog Mountain, the bridge is now on the National Register of Historic Places. It also offers a dogtrot cabin and gristmill, a nature trail and picnic facilities. Daily.

HURRICANE CREEK PARK

22600 U.S. Highway 31, Vinemont, 256-734-2125;
www.hurricanecreek.homestead.com
Come see the park's 500-foot-deep gorge with observation platform, trail over the swinging bridge, unusual rock formations, earthquake fault and waterfalls. Picnic tables are available. Tuesday-Saturday 9 a.m.-5 p.m., Sunday 1-5 p.m.

SPORTSMAN LAKE PARK

1536 Sportsman Lake Road N.W., Cullman, 256-734-3052;
www.cullmancountyparks.com
Stocked with bream, bass, catfish and other fish, the lake also offers land-based activities such as miniature golf, kiddie rides (Thursday-Sunday), picnicking and primitive camping. Fee for some activities. April-September: daily.

WILLIAM B. BANKHEAD NATIONAL FOREST

Highway 278, Double Springs, 205-489-5111; www.fs.fed.us/r8/alabama
A place primed for adventure, the 180,000 acres contain bubbling streams, diverse wildlife and plenty of space to wander. The forest's crown jewel is Sipsey Wilderness, often called the "Land of a Thousand Waterfalls." Trek through the Sipsey to find the state's last remaining stand of old-growth hardwood. Swimming, fishing (bass, bream), boating; hunting (deer, turkey, squirrel), hiking, horseback riding. Fee for some activities.

ALABAMA

★ ★ ★ ★

RESTAURANT
★★ALL STEAK
314 Second Ave. Southwest, Cullman, 256-734-4322; www.theallsteak.com
Seafood, steak menu. Breakfast, lunch, dinner. Children's menu. **$$**

DAUPHIN ISLAND

A barrier island with white sandy beaches and about 1,200 residents, Dauphin Island is rich in history. Native Americans first inhabited the island and built shell middens from discarded oyster shells and other waste from the sea. The Shell Mound still stands as a testament to Native American presence on the island. Later, Spaniards visited and mapped the area in the 16th century. French explorer Pierre le Moyne, Sieur d'Iberville, used the island as his base for a short time in 1699 as he scouted out French Louisiana. Today, the island is part of Mobile County and a playground for its citizens. It is also a haven for birds; a 60-acre sanctuary is home to many local and migratory species.

Reach Dauphin Island from the north on Highway 193, via a four-mile-long, high-rise bridge and causeway, that crosses Grants Pass. The island also has a 3,000-foot paved airstrip. A ferry service to Fort Morgan operates year-round.
Information: 251-861-3607; www.dauphinisland.org

WHAT TO SEE AND DO
FORT GAINES
109 Bienville Blvd., Dauphin Island, 251-861-3607; www.dauphinisland.org
This five-sided fort was begun in 1821 and completed in the 1850s. Union forces captured the fort from the Confederates on August 23, 1864. Check out the museum on the premises. Daily.

DAUPHIN ISLAND CAMPGROUND
Dauphin Island, 251-861-2742; www.dauphinisland.org
A private path leads to secluded Gulf beaches, fishing piers and boat launches; a hiking trail brings you to the Audubon Bird Sanctuary. The campground also has recreation areas and tent and trailer sites.

DECATUR

Decatur, center of northern Alabama's mountain lakes recreation area, is a thriving manufacturing and market city with historic districts and sprawling public parks.

President Monroe selected the town site in 1820, and Decatur, named for U.S. naval officer Commodore Stephen Decatur, was born. The Civil War was hard on the town, which found itself seesawing between invasion and resistance, frequently attacked and then abandoned. Only three buildings were left standing at war's end.

On the edge of the Tennessee River, Decatur today is a busy port and a bustling town where residents and visitors enjoy the area's many recreational activities.
Information: Convention & Visitors Bureau, 719 Sixth Ave. S.E.,
256-350-2028, 800-232-5449; www.decaturcvb.org

WHAT TO SEE AND DO
MOORESVILLE
Six miles east on Highway 20, 413 N. Main St., Mooresville, 704-663-3800;
www.ci.mooresville.nc.us
History buffs must visit Mooresville for a glimpse of the South circa 1818. The state's oldest incorporated town, Mooresville is (not surprisingly) home to Alabama's oldest operational post office, which has original wooden call boxes and still hand-stamps the mail. Ghosts of presidents past linger here: President Andrew Johnson was a tailor's apprentice before his rise to the presidency, and President James Garfield preached here during the Civil War. Monday-Saturday.

OLD DECATUR AND ALBANY HISTORIC DISTRICTS
719 Sixth Ave. S.E., Decatur, 256-350-2028; www.historicalbanyalabama.com
The walking tour of this Victorian neighborhood begins at the restored Old Bank on historic Bank Street and includes three antebellum and 194 Victorian structures. Contact the Convention & Visitors Bureau.

POINT MALLARD PARK
2901 Point Mallard Drive, Decatur, 256-341-4900, 800-350-3000;
www.pointmallardpark.com
On the Tennessee River, this 500-acre park offers plenty of fun for families. It includes a swimming pool, a wave pool, a water slide, a beach (mid-May to Labor Day), hiking, bicycle trails, an 18-hole golf course, tennis courts, an indoor ice rink, camping (hookups) and a recreation center. Fee for activities.

PRINCESS THEATRE
112 Second Ave. N.E., Decatur, 256-340-1778; www.princesstheatre.org
The renovated Art Deco-style theater features musical and dramatic performances and children's theater.

WHEELER NATIONAL WILDLIFE REFUGE
2700 Refuge Headquarters Road, Decatur, 256-353-7243; wheeler.fws.gov
This is Alabama's oldest and largest (34,500 acres) wildlife refuge. It's a wintering ground for waterfowl and home to numerous species of animal and plant life. Fishing, boating, hunting (limited, permit required), picnicking, bird study and photography are all available here. There's a visitor center and Waterfowl Observation Building. March-September: Tuesday-Saturday, rest of year: daily.

SPECIAL EVENTS
ALABAMA JUBILEE HOT AIR BALLOON CLASSIC
Point Mallard Park, 1800 Point Mallard Drive S.E., Decatur, 800-524-6181;
www.alabamajubilee.net
Since its beginnings in 1977, the Alabama Jubilee has become one of the most popular events in the state. Over the three-day Memorial Day weekend, more than 50,000 spectators gather to watch 60 pilots compete in five hot-air balloon races. The festival also offers a fireworks display, an antique tractor and classic car shows, entertainment and arts and crafts. Memorial Day weekend.

ALABAMA

CIVIL WAR REENACTMENT/SEPTEMBER SKIRMISH

Point Mallard Park, 1800 Point Mallard Drive S.E., Decatur, 800-524-6181;
www.decaturcvb.org

This historical reenactment is held in honor of Confederate Gens. "Fighting Joe" Wheeler and John Hunt. Events include craft fairs, displays of Civil War relics, a living history of daily camp life, and battles between Confederate and Union "troops" dressed in authentic Civil War uniforms. Labor Day weekend.

RACKING HORSE WORLD CELEBRATION

Celebration Arena, 67 Horse Center Road, Decatur, 256-353-7225;
www.rackinghorse.com

Horses show off their high-stepping four-beat gait at this annual competition. Last full week in September.

SOUTHERN WILDLIFE FESTIVAL

6250 Highway 31, Decatur, 800-524-6181; www.decaturcvb.org

The fest holds competition and exhibits of wildlife carvings, artwork, photography and duck calling. Third weekend in October.

SPIRIT OF AMERICA FESTIVAL

Point Mallard Park, 1800 Point Mallard Drive S.E., Decatur, 800-524-6181;
www.spiritofamericafestival.com

One of the South's largest free Fourth of July celebrations, the Spirit of America Festival offers games, contests, a beauty pageant, concerts, exhibits and fireworks. Early July.

HOTEL

★★COUNTRY INN & SUITES BY CARLSON DECATUR

807 Bank St. N.E., Decatur, 256-355-6800, 800-456-4000, 888-201-1746;
www.countryinns.com

110 suites. Restaurant, bar. Airport transportation available. $

RESTAURANTS

★★SIMP MCGHEE'S

725 Bank St., Decatur, 256-353-6284; www.simpmcghees.com

Cajun/Creole, seafood menu. Dinner. Closed Sunday. $$

★★WATERSHED

406 W. Ponce De Leon Ave., Decatur, 404-378-4900; www.watershedrestaurant.com

American menu, other. Brunch, lunch, dinner. $$

DEMOPOLIS

A group of French exiles settled in Demopolis in 1817 after Congress granted them four townships, and dubbed them the "French Emigrants for the Cultivation of the Vine and Olive." Unfortunately, the grapes and olives did not flourish, and the wilderness prevailed over the settlers and their plants. By the mid-1820s, many scattered or were killed by disease. Much of Demopolis, however, has a French flair today, and in an ironic twist of fate, the olive trees bear fruit each year.

Information: Demopolis Area Chamber of Commerce, 102 E. Washington St.,
334-289-0270; www.demopolischamber.com

WHAT TO SEE AND DO

BLUFF HALL

405 N. Commissioners St., Demopolis, 334-289-9644

This restored antebellum mansion was built by the slaves of Allen Glover, a planter and merchant, as a wedding gift for his daughter. The interior has Corinthian columns in the drawing room, period furniture and marble mantels. There's also a clothing museum and a craft shop. Tuesday-Sunday.

FORKLAND PARK

12 miles north on Highway 43, one mile west of Forkland on River Road, 334-289-5530

This park is on 10,000-acre Lake Demopolis, which was formed by a 40-foot-high dam on the Tombigbee River. There, you can do some waterskiing, fishing, boating (ramp) or camping (hookups, dump station; fees). Daily.

FOSCUE CREEK PARK

384 Rescue Management Drive, Demopolis, 334-289-3540; bwt.sam.usace.army.mil

On Lake Demopolis, this park offers boating (ramps), trails, picnic areas, a pavilion, a playground, ball fields and camping (hookups, dump station; fees). Daily.

GAINESWOOD

805 S. Cedar Ave., Demopolis, 334-289-4846

This restored 20-room Greek Revival mansion is furnished with many original pieces. Daily.

MAGNOLIA GROVE

1002 Hobson St., Greensboro, 334-624-8618

Built for wealthy planter Col. Isaac Croom, Magnolia Grove was also the home of the builder's nephew, Richmond Pearson Hobson, a congressman and an admiral who was responsible for sinking the *Merrimac* and for blockading the Spanish fleet in Santiago Harbor in June 1898. The Greek Revival house features an unsupported winding stairway and original furnishings. Tuesday-Sunday.

SPECIAL EVENT

CHRISTMAS ON THE RIVER

102 E. Washington St., Demopolis, 334-289-0270; www.demopolischamber.com

Christmas on the River has been a tradition in this Alabama town since 1972. The weeklong celebration kicks off with the lighting of the Love Light Tree and continues with live entertainment, a candlelight antebellum home tour, a barbecue cook-off, the Jingle Bells Run/Walk, parades and a free screening of a Christmas-themed movie. Thousands of spectators gather along the river on the festival's final night to watch the nautical parade, where floats decorated with dazzling lights glide down the water. The evening ends with fireworks. Late November-early December.

ALABAMA

DOTHAN

The self-proclaimed "Peanut Capital of the World," Dothan has more going for it than just nuts. It's enjoying an economic boom, thanks to growth in retail shops and restaurants. And its prime locale—almost equidistant from Atlanta, Birmingham, Jacksonville and Mobile—makes it a popular stop for visitors, so local businesses cater to out-of-towners.

Information: Dothan Area Convention & Visitors Bureau,
3311 Ross Clark Circle N.W., 334-794-6622; www.dothanalcvb.com

WHAT TO SEE AND DO

ADVENTURELAND THEME PARK

3738 W. Main St., Dothan, 334-793-9100; www.adventurelandthemepark.com

A kid's dream, this park offers two 18-hole miniature golf courses, a go-cart track, bumper boats, batting cages, a snack bar and a game room. Bring your quarters. November-March: Monday-Friday noon-10 p.m., Saturday 10 a.m.-midnight, Sunday noon-10 p.m.; rest of year: Monday-Saturday 10 a.m.-midnight, Sunday noon-midnight.

LANDMARK PARK

430 Landmark Drive, Dothan, 334-794-3452; www.landmarkpark.com

This 100-acre park features a living-history farm from the 1890s, a natural science and history center, turn-of-the-century buildings (including a drug store with an old-fashioned soda fountain). Star gaze in the planetarium or meander along the nature trails and elevated boardwalk. Monday-Saturday 9 a.m.-5 p.m., Sunday noon-6 p.m.

★
★
★
★
★

OPERA HOUSE

115 N. St. Andrews St., Dothan, 334-793-0127

Built in 1915 and recently refurbished, this 590-seat theater hosts concerts, dance recitals and choral performances.

WESTGATE PARK

501 Recreation Road, Dothan, 334-615-3760

This recreation complex has a little something for everyone. Water World water park offers a children's pool, triple-flume slide and wave pool. The recreation center has an indoor pool and ball fields, and tennis, racquetball and basketball courts. Early May-Labor Day: daily.

SPECIAL EVENTS

AZALEA DOGWOOD FESTIVAL

Dothan Garden District, Dothan, 334-794-6622; www.dothanalcvb.com

Stroll through residential areas in late March when the flowers reach peak bloom. Late March.

NATIONAL PEANUT FESTIVAL

National Peanut Festival Fairgrounds, 5622 Highway 231 S., Dothan, 334-793-4323;
www.nationalpeanutfestival.com

Celebrate America's peanuts, half of which are grown within 100 miles of Dothan. The festival includes entertainment, sports events, arts and crafts, livestock exhibits and a parade. Late October-early November.

HOTELS

★★COMFORT INN

3593 Ross Clark Circle N.W., Dothan, 334-793-9090, 800-474-7298;
www.choicehotels.com

122 rooms. High-speed Internet access. Complimentary continental breakfast. Restaurant. Outdoor pool. Pets accepted. **$**

★★HOLIDAY INN

2195 Ross Clark Circle S.E., Dothan, 334-794-8711, 800-777-6611;
www.holiday-inn.com

144 rooms. High-speed Internet access. Complimentary full breakfast. Restaurant, bar. Outdoor pool. **$**

★★QUALITY INN

3053 Ross Clark Circle, Dothan, 334-794-6601, 800-228-5151; www.qualityinn.com

102 rooms. High-speed Internet access. Restaurant, bar. Complimentary continental breakfast. Outdoor pool. Pets accepted. **$**

EUFAULA

This city stands on a bluff rising 200 feet above Lake Eufaula, a 45,000-acre lake known throughout the area for its excellent bass fishing.

Information: Chamber of Commerce, 102 N. Orange St., 334-687-6664, 334-687-6665;
www.eufaulaalabama.com

WHAT TO SEE AND DO

EUFAULA NATIONAL WILDLIFE REFUGE

509 Old Highway 165, Eufaula, 334-687-4065; www.eufaula.fws.gov

Stretching from Alabama to Georgia, the refuge offers a feeding and resting area for waterfowl migrating between the Tennessee Valley and the Gulf Coast. See ducks, geese, egrets and herons—along with more than 275 other species of birds. The grounds also boast an observation tower, a nature trail, hunting, and great photography. Daily.

LAKEPOINT RESORT STATE PARK

104 Lakepoint Drive, Eufaula, 334-687-6676; www.dcnr.state.al.us

This 1,220-acre picturesque park rests on the shores of Lake Eufaula. Swimming, fishing, boating (marina), hiking, 18-hole golf (fee), tennis, picnicking, concessions, a restaurant, a resort inn, camping and cottages are among the park's offerings.

SETH LORE AND IRWINTON HISTORIC DISTRICT

211 N. Eufaula Ave., Eufaula

Architecture buffs should walk through the district for a look at Greek Revival, Italianate and Victorian homes, churches and commercial structures built between 1834 and 1911. Pick up a brochure of a driving tour from the Chamber of Commerce.

SHORTER MANSION

340 N. Eufaula Ave., Eufaula, 334-687-3793; www.eufaulapilgrimage.com

Built in 1906, this neoclassical mansion houses antique furnishings, Confederate relics and memorabilia of six state governors from Barbour County. Daily. Mini tours are available by appointment.

ALABAMA

★
★
★
★
★

EUFAULA PILGRIMAGE

917 W. Barbour St., Eufaula, 334-687-3793; www.eufaulapilgrimage.com

This event features daytime and candlelight tours of antebellum houses and churches, an antiques show and sales, historic reenactments and Civil War displays. First weekend in April.

INDIAN SUMMER DAYS

N. Randolph Ave., Eufaula Historic District, 334-687-6664; www.eufaulachamber.com

The festival offers arts and crafts, music, food and children's activities. First or second weekend in October.

EVERGREEN

Not surprisingly, Evergreen is named for its abundance of evergreen trees, which means it's a popular place for Alabamians in search of Christmas trees.

Information: Chamber of Commerce, 28065 Highway 74, 334-674-3412;
www.evergreenchamber.org

WHAT TO SEE AND DO

CONECUH NATIONAL FOREST

Highway 29 S., Andalusia, 334-222-2555; klat.com

This 84,400-acre forest, mostly of Southern pine, offers swimming (at Blue Pond, fee per vehicle), fishing, boating, hunting, hiking (including 20 miles of the Conecuh Trail) and campsites at Open Pond only (fee for overnight).

HOTEL

★COMFORT INN

1571 Ted Bates Road, Evergreen, 251-578-4701, 800-228-5150; www.comfortinn.com

58 rooms. Outdoor pool. Pets accepted. **$**

FLORENCE

A small town with a rich cultural life, Florence lays claim to some of Alabama's most famous residents: W.C. Handy, "Father of the Blues," was born here, and Helen Keller grew up nearby. The town is also the site of Alabama's only structure designed by Frank Lloyd Wright: the Rosenbaum House.

Information: Florence/Lauderdale Tourism, 1 Hightower Place,
256-740-4141, 888-356-8687; www.flo-tour.org

WHAT TO SEE AND DO

ELK RIVER

Florence, 15 miles west of Athens

The river provides a prime spot for fishing, boating (launch), picnicking, a playground and a group lodge. Daily; standard fees.

FIRST CREEK

Highway 72, Florence

Head to First Creek to do some beachfront swimming, boating (marina), nature and hiking trails, 18-hole golf, tennis or picnicking. The resort lodge overlooks the Tennessee River; or you can rough it at one of the camping sites (primitive and improved).

INDIAN MOUND AND MUSEUM

1028 S. Court St., Florence, 256-760-6427; www.florenceal.org

Archeologists believe the mound—the largest in the Tennessee Valley—was the site of ceremonies and other tribal exercises. Visit the museum to see artifacts thought to be thousands of years old. Tuesday-Saturday.

JOE WHEELER STATE PARK

201 Mclean Drive, Rogersville, 256-247-1184; www.joewheelerstatepark.com

Named for Confederate Gen. Joseph Wheeler of the Army of Tennessee, the 2,550-acre park is divided into three parts: Elk River, First Creek and Wheeler Dam. There's also a restaurant at the park.

NATCHEZ TRACE PARKWAY

This 444-mile parkway traces an ancient trail used by Natchez, Choctaw and Chickasaw Indians. The trail connected southern portions of the Mississippi River to central Tennessee through Alabama. Visitors can hike, bike, drive, ride horseback and camp along the trail. Stop by historic sites such as Colbert Ferry Park. Legend says George Colbert, a leading Chickasaw of the area, charged Andrew Jackson $75,000 to ferry Jackson's army across the river.

POPE'S TAVERN

203 Hermitage Drive, Florence, 256-760-6439; www.florenceal.org

Gen. Andrew Jackson stayed in this stage stop, which served as a hospital for both Union and Confederate soldiers during the Civil War. Tuesday-Saturday 10 a.m.-4 p.m.

UNIVERSITY OF NORTH ALABAMA

600 Wesleyan Ave., Florence, 256-765-4100; www.una.edu

Tours are available. Noteworthy campus spots include the University Art Gallery (Monday-Friday) and the Planetarium-Observatory (open by appointment, 256-760-4284).

W. C. HANDY HOME, MUSEUM AND LIBRARY

620 W. College St., Florence, 256-760-6434; www.florenceal.org

Blues lovers take note: The restored birthplace of the famous composer and the "Father of the Blues" houses handwritten sheet music, Handy's famous trumpet and the piano on which he composed "St. Louis Blues." Tuesday-Saturday 10 a.m.-4 p.m.

ALABAMA

★
★
★
★

WHEELER DAM

Highway 101, Elgin, 256-685-3306; www.alapark.com/JoeWheeler

Part of the Muscle Shoals complex, the dam is 72 feet high and stretches 6,342 feet across the Tennessee River. It's a good setting for swimming, fishing, boat liveries, tennis, picnic facilities and cabins.

WILSON DAM

704 S. Wilson Dam Road, Florence, 256-386-2327

Completed in 1924 and named after President Woodrow Wilson, the dam is owned and operated by the Tennessee Valley Authority. It is the TVA's only neo-classical dam; it combines hints of Greek and Roman architecture into a modern structure. Stretching 4,541 feet across the Tennessee River, the dam prevents floods, provides 650 miles of navigable channel and produces electricity for the area's residents, farms and industry.

WILSON LAKE

719 Highway 72 W., Tuscumbia, 256-383-0783; www.colbertcountytourism.org

The lake extends more than 15 miles upstream to Wheeler Dam. Go there for swimming, fishing or boating. Monday-Friday 8:30 a.m.-5 p.m., Saturdays 9 a.m.-4 p.m.

SPECIAL EVENTS

ALABAMA RENAISSANCE FAIRE

Wilson Park, 541 Riverview Drive, Florence, 256-740-4141; www.visitflorenceal.com

Renaissance-era arts and crafts, music, food, entertainment bring you back to the olde days. Fair workers in period costumes also set the mood. October.

FESTIVAL OF THE SINGING RIVER

McFarland Park, 2500 Chisholm Road, Florence,
256-760-6416, 888-356-8687; www.florenceal.org

The fest honors the history and culture of Native American. There's also a traditional dance competition and arts and crafts. October.

HELEN KELLER FESTIVAL

Spring Park, 719 Highway 72 W., Florence, 256-383-0783; www.colbertcounty.org

Celebrate Keller's legacy of courage during this three-day celebration. Music, crafts and a parade are among the festivities. Last full weekend in June.

W. C. HANDY MUSIC FESTIVAL

115 1/2 E. Mobile, Florence, 256-766-7642; www.wchandyfest.com

This weeklong festival celebrates the musical heritage of northwest Alabama, particularly Handy's legacy. The offerings are impressive: See musical performances from jazz, blues and gospel groups. First full week in August.

FOLEY

This city earns its title as the "Golf" Coast with more than a dozen golf courses. The nearby estuary ensures an abundance of hummingbirds, butterflies and flycatchers.

Information: 407 E. Laurel Ave., Foley, 251-943-1545; www.cityoffoley.org

RESTAURANT
★GIFT HORSE
209 W. Laurel, Foley, 251-943-3663; www.thegifthorserestaurant.com
American menu. Lunch, dinner, Sunday brunch. $$

FORT PAYNE
Fort Payne is in an area celebrated for natural wonders and Native American history. Sequoyah, who invented the Cherokee alphabet, lived in Will's Town, a Cherokee settlement near Fort Payne.
Information: DeKalb County Tourist Association, 2201-J Gault Ave. N.,
256-845-3957; www.fortpayne.com

WHAT TO SEE AND DO
CLOUDMONT SKI AND GOLF RESORT
721 County Road 614, Mentone, 256-634-4344; www.cloudmont.com
Skiing in the South? You bet. Cloudmont doesn't let a little thing like the weather stand in the way of a great run. It manufactures its own snow for about three months a year (mid-December to early March). The longest run is 1,000 feet, and the vertical drop 150 feet. The resort offers ski school, rentals, concessions, a snack bar and snow patrol. In the summer, visit Cloudmont for swimming, horseback riding, fishing, hiking and golf. Monday-Friday 10 a.m.-4 p.m., 6-10 p.m.

DESOTO STATE PARK
13883 County Road 89, Fort Payne, 256-845-5380; www.desotostatepark.com
This 3,502-acre park includes Lookout Mountain, Little River Canyon and DeSoto Falls and Lake. Twenty miles of hiking trails cross the mountain top and a scenic drive skirts the canyon. Enjoy the wildflowers and waterfalls, both in abundance. The park also offers a swimming pool, a bathhouse, fishing, a hiking trail, tennis, a playground, picnicking, a restaurant, a country store, a resort inn, a nature center, camping (all year) and cabins (reservations required for both).

FORT PAYNE OPERA HOUSE
510 Gault Ave. N., Fort Payne, 256-845-2741; www.fortpaynechamber.com
Alabama's oldest opera house still in use, the building was restored and reopened in 1970 as a cultural arts center. Tours of the theater include historic murals (by appointment).

LANDMARKS OF DEKALB MUSEUM
105 Fifth St. N.E., Fort Payne, 256-845-5714; www.fortpaynedepotmuseum.org
The museum features Native American artifacts from several different tribes, a turn-of-the-century house and farm items, railroad memorabilia and photographs and artwork of local historical significance. Monday, Wednesday, Friday 10 a.m.-4 p.m., Sunday 2-4 p.m.

SEQUOYAH CAVERNS
1438 County Road 731, Fort Payne, 256-635-0024; www.sequoyahcaverns.com
Tour the caverns—once occupied by local Native Americans seeking shelter—and gaze into the Looking Glass Lakes. The caverns hold thousands of rock formations, and the homestead around the caverns are home to deer, buffalo and rainbow trout

33

ALABAMA

★
★
★
★

pools. The caverns also have a swimming pool, a picnic area and camping. Guided tours are available. March-November: daily; rest of year: weekends.

SPECIAL EVENT

DEKALB COUNTY VFW AGRICULTURAL FAIR

VFW Fairgrounds, 600 Golf Ave., Fort Payne, 256-845-4752; www.fortpayne.com

The fair attracts nearly 45,000 visitors annually and features live music, a beauty pageant for ladies 65 years and older and special events for kids. Late September-early October.

GADSDEN

Named for James Gadsden, who negotiated the purchase of Arizona and New Mexico in 1853, Gadsden has a charming downtown district, and plenty of natural beauty and a few fascinating historic tales.

Information: Gadsden-Etowah Tourism Board, 256-549-0351; www.cityofgadsden.com

WHAT TO SEE AND DO

CENTER FOR CULTURAL ARTS

501 Broad St., Gadsden, 256-543-2787; www.culturalarts.com

The center offers visual art exhibits from the U.S. and Europe, concerts and theatrical performances and the renowned Etowah Youth Orchestras. Imagination Place, the children's museum, keeps kids entertained with hands-on exhibits such as a tree house and miniature "walk-through" city. Monday, Wednesday-Friday 9 a.m.-6 p.m., Tuesday 9 a.m.-9 p.m., Saturday 10 a.m.-6 p.m., Sunday 1-5 p.m.

GADSDEN MUSEUM OF ART

2829 W. Meighan Blvd., Gadsden, 256-546-7365; www.gadsdenmuseum.com

Dedicated to celebrating Southern artists and preserving the region's history, the museum is home to numerous paintings, sculptures and prints. Monday-Saturday.

HORTON MILL COVERED BRIDGE

Highway 75, Hendrix

This 22-foot-long structure is the highest covered bridge built over water in the U.S., in this case over the Black Warrior River. Daily.

NOCCALULA FALLS PARK

1500 Noccalula Road, Gadsden, 256-549-4663;
www.gadsden-etowahtourismboard.com

This 100-foot waterfall comes with a tale of star-crossed love: according to local legend, an Indian chief's daughter, named Noccalula, leaped to her death instead of betraying her true love and marrying a man of her father's choosing. Lookout Mountain Parkway, a scenic drive that stretches all the way to Chattanooga, originates here. A swimming pool, a bathhouse, nature and hiking trails, miniature golf, a picnic area, a playground, camping, hookups (fee), a petting zoo and an animal habitat house are all on offer. There's also a pioneer homestead and museum and botanical gardens. Daily.

34

ALABAMA

★
★
★
★
★

WEISS DAM AND LAKE
590 E. Main St., Centre, 256-526-8467
Swim or fish on this 30,200-acre lake. When you tire of the sun and water, you can tour the nearby power plant, which harnesses the energy produced by the dam.

GREENVILLE
Located just a half-hour south of Montgomery, Greenville is best known for being the hometown of Hank Williams Sr. Modern movement comes from the city's small business district, which offers everything from ballet and Broadway-style musicals to down-home cooking and great used bookstores.
Information: 119 E. Commerce St., Greenville, 334-382-2647;
www.greenville-alabama.com

WHAT TO SEE AND DO
HANK WILLIAMS, SR., BOYHOOD HOME & MUSEUM
127 Rose St., Georgiana, 334-376-2396
Country music legend Hank Williams Sr. lived here as a young boy. Boot-scoot your way through memorabilia, including recordings, posters and sheet music. Monday-Saturday, Sunday.

GULF SHORES
Postcard-perfect beaches are the main attraction in Gulf Shores, located on the aptly named Pleasure Island. Swimming and fishing in the Gulf are excellent, and golfers will find plenty of nearby courses to keep them busy. Nature lovers will enjoy bike paths, hiking trails and even a few prime spots for canoeing.
Information: Alabama Gulf Coast Convention & Visitors Bureau,
3150 Gulf Shores Parkway, 251-968-7511, 800-745-7263; www.gulfshores.com

★
★
★
★
☆

WHAT TO SEE AND DO
ALABAMA GULF COAST ZOO
1204 Gulf Shores Parkway, Gulf Shores,
251-968-5731; www.alabamagulfcoastzoo.com
Located a few miles from the beach, this zoo has endured violent visits from hurricanes Ivan, Dennis and Katrina in recent years, but its comeback landed it a series called *The Little Zoo That Could* on Animal Planet. Daily 9 a.m.-4 p.m.

BON SECOUR NATIONAL WILDLIFE REFUGE
12295 State Highway 180, Gulf Shores, 251-540-7720; www.fws.gov/bonsecour
One of Alabama's 10 natural wonders, Bon Secour's 7,000 acres are home to endangered and threatened animals such as the nesting sea turtles and the Alabama beach mouse. Visitors can commune with nature by swimming, hiking and even fishing here. Visitor center daily.

FORT MORGAN
Gulf Shores, 251-540-7125
Fort Morgan's most famous moment came during the Civil War's Battle of Mobile Bay, when Union Adm. Farragut commanded his troops: "Damn the torpedoes, full

speed ahead!" (Farragut was referring to the Confederates' use of mines, known then as torpedoes.) Following the battle, the fort withstood a two-week siege before surrendering to Union forces. The fort was in active use during the Spanish-American War, World War I and World War II. Daily.

FORT MORGAN MUSEUM
Gulf Shores, 251-540-7127
Just can't get enough military history? The museum, built in 1967 and designed after the 10-sided citadel damaged in 1864, displays military artifacts from the War of 1812 through World War II. Daily.

FORT MORGAN PARK
51 Highway 180, Gulf Shores
Explored by the Spanish in 1519, this area on the western tip of Mobile Point is a history buff's dream. Between 1519 and 1813, Spain, France, England and finally the U.S. held this strategic point. The park also has a fishing pier, picnicking and concessions.

GULF STATE PARK
20115 State Highway 135, Gulf Shores, 251-948-7275; www.dcnr.state.al.us
The 6,000-acre park boasts more than two miles of white-sand beaches on the Gulf and freshwater lakes. There's swimming, a bathhouse, waterskiing, surfing, fishing in Gulf of Mexico (825-foot pier) and in lakes, a marina, a boathouse, rentals, hiking, bicycling, tennis, 18-hole golf (fee), a picnic area, a pavilion, grills, a restaurant, a resort inn, cabins (for reservations, call cabin reservations at 251-948-7275) and camping (14-day maximum in season, 251-948-6353 Monday-Friday for reservations). Daily.

SPECIAL EVENTS
MARDI GRAS CELEBRATION
3150 Gulf Shores Parkway, Gulf Shores, 251-968-6904; www.gulfshores.com
Don't let New Orleans fool you: Alabama was actually the site of the first Mardi Gras celebration in this neck of the woods. In Gulf Shores, catch a parade of boats on the water and rock bands on flatbed trailers on the roads. Late February.

NATIONAL SHRIMP FESTIVAL
Highways 59 and 182, Gulf Shores, 251-968-6904; www.gulfshores.com
Although fabulous seafood is the main draw at this annual festival, visitors will also enjoy live music, a kids' art show and a sandcastle contest. Second full weekend of October.

HOTELS
★AMERICA'S BEST INN & SUITES
1517 S. McKenzie St., Foley, 251-943-3297, 888-800-8000; www.foleyabis.com
86 rooms. Wireless Internet access. Complimentary continental breakfast. Fitness center. Outdoor pool. $

★★BEST WESTERN ON THE BEACH

337 E. Beach Blvd., Gulf Shores, 251-948-2711, 800-788-4557; www.bestwestern.com
111 rooms. High-speed Internet access. Restaurant. Indoor pool, outdoor pool. **$**

RESTAURANTS

★MIKEE'S SEAFOOD

First Street and Second Avenue, Gulf Shores, 251-948-6452; www.mikeesseafood.com
Lunch, dinner. **$$**

★ORIGINAL OYSTER HOUSE

701 Gulf Shores Parkway, Gulf Shores, 251-948-2445; www.theoysterhouse.com
Seafood menu. Lunch, dinner. **$$**

★SEA-N-SUDS

405 E. Beach Blvd., Gulf Shores, 251-948-7894; www.sea-n-suds.com
Lunch, dinner. Closed Sunday (off-season). **$$**

GUNTERSVILLE

On a peninsula surrounded by water, Guntersville is a beautiful backdrop for plenty of recreational activities. Landlubbers will enjoy hiking or mountain biking in the Appalachian foothills. Visitors who prefer to play in the water will be thrilled by the sparking waters of Lake Guntersville.

The town has a unique history: Cherokee Indians and European settlers lived together peacefully here for many decades. The Cumberland River Trail, the route Andrew Jackson took on his way to the Creek War in 1813, passed through Guntersville, and Cherokees from this area joined and fought bravely with Jackson's troops against the Creeks. But in 1837, Gen. Winfield Scott—under the direction of Andrew Jackson—rounded up the area's Cherokees and moved them westward.

Information: Chamber of Commerce, 200 Gunter Ave.,
205-582-3612, 800-869-5253; www.lakeguntersville.org

WHAT TO SEE AND DO

BUCK'S POCKET STATE PARK

393 County Road 174, Guntersville, 256-659-2000; www.dcnr.state.al.us
A secluded natural pocket of the Appalachian mountain chain, this park offers breathtaking vistas. Fishing, a boat launch, hiking trails, picnic facilities, a playground, a concession, primitive and improved camping and a visitor center are all available at the park.

GUNTERSVILLE DAM AND LAKE

1155 Lodge Drive, Guntersville, 256-582-3263; www.tva.gov/sites/guntersville.htm
A playground for fishermen, swimmers and boaters, Guntersville Lake is Alabama's largest lake. The lake holds largemouth bass, bream, crappie and catfish, among other species of fish.

LAKE GUNTERSVILLE STATE PARK

Highway 227, Guntersville, 256-571-5440, 800-548-4553; www.dcnr.state.al.us
Overlooking the Guntersville Reservoir, the 6,000-acre park is a nature lover's dream. A beach, waterskiing, a fishing center, boating, hiking, bicycling, golf (18 holes),

ALABAMA

★
★
★
★

tennis, nature programs, picnicking, camping, a playground, a concession, a restaurant, chalets, lakeside cottages and a resort inn on Taylor Mountain keep the park busy.

HOTELS

★COVENANT COVE LODGE AND MARINA

7001 Val Monte Drive, Guntersville, 256-582-1000; www.covenantcove.com
53 rooms. Complimentary continental breakfast. Bar. **$**

★★HOLIDAY INN

2140 Gunter Ave., Guntersville, 256-582-2220, 888-882-1160; www.holiday-inn.com
100 rooms. High-speed Internet access. Restaurant, bar. Outdoor pool. **$**

HAMILTON

Settled in the 1880s, Hamilton spans "Military Road," a passage carved out of the wilderness by volunteer soldiers from Tennessee returning to their homes after fighting the British in New Orleans in 1815. General. Andrew Jackson ordered the road created as a shortcut between New Orleans and Nashville and today a bike and hiking path is under way to commemorate this historic path.

Information: Hamilton, 205-921-2121; www.cityofhamilton.org

WHAT TO SEE AND DO

HORSESHOE BEND NATIONAL MILITARY PARK

11288 Horseshoe Bend Road, Daviston, 256-234-7111; www.nps.gov/hobe
The park is the site of a 1814 clash between General Andrew Jackson's army and Upper Creek Indian warriors—the bloodiest battle of the Creek War. Jackson's army of 3,300 men attacked about 1,000 Upper Creek warriors, who had vowed to defend their land and their customs from the growing number of white settlers. More than 800 Upper Creeks died, making this the deadliest single battle for Native Americans in U.S. history. The peace treaty that followed cost the Creeks more than 20 million acres of land, opening a vast and rich domain to settlement—a move that eventually led to Alabama's statehood in 1819. For Jackson, Horseshoe Bend was the beginning; for the Creek Nation, it was the beginning of the end. Thanks in part to his military fame, Jackson was elected president of the United States in 1829. A year later, he signed the Indian Removal Bill, which forced all Native American tribes living east of the Mississippi River to move to Oklahoma. The Cherokees named this trek the "Trail of Tears." Located on the banks of the Tallapoosa River, the park contains 2,040 acres of forested hills. A museum at the visitor center depicts the battle with a slide presentation and an electric map exhibit. A three-mile loop road tour with seven interpretive markers crosses the battle area. Nature trails, picnic areas and a boat ramp are all available. Daily.

NATURAL BRIDGE OF ALABAMA

Highway 278 W. Natural Bridge, 205-486-5330
Two spans of sandstone, the longest 148 feet, were created by natural erosion of a tributary stream more than 200 million years ago. Picnicking is available. Daily.

★
★
★
★
★

HOTEL

★★ECONO LODGE INN & SUITES

2031 Military St. S., Hamilton, 205-921-7831, 800-553-2666; www.econolodge.com

80 rooms. High-speed Internet access. Restaurant. Pets accepted. **$**

HUNTSVILLE

Huntsville might deceive you. This little city at the foot of a mountain in northern Alabama is intimately involved in space exploration, thanks to NASA's Space and Rocket Center, which is headquartered here. Aspiring astronauts (or just curious earth-bound folks) head to Huntsville for Space Camp, where kids and families learn what it takes to cruise the universe. But rockets aren't the only attraction here. Huntsville is rich in Civil War history, natural beauty, golf courses and good ol' Southern cooking. Don't miss the hush puppies, fried catfish and pecan pie.

Information: Convention & Visitors Bureau, 700 Monroe St., 256-551-2230,
800-772-2348; www.huntsville.org

WHAT TO SEE AND DO

ALABAMA CONSTITUTION VILLAGE

109 Gates Ave., Huntsville, 256-564-8100; www.earlyworks.com

This re-created complex of buildings commemorates Alabama's entry into the Union at the 1819 Constitutional Convention. The village offers period craft demonstrations and activities, and guides in period dress. Saturday 9 a.m.-4 p.m.; June-August: Saturday 10 a.m.-5 p.m.

BIG SPRING INTERNATIONAL PARK

500 Church St., Huntsville, 256-533-5723; www.huntsville.org

This natural spring produces 24 million gallons daily, and is the town's water supply. John Hunt—Huntsville's namesake—built the town around this spring.

BURRITT MUSEUM & PARK

3101 Burritt Drive, Huntsville, 256-536-2882; www.burrittonthemountain.com

The 167-acre park atop Round Top Mountain offers a little something for everyone. The former home of eccentric Dr. William Henry Burritt, the mansion houses rotating exhibits, most of which have regional or local themes. The historic park has restored 19th-century buildings—including a blacksmith shop and a smokehouse—and volunteers in period dress. You'll also find nature trails, gardens and a panoramic view of city. Museum: April-October: Tuesday-Saturday 9 a.m.-5 p.m., Sunday 9 a.m.-noon; November-March: Tuesday-Saturday 10 a.m.-4 p.m., Sunday 9 a.m.-noon. Grounds: daily.

HISTORIC HUNTSVILLE DEPOT

320 Church St., Huntsville, 256-564-8100, 800-678-1819; www.earlyworks.com

Opened in 1860 as a "passenger house" and eastern division headquarters for the Memphis & Charleston Railroad Company, the Huntsville depot was captured by Union troops and used as a prison; Civil War graffiti is still there. Kids can climb aboard real trains and Huntsville's first ladder truck. Tuesday-Saturday 10 a.m.-4 p.m.; closed thaks giving, December 24-25; also January and February.

ALABAMA

★
★
★
★

HUNTSVILLE MUSEUM OF ART

300 Church St., Huntsville, 256-535-4350; www.hsvmuseum.org

Named one of the state's top 10 destinations by the Alabama Bureau of Tourism and Travel, the museum has seven galleries, which host traveling exhibits and display work from the museum's own collection. Tours, lectures, concerts, films round out the offerings. Monday-Wednesday, Friday-Saturday 10 a.m.-5 p.m., Sunday 1-5 p.m.

MADISON COUNTY NATURE TRAIL

5000 Nature Trail Road, Huntsville, 256-883-9501;
www.co.madison.al.us

This was the original house on the first homestead. The grounds include a chapel, a covered bridge, a 16-acre lake, a waterfall, spring houses, wooded hiking trails and a Braille trail. Daily.

MONTE SANO STATE PARK

5105 Nolan Ave., Huntsville, 256-534-3757; www.dcnr.state.al.us

Spanish for "mountain of health," Monte Sano reaches 1,600 feet above sea level. Hiking trails, picnicking (tables, shelters, barbecue pits, fireplaces), a playground, concessions, camping, cabins and an amphitheater keep the park humming. Park open all year.

TWICKENHAM HISTORIC DISTRICT

500 Church St., Huntsville, 256-551-2230; www.huntsville.org

A living museum of antebellum architecture, the district contains Alabama's largest concentration of antebellum houses. Several of the houses are occupied by descendants of original builders or owners. Tours can be self-guided; guided tours available for groups. Contact the Convention and Visitors Bureau.

★
★
★
★
★

U.S. SPACE AND ROCKET CENTER

1 Tranquility Base, Huntsville, 256-837-3400, 800-637-7223; www.spacecamp.com

If you've ever dreamed of climbing aboard a rocket and blasting off, this is the place for you. Experience a rocket launch in Space Spot, a simulated ride that shoots riders 140 feet in the air in 2.5 seconds. Visit the Mars exhibit, where you can climb Olympus Mons, the tallest volcano in the solar system. In the museum, check out the Apollo capsule and space shuttle objects returned from orbit. The Omnimax Theater, with a tilted dome screen, seats 280 and shows 45-minute space shuttle and science films photographed by astronauts. NASA bus tours take visitors through Marshall Space Flight Center, featuring mission control, space station construction and the tank where astronauts simulate weightlessness. The U.S. Space Camp offers programs for children fourth grade and up, families and even corporate executives. Daily 9 a.m.-5 p.m.

VON BRAUN CENTER

700 Monroe St., Huntsville, 256-533-1953; www.vonbrauncenter.com

This is the largest multipurpose complex in northern Alabama, named for noted space pioneer Dr. Wernher von Braun. The center hosts concerts, touring Broadway performances, ballets and other shows. For information on upcoming events, call the Tourist Information Center at 256-533-5723.

SPECIAL EVENTS

BIG SPRING JAM

Big Spring International Park, 700 Monroe St., Huntsville, 256-533-1953;
www.bigspringjam.org

Three days, five stages, more than 80 musical acts—what else do you want? Wynonna Judd, Lynyrd Skynyrd and Jewel have performed in recent years. Late September.

PANOPLY ARTS FESTIVAL

Big Spring International Park, 700 Monroe St., Huntsville, 256-519-2787;
www.panoply.org

A haven for art lovers of all kinds, the festival showcases work by visual artists, dancers, musicians and actors. Enjoy dance performances at the choreography competition and interactive art activities at Artrageous. Don't miss the final round of excitement at Panoply Idol. Last full weekend of April.

HOTELS

★★COURTYARD BY MARRIOTT

4804 University Drive, Huntsville, 256-837-1400, 800-321-2211; www.marriott.com
149 rooms. High-speed Internet access. Restaurant, bar. Outdoor pool, whirlpool. **$**

★★FOUR POINTS BY SHERATON

1000 Glenn Hearn Blvd., Huntsville, 256-772-9661, 888-625-5144;
www.fourpoints.com
148 rooms. Restaurant, bar. **$**

★GUESTHOUSE INTERNATIONAL

4020 Independence Drive N.W., Huntsville, 256-837-8907, 800-331-3131;
www.guesthouseintl.com
112 rooms. Complimentary continental breakfast. Airport transportation available. Pets accepted, fee. **$**

★★HOLIDAY INN EXPRESS

3808 University Drive, Huntsville, 256-721-1000, 800-345-7720; www.hiexpress.com
112 rooms. Restaurant, bar. Airport transportation available. **$**

★★HOLIDAY INN HUNTSVILLE

401 Williams Ave., Huntsville, 256-533-1400; www.holidayinn.com
279 rooms. Restaurant, bar. Airport transportation available. **$**

★LA QUINTA INN

3141 University Drive N.W., Huntsville, 256-533-0756, 800-687-6667;
www.laquinta.com
130 rooms. Complimentary continental breakfast. **$**

ALABAMA

★★★MARRIOTT HUNTSVILLE

5 Tranquility Base, Huntsville, 256-830-2222; www.marriott.com

Enjoy the comfort of this fine hotel, with rooms specifically designed for the business traveler. The Space and Rocket Museum is next door. 290 rooms. High-speed Internet access. Restaurant, bar. Airport transportation available. $

★QUALITY INN UNIVERSITY

3788 University Drive, Huntsville, 256-533-3291, 800-228-5150; www.qualityinn.com

67 rooms. Complimentary continental breakfast. $

★★RADISSON SUITE HOTEL HUNTSVILLE

6000 Memorial Parkway S., Huntsville, 256-882-9400, 800-333-3333;
www.radisson.com

153 suites. Restaurant, bar. Airport transportation available. $

RESTAURANT

★★OL' HEIDELBERG

6125 University Drive N.W., Huntsville, 256-922-0556

American, German menu. Dinner. $$

MOBILE

Mobile, Alabama's largest port city, blends old Southern grace with new Southern enterprise. The city began in 1702 as the first capital of French Louisiana. Thanks to its prime location on the water and easy access to the Gulf of Mexico, it flourished. After the Civil War, Mobile grew into a shipbuilding port, and increased military production buoyed the town's economy during World War II. In fact, one of the nation's first submarines was built in Mobile. Today, Mobile is a vibrant industrial seaport that has preserved its air of antebellum graciousness. Its historic charm is on display in the Church Street, DeTonti Square, Oakleigh Garden and Old Dauphinway historical districts. So indulge in some fresh Gulf seafood, enjoy the city's diverse architectural styles and breathe in the salty air of Alabama's "Port City."

Information: Convention & Visitors Corporation, 1 S. Water St., 251-208-2000,
800-566-2453; www.mobile.org

WHAT TO SEE AND DO

BATTLESHIP MEMORIAL PARK, USS *ALABAMA*

2703 Battleship Parkway, Mobile bay, 251-433-2703; www.ussalabama.com

Visitors may tour the 35,000-ton USS *Alabama*, which serves as a memorial to the state's men and women who served in World War II, the Korean conflict, Vietnam and Desert Storm. Don't miss the submarine USS *Drum*, World War II aircraft, a B-52 bomber and an A-12 Blackbird spy plane. October-March: daily 8 a.m.-4 p.m.; April-September: daily 8 a.m.-6 p.m.

BELLINGRATH GARDENS AND HOME

12401 Bellingrath Gardens Road, Mobile, 251-973-2217, 800-247-8420;
www.bellingrath.org

Travels to world-famous gardens abroad inspired the Bellingraths to create these majestic gardens in the 1920s. Approximately 250,000 azalea plants of 200 varieties bloom on the estate alongside camellias, roses and water lilies. In the center of the gardens, you'll find the Bellingrath house, furnished with antiques, fine china and rare porcelain. The riverboat *Southern Belle* provides 45-minute cruises along the nearby Fowl River. Daily 8 a.m.-5 p.m.

BRAGG-MITCHELL MANSION

1906 Springhill Ave., Mobile, 251-471-6364; www.braggmitchellmansion.com
This Greek Revival 20-room mansion sits amid 12 acres of landscaped grounds. The restored interior includes extensive faux-grained woodwork and stenciled moldings as well as period furnishings. Tours: Tuesday-Friday 10 a.m.-4 p.m.

CATHEDRAL OF THE IMMACULATE CONCEPTION

2 S. Claiborne, Mobile, 251-434-1565; www.mobilecathedral.org
Begun in 1835 and consecrated in 1850, the cathedral has German art-glass windows, a bronze canopy over the altar and hand-carved stations of the cross. Daily; limited hours Monday-Friday.

CLAUDE D. KELLEY STATE PARK

580 H. Kyle, Atmore, 251-862-2511; www.dcnr.state.al.us
A 25-acre lake sits beneath the towering pines of this 960-acre park. Swimming, fishing, boating (ramps, rentals), picnicking, primitive camping and cabins are among some of the offerings.

CONDE-CHARLOTTE MUSEUM HOUSE

104 Theatre St., Mobile, 251-432-4722; www.condecharlottemuseum.com
Mobile's first jail, the museum house now gives visitors a quick look at Mobile through its history, period kitchen and Spanish garden. Tuesday-Saturday 10 a.m.-4 p.m.

43

MALBIS GREEK ORTHODOX CHURCH

10145 Highway 90, Daphne, 251-626-3050
Inspired by a similar church in Athens, Greece, this Byzantine church is a Greek wonder. Pentelic marble is from the same quarries that supplied the Parthenon. Skilled artists from Greece created the authentic paintings; hand-carved figures and ornaments were brought from Greece. Visitors enjoy the stained-glass windows, dome with murals and many works of art depicting the life of Christ. Guided tours are by appointment. Daily.

MOBILE MEDICAL MUSEUM

1664 Springhill Ave., Mobile, 251-415-1109; www.mobilemedicalmuseum.com
Prepare to be fascinated—and a little grossed out. The museum houses rare medical artifacts, tools and photographs. Imagine life as a Civil War solider when you see the tools a Civil War surgeon used, including bullet extractors and amputation saws. Monday-Friday 10 a.m.-4 p.m.

ALABAMA

★
★
★
★

MOBILE MUSEUM OF ART

4850 Museum Drive, Mobile, 251-208-5200; www.mobilemuseumofart.com

The permanent collection includes African and Asian art, contemporary glass as well as American and European 19th-century paintings and prints. It also houses traveling exhibits. Monday-Saturday 10 a.m.-5 p.m., Sunday 1-5 p.m.

MUSEUM OF MOBILE

111 S. Royal St., Mobile, 251-208-7569; www.museumofmobile.com

See 300 years of history in one place: You'll find artifacts from Mobile's French, British, Spanish and Confederate periods; costumes from Mardi Gras celebrations; ship models and arms collection. Guided tours are by appointment. It's in the Bernstein-Bush House (1872), an Italianate town house. Free admission first Sunday of each month. Monday-Saturday 9 a.m.-5 p.m., Sunday 1-5 p.m.

PHOENIX FIRE MUSEUM

111 S. Royal St., Mobile, 251-208-7569; www.museumofmobile.com

This museum showcases firefighting equipment, memorabilia dating from Mobile's first volunteer company, steam fire engines and a collection of silver trumpets and helmets. It's housed in a restored fire station from the 1800s. Guided tours are available by appointment. Tuesday-Saturday 10 a.m.-5 p.m., Sunday from 1-5 p.m.

RICHARDS-DAR HOUSE

256 N. Joachim St., Mobile, 251-208-7320; www.richardsdarhouse.com

This restored Italianate town house features elaborate ironwork, a curved suspended staircase and period furniture. Monday-Friday 11 a.m.-3:30 p.m., Saturday 10 a.m.-4 p.m., Sunday 1-4 p.m.

UNIVERSITY OF SOUTH ALABAMA

307 University Blvd., Mobile, 251-460-6101; www.southalabama.edu

Theater productions are presented during the school year at Laidlaw Performing Arts Center (334-460-6305) and at Saenger Theatre (334-438-5686). Of architectural interest on campus are Seaman's Bethel Theater (1860); the Plantation Creole House (1828), a reconstructed Creole cottage; and Mobile town house (1870), a federal-style building showing Italianate and Greek Revival influences that also houses the USA campus art gallery. Tours of campus are available.

SPECIAL EVENTS

AZALEA TRAIL RUN FESTIVAL AND FESTIVAL OF FLOWERS

1 S. Water St., Mobile, 800-566-2453; www.mobilebay.org

Strap on your running shoes and enjoy the Azalea Trail 10 K Run, one of the nation's premier road races. Not much of an athlete? You can still enjoy this fragrant event. A 35-mile-long driving tour winds through the floral streets in and around Mobile; printed guides are available. The Convention & Visitors Corporation has further details and maps for self-guided tours of the Azalea Trail and local historic sites. Late March.

BAY FEST

2900 Dauphin St., Mobile, 251-470-7730; www.bayfest.com

Musicians occupy nine stages for three days every fall. Past performers include B.B. King, 3 Doors Down and Keith Urban. First full weekend in October.

BLESSING OF THE FLEET

13790 S. Wintzell, Bayou La Batre, 251-824-2415; www.fleetblessing.org

A special Mass, a live crab race and a parade are just some of the activities at this annual church festival. Early May.

GREATER GULF STATE FAIR

1035 Cody Road, Mobile, 251-344-4573; www.mobilefair.com

The state fair has all the makings of a great time: carnival rides, a rodeo, livestock shows, food and entertainment. Late October.

SENIOR BOWL FOOTBALL GAME

Ladd-Peebles Stadium, 1621 Virginia St., Mobile, 251-438-2276, 888-736-2695; www.seniorbowl.com

This unique annual football game stars all of the nation's leading NFL draft prospects on teams coached by NFL coaches. Late January.

HOTELS

★★ASHBURY HOTELS AND SUITES

600 W I-65 Service Road S., Mobile, 251-344-8030; www.ashburyhotel.com

236 rooms. Restaurant, bar. Airport transportation available. **$**

★DAYS INN AND SUITES MOBILE

5472-A Inn Road, Mobile, 251-660-1520; www.daysinn.com

118 rooms. High-speed Internet access. Fitness center. Outdoor pool. Business center. **$**

★HAMPTON INN

930 S. Beltline Highway, Mobile, 251-344-4942, 800-426-7866; www.hamptoninn.com

118 rooms. High-speed Internet access. Complimentary continental breakfast. Fitness center. Outdoor pool. Spa. Business center. **$**

★★HOLIDAY INN

5465 Highway 90 W., Mobile, 251-666-5600, 800-465-4329; www.holiday-inn.com

160 rooms. High-speed Internet access. Restaurant, bar. Airport transportation available. Fitness center. Outdoor pool. Business center. **$**

★LA QUINTA INN

816 S. Beltline Highway, Mobile, 251-343-4051, 800-531-5900; www.laquinta.com

122 rooms. High-speed Internet access. Complimentary continental breakfast. Fitness center. Outdoor pool. Pets accepted. **$**

★
★
★
★

★★★MARRIOTT GRAND HOTEL
1 Grand Blvd., Point Clear, 251-928-9201, 800-544-9933; www.marriott.com
Guests can indulge in fun and relaxation at this hotel on 550 landscaped acres on Mobile Bay. A historic Civil War cemetery is onsite. 306 rooms. High-speed Internet access. Restaurant, bar. Children's activity center. Airport transportation available. **$**

★★RADISSON ADMIRAL SEMMES HOTEL
251 Government St., Mobile, 251-432-8000, 800-333-3333; www.radisson.com
170 rooms. High-speed Internet access. Restaurant, bar. Outdoor pool. **$**

★★RIVERVIEW PLAZA
64 S. Water St., Mobile, 251-438-4000, 800-922-3298; www.marriott.com
375 rooms. High-speed Internet access. Restaurant, bar. **$$**

RESTAURANTS
★★★THE PILLARS
1757 Government St., Mobile, 251-471-3411; www.thepillarsmobile.com
Treat yourself to a delicious meal in a beautiful historic house. The menu reads like a surf-and-turf lover's dream: Gulf crab, shrimp, plenty of fresh fish and any cut of steak you could want. Owner Filippo Milone is the perfect host, warmly greeting guests and watching over his excellent staff. American menu. Dinner. Closed Sunday. **$$**

★★★RUTH'S CHRIS STEAK HOUSE
271 Glenwood St., Mobile, 251-476-0516; www.ruthschris.com
Now an international presence, this restaurant group started in New Orleans, so portions are generous and the menu is dotted with food inspired by the founder's hometown. The custom-aged Midwestern beef is never frozen and cooked in a 1,800-degree broiler to customers' tastes. Steak menu. Dinner. **$$$**

★
★
★
★
★

MONTGOMERY
Known as the birthplace of the Civil War and civil rights, Montgomery is not just Alabama's state capital; it is a city that holds history important to the entire nation. It served as the Confederacy's first capital, from which Confederate leaders sent the "Fire on Fort Sumter" telegram that began the Civil War. About 100 years later, when black seamstress Rosa Parks refused to give up her bus seat to a white man, Montgomery again found itself embroiled in battle, this time for civil rights.

Montgomery has turned that turbulent history into rich cultural offerings. Here you'll find the nation's first Civil Rights Memorial, the famed Alabama Shakespeare Festival, fine art museums and historic buildings.
Information: Montgomery Area Chamber of Commerce, 41 Commerce St., Montgomery, 334-834-5200; www.montgomerychamber.com

WHAT TO SEE AND DO
ALABAMA DEPARTMENT OF ARCHIVES AND HISTORY
624 Washington Ave., Montgomery, 334-242-4363; www.archives.state.al.us
This place houses a historical museum and genealogical research facilities. Artifact collections include exhibits on the 19th century, the military and early Native American. It also has an interactive children's gallery. Monday-Friday 8.30 a.m.-4.30 p.m., first Saturday of the month 8.30 a.m.-4.30 p.m.

ALABAMA SHAKESPEARE FESTIVAL

1 Festival Drive, Montgomery, 800-841-4273; www.asf.net

What started as a six-week summer festival held in a stuffy high school auditorium has become one the nation's finest year-round theaters. Each year, ASF actors perform three Shakespearean plays in addition to other classics by playwrights such as Tennessee Williams, George Bernard Shaw and Thornton Wilder. The company also produces musicals and commissions new works.

CIVIL RIGHTS MEMORIAL

400 Washington Ave., Montgomery; www.tolerance.org/memorial

Designed by Vietnam Veterans Memorial artist Maya Lin, the memorial is inscribed with the names of people who lost their lives in the fight for civil rights.

DEXTER AVENUE KING MEMORIAL BAPTIST CHURCH

454 Dexter Ave., Montgomery, 334-263-3970; www.dexterkingmemorial.org

See the pulpit from which Dr. Martin Luther King Jr. first preached his message of nonviolent activism. King directed the Montgomery bus boycott from this church, where he served as pastor from 1954 to 1960. The church is now home to the mural and original painting "The Beginning of a Dream." To see the church, go on a guided tour (Monday-Thursday 10 a.m. and 2 p.m.), walk through (Friday 10 a.m.) or make an appointment (Saturday 10:30 a.m.-1:30 p.m.). Sunday worship is at 10:30 a.m.

F. SCOTT AND ZELDA FITZGERALD MUSEUM

919 Felder Ave., Montgomery, 334-264-4222

The famous author and his wife lived in this house from 1931 to 1932. The museum contains personal artifacts detailing the couple's public and private lives. It includes paintings by Zelda, letters and photographs, plus a 25-minute video presentation. Wednesday-Sunday.

FIRST WHITE HOUSE OF THE CONFEDERACY

644 Washington Ave., Montgomery, 334-242-1861

Confederacy President Jefferson Davis and his family lived here while Montgomery was the Confederate capital. Moved from its original location at Bibb and Lee streets in 1920, it is now a Confederate museum containing period furnishings, Confederate mementos, personal belongings and paintings of the Davis family. Monday-Friday 8 a.m.-4:30 p.m.

FORT TOULOUSE/JACKSON PARK NATIONAL HISTORIC LANDMARK

2521 W. Fort Toulouse Road, Montgomery, 334-567-3002; www.fttoulousejackson.org

At the confluence of the Coosa and Tallapoosa rivers, Fort Toulouse was originally a French fort, built in 1717 to keep those pesky Brits at bay. The French abandoned it in 1763, and more than 50 years later, Andrew Jackson built a fort on the same site. Today, visitors can see a reconstructed Fort Toulouse and a partially reconstructed Fort Jackson. Don't miss the mounds, nearly 1,000 years old. The park features a boat ramp, nature walks, picnicking, improved camping and a museum. A living history program can be seen the third weekend of each month. Daily.

ALABAMA

★
★
★
☆
☆

HANK WILLIAMS' GRAVE

Oakwood Cemetery, 1305 Upper Wetumpka Road,
Montgomery
This is the gravesite memorial to the country music legend.

LOWER COMMERCE STREET HISTORIC DISTRICT

100 block of Commerce St., Montgomery
The wholesale and railroad district sits along the Alabama River. Its buildings, primarily Victorian in style, date from the 1880s to the turn of the century.

MAXWELL AIR FORCE BASE

55 S. LeMay Plaza, Montgomery, 334-953-1110; www.au.af.mil
Wilbur Wright began the world's first flying school on this site in 1910. His brother Orville made his first flight in Montgomery on March 26, 1910. Named in 1922 for Lieutenant William C. Maxwell of Alabama, who was killed while serving in the Third Aero Squadron in the Philippines, it is now the site of Air University. Daily.

MONTGOMERY MUSEUM OF FINE ARTS

1 Museum Drive, Montgomery, 334-244-5700; www.mmfa.org
The museums holds collections of 19th- and 20th-century American art, European works on paper, regional and decorative arts. It also offers hands-on children's exhibits, lectures and concerts. Admission: free. Tuesday, Friday-Saturday 10 a.m.-5 p.m., Thursday 10 a.m.-9 p.m., Saturday noon-5 p.m.

MONTGOMERY ZOO

2301 Coliseum Parkway, Montgomery, 334-240-4900; www.montgomeryal.gov
More than 500 animals from five continents reside here in natural, barrier-free habitats. The zoo's Overlook Café gives visitors a unique peek at the zoo, and a train ride helps them get a lay of the land. Daily 9 a.m.-5 p.m.

MURPHY HOUSE

22 Bibb St., Montgomery, 334-206-1600; www.mobilebay.org
This fine example of Greek Revival architecture with fluted Corinthian columns and wrought-iron balcony is now the headquarters of the Montgomery Water Works. Monday-Friday.

OLD ALABAMA TOWN

301 Columbus St., Montgomery, 334-240-4500, 888-240-1850;
www.oldalabamatown.com
In the heart of historic Montgomery, this six-block stretch of restored 19th- and 20th-century buildings includes an 1820s log cabin, an urban church circa 1890, a country doctor's office and a corner grocer, among many others. Hosts in period dress give visitors an inside look into Alabama's history. A taped driving tour of historic Montgomery also available. Monday-Saturday 9 a.m.-3 p.m.

ST. JOHN'S EPISCOPAL CHURCH

113 Madison Ave., Montgomery, 334-262-1937; www.stjohnsmontgomery.org

Built in 1855, this church has seen much of Alabama's history up close. Confederacy President Jefferson Davis worshipped here with his family. Today, visitors come to see the church's stained-glass windows, Gothic pipe organ and Jefferson's pew. Sunday-Friday.

STATE CAPITOL

468 S. Perry St., Montgomery, 334-242-3935; www.preserveala.org

This has been the seat of Alabama's government for more than 100 years.

SPECIAL EVENTS

ALABAMA NATIONAL FAIR

Garrett Coliseum, 1555 Federal Drive, Montgomery, 334-272-6831; www.alnationalfair.org

Don't miss the festivities, which include concerts, a circus, children's rides and the famed pig races. October.

JUBILEE CITY FEST

640 S. McDonough St., Montgomery, 334-834-7220; www.jubileecityfest.org

This annual festival features national musical acts as well as cultural events and children's activities. Mid-spring.

SOUTHEASTERN LIVESTOCK EXPOSITION AND RODEO

Garrett Coliseum, 1555 Federal Drive, Montgomery, 334-265-1867; www.bamabeef.org

Some of the nation's best cowboys and cowgirls compete in this PRCA event, the largest rodeo east of the Mississippi. Mid-March.

HOTELS

★ECONO LODGE & SUITES

5924 Monticello Drive, Montgomery, 334-272-1013; www.choicehotels.com

46 suites. Complimentary continental breakfast. Fitness center. Outdoor pool. Business center. Pets accepted. **$**

★FAIRFIELD INN

5601 Carmichael Road, Montgomery,
205-270-0007, 800-228-2800; www.fairfieldinn.com

133 rooms. High-speed Internet access. Complimentary continental breakfast. **$**

★★HOLIDAY INN

1185 Eastern Bypass, Montgomery, 334-272-0370, 800-465-4329; www.himontgomery.com

211 rooms. Restaurant, bar. **$**

★KINGS INN

1355 East Blvd., Montgomery, 334-277-2200, 800-240-2200; www.ramada.com

152 rooms. High-speed Internet access. Complimentary full breakfast. Bar. Pets accepted. **$**

★LA QUINTA INN

1280 Eastern Blvd., Montgomery, 334-271-1620, 800-531-5980; www.laquinta.com

130 rooms. High-speed Internet access. Complimentary continental breakfast. Outdoor pool. Pets accepted. **$**

★★RAMADA

1100 W. South Blvd., Montgomery, 334-281-1660, 800-272-6232; www.ramada.com

150 rooms. Restaurant, bar. Airport transportation available. **$**

SPECIALITY LODGINGS

LATTICE INN

1414 S. Hull St., Montgomery, 334-262-3388; www.latticeinn.com

Located in the historic Garden District, this home was built in 1906 and is furnished with antiques and family pieces. A large Southern breakfast is served each morning. Four rooms. **$**

RED BLUFF COTTAGE BED AND BREAKFAST

551 Clay St., Montgomery, 334-264-0056, 888-551-2529; www.redbluffcottage.com

This 19th-century Victorian cottage in downtown Montgomery has six rooms with Southern themes. The large veranda offers a panoramic view of the Alabama River plain and the state capital. Guests enjoy a hearty Southern breakfast each morning. Six rooms. High-speed Internet access. **$**

RESTAURANTS

★★ALA THAI

1361 Federal Drive, Montgomery, 334-262-5830; www.thaicuisine.com

Thai menu. Lunch, dinner. **$**

★MARTHA'S PLACE

458 Sayre St., Montgomery, 334-263-9135; www.mgm4lunch.com/marthas.htm

American menu. Breakfast, lunch. Saturday-Sunday by reservation only. **$**

★★★VINTAGE YEAR

405 Cloverdale Road, Montgomery, 334-264-8463

Located in Montgomery's historic Cloverdale District, this restaurant serves unique appetizers and desserts. The modern décor with intimate lighting makes it a great spot for a romantic dinner. Seafood menu. Dinner. Closed Sunday-Monday. **$$**

ORANGE BEACH

This town on the Gulf Coast offers plenty of white sand and warm breezes. Orange Beach and its neighbor town, Gulf Shores, make up one of Alabama's best playgrounds. Golf, hike, swim, fish—or just lounge on the beach.

Information: Orange Beach, 251-981-6979; www.cityoforangebeach.com

HOTELS

★★HILTON GARDEN INN ORANGE BEACH BEACHFRONT

23092 Perdido Beach Blvd., Orange Beach, 251-974-1600; www.hiltongardeninn.com
137 rooms. High-speed Internet access. Fitness center. Outdoor pool. Business center. **$**

★★★PERDIDO BEACH RESORT

27200 Perdido Beach Blvd., Orange Beach, 251-981-9811, 800-634-8001;
www.perdidobeachresort.com
Directly on the Gulf of Mexico, this wonderful Mediterranean-style resort offers everything you need for a relaxing beachside vacation. Enjoy the white sand beaches, boating, deep-sea fishing, parasailing and scuba diving. 345 rooms. Restaurant, bar. Children's activity center. **$$**

RESTAURANTS

★HAZEL'S FAMILY RESTAURANT

25311 Perdido Beach Blvd., Orange Beach, 251-981-4628;
www.hazelsseafoodrestaurant.com
American menu. Breakfast, lunch, dinner. **$$**

★★ZEKE'S LANDING

26619 Perdido Beach Blvd., Orange Beach, 251-981-4044; www.zekeslanding.com
Seafood menu. Dinner, Sunday brunch. **$$**

OZARK

Named one of the top 25 places to retire by *Consumer's Digest*, Ozark is a small town dotted with Antebellum buildings and a large lake, complete with lakeside park and walking trails.
Information: Ozark Area Chamber of Commerce, 308 Painter Ave., 334-774-9321,
800-582-8497; www.ozarkalabama.org

WHAT TO SEE AND DO

BLUE SPRINGS STATE PARK

2595 Highway 10, Clio, 334-397-4875; www.dcnr.state.al.us
This 103-acre park features a spring-fed pool, a swimming pool, a bathhouse, tennis, picnic facilities, a playground, a softball field and primitive and improved campsites.

RUSSELL CAVE NATIONAL MONUMENT

3729 County Road 98, Bridgeport, 256-495-2672; www.nps.gov/ruca
Archeological field studies show that this cave shelter was home to North American inhabitants for more than 10,000 years, from about 6,500 B.C. to A.D. 1650 The visitor center has displays detailing the daily life of the cave's prehistoric occupants, including exhibitions of weapons, tools and cooking processes. Visitors can tour the cave shelter and, with a special permit, three miles of the Russell Caves. Area and visitor center daily.

ALABAMA

★
★
★
★

★★★THE GRAND DINING ROOM

1 Grand Blvd., Point Clear, 251-928-9201; www.marriott.com

Part of the Marriott's Grand Hotel Resort & Golf Club, this signature restaurant with a view offers generous buffet dining during breakfast and lunch and romantic, festive dinners. American menu. Breakfast, lunch, dinner. Closed Sunday-Monday. **$$**

RUSSELLVILLE

Calling itself a "big small city," Russellville boasts a popular fine arts center and plenty of options to keep you busy in the great outdoors.

Information: Franklin County Area Chamber of Commerce, 256-332-1760;
www.russellvillegov.com

WHAT TO SEE AND DO

CEDAR CREEK

Highway 24 and County 41, Russellville, 256-332-9809; www.cedarcreekwings.org

The 4,300-acre reservoir has five recreation areas where you can do swimming, use bathhouses (Slick Rock Ford), do boat launches (at dam, Slick Rock Ford, Lost Creek, Hellums Mill, Britton Bridge); picnic and camp.

UPPER BEAR CREEK

I-43, Russellville

The 1,850-acre reservoir Offers a boat launch (Twin Forks, Quarter Creek, Batestown, Mon Dye), picnicking, camping, tables and grills (Twin Forks). The float stream is 28 miles below the dam.

52

ALABAMA

★
★
★
★

SELMA

High on a bluff above the Alabama River, Selma has had a front-row seat to some of American history's most tumultuous battles. During the Civil War, Selma was one of the Confederacy's prime military manufacturing centers, which made it a target for Union armies. The city fell on April 2, 1865, during a bloody siege by Union forces, which destroyed Selma's arsenal and factories, along with much of the city. With defeat came an end to the era of wealthy plantation owners and leisurely living. One hundred years after Selma fell to Union forces, it was entangled in another battle. On March 7, 1965, nearly 600 African-American residents of Selma marched east toward Montgomery. In the weeks before the march, discrimination and intimidation had prevented much of Selma's black population from registering to vote, and the marchers hoped Gov. George Wallace would take notice of their plight when they arrived in the state's capital. Instead, Wallace declared the march a threat to public safety, and the marchers only made it as far as Selma's Edmund Pettus Bridge before they were driven back into town by police officers with clubs, whips and tear gas. This violence gave the day its name: "Bloody Sunday." Marchers, led by Dr. Martin Luther King Jr. tried again unsuccessfully two days later. They finally made it to Montgomery on their third attempt.

Information: Chamber of Commerce, 513 Lauderdale St., 334-875-7241, 800-457-3562;
www.selmaalabama.com

WHAT TO SEE AND DO

BLACK HERITAGE TOUR

Chamber of Commerce, 513 Lauderdale St., Selma, 334-875-7241;
www.selmaalabama.com

Learn about Selma's role in the fight for civil rights. Visit Brown Chapel A. M. E. Church (also a part of the Martin Luther King Jr. self-guided Street Walking Tour), the Edmund Pettus Bridge, the National Voting Rights Museum, Selma University, the Dallas County Courthouse and the Wilson Building.

CAHAWBA

9518 Cahaba Road, Selma, 334-872-8058; www.selmaalabama.com

This ghost town has a fascinating history. From 1820 to 1826, Cahawba served as Alabama's first permanent capital. Its low elevation made it vulnerable to frequent flooding, and the capital was moved to Tuscaloosa in 1826. The town survived until the Civil War, when the Confederate government tore up the railroad to extend a railroad nearby and established a lice-infested prison for captured Union troops. After the war, freemen used the courthouse as a meeting place to discuss how to gain political power, and former slave families created a new rural community. By 1900, the town was again abandoned and most of the buildings had collapsed or been burned. Today, visitors can stroll the deserted streets, chat with archeologists onsite and view the town's ruins. Daily

JOSEPH T. SMITHERMAN HISTORIC BUILDING

109 Union St., Selma, 334-874-2174; www.selmaalabama.com

The building has been restored and furnished with artifacts and antiques. It also has an art pavilion. Tuesday-Friday 9 a.m.-4 p.m., Saturday 8 a.m.-4 p.m.; also by appointment.

NATIONAL VOTING RIGHTS MUSEUM AND INSTITUTE

1012 Water Ave., Selma, 334-418-0800

Located near the foot of Edmund Pettus Bridge, this museum offers a pictorial history of the voting-rights struggle. It displays an exceptional record of events and participants, including Viola Liuzzo, who was killed by Ku Klux Klan members after the voting-rights march, and Marie Foster, who made voting rights history. Monday-Friday 9 a.m.-5 p.m., Saturday 10 a.m.-3 p.m., Sunday by appointment only.

OLD DEPOT MUSEUM

4 Martin Luther King Jr. St., Selma, 334-874-2197; www.selmaalabama.com

Visit this interpretive history museum to see artifacts from Selma and Alabama's "black belt" region. Monday-Saturday 10 a.m.-4 p.m.; also by appointment.

OLD TOWN HISTORIC DISTRICT

Chamber of Commerce, 513 Lauderdale St., Selma, 334-875-7241;
www.selmaalabama.com

Alabama's largest historic district, Old Town comprises more than 1,200 structures, including museums, specialty shops and restaurants. Self-guided tours are available (cassette; deposit required).

53

ALABAMA

★
★
★
★

PAUL M. GRIST STATE PARK

1546 Grist Road, Selma, 334-872-5846; www.alapark.com

This 1,080-acre park has a 100-acre lake. The park also has swimming, a bathhouse, fishing, boating (launch rentals), hiking, picnic facilities (grills, shelters), a playground and primitive camping.

STURDIVANT HALL

713 Mabry St., Selma, 334-872-5626; www.sturdivanthall.com

This beautiful home is an excellent example of Greek Revival architecture. Designed by Thomas Helm Lee, cousin of Robert E. Lee, it features massive Corinthian columns, original wrought iron on the balconies and belvedere on the roof. It's fully restored with period furnishings; the kitchen has slave quarters above; plus there's a smokehouse, wine cellar, carriage house and garden. One-hour guided tours are available. Tuesday-Saturday 10 a.m.-4 p.m.

SPECIAL EVENTS

HISTORIC SELMA PILGRIMAGE

109 Union St., Selma, 800-457-3562; www.pilgrimage.selmaalabama.com

If you want to wander through Selma's beautiful historic homes, this is your chance. Each year, guides take curious onlookers through privately owned historic homes. At twilight, take the living history tour at Old Live Oak cemetery. The event also includes an antiques show. Contact Chamber of Commerce. Mid-March.

REENACTMENT OF THE BATTLE OF SELMA

Battlefield Park, 205-755-1990

The Yankees are coming! One weekend each year, residents of Selma relive the battle between Union troops and the Confederacy. The battles take place on Saturday and Sunday, and other activities include a ladies' home tour and the Grand Military Ball. Late April.

TALE TELLIN' FESTIVAL

Pickard Auditorium, 400 Washington St., Selma, 334-875-7241, 800-457-3562; www.taletellin.selmaalabama.com

Each year, three featured storytellers thrill audiences with ghost stories, historical tales and traditional fables. Early October.

HOTEL

★★HOLIDAY INN

Highway 80 W., Selma, 334-872-0461, 800-465-4329; www.holiday-inn.com

165 rooms. High-speed Internet access. Restaurant, bar. Fitness center. Outdoor pool. Business center. **$**

SPECIAL LODGING

BRIDGE TENDERS HOUSE

127 Deep Woods Circle, Selma, 334-875-5517

This small cottage sits in the shadow of Pettus Bridge on the Alabama River. Each suite is private with a full kitchen, living room, bedroom and bath. Two suites. **$**

RESTAURANT

★★TALLY-HO

509 Mangum Ave., Selma, 334-872-1390

Seafood, steak menu. Dinner. Closed Sunday. $$

SHEFFIELD

Sheffield sits on the edge of the Tennessee River, a perfect spot for swimmers, fishermen and boaters. Locals are particularly proud of the area's musical heritage. Legends such as the Rolling Stones, Cher and Lynyrd Skynyrd recorded their music at Muscle Shoals Sound Studio, and musicians still trek to this northwest corner of Alabama to record their work.

Information: Colbert County Tourism and Convention Bureau, Tuscumbia, 256-383-0783; www.sheffieldalabama.org

WHAT TO SEE AND DO

ALABAMA MUSIC HALL OF FAME

617 Highway 72 W., Tuscumbia, 256-381-4417, 800-239-2643; www.alamhof.org

Rock on, Alabama: The Hall of Fame honors the contributions Alabamians have made to music of all genres—rock, rhythm and blues, gospel, contemporary and country music. Exhibits celebrate the accomplishments of performers such Hank Williams, also Nat King Cole and Lionel Richie. Think you're the next Jimmy Buffett (who also grew up in Mobile)? A recording studio is available to record personal cassettes or videos. Monday-Saturday 9 a.m.-5 p.m., Sunday 1-5 p.m.

IVY GREEN

300 W. North Commons, Tuscumbia, 256-383-4066; www.helenkellerbirthplace.org

Helen Keller was born here in 1880. Deaf and blind from the age of 19 months, she learned to sign her first words at the water pump out back from her teacher Annie Sullivan. The play *The Miracle Worker* captures the turbulent and eventually triumphant relationship between Sullivan and Keller. Monday-Saturday 8:30 a.m.-4 p.m., Sunday 1-4 p.m.

SPECIAL EVENTS

HELEN KELLER FESTIVAL

Ivy Green, 300 N. Commons St. W., Tuscumbia, 256-383-4066; www.helenkellerfestival.com

First held in 1979, this festival includes Braille and sign language lessons as well as performances of *The Miracle Worker*. Late June.

THE MIRACLE WORKER

300 N. Commons St. W., Tuscumbia, Ivy Green, 256-383-4066; www.helenkellerbirthplace.org

This is an outdoor performance of William Gibson's prize-winning play based on Helen Keller's life. A limited number of tickets are available at the gate; advance purchase is recommended. Price includes tour of Ivy Green preceding the play. Mid-June to July: Friday-Saturday.

55

ALABAMA

★
★
★
★

HOTEL

★★HOLIDAY INN

4900 Hatch Blvd., Sheffield, 256-381-4710, 800-465-4329, 800-111-000;
www.holiday-inn.com

204 rooms. High-speed Internet access. Restaurant, bar. Airport transportation available. Outdoor pool, whirlpool. **$**

RESTAURANTS

★★GEORGE'S STEAK PIT

1206 Jackson Highway, Sheffield, 256-381-1531; www.georgessteakpit.com

American menu. Dinner. Closed Sunday-Monday. **$$$**

★SOUTHLAND

1309 Jackson Highway, Sheffield, 256-383-8236; www.thesouthlandrestaurant.com

Lunch, dinner. Closed Monday. **$$**

SYLACAUGA

The city's fortune is literally its foundation—a bed of prized translucent white marble estimated to be 32 miles long, one-and-a-half miles wide and about 400 feet deep. Marble from Sylacauga has been used in the U.S. Supreme Court Building, the Al Jolson shrine in California and many other famous buildings in the United States.

Information: Sylacauga Chamber of Commerce, 17 W. Fort Williams St.,
256-249-0308; www.sylacauga.net

WHAT TO SEE AND DO

DESOTO CAVERNS PARK

5181 DeSoto Caverns Parkway, Childersburg, 256-378-7252, 800-933-2283;
www.desotocavernspark.com

This attraction mixes natural beauty with man-made fun. The 80-acre wooded park is famous for its historic caverns, which Hernando de Soto visited in 1540. The largest cavern, the Great Onyx Cathedral, is larger than a football field and taller than a 12-story building. A sound, light and water show happens here each summer between Flag Day (June 13) and the Fourth of July. Featured at the park is DeSoto's Lost Trail, a three-quarter-mile path. Visitors can also pan for gold and gemstones, visit the Bow and Arrow Arcade and enjoy other games. Other facilities include picnic areas, a shipboard playground and an RV campground. Guided tours are also available. April-October: Monday-Saturday 9 a.m.-5:30 p.m., Sunday 1-5:30 p.m.; November-March: Monday-Saturday 9 a.m.-4:30 p.m., Sunday 1-4:30 p.m.

ISABEL ANDERSON COMER MUSEUM &ARTS CENTER

711 N. Broadway, Sylacauga, 256-245-4016; www.comermuseum.freeservers.com

The museum features permanent exhibits of local and Native American artifacts and hosts special visiting exhibitions. Tuesday-Friday 10 a.m.-5 p.m.

TALLADEGA

Famous for its Talladega Speedway, this town is also home to Talladega College, founded by two former slaves. Love the great outdoors? Check out Logan Martin Lake to the northwest of Talladega and Talladega National Forest to the east.

Information: Chamber of Commerce, 210 East St. S., 256-362-9075; www.talladegachamber.com

WHAT TO SEE AND DO

CHEAHA STATE PARK

19 Bunker Loop, Delta, 256-488-5111; www.dcnr.state.al.us

Visit the observation tower at the top of Mount Cheaha (2,407 feet above sea level), the state's highest point. Nearly 2,800 acres of rugged forest country surround the mountain. But you may want to stick to the swimming in Lake Cheaha, sand beach, wading area, swimming pool, bathhouse, fishing, boating, picnicking, motel, restaurant, camping and cabins. Park: daily.

INTERNATIONAL MOTORSPORTS HALL OF FAME

3198 Speedway Blvd., Talladega, 256-362-5002; www.motorsportshalloffame.com

This is the official hall of fame of motor sports, with memorabilia and displays of more than 100 vehicles. Try the race car simulator and then go to the gift shop. The annual hall of fame induction ceremony takes place in late April. Daily 8 a.m.-5 p.m.

PINHOTI HIKING TRAIL

45 Highway 281, Talladega, 256-463-2272; www.fs.sed.us/rh/alabama

Alabama's premier long-distance recreational trail stretches 102 miles through the Talladega Mountains. It starts at the southern end of the Talladega National Forest and extends through Calhoun County to the Georgia line. Daily.

SILK STOCKING DISTRICT

25 W. 11th St., Talladega, 256-761-2108

Stroll by antebellum and turn-of-the-century houses along tree-lined streets. Talladega Square, in the heart of town, dates to 1834 and includes the renovated Talladega County Courthouse, the oldest courthouse in continuous use in the state.

TALLADEGA NATIONAL FOREST

Forest Supervisor, 2946 Chestnut St., Montgomery, 256-362-2909; www.fs.fed.us

On the Southern edge of the Appalachian Mountains, this forest comprises more than 360,000 acres of beauty. The forest has high ridges with spectacular views of wooded valleys, waterfalls and streams. There's lake swimming (fee), fishing and hiking trails, including the 100-mile Pinhoti National Recreation Trail, a national byway extending from Highway 78 to Cheaha State Park. Camping is also available (no electric hookup; fee).

ALABAMA

TALLADEGA SUPERSPEEDWAY

5200 Speedway Blvd., Eastaboga, 256-362-5002, 877-462-3342;
www.talladegasuperspeedway.com

Race mavericks say this is one of the world's fastest speedways, with 33-degree banks in the turns. Stock-car races include the EA Sports 500, Aaron's 499, and Aaron's 312. Daily 8 a.m.-4 p.m.

TALLADEGA-TEXACO WALK OF FAME

Downtown Talladega, 256-362-4261; www.talladegawalk.com

The walk of fame is an outdoor tribute to stock-car racers, including a memorial for Davey Allison, one of NASCAR's greatest champions.

TROY

Once home to country music singer Hank Williams Jr., Troy was originally known as Deer Stand Hill, a Native American hunting ground, before being settled and renamed in 1838.

Information: Pike County Chamber of Commerce, 246 US 231 N., 334-566-2294;
www.pikecountychamber.com

WHAT TO SEE AND DO

PIONEER MUSEUM OF ALABAMA

248 Highway 231 N., Troy, 334-566-3597; www.pioneer-museum.org

An antique farm and household implements, a reconstructed log house, a country store and other buildings hint at 19th-century life. Monday-Saturday 9 a.m.-5 p.m., Sunday 1-5 p.m.

HOTEL

★SUPER 8

1013 Highway 231, Troy, 334-566-4960, 800-800-8000; www.super8.com

69 rooms. High-speed Internet access. Complimentary continental breakfast. Outdoor pool. $

RESTAURANT

★MOSSY GROVE SCHOOLHOUSE

1841 Elba Highway, Troy, 334-566-4921

American menu. Dinner. Closed Sunday-Monday. $$

TUSCALOOSA

The Crimson Tide—otherwise known as the University of Alabama—calls Tuscaloosa home, and college football rules supreme here. But the city, located on the Black Warrior River, has a strong sense of history beyond its football traditions. Tuscaloosa was the capital of Alabama from 1826 to 1846, when profits from cotton padded farmers' pockets funded extravagant parties. But cotton prices fell, the capital moved to Montgomery and the Civil War ravaged Tuscaloosa (Choctaw for "black warrior"). Thanks to the expansion of the university and growing industry, today the city is a vibrant community, especially when the Tide is rollin'.

Information: Convention & Visitors Bureau, 205-391-9200, 800-538-8696;
www.tcvb.org

WHAT TO SEE AND DO

BATTLE-FRIEDMAN HOUSE

1010 Greensboro Ave., Tuscaloosa, 205-758-6138; www.historictuscaloosa.org

Local plantation owner Alfred Battle built this magnificent house when Tuscaloosa was the capital of Alabama. Financially ravaged by Confederate investments, Battle was forced to sell the house to Hungarian immigrant Bernard Friedman. Preserved and restored, today it contains fine antiques and its period gardens occupy a half block. Tuesday-Saturday 10 a.m.-noon, 1-4 p.m.; Sunday 1-4 p.m.

CHILDREN'S HANDS-ON MUSEUM

2213 University Blvd., Tuscaloosa, 205-349-4235; www.chomonline.org

The exhibit highlights at this kiddie museum include a Choctaw Indian Village, an art studio, a planetarium, a beaver's den and a TV studio. There's also a computer and science lab resource center for enterprising little minds. Monday-Friday 9 a.m.-5 p.m., Saturday 10 a.m.-4 p.m.

DENNY CHIMES

Tuscaloosa, opposite President's Mansion, 205-348-6010

The 115-foot-high tower was erected in honor of former university president Dr. George H. Denny. On the quarter-hour, the Westminster Chimes are struck, and selections are played each afternoon on the campanile (carillon).

GORGAS HOUSE

Tuscaloosa, Ninth Avenue and Capstone Drive, 205-348-6010; gorgashouse.ua.edu

The three-story brick structure was named for General Josiah Gorgas, a former university president. One of the school's original structures, Gorgas now houses a museum with historical exhibits. Get a look at the Spanish Colonial silver display. Tuesday-Saturday 10 a.m.-4 p.m.

LAKE LURLEEN STATE PARK

13226 Lake Lurleen Road, Coker, 205-339-1558; www.dcnr.state.al.us

The peaceful retreat rests on the banks of a 250-acre lake. Head there for swimming, bathhouses, fishing (piers), a bait and tackle shop, boating (ramps, rentals), hiking, picnic shelters, playgrounds and camping.

MOUNDVILLE ARCHAEOLOGICAL PARK

100 Mound Parkway, Moundville, 205-371-2234; www.moundville.ua.edu

The park maintains a group of more than 20 Native American ceremonial mounds (A.D. 1000-1450). The Jones Archaeological Museum (daily 9 a.m.-5 p.m.) traces the prehistory of southeastern Native Americans and exhibits products of this aboriginal culture. There are also nature trails along river, picnic facilities and tent and trailer sites (fee). Daily 8 a.m.-8 p.m.

NATIONAL HEADQUARTERS OF GULF STATES PAPER CORPORATION

1400 Jack Warner Parkway N.E., Tuscaloosa, 205-553-6200; www.westervelt.com

Four Asian buildings house an outstanding collection of sculpture and art, including primitive artifacts from Africa and the South Pacific; Asian art; a large collection of paintings including works by Georgia O'Keeffe, Mary Cassatt and James

★
★
★
★

A. M. Whistler. Guided tours are on offer. Tours: Monday-Friday 5:30 and 6:30 p.m., Saturday 10 a.m.-4 p.m., Sunday 1-4 p.m.

THE OLD OBSERVATORY
Tuscaloosa, 205-348-6010
This is the only pre-Civil War classroom building still standing.

OLD TAVERN
500 28th Ave., Tuscaloosa, 205-758-2238; www.historictuscaloosa.org
Governor Gayle and members of the Alabama legislature frequented this former inn and stagecoach stop when Tuscaloosa was the state's capital. Tuesday-Friday 10 a.m.-noon, 1-4 p.m.

UNIVERSITY OF ALABAMA
801 University Blvd. E., Tuscaloosa, 205-348-6010; www.ua.edu
Roll Tide! Alabama's first public university, Bama has 21,000 students. Visitors can arrange tours of the 850-acre campus in the Students Services Center, Room 203 (Monday-Saturday). On the campus is an art gallery in Garland Hall with changing exhibits, a museum of natural history, a 60-acre arboretum and the Paul W. Bryant Museum. The Frank Moody Music Building holds concerts and is the home of the largest pipe organ in the Southeast.

WILL T. MURPHY AFRICAN AMERICAN MUSEUM
2601 Paul W. Bryant Drive, Tuscaloosa, 205-758-2861
The house features two rooms with changing exhibits relating to culture and heritage of African-Americans. It also holds an antique doll collection, rare books and some period furnishings. By appointment only.

SPECIAL EVENT
MOUNDVILLE NATIVE AMERICAN FESTIVAL
Moundville Archaeological Park, 100 Mound Parkway, Tuscaloosa, 205-371-2572; www.moundville.ua.edu/festival.html
Celebrate the culture of the southeastern Native American with craft demonstrations, songs, dances and folktales. The final day (Saturday) is Indian Market Day, when artisans exhibit their wares. Early October.

HOTELS
★BEST WESTERN PARK PLAZA MOTOR INN
3801 McFarland Blvd., Tuscaloosa, 205-556-9690, 800-235-7282; www.bestwestern.com
118 rooms. High-speed Internet access. Complimentary continental breakfast. Outdoor pool. **$**

★★FOUR POINTS BY SHERATON
320 Paul Bryant Drive, Tuscaloosa, 205-752-3200, 888-625-5144; www.fourpoints.com
152 rooms. High-speed Internet access. Complimentary breakfast. Restaurant, bar. Airport transportation available. **$**

★
★
★
★
★

★HAMPTON INN

600 Harper Lee Drive, Tuscaloosa, 205-553-9800, 800-426-7866;
www.hamptoninn.com

102 rooms. High-speed Internet access. Complimentary continental breakfast. Fitness center. Outdoor pool. Business center. **$**

RESTAURANT

★★HENSON'S CYPRESS INN

501 Rice Mine Road N., Tuscaloosa, 205-345-6963; www.cypressinnrestaurant.com
Steak menu. Lunch, dinner. **$$**

TUSKEGEE

For more than 100 years, Tuskegee has witnessed great accomplishments by African-Americans. In 1881, Booker T. Washington founded the Tuskegee Normal School for Colored Teachers, which eventually became the Tuskegee Institute and then Tuskegee University. One of the institute's most famous instructors, George Washington Carver taught former slaves how to farm and be self-sufficient. In the early 1940s, the town's famous Tuskegee Airmen became America's first black military airmen.

Information: Office of the Mayor, City Hall, 101 Fonville St., 334-727-2180;
www.tuskegeealabama.org

WHAT TO SEE AND DO

BOOKER T. WASHINGTON MONUMENT

Tuskegee, 540-721-2094; www.nps.gov/bowa

The larger-than-life bronze figure honors the institute's first principal, who advocated "lifting the veil of ignorance" from the heads of freed slaves.

CHAPEL, TUSKEGEE UNIVERSITY

Tuskegee University campus, Tuskegee, 334-727-8322;
www.tuskegee.edu

Paul Rudolph designed this unusual structure with saw-toothed ceilings and deep beams. Adjacent are the graves of George Washington Carver and Booker T. Washington.

GEORGE WASHINGTON CARVER MUSEUM

Tuskegee, 334-727-3200; www.nps.gov

Born a slave, George Washington Carver eventually earned an advanced degree in agriculture from Iowa Agricultural College (which became Iowa State University). He accepted a position at Tuskegee Institute in 1896, where he taught and researched for 47 years. The museum includes Carver's original laboratory, the array of products he developed, and his extensive collection of native plants, minerals, needlework, paintings, drawings and personal belongings. Daily 9 a.m.-4:30 p.m.

ALABAMA

TUSKEGEE INSTITUTE NATIONAL HISTORIC SITE

1212 W. Montgomery Road, Tuskegee, 334-727-6390; www.nps.gov/tuin

The Tuskegee Institute opened on July 4, 1881—a date that celebrated freedom for all citizens, including the black students who enrolled. The institute focused on giving students the skills they would need to find work and on building its students' moral character. Many of these students went on to become educators who took their knowledge and skills to rural areas, where they taught people how to implement these ideas. The school's reputation as a progressive institution grew, and in 1974, Congress established Tuskegee Institute National Historic Site to include "The Oaks," home of Booker T. Washington; the George Washington Carver Museum; and the Historic Campus District. The 5,000-acre campus comprises more than 160 buildings. Daily 9 a.m.-4:30 p.m.

TUSKEGEE NATIONAL FOREST

125 National Forest Road 949, Tuskegee, 334-727-2652; www.stateparks.com

This beautiful slice of southeastern country offers plenty of outdoor fun. There's fishing, hunting and hiking on Bartram National Recreation Trail; Atasi and Taska picnic sites; and camping. See the area's native animals at the Tsinia Wildlife Viewing Area. Daily.

HOTEL

★★KELLOGG CONFERENCE CENTER

Tuskegee University, Tuskegee Institute, 334-727-3000, 800-949-6161;
www.tuskegeekelloggcenter.com

110 rooms. High-speed Internet access. Restaurant, bar. Airport transportation available. $

ALABAMA

ARKANSAS

OUTDOOR ENTHUSIASTS OF EVERY STRIPE THINK ARKANSAS IS HEAVEN ON EARTH—AND THEY just might be right. The Natural State has been well endowed by Mother Nature, and its beautiful terrain inspires people to trade in laptops and cell phones for mountain bikes and spelunking lanterns. The Ozark and Ouachita mountain ranges, separated by the Arkansas River, offer splendid forests. Pine and hardwood trees shade streams filled with enough black bass, bream and trout to restore any angler's faith. There are deer, geese, ducks and quail to hunt and feast on in season, and if you just want to see wildlife, the White River National Wildlife Refuge is a haven for a diverse population of animals and plants. Caves, springs, meadows, valleys, bayous, rice and cotton fields and magnificent lakes and rivers dot the state. For an enjoyable backwoods vacation, a visitor can't go wrong bunking in a quiet rustic resort or indulging in cosmopolitan Hot Springs National Park—the renowned spa dedicated to sophisticated pleasures and therapeutic treatment.

For much of its early American history, Arkansas was rugged land on the western frontier, and a spirit of adventure still lives here, as does an appreciation for the cultural offerings that make Arkansas unique. Bluegrass music rules, and it's almost as necessary as good food at many of the town's annual festivals.

Arkansas also has several great cities and towns. Hot Springs, in the midst of wooded hills and valleys, has been a vacation hot spot—literally—since the 19th century. The town offers a mixture of spa-inspired luxury and hearty outdoor fun. Little Rock, the state's capital, enjoyed its time in the nation's spotlight when the 42nd president of the United States, Bill Clinton, once the governor, moved into the White House. Today, Little Rock—so named for its place on the Arkansas River—has a revived downtown scene that attracts fun-seekers looking for live entertainment, eclectic dining and a healthy dose of retail therapy. For a totally different scene, check out Eureka Springs, a tourist destination admired for its European flavor, Victorian homes and steep, winding streets.

People who have already discovered Arkansas' rich offerings don't want the secret to get out, but there's plenty of room in Arkansas' wide-open spaces for a few more guests. So regardless of whether you come to party at Little Rock's riverfront, indulge in a hot-spring-fed spa or wander along quiet mountain trails, you'll find a surprising slice of paradise in Arkansas.

Information: www.arkansas.com

 FUN FACTS The Arkansas Blues Heritage Festival (formerly King Biscuit Blues Festival), held in Helena the second weekend in October each year, is the largest free blues fest in the world.

ALTUS

This itty-bitty town (population about 800) packs a serious punch for lovers of wine and Paris Hilton. The first season of *The Simple Life*, starring Hilton and Nicole Richie, was filmed here.

Information: Chamber of Commerce, Altus, 479-468-4684; www.arkansas.com

A CLINTON DRIVING TOUR

Former President Bill Clinton may reside in New York now, but much of his history lives in Arkansas. Little Rock is the place to learn about Clinton's political career, but to explore his life before he stepped into the limelight, you'll need to visit Hope, Clinton's birthplace, and Hot Springs, where he spent much of his childhood.

From I-30 in Hope, follow signs to the visitor center at the train depot on Main and Division Streets. (You might recognize the small depot with a large green "HOPE" sign from Clinton's presidential campaign videos.) Four blocks from the visitor center, Clinton's birthplace—a modest home on Hervey Street where he lived until he was eight years old—is now an historic site and museum.

Next, head east on I-30 toward Hot Springs; once in town, head north on Highway 278 toward downtown. Clinton went to grade school and high school here, and the town is full of sites where he studied, worked and played long before he moved into the White House. Off Highway 7, at the south end of Bathhouse Row, a city visitor center distributes a map of 16 Clinton-related sites, including his church, a local bowling alley and his favorite hamburger joint. Hot Springs High School, from which Clinton graduated in 1964, is now the William Jefferson Clinton Cultural Campus, a residential community art center that features a restored theater and presidential museum from Clinton's high school days. And if you still haven't gotten enough presidential history, take I-30 east to Little Rock, where Clinton made his political debut as attorney general of Arkansas in 1976. *Approximately 150 miles.*

WHAT TO SEE AND DO
WIEDERKEHR WINE CELLARS

3324 Swiss Family Drive, Altus, 501-468-9463, 800-622-9463;
www.wiederkehrwines.com

Take a guided wine-tasting tour (there's a gourmet and nonalcoholic beverage tasting for visitors under 21) or a self-guided tour of the vineyards. Stop by the observation tower, restaurant and gift shop along the way. Daily 9 a.m.-4:30 p.m.

RESTAURANT
★★★WEINKELLER RESTAURANT

3324 Swiss Family Drive, Altus, 479-468-3551; www.wiederkehrwines.com

Listed on the National Register of Historic Places, this restaurant sits on the site of the first Wiederkehr wine cellar, dug in 1880. The menu offers Old World cuisine with classic European favorites. Swiss, European menu. Lunch, dinner. $$

ARKADELPHIA

On a bluff overlooking the Ouachita River, Arkadelphia is an outdoor lover's dream: Hikers trek along Ouachita National Forest, the South's oldest national forest, while others take to the woods with a mountain bike or via horseback. Arkadelphia will also delight fishermen, boaters and swimmers, thanks to DeGray Lake and Ouachita River.

Information: Chamber of Commerce, 107 N. Sixth St., 870-246-5542, 800-874-4289;
www.arkadelphia.org

WHAT TO SEE AND DO

ARKANSAS POST MUSEUM

5530 Highway 165 S., Gillett, 870-548-2634; www.arkansas.com

The museum and five buildings house artifacts of early settlers on the grand prairie of Arkansas. Highlights include a colonial kitchen, an 1877 log house with period furnishings, Civil War memorabilia and a child's three-room finished playhouse. Daily.

ARKANSAS POST NATIONAL MEMORIAL

1741 Old Post Road, Gillett, 501-548-2207; www.nps.gov/arpo

The Arkansas Post began as a trading post, established by French lieutenant Henri De Tonti in 1686. The French's first semi-permanent settlement in the lower Mississippi River Valley, the Post grew to an impressive garrison of 40 men by 1759. As European forces fought for control over the expanding American territory, Spain, England and France controlled this land at different points in American history until the U.S. bought it as part of the Louisiana Purchase in 1803. It became the capital of the new Arkansas Territory and home of Arkansas' first newspaper, *The Arkansas Gazette*. Both moved to Little Rock in 1821, and eventually, the Civil War and numerous floods finally destroyed the little town. Today, visitors enjoy fishing, hiking and picnicking on the 389 acres of this wildlife sanctuary. Personnel and exhibits, including a partial replica of a 1783 Spanish fort, tell the story of the post.

DEGRAY LAKE

2027 State Park Entrance Road, Bismark, 870-246-5501; www.degray.com

More than 200 miles of shoreline make this 13,000-acre lake a perfect place to water-ski, fish or swim, or simply lounge on the shoreline. DeGray is one of Arkansas' "diamond lakes," renowned for their clear water. Camping (fee) is also available. Daily.

DEGRAY LAKE RESORT STATE PARK

Highway 7, Arkadelphia, 870-865-2801; www.arkansas.com

A great spot for family fun, this resort park offers something for everyone. Where else can you golf, fish, hike, camp and even square dance all in one place? Activities include swimming, fishing, boating (houseboat and sailboat rentals, marina, launch), hiking on a nature trail, 18-hole golf (and a pro shop), tennis, picnicking and playing on the playground. If you want to do camping (many water, electric hookups, dump station; reservations available April-October), a store, laundry facility, restaurant and lodge may come in handy. The visitor center offers interpretive programs. Guided hikes, lake cruises, square dances, hay rides, live animal demonstrations, evening slides and films round out the offerings.

HENDERSON STATE UNIVERSITY MUSEUM

1100 Henderson St., Arkadelphia, 870-246-7311; www.hsu.edu

The Victorian house of C.C. Henderson showcases displays of Caddo artifacts and items of historic interest. Monday, Wednesday, Friday.

65

ARKANSAS

★
★
★
★

OUACHITA BAPTIST UNIVERSITY
410 Ouachita St., Arkadelphia, 870-245-5206; www.obu.edu

Located on the banks of the Ouachita River, and surrounded by the foothills of the Ouachita Mountains, McClellan Hall contains the official papers and memorabilia of U.S. Senator John L. McClellan. Campus tours are available.

SPECIAL EVENTS
CLARK COUNTY FAIR
Clark County Fairgrounds, Arkadelphia, 870-246-5542; www.arkadelphia.org

September.

FESTIVAL OF THE TWO RIVERS
Clay and Fourth streets, Arkadelphia, 870-246-5542

The fest features arts and crafts, a juried art show, contests, games and food. Mid-April.

HOTEL
★★BEST WESTERN CONTINENTAL INN
136 Valley St., Arkadelphia, 870-246-5592, 800-780-7234; www.bestwestern.com

59 rooms. Restaurant. Fitness center. Outdoor pool. $

ASHDOWN

Smack-dab in the middle of Little River County, Ashdown attracts local and visiting fishermen.

Information: 180 E. Whitaker St., Ashdown, 870-898-2758; www.ashdownar.org

WHAT TO SEE AND DO
MILLWOOD STATE PARK
Ashdown, 870-898-2800; www.arkansas.com

A haven for bass, Millwood Lake is also home to catfish, crappie and bream. Aside from fishing, you can do some boating (rentals, marina), hiking, picnicking and camping (hookups, dump station). Millwood Dam and Reservoir is adjacent (1564 Highway 32 E., Ashdown, 870-898-3343).

BATESVILLE

The largest city in Independence County, Batesville is also the second-oldest municipality in Arkansas (behind Georgetown). It may not be a sprawling metropolis, but this small city boasts plenty of access to water sports.

Information: Batesville Area Chamber of Commerce, 409 Vine St., 870-793-2378; www.mybatesville.org

SPECIAL EVENTS
NATIONAL INVITATIONAL EXPLORER CANOE RACE
409 Vine St., Batesville, 870-793-2378, 870-793-2378; www.mybatesville.org

The race takes place on the last day of Water Carnival.

OZARK SCOTTISH FESTIVAL

Lyon College, 2300 Highland Road, Batesville, 870-793-9813; www.mybatesville.org

The fest gets samples Scottish culture with pipe bands, Highland dancing, a Parade of Clans and, of course, a Scottish feast. Late April.

WHITE RIVER WATER CARNIVAL

409 Vine St., Batesville, 870-793-2378; www.mybatesville.org,
www.batesvillepromotions.com

The carnival festivities include a parade, arts and crafts and a beauty pageant. First weekend in August.

HOTEL
★★RAMADA

1325 N. St. Louis St., Batesville, 870-698-1800, 800-298-2054; www.ramada.com

124 rooms. High-speed Internet access. Restaurant. Outdoor pool. Pets accepted. **$**

BENTON

Benton is close to Arkansas' famed Hot Springs, a short drive from Little Rock and close to plenty of the state's beautiful natural landscapes.

Information: Chamber of Commerce, 607 N. Market St., 501-315-8272, 501-315-8290;
www.bentonchamber.com

WHAT TO SEE AND DO
GANN MUSEUM

218 S. Market St., Benton, 501-778-5513; www.arkansas.com

One of the most beautiful buildings in town, the Gann Museum was originally a medical office built for Dr. Dewel Gann by patients who could not afford to pay him for his services. It contains furniture and artifacts reflecting local pioneer, Native American and church history. Tuesday-Thursday 10 a.m.-4 p.m., tours by appointment.

RESTAURANT
★BROWN'S

18718 I-30, Benton, 501-778-5033; www.brownscountryrestaurant.com

Buffet menu. Breakfast, lunch, dinner. **$**

BENTONVILLE

Bentonville is the headquarters for Wal-Mart. But that's not the only thing it has going. Cultural events, nearby state parks and a historic town square give visitors plenty to do.

Information: Bentonville-Bella Vista Chamber of Commerce, 412 S. Main St.,
479-273-2841; www.bentonvilleusa.org

WHAT TO SEE AND DO
PEEL MANSION & HISTORIC GARDENS

400 S. Walton Blvd., Bentonville, 479-273-9664; www.peelmansion.org

This villa tower Italianate mansion—built by Colonel Samuel West Peel, the first native-born Arkansan to serve in the U.S. Congress—has been restored and refurnished in Victorian style. The 180-acre site also has an outdoor museum of historic

★
★
★
★

roses, perennials and native plants. The pre-Civil War Andy Lynch log cabin serves as gatehouse and gift shop. Tuesday-Saturday 10 a.m.-4 p.m.

SPECIAL EVENT
SUGAR CREEK ARTS & CRAFTS FAIR
805 S. Main St., Bentonville, 479-273-3270
Nearly 200 exhibitors come to display their works. Third weekend in October.

HOTELS
★BEST WESTERN BENTONVILLE INN
2307 S.E. Walton Blvd., Bentonville, 479-273-9727, 800-780-7234;
www.bestwestern.com
54 rooms. High-speed Internet access. Complimentary continental breakfast. Outdoor pool. Business center. $

★HOLIDAY INN EXPRESS
2205 S.E. Walton Blvd., Bentonville, 479-271-2222; www.holiday-inn.com
84 rooms. Wireless Internet access. Complimentary continental breakfast. $

RESTAURANT
★★FRED'S HICKORY INN
1502 N. Walton Blvd., Bentonville, 479-273-3303; www.fredshickoryinn.net
Steak menu. Lunch, dinner. $$

BERRYVILLE
Book worms, rejoice! Berryhill is a great place to find rare or unusual books, thanks to many antique shops and flea markets that specialize in collectible or used tomes. Some of Arkansas' beloved writers spend time here, too.
Information: Chamber of Commerce, Highway 62 E., 870-423-3704;
www.berryvillear.com

WHAT TO SEE AND DO
CARROLL COUNTY HERITAGE CENTER
403 Public Square, Berryville, 870-423-6312; www.rootsweb.com
Local historical exhibits and genealogical material are housed in this old courthouse, which dates back to 1880. April-October: Monday-Friday 9 a.m.-4 p.m.; closed Monday from November-March.

COSMIC CAVERN
6386 Highway 21, Berryville, 870-749-2298; www.cosmiccavern.com
This limestone cave in the Ozarks has two "bottomless" lakes—cave divers have never found the bottom. One section of the cave, discovered in 1993, has one of the longest soda-straw formations—beautiful and fragile mineral tubes. A visitor center and picnic area are also on the premises. One-hour guided tours are available. Days and times vary.

SAUNDERS MEMORIAL MUSEUM

115 E. Madison, Berryville, 870-423-2563; www.arkansas.com

Here you'll find an eclectic collection of loot collected by C. Burton Saunders during a lifetime of adventure. See guns once used by Jesse James, Billy the Kid and Buffalo Bill Cody. You'll also find items as diverse as Sitting Bull's war bonnet and an Arab sheik's tent. April-October: Monday-Saturday.

SPECIAL EVENTS

CARROLL COUNTY FAIR

Carroll County Fairgrounds, Highway 21 N., Berryville, 870-423-3704;
www.berryvillear.com

A parade and the Miss Carroll County competition are highlights of the week's events. Week of Labor Day.

ICE CREAM SOCIAL

Public Square, Highways 62 E. and 21 S., Berryville, 870-423-3704;
www.berryvillear.com

Browse the arts and crafts booths, purchase some baked goods, or join the 5K fun run. Second weekend in June.

SAUNDERS MEMORIAL MUZZLELOADING AND FRONTIER GUN SHOOT & HANDCRAFTERS' SHOW

Luther Owens Muzzleloading Range and Park, Berryville

Costumed contestants compete in a gun show. Last full weekend in September.

BLYTHEVILLE

Duck hunters and fishermen love Blytheville. The Mississippi Flyway, a popular migration route for birds, is nearby, and Mallard Lake (12 miles west on Highway 18) has good bass, bream and crappie fishing.

Information: Chamber of Commerce, 870-762-2012; www.blythevillegosnell.com

WHAT TO SEE AND DO

BUFFALO NATIONAL RIVER

Buffalo Point Contact Station, 17 miles south of Yellville via Highway 14; Tyler Bend Visitor Center, 11 miles north of Marshall via Highway 65; www.nps.gov/buff

This is an outdoor enthusiast's dream: For 135 miles, the river flows freely, creating thrilling rapids and tranquil pools. In the spring, white-water rafters float the upper river from Ponca to Pruitt, stopping at primitive campgrounds along the way. Springs, waterfalls, streams and woods along the river attract hikers. Because river levels fluctuate, contact park headquarters about floatable areas. Visitor information is available at Buffalo Point Contact Station, Tyler Ben Visitor Center and Pruitt Ranger Station. The park offers swimming, fishing, canoe rentals, self-guided hikes, picnicking and camping (fee). Ask about trips and special presentations led by park staff. Rustic and modern cabins are available from April to November. For information, call Buffalo Point Concession at 870-449-6206.

ARKANSAS

BULL SHOALS LAKE AREA

Bull Shoals, 11 miles west of Mountain Home via Highways 5, 870-425-2700; www.bullshoals.com

Bull Shoals Lake, on the White River in the Ozarks, is an ideal place to indulge in all of your favorite water sports. Visitors come to fish, water ski, swim and even scuba dive in the lake's clear water. Boat docks and recreation areas line the shore.

BULL SHOALS STATE PARK

129 Bull Shoals Park, Lakeview, 870-431-5521; www.bullshoals.com

The park takes up more than 680 acres at the southeast corner of the lake below the dam. There you can fish for trout, go boating (ramp, rentals, dock), hike trails, picnic and camp (hookups, dump station; daily).

HOTELS

★HAMPTON INN

301 Frontage Road, Blytheville, 870-763-5220, 800-426-7866; www.hamptoninn.com

87 rooms. Wireless Internet access. Complimentary continental breakfast. Outdoor pool. Business center. Pets accepted. $

★★HOLIDAY INN

1121 E. Main, Blytheville, 870-763-5800; www.holiday-inn.com

153 rooms. Restaurant, bar. Fitness center. Outdoor pool. Business center. $

RESTAURANTS

★★CLUB 178

2109 Central Blvd., Bull Shoals, 870-445-4949; www.178club.com

Seafood menu. Lunch, dinner, Sunday brunch. Closed Monday. $$

★VILLAGE WHEEL

1400 E. Central Blvd., Bull Shoals, 870-445-4414; www.bullshoals.org

American menu. Breakfast, lunch, dinner. $$

CAMDEN

This little town on the Ouachita River has seen its fair share of historical events—including the Civil War Battle of Poison Springs in 1864, three performances by Elvis Presley in 1955 and a parade of politicians stumping for different causes over the last 200 years.

Information: Camden Area Chamber of Commerce, 141 Jackson S.W., 870-836-6426

WHAT TO SEE AND DO

CONFEDERATE CEMETERY

Adams Avenue and Pearl Street, Camden

More than 200 veterans of the Civil War and many unknown soldiers are buried here.

MCCOLLUM-CHIDESTER HOUSE
926 Washington St. N.W., Camden
Once a stage coach headquarters, this historic house was used as headquarters at various times by Confederate General Sterling Price and Union General Frederick Steele. It contains original furnishings and mementos of the Civil War period. It was the setting for segments of the TV miniseries *North and South*.

LEAKE-INGHAM BUILDING
Camden, 870-836-6426
The building was used as a law office before the Civil War and as a freedmen's bureau during Reconstruction. Now it houses books and other memorabilia of the antebellum South.

POISON SPRING BATTLEGROUND HISTORICAL MONUMENT
Highway 76, Bluff City, 870-836-6426
This was the site of Union defeat during Union General Frederick Steele's "Red River Campaign" into southwest Arkansas. Exhibits and dioramas trace troop movement. There's also a trail to a small spring and a picnic area.

WHITE OAK LAKE STATE PARK
986 Highway 387, Bluff City, 870-685-2748; www.arkansasstateparks.com/whiteoaklake
Go swimming; fishing for bass, crappie and bream; or boating (rentals) on this 2,765-acre lake. Land-based fun abounds with hiking trails, picnicking and camping (hookups, dump station). Head to the visitor center for interpretive programs (summer only). Daily.

SPECIAL EVENT
OUACHITA COUNTY FAIR AND LIVESTOCK SHOW
Camden
The fair includes carnival rides, food and live music. September.

CONWAY
"The City of Colleges," Conway is home to the University of Central Arkansas, Central Baptist College and Hendrix College. Like many towns in Arkansas, Conway offers residents and visitors opportunities to enjoy the outdoors, and the colleges and community groups provide cultural activities, such as theatrical performances and concerts.
Information: Chamber of Commerce, 900 Oak St., 501-327-7788, 501-327-7789; www.conwayarkcc.org

WHAT TO SEE AND DO
CADRON SETTLEMENT PARK
6298 Highway 60 W. Conway, 501-329-2986;
www.swl.usace.army.mil
Part of the Cherokee Trail of Tears runs through the park. You'll also find a replica of blockhouse built by early settlers in the 1770s. Daily.

71

ARKANSAS

★
★
★
★

HENDRIX COLLEGE

1600 Washington Ave., Conway, 501-450-1349; www.hendrix.edu

This private liberal arts college has long been a favorite of college guides. Stroll the campus and see why. The Mills Center houses congressional office contents and some personal papers of former Congressman Wilbur D. Mills, chairman of the House Ways and Means Committee and graduate of Hendrix College. Monday-Friday.

TOAD SUCK FERRY LOCK AND DAM

6298 Highway 60 W., Conway, 501-329-2986;
www.wildernet.com

The dam is the site of the 1820 river crossing. It has a public viewing platform and historical markers. The adjacent park offers fishing, boating, picnicking and camping (fee; electricity and water available). All year.

WOOLLY HOLLOW STATE PARK

82 Woolly Hollow Road, Greenbrier, 501-679-2098;
www.arkansasstateparks.com/wollyhollow

A peaceful getaway in the Ozark foothills, the park surrounds Lake Bennett, where visitors can fish and swim. Woolly Cabin, a restored one-room log structure built in 1882, gives visitors a glimpse of early settlers' lives. Swimming beach, fishing, boating (rentals), hiking trails, picnicking, a playground, camping (hookups), and a snack bar are available.

SPECIAL EVENTS

FAULKNER COUNTY FAIR

Conway

The Faulkner County Fair has everything you'd expect from a small-town county fair, from Ferris wheels to gobs of cotton candy. Mid-September.

TOAD SUCK DAZE

1234 Main St., Conway, 501-327-7788; www.toadsuck.org

According to local lore, the name "Toad Suck" comes from a description locals used to describe steamboat captains and crews who traveled down the Arkansas River and stopped to imbibe at the local tavern. Wary locals said the visitors sucked on liquor bottles "until they swelled up like toads." The festival features carnival rides; arts and crafts; bluegrass, country and gospel music; and of course, toad races. First weekend of May.

HOTELS

★★BEST WESTERN CONWAY

Conway, 501-329-9855, 800-780-7234; www.bestwestern.com

70 rooms. High-speed Internet access. Complimentary continental breakfast. Restaurant. Outdoor pool. Pets accepted. $

★COMFORT INN

150 Highway 65 N., Conway, 501-329-0300, 800-228-5150; www.choicehotels.com

60 rooms. Complimentary continental breakfast. Outdoor pool. $

RESTAURANT
★FU LIN
195 Farris Road, Conway, 501-329-1415
Chinese menu. Lunch, dinner. $$

DUMAS

Dumas, Ark., and Dumas, Texas, have been in a bit of a scuffle over a song written in the 1930s. Both towns lay claim to the song "I'm a Ding Dong Daddy From Dumas," a knee-slapping song written by Phil Baxter and Carl Moore. The tune, which was a big hit, prompted the town to erect big signs on the highway entrances to Dumas, proclaiming "Welcome to Dumas, home of the Ding Dong Daddies."
Information: Chamber of Commerce, 165 S Main, 870-382-5447

WHAT TO SEE AND DO
DESHA COUNTY MUSEUM
Highway 54 E., Dumas, 870-382-4222; www.arkansas.com
The museum spotlights artifacts depicting the history of the area, an agricultural display and an arrowhead collection. There's also a log house farmstead. Tuesday, Thursday, Sunday.

LAKE CHICOT STATE PARK
2542 Highway 257, Lake Village, 870-265-5480; www.arkansas.com
The park surrounds Arkansas' largest natural lake (formed centuries ago when the Mississippi changed its course), which is famous for its bream, crappie, catfish and bass fishing. But you also have your choice of swimming in a pool, boating (rentals, ramp, marina), picnicking, frolicking on the playground, camping (hookups, dump station) or staying in cabins (there's a store and coin laundry onsite for campers). Sporty types can take archery lessons in the summer.

NORRELL AND NO. 2 LOCKS AND DAMS
628 Wild Goose Lane, Tichnor, 870-548-2291; www.arkansas.com
The major recreation areas are Wild Goose Bayou, north of Norrell Lock; Merrisach Lake, west of Lock No. 2; Pendleton Bend, west of Dam No. 2; Moore Bayou, south of Gillet on Highway 165; Notrebes Bend, east of Dam No. 2. All areas offer fishing, boating, picnicking and playgrounds. Camping is only available at Merrisach Lake, Notrebes Bend, Moore Bayou and Pendleton Bend (electric hookups, dump stations). Fees charged at some areas. Daily.

EL DORADO

Legend tells us that one day around 1830, pioneer Matthew F. Rainey's wagon broke down in a forest of hardwood and pine. Discouraged and tired, he offered his goods for sale. The farmers in the area were such eager customers that Rainey decided to open a store on the spot and call the place El Dorado. The town led a quiet existence until oil was discovered in 1921. Soon it was inundated with drillers, speculators, engineers and merchants. The vivacity of the '20s continues today in El Dorado, especially in its lively and beautiful downtown district.
Information: Chamber of Commerce, 201 N Jackson, 870-863-6113; www.goeldorado.com

ARKANSAS

★
★
★
★

WHAT TO SEE AND DO
ARKANSAS MUSEUM OF NATURAL RESOURCES
3853 Smackover Highway, Smackover, 870-725-2877; www.amnr.org

The 10-acre outdoor exhibit depicts working examples of oil production from 1920s to the present. Aside from the museum exhibits, there's a research center, gift shop and picnic area. Monday-Saturday 8 a.m.-5 p.m., Sunday 1-5 p.m.

MORO BAY STATE PARK
6071 Highway 600, Jersey, 870-463-8555; www.arkansasstateparks.com/morobay

Fishing, boating, hiking, picnicking, a playground and camping (hookups, dump station) make this park a draw. Daily.

SOUTH ARKANSAS ARBORETUM
501 Timberlane, El Dorado, 870-862-8131; www.goeldorado.com

The 17-acre arboretum features indigenous trees and plants. The grounds also have nature trails and wooden bridges. Daily 8 a.m.-5 p.m.

SPECIAL EVENT
UNION COUNTY FAIR
3853 Smackover Highway, Smackover, 870-725-2877; www.arkansassouth.com

The county fair gets under way with a carnival, food booths and a livestock auction. Mid-September.

HOTEL

★★BEST WESTERN KING'S INN CONFERENCE CENTER
1920 Junction City Road, El Dorado, 870-862-5191; www.bestwestern.com

131 rooms. Restaurant. Airport transportation available. Outdoor pool. Business Center. Reservation recommended. $

ARKANSAS

★
★
★
★
★

EUREKA SPRINGS

Eureka Springs is one of Arkansas' most popular tourist destinations. Visitors are drawn to its European flavor, Victorian buildings and steep, winding streets. In the 19th century, Eureka Springs was a well-known health spa. Thousands of people flocked to the city because its springs, which gushed from limestone crevices, had a reputation for healing a wide variety of illnesses. Today, the town attracts tourists who simply want to enjoy the town's many art galleries, boutiques, restaurants and charm.

Information: Chamber of Commerce, 137 W. Van Buren, Highway 62 W.,
479-253-8737, 800-638-7352; www.eurekasprings.org

WHAT TO SEE AND DO
BLUE SPRING HERITAGE CENTER
1537 County Road 210, Eureka Springs, 479-253-9244; www.eurekagardens.com

More than a mile of trails wind through the gardens. April-October: daily 9 a.m.-6 p.m.; November-March: daily 9 a.m.-5 p.m.

EUREKA SPRINGS & NORTH ARKANSAS RAILWAY

299 N. Main St. (Highway 23), Eureka Springs, 479-253-9623; www.esnarailway.com

Travel through the hills of the Ozarks and imagine life in the 19th century, when the first settlers rode into Eureka Springs. Dining cars are available on certain trips. April-October: Monday-Saturday.

EUREKA SPRINGS HISTORICAL MUSEUM

95 S. Main St., Eureka Springs, 479-253-9417; www.eshm.org

Eureka Springs has a history worth investigating, and the museum is a good spot to begin your exploration. Artifacts from the 19th century, including photographs and furniture, are on display in this beautiful house. Monday-Saturday 9:30 a.m.-4 p.m., Sunday 11 a.m.-4 p.m.

EUREKA SPRINGS TROLLEY

95 S. Main St., Eureka Springs, 479-253-9572; www.eurekatrolley.org

The trolley makes regularly scheduled trips through the city, the historic district and many points of interest. April-November.

FROG FANTASIES

151 Spring St., Eureka Springs, 479-253-7227; www.arkansas.com

This museum displays more than 7,000 man-made frog trinkets, from Christmas ornaments and plush toys to a diamond-encrusted pin. There's also a gift shop so you can pick up your own froggie souvenirs. Daily.

HAMMOND MUSEUM OF BELLS

2 Pine St., Eureka Springs, 479-253-7411

More than 30 lighted exhibits trace the history and structure of bells from 800 B.C. to the present. More than 1,000 primitive, antique and fine art bells are on display. There's a narrated audio tour. Monday-Friday 9:45 a.m.-5 p.m., Sunday 11:30 a.m.-4 p.m.

ONYX CAVE PARK

338 Onyx Cave Road, Eureka Springs, 479-253-9321; www.eurekaspringschamber.com

The park has unusual onyx formations in its cave, a blind cave fish display, a gift shop and places for picnicking. Continuous tours are given throughout the day.

PIVOT ROCK AND NATURAL BRIDGE

1708 Pivot Rock Road, Eureka Springs, 479-253-8982; www.arkansas.com

Hidden in a forest, these unusual rock formations will surprise you. The top of Pivot Rock is 15 times as wide as the bottom yet it is perfectly balanced. Nearby are a natural bridge and caves, where locals believe Jesse James once hid. April to mid-November.

ROSALIE HOUSE

282 Spring St., Eureka Springs, 479-253-7377; www.estc.net/rosalie

The house was built of handmade brick with gingerbread trim. It has its original interior, with gold leaf molding, ceiling frescoes, handmade woodwork and period furnishings. Guided tours: Thursday-Monday 11 a.m.-5 p.m.

★
★
★
★
★

SACRED ARTS CENTER

935 Passion Play Road, Eureka Springs, 479-253-9200; www.greatpassionplay.com

The center showcases more than 1,000 works of Christian art. Tuesday-Sunday.

BIBLE MUSEUM

Eureka Springs; www.greatpassionplay.com

This museum carries rare Bibles, artifacts and more than 6,000 volumes in 625 languages, including works on papyrus, parchment and clay cylinders and cones dating from 2000 B.C. Tuesday-Sunday.

CHRIST OF THE OZARKS

Eureka Springs; www.greatpassionplay.com

Erected in 1966, this seven-story-tall statue of Jesus weighs more than 1 million pounds and has an arm span of 65 feet.

NEW HOLY LAND

Eureka Springs; www.greatpassionplay.com

This facility contains Old and New Testament exhibits with costumed guides, including full-size replica of Moses' tabernacle and Last Supper re-creation. Monday-Saturday.

THORNCROWN CHAPEL

12968 Highway 62 W., Eureka Springs, 479-253-7401; www.thorncrown.com

This sensational glass chapel structure is tucked in the woods in the Ozarks. It was designed by noted Arkansas architect E. Fay Jones.

WITHROW SPRINGS STATE PARK

Highway 23 N., Huntsville, 479-559-2593; www.arkansasstateparks.com

This 700-acre recreation area stretches across mountains and valleys along the bluffs of War Eagle River. The waters of a large spring gush from a shallow cave at the foot of a towering bluff. Get active in the swimming pool (Memorial Day-mid-August: daily; also Labor Day weekend), canoeing (rentals), hiking, playing tennis, picnicking or camping. Daily.

SPECIAL EVENTS

CANDLELIGHT TOUR OF HOMES

137 W. Van Buren, Eureka Springs, 479-253-9417; www.eurekasprings.com

The Eureka Springs Preservation Society annually sponsors this tour of historic Victorian homes. Sunday in mid-December.

COUNTRY MUSIC SHOWS

137 W. Van Buren, Eureka Springs, 479-253-8737; www.eurekaspringschamber.com

You can catch various productions with country music, comedy skits and other family entertainment. Most shows April-December.

THE GREAT PASSION PLAY

Mount Oberammergau, Passion Play Road, Eureka Springs,
479-253-9200, 866-566-3565; www.greatpassionplay.com

Performed five nights a week from late April to late October, the play portrays the life of Jesus from Palm Sunday through the Ascension in an outdoor amphitheater. Monday-Tuesday, Thursday-Saturday.

OZARK FOLK FESTIVAL

36 S. Main St., Eureka Springs, 888-855-7823; www.ozarkfolkfestival.com

The festival attracts national headliners and other musical acts, and also offers a beauty pageant, Gay '90s costume parade and other events. Early October.

HOTELS

★★★1886 CRESCENT HOTEL & SPA

75 Prospect Ave., Eureka Springs, 479-253-9766, 800-342-9766;
www.crescent-hotel.com

Built atop Eureka Springs' highest point, this grand hotel offers gorgeous views of the valley. Guests will feel as if they have traveled back in time when they pass through the front door into the opulent lobby. The guest rooms are decorated in Victorian style with wallpaper and period furnishings, but they also offer modern conveniences like Wireless Internet access. Stake out a spot by the pool or indulge in a spa treatment at the property's New Moon Spa and Salon. Adventure seekers will find plenty of activities in the area such as ghost tours, fishing, hiking, kayaking, canoeing, and car and motorcycle tours. After a busy day, The Crystal Dining Room is the perfect spot for an elegant meal, followed by drinks at Dr. Baker's Lounge, where guests can enjoy panoramic views of the Ozarks and live entertainment on the weekends. 72 rooms. Two restaurants, bar. Airport transportation available. Spa. $

★★BEST WESTERN INN OF THE OZARKS

207 W. Van Buren, Eureka Springs, 479-253-9768, 800-780-7234;
www.innoftheozarks.com

122 rooms. Restaurant. Children's activity center. Outdoor pool. Business center. Wireless Internet access. Tennis. Pets accepted. Reservations recommended. $

★DAYS INN

120 W. Van Buren St., Eureka Springs, 479-253-8863, 800-329-7466; www.daysinn.com

24 rooms. High-speed Internet access. Complimentary continental breakfast. Outdoor pool. Pets accepted. $

★★NEW ORLEANS HOTEL & SPA

63 Spring St., Eureka Springs, 479-253-8630, 800-243-8630;
www.neworleanshotelandspa.com

20 rooms. High-speed Internet access. Restaurant, bar. Spa. $

★
★
★
★

SPECIALTY LODGINGS

1881 CRESCENT COTTAGE INN

211 Spring St., Eureka Springs, 479-253-6022, 800-223-3246;
www.1881crescentcottageinn.com

Four rooms. Children over 16 years only. Complimentary full breakfast. Reservation recommended. **$**

ARSENIC & OLD LACE BED AND BREAKFAST INN

60 Hillside Ave., Eureka Springs, 479-253-5454, 800-243-5223;
www.arsenicoldlace.com

This elegant Queen Anne mansion (built in 1992) has old-fashioned bed-and-breakfast charm with modern conveniences. Just a 10-minute walk from the downtown area, the house is set back from the road in a quiet neighborhood. The large, welcoming porch invites you to stay awhile, and each room has a whirlpool tub. The gourmet breakfast will start each day off right. Five rooms. Wireless Internet access. Children over 12 years only. Complimentary full breakfast. Pets accepted. **$$**

BRIDGEFORD HOUSE

263 Spring St., Eureka Springs, 479-253-7853, 888-567-2422;
www.bridgefordhouse.com

Listed on the National Register of Historic places, this 1884 Victorian mansion is in a charming historic neighborhood. Walk to downtown shops and cafés, or lounge on the house's large porch. The owners have preserved the house's history by decorating with antiques and period furniture. The comfortable rooms feature fireplaces and whirlpool tubs. This is a perfect destination for a weekend escape. Five rooms. Children over 8 years only. Complimentary full breakfast. **$**

HEARTSTONE INN AND COTTAGES

35 Kings Highway, Eureka Springs, 479-253-8916, 800-494-4921;
www.heartstoneinn.com

In the town's Historic Loop—and only four blocks from downtown—this Victorian inn provides comfortable rooms, charming service and delicious breakfasts. 11 rooms. Children over 10 years only. Complimentary full breakfast. Spa. **$**

THE INN AT ROSE HALL

56 Hillside Ave., Eureka Springs, 479-253-8313, 800-544-7734; www.innatrosehall.com

Escape the rat race by booking a room at the Inn at Rose Hall. On a quiet, tree-lined street, this reproduction Victorian house offers spacious rooms with fireplaces and whirlpool tubs. Wake up to gourmet breakfasts, which you'll enjoy while admiring the inn's beautiful stained-glass windows and elegant Victorian furniture. Five rooms. Children not allowed. Complimentary full breakfast. Reservations recommended. **$$**

PALACE HOTEL & BATH HOUSE

135 Spring St., Eureka Springs, 479-253-7474; www.palacehotelbathhouse.com

Built in 1901, this historic Victorian-era property was fully restored to its original beauty. Large guest suites are beautifully decorated and include whirlpool tubs, wet bars and refrigerators. The bathhouse has been in operation for more than 100 years and offers services such as natural clay masks and Swedish massage therapy. Eight rooms. Children not allowed. Complimentary continental breakfast. Spa. Reservations recommended. **$$**

★
★
★
★
★

RESTAURANTS

★BUBBA'S BARBECUE
166 W. Van Buren, Eureka Springs, 479-253-7706
Barbecue menu. Lunch, dinner. Closed Sunday. $$

★CENTER STREET PUB
10 Center St., Eureka Springs, 479-253-7147
American menu. Lunch, dinner. $$

★★★THE CRYSTAL DINING ROOM
75 Prospect Ave., Eureka Springs, 479-253-9766, 800-342-9766;
www.crescent-hotel.com/dining
Located off the lobby of the historic 1886 Crescent Hotel & Spa, The Crystal Dining Room offers beautiful Victorian-style surroundings with hardwood floors, high ceilings and sparkling chandeliers, formal but friendly service and a stellar menu of inventive American cuisine. Dinner options may include espresso-glazed filet of sirloin or mesquite-seared salmon. Enjoy a selection from the impressive wine list, which has been the recipient of the *Wine Spectator* Award of Excellence and is the most expansive in the area. Breakfast, lunch and a Sunday champagne brunch are also served; dishes like three-layer pancakes with wild berry compote and a classic Reuben on marble rye satisfy every palate. American menu. Breakfast, lunch, dinner, brunch. Children's menu. Business casual attire. Reservations recommended. $$$

FAYETTEVILLE

Home of the University of Arkansas Razorbacks, Fayetteville is often ranked among the nation's best places to live, thanks to its reputation for affordable living, natural beauty, temperate climate and easy access to outdoor activities.
Information: Chamber of Commerce, 123 W. Mountain St.,
479-521-1710, 800-766-4626; www.fayettevillear.com

WHAT TO SEE AND DO

ARKANSAS AIR MUSEUM
4290 S. School St., Fayetteville, 479-521-4947; www.arkairmuseum.org
Aspiring pilots and curious air travelers will enjoy the exhibits here, which span the history of manned flight. Don't miss the racing planes from the 1920s and '30s, the Lear Jet 23 and the Cobra Helicopter, one of the first modern combat helicopters. Sunday-Friday 11 a.m.-4:30 p.m., Saturday 10 a.m.-4:30 p.m.

DEVIL'S DEN STATE PARK
11333 Highway 74 W., West Fork, 479-761-3325; www.arkansasstateparks.com
In a scenic valley in the Boston Mountains, this 2,000-acre park in the heart of rugged Ozark terrain includes unusual sandstone formations and the Devil's Icebox, where the temperature never goes above 60 F. If you want to get moving, go swimming in the pool (summer; lifeguard), fishing, canoeing (rentals), hiking, mountain biking on trails, picnicking and camping (electric hookups, dump station; standard fees). There's also a horse camp and a visitor center with exhibits, camping and backpack equipment rentals. Daily.

FINE ARTS CENTER

Garland St., Fayetteville, 479-575-4752; www.art.uark.edu

The center includes a theater, a concert hall, a library and an exhibition gallery. Daily.

HEADQUARTERS HOUSE

118 E. Dickson St., Fayetteville, 479-521-2970; www.washcohistoricalsociety.org

Union and Confederate forces used this Greek Revival house, at different times during the Civil War. Inside, you'll find period furnishings, local historical artifacts and Civil War relics. By appointment.

PRAIRIE GROVE BATTLEFIELD STATE PARK

14262 Highway 62, Prairie Grove, 479-846-2990; www.arkansasstateparks.com

Here you'll find the site where more than 22,000 Union and Confederate forces fought on December 7, 1862. The armies suffered a combined loss of 2,700 dead, wounded or missing. The Hindman Hall Museum houses a visitor center with exhibits, a battle diorama, artifacts and an audiovisual presentation. The park is also home to historic structures. There are guided tours daily.

UNIVERSITY OF ARKANSAS

1125 W. Maple St., Fayetteville, 479-575-2000; www.uark.edu

This university, which is home to 15,800 students, includes a fine arts center, a museum and an arts center.

UNIVERSITY MUSEUM

Garland Ave., Museum Building, Fayetteville, 479-575-3466; www.arkansas.com

The museum houses science, natural history and ethnological exhibits. Monday-Saturday.

WALTON ARTS CENTER

495 W. Dickson St., Fayetteville, 479-443-5600; www.waltonartscenter.org

Come to the arts center for your fill of musicals, opera, plays and symphonies.

SPECIAL EVENT
BATTLE REENACTMENT

Prairie Grove Battlefield State Park, Highway 62, Prairie Grove,
479-846-2990; www.arkansas.com

Costumed volunteers reenact historic battle and demonstrate war tactics and the life of a Civil War soldier. First full weekend in December on even-numbered years.

HOTELS
★BEST WESTERN WINDSOR SUITES

1122 S. Futrall, Fayetteville, 479-587-1400, 800-780-7234; www.bestwestern.com

68 rooms. High-speed Internet access. Complimentary continental breakfast. Outdoor pool. Business center. **$**

★★CLARION CARRIAGE HOUSE INN AT THE MILL

3906 Great House Springs Road, Johnson, 479-443-1800; www.innatthemill.com

48 rooms. Complimentary continental breakfast. Restaurant. **$**

★DAYS INN

2402 N. College Ave., Fayetteville, 479-443-4323, 800-329-7466; www.daysinn.com

149 rooms. High-speed Internet access. Complimentary continental breakfast. Outdoor pool. **$**

★★RADISSON HOTEL FAYETTEVILLE

70 N. East Ave., Fayetteville, 479-442-5555, 800-333-3333;
www.radisson.com/fayettevillear

235 rooms. Wireless Internet access. Restaurant, bar. **$**

FORREST CITY

Named for Confederate General Nathan Bedford Forrest, the town stands on Crowley's Ridge, an unusual geological formation that rises 250 to 500 feet above the Mississippi Delta; the ridge runs nearly 200 miles from Missouri to Helena, Ark.
Information: Chamber of Commerce, 203 N. Izard, 870-633-1651;
www.forrestcitychamber.com

WHAT TO SEE AND DO
VILLAGE CREEK STATE PARK

201 CR 754, Wynne, 870-238-9406; www.arkansasstateparks.com

The park, with its two lakes and miles of hiking and horse trails, offers plenty of ways to play on the unique geology of Crowley's Ridge. Activities abound: swimming, fishing, boating (rentals), hiking trails, tennis, picnicking, playing on the playground, camping (hookups, dump station), sleeping in one of 10 fully equipped cabins. The visitor center offers history, geology and botany exhibits; audiovisual presentations; and interpretive programs (summer). Daily.

HOTEL
★★DAYS INN

350 Barrow Hill Road, Forrest City, 870-633-0777, 800-329-7466; www.daysinn.com

53 rooms. High-speed Internet access. Complimentary full breakfast. Restaurant. Outdoor pool. Pets accepted. **$**

FORT SMITH

It's hard to imagine today, but Fort Smith was once the edge of the Wild West. The original fort was built on the Arkansas River in 1817 to promote peace between the warring Osages and the Cherokees. It also gave protection to traders, trappers and explorers.

In 1848, when gold was discovered in California, Fort Smith immediately became a thriving supply center and starting point for gold rush wagons heading south across the plains. Bandits, robbers and gamblers moved in. Without peace officers, the territory was wild and tough until 1875, when Judge Isaac C. Parker—known later as "The Hanging Judge"—arrived to clean it up. Parker was judge of the Federal District Court at Fort Smith for 21 years; during his first 14 years, there were no appeals of his decisions. Under Parker's rule, 151 men were sentenced to die and about 80 hanged, sometimes as many as six at a time. The town has preserved much of its history, which makes it a great stop for travelers who want to see the place where the Old West meets the Old South.
Information: Chamber of Commerce, 612 Garrison Ave., 501-783-6118;
www.fschamber.com

ARKANSAS

WHAT TO SEE AND DO

FORT SMITH ART CENTER

423 N. Sixth St., Fort Smith, 479-784-2787; www.ftsartcenter.com

Originally built in 1879 as a residence, the art center now offers changing monthly exhibits and art classes. Guided tours are available by appointment. Tuesday-Saturday 9:30 a.m.-4:30 p.m., Sunday 1-4 p.m.

FORT SMITH MUSEUM OF HISTORY

320 Rogers Ave., Fort Smith, 479-783-7841; www.fortsmithmuseum.com

The museum gives a glimpse into regional history with a period pharmacy with a working soda fountain and a transportation exhibit with an 1899 steam fire pumper. Tuesday-Saturday 10 a.m.-5 p.m.; June-August: Tuesday-Saturday 9 a.m.-5 p.m.; Sunday 1-5 p.m.

FORT SMITH NATIONAL HISTORIC SITE

301 Parker Ave., Fort Smith, 501-783-3961; www.nps.gov/fosm

The park includes foundations of the first Fort Smith, the famous Judge Parker's courtroom, jail (known during Judge Parker's reign as "Hell on the Border") and reconstructed gallows. Daily 9 a.m.-5 p.m.

WHITE ROCK MOUNTAIN RECREATION AREA

Highway 215, in the Boston Mountain range of the Ozark National Forest, Alma,
501-369-4128; www.whiterockmountain.com

At the summit of 2,287-foot White Rock peak, this primitive area has beautiful panoramic views. It's a great spot for picnicking and camping. Daily.

SPECIAL EVENTS

ARKANSAS-OKLAHOMA STATE FAIR

Kay Rodgers Park, 4400 Midland Blvd., Fort Smith, 479-783-6176, 800-364-1080;
www.kayrodgerspark.com

Kay Rodgers Park is home to a number of events throughout the year, including the Arkansas-Oklahoma State Fair, held nine days in September and October. The fair features live musical entertainment, a youth talent contest, a circus, a demolition derby, monster-truck racing, a carnival, and livestock, poultry and horticulture exhibits. Late September-early October.

OLD FORT DAYS RODEO

Kay Rodgers Park, 4400 Midland Blvd., Fort Smith, 479-783-6176, 800-364-1080;
www.oldfortdaysrodeo.com

This fast-paced rodeo has it all: calf roping, wild-horse racing, steer wrestling and rodeo clown bullfighting. Late May-early June.

HOTELS

★ASPEN HOTEL & SUITES

2900 S. 68th, Fort Smith, 501-452-9000, 800-627-9417;
www.aspenhotelandsuites.com

49 rooms. High-speed Internet access. Complimentary continental breakfast. Airport transportation available. Business center. $

★
★
★
★

★★HOLIDAY INN

700 Rogers Ave., Fort Smith, 479-783-1000, 800-465-4329; www.holiday-inn.com
255 rooms. High-speed Internet access. Restaurant. Airport transportation available. Outdoor pool. **$**

RESTAURANT
★CALICO COUNTY

2401 S. 56th St., Fort Smith, 501-452-3299; www.calicocounty.net
Breakfast, lunch, dinner. **$$**

GREERS FERRY LAKE AREA

Shortly before his assassination in November 1963, President John F. Kennedy dedicated this 50-mile-long lake. Since then, the area has developed rapidly, now offering 15 public recreation areas on more than 31,000 acres. Swimming, waterskiing, scuba diving, boating (rentals, marina, ramps), hunting, hiking up Sugar Loaf Mountain, picnicking and camping are some of the activities available.
Information: Heber Springs Chamber of Commerce, 1001 W. Main, Heber Springs, 501-362-2444, 800-774-3237; www.greers-ferry.com

WHAT TO SEE AND DO
LITTLE RED RIVER
Greers Ferry Lake Area
One of the finest trout streams in the area, Little Red River is stocked weekly. Lucky fishermen have caught trout weighing more than 15 pounds. There are five commercial docks.

WILLIAM CARL GARDNER VISITOR CENTER
700 Heber Springs Road N., Heber Springs, 501-362-9067; www.greersferrylake.org
The center provides tourist information and houses exhibits interpreting history and culture of the southern Ozark region; displays relate history of the Corps of Engineers and their projects in Arkansas. You can opt for a guided tour of Greers Ferry Dam and Powerhouse, which depart from the visitor center (Memorial Day-Labor Day: Monday-Friday). Visitor center: March-October: daily; February, November-December: Saturday-Sunday.

HOTEL
★★RED APPLE INN
Highway 110, Heber Springs, 501-362-3111, 800-733-2775; www.redappleinn.com
59 rooms. Restaurant, bar. Airport transportation available. **$**

HARRISON

Scenic Harrison, headquarters for a rustic resort area in the wild and beautiful Ozarks, is an excellent vacation spot. Don't miss the gorgeous drive along Highway 7.
Information: Chamber of Commerce, 621 E. Rush, 870-741-2659, 800-880-6265; www.harrison-chamber.com

★
★
★
★

WHAT TO SEE AND DO

BOONE COUNTY HERITAGE MUSEUM

110 S. Cherry, Harrison, 870-741-3312; www.bchrs.org

The museum preserves history and antiques from the Civil War and the Missouri and North Arkansas Railroad Co., Native American artifacts, old clocks, and medical and domestic tools from the 1800s. March-December: Monday-Friday.

FLOAT TRIPS

Walnut and Erie streets, Harrison, 870-741-5443; www.harrisonanglers.com

Take an excursion down the Buffalo River through the Ozark Mountains and the forested hill country.

MYSTIC CAVERNS

Highway 7 S., Dogpatch, 870-743-1739; www.mysticcaverns.com

Mystic has two caves with large formations, a 35-foot "pipe organ" formation and an eight-story crystal dome. The one-hour guided tours cover ³⁄₈ mile of lighted walks (may be strenuous). March-December: Monday-Saturday 9 a.m.-5 p.m.; February: Wednesday-Saturday 10 a.m.-5 p.m.

SPECIAL EVENTS

CROOKED CREEK CRAWDAD DAYS

Harrison

This annual spring festival celebrates the crawdads of Crooked Creek with arts, crafts, music, a fishing derby, a crawdad-eating contest and a cardboard boat race. May.

★
★
★
★
★

HARVEST HOMECOMING

Harrison, 870-741-1789; www.arkansas.com

During the first weekend in October, the people of Harrison flock to the downtown area to take part in the city's largest festival. The Harvest Homecoming celebrates Harrison's history with activities the whole family can enjoy. In addition to autumn food and live entertainment, the festival features a farmers' market, working craftsmen, children's activities, sports-related activities, a car show, tractor races and a scarecrow-decorating contest. October.

NORTHWEST ARKANSAS BLUEGRASS MUSIC FESTIVAL

Northwest Arkansas Fairgrounds, 1400 Fairgrounds Road, Harrison, 870-427-3342; www.southshore.com

Festivalgoers camp out and enjoy impromptu jam sessions when they're not busy catching the scheduled stage acts. August.

NORTHWEST ARKANSAS DISTRICT FAIR

1400 Fair Ground Road, Harrison, 870-743-1011; www.harrison-chamber.com

The fair gets festive with a livestock show and rodeo. September.

HOTELS

★COMFORT INN

1210 Highway 62-65 N., Harrison, 870-741-7676, 800-228-5150; www.choicehotels.com

93 rooms. High-speed Internet access. Complimentary continental breakfast. Outdoor pool. $

★DAYS INN
1425 Highway 62/65 N., Harrison, 870-391-3297, 800-329-7466; www.daysinn.com
82 rooms. High-speed Internet access. Complimentary continental breakfast. Bar. Outdoor pool. **$**

★★RED APPLE INN
Highway 110, Heber Springs, 501-362-3111, 800-733-2775; www.redappleinn.com
59 rooms. Restaurant, bar. Airport transportation available. **$**

RESTAURANTS
★★CAFE KLASER
600 W. Main St., Heber Springs, 501-206-0688; www.cafeklaser.com
French, German menu. Lunch, dinner. Closed Sunday-Monday. **$$**

★★OL' ROCKHOUSE
416 S. Pine St., Harrison, 870-741-8047
American menu. Lunch, dinner. **$$**

★★RED APPLE DINING ROOM
1000 Club Road, Heber Springs, 501-362-3111; www.redappleinn.com
American menu. Breakfast, lunch, dinner, Sunday brunch. **$$**

HELENA

Mark Twain once described Helena as occupying "one of the prettiest situations on the Mississippi." This spot has more than good looks: Some of the nation's best blues musicians cut their teeth here. Sunnyland Slim, Memphis Slim and Roosevelt Sykes all played here in the 1940s and '50s.

Information: Phillips County Chamber of Commerce, 870-338-8327; www.phillipscountychamber.org

WHAT TO SEE AND DO
DELTA CULTURAL CENTER
141 Cherry St., Helena, 870-338-4350; www.deltaculturalcenter.com
Housed in a 1912 Missouri Pacific rail depot, the center has exhibits on the history of the Delta. Tuesday-Sunday.

OZARK NATIONAL FOREST
Highway 44, Helena, 870-295-5278; www.fs.fed.us/oonf/ozark
In beautiful Ozark National Forest, you'll find the Boston Mountains, the state's tallest mountain—Mount Magazine—and an amazing underground cave, Blanchard Springs Caverns. The park's 1.2 million acres are the perfect playground for outdoor enthusiasts. Trek the 165-mile Ozark Highlands Trail, paddle Richland Creek and check out the waterfalls and camp along Shores Lake (especially in April, when dogwoods are in bloom). Fees may be charged at recreation sites. Daily.

PHILLIPS COUNTY MUSEUM
623 Pecan St., Helena, 870-338-7790; www.arkansas.com
At this museum, you'll find Native American artifacts, Civil War relics, a local history collection, glass, china, paintings and costumes. Tuesday-Saturday.

85

ARKANSAS

★
★
★
★

SPECIAL EVENTS

ARKANSAS BLUES HERITAGE FESTIVAL

Cherry St., Helena, 870-338-8798; www.bluesandheritage.org

Formerly the King Biscuit Blues Festival, this celebration of blues is one of the South's best. For three full days, nearly 100,000 people enjoy blues music and culture. October.

WARFIELD CONCERT SERIES

1000 Campus Drive, Helena, 870-338-6474; www.arkansas.com

A series of concerts features internationally known artists. Tickets are available at the Chamber of Commerce. Fall shows.

HOTEL

★DELTA INN

1207 Highway 49 W., West Helena, 870-572-7915; www.motel6.com

94 rooms. Complimentary continental breakfast. $

SPECIALTY LODGINGS

EDWARDIAN INN

317 Biscoe St., Helena, 870-338-9155, 800-598-4749; www.edwardianinn.com

This restored historic mansion, built in 1904, is near the Mississippi River. 12 rooms. Wireless Internet access. Complimentary full breakfast. $

MAGNOLIA HILL BED AND BREAKFAST

608 Perry St., Helena, 870-338-6874; www.magnoliahillbnb.com

8 rooms. Complimentary full breakfast. $

★
★★
★★
★

WHERE THE MISSISSIPPI RIVER DELTA GOT THE BLUES

A tiny town with a giant legacy, Helena is home to the longest-running blues radio program in the United States: *King Biscuit Time*, named after its local sponsor. First broadcast on November 21, 1941, the show featured blues musicians Sonny Boy Williamson and Robert Junior Lockwood playing live in the studio. Since 1951, Sunshine Sonny Payne has hosted the show, and generations of musicians credit the blues and *King Biscuit Time* with inspiring their work.

The radio show's success inspired another celebration of the blues. Every October, tens of thousands of people invade this isolated Delta outpost to enjoy the King Biscuit Blues Festival, recently renamed the Arkansas Blues Heritage Festival.

Visit the Delta Cultural Center, a converted 1913 train depot in downtown Helena, to see Sunshine Sonny Payne work his magic (at 95 Missouri St., weekdays only). The center also chronicles the rise of the blues in this Mississippi Delta town. When you're finished, stroll up to Cherry Street, a four-block stretch in the heart of downtown Helena. Here you'll find the Sonny Boy Blues Society, which occasionally hosts live performances by local artists.

If all this makes you hungry, walk down Cherry Street to find the candlelit Bells Ducks by the Levee (870-338-6655), which serves steak, catfish and surf-and-turf combos.

HOPE

Before he was the 42nd president of the United States, William Jefferson Clinton was a little kid in Hope, Ark. Today, the town celebrates its native son who told delegates at the 1992 Democratic National Convention: "I still believe in a place called Hope." Hope's second claim to fame is its Watermelon Festival, where farmers compete to win awards for the largest melon.

Information: Chamber of Commerce, 108 E. Third, 870-777-3640; www.hopeusa.com

WHAT TO SEE AND DO
CLINTON BIRTHPLACE HOME

117 S. Hervey, Hope, 870-777-4455; www.clintonbirthplace.com

This was the first home of President Bill Clinton; he lived here from the time of his birth in 1946 until his mother married Roger Clinton in 1950. It's a National Register Historic Site. There's also a visitor center and gift shop. Tuesday-Saturday 10 a.m.-4:30 p.m.; also Sunday 1-5 p.m. in spring and summer.

HOPE WATERMELON FESTIVAL

108 W. Third St., Hope, 870-777-3640; www.hopemelonfest.com

Celebrate the great melon for four days. The festival tradition began in the 1920s, when trains cut through this small town and local watermelon growers would sell their fruit to parched travelers. These days, people flock to the four-day festival to enjoy good food, buy arts and crafts, attend the antique car show and compete in the Watermelon Olympics, which includes a seed-spitting contest and a melon toss. The big event, though, is the competition to see the biggest watermelon. Most years, the winner weighs between 150 and 200 pounds. Early August.

OLD TAVERN

Highways 195 and 278, Hope, 870-983-2733

The 1874 Courthouse now serves as a park information center; Royston House, restored residence of Arkansas Militia General Grandison D. Royston, president of Arkansas Constitutional Convention of 1874; Sanders House, restored Greek Revival house; Purdom House, which served as the medical offices of Dr. James Purdom; gun museum with more than 600 antique weapons; and the Goodlett Cotton Gin and more.

HOTEL
★BEST WESTERN OF HOPE

I-30 and Highway 278, Hope, 870-777-9222, 800-429-4494; www.bestwestern.com

75 rooms. High-speed Internet access. Complimentary breakfast. Outdoor pool. $

HOT SPRINGS AND HOT SPRINGS NATIONAL PARK

One of the most popular destinations in the United States, the colorful city of Hot Springs surrounds portions of Hot Springs National Park. Known as "America's spa," Hot Springs has long attracted vacationers in search of healing or relaxation.

Nearly 1 million gallons of thermal water flow daily from the 47 springs within the park. At an average temperature of 147 F, the water flows to a reservoir under

★
★
★
★

the city's headquarters building; here it is distributed to bathhouses and spas through insulated pipes. Bathhouses mix cooled and hot thermal water to regulate bath temperatures.

Hot Springs, however, is more than a spa. It is a cosmopolitan city in the midst of beautiful wooded hills, valleys and lakes of the Ouachita region. The town's art scene is one of the best in the South, and its downtown area offers delicious restaurants and charming shops. Swimming, boating and water sports are available at nearby Catherine, Hamilton and Ouachita lakes. All three offer good year-round fishing for bream, crappie, bass and rainbow trout.

Information: Convention & Visitors Bureau, 134 Convention Blvd.,
501-321-2277, 800-772-2489; www.nps.gov/hosp and www.hotsprings.org

WHAT TO SEE AND DO
ARKANSAS ALLIGATOR FARM & PETTING ZOO
847 Whittington Ave., Hot Springs, 501-623-6172; www.arkansasalligatorfarm.com
We're not sure you'll actually want to pet the alligators, but this stop has plenty for you to see. It's also home to rhesus monkeys, mountain lions, llamas, pygmy goats, ducks and other animals. Daily.

AUTO TOURS
Fountain Street and Hot Springs, Mountain Drive, Hot Springs, 501-321-2277;
www.hotsprings.org
Just north of Bathhouse Row, drive from the end of Fountain Street up Hot Springs Mountain Drive to scenic overlooks at Hot Springs Mountain Tower and a picnic area on the mountaintop. West Mountain Drive, starting from either Prospect Avenue (on the south) or from Whittington Avenue (on the north), also provides excellent vistas of the city and surrounding countryside.

BATHHOUSE ROW
Central Avenue, Hot Springs, 501-624-3383; www.hotsprings.org
Self-guided tours of the Fordyce Bathhouse are offered. Daily.

BELLE OF HOT SPRINGS
5200 Central Ave., Hot Springs, 501-525-4438; www.belleriverboat.com
Take a sightseeing, lunch or dinner cruise along Lake Hamilton on the 400-passenger vessel (February-November: daily). Charter cruises are also available.

COLEMAN'S CRYSTAL MINE
5386 N. Highway 7, Jesseville, 501-984-5328; www.jimcolemancrystals.com
Visitors may dig for quartz crystals; tools are supplied. Daily.

DRYDEN POTTERIES
341 Whittington Ave., Hot Springs, 501-623-4201; www.drydenpottery.com
Check out pottery-making demonstrations. Monday-Friday 9 a.m.-3:30 p.m., Saturday 9:30 a.m.-3:30 p.m.

FORDYCE BATHHOUSE MUSEUM & HOT SPRINGS NATIONAL PARK VISITOR CENTER

300 Central Ave., Hot Springs, 501-624-2308; www.hotsprings.org
Luxuriate in the hot springs at this remodeled bathhouse.

GRAND PROMENADE

Grand Promenade and Fountain streets, Hot Springs, 501-624-3383;
www.nps.gov/hosp
Catch beautiful vistas of the city by following this path through a landscaped park above and behind Bathhouse Row.

HOT SPRINGS MOUNTAIN TOWER

401 Hot Springs Mountain Drive, Hot Springs, 501-623-6035; www.hotspringsar.com
The tower rises 216 feet above Hot Springs National Park. Ride its glass-enclosed elevator up 1,256 feet above sea level for spectacular view of the Ouachita Mountains. Enjoy the fully enclosed viewing area and higher up, an open-air deck. Daily.

JOSEPHINE TUSSAUD WAX MUSEUM

250 Central Ave., Hot Springs, 501-623-5836; www.rideaduck.com
Set in the former Southern Club, which was the city's largest casino and supper club until the late 1960s, this museum displays more than 100 wax figures. Summer: Sunday-Thursday 9 a.m.-8 p.m., Friday-Saturday 9 a.m.-9 p.m.; winter: Sunday-Thursday 9:30 a.m.-5 p.m., Friday-Saturday 9:30 a.m.-8 p.m.

LAKE CATHERINE STATE PARK

5386 N. Highway 7, Hot Springs Village, 501-984-5396; www.arkansasstateparks.com

LAKE OUACHITA STATE PARK

5451 Mountain Pine Road, Mountain Pine, 501-767-9366; www.arkansasstateparks.com
Set on approximately 400 acres, the park offers swimming, fishing, boating (rentals, marina), hiking trails, picnicking and camping (hookups, dump station). Daily.

MID-AMERICA SCIENCE MUSEUM

500 Mid-America Blvd., Hot Springs, 71913; 501-767-3461;
www.midamericamuseum.org
Spend a day contemplating the wonders of the world—or at least, of Arkansas. Travel through "Underground Arkansas," an indoor cave with bridges, chambers, tunnels and slides. Catch the laser light show and trap your shadow—à la Peter Pan—in the Shadow Trapper. Before you leave, check out the 35,000-gallon freshwater aquarium. There's also a snack bar (seasonal) and a gift shop. Memorial Day-Labor Day: daily 9:30 a.m.-6 p.m.; rest of year: Tuesday-Sunday 10 a.m.-5 p.m.

NATIONAL PARK & HOT SPRINGS DUCK TOURS

406 Central Ave., Hot Springs, 501-321-2911, 800-682-7044; www.rideaduck.com
The "Amphibious Duck" travels on both land and water. Board in the heart of Hot Springs and proceed onto Lake Hamilton and around St. John's Island. March-October: daily; November-February: weather permitting.

ARKANSAS

★
★
★
★

OUACHITA NATIONAL FOREST

100 Reserve St., Hot Springs, 501-321-5202; www.fs.fed.us.oonf/ouachita.htm

The Ouachita ("WASH-i-taw") is 1.8 million acres of natural beauty in west central Arkansas and southeast Oklahoma. Hike, mountain bike or ride horseback along the park's many trails. Fish, swim or boat in any one of eight lakes, or canoe down one of its nine navigable rivers. Some recreation areas charge fees. Daily.

PARK HEADQUARTERS AND VISITOR CENTER

101 Reserve St., Hot Springs, 501-624-3383; www.hot.springs.national-park.com

The center offers an exhibit on the workings and origin of the hot springs. A self-guided nature trail starts here and follows the Grand Promenade. The visitor center is in the Hill Wheatley Plaza at the park entrance (Daily). Gulpha Gorge Campground is available for stays limited to 14 days April to October, and to 30 days the rest of the year (fee). Inquire at National Park Fordyce Visitor Center on Bathhouse Row.

TINY TOWN

374 Whittington Ave., Hot Springs, 501-624-4742; www.hotsprings.org

Handmade miniatures make up this indoor train town with locomotives across America. April-November, Monday-Saturday.

SPECIAL EVENT

THOROUGHBRED RACING

Oaklawn Jockey Club, 2705 Central Ave., Hot Springs,
501-623-4411, 800-625-5296; www.oaklawn.com

Wager on live races at Oaklawn, where you can also follow simulcast races or dine on a variety of tasty treats. January-April: daily.

HOTELS

★★★ARLINGTON RESORT HOTEL AND SPA

239 Central Ave., Hot Springs, 501-623-7771, 800-643-1502; www.arlingtonhotel.com

Guests will find total relaxation and enjoyment at this resort in the beautiful Ouachita Mountains of Hot Springs National Park. Guests can unwind in twin cascading pools or in the refreshing outdoor mountainside hot tub. 484 rooms. Restaurant, bar. **$**

★★★THE AUSTIN HOTEL & CONVENTION CENTER

305 Malvern Ave., Hot Springs, 501-623-6600, 877-623-6697; www.theaustinhotel.com

This wonderful getaway is in Hot Springs Park with a spectacular view of the Ouachita Mountains. Guests can rejuvenate with a visit to the famous spa in the park or enjoy art galleries and music shows only a few miles away. The hotel is connected to the Hot Springs Convention Center via covered walkway. 200 rooms. High-speed Internet access. Restaurant, bar. Spa. **$$**

★DAYS INN

106 Lookout Point, Hot Springs, 501-525-5666, 800-995-9559; www.daysinn.com

58 rooms. **$**

★HAMPTON INN

151 Temperance Hill Road, Hot Springs, 501-525-7000, 800-426-7866;
www.hamptoninn.com
82 rooms. Complimentary continental breakfast. **$**

RESTAURANTS
★★BOHEMIA

517 Park Ave., Hot Springs, 501-623-9661
Czech, German menu. Lunch, dinner. Closed Sunday. **$**

★CAJUN BOILERS

2806 Albert Pike Highway, Hot Springs, 501-767-5695
Cajun menu. Dinner. Closed Sunday-Monday. **$$**

★★COY'S STEAK HOUSE

300 Coy St., Hot Springs, 501-321-1414; www.coyssteakhouse.com
Seafood, steak menu. Dinner. **$$$**

★★★HAMILTON HOUSE

132 Van Lyell Trail, Hot Springs, 501-520-4040; www.hamiltonhouseestate.com
The town's best fine-dining experience, the restaurant occupies four stories of an old
estate home. The cozy dining rooms will charm you. The house sits on a quiet penin-
sula on beautiful Lake Hamilton. American menu. Dinner. **$$$**

★★HOT SPRINGS BRAU-HOUSE

801 Central Ave., Hot Springs, 501-624-7866
German menu. Dinner. Closed Monday. **$**

★MCCLARD'S BAR-B-Q

505 Albert Pike, Hot Springs, 501-624-9665; www.mcclards.com
Lunch, dinner. Closed Sunday-Monday. **$**

★MOLLIE'S

538 W. Grand Ave., Hot Springs, 501-623-6582
American menu. Lunch, dinner. Closed Sunday. **$$**

JONESBORO

The largest city in northeast Arkansas, Jonesboro is on Crowley's Ridge, an unusual
geological formation that rises 250 to 500 feet above the Mississippi Delta; the
ridge runs nearly 200 miles from Missouri to Helena, Ark., more or less parallel to
the Mississippi. Jonesboro is home to Arkansas State University and to more than
75 churches, earning it the nickname "The City of Churches."
Information: Greater Jonesboro Chamber of Commerce, 1709 E. Nettleton,
870-932-6691; www.jonesboro.org

★
★
★
★

WHAT TO SEE AND DO
ARKANSAS STATE UNIVERSITY
106 N. Caraway, Jonesboro, 870-972-2100; www.astate.edu
Nine colleges and a graduate school are spread throughout the 941-acre campus. Tours of campus are available.

CRAIGHEAD FOREST PARK
4910 S. Culberhouse, Jonesboro, 870-933-4604; www.mapquest.com
The 600-acre park is the place to go for swimming, fishing, paddleboats, picnicking and camping (hookups, showers, dump station). Fee for most activities. Daily.

CROWLEY'S RIDGE STATE PARK
2092 Highway 168, Walcott, 870-573-6751; www.arkansasstateparks.com
Once a campground for the Quapaw, this park has two lakes and miles of wooded hills. The ridge is named for Benjamin Crowley, whose homestead and burial place are here. You also have your choice of swimming (lifeguard), fishing, boating (paddleboat rentals), hiking trails, picnicking, camping and renting cabins. Daily.

DEAN B. ELLIS LIBRARY, CONVOCATION CENTER AND MUSEUM
Arkansas State University, Jonesboro
The museum houses natural and state history displays. Daily.

LAKE FRIERSON STATE PARK
7904 Highway 141, Jonesboro, 870-932-2615; www.arkansasstateparks.com
Famous for its brilliant array of dogwood blossoms in spring, this 135-acre park is on the eastern shore of Lake Frierson, which fronts the western edge of Crowley's Ridge. Activities include fishing, boating (rentals, ramp), hiking trails, picnicking and camping. Daily.

HOTELS
★★HOLIDAY INN
3006 S. Caraway Road, Jonesboro, 870-935-2030; www.holiday-inn.com
179 rooms. Restaurant, bar. Airport transportation available. $

★HOLIDAY INN EXPRESS
2407 Phillips Drive, Jonesboro, 870-932-5554, 800-465-4329; www.hiexpress.com
103 rooms. Wireless Internet access. Complimentary continental breakfast. Airport transportation available. $

RESTAURANT
★FRONT PAGE CAFE
2117 E. Parker, Jonesboro, 870-932-6343
Breakfast, lunch, dinner. $

LITTLE ROCK
Little Rock, the state capital, got its name from French explorers who dubbed this site on the Arkansas River "La Petite Roche" to distinguish it from larger rock outcroppings up the river. By 1831, the town was incorporated.

★
★
★
★
★

More than 175 years later, Little Rock is a historic city with the sophistication and spunk of a metropolitan mecca. Little Rockers—as the city's residents are called—enjoy beautiful river walks, chic restaurants, fine museums and plenty of recreational and cultural activities. One of the hottest spots in town is River Market in downtown Little Rock, home to a large indoor market where shoppers can buy everything from fresh vegetables to instruments. At night, River Market is the place to find live entertainment, often provided by the city's up-and-coming musicians.

Another lively neighborhood, the Heights on the north central side of town has a good vibe. Exclusive boutiques, antique shops, coffee houses and cafés—all frequented by the yuppies who live nearby—are worth a visit. The area gets its name from the bluffs on which many of the posh residential homes sit.

Information: Little Rock Convention & Visitors Bureau, Robinson Center, Markham & Broadway, 501-376-4781, 800-844-4781; www.littlerock.com

WHAT TO SEE AND DO

ARKANSAS ARTS CENTER

MacArthur Park, 501 E. 9th St., Little Rock, 501-372-4000; www.arkarts.com
Exhibits at this arts center include paintings, drawings, prints, sculpture and ceramics. Public classes in visual and performing arts are also available. Plus, the facility also feature a library, restaurant and theater. You can catch a performance by the Arkansas Arts Center Children's Theater here. Tuesday-Saturday 10 a.m.-5 p.m., Sunday 11 a.m.-5 p.m.

ARKANSAS REPERTORY THEATRE

601 Main St., Little Rock, 866-684-3737; www.therep.org
See professional theatrical productions at this theater.

ARKANSAS SYMPHONY ORCHESTRA

Robinson Center Music Hall, 2417 N. Tyler St., Little Rock, 501-666-1761; www.arkansassymphony.org
September-May.

BURNS PARK

1 Eldor Johnson Drive, North Little Rock, 501-791-8537; www.northlittlerock.ar.gov
One of the largest city-owned parks in the country, 1,500-acre Burns Park offers a little something for everyone. Fishing, boating, wildlife-trail hiking, 27-hole golf, miniature golf, tennis and even camping (10-day maximum) are available. The park's more unusual activities include amusement rides and nine-hole Frisbee golf. Fee for some activities. Daily.

DECORATIVE ARTS MUSEUM

501 E. Ninth St., Little Rock, 501-372-4000; www.arkarts.com
The restored 1839 Greek Revival mansion houses decorative art objects ranging from Greek and Roman period to contemporary American. You'll see ceramics, glass, textiles, crafts and Asian works of art. Tuesday-Saturday.

★
★
★
★

HISTORIC ARKANSAS MUSEUM

200 E. Third St., Little Rock, 501-324-9351; www.arkansashistory.com

Built between the 1820s and 1850s, the restoration includes four houses, outbuildings and a log house arranged to give a realistic picture of pre-Civil War Arkansas. The museum houses Arkansas-made exhibits and a crafts shop. Guided tours are available. Monday-Saturday 9 a.m.-5 p.m., Sunday 1-5 p.m.

LITTLE ROCK ZOO

Little Rock, 501-666-2406; www.littlerockzoo.com

What began in 1926 with an abandoned timber wolf and a circus-trained brown bear has grown into one of Little Rock's best attractions. More than 500 animals live here, many of them on the endangered species list. November-March: daily 9:30 a.m.-4:30 p.m., rest of year 9:30 a.m.-5 p.m.

MUSEUM OF DISCOVERY

500 President Clinton Ave., Little Rock, 501-396-7050, 800-880-6475; www.amod.org

This hands-on museum houses exhibits that will fascinate you and your kids. Check out the eerily empty mummy's coffin; its owner hasn't been found. Or chill out with a tarantula, an alligator or even the famed blue-tongued skink. Other exhibits cover energy, technology, the human body, other nations and much more. Monday-Saturday.

OLD MILL

Lakeshore and Fairway avenues, North Little Rock, 501-791-8537;
www.northlr.org

This scenic city park is famous for its cameo in the opening scene of *Gone with the Wind*. On the road to the mill are original milestones laid out by Confederate President Jefferson Davis. Daily.

★
★★
★★★
★★★★

THE OLD STATE HOUSE

300 W. Markham St., Little Rock, 501-324-9685; www.oldstatehouse.com

Originally designed by Kentucky architect Gideon Shryock, this beautiful Greek Revival building was the capitol from 1836 to 1911. It now houses a museum of Arkansas history. Features include the restored governor's office and legislative chambers; Granny's Attic, a hands-on exhibit; a President William J. Clinton exhibit; and an interpretive display of Arkansas' first ladies' gowns. Self-guided tours are available. Monday-Saturday 9 a.m.-5 p.m., Sunday 1-5 p.m.

PINNACLE MOUNTAIN STATE PARK

9420 Highway 300, Roland, 501-868-5806; www.arkansasstateparks.com

A cone-shaped mountain juts 1,000 feet above this heavily forested, 1,800-acre day-use park, bordered on the west by 9,000-acre Lake Maumelle. Fishing, boating (ramps), hiking, backpacking, picnicking and a playground provide lots to do. There's also a gift shop and visitor center with natural history exhibits. Daily.

QUAPAW QUARTER HISTORIC NEIGHBORHOODS

1315 Scott St., Little Rock and North Little Rock, 501-371-0075; www.quapaw.com

Named for Arkansas' native Quapaw Indians, this nine-square-mile area oozes charm and old-fashioned style. The neighborhoods contain sites and structures from the

1820s to the present. The original town of Little Rock grew up here, and you'll find more than 150 buildings listed on the National Register of Historic Places. A tour of historic houses in the area is held the first weekend of May.

STATE CAPITOL

1 State Capitol, Little Rock, 501-682-5080; www.sosweb.state.ar.us

This slightly smaller replica of the nation's capitol has stood in for its big brother in several films, including the 1986 TV movie *Under Siege*. You can explore some of the grounds on your own, but you might opt for the free guided tour to get the scoop on the building's history and some of the state's liveliest politicians. When the legislature is in session—beginning the second Monday in January of odd-numbered years—take a seat in the House or Senate chamber and watch the politicos debate. If you get tired of the wrangling, escape to the south lawn's 1,600-bush rose garden. Monday-Friday.

TOLTEC MOUNDS ARCHEOLOGICAL STATE PARK

490 Toltec Mounds Road, Scott, 501-961-9442; www.arkansasstateparks.com

The park is one of the largest and most complex prehistoric Native American settlements in the Lower Mississippi Valley. Native Americans inhabited this site from A.D. 600 to 1050, and the park preserves several mounds and a remnant of an embankment. Guided onsite tours (by appointment; fee) are available. A paved trail is accessible to the disabled. Tours depart from the visitor center, which has exhibits that explain the site's history. The center also offers audiovisual programs and an archaeological laboratory. Tuesday-Sunday.

VILLA MARRE

1321 Scott St., Little Rock, 501-371-0075; www.littlerock.com

If this beautiful restored Italianate mansion looks familiar, you'll have to own up to watching the 1980s TV hit *Designing Women*; the show's opening credits featured the home. Built in 1881 by Angelo and Jennie Marre in one of Little Rock's swankiest neighborhoods, Villa Marre reflects the opulence of the late 19th century, with ornate parquet floors, walnut woodwork and crystal chandeliers. Tours: Monday-Friday mornings, Sunday afternoons.

ARKANSAS

WAR MEMORIAL PARK

1 Jonesboro Drive, Little Rock, 501-664-6976; www.lrpr.org

One of the city's most popular parks offers playgrounds, bike trails, tennis courts, a golf course, a fitness center and amusement rides. Daily.

WILD RIVER COUNTRY

6820 Crystal Hill Road, North Little Rock, 501-753-8600; www.wildrivercountry.com

Cool off in Arkansas' largest water park and enjoy rides with names like Vertigo, Vortex and Cyclone. June-Labor Day: daily; May: weekends.

SPECIAL EVENTS

ARKANSAS ALL-ARABIAN HORSE SHOW

Barton Coliseum, 2600 Howard St., Little Rock, 501-372-8341; www.asfg.net

Second full weekend in April.

ARKANSAS STATE FAIR AND LIVESTOCK SHOW
2300 W. Roosevelt Road, Little Rock, 501-372-8341; www.arkansasstatefair.com
Enjoy some down-home fun at this popular fair, which attracts more than 400,000 people during its 10-day run. Live music, motor sports, rodeos and children's shows, as well as a 10-acre Midway with carnival rides, food and games will thrill every member of the family. Early to mid-October.

RIVERFEST
Riverfront Park, Little Rock, 501-255-3378; www.riverfestarkansas.com
This arts and music festival brings some of the nation's best performers to Little Rock. There's something for art lovers of all kinds: ballet, symphony, opera, theater, jazz, bluegrass and rock groups. There's also a children's area, bike race and five-mile run. Memorial Day weekend.

WILDWOOD FESTIVAL
20919 Denny Road, Little Rock, 501-821-7275, 888-278-7727; www.wildwoodpark.org
This series of musical programs, exhibits, lectures and events focuses on the performing arts. Late May-June.

HOTELS
★BEST WESTERN GOVERNORS SUITES
1501 Merrill Drive, Little Rock, 501-224-8051, 800-422-8051; www.bestwestern.com
49 rooms, all suites. Complimentary full breakfast. $

★★★THE CAPITAL HOTEL
111 W. Markham St., Little Rock, 501-374-7474, 800-766-7666;
www.thecapitalhotel.com
Built in 1876, this hotel is at home amid Little Rock's historical district. Turn-of-the-century ambience and attentive service will be found throughout the hotel. 125 rooms. Restaurant, bar. $$

★★COURTYARD BY MARRIOTT
10900 Financial Centre Parkway, Little Rock, 501-227-6000, 800-321-2211;
www.courtyard.com
149 rooms. Restaurant, bar. Fitness room. Outdoor pool, whirlpool. $

★★★EMPRESS OF LITTLE ROCK
2120 S. Louisiana, Little Rock, 501-374-7966, 877-374-7966; www.theempress.com
Scarlett O'Hara would approve of this 1888 Queen Anne-style mansion, carefully restored in the 1990s. This Victorian masterpiece offers antique-filled suites and gourmet breakfasts. Ask the innkeeper about the house's fascinating history. All rooms are named after historic Arkansas figures. Five rooms, three suites. Complimentary full breakfast. $$

★HAMPTON INN
6100 Mitchell Drive, Little Rock, 501-562-6667, 800-426-7866; www.hamptoninn.com
122 rooms. Complimentary continental breakfast. $

★★LA QUINTA INN
11701 Interstate-30, Little Rock, 501-455-2300, 800-687-6667; www.laquinta.com
145 rooms. Complimentary continental breakfast. Restaurant, bar. **$**

★★★THE PEABODY LITTLE ROCK
Three Statehouse Plaza, Little Rock, 501-375-5000; www.peabodylittlerock.com
Travelers to historic Little Rock would be hard-pressed to find a place more luxurious
than The Peabody, located on the banks of the Arkansas River. One of Little Rock's
most unusual—and endearing—spectacles happens here: At 11 a.m. each day, the
hotel's beloved ducks march on a red carpet from their duck palace in the lobby to the
fountain, while John Philip Sousa's *King Cotton March* plays. At 5 p.m., they march
back to their digs. If the ducks are treated this well, imagine how much pampering the
hotel's human guests enjoy. One treat not to be missed: gourmet dining at Capriccio,
famous for steaks and Italian favorites. 417 rooms. Three restaurants, bar. Airport
transportation available. **$$**

RESTAURANTS

★★1620
1620 Market St., Little Rock, 501-221-1620; www.1620restaurant.com
American menu. Dinner. **$$**

★BROWNING'S
5805 Kavanaugh Blvd., Little Rock, 501-663-9956
Mexican, American menu. Lunch, dinner. Closed Sunday-Monday. **$$**

★BRUNO'S LITTLE ITALY
315 N. Bowman Road, Little Rock, 501-224-4700; www.brunoslittleitaly.com
Italian menu. Dinner. Closed Sunday. **$$**

★BUFFALO GRILL
1611 Rebsamen Park Road, Little Rock, 501-663-2158
American menu. Lunch, dinner. Closed Sunday. **$**

★CHIP'S BARBECUE
9801 W. Markham St., Little Rock, 501-225-4346
American, Southern menu. Lunch, dinner. Closed Monday. **$**

★FADED ROSE
1619 Rebsamen Park Road, Little Rock, 501-663-9734; www.thefadedrose.com
American, Cajun menu. Lunch, dinner. **$$**

★★GRAFFITI'S
7811 Cantrell Road, Little Rock, 501-224-9079
Italian menu. Dinner. Closed Sunday. **$$**

★★SIR LOIN'S INN
801 W. 29th St., North Little Rock, 501-753-1361
Steak menu. Dinner. Closed Sunday. **$$$**

ARKANSAS

★
★
★
★

MAGNOLIA

Named for the fragrant white blossoms that dot its landscape, Magnolia is home to Southern Arkansas University (the Muleriders). The small town's other big claim to fame is the World Championship Steak Cook-Off, held each May during the Magnolia Blossom Festival.

Information: Magnolia-Columbia County Chamber of Commerce, 202 N. Pine, 870-234-4352; www.magnoliachamber.com

WHAT TO SEE AND DO

LOGOLY STATE PARK

31 Columbia 459, McNeil, 870-695-3561; www.arkansasstateparks.com/logoly

Logoly is the first state park in Arkansas dedicated to environmental education. The 368 acres of forested coastal plain offer a "living laboratory" for students and researchers. Enjoy well-marked hiking trails, observation stands, photo blinds and the park's 11 natural springs. Picnicking and tent camping are available. The visitor center displays flora, fauna and history of the area. Daily.

SOUTHERN ARKANSAS UNIVERSITY

100 E. University St., Magnolia, 870-235-4000; www.saumag.edu

On the north edge of Magnolia, the campus is home to a Greek theater and model farm. The Carl White Caddo Native American Collection is on permanent display in Magale Library. Campus tours are available.

HOTEL

★★BEST WESTERN COACHMAN'S INN

420 E. Main St., Magnolia, 870-234-6122, 800-237-6122; www.bestwestern.com

80 rooms. Complimentary continental breakfast. Restaurant. $

MALVERN

Established in 1870 by the Cairo & Fulton Railroad, Malvern was a popular destination with travelers who were heading to the spas in Hot Springs. Today, it is known as the "Brick Capital of the World" for its brick manufacturing.

Information: Chamber of Commerce, 213 W. 3rd St., 501-332-2721; www.malvernchamber.com

WHAT TO SEE AND DO

JENKINS' FERRY STATE HISTORIC MONUMENT

Sixteen miles east on Highway 270, six miles south on Highway 291, two miles southwest on Highway 46, Malvern, 501-844-4176; www.stateparks.com/jenkins_ferry.html

See exhibits on this Civil War battleground site.

SPECIAL EVENTS

BRICKFEST

Courthouse grounds, 305 Locust St., Malvern, 501-332-2721; www.malvernbrickfest.com

The three-day event offers the usual fare: concerts, arts and crafts and plenty of food. There's also the contest for "Best Dressed Brick," a brick toss and a brick car derby. You have to see it to believe it. Last weekend in June.

HOT SPRING COUNTY FAIR AND RODEO

Fairgrounds, Malvern, 501-332-5267

Weekend after Labor Day.

HOTEL

★SUPER 8

Highway 270 W., Malvern, 501-332-5755, 800-800-8000; www.super8.com

74 rooms. Complimentary continental breakfast. **$**

MENA

This pretty little town sits at the base of Rich Mountain in the Ouachita Mountains.

Information: Mena/Polk County Chamber of Commerce, 524 Sherwood Ave.,
501-394-2912; www.menapolkchamber.com

WHAT TO SEE AND DO

QUEEN WILHELMINA STATE PARK

3877 Highway 88 W., Mena, 479-394-2863, 800-264-2477; www.queenwilhelmina.com

With views fit for royalty, this park atop Rich Mountain is the perfect antidote to cabin fever or too much time in the office. The Kansas City Railroad company built the original inn here in 1898 as a luxurious retreat; financed by Dutch investors, the inn was named for the reigning queen of the Netherlands, Queen Wilhelmina. The current building is a reconstruction of the original. The park also offers hiking trails, miniature golf, picnicking, a playground, a store, a restaurant, camping (electric and water hookups) and shower facilities. Daily.

TALIMENA SCENIC DRIVE

524 Sherwood Ave., Mena, 501-394-2912; www.talimenascenicdrive.com

This 54-mile roller-coaster drive through the Ouachita National Forests to Talihina, Okla., passes through the park and other interesting and beautiful areas. In addition to campgrounds in the park, there are other camping locations along the drive (fees may be charged). The drive may be difficult in winter.

SPECIALTY LODGING

QUEEN WILHELMINA LODGE

3877 Highway 88 W., Mena, 479-394-2863; www.queenwilhelmina.com

38 rooms. Restaurant. Children's activity center. Airport transportation available. **$**

MORRILTON

The common story on how Morrilton got its name is that two farmers donated some land to the railroad being built here in the late 1800s. Each farmer wanted the train stop to bear his name and the two flipped a coin. Mr. Morrill won (hence Morrilton), though if you swing through the downtown streets, you'll also see Mr. Moose's name.

Information: Chamber of Commerce, 120 N. Division, 501-354-2393;
www.morrilton.com

★
★
★
★

WHAT TO SEE AND DO

MUSEUM OF AUTOMOBILES

8 Jones Lane, Morrilton, 501-727-5427; www.museumofautos.com

Founded by former Arkansas Governor Winthrop Rockefeller, the museum features impressive antique and classic cars. There are autos from Rockefeller's personal collection as well as changing exhibits of privately owned cars. Daily.

PETIT JEAN STATE PARK

Highway 9, Morrilton, 501-727-5431, 800-264-2462; www.petitjeanstatepark.com

This rugged area is the oldest, and one of the most beautiful, of the Arkansas parks. The park and its forested Petit Jean Mountain are named for a French girl who disguised herself as a boy to accompany her sailor sweetheart to America. In the New World, she got sick and died, and legend tells us that friendly Native Americans buried her on the mountain. Among the park's most spectacular sights are Cedar Falls—a magnificent waterfall—and Cedar Creek Canyon. More than 20 miles of hiking trails will take you to these and other jewels of the park. The park also offers a swimming pool (lifeguard), boating (paddleboat, fishing boat rentals), hiking trails, tennis, picnicking, playgrounds, a restaurant, a snack bar (Memorial Day-Labor Day), camping, trailer sites, cabins and a lodge.

SPECIAL EVENT

GREAT ARKANSAS PIGOUT FESTIVAL

120 N. Division St., Morrilton, 501-354-5400

The name says it all. After you stuff yourself silly, enjoy softball, volleyball and three-on-three basketball tournaments. Don't miss the hog-calling competition and the famed pig chase. Local and nationally known entertainment also take the stage. First full weekend in August.

MOUNTAIN HOME

Mountain Home is a popular vacation spot midway between Arkansas' two big Ozark lakes: Bull Shoals and Norfolk. People come here for the outdoor sports, scenic views and quiet hospitality that define this unique place.

Information: Chamber of Commerce, 870-425-5111, 800-822-3536; www.mtnhomechamber.com

WHAT TO SEE AND DO

NORFORK LAKE

324 W. Seventh St., Mountain Home, 870-425-2700; www.norfork.com

Worth the 15-minute drive from Mountain Home, this 40-mile lake is one of Arkansas' most attractive water vacation areas. It offers water sports and boating (ramps, rentals, ten marinas). Fishing is great for largemouth, striped and white bass, plus walleye, crappie, bream, bluegill and catfish. Rainbow and brown trout are found in the North Fork River below the dam. If fishing isn't your thing, there's also hunting and camping. Daily.

NORFORK NATIONAL FISH HATCHERY
1414 Highway 177 S., Mountain Home, 870-499-5255; www.arkansas.com
One of the largest federal trout hatcheries in the country, this place annually distributes more than 2 million rainbow, brown, cutthroat and brook trout. Daily.

SPECIAL EVENTS
BAXTER COUNTY FAIR
Baxter County Fairgrounds, Mountain Home, 870-425-6828; www.baxtercountyfair.org
A quintessential county fair, the Baxter County bash offers a carnival, live bands, a pageant and livestock shows. The kids can participate in a hula-hoop contest, treasure hunt and pogo jump. Mid-September.

RED, WHITE AND BLUE FESTIVAL
Mountain Home, 870-425-5111; www.redwhitebluefestival.com
This patriotic festival has good food, great music and plenty of activities for all members of the family to enjoy. Late June.

HOTEL
★★BEST WESTERN CARRIAGE INN
963 Highway 62, Mountain Home, 870-425-6001, 800-780-7234;
www.bestwesternmtnhome.com
80 rooms. Outdoor pool. $

RESTAURANT
★FRED'S FISH HOUSE
44 Highway 101 Cutoff., Mountain Home, 870-492-5958
Seafood, steak menu. Lunch, dinner. Closed Sunday. $$

MOUNTAIN VIEW
This retreat will provide a unique soundtrack to your vacation: The folk music heritage that early settlers brought to these mountains is still an important part of the community. Almost every night of the summer, if the weather is nice, people gather in Courthouse Square with chairs and instruments to hear and play music.
Information: Mountain View Area Chamber of Commerce, 870-269-8098;
www.ozarkgetaways.com

★
★★
★★
★

WHAT TO SEE AND DO
BLANCHARD SPRINGS CAVERNS
Highway 14, Mountain View, 870-757-2211, 888-757-2246; www.tripadvisor.com
These spectacular living caverns feature crystalline formations, an underground river and huge chambers. Guided tours depart from visitor information center, which has an exhibit hall and free movie. There's a one-hour tour of the half-mile Dripstone Trail (year-round) and a 1¾-hour tour of the more strenuous 1¼-mile Discovery Trail (summer only). April-October: daily; November-March: Wednesday-Sunday.

OZARK FOLK CENTER STATE PARK

Highway 382, Mountain View, 870-269-3851, 800-264-3655;
www.ozarkfolkcenter.com

Established to preserve and share the crafts, music and heritage of the Ozark region, the park hosts fascinating events, such as a cowboy folk humor and storytelling weekend and crafts workshops. In the living museum, artisans demonstrate basketry, quiltmaking and woodcarving. The park also includes a lodge, restaurant, music auditorium and an outdoor stage with 300 covered seats. Special events are held all year. Crafts area: daily. Music shows: Monday-Saturday. Park: mid-April to October: daily.

SPECIAL EVENTS

ARKANSAS FOLK FESTIVAL

Mountain View, 870-269-8068; www.ozarkgetaways.com

Relax in the shade of blooming dogwood trees, browse the arts and crafts, and delight in local fare, all the while listening to acoustic music. Third weekend in April.

ARKANSAS STATE OLD-TIME FIDDLE CONTEST

Ozark Folk Center, Highway 382, Mountain View, 870-269-3851, 800-264-3655;
www.ozarkfolkcenter.com

This annual event celebrates the talent of fiddlers from the state. Early October.

BEAN FEST AND GREAT ARKANSAS CHAMPIONSHIP OUTHOUSE RACE

Courthouse Square, Mountain View, 870-269-8068;
www.ozarkgetaways.com

This three-day festival mixes traditional events—music, food and fun—with the unorthodox Parade of Outhouses and subsequent homemade outhouse races around Courthouse Square. Music, a bean cook-off and games add to the festivities. Last Saturday in October.

HERB HARVEST FALL FESTIVAL

Ozark Folk Center, Highway 382, Mountain View, 870-269-3851;
www.ozarkfolkcenter.com

The fest ushers in the harvest with concerts, crafts demonstrations, races, a fiddlers' jamboree and contests. Early October.

TRIBUTE TO MERLE TRAVIS: NATIONAL THUMBPICKING GUITAR CONTEST

Ozark Folk Center, Highway 382, Mountain View, 870-269-3851;
www.ozarkfolkcenter.com

This two-day event and contest honors Merle Travis, the guitarist, singer and composer who mastered the thumb and finger guitar technique. Mid-May.

HOTEL

★BEST WESTERN FIDDLERS INN

601 Sylamore Ave., Mountain View, 870-269-2828, 800-780-7234;
www.bestwestern.com

28 rooms. $

INN AT MOUNTAIN VIEW

P.O. Box 812, Mountain View, 870-269-4200, 800-535-1301;
www.innatmountainview.com

10 rooms. No children accepted. Complimentary full breakfast. **$**

NEWPORT

The White River, Black River and 35 lakes are nearby, making Newport a popular place for hunting, boating and fishing.

Information: Newport Area Chamber of Commerce, 210 Elm, 870-523-3618;
www.newportarchamber.org

WHAT TO SEE AND DO

COURTHOUSE MUSEUM

205 Avenue St., Newport, 870-523-2143

Inside the restored courthouse, the furniture represents various periods of Delta life. The Indian Room and War Memorial Room have uniforms and relics. Tuesday-Sunday.

JACKSONPORT STATE PARK

205 Avenue St., Jacksonport, 870-523-2143; www.arkansasstateparks.com

At the park, there's swimming, fishing, picnicking and camping. Daily.

MARY WOODS NO. 2

205 Avenue St., Newport, 870-523-2143

The refurbished White River steamboat, berthed at Jacksonport Landing, houses a maritime museum. May-early September: Tuesday-Sunday; September and October: Saturday-Sunday.

SPECIAL EVENT

PORTFEST & STATE CATFISH COOKING CONTEST

205 Avenue St., Newport, 870-523-2143; www.arkansasstateparks.com

National headliners come to tiny Newport for this annual music festival, which also offers catfish dinners, an arts and crafts show, races and a water-ski show. First weekend in June.

HOTEL

★★FORTUNE INN AND SUITES

901 Highway 367 N., Newport, 870-523-5851

58 rooms. Restaurant, bar. **$**

PARIS

Sure, France may have baguettes and Brie, but this Paris is home to some staggering natural beauty, nestled in a river valley near the Arkansas River and the Ozark Mountain region.

Information: Paris Area Chamber of Commerce, 301 W. Walnut,
479-963-2244, 800-980-8660; www.parisaronline.com

103

ARKANSAS

★
★
★
★

WHAT TO SEE AND DO
BLUE MOUNTAIN LAKE
Highway 10, Waveland, 501-947-2372; www.us-parks.com
Come to this park for swimming, waterskiing, fishing and boating. Landlubbers can opt for hunting, picnicking and camping. Daily.

COVE LAKE RECREATION AREA
3001 E. Walnut St., Paris, 501-963-3076; www.fs.fed.us
This area is near Magazine Mountain, the highest point in the state. The 160-acre lake is perfect for swimming (fee), fishing and boating (ramps). Picnicking and camping (fee) are also available. Daily.

LOGAN COUNTY MUSEUM
202 N. Vine St, Paris, 501-963-3936; www.loganso.com
The museum highlights historical information and artifacts from Paris and Logan County. Monday-Saturday afternoons.

PINE BLUFF
Any loyal citizen of Pine Bluff will tell you that the Civil War began right here. In April 1861, several days before the war's first official shots rang out at Fort Sumter, a musket shot was fired across the bow of a federal gunboat in the Arkansas River. The vessel and its supplies were confiscated. On October 25, 1863, Union troops took control of Pine Bluff and it remained in Union hands until the end of the Civil War.

Today Pine Bluff anchors the southeast corner of Arkansas. The "Bass Capital of the World," this area hosts as many as 35 bass-fishing tournaments each year.
Information: Convention Center & Visitors Bureau, One Convention Center Plaza, 870-536-7600, 800-536-7660; www.pinebluff.com

WHAT TO SEE AND DO
ARKANSAS ENTERTAINERS HALL OF FAME
1 Convention Center Plaza, Pine Bluff, 870-536-7600, 800-536-7600; www.pinebluffcvb.org
Arkansas has given the world entertainment greats Johnny Cash, Glenn Campbell, Billy Bob Thornton and Al Green, among many others. Trace their careers and check out stars' personal memorabilia. Monday-Friday, Saturday-Sunday (seasonal).

ARTS & SCIENCE CENTER FOR SOUTHEAST ARKANSAS
701 Main St., Pine Bluff, 870-536-3375; www.artssciencecenter.org
The center houses visual arts and science exhibits. Educational workshops are available for children. Daily.

DEXTER HARDING HOUSE
110 N. Pine St., Pine Bluff, 870-536-8742; www.arkansas.com
A tourist information center is in this 1850s house. Daily.

JEFFERSON COUNTY HISTORICAL MUSEUM

201 E. Fourth St., Pine Bluff, 870-541-5402; www.planetware.com

The museum features exhibits on the history of Pine Bluff and Jefferson County; development of area transportation, including river, roads and rail; displays of Victorian artifacts; and clothing used by early settlers. There's also a gift shop. Monday-Saturday.

NAVIGATION POOL (LOCK) NO. 3

Fifteen miles southeast via Highways 65 and 11, Altheimer, 870-534-0451

Visit Huffs Island, Rising Star (fee) and Trulock, which have fishing, boat-launching facilities, picnicking (fee for group picnicking in Rising Star and Trulock) and camping (Rising Star has electrical hookups, showers and dump station; fee). Some facilities are closed during winter. Daily.

NAVIGATION POOL (LOCK) NO. 4

Highways 425 and 65, Altheimer, 870-534-0451

Sainte Marie and Sheppard Island have fishing and boat-launching facilities. Sainte Marie also has a fishing dock designed for use by the disabled. Some facilities are closed during winter.

HOTEL

★★RAMADA

Two Convention Center Drive, Pine Bluff, 870-535-3111; www.ramada.com

84 rooms. Restaurant, bar. **$**

SPECIALTY LODGING

MARGLAND BED AND BREAKFAST

703 W. Second St., Pine Bluff, 870-536-6000, 800-545-5383; www.margland.net

22 rooms. Complimentary continental breakfast. **$**

POCAHONTAS

Even the most active visitors won't have trouble filling their time here whether fishing, boating or taking in the breathtaking vistas on a hike. Of course, those who prefer to lounge can soak in plenty of beauty from a sun chair.

Information: Randolph County Chamber of Commerce, 121 E. Everett St.,
870-892-3956; www.cityofpocahontas.com

WHAT TO SEE AND DO

MAYNARD PIONEER MUSEUM & PARK

13052 Highway 115, Maynard, 870-647-2701

Check out the log-cabin museum, which has displays of antique farm equipment. June-September: Tuesday-Sunday.

OLD DAVIDSONVILLE STATE PARK

7953 Highway 166 S., Pocahontas, 870-892-4708; www.arkansasstateparks.com

This 163-acre park on the Black River was the site of historic Davidsonville, a small town established by French settlers in 1815. The first post office and courthouse in the state were located here. Fishing, canoeing, boating (no motors; rentals), hiking trails, picnicking, a playground and camping (tent sites, hookups, dump station; fee) are also on offer. The visitor center exhibits local artifacts. Daily.

ROGERS

This pleasant town in the Ozark area is where Sam Walton built the first Wal-Mart. Its proximity to the mountains makes it a prime spot for outdoor sports year-round.
Information: Chamber of Commerce, 317 W. Walnut, 479-636-1240, 800-364-1240; www.rogerslowell.com

WHAT TO SEE AND DO
BEAVER LAKE
2260 N. Second St., Rogers, 479-636-1210
A huge reservoir with a 500-mile shoreline is a prime spot for swimming, waterskiing, fishing and boating (ramp, marine station, rental boats, motors). The lake also offers hunting, picnicking, a playground and camping (hookups, dump station). Fee for some activities. Daily.

DAISY INTERNATIONAL AIRGUN MUSEUM
202 W. Walnut, Rogers, 479-986-6873; www.daisymuseum.com
Daisy Outdoor Products, which manufactures the famed Red Ryder B-B Gun ("You'll shoot your eye out!"), established this museum, which has a large display of guns, some dating to the late 18th century. Tuesday-Saturday.

PEA RIDGE NATIONAL MILITARY PARK
15930 E. Highway 62, Garfield, 479-451-8122; www.nps.gov/peri
More than 26,000 troops clashed here on March 7 and 8, 1862, in a decisive Civil War battle that gave the Union control of Missouri. Three Confederate generals—McCulloch, McIntosh and Slack—died in the battle. The park preserves the battles site and a 2½-mile section of the Trail of Tears. Daily.

ROGERS HISTORICAL MUSEUM (HAWKINS HOUSE)
322 S. Second St., Rogers, 479-621-1154; www.rogersarkansas.com/museum
The museum shows exhibits on local history, re-created turn-of-the-century businesses and Victorian-era furnishings. There's also a hands-on children's discovery room. Tuesday-Saturday.

WAR EAGLE CAVERN
21494 Cavern Road, Rogers, 479-789-2909; www.wareaglecavern.com
The cavern's spectacular natural entrance leads to huge rooms full of interesting geologic formations. Learn about the cave's history and the bandits, warriors, squatters and draft dodgers who've holed up in the cavern over the years. Guided tours are available. Mid-March to November: daily.

WAR EAGLE MILL
11045 War Eagle Road, Rogers, 479-789-5343; www.wareaglemill.com
This picturesque little community is the site of one of the state's largest and most popular arts and crafts shows (May and October). Take a tour of the working, water-powered gristmill. Daily.

★★THE BEAN PALACE

11045 War Eagle Road, Rogers, 479-789-5343; www.wareaglemill.com
American menu. Breakfast, lunch. Closed weekdays (January-February). **$**

RUSSELLVILLE

Headquarters for the Ozark and St. Francis National Forests, Russellville is a haven for people who love the great outdoors. Nearby state parks, a wildlife refuge and the scenic Highway 7 make this town a popular destination for travelers.

Information: Chamber of Commerce, 708 W. Main St., 479-967-1763;
www.discoverrussellville.org

WHAT TO SEE AND DO

HOLLA BEND NATIONAL WILDLIFE REFUGE

Highway 1, Dardanelle, 479-229-4300; www.fws.gov/southeast/HollaBend
The refuge provides a safe home for thousands of migratory birds that fly south each winter, so the best time to visit is between late November and February. Ducks, geese, golden and bald eagles, herons, egrets, sandpipers and scissor-tailed flycatchers call this spot home for at least part of the year. Fishing is available (March-October) as is a self-guided auto tour. Daily.

LAKE DARDANELLE

2428 Marina Road, Russellville, 479-967-5516
More than 300 miles of shoreline on the lake are formed by Dardanelle Dam.

LAKE DARDANELLE STATE PARK

100 State Park Drive, Russellville, 479-967-5516
The park offers swimming, fishing, boating (rentals), bicycling, hiking, miniature golf, picnicking and camping (hookups, dump station). Daily.

MOUNT NEBO STATE PARK

1 State Park Drive, Dardanelle, 479-229-3655, 800-264-2458;
www.arkansasstateparks.com
Mount Nebo has gorgeous vistas, miles of hiking trails and several campsites. It is also one of two state parks that offer launch sites for hang gliders. Bench Trail, a 4½-mile mountain bike path is perfect for novice bikers. The drive from the base to the summit winds up the eastern side of the mountain; the drive is not recommended for trailers over 15 feet, thanks to a few hairpin turns. There's also a swimming pool, fishing (nearby), bicycling (rentals), hiking trails, tennis, picnicking, a playground, a store, camping (electric hookups) and cabins. The visitor center provides exhibits and interpretive programs. Daily.

NIMROD LAKE

Highway 60 E. Plainview, 28 miles south on Highway 7 at Fourche junction, 479-272-4324
This reservoir was formed by a dam on the Fourche La Fave River. Head there for swimming, waterskiing, fishing, boating, hunting, picnicking and tent and trailer camping. Quarry Cove, County Line and Sunlight Bay parks have showers. There's free camping at Carden Point Park (all year). Daily.

107

ARKANSAS

★
★
★
★

OZARK NATIONAL FOREST

605 W. Main St., Russellville, 479-968-2354; www.fs.fed.us/oonf/ozark/index_more.html

In beautiful Ozark National Forest, you'll find the Boston Mountains, the state's tallest mountain—Mount Magazine—and an amazing underground cave, Blanchard Springs Caverns. The park's 1.2-million acres are the perfect playground for outdoor enthusiasts. Fees may be charged at recreation sites. Daily.

SPECIAL EVENTS
POPE COUNTY FAIR

Pope County Fairgrounds, 479-967-0320; www.pcfg.org

The fair features a youth horse show, arts, crafts and horticulture exhibits, a carnival and a talent show. Mid-September.

VALLEY FEST

300 E. Third St., Russellville, 479-968-7819; www.valley-fest.org

Have fun and support a worthy cause: Proceeds from the event go to the Boys and Girls Club of the Arkansas River Valley. Festivities include a barbecue cook-off, three-on-three basketball, volleyball, fishing derby rides, live music and games such as horseshoes and hoop shooting (entry fees for most).

HOTEL
★★HOLIDAY INN

2407 N. Arkansas, Russellville, 479-968-4300, 800-465-4329; www.holiday-inn.com

149 rooms. Complimentary continental breakfast. Restaurant. Airport transportation available. $

SPRINGDALE

Springdale calls itself the heart of northwest Arkansas. It has much of Arkansas' natural beauty and—as a bonus—colorful vineyards nearby. The best are a few miles west on Highway 68 near Tontitown, a community settled by Italian immigrants in 1897.

Information: Chamber of Commerce, 202 W. Emma Ave.,
479-872-2222, 800-972-7261; www.springdale.com

★
★
★
★

WHAT TO SEE AND DO
ARTS CENTER OF THE OZARKS

214 S. Main, Springdale, 479-751-5441; www.artscenteroftheozarks.org

"Come play with us" is the center's motto—a tempting invitation for art lovers of any kind. Catch a show or concert in the theater, amble through the art gallery or take an art or a music class. Monday-Saturday.

SHILOH HISTORIC DISTRICT

118 W. Johnson Ave., Springdale, 479-750-8165; www.springdaleark.org/shiloh

The Shiloh Museum, Shiloh Church, Shiloh Memorial Park and early residences compose this district. Markers in the park show locations of historic Springdale buildings, streets and sites.

SHILOH MUSEUM OF OZARK HISTORY
118 W. Johnson Ave., Springdale, 479-750-8165

Long before Angelina Jolie and Brad Pitt named their baby Shiloh, the title belonged to a community that would become Springdale. The museum tells the history of the Ozarks through interactive exhibits, photographs, Native American artifacts and other historic items. Check out the log cabin (circa 1855), post office/general store (1871), country doctor's office (circa 1870) and farm machinery. Monday-Saturday.

SPECIAL EVENT
RODEO OF THE OZARKS
Parsons Stadium, 1433 E. Emma Ave., Springdale, Old Missouri Road, 877-927-6336;
www.rodeooftheozarks.org

Nothing says Independence Day quite like a rodeo, so the folks in Springdale celebrate each July with a professional one. Spectators watch seven professional events, including steer wrestling, bareback riding and the ever-popular bull riding. A parade, pageant, "denim & lace" dance and other activities round out the festivities. Early July.

HOTELS
★HAMPTON INN
1700 S. 48th St., Springdale, 479-756-3500, 800-426-7866;
www.hamptoninnspringdale.com

102 rooms. Wireless Internet access. Complimentary full breakfast. Airport transportation available. $

★★HOLIDAY INN
1500 S. 48th St., Springdale, 479-751-8300, 800-465-4329; www.holiday-inn.com

206 rooms. Wireless Internet access. Two restaurants, two bars. Airport transportation available. $

RESTAURANT
★A. Q. CHICKEN HOUSE
1207 N. Thompson, Springdale, 501-751-4633; www.aqchicken.com

American menu. Lunch, dinner. $$

STUTTGART

If you show up in Stuttgart and everyone's wearing camouflage, don't panic. The small town is one of the nation's best areas for duck hunting, and from November until January, duck hunters from around the world descend on Stuttgart.

Information: Chamber of Commerce, 507 S. Main, 870-673-1602;
www.stuttgartarkansas.com

WHAT TO SEE AND DO
MUSEUM OF THE ARKANSAS GRAND PRAIRIE
921 E. Fourth St., Stuttgart, 870-673-7001; www.tripadvisor.com

The museum tells the history of pioneer life and prairie farming with unique displays, including a replica prairie village, a scale model of an early newspaper office with a working printing press, a wildlife exhibit and a simulated duck hunt. Tuesday-Saturday.

ARKANSAS

★
★
★
★

WHITE RIVER NATIONAL WILDLIFE REFUGE

57 S. CC Camp Road, St. Charles, 870-282-8201

Migratory birds make their home here, which makes the refuge an excellent spot to bird-watch. Keep an eye out for the other animals that live here, including raccoons, alligators, deer and bears. Hunting is permitted for duck, deer, turkey, squirrel and raccoon. There's also fishing, boat access, picnicking and primitive camping. March-October: daily.

SPECIAL EVENT
WINGS OVER THE PRAIRIE FESTIVAL

Downtown Stuttgart, 870-673-1602

The kick-off to duck-hunting season, the festival includes the famous World Championship Duck Calling Contest, which is featured in the bestselling *1,000 Places to See Before You Die* by Patricia Schultz. Other highlights include a carnival, the 10-K Great Duck Race (for people, not birds) and the Duck Gumbo Cook-off. Thanksgiving week.

HOTEL
★BEST WESTERN DUCK INN

704 W. Michigan St., Stuttgart, 870-673-2575; www.bestwestern.com

70 rooms. High-speed Internet access. Complimentary continental breakfast. Pets accepted. **$**

TEXARKANA

Folks flock from surrounding states to Texarkana each year to attend the annual fair and rodeo. Cowboy hat not required.

Information: www.txkusa.org

SPECIAL EVENT
FOUR STATES FAIR & RODEO

Fairgrounds, Loop 245 and East 50th St., Texarkana,
870-773-2941, 800-776-1836; www.fourstatesfair.com

The rodeo features live entertainment, livestock exhibits and a Demolition Derby (fee). September.

HOTEL
★★AMERICA'S BEST VALUE KINGS ROW INN & SUITES

4200 State Line Ave., Texarkana, 870-774-3851, 800-643-5464;
www.kingsrowinn.com

116 rooms. Restaurant. Airport transportation available. **$**

WASHINGTON

Soak up a bit of history by stepping foot in Washington, which became the Confederate capital for the state after Little Rock was captured in 1863.

OLD WASHINGTON HISTORIC STATE PARK

Highways 195 and 278, Washington, 870-983-2684;
www.oldwashingtonstatepark.com

This historic village will transport you to the 19th century, when the town of Washington was a convenient stop on the Southwestern Trail and visitors such as Stephen Austin, Sam Houston and Davy Crockett strolled the streets. The park preserves and interprets the town's past from 1824 to 1875. Daily 8 a.m.-5 p.m.

SPECIAL EVENTS
FRONTIER DAYS

Old Washington Historic State Park, Highways 195 and 278,
Washington, 870-983-2684

Curious about what 19th-century pioneers did for fun? Visit this festival, where you'll see park staff create and throw knives, make lye soap, render lard and shoot turkeys. Third weekend in October.

JONQUIL FESTIVAL

Old Washington Historic State Park, Highways 195 and 278,
Washington, 870-983-2684

The fest coincides with blooming of jonquils planted by early settlers. It also has craft demonstrations and bluegrass music. Mid-March.

WEST MEMPHIS

Just across the Mississippi River from Memphis, West Memphis offers big-city charm with plenty of nature.

Information: 108 W. Broadway, West Memphis, 870-735-1134; www.westmemphis.org

WHAT TO SEE AND DO
TOM SAWYER'S MISSISSIPPI RIVER RV PARK

1286 S. Eighth St., West Memphis, 870-735-9770

The RV park has 80 sites and a pavilion.

111

ARKANSAS

★
★
★
★
☆

KENTUCKY

FAMOUS FOR HORSERACING, MINT JULEPS AND THE BLUEGRASS, KENTUCKY SPENDS A FEW minutes each May in the world's spotlight when all eyes turn to Louisville's Churchill Downs and the Derby. But the commonwealth offers much more than "the most exciting two minutes in sports." This is the place where President Abraham Lincoln was born, where explorer Daniel Boone carved out a path on young America's western edge for pioneers, and where Harriet Beecher Stowe witnessed the auctioning of slaves and found inspiration for *Uncle Tom's Cabin*. It's also home to flourishing art communities, hip urban neighborhoods and an eclectic music scene. And even though the Derby might be Kentucky's biggest party, the rest of the year, Kentuckians celebrate everything from bluegrass music and barbecue to beauty queens and Scottish traditions. The pioneer spirit meets Southern charm in this diverse state. Kentucky stretches from Virginia to Missouri, a geographic and historic bridge in the westward flow of American settlement. The commonwealth can be divided into four sections: the Bluegrass, the south-central cave country, the eastern mountains and the western lakes. Each region will surprise visitors with its unique geography and culture. The Lexington plain, a circular area in the north-central part of Kentucky, is bluegrass country, home of fast horses and gentlemen farmers. South of this region is cave country, where you'll find Mammoth Cave National Park, the world's longest cave system. And outdoor enthusiasts will enjoy the Appalachian Mountains in the east, which provide a beautiful backdrop for outdoor activities, and the western lakes, an ideal place for boating, fishing and canoeing.

The Cumberland Gap, a natural passageway through the mountains that sealed the Kentucky wilderness off from Virginia, was the gateway of the pioneers. Dr. Thomas Walker, the first recorded explorer to make a thorough land expedition into the area, arrived in 1750. Daniel Boone and a company of axmen hacked the Wilderness Road through the Cumberland Gap and far into the wilds. The first permanent settlement was at Harrodsburg in 1774, and less than 20 years later in 1792, Congress admitted Kentucky into the Union. During the Civil War, Kentucky supported the Union but opposed abolition, a position that highlights its place as a bridge between the Old South and the Yankee North. Ironically, President Abraham Lincoln and Confederate President Jefferson Davis were both born in Kentucky—less than one year and 100 miles apart. Countless museums,

FUN FACTS

Mammoth Cave is the world's longest cave and was first promoted in 1816, making it the second-oldest tourist attraction in the United States. Niagara Falls, N.Y. is the first.

Two of Kentucky's biggest claims to fame are horses and bourbon. They come together at the Kentucky Derby each year, where folks mix mint juleps and watch the nation's oldest continuously held horse race. Some of the world's best horses come from Kentucky's farms, and 95 percent of the world's bourbon comes from its distilleries.

restored historical sites and festivals pay tribute to Honest Abe, the commonwealth's most famousnative son.

Of course, Kentucky didn't just give the nation bourbon, horses and politicians. Heavyweight boxing champion Muhammad Ali, actor Johnny Depp, TV journalist Diane Sawyer and country music legend Loretta Lynn all hail from the Bluegrass State. As if that weren't enough, this is where Kentucky Fried Chicken got its start, where Louisville Slugger baseball bats were born and where all the Corvettes in the world are produced.

So if you miss the most exciting two minutes in sports each May, you'll still find plenty of ways to fill the time until the next Derby Day.

Information: www.kentuckytourism.com

ASHLAND

Set in the highlands of northeastern Kentucky, Ashland enjoys a prime spot on the Ohio River. The small town is the first unofficial stop on the Country Music Highway (Highway 23).

Information: Ashland Area Convention & Visitors Bureau, 1509 Winchester Ave., Ashland, 606-329-1007, 800-377-6249; www.visitashlandky.com

THE COUNTRY MUSIC HIGHWAY

A stretch of Highway 23 that runs almost the entire length of Eastern Kentucky is the perfect introduction to the state's rich history and musical heritage. Dubbed the "Country Music Highway," the path will take you by towns where country music stars such as Loretta Lynn, Wynona and Naomi Judd, Dwight Yoakam and Patty Loveless once lived. You'll also learn about Kentucky's fascinating history, so find a little country music on the radio and explore, y'all.

Begin in Ashland at the Paramount Art Center (606-324-3175), where music legends including Kentucky natives Billy Ray Cyrus and Wynona and Naomi Judd have played. Originally a movie theater, this restored theater also hosts up-and-comers in its intimate space. Not far away, the Highlands Museum and Discovery Center (606-329-8888) celebrates Eastern Kentucky heritage. Kids will enjoy the Karaoke Korner, where they can make their own music.

Head south to Louisa and Kentucky Paveillon (606-638-9998), a shrine to country music. The five-story building houses country stars' costumes, signed guitars, photographs—even Elvis Presley's Exxon gas card.

Continue south to the remote mining town of Butcher Hollow, where Loretta Lynn was born. Visitors can stop by the cabin where Lynn grew up. (Her autobiographical song "Coal Miner's Daughter" is based on her life here.)

Your next stop is Prestonburg, about 15 miles from Butcher Hollow. Here you'll find the Kentucky Opry (888-459-8704) at the Mountain Arts Center. Catch a country, bluegrass or gospel show by local favorites or national headliners to round out your trip along one of America's most historic highways. (Approximately 90 miles.)

KENTUCKY

★
★
★
★

WHAT TO SEE AND DO

BENNETT'S MILL BRIDGE

Ashland, eight miles west on Highway 125 off Highway Seven

One of Kentucky's longest single-span covered bridges (195 feet), Bennett's Mill Bridge was built in 1855 to serve mill customers. Its original footings and frame are intact, but it's closed to traffic.

CENTRAL PARK

Ashland, 606-327-2046

This 47-acre park has prehistoric Native American mounds, sports facilities, playgrounds and a picnicking area.

GREENBO LAKE STATE RESORT PARK

Ashland, 18 miles west via Highway 23 to Highway 1, 606-473-7324;
www.parks.ky.gov/findparks/resortparks/go

Get active at this state park with a swimming pool (Memorial Day-Labor Day), fishing, boating (marina), hiking, bicycle rentals and tennis. If you want to stay awhile, check out the lodge, tent and trailer sites (April-October). The new amphitheater offers concerts and shows and there's a recreation program for children.

HIGHLANDS MUSEUM & DISCOVERY CENTER

1620 Winchester Ave., Ashland, 606-329-8888; www.highlandsmuseum.com

Visit this interactive museum to learn about Kentucky's unique heritage. Exhibits include a tribute to country music's history in the state, a glimpse at life in the 19th century and a look at the Kentuckians who fought in the wars of the 20th century. There's also a gift shop. Admission: adults $5.50, seniors and children 2 and older $4.50, children under 2 free. Tuesday-Saturday 10 a.m.-5 p.m.

PARAMOUNT ARTS CENTER

1300 Winchester Ave., Ashland, 606-324-3175; www.paramountartscenter.com

This intimate theater hosts all kinds of performances, from country music concerts to touring Broadway shows. The center also prides itself on sharing the arts with the rest of the community, especially youths. The restored 1930s Art Deco theater was originally a movie theater. Tours are available. Daily.

SPECIAL EVENT

POAGE LANDING DAYS FESTIVAL

Central Park, Winchester Avenue, Ashland, 606-329-1007, 800-377-6249;
www.poagelandingdays.com

This fiddle festival features national and local entertainers. Also on offer are arts and crafts and children's activities. Third weekend in September.

HOTELS

★DAYS INN

12700 Highway 180, Ashland, 606-928-3600, 800-329-7466; www.daysinn.com

63 rooms. High-speed Internet access. Complimentary continental breakfast. Outdoor pool. Pets accepted. **$**

KENTUCKY

★
★
★
★
★

★FAIRFIELD INN

10945 Highway 60, Ashland, 606-928-1222, 800-228-2800; www.fairfieldinn.com
63 rooms. High-speed Internet access. Complimentary continental breakfast. **$**

★★JESSE STUART LODGE AT GREENBO LAKE STATE RESORT

Ashland, 606-473-7324, 800-325-0083; www.parks.ky.gov/greenbo2.htm
36 rooms. Restaurant. Children's activity center. **$**

BARBOURVILLE

There's something in the water in Barbourville: The city has produced two Kentucky governors, a lieutenant governor, three U.S. congressmen and a slew of politicians who serve outside of Kentucky. Thanks to its location in the valley of the scenic Cumberland River, this little town has opportunities for fishing, swimming and other outdoor activities.

Information: Knox County Chamber of Commerce, 205 Municipal Building, Barbourville, 606-546-4300; www.barbourvilleky.com

WHAT TO SEE AND DO

DR. THOMAS WALKER STATE HISTORIC SITE

4929 Kentucky 459, Barbourville, 606-546-4400;
www.parks.ky.gov/findparks/histparks/tw
See a replica of original log cabin built in 1750 by Dr. Thomas Walker surrounded by 12 acres of parkland. The site also includes a miniature golf course (fee), picnic area and playground. Daily.

SPECIAL EVENT

DANIEL BOONE FESTIVAL

Knox and Daniel Boone Drive, Barbourville, 606-546-4300
Get a little pioneer spirit at this annual celebration of Boone's adventures in Kentucky. Activities include square dancing, musket shooting, a reenactment of Native American treaty signing, a horse show, a parade, old-time fiddling, antique displays, arts and crafts and entertainment. The Cherokee make an annual pilgrimage to the city. Seven days in early October.

KENTUCKY

★
★
★
★
★

BARDSTOWN

Folks in Bardstown are proud of their town's Southern charm, their beautiful city— and their bourbon. In fact, Bardstown is the heart of the Kentucky Bourbon Trail, featured in Patricia Schultz's bestseller *1,000 Places to See Before You Die.*

Information: Bardstown-Nelson County Tourist & Convention Commission,
107 E. Stephen Foster Ave., Bardstown, 502-348-4877, 800-638-4877;
www.bardstowntourism.com

WHAT TO SEE AND DO

BARDSTOWN HISTORICAL MUSEUM

114 N. Fifth St., Bardstown, 502-348-2999; www.whiskeymuseum.com
The museum features items covering 200 years of local history. Exhibits include Native American artifacts, Lincoln documents, Stephen Foster memorabilia, Civil War artifacts, gifts from King Louis Philippe and King Charles X of France, pioneer

items, period costumes (1850s-1890s) and a natural science display. May-October: daily; rest of year: Tuesday-Sunday.

BERNHEIM FOREST

State Highway 245,14 miles northwest on Highway 245, Shepherdsville, 502-955-8512; www.bernheim.org

This arboretum is an ideal spot to relax, take a walk and admire Kentucky's foliage.

JIM BEAM AMERICAN OUTPOST

149 Happy Hollow Road, Shepherdsville, 502-543-9877; www.jimbeam.com

Visitors can tour the historic Beam family home and stroll the grounds. Check out the craft shop. Daily.

LINCOLN HOMESTEAD STATE PARK

5079 Lincoln Park Road, Bardstown, 859-336-7461; www.e-archives.ky.gov

This park is full of Lincoln family history. See the Berry House, where Nancy Hanks, Abe's mother, lived while Thomas Lincoln was courting her. You'll also find replicas of the cabin and blacksmith shop where Thomas Lincoln grew up and learned his trade. And if that's not enough, stop by the house where Lincoln's favorite uncle—Mordecai Lincoln—lived (on its original site). The houses are open May to September daily. The 150-acre park also offers 18-hole golf (daily, fee), picnic facilities and a playground.

MY OLD KENTUCKY DINNER TRAIN

602 N. Third St., Bardstown, 502-348-7300; www.kydinnertrain.com

Go on a scenic dining excursion aboard elegant restored dining cars from the 1940s. A round-trip ride through the countryside includes a three-course lunch or four-course dinner. February-December: Tuesday-Saturday.

MY OLD KENTUCKY HOME STATE PARK

501 E. Stephen Foster Ave., Bardstown, 502-348-3502; www.myoldkentuckyhome.com

Costumed guides lead visitors through this beautiful Georgian-style mansion and its gardens. The composer Stephen Foster occasionally visited his cousin, Judge John Rowan, at the stately 1795 house, Federal Hill. These visits may have inspired him in 1852 to write "My Old Kentucky Home," Kentucky's state song. The grounds include a golf course, picnic area, playground, tent and trailer sites (standard fees), gardens and an amphitheater. A guided tour is available for a fee. Admission: $50. Daily.

OSCAR GETZ MUSEUM OF WHISKEY HISTORY

114 N. Fifth St., Bardstown, 502-348-2999; www.whiskeymuseum.com

Whiskey is a big deal in Kentucky, and this museum chronicles the history of the liquor from pre-colonial days to the Prohibition era. Check out copper stills, manuscripts, old advertising art, a moonshine still and even Abe Lincoln's liquor license. May-October: daily, rest of year: Tuesday-Sunday.

SPALDING HALL

114 N. Fifth St., Bardstown, 502-348-2999; www.whiskeymuseum.com

Once part of St. Joseph College, Spalding Hall was used as a hospital in the Civil War. The former dormitory now houses art. May-October: daily, rest of year: Tuesday-Sunday.

ST. JOSEPH PROTO-CATHEDRAL

310 W. Stephen Foster Ave., Bardstown, 502-348-3126; www.bardstown.com

This is the first Catholic cathedral west of the Allegheny Mountains. Paintings were donated by Pope Leo XII. Daily 9 a.m.-5 p.m.

SPECIAL EVENTS

KENTUCKY BOURBON FESTIVAL

1 Court Square, Bardstown, 800-638-4877; www.kybourbonfestival.com

Folks in Bardstown have been making bourbon since 1776, and at this annual festival, they celebrate their favorite spirit. Festivities include art exhibits, a black-tie gala and, of course, plenty of bourbon tasting. Mid-September.

STEPHEN FOSTER, THE MUSICAL

J. Dan Talbott Amphitheater, My Old Kentucky Home State Park, Bardstown, 502-348-5971, 800-626-1563; www.stephenfoster.com

More than 50 songs in this musical tell the story of American composer Stephen Foster's triumphs and romance. The show is performed in an outdoor amphitheater. In the event of rain, indoor theater is used. Admission: adults $23, children ages 6-12 $10, children ages 5 and under free. Early June-late August: Tuesday-Sunday, Saturday also matinee.

HOTELS

★BEST WESTERN GENERAL NELSON

114 W. Stephen Foster Ave., Bardstown, 502-348-3977, 800-225-3977; www.generalnelson.com

48 rooms. Wireless Internet access. Complimentary continental breakfast. Outdoor pool. Spa. Business center. Pets accepted. $

★HAMPTON INN

985 Chambers Blvd., Bardstown, 502-349-0100; www.hamptoninn.com

106 rooms. High-speed Internet service. Complimentary continental breakfast. Fitness center. Outdoor pool. $

★★QUALITY INN

1875 New Haven Road, Bardstown, 502-348-9253, 800-329-7466; www.qualityinnofbardstown.com

102 rooms. Restaurant, bar. $

★
★
★
★
★

SPECIALTY LODGING

JAILER'S INN BED AND BREAKFAST

111 W. Stephen Foster Ave., Bardstown, 502-348-5551, 800-948-5551; www.jailersinn.com

Six rooms. Complimentary full breakfast. $

RESTAURANT

★★KURTZ

418 E. Stephen Foster Ave., Bardstown, 502-348-8964, 800-732-2384; www.bardstownparkview.com/index.html

American menu. Lunch, dinner. $$

BEREA

This community in the foothills of the Cumberland Mountains is known as the "Folk Arts and Crafts Capital of Kentucky." Antique shops, craft stores and working studios line the streets; if you're looking for a handmade souvenir from your trip through Kentucky, Berea is a good place to look.

Information: Welcome Center, 201 N. Broadway, Berea, 859-986-2540, 800-598-5263; www.berea.com

WHAT TO SEE AND DO
BEREA COLLEGE
107 Jackson St., Berea, 859-985-3500, 800-326-5948; www.berea.edu

Berea College, the first coeducational, integrated college in the South, mirrors the town's unique approach to hard work and creativity. The college charges no tuition; instead, students work in the college's Labor Program to cover the cost of their education.

CHURCHILL WEAVERS
100 Churchill Court, Berea, 859-986-3127; www.churchillweavers.com

Established in 1922, Churchill is one of the nation's oldest producers of hand-woven goods. Take a self-guided tour through the loom house. Monday-Thursday.

STUDIO CRAFTSPEOPLE OF BEREA
Berea, 859-986-2540; www.berea.com

An organization of craftspeople working in various media invites visitors to their studios. The Tourist and Convention Commission has a list of studios that are open to the public.

SPECIAL EVENTS
BEREA CRAFT FESTIVAL
Indian Fort Theater at Berea College, Berea, 859-986-2258, 800-598-5263; www.bereacraftfestival.com

For more than 25 years, artisans from across the country have presented their work at this annual festival. Three days in mid-July.

CELEBRATION OF TRADITIONAL MUSIC FESTIVAL
Berea College, 107 Jackson St., Berea, 859-985-3500, 800-326-5948; www.berea.edu/appalachiancenter/ctm/default.asp

This fest features traditional music, dancers and concerts. Last weekend in October.

KENTUCKY GUILD OF ARTISTS AND CRAFTSMEN'S FAIRS
Indian Fort Theater, Highway 21 E., Berea, 859-986-3192, 800-598-0334; www.kyguild.org

At these events, you'll find crafts, art, folk dances and singing. Third weekend in May and second weekend in October.

HOTEL
★★BOONE TAVERN HOTEL
Main and Prospect Streets, Berea, 859-986-9358, 800-366-9358; www.boonetavernhotel.com.

58 rooms. Restaurant. **$**

★DINNER BELL
Interstate-75 Plaza, Berea, 859-986-2777
American menu. Breakfast, lunch, dinner. **$**

★PAPALENO'S
108 Center St., Berea, 859-986-4497; www.papalenos.com
Italian menu. Lunch, dinner. **$$**

BOWLING GREEN

This city is where Corvettes are born: every Corvette made in the world today is produced in Bowling Green, so there are plenty of attractions for car lovers. But if motors and chrome aren't your thing, don't dismay. Bowling Green is also home to beautiful historic mansions, natural wonders (think underground boat tour) and even an amusement park.

Information: Bowling Green Area Chamber of Commerce, 710 College St., Bowling Green, 270-781-3200; www.bgchamber.com

WHAT TO SEE AND DO
BEECH BEND PARK & SPLASH LAGOON
798 Beech Bend Road, Bowling Green, 270-781-7634; www.beechbend.com
This amusement park has more than 40 rides, including the Kentucky Rambler—the self-proclaimed "most twisted wooden roller coaster in seven states." The park's watery counterpart, Splash Lagoon, gives families a chance to cool off in its giant swimming pool, water slides and children's splash pool. The park also includes areas for miniature golf, picnicking and camping (separate fee for each activity). Late May-early September: Sunday-Friday 10 a.m.-7 p.m., Saturday 10 a.m.-8 p.m.

CAPITOL ARTS CENTER
416 E. Main St., Bowling Green, 270-782-2787; www.capitolarts.com
In this restored Art Deco building are national and local live presentations and gallery exhibits. Monday-Friday.

HARDIN PLANETARIUM
Western Kentucky University, Bowling Green, 270-745-4044; www.physics.wku.edu/planetarium
Different programs are offered year-round.

HISTORIC RIVERVIEW AT HOBSON GROVE
Hobson Grove Park, 1100 W. Main St., Bowling Green, 270-843-5565; www.bgky.org/riverview
Housed in Italianate style, this home is furnished with a collection of Victorian furniture from 1860-1890. Admission: adults $5, students $2.50, children under 6 free. February to mid-December: Tuesday-Sunday 10 a.m.-4 p.m.

119

KENTUCKY

★
★
★
★

KENTUCKY LIBRARY

Western Kentucky University, Bowling Green, 270-745-2592;
www.wku.edu/Library/museum

The library contains 30,000 books, manuscripts, maps, broadsides, photographs, sheet music, scrapbooks and materials relating to Kentucky and genealogical research of Kentucky families. Tuesday-Saturday.

KENTUCKY MUSEUM

Western Kentucky University, Kentucky Building, Bowling Green,
270-745-2592; www.wku.edu/Library/museum

Collections here include costumes, implements, art works and textiles relating to the cultural history of Kentucky and the region. Exhibits, tours, special programs and a gift shop are available. Tuesday-Saturday 9:30 a.m.-4 p.m., Sunday until 1 p.m.

NATIONAL CORVETTE MUSEUM

350 Corvette Drive, Bowling Green, 270-781-7973; www.corvettemuseum.com

Sports car aficionados drool over this place, which has hands-on educational exhibits and displays about the history of this classic American car. More than 50 vintage cars are available for viewing. Daily 8 a.m.-5 p.m.

WESTERN KENTUCKY UNIVERSITY

1906 College Heights Blvd., Bowling Green, 270-745-0111; www.wku.edu

High on a hill, Western Kentucky University was built around the site of a Civil War fort.

★
★
★
★
☆

HOTELS

★★BEST WESTERN MOTOR INN

166 Cumberland Trace Road, Bowling Green, 270-782-3800, 800-780-7234;
www.bestwestern.com

177 rooms. High-speed Internet access. Restaurant. Outdoor pool. Spa. **$**

★FAIRFIELD INN

1940 Mel Browning St., Bowling Green, 270-782-6933, 800-228-2800;
www.fairfieldinn.com

105 rooms. Complimentary continental breakfast. High-speed Internet access. **$**

★HAMPTON INN

233 Three Springs Road, Bowling Green, 270-842-4100, 800-426-7866;
www.hamptoninn.com

131 rooms. Complimentary continental breakfast. Fitness center. Outdoor pool. **$**

RESTAURANT

★★MARIAH'S

801 State St., Bowling Green, 270-842-6878; www.mariahs.com

American menu. Lunch, dinner. **$$**

BREAKS INTERSTATE PARK

This park's main attraction is the "Grand Canyon of the South," where the Russell Fork of the Big Sandy River plunges through the mountains. The 1,600-foot-deep gorge stretches for five miles through this park on the Kentucky-Virginia border. From the park's entrance, a paved road winds through an evergreen forest and then skirts the canyon rim. Overlooks along the route provide spectacular views of the "Towers," a huge pyramid of rocks. You'll also find caves, springs and fields of rhododendron in this natural wonder.

The visitor center houses historical and natural exhibits (April-October: daily). Laurel Lake is stocked with bass and bluegill. It also has a swimming pool, pedal boats, hiking, bridle and mountain bike trails, picnicking, playground and camping (April-October, fee). In addition, a motor lodge and cottages (year-round) are available.

Information: Breaks Interstate Park, Breaks, 276-865-4413, 800-982-5122; www.breakspark.com

HOTEL
★★BREAKS INTERSTATE
Highway 1, Breaks, 540-865-4414, 800-982-5122; www.breakspark.com
34 rooms. High-speed Internet access available. Restaurant. Outdoor pool. Pets accepted.

CADIZ

Time has almost stopped in this small town. Many of Cadiz's original buildings are preserved, making it a great place to see architecture from the 19th century. Its location on a 170,000-acre wooded peninsula between Kentucky Lake and Lake Barkley gives this pretty town a gorgeous backdrop.

Information: Cadiz-Trigg County Chamber of Commerce, 22 Main St., Cadiz, 270-522-3892; www.barkleylake.com

WHAT TO SEE AND DO
HURRICANE CREEK PUBLIC USE AREA
Cadiz, 12 miles northwest via Highway 274, 270-522-8821
Swimming, a launching ramp, a playground and campsites (fee) are all available here. April to mid-October: daily.

LAKE BARKLEY STATE RESORT PARK
3500 State Park Road, Cadiz, 270-924-1131, 800-325-1708; www.parks.ky.gov
This park on the shores of Lake Barkley provides almost every outdoor activity you can imagine: swimming beach, pool, bathhouse (seasonal), fishing, boating, canoeing (ramps, rentals, marina), hiking, backpacking, horseback riding (seasonal), 18-hole golf (year-round), tennis, trapshooting, shuffleboard, basketball, picnicking, restaurant, cottages, lodge and camping (fee). Children's programs are offered as well.

ORIGINAL LOG CABIN
22 Main St., Cadiz, 270-522-3892; www.gocadiz.com
This four-room log cabin, furnished with 18th- and 19th-century artifacts, was occupied by a single family for more than a century. Monday-Friday.

121

KENTUCKY

HOTEL
★★LAKE BARKLEY STATE RESORT PARK
3500 State Park Road, Cadiz, 270-924-1131, 800-325-1708;
www.parks.ky.gov
The lodge proves that you can enjoy Mother Nature without having to sleep on the ground. Most of the lodge's rooms have views of beautiful Lake Barkley from the balconies. 124 rooms. Restaurant. Airport transportation available.

CAMPBELLSVILLE
In the heart of Kentucky, this little town is where the Pennyrile, Bluegrass and Knobs regions come together. This area is full of interesting history. Don't miss nearby Greensburg's historic district, which dates back to the 18th century.
Information: Taylor County Tourism Commission, 107 W. Broadway, Campbellsville,
270-465-3786, 800-738-4719; www.campbellsvilleky.com

WHAT TO SEE AND DO
GREEN RIVER LAKE STATE PARK
179 Park Office Road, Campbellsville, 270-465-8255;
www.state.ky.us/agencies/parks/greenriv.htm
In Kentucky's cave country, this lake provides the perfect spot for water sports of any kind. Plus it's ideal for fishing, picnicking and camping. Daily.

HOTEL
★BEST WESTERN CAMPBELLSVILLE LODGE
1400 E. Broadway, Campbellsville, 270-465-7001, 800-770-0430;
www.bestwesternlodge.com
60 rooms. High-speed Internet access. Complimentary continental breakfast. Fitness center. Outdoor pool. $

★
★
★
★

CARROLLTON
Where the Ohio and Kentucky rivers meet, Carrollton was named in honor of Charles Carroll, one of the signers of the Declaration of Independence. Today, this place has small-town charm, a beautiful state park and several great antique shops.
Information: Carroll County Tourism Commission, 515 Highland Ave., Carrollton,
502-732-7036, 800-325-4290; www.carrolltontourism.com

WHAT TO SEE AND DO
EDGE OF SPEEDWAY CAMPGROUND
4125 Highway 1130, Sparta, 859-576-2161; www.edgeofspeedway.com
This well-manicured campground overlooks the Kentucky Speedway and has space for 200 campers. Gravel roads and large sites set it apart from other camping spots in the area. The walk to track shuttlebuses is a half mile; the drive to the track parking area, 1½ miles. Water stations and showers (fee) are available.

GENERAL BUTLER STATE RESORT PARK
1608 Highway 227, Carrollton, 502-732-4384; www.parks.ky.gov
The Ohio and Kentucky Rivers meet here, making the park a scenic site for outdoor activities of all kinds. Swim, fish and boat (rentals available) at the 30-acre lake; or

play nine-hole golf (fee) or tennis. Picnic sites, playground, cottages, lodge, dining room, tent and trailer camping are also available. Daily.

HISTORIC DISTRICT
Highland and Court Streets, Carrollton
A self-guided auto tour of historic sites and houses begins at Old Stone Jail. The tourist center on the second floor houses a small museum on local history.

SPECIAL EVENTS
BLUES TO THE POINT—TWO RIVERS BLUES FESTIVAL
Point Park Pavilion in downtown Carrollton, 502-732-7036; www.bluesthepoint.net
This two-day event showcases regional and national blues performances. Early September.

KENTUCKY SCOTTISH WEEKEND
Carrollton, 502-239-2665; www.kyscottishweeekend.org
At this celebration of Scottish heritage, you'll find bands and bagpipers, the Scottish Athletic Competition (where athletes wear kilts), Celtic music, a Highland dance competition (where dancers wear kilts) and a British auto show. Second weekend in May.

HOTELS
★★GENERAL BUTLER STATE RESORT PARK
1608 Highway 227, Carrollton, 502-732-4384, 800-325-0078;
www.parks.ky.gov
77 rooms. Wireless Internet access. Restaurant. Children's activity center. $

★HOLIDAY INN EXPRESS
141 Inn Road, Carrollton, 502-732-6661, 800-465-4329; www.holiday-inn.com
62 rooms. Wireless Internet access. Complimentary continental breakfast. $

CAVE CITY
True to its name, the city in the heart of Cave Country primarily serves tourists passing through the region en route to Mammoth Cave and other commercially operated caves nearby.
Information: Cave City Convention Center, 270-773-3131, 800-346-8908;
www.cavecity.com

WHAT TO SEE AND DO
CRYSTAL ONYX CAVE
8709 Happy Valley Road, Cave City, 270-773-2359; www.cavecity.com/cavetours.html
Geologic wonders of all kinds fill this cave. Helectites, stalagmites, stalactites, onyx columns and rare crystal onyx rimstone formations will amaze you. So will the knowledge that Native Americans used the 54-degree cave as a burial site more than 2,700 years ago. Guided tours depart every 45 minutes. Also available are improved and primitive camping, adjacent (fee). June-August: 8 a.m.-6 p.m.; early August-late May: 9 a.m.-5 p.m.

KENTUCKY

★
★
★
★

KENTUCKY ACTION PARK

3057 Mammoth Cave Road, Cave City, 270-773-2560, 800-798-0560;
www.kentuckyactionpark.com

Ride to the top of the mountain on a chairlift and slide ¼ mile down in an alpine sled. The action keeps going with go-karts, bumper boats, bumper cars and horseback riding. Admission: $5. Days and times vary.

HOTELS

★BEST WESTERN KENTUCKY INN

1009 Doyle Ave., Cave City, 270-773-3161, 800-780-7234; www.bestwestern.com

50 rooms. High-speed Internet access. Complimentary continental breakfast. Outdoor pool. $

★★QUALITY INN

Mammoth Cave Road, Cave City, 270-773-2181, 800-321-4245; www.qualityinn.com

100 rooms. Restaurant. $

RESTAURANT

★SAHARA STEAK HOUSE

413 E. Happy Valley St., Cave City, 270-773-3450

Steak menu. Lunch, dinner. $$

CORBIN

124

KENTUCKY

★
★
★
★
☆

Feel like some finger-lickin' good chicken? There's plenty to eat in Corbin, home to the first Kentucky Fried Chicken restaurant. Just make sure to wait an hour before diving into the nearby 5,600-acre lake.

Information: Tourist & Convention Commission, 101 N. Depot St.,
606-528-6390, 800-528-7123; www.corbinkycityguide.com

WHAT TO SEE AND DO

COLONEL HARLAND SANDERS' ORIGINAL RESTAURANT

Corbin, two miles north on Highway 25, 606-528-2163; www.chickenfestival.com

There really was a Colonel Sanders. See this authentic restoration of his first Kentucky Fried Chicken restaurant. Displays include an original kitchen, artifacts and the motel where Sanders worked as a chef. The original dining area is still in use. Daily 10 a.m.-10 p.m.

LAUREL RIVER LAKE

1433 Laurel Lake Road, London, 606-864-6412

A 5,600-acre lake offers fishing, boating (launch, rentals). Hiking, recreation areas, picnicking and camping (fee) are also available.

SPECIAL EVENT

NIBROC FESTIVAL

101 N. Depot St., Corbin, 800-528-7123; www.corbinky.org

This fest highlights mountain arts and crafts. A parade, square dancing, a beauty pageant, a midway and entertainment round out the event. Early August.

m o b i l t r a v e l g u i d e . c o m

HOTELS

★BEST WESTERN CORBIN INN

2630 Cumberland Falls Highway, Corbin, 606-528-2100, 800-780-7234;
www.bestwestern.com

63 rooms. High-speed Internet access. Complimentary continental breakfast. Pets accepted. **$**

★★CUMBERLAND FALLS STATE PARK

7351 Highway 90, Corbin, 606-528-4121, 800-325-0063; www.parks.ky.gov

78 rooms. Wireless Internet access. Restaurant. **$**

★HAMPTON INN

125 Adams Road, Corbin, 606-523-5696, 800-426-7866; www.hamptoninn.com

82 rooms. Complimentary continental breakfast. Fitness center. Outdoor pool. Business center. **$**

COVINGTON (CINCINNATI AIRPORT AREA)

Five broad bridges spanning the Ohio River link Covington to Cincinnati, but this city doesn't need help from Ohioans to have fun. Covington, named for a hero of the War of 1812, has had a renaissance in the last 20 years. Real estate developers and the city government invested in the city's riverfront and infrastructure, and funky restaurants and cool shops followed. To experience this revival, check out Covington Landing, a floating restaurant and entertainment complex.

Information: Northern Kentucky Convention and Visitors Bureau, 50 E. River Center Blvd.,
859-261-4677, 800-782-9659; www.nkycvb.com

WHAT TO SEE AND DO

CARROLL CHIMES BELL TOWER

Covington, west end of village

Completed in 1979, this 100-foot tower has a 43-bell carillon and mechanical figures that portray the legend of the Pied Piper of Hamelin.

CATHEDRAL BASILICA OF THE ASSUMPTION

Madison Avenue and 12th Street, Covington, 859-431-2060; www.covcathedral.com

Patterned after the Abbey of St. Denis and the Cathedral of Notre Dame in France, the basilica has massive doors, classic stained-glass windows (including one of the largest in the world), murals and mosaics by local and foreign artists. Daily. Guided tours Sunday after 10 a.m. mass; also by appointment.

DEVOU PARK

Park Drive and Montague Road, Covington, 859-292-2151

A 550-acre park has a lake overlooking the Ohio River. Available activities include golf (fee), tennis And picnicking. A number of outdoor concerts are held here as well (mid-June to mid-August). Daily.

BEHRINGER-CRAWFORD MUSEUM

1600 Montague Road, Covington, 859-491-4003; www.bcmuseum.org

The museum keeps exhibits on local archaeology, paleontology, history, fine art and wildlife. Admission: adults $7, seniors $6, children $4. Tuesday-Saturday 10 a.m.-5 p.m.

KENTUCKY

MAINSTRASSE VILLAGE

406 W. Sixth St., Covington, 859-491-0458; www.mainstrasse.org

Approximately five square blocks in Covington's old German area make up this historic district of residences, shops and restaurants. It has more than 20 restored buildings dating back to the mid to late 1800s. Monday-Saturday 11 a.m.-5 p.m., Sunday noon-5 p.m.

NEWPORT ON THE LEVEE

1 Levee Way, Newport, 859-750-4995; www.newportonthelevee.com

This 10-acre entertainment district on the river includes a trendy shopping center; 12 stylish restaurants; a state-of-the-art, 20-screen movie theater; and the acclaimed Newport Aquarium. Days and times vary.

VENT HAVEN MUSEUM

33 W. Maple Ave., Fort Mitchell, 859-341-0461; www.venthavenmuseum.net

The only one of its kind in the world, this quirky museum houses more than 700 ventriloquist figures—"dummies"—who stare wide-eyed at visitors. The museum also contains pictures and collectibles. By appointment only, May-September.

WORLD OF SPORTS

7400 Woodspoint Drive, Florence, 859-371-8255; www.landrumgolf.com

Grab your clubs and check out this family entertainment complex, which has an 18-hole golf course (daily 7 a.m.-dark), a 25-station lighted practice range, nine covered tees and a miniature golf course. When you tire of the woods and irons, you can play at the billiard hall, video arcade, five racquetball/walleyball courts and three slam-dunk basketball courts. A snack bar is available for refueling. Sunday-Thursday 9 a.m.-11 p.m., Friday-Saturday 9 a.m.-1 p.m.

SPECIAL EVENTS

MAIFEST

MainStrasse Village, 605 Philadelphia St., Covington, 859-491-0458;
www.mainstrasse.org

Organizers say this traditional festival celebrates the spring's first wines, but you'll find plenty of that other German brew here, too. Maifest meshes traditional German fare—like polka bands and sauerkraut—with Kentucky treats, like Southern rock bands and artisans' crafts. Third weekend in May.

OKTOBERFEST

MainStrasse Village, 605 Philadelphia St., Covington

Any self-respecting German historic neighborhood must celebrate Oktoberfest, and MainStrasse doesn't disappoint. Grab a beer and a brat and enjoy the full schedule of German music, ranging from rock 'n' roll to oompah music. Each day begins with the legendary Keg Tapping Ceremony. Early September.

RIVERFEST

Covington, banks of Ohio River, 859-261-4677; www.nkycvb.com

One of the largest fireworks displays in the country, Riverfest shoots its pyrotechnics from barges moored on the river. Labor Day weekend.

HOTELS

★★BEST WESTERN FT. MITCHELL INN

2100 Dixie Highway, Fort Mitchell, 859-331-1500, 800-780-7234;
www.bestwestern.com

214 rooms. Restaurant. Airport transportation available. **$**

★★DRAWBRIDGE INN

2477 Royal Drive, Fort Mitchell, 859-341-2800, 800-354-9793;
www.drawbridgeinn.com

488 rooms. Wireless Internet access. Restaurant, bar. Airport transportation available.
Fitness center. Outdoor pool. **$**

★★EMBASSY SUITES

10 E. River Center Blvd., Covington, 859-261-8400, 800-362-2779;
www.embassysuites1.hilton.com

226 suites. Wireless Internet access. Complimentary full breakfast. Restaurant, bar.
Fitness center. Outdoor pool. Business center. Pets accepted. **$**

★HAMPTON INN

200 Crescent Ave., Covington, 859-581-7800; www.hamptoninn.com

151 rooms. High-speed Internet access. Complimentary continental breakfast. Fitness
center. Outdoor pool. Business center. **$**

★★★MARRIOTT AT RIVERCENTER

10 W. River Center Blvd., Covington, 859-261-2900, 800-228-9290; www.marriott.com

321 rooms. Wireless Internet access. Restaurant, bar. Airport transportation available.
Fitness center. **$**

★★★RADISSON HOTEL CINCINNATI RIVERFRONT

668 W. Fifth St., Covington, 859-491-1200; www.radisson.com

The guest rooms offer views of the beautiful Ohio River, the lush wooded hills of
northern Kentucky or scenic downtown Cincinnati. Nearby attractions include
the Cincinnati Reds and Bengals, the Newport Aquarium and the Cincinnati Zoo.
220 rooms. High-speed Internet access. Restaurant, bar. Airport transportation available. Fitness center. Outdoor pool. **$**

★★RESIDENCE INN BY MARRIOTT

2811 Circleport Drive, Erlanger, 859-282-7400, 800-331-3131;
www.residenceinn.com

150 rooms. High-speed Internet access. Complimentary continental breakfast. Airport
transportation available. Fitness center. Outdoor pool. Pets accepted. **$**

RESTAURANTS

★★DEE FELICE CAFE

529 Main St., Covington, 859-261-2365; www.deefelice.com

Cajun/Creole menus. Dinner, Sunday brunch. **$$**

KENTUCKY

★
★
★
★

★★MIKE FINK

One Ben Bernstein Place, Covington, 859-261-4212; www.mikefink.com

Seafood menu. Lunch, dinner, Sunday brunch. **$$**

★★RIVERVIEW

668 W. Fifth St., Covington, 859-491-5300

American menu. Breakfast, lunch, dinner. **$$**

★★★WATERFRONT

14 Pete Rose Pier, Covington, 859-581-1414; www.jeffruby.com

This bustling steak and lobster house has a stunning view of the Cincinnati skyline and a sit-down sushi bar. Steak menu. Dinner. Closed Sunday. **$**

CUMBERLAND FALLS STATE RESORT PARK

The park's main attraction is a magnificent waterfall, 65 feet high and 125 feet wide. Surrounded by Daniel Boone National Forest, this awesome waterfall is the second largest east of the Rockies. By night, when the moon is full and the sky clear, a mysterious moonbow appears in the mist—a phenomenon you can't find anywhere else in the Western Hemisphere. The park also offers a swimming pool (seasonal), fishing, nature trails, a nature center, riding (seasonal), tennis, picnicking, a playground, a lodge, cottages, tent and trailer campsites (standard fees).

Information: 7351 Highway 90, Corbin, 606-528-4121; www.parks.ky.gov

WHAT TO SEE AND DO

BLUE HERON MINING COMMUNITY

Cumberland, in Big South Fork National River/Recreation Area (KY side), south via Highways 27 and 92 to Stearns, then nine miles west on Highway 742 (Mine 18 Road), 606-376-3787; www.nps.gov/biso/bheron.htm

Once a thriving mining community, Blue Heron was abandoned when the mine was closed in 1962. Today, the re-created town comprises metal-frame "ghost structures" that tell the stories of life here in the mid-20th century. Begin your tour at the depot, which has exhibits on the town's history. A snack bar and gift shop (April-October) are on the premises. A scenic railway line connects Blue Heron with the town of Stearns.

SHELTOWEE TRACE OUTFITTERS

117 Hawkins Ave., Somerset, 606-376-5567, 800-541-7238;
www.ky-rafting.com

Go on river rafting, canoeing and "funyak" trips in the scenic Cumberland River below the falls. Appointments are required for the five- to seven-hour trips. Memorial Day-September: daily; mid-March to mid-May and October: Saturday and Sunday.

HOTEL

★★CUMBERLAND FALLS STATE PARK

7351 Highway 90, Corbin, 606-528-4121, 800-325-0063; www.parks.ky.gov

78 rooms. Restaurant. **$**

CUMBERLAND GAP NATIONAL HISTORICAL PARK

The famous Cumberland Gap served as the early pioneers' primary route through the central Appalachian Mountains. Long before settlers used the passage, Native Americans followed migratory animals along the gap, which was prime hunting territory. Then in 1775, Daniel Boone and 30 axmen cut a 208-mile swath through the forests from Kingsport, Tenn. to the Kentucky River, passing through the Cumberland Gap. Settlers poured through the pass and along Boone's "Wilderness Road," and in 1777, Kentucky became Virginia's westernmost county. After the Revolution, the mainstream of western settlement went through Cumberland Gap and slowed only when more direct northerly routes opened.

The park captures the gap's history with several historic buildings and structures preserved on 22,000 acres. Visitors will be amazed by the park's dramatically beautiful countryside, ready to be explored on more than 70 miles of hiking trails. Daily.
Information: Park Superintendent, Highway 25E, Middlesboro, 606-248-2817;
www.nps.gov/cuga

WHAT TO SEE AND DO

CIVIL WAR FORTIFICATIONS
Corbin
These are available throughout the Gap area.

HENSLEY SETTLEMENT
Cumberland Gap, National Historical Park, Highway 25E, Corbin, 606-248-2817;
www.nps.gov/cuga
An isolated mountain community until 1951, Hensley is now a restored historic site. To get here, hike 3½ miles up the Chadwell Gap trail or take the shuttle from the visitor center.

PINNACLE OVERLOOK
Cumberland Gap, National Historical Park, Highway 25E, Corbin, 606-248-2817;
www.nps.gov/cuga
The overlook (at 2,440 feet) offers spectacular views into Kentucky, Virginia and Tennessee. To get there, take four-mile-long Skyline Road up the mountain. Vehicles more than 20 feet in length and all trailers are prohibited.

TRI-STATE PEAK
Cumberland Gap, National Historical Park, Highway 25E, Corbin, 606-248-2817;
www.nps.gov/cuga
The peak gives a view of the meeting point of Kentucky, Virginia and Tennessee.

VISITOR CENTER
Cumberland Gap, National Historical Park, Highway 25E, Corbin, 606-248-2817;
www.nps.gov/cuga
At west end of the park (near Middlesboro), the visitor center shows historical exhibits and offers an audiovisual program.

DANVILLE

The birthplace of Kentucky government, Danville has had a front-row seat for much of the state's history. Ten years after the city was founded, it became the first capital of

KENTUCKY

★
★
★
★
★

DANIEL BOONE NATIONAL FOREST

These 707,000 acres contain some of Kentucky's most spectacular scenery. Among the park's famous attractions is Red River Gorge Geological Area, known for its natural arches and colorful rock formations as tall as 300 feet. A scenic loop drive of the gorge begins north of Natural Bridge State Resort Park on Highway 77. The nearest camping facilities (fee) are at Koomer Ridge, on Highway 15 between the Slade (33) and Beattyville (40) exits of Mount Parkway.

Another must-see is the forest's section of Sheltowee Trace National Recreation Trail, which runs the length of the national forest (and stretches more than 260 miles from Morehead, Kentucky, to Pickett State Rustic Park in Tennessee). If you're looking for a spectacular drive, take Forest Development Road 918—the main road to Zilpo Recreation Area on Cave Run Lake. The 11.2-mile road winds through hardwood forests and offers great views of Cave Run Lake.

After glimpsing it from afar, don't miss Cave Run Lake. It has swimming beaches, boat ramps and camping at Twin Knobs and Zilpo recreation areas. Laurel River Lake has boat ramps and camping areas at Holly Bay and Grove (vehicle access). Clay Lick (Cave Run Lake), Grove and White Oak (Laurel River Lake) have boat-in camping. Hunting and fishing are permitted in most parts of the forest under Kentucky regulations; backpacking is permitted on forest trails. For details, contact the forest supervisor, 1700 Bypass Road, Winchester 859-745-3100, 800-255-7275.

Information: 859-745-3100, 800-255-7275; www.southernregion.fs.fed.us/boone.

★
★
★
★

the Kentucky district of Virginia. The state constitution was signed here in 1792, and in the years leading up to statehood, Danville was one of the largest settlements on the Wilderness Road. Danville is the site of the state's first college, first log courthouse, first post office, first school for the deaf and first law school.

Information: Danville-Boyle County Convention & Visitors Bureau, 304 S. Fourth St., Danville, 859-236-7794, 800-755-0076; www.danville-ky.com

WHAT TO SEE AND DO

CONSTITUTION SQUARE STATE SHRINE

134 S. Second St., Danville, 859-239-7089;
www.parks.ky.gov/findparks/histparks/cs/
An authentic reproduction of Kentucky's first courthouse square stands at the exact site where the first state constitution was framed and adopted in 1792. The original post office is here as well as replicas of the jail, courthouse and meetinghouse. Governor's Circle has a bronze plaque of each Kentucky governor. A museum store and art gallery are also on the grounds. Daily.

HERRINGTON LAKE

1200 Gwinn Island Road, Danville, 859-236-4286; gwinnmarina.com
Formed by Dix Dam, one of the world's largest rock-filled dams, Herrington has 333 miles of shoreline. A balanced fish population is maintained through a

conservation program. Fishing (fee), a boat launch (fee, rentals), camping hookups and cabins are all available.

KIDS FARM EDUCATION CENTER
636 Quirks Run Road, Danville
This working farm reveals wildlife management techniques, exotic animals and wild game in a natural setting. Daily.

MCDOWELL HOUSE AND APOTHECARY SHOP
125 S. Second St., Danville, 859-236-2804; www.mcdowellhouse.com
On Christmas Day 1809, Dr. Ephraim McDowell removed a 22.5-pound ovarian tumor from a woman without the benefit of anesthesia or antisepsis, neither of which had been invented yet. Amazingly, the surgery was a success. McDowell's residence and shop are restored and refurbished with period pieces. You'll see a large apothecary-ware collection. The surrounding gardens include trees, wildflowers and herbs of the period. Monday-Saturday 10 a.m.-noon, 1-4 p.m.

PERRYVILLE BATTLEFIELD STATE HISTORIC SITE
1825 Battlefield Road, Perryville, 859-332-8631; www.parks.ky.gov
A 300-acre park, once a field, appears much as it did October 8, 1862, when Confederate forces and Union troops clashed. A total of 4,241 Union soldiers and 1,822 Confederate troops were killed, wounded or missing. Still standing are the Crawford House, used by Confederate Gen. Bragg as headquarters, and Bottom House, the site of some of the heaviest fighting. A mock battle is staged each year (weekend nearest October 8). At the north end of the battle line is a 1902 memorial to remember the Confederate dead and one built in 1931 to honor the Union dead. A museum houses artifacts from the battle. Take a gander at a 9-by-9-foot detailed battle map and battle dioramas (fee). Hiking, picnicking and a playground are available, as are self-guided tours. April-October: daily; rest of year: by appointment.

PIONEER PLAYHOUSE VILLAGE-OF-THE-ARTS
840 Stanford Road, Danville, 859-236-2747; www.pioneerplayhouse.com
This reproduction of an 18th-century Kentucky village features a drama school and museum on its on a 200-acre site. Camping (fee) is available. May to mid-October: daily.

SPECIAL EVENT
PIONEER PLAYHOUSE
Pioneer Playhouse Village-of-the-Arts, 840 Stanford Road, Danville, 859-236-2747; www.pioneerplayhouse.com
Kentucky's oldest outdoor theater, this summer stock theater puts on five shows each summer. June-August: Tuesday-Saturday.

HOTELS
★★COUNTRY HEARTH INN-DANVILLE
Highway 127, Danville, 859-236-8601; www.countryhearth.com
81 rooms. High-speed Internet access. Restaurant. Fitness center. Outdoor pool. Pets accepted. **$**

KENTUCKY

★
★
★
★
★

★HOLIDAY INN EXPRESS
96 Daniel Drive, Danville, 859-236-8600; www.hiexpress.com

63 rooms. High-speed Internet access. Complimentary continental breakfast. Outdoor pool. Pets accepted. **$**

ELIZABETHTOWN

With a starring role in Cameron Crowe's 2005 movie, Elizabethtown could have gotten a Hollywood-sized ego. Instead, this little town is as laid-back and charming as it ever was. The town plays a big role in President Abraham Lincoln's family story: Thomas Lincoln, the president's father, owned property and worked here, and he brought his bride Nancy Hanks to the area after their wedding. Honest Abe's older sister Sarah was born here, and after his first wife's death, Thomas returned here to marry Sarah Bush Johnston.

Information: Elizabethtown Tourism & Convention Bureau, 1030 N. Mulberry St., Elizabethtown, 270-765-2175, 800-437-0092; www.touretown.com

WHAT TO SEE AND DO
BROWN-PUSEY COMMUNITY HOUSE
128 N. Main St., Elizabethtown, 270-765-2515; www.touretown.com

This former stagecoach inn is an excellent example of Georgian Colonial architecture; Gen. George Custer lived here from 1871 to 1873. It's restored as a historical genealogy library (fee) and community house. Monday-Saturday 10 a.m.-4 p.m.

LINCOLN HERITAGE HOUSE
Elizabethtown, one mile north on Highway 31 W., in Freeman Lake Park, 270-765-2175, 800-437-0092; www.touretown.com/heritagehouse.html

Pioneer Hardin Thomas lived in this double log cabin, and Thomas Lincoln, father of the President Abraham Lincoln, created the unusual trim work. It showcases pioneer implements, early surveying equipment and period furniture. Park facilities include pavilions, paddle and row boats and canoes. June-September: Tuesday-Sunday 10 a.m.-5 p.m.

SCHMIDT MUSEUM OF COCA-COLA MEMORABILIA
109 Buffalo Creek Drive, Elizabethtown, 270-234-1100;
www.schmidtmuseum.com

Have a Coke and a smile at this museum, the world's largest private collection of Coca-Cola memorabilia with more than 80,000 items, some dating back to 1886. More than 1,100 pieces are on display at this museum at any given time. Expect to see artifacts like old Coca-Cola toys, bottles, Santas, trays and vending machines. Monday-Saturday 10 a.m.-6 p.m., Sunday 1-5 p.m.

SPECIAL EVENTS
HARDIN COUNTY FAIR
Hardin County Fairgrounds, Elizabethtown. South on Highway 31 W., 270-765-2175; www.touretown.com
Mid-July.

KENTUCKY

★
★
★
★
★

KENTUCKY HEARTLAND FESTIVAL

Freeman Lake Park, 111 W. Dixie Ave., Elizabethtown, 270-765-4334;
www.touretown.com

The festival offers an antique auto show, arts and crafts, a canoe race, a running event, a hot-air balloon, bluegrass music, games and lots of food. Last full weekend in August.

HOTELS

★BEST WESTERN ATRIUM GARDENS

1043 Executive Drive, Elizabethtown, 270-769-3030; www.bestwestern.com

133 rooms. High-speed Internet access. Complimentary continental breakfast. Fitness center. Pets accepted. **$**

★BEST WESTERN CARDINAL INN

642 E. Dixie Ave., Elizabethtown, 270-765-6139, 800-528-1234; www.bestwestern.com

54 rooms. High-speed Internet access. Complimentary continental breakfast. Fitness center. Outdoor pool. Pets accepted. **$**

RESTAURANTS

★JERRY'S

654 E Dixie Ave., Elizabethtown, 270-769-2336

American menu. Breakfast, lunch, dinner. **$$**

★★STONE HEARTH

1001 N. Mulberry St., Elizabethtown, 270-765-4898; www.stonehearthetown.com

Lunch, dinner. **$$**

FLORENCE

It doesn't take a genius to figure out everyone's favorite animal in Florence. Here, it's all about the horses.

Information: 300 Buttermilk Pike, Fort Mitchell, 859-578-8800; www.florence-ky.gov

KENTUCKY

SPECIAL EVENTS

HORSE RACING

Turfway Park, 7500 Turfway Road, Florence, 859-371-0200, 800-733-0200;
www.turfway.com

Thoroughbred racing takes place Wednesday to Sunday. Early September-early October, late November-early April.

LANES END SPIRAL STAKES RACE

Turfway Park, 7500 Turfway Road, Florence, 859-371-0200; www.spiralstakes.com

A testing ground for the Kentucky Derby, this race is one of the sport's largest pursed thoroughbred races for 3-year-olds. The race is the final event of a weeklong festival of parties, charity events and a special crawfish boil.

HOTELS

★ASHLEY QUARTERS

4880 Houston Road, Florence, 859-525-9997, 888-525-9997; www.ashleyquarters.com

70 rooms. Wireless Internet access. Continental breakfast. Outdoor pool. **$**

★BEST WESTERN INN FLORENCE
7821 Commerce Drive, Florence, 859-525-0090, 800-780-7234; www.bestwestern.com
51 rooms. High-speed Internet access. Complimentary continental breakfast. Fitness center. Outdoor pool. Pets accepted. **$**

★★★HILTON GREATER CINCINNATI AIRPORT
7373 Turfway Road, Florence, 859-371-4400, 800-932-3322; www.hilton.com
206 rooms. Restaurant, bar. Airport transportation available. Fitness center. Outdoor pool. Business center. **$**

FORT KNOX
This military post established in 1918 is home to the U.S. Army Armor Center and School and the Army's home of Mounted Warfare. Named for Maj. Gen. Henry Knox, the first secretary of war, the post has been a major installation since 1932.
Information: Public Affairs Office, US Army Armor Center & Fort Knox, 270-624-4788;
www.knox.army.mil

WHAT TO SEE AND DO
PATTON MUSEUM OF CAVALRY AND ARMOR
4554 Fayette Ave., Fort Knox, 502-624-3812; www.generalpatton.org
The Armor Branch Museum was named in honor of Gen. George S. Patton Jr. The collection includes U.S. and foreign armored equipment, weapons, art and uniforms as well as mementos of Gen. Patton's military career, including the sedan in which he was riding when he was fatally injured in 1945. Also on display are a 10-by-12-foot section of the Berlin Wall and foreign armored equipment from Operation Desert Storm. Monday-Friday 9 a.m.-4:30 p.m., Saturday-Sunday 10 a.m.-4:30 p.m.

UNITED STATES BULLION DEPOSITORY
Fort Knox, Gold Vault Road, www.usmint.gov
It turns out that the old saw about "all the gold in Fort Knox" refers to real gold. Opened in 1937, this two-story granite, steel and concrete building houses part of the nation's gold reserves. The depository and the surrounding grounds are not open to the public.

HOTEL
★RADCLIFF INN
438 S. Dixie Blvd., Radcliff, 270-351-8211, 800-421-2030; www.radcliffinn.com
83 rooms. Complimentary continental breakfast. Fitness center. Outdoor pool. **$**

FRANKFORT
The Kentucky River runs through the heart of Frankfort, and wooded hills rise up around it, making the city one of the most picturesque state capitals in the country. But don't let the scenery fool you: Against this serene backdrop, politics rule when the legislature is in session. Catch the politicos at play and tour the city's historic sites. This place has real charm, good stories and plenty for visitors to do.
Information: Frankfort/Franklin County Tourist and Convention Commission,
100 Capital Ave., Frankfort 502-875-8687, 800-960-7200; www.visitfrankfort.com

KENTUCKY

★
★
★
★
★

WHAT TO SEE AND DO

DANIEL BOONE'S GRAVE

215 E. Main St., in Frankfort Cemetery, Frankfort,

This monument is for Boone and his wife. Boone died in Missouri but his remains were brought here in 1845.

FLORAL CLOCK

300 Capitol Ave., Frankfort, 502-564-3449; www.lrc.state.ky.us

This functioning outdoor timepiece is adorned with thousands of plants and elevated above a reflecting pool. The mechanism moves a 530-pound minute hand and a 420-pound hour hand. Visitors toss thousands of dollars in coins into the pool, all of which are donated to state child-care agencies.

KENTUCKY HISTORY CENTER

100 W. Broadway St., Frankfort, 502-564-3016; www.history.ky.gov

The center features exhibits pertaining to the history and development of the state and the culture of its people. Tuesday-Saturday 10 a.m.-5 p.m.

KENTUCKY MILITARY HISTORY MUSEUM

Main Street and Capital Avenue, Frankfort, 502-564-1792; www.history.ky.gov

Exhibits in this museum trace Kentucky's involvement in military conflicts through two centuries. Items on display include weapons, flags and uniforms. Tuesday-Friday 10 a.m.-5 p.m.

KENTUCKY STATE UNIVERSITY

400 E. Main St., Frankfort, 502-597-6000; www.kysu.edu

Historically, KSU was a black liberal studies institution. Jackson Hall (1887) has art and photo gallery exhibits (September to mid-May); Carver Hall features the King Farouk butterfly collection.

KENTUCKY VIETNAM VETERANS MEMORIAL

300 Coffee Tree Road, Frankfort; www.kyvietnammemorial.net

This unique memorial is a 14-foot sundial that casts a shadow across veterans' names on the anniversaries of their deaths. The memorial contains more than 1,000 names.

LIBERTY HALL

218 Wilkinson St., Frankfort, 502-227-2560; www.libertyhall.org

The first U.S. senator from Kentucky, John Brown, built this home near the end of the 18th century. It has been restored to its original state and furnished with family heirlooms. Take a stroll through the surrounding period gardens.

LIBRARY

100 W. Broadway, Frankfort, 502-564-3016; www.history.ky.gov

The library has manuscripts, maps, photographs and special collections covering Kentucky's history, as well as a genealogy section. Tuesday-Saturday 8 a.m.-4 p.m.

KENTUCKY

★
★
★
★
★

OLD GOVERNOR'S MANSION

420 High St., Frankfort, 502-564-3449; kentucky.gov/Pages/home.aspx

The official residence of the governor is styled after the Petit Trianon, Marie Antoinette's villa at Versailles. Guided tours are given Tuesday and Thursday 1:30-3:30 p.m.

OLD STATE CAPITOL BUILDING

Broadway and Lewis streets, Frankfort; www.history.ky.gov

Kentucky's third capitol building was used as the capitol from 1830 to 1909 and was the first Greek Revival statehouse west of the Alleghenies. Completely restored and furnished in period style, the building features an unusual self-balanced double stairway. Tuesday-Friday 10 a.m.-5 p.m.

ORLANDO BROWN HOUSE

202 Wilkinson St., Frankfort, 502-227-2560; www.libertyhall.org

This early Greek Revival house was built for Orlando Brown, son of Senator John Brown. The home has its original furnishings and artifacts. March-December: Tuesday-Sunday.

STATE CAPITOL

702 Capitol Ave., Frankfort, 502-564-3590; www.finance.ky.gov/properties/capitol.htm

The stately Beaux-Arts building has French influences. The dome over the rotunda was designed to look like the one over Napoleon's tomb in Paris, and the Paris Grand Opera House inspired the massive marble stairways to the second floor. You can watch the politicians do their thing when the legislature is in session (check www.lrc.ky.gov for session details). Admire great men of history when you walk by the rotunda's statues of Abraham Lincoln, Jefferson Davis, Henry Clay, Dr. Ephraim McDowell and Alben Barkley, vice president under Harry S. Truman. Guided tours are available. Monday-Friday 8:30 a.m.-3:30 p.m., Saturday 10 a.m.-2 p.m., Sunday 1-4 p.m.

SPECIAL EVENTS

CAPITAL EXPO FESTIVAL

405 Mero St., Capital Plaza Complex, Frankfort, 502-695-7452;
www.capitalexpofestival.com

Traditional music, country music and fiddling fill the air at this fest. Workshops, demonstrations, arts and crafts, balloon races, dancing, games, contests, puppets, museum exhibitions, ethnic and regional foods all add to the fun. First full weekend in June.

GOVERNOR'S DERBY BREAKFAST

700 Capitol Ave., Frankfort, 502-564-2611

Kentuckians, nearly 13,000 of them, start Derby Day right with a hearty breakfast served on the Capitol grounds. The staff here serves 2,080 pounds of country ham, 20,000 eggs and 15,000 cups of coffee. Music and crafts round out the festivities. First Saturday in May.

HOTELS

★BEST WESTERN PARKSIDE INN

80 Chenault Road, Frankfort, 502-695-6111, 800-938-8376; www.bestwestern.com

99 rooms. High-speed Internet access. Complimentary continental breakfast. Airport transportation available. Fitness center. Outdoor pool. Pets accepted. **$**

★★HOLIDAY INN

405 Wilkinson Blvd., Frankfort, 502-227-5100; www.holiday-inn.com
189 rooms. Restaurant, bar. **$**

RESTAURANT
★JIM'S SEAFOOD

950 Wilkinson Blvd., Frankfort, 502-223-7448
Seafood menu. Lunch, dinner. Closed Sunday. **$$**

GEORGETOWN

Georgetown may be small, but it has one big claim to fame: This is the place where Kentucky bourbon whiskey was first produced. Baptist minister the Rev. Elijah Craig invented the spirit in 1789 using water from Royal Spring, which still flows in the center of the city.

Information: Georgetown/Scott County Chamber of Commerce, 399 Outlet Center Drive, 502-863-2547, 888-863-8600; www.georgetownky.com

WHAT TO SEE AND DO
CARDOME CENTRE

800 Cincinnati Pike, Georgetown, 502-863-1575; www.cardomecentre.com
This place was the former house of Civil War Governor J. F. Robinson and later the home of the Academy of the Sisters of the Visitation. Now it houses Georgetown and Scott County Museum and serves as a community center. Monday-Friday, also by appointment.

ROYAL SPRING PARK

West Main and South Water streets, Georgetown, 502-863-2547; www.georgetownky.com
Kentucky's largest spring and the city's water source since 1775, Royal Spring is the site of the first bourbon distillation (1789). It's also the former site of McClelland's Fort (1776), the first paper mill in the West, a pioneer classical music school and state's first ropewalk. A cabin of a former slave was relocated and restored here for use as an information center. Mid-May to mid-October: Tuesday-Sunday.

SCOTT COUNTY COURTHOUSE

101 E. Main St., Georgetown, 502-863-7850
The courthouse was designed in Second Empire style by Thomas Boyd of Pittsburgh. It's part of the historic business district. Monday-Friday.

TOYOTA MOTOR MANUFACTURING, KENTUCKY, INC

1001 Cherry Blossom Way, Georgetown, 502-868-3027, 800-866-4485; www.toyotageorgetown.com
About 400,000 cars and 350,000 engines are made here annually. The visitor center has interactive exhibits. One-hour tours of the plant (ages 6 and up) include a video presentation and tram ride through different levels of production. Visitor center: Monday-Friday, Tours: Monday-Friday (reservations required).

KENTUCKY

★
★
★
★

GILBERTSVILLE

Fishing parties heading for Kentucky Lake stop in tiny Gilbertsville for last-minute provisions. The area also caters to tourists bound for the resorts and state parks.

Information: Marshall County Chamber of Commerce, 17 Highway 68 W. Benton, Gilbertsville, 270-527-7665; www.marshallcounty.net

WHAT TO SEE AND DO

BARKLEY LOCK AND DAM

Highways 62 and 641, Gilbertsville, 270-362-4236

Play on more than 1,000 miles of shoreline. Navigation lock, canal, hydroelectric generating plant and recreation areas are available; get more information at the visitor center.

KENTUCKY DAM

Gilbertsville, 270-362-4221; www.kentuckylake.org.com

The dam stretches 8,422 feet and stands 206 feet tall. It creates a lake and regulates the flow of water from the Tennessee River into the Ohio River. Viewing balcony (daily); tours of powerhouse (by appointment).

KENTUCKY DAM VILLAGE STATE RESORT PARK

Gilbertsville, 113 Administration Drive, 270-362-4271, 800-325-0146; www.parks.ky.gov.com

The park, on Kentucky Lake, provides many ways to play: swimming beach, pool, bathhouse (seasonal), waterskiing, boating (rentals, launching ramps, docks), hiking, 18-hole and miniature golf (seasonal fee), tennis, picnicking, playground, shops, camping, lodge and cottages.

HOTEL

★★KENTUCKY DAM STATE RESORT

Gilbertsville, 270-362-4271, 800-325-0146; www.parks.ky.gov

156 rooms. Restaurant. Airport transportation available. **$**

RESTAURANT

★PATTI'S

1759 J. H. O'Bryan Ave., Grand River, 270-362-8844, 888-736-2515; www.pattis-settlement.com

Lunch, dinner. **$$**

GLASGOW

Not surprisingly, Glasgow has a bit o' Scottish flavor. It's famous for its Highland Games, which celebrate Celtic heritage and culture.

Information: Glasgow-Barren County Chamber of Commerce, 118 E. Public Square, Glasgow, 270-651-3161; www.glasgowbarrenchamber.com

WHAT TO SEE AND DO

BARREN RIVER LAKE STATE RESORT PARK

1149 State Park Road, Lucas, 270-646-2151, 800-325-0057; www.parks.ky.gov

Near Mammoth Cave National Park, this resort park is near the 10,000-acre Barren River Lake. You'll have your choice of activities: swimming at the beach or pool, fishing, boating (rentals), hiking, horseback riding, riding bicycle trails, playing on the 18-hole golf course, tennis, picnicking and hanging around the playground. If you want to stay the night, tent and trailer sites (April-October, standard fees), cottages and a lodge are available.

SPECIAL EVENT
HIGHLAND GAMES AND GATHERING OF SCOTTISH CLANS
1149 State Park Road, Lucas, 270-651-3161
There's something captivating about watching grown men in plaid kilts compete in the historic Highland Games. Athletic events include the stone toss, hammer throw and the caber throw, in which contestants toss a 19-foot, 120-pound pole end-over-end. The four-day festival also hosts live entertainment, food vendors and a banquet. Weekend following Memorial Day.

HOTELS
★★BARREN RIVER LAKE STATE RESORT PARK
1149 State Park Road, Lucas, 270-646-2151, 800-325-0057;
www.parks.ky.gov/findparks/resortparks/br
51 rooms. Restaurant. Children's activity center. $

★DAYS INN
105 Days Inn Blvd., Glasgow, 270-651-1757; www.daysinn.com
59 rooms. High-speed Internet access. Complimentary breakfast. Outdoor pool. Business center.

SPECIALTY LODGING
FOUR SEASONS COUNTRY INN
4107 Scottsville Road, Glasgow, 270-678-1000; www.fourseasonscountryinn.com
The atmosphere in this Victorian-style bed and breakfast is comfortable and laid-back. Sit by the fireplace on chilly nights, or relax with a good book on the large porch. 21 rooms. Complimentary continental breakfast. $

RESTAURANT
★★BOLTON'S LANDING
2433 Scottsville Road, Glasgow, 270-651-8008
Lunch, dinner. Closed Sunday. $$

GREENVILLE
Located in the heart of the western Kentucky coal, oil and natural gas fields, Greenville is also close to areas popular with hunters and fishermen.
Information: Chamber of Commerce, 200 Court St., Greenville, 270-338-5422;
www.greenvillechamber.org

WHAT TO SEE AND DO
LAKE MALONE STATE PARK
331 Highway 8001, Dunmore, 270-657-2111; www.parks.ky.gov
Steep sandstone bluffs and a wooded shoreline surround Lake Malone, making it a beautiful place to relax. If you get the urge to hike, take the easy 1½-mile trek on Laurel Trail. Swimming; fishing for bass, bluegill and crappie; boating (ramp, rentals,

motors); hiking and picnicking are some of the offerings. Tent and trailer camping (April to mid-November) are also available. Daily.

HARRODSBURG

Settled in 1774, Harrodsburg (named for pioneer James Harrod) is Kentucky's oldest town. Its sulfur springs and historical sites make it a busy tourist town.

Information: Harrodsburg/Mercer County Tourist Commission, 103 S. Main St., 859-734-2364, 800-355-9192; www.harrodsburgky.com

WHAT TO SEE AND DO

MORGAN ROW

220-222 S. Chiles St., Harrodsburg, 859-734-5985

Probably the oldest standing row house west of the Alleghenies, Morgan Row once was a stagecoach stop and tavern. Now it houses the Harrodsburg Historical Society Museum. Tuesday-Saturday.

OLD FORT HARROD STATE PARK

100 S. College, Harrodsburg, 859-734-3314; www.parks.ky.gov/findparks/recparks/fh

This 28-acre park includes a reproduction of Old Fort Harrod, near where the original fort was built in 1774. Other structures on the site include pioneers' homes, which hold authentic cooking utensils, tools and furniture. The Mansion Museum includes the Lincoln Room, the Confederate Room, a gun collection and Native American artifacts. Lincoln Marriage Temple shelters the log cabin in which Abraham Lincoln's parents were married on June 12, 1806 (moved from its original site in Beech Fork). Picnic facilities, playground and gift shop are there as well. Living history crafts program are held in the fort (mid-April-late October). Days and times vary.

OLD MUD MEETING HOUSE

Harrodsburg, four miles south off Highway 68, 859-734-5985

This is the first Dutch Reformed Church west of the Alleghenies. The original mud-thatch walls have been restored. By appointment only.

SHAKER VILLAGE OF PLEASANT HILL

3501 Lexington Road, Harrodsburg, 859-734-5411; www.shakervillageky.org

What was once a flourishing society is now the nation's largest restored Shaker community. In the heart of horse country, this village has 34 buildings and 3,000 acres of farmland, much of which visitors can explore on foot, bike or horseback. Costumed interpreters in the village tell the stories of Shaker life. Craft shops offer reproductions of Shaker furniture and Kentucky craft items. A year-round calendar of special events includes music, dance and workshops. Daily. Sternwheeler offers one-hour excursions on the Kentucky River (late April-October; fee).

SPECIAL EVENTS

THE LEGEND OF DANIEL BOONE

Harrodsburg

This outdoor drama tells the story of Boone, one of America's great explorers. James Harrod Amphitheater, in Old Fort Harrod State Park. Mid-June-August: Tuesday-Sunday.

PIONEER DAYS FESTIVAL

Charles Street, Harrodsburg, 859-734-2365

Celebrate Pioneer Days with music, arts and crafts, carnival and a car show. Second weekend August.

HOTELS

★★★BEAUMONT INN

Harrodsburg, 859-734-3381, 800-352-3992; www.beaumontinn.com

Maintaining the style and tradition of the past, this property offers unique accommodations that reflect the area's rich heritage. Guests experience the meaning of "Southern decadence" when they treat themselves to dinner here. 31 rooms. Restaurant. **$**

★BEST WESTERN OF DANVILLE & HARRODSBURG

1680 Danville Road, Harrodsburg, 859-734-9431; www.daysinn.com

69 rooms. Complimentary continental breakfast. **$**

SPECIALTY LODGING

SHAKER VILLAGE OF PLEASANT HILL

3501 Lexington Road, Harrodsburg, 859-734-5411; www.shakervillageky.org

81 rooms. Restaurant. **$**

RESTAURANT

★★TRUSTEES' HOUSE AT PLEASANT HILL

3501 Lexington Road, Harrodsburg, 859-734-5411; www.shakervillageky.org

Lunch, dinner. **$$**

HAZARD

In rugged mountain country, Hazard is a coal-mining town that earned a little name recognition from the 1980s TV hit *Dukes of Hazzard*, although the fictional Hazzard County was set in Georgia.

Information: Hazard-Perry County Chamber of Commerce & Tourism Commission, 601 Main St., 606-439-2659; www.hazardperrychamber.com

WHAT TO SEE AND DO

BOBBY DAVIS MEMORIAL PARK

Walnut Street, Hazard

Head to the park for its picnic area, reflecting pool, World War II Memorial and 400 varieties of shrubs and plants. Daily. In the park is Bobby Davis Park Museum, which houses local historical artifacts and photographs about life on Kentucky River waterways. Monday-Friday.

BUCKHORN LAKE STATE RESORT PARK

4441 Highway 1833, Hazard, 606-398-7510;
www.parks.ky.gov/findparks/resortparks/bk

Visitors enjoy canoeing, fishing (especially for muskie), swimming in the pool, relaxing in the bathhouse (seasonal), boating (ramp, motors, rentals), hiking, renting bikes, playing miniature golf, hitting some tennis balls and picnicking at this park. A lodge and cottages are also available.

CARR FORK LAKE

843 Sassafras Creek Road, Sassafras, 606-642-3308; www.lrl.usace.army.mil/cfl/ - 21k

The 710-acre lake make for good fishing, boating (ramps, marina) and camping. Check out the observation points. Some facilities are seasonal.

SPECIAL EVENT
BLACK GOLD FESTIVAL

Main Street, Hazard, 606-436-0161; www.blackgoldfestival.com

The festival celebrates local coal resources with food and craft booths, games, an ugliest lamp contest, entertainment, a carnival and a parade. Third full weekend in September.

HOTELS
★★BUCKHORN LAKE STATE RESORT PARK

4441 Highway 1833, Buckhorn, 606-398-7510, 800-325-0058; www.parks.ky.gov

36 rooms. Restaurant. Children's activity center. $

★SUPER 8

125 Village Lane, Hazard, 606-436-8888, 800-800-8000; www.super8.com

86 rooms. High-speed Internet access. Complimentary continental breakfast. Pets accepted. $

HENDERSON

On a bluff overlooking the Ohio River, Henderson is a town of great natural beauty. It was once home to artist and naturalist John James Audubon, who lived here for nine years and painted life-size pictures of the wildlife nearby.

Information: Tourist Commission, 2961 Highway 41 North, Henderson, 270-826-3128, 800-648-3128; www.hendersonky.org

WHAT TO SEE AND DO
JOHN JAMES AUDUBON STATE PARK

3100 I-41 North, Henderson, 270-826-2247; www.parks.ky.gov/findparks/recparks/au

See the massive hardwood forests, woodland plants and two lakes that inspired Audubon's writings. The museum here holds the celebrated naturalist's art and personal memorabilia. The park also has a bathhouse (seasonal), fishing, paddleboat rentals (seasonal), nine-hole golf (year-round; fee), picnicking, a playground, tent and trailer camping (standard fees) and cottages (year-round). Supervised recreation (seasonal) and guided nature walks (by appointment) are also available.

SPECIAL EVENTS
BIG RIVER ARTS & CRAFTS FESTIVAL

Audubon State Park, 2910 Highway 41 North, Henderson, 42420

More than 250 exhibitors turn out for this arts and crafts fair. Early October.

BLUEGRASS IN THE PARK

Henderson, 270-826-3128; www.bluegrassintheparkfestival.com

On the banks of the Ohio River, in Audubon Mill Park, this free festival hosts bluegrass acts from across the country. The festival includes a Folklife Festival, where locals celebrate folk music, crafts, cooking and storytelling. Early August.

HORSE RACING

Ellis Park, 3300 Highway 41 North, Henderson, 800-333-8110;
www.ellisparkracing.com

Head to Ellis Park to see some thoroughbred racing. Early July-Labor Day: Tuesday-Sunday.

W. C. HANDY BLUES & BARBECUE FESTIVAL

Atkinson Park, Elm St., Henderson, 270-826-3128; www.handyblues.org

Local legends says that W.C. Handy, the "father of the blues," was traveling back from the Chicago World's Fair in 1893 when he ran out of money in St. Louis and joined a band that played in the region. At a gig in Henderson, Handy met Elizabeth Price, the woman who would become his wife. W.C. Handy lived in Henderson for 10 years, and this festival celebrates the musical genre he helped create. Mid-June.

HOTEL
★COMFORT INN

2820 Highway 41 N., Henderson, 270-827-8191, 877-417-3251;
www.choicehotels.com

55 rooms. High-speed Internet access. Complimentary continental breakfast. Outdoor pool. $

HODGENVILLE

Admirers of Abraham Lincoln will appreciate Hodgenville, where the 16th president of the United States was born in 1809. Almost all of the tourist attractions here relate to the city's most famous native son.

Information: LaRue County Chamber of Commerce, 60 Lincoln Square, Hodgenville,
270-358-3411; www.laruecounty.org/civicclubs.shtml

WHAT TO SEE AND DO
LINCOLN JAMBOREE

2579 Lincoln Farm Road, Hodgenville, 270-358-3545; www.lincolnjamboree.com

This family entertainment event features traditional and modern country music. Saturday evenings; reservations recommended in summer.

ABRAHAM LINCOLN BIRTHPLACE NATIONAL HISTORIC SITE

Honest Abe was born here on February 12, 1809, at his father's Sinking Spring Farm. Less than three years later, the Lincolns moved to Knob Creek Farm, about 10 miles northeast. Eventually the family moved to Indiana and then Illinois. The park preserves much of Sinking Spring Farm and part of Knob Creek.

Inside the granite and marble Memorial Building is a log cabin that symbolizes the cabin where the 16th president was born. More than 100,000 citizens contributed funds to build the Memorial Building in 1911. Today, visitors can also see a cabin much like Lincoln's boyhood home at Knob Creek.

Don't miss the visitor center audiovisual program (18 minutes) and exhibits that explore Lincoln's childhood and background. Daily.

Hodgenville, three miles south on Highway 31 East/Highway 61; www.nps.gov/abli

143

KENTUCKY

LINCOLN MUSEUM

66 Lincoln Square, Hodgenville, 270-358-3163; www.lincolnmuseum-ky.org
Dioramas at the museum tell the story of Lincoln's life, from his early childhood in Kentucky to his assassination at Ford's Theatre. The second floor holds rare newspaper clippings, memorabilia, campaign posters and an art gallery. Daily.

SPECIAL EVENTS
FOUNDER'S DAY

2995 Lincoln Farm Road, Hodgenville, 270-358-3137; www.nps.gov/abli
The event offers arts, crafts and music. Weekend nearest July 17.

LINCOLN DAYS CELEBRATION

Lincoln Square, Hodgenville, 270-358-3411; www.laruecounty.org/civicclubs.shtml
Lincoln Days has a rail-splitting competition, pioneer games, a classic car show, arts and crafts exhibits and a parade. Second weekend in October.

LINCOLN'S BIRTHDAY

2995 Lincoln Farm Road, Hodgenville, 270-358-3137; www.nps.gov/abli
A wreath-laying ceremony marks Abraham Lincoln's birthday. Afternoon of February 12.

MARTIN LUTHER KING'S BIRTHDAY

2995 Lincoln Farm Road, Hodgenville, 270-358-3137; www.nps.gov/abli
Sunday, mid-January.

144 HOPKINSVILLE

The tobacco auctioneers' chant has long been the theme song of Hopkinsville. The town was the infamous site of the Night Rider War, brought on by farmers' discontent at the low prices they received for their dark tobacco. They raided the town in December 1907, burning several warehouses. In 1911, the culprits were tried and their group disbanded.

Hopkinsville was also a stop on the "Trail of Tears." The site of the Cherokee encampment is now a park with a museum and memorial dedicated to those who lost their lives.

Information: Hopkinsville-Christian County Convention & Visitors Bureau, 2800 Fort Campbell Blvd., Hopkinsville, 270-885-9096, 800-842-9959; www.hopkinsville.info/QCMS

WHAT TO SEE AND DO
FORT CAMPBELL

2334 19th St., Hopkinsville, 270-798-2151; www.campbell.army.mil/campbell.htm
The fort is one of the nation's largest military installations (105,000 acres) and home of 101st Airborne Division (Air Assault). Wickham Hall houses the Don F. Pratt Museum, which displays historic military items. Daily.

PENNYRILE FOREST STATE RESORT PARK

20781 Pennyrile Lodge Road, Dawson Springs, 270-797-3421; www.parks.ky.gov/findparks/resortparks/pf
You'll stay busy at the park with swimming at the beach and pool, a bathhouse (seasonal), fishing, boating (no motors), hiking, riding, nine-hole and miniature golf

(seasonal, rentals), tennis, picnicking and a playground. The grounds also have a grocery, cottages, a lodge, and tent and trailer sites (April-October, standard fees).

PENNYROYAL AREA MUSEUM
217 E. Ninth St., Hopkinsville, 270-887-4270; www.hoptown.org
Exhibits feature the area's agriculture and industries, a miniature circus and old railroad items. The museum also highlights Civil War items, 1898 law office furniture and an Edgar Cayce exhibit. Monday-Saturday.

SPECIAL EVENTS
LITTLE RIVER DAYS
1209 S. Virginia St., Hopkinsville, 270-885-9096; www.campbell.army.mil/hopkinsville.htm
The festival consists of road races, canoe races, arts and crafts, entertainment and children's events. Early May.

WESTERN KENTUCKY STATE FAIR
Hopkinsville, 270-885-9096; www.hopkinsvillechamber.com
The state fair keeps it festive with a midway, rides, concerts, local exhibits and events. First week in August.

HOTELS
★BEST WESTERN HOPKINSVILLE
4101 Fort Campbell Blvd., Hopkinsville, 270-886-9000; www.bestwestern.com
107 rooms. High-speed Internet access. Complimentary continental breakfast. Bar. Business center. Outdoor pool. $

★★HOLIDAY INN
2910 Fort Campbell Blvd., Hopkinsville, 270-886-4413; www.holiday-inn.com
101 rooms. High-speed Internet access. Restaurant, bar. Indoor pool. Pets accepted. $

HORSE CAVE
On the south side of Main Street, you'll find the reason for this city's unusual name: a large natural cave opening. Legend suggests that in the 19th century, *horse* was a synonym for *large*, hence the cave's—and the city's—unusual name.
Information: www.horsecaveky.com

WHAT TO SEE AND DO
KENTUCKY DOWN UNDER/KENTUCKY CAVERNS
3700 Land Turnpike Road N., Horse Cave, 270-786-2634, 800-762-2869; www.kdu.com
This Australian-themed animal park features free-roaming kangaroos, wallabies, emus and other animals native to Down Under. Walk into the exotic bird garden and feed colorful lorikeets while they sit on your head and shoulders. Learn about sheep herding in the sheep station area, or find out about Australia's aborigines and their way of life at Camp Corroboree. View bison from the Overlook Deck and then try not to feel guilty as you munch on a bison burger at the Outback Cafe. Admission to Kentucky Caverns (formerly Mammoth Onyx Cave) is included and lets visitors get

★
★
★
★
☆

up close and personal with the beautiful onyx formations found underground here in Kentucky's "Cave Country." The 45-minute guided cave tour reveals colorful stalactites and stalagmites, flowstone and hanging bridges and is leisurely enough to accommodate most people (though not those in wheelchairs). Best of all, the cave keeps to a comfortable 60 degrees year-round, so it stays open through the winter. Mid-March to October: daily 8 a.m.-5 p.m.

KENTUCKY REPERTORY THEATRE AT HORSE CAVE

107 E. Main St., Horse Cave, 800-342-2177; www.kentuckyrep.org

This is Southern Kentucky's resident professional festival theater. Six of the season's plays run in rotating repertory during the summer. An art gallery is also on the premises. Days and times vary.

JAMESTOWN

It was here that Lake Cumberland was created, with the help of a 101-mile-long dam. Look for plenty of water sports, and more than a few activities—from golf to shuffleboard—for the landlubbers among us.

Information: Russell County Tourist Commission, 650 S. Highway 127, Russell Springs, 270-866-4333; www.russellcountyky.com

WHAT TO SEE AND DO

LAKE CUMBERLAND STATE RESORT PARK

5465 State Park Road, Jamestown, 270-343-3111, 800-325-1709; www.parks.ky.gov/findparks/resortparks/lc

This lake resort is a water sportsman's dream. It has a reputation as one of the best fishing spots in the eastern United States. The park also has swimming pools, fishing, boating (ramps, rentals, dock), hiking, riding (seasonal), nine-hole par-3 and miniature golf (seasonal), tennis, shuffleboard, bicycling, picnicking, a playground, a lodge, rental houseboats, cottages and tent and trailer camping (April-November). Check out the nature center.

JEFFERSON DAVIS MONUMENT STATE SHRINE

In 1808, Jefferson Davis, the only president of the Confederate States of America, was born in Fairview, Ky. (Ironically, less than a year later, President Abraham Lincoln was born about 100 miles away.) This monument to Davis, a cast-concrete obelisk more than 350 feet tall, overlooks a 19-acre park. Visitors may take an elevator to the observation area at the top (fee).

The son of a Revolutionary War officer, Davis graduated from West Point, became a successful cotton planter in Mississippi, was elected to the U.S. Senate, and served as secretary of war in President Franklin Pierce's cabinet. He had returned to the Senate when Mississippi seceded from the Union in 1860, a move that prompted Davis to resign his seat. Elected president of the Confederacy, he served for the duration of the war—about four years. Union troops captured him in Georgia, and Davis lost his citizenship and served two years in prison. May-October: daily.

Information: 10 miles east of Hopkinsville on Highway 68, Fairview, 270-886-1765; www.parks.ky.gov/findparks/histparks/jd/history

KENTUCKY

★
★
★
★
★

HOTEL
★★LAKE CUMBERLAND STATE RESORT PARK
5465 State Park Road, Jamestown, 270-343-3111, 800-325-1709;
www.parks.ky.gov/findparks/resortparks/lc
106 rooms. Restaurant. Children's activity center. **$**

KENLAKE STATE RESORT PARK

This park on Kentucky Lake has it all: beautiful scenery, four miles of shoreline and so many amenities you won't know where to begin your vacation. A pool, a bathhouse (seasonal), waterskiing, fishing, boating (ramps, rentals, marina), hiking, nine-hole golf (rentals), shuffleboard, tennis (indoor, outdoor, shop), picnicking, playgrounds, cottages, a dining room, a lodge and tent and trailer sites are all available here. April-October.

Information: 16 miles northeast of Murray on Highway 94,
270-474-2211, 800-325-0143; www.parks.ky.gov/findparks/resortparks/kl

HOTEL
★★KENLAKE STATE RESORT PARK
542 Kenlake Road, Hardin, 270-474-2211, 800-425-0143;
www.parks.ky.gov/findparks/resortparks/kl
82 rooms. Restaurant. **$**

LAND BETWEEN THE LAKES

Welcome to one of the nation's biggest outdoor recreation areas. More than 170,000 acres make up this wooded peninsula that runs 40 miles from north to south between Kentucky Lake and Lake Barkley.

There are four major family campgrounds: Hillman Ferry, Piney, Energy Lake (year-round; electric hookups; fee) and Wranglers Campground, which is equipped for horseback riders. Eleven other lake-access areas offer more primitive camping (fee). All areas offer swimming, fishing, boating, ramps and picnic facilities. Family campgrounds have planned recreation programs (summer).

There is a 5,000-acre wooded Environmental Education Area that includes the Nature Station, which presents interpretive displays of native plant and animal life. Within this area are several nature trails. Elk and Bison Prairie is a drive-through viewing area where you'll see native plants and wildlife (Daily; fee). Nature center: March-November: daily; fee.

Information: 100 Van Morgan Drive, Murray, 270-924-5897; www.lbl.org

WHAT TO SEE AND DO
GOLDEN POND VISITOR CENTER
Land Between the Lakes, 100 Van Morgan Drive,
Golden Pond, 270-924-2233; www.lbl.org
This is the main orientation center for Land Between the Lakes visitors. Planetarium presentations take place here (March-December, fee). Daily.

THE HOMEPLACE

Land Between the Lakes, 100 Van Morgan Drive, Golden Pond,
270-924-270-2000; www.lbl.org

This working history farm provides an authentic look at farm life in the 19th century. Corn and tobacco are grown and harvested using tools and techniques of the era. The livestock and farm animals are "minor breeds"—historic breeds of domestic animals that are endangered species. April-November: daily.

WOODLANDS NATURE STATION

Land Between the Lakes, 100 Van Morgan Drive, Golden Pond,
270-924-270-2000; www.lbl.org

Inside you'll find the station's discovery center, and outside in "the Backyard," you'll see plants and animals from this corner of the world. Catch sight of a bobcat, red wolf and maybe even a bald eagle. March-November: daily 9 a.m.-5 p.m.

LEXINGTON

Lexington might be the "Horse Capital of the World," but don't mistake this city for a simple horse town. In the heart of Kentucky's Bluegrass region, Lexington benefits from smart urban planning, Southern sophistication and the allure of bourbon and horse racing. (Don't be fooled by the region's name: The legendary steel-blue tint of the bluegrass is visible only in May's early morning sunshine.) In 1775, an exploring party was camping here when members got news of the colonists' triumph at the Battle of Lexington in Massachusetts and decided to name their campsite in honor of the victory. Four years later, the city was established, and it quickly gained prominence in the expanding western territory. Pioneers who settled here brought their best horses from Maryland and Virginia, and as the citizens' wealth grew, they imported horses from abroad to improve the breed. The first races were held in Lexington in 1780, and the first jockey club was organized in 1797.

In the early 19th century, Lexington earned the nickname "Athens of the West," thanks to its vibrant cultural life—a spirit that continues today. The city's offerings include two ballet companies, a professional theater group and an outstanding opera program at the University of Kentucky.

Information: Lexington Convention & Visitors Bureau, 301 E. Vine St., Lexington,
859-233-7299, 800-845-3959; www.visitlex.com

WHAT TO SEE AND DO

AMERICAN SADDLEBRED MUSEUM

4093 Iron Works Parkway, Lexington, 859-259-2746;
www.americansaddlebredmuseum.org

The museum is dedicated to the American Saddlebred horse, Kentucky's only native breed. Contemporary exhibits look at the development and uses of the American Saddlebred. There's also a gift shop. Days and times vary.

ART MUSEUM

Singletary Center for the Arts, Euclid Avenue and Rose Street, Lexington,
859-257-5716; www.uky.edu

The museum has both permanent collections and special exhibitions. Tuesday-Thursday, Saturday-Sunday noon-5 p.m., Friday noon-8 p.m.

ASHLAND

Richmond and Sycamore Roads, Lexington, 859-266-8581; www.henryclay.org

This estate on 20 acres of woodland was the home of Henry Clay, statesman, orator, senator and would-be president. Occupied by the Clay clan for five generations, Ashland is furnished with family possessions. The estate was named for the ash trees that surround it. A number of outbuildings still stand. Days and times vary.

HEADLEY-WHITNEY MUSEUM

4435 Old Frankfort Pike, Lexington, 859-255-6653; www.headley-whitney.org

This museum exhibits decorative arts—furniture, metalwork, textiles and ceramics. Unusual buildings house displays of bibelots (small decorative objects) created with precious metals and jewels, Oriental porcelains, paintings, decorative arts, shell grotto and special exhibits. Tuesday-Friday 10 a.m.-5 p.m., Saturday-Sunday noon-5 p.m.

HORSE FARMS

Lexington

More than 400 horse farms are in the area, most of them concentrated in Lexington-Fayette County. Although the majority are thoroughbred farms, some farms breed other varieties such as standardbreds, American saddle horses, Arabians, Morgans and quarter horses. Visitors can see the farms by taking one of many tours offered by tour companies in Lexington.

HUNT-MORGAN HOUSE

201 N. Mill St., Lexington, 859-253-0362; www.bluegrasstrust.org

This mansion has been home to several of Kentucky's famous sons. Built for John Wesley Hunt, Kentucky's first millionaire, it was later occupied by his grandson, Gen. John Hunt Morgan, known as the "Thunderbolt of the Confederacy" for his guerilla tactics behind enemy lines. In 1866, Nobel Prize-winning geneticist Thomas Hunt Morgan was born in this house. Inside it, you'll see family furniture, portraits and porcelain. There's also a walled courtyard garden and gift shop. Days and times vary.

KENTUCKY

★
★
★
★

KENTUCKY HORSE PARK

4089 Iron Works Parkway, Lexington, 859-233-4303, 800-568-8813; www.imh.org

Dedicated to "man's relationship with the horse," this park has more than 1,000 acres of beautiful bluegrass. Its diverse offerings include the Man O' War grave and memorial, in honor of one of the world's greatest thoroughbred horses of all time. The visitors' information center shows a widescreen film presentation, *Thou Shalt Fly Without Wings.* Also located within the park are the International Museum of the Horse, Parade of Breeds (seasonal), Calumet Trophy Collection, Sears Collection of hand-carved miniatures, Hall of Champions stable that houses famous thoroughbreds and standardbreds, walking farm tour and antique carriage display. In addition, the park offers swimming, tennis, ball courts, picnic areas, playgrounds and a campground (fee). Special events include horse-drawn rides (fee). Days and times vary.

LEXINGTON CEMETERY

833 W. Main St., Lexington, 859-255-5522; www.lexcem.org

Buried on these 170 acres are Henry Clay, John C. Breckinridge, Gen. John Hunt Morgan, the Todds (Mrs. Abraham Lincoln's family), coach Adolph Rupp (one of college basketball's most successful coaches) and many other notable persons, including 500 Confederate and 1,110 Union veterans. The grounds have sunken gardens, lily pools, a four-acre flower garden, extensive plantings of spring-flowering trees and shrubs. Daily.

MARY TODD LINCOLN HOUSE
578 W. Main St., Lexington, 859-233-9999; www.mtlhouse.org
The childhood residence of Mary Todd Lincoln is authentically restored and has period furnishings and personal items. Mid-March to November: Monday-Saturday 10 a.m.-4 p.m.

OPERA HOUSE
430 W. Short St., Lexington, 859-233-4567; www.lexingtonoperahouse.com
This restored and reconstructed opera house is a regional performing arts center; performances include Broadway shows and special events. September-June.

TRANSYLVANIA UNIVERSITY
300 N. Broadway, Lexington, 859-233-8300; www.transy.edu
The oldest institution of higher learning west of the Allegheny Mountains, Transylvania has a list of distinguished alumni: two U.S. vice presidents, 36 state and territorial governors, 34 ambassadors, 50 senators, 112 members of the U.S. House of Representatives and Confederate President Jefferson Davis. Thomas Jefferson was one of Transylvania's early supporters. Henry Clay taught law courses and was a member of the university's governing board. The administration building, "Old Morrison" (1833), was used as a hospital during the Civil War. Tours of campus are available by appointment.

UNIVERSITY OF KENTUCKY
104 Administration Building, Lexington, 859-257-9000; www.uky.edu

VICTORIAN SQUARE
401 W. Main St., Lexington, 859-252-7575; www.victoriansquareshoppes.com
This shopping area is in the downtown restoration project. Head there for specialty stores, restaurants and a children's museum (859-258-3253).

WAVELAND STATE HISTORIC SITE
225 Waveland Museum Lane, Lexington, 859-272-3611;
www.parks.ky.gov/findparks/histparks/wl
For a glimpse into plantation life in the 19th century, visit this Greek Revival mansion. Slave quarters, outbuildings, an icehouse and a smokehouse still stand. There's also a playground. Days and times vary.

WILLIAM S. WEBB MUSEUM OF ANTHROPOLOGY
S. Limestone Street and Euclid Avenue, Lexington, 859-257-7112;
www.uky.edu/AS/Anthropology/Museum/museum.htm
Exhibits include the cultural history of Kentucky and the evolution of man. Monday-Friday.

SPECIAL EVENTS

BLUE GRASS STAKES

Keeneland Race Course, 4201 Versailles Road, Lexington, 859-254-3412;
www.keeneland.com

The top contenders for the Derby face off in one of the last major prep races before Derby Day. Mid-April.

EGYPTIAN EVENT

Kentucky Horse Park, 4089 Iron Works Parkway, Lexington, 859-231-0771;
www.pyramidsociety.org/event.htm

The event celebrates rare Egyptian Arabian horses, whose lineage can be traced back at least 3,500 years. There are show classes, a walk of stallions, a breeder's sale, native costumes, seminars, an art auction and an Egyptian bazaar. Early June.

FESTIVAL OF THE BLUEGRASS

Kentucky Horse Park, 4089 Iron Works Parkway, Lexington, 859-846-4995;
www.festivalofthebluegrass.com

The festival attracts top names in bluegrass music with more than 20 bands appearing. It includes special shows for children and workshops with the musicians. The 600-acre park has more than 750 electric hookups for campers. Second full weekend in June.

GRAND CIRCUIT MEET

The Red Mile Track, 1200 Red Mile Road, Lexington, 859-255-0752;
www.theredmile.com

The Red Mile has been hosting harness racing since 1875, which makes it Lexington's oldest track. The Grand Circuit Meet features the Kentucky Futurity race, the final leg of harness racing's Triple Crown. Two weeks, late September-early October.

HARNESS RACING

The Red Mile Harness Track, 1200 Red Mile Road, Lexington, 859-255-0752;
www.theredmile.com

This is also the site of Grand Circuit racing. Night racing takes place on the grounds as well. May-June: Thursday-Saturday; September-October: Monday-Tuesday, Friday-Saturday.

HIGH HOPE STEEPLECHASE

Kentucky Horse Park, 4089 Iron Works Parkway, Lexington, 859-967-9444;
www.highhopesteeplechase.com

Mid-May.

JUNIOR LEAGUE HORSE SHOW

The Red Mile Harness Track, 1200 Red Mile Road, Lexington, 859-252-8014;
www.lexjrleague.com

The Junior League puts on an outdoor saddlebred-horse show. Six days in early to mid-July.

KENTUCKY

★
★
★
★

ROLEX KENTUCKY THREE-DAY EVENT

Kentucky Horse Park, 4080 Iron Works Parkway, Lexington, 859-233-2362;
www.rk3de.org

This is a three-day endurance test for horses and riders in dressage, cross-country and stadium jumping. The fair also features boutiques. Late April.

THOROUGHBRED RACING

Keeneland Race Course, 4201 Versailles Road, Lexington, 859-254-3412;
www.keeneland.com

Three weeks in April and three weeks in October.

HOTELS

★★BEST WESTERN LEXINGTON CONFERENCE CENTER HOTEL

5532 Athens Boonesboro Road, Lexington, 859-263-5241, 800-780-7234;
www.bestwestern.com

150 rooms. High-speed Internet access. Complimentary breakfast. Restaurant, bar. Children's activity center. **$**

★BEST WESTERN REGENCY/LEXINGTON

2241 Elkhorn Road, Lexington, 859-293-2202; www.bestwestern.com

112 rooms. High-speed Internet access. Complimentary continental breakfast. Outdoor pool. **$**

★COMFORT INN

2381 Buena Vista Drive, Lexington, 859-299-0302; www.choicehotels.com

122 rooms. Complimentary continental breakfast. Indoor pool. **$**

★★CROWNE PLAZA HOTEL LEXINGTON-THE CAMPBELL HOUSE

1375 S. Broadway, Lexington, 859-255-4281; www.crowneplaza.com

370 rooms. High-speed Internet access. Restaurant, bar. Fitness center. Airport transportation available. Business center. **$**

★★★DOUBLETREE GUEST SUITES LEXINGTON

2601 Richmond Road, Lexington, 859-268-0060, 800-262-3774; www.doubletree.com

155 suites. Wireless Internet access. Restaurant, bar. Airport transportation available. Fitness center. Outdoor pool. Business center. Pets accepted. **$**

★★★GRATZ PARK INN

120 W. Second St., Lexington, 606-231-1777, 800-752-4166;
www.gratzparkinn.com

Just steps from many of Lexington's attractions, this boutique inn pampers guests with distinctive charm. Each room is decorated differently with 19th-century antique reproductions, stately mahogany furniture and regional artwork. Guests can relax in the lobby, retreat to the library or enjoy a mouthwatering meal at Chef Lundy's five-star restaurant, Jonathan at Gratz Park Inn. 41 rooms. Restaurant. Wireless Internet access. Airport transportation available. **$$**

152

KENTUCKY

★
★
★
★
★

★HAMPTON INN
2251 Elkhorn Road, Lexington, 859-299-2613, 800-426-7866; www.hamptoninn.com
125 rooms. Wireless Internet access. Complimentary continental breakfast. Fitness center. Outdoor pool. Business center. Pets accepted. **$**

★★★HILTON SUITES
245 Lexington Green Circle, Lexington, 859-271-4000, 800-774-1500; www.hilton.com
This hotel features deluxe two-room suites. It's near restaurants and a shopping mall and it is also less than seven miles from Bluegrass Airport. 174 suites. High-speed Internet access. Restaurant, bar. Airport transportation available. Fitness center. Outdoor pool. Business center. Pets accepted. **$**

★★★HYATT REGENCY LEXINGTON
401 W. High St., Lexington, 859-253-1234; www.hyatt.com
This hotel is perfectly situated in the downtown business district at Triangle Park and Lexington Center, near shopping, restaurants, a convention center, sports and entertainment. 365 rooms. Restaurant, bar. Airport transportation available. Indoor pool. Business center. **$$**

★★LEXINGTON DOWNTOWN HOTEL & CONFERENCE CENTER
369 W. Vine St., Lexington, 859-231-9000; www.lexingtondowntownhotel.com
367 rooms. Wireless Internet access. Complimentary continental breakfast. Restaurant, bar. Airport transportation available. Business center. **$$**

★★★MARRIOTT'S GRIFFIN GATE RESORT
1800 Newtown Pike, Lexington, 859-231-5100, 888-236-2427; www.marriott.com
This resort sits in the heart of Kentucky Bluegrass Country. Leisure guests will enjoy recreational facilities such as a championship golf course, tennis courts and an indoor and outdoor pool. Business travelers will appreciate the dataport-equipped phones, voicemail services, business center and corporate-team-challenge programs. 409 rooms. High-speed Internet access. Four restaurants, bar. Airport transportation available. Children's activity center. Tennis. Pool. Business center **$**

SPECIALTY LODGINGS

1823 HISTORIC ROSE HILL INN
233 Rose Hill Ave., Versailles, 859-873-5957, 800-307-0460; www.rosehillinn.com
Seven rooms. Wireless Internet access. Complimentary full breakfast. **$$**

MONTGOMERY INN
270 Montgomery Ave., Versailles, 859-251-4103; www.montgomeryinnbnb.com
In the center of horse-farm country, this restored Victorian inn is filled with Kentucky antiques and quiet charm. 10 rooms. Wireless Internet access. Complimentary full breakfast. Airport transportation available. **$**

KENTUCKY

★
★
★
★

RESTAURANTS

★★A-LA LUCIE
159 N. Limestone St., Lexington, 859-252-5277; www.alalucie.com
American menu. Lunch, dinner. Closed Sunday. $$

★★DESHA'S GRILLE AND BAR
101 N. Broadway, Lexington, 859-259-3771; www.deshas.com
American menu. Lunch, dinner. $$

★★DUDLEY'S
380 S. Mill St., Lexington, 859-252-1010; www.dudleysrestaurant.com
Mediterranean menu. Lunch, dinner. $$

★★MALONE'S
3347 Tates Creek Road, Lexington, 859-335-6500; www.malonesrestaurant.com
American menu. Lunch, dinner. $$$

★★★MANSION AT GRIFFIN GATE
1800 Newtown Pike, Lexington, 859-288-6142; www.mansionrestaurant.com
In this antebellum mansion, executive chef Brian Hove serves elegant entrées such as Kurobuta pork chops (served with baked grits and apricot bourbon glaze) and sesame-crusted ahi with coconut risotto, pineapple salsa and a sesame-soy sauce. The wine list is extensive, and the service professional. American menu. Dinner. $$$

★★MERRICK INN
1074 Merrick Drive, Lexington, 859-269-5417; www.murrays-merrick.com
American menu. Lunch, dinner. Closed Sunday. $$

★★MURRAY'S
3955 Harrodsburg Road, Lexington, 859-219-9922; www.murrays-merrick.com
American menu. Dinner. Closed Sunday. $$$

★★REGATTA SEAFOOD GRILLE
161 Lexington Green Circle, Lexington, 859-273-7875; www.regattaseafood.com
Seafood menu. Lunch, dinner. $$

LONDON
In the foothills of the Appalachian Mountains, London is close to the beautiful Daniel Boone National Forest, a prime spot for outdoor recreation.
Information: London-Laurel County Tourist Commission, 140 W. Daniel Boone Parkway, London, 606-878-6900, 800-348-0095; www.laurelkytourism.com

WHAT TO SEE AND DO

LEVI JACKSON WILDERNESS ROAD STATE PARK

998 Levi Jackson Mill Road, London, 606-330-2130;
www.parks.ky.gov/findparks/recparks/lj

Descendants of pioneer farmer Levi Jackson deeded some of this land to the state as a historical shrine to those who carved homes out of the wilderness. Boone's Trace and Wilderness Road pioneer trails converge in the park. Recreational facilities include a swimming pool (fee), a bathhouse, hiking, an archery range, miniature golf (April-October, fee), picnicking, playgrounds and camping (tent and trailer sites).

MCHARGUE'S MILL

998 Levi Jackson Mill Road, London, 606-330-2130;
www.parks.ky.gov/findparks/recparks/lj

This is one of the largest collections of millstones in the world. The mill was built in 1812 and reconstructed on the present site in 1939. Tours and demonstrations are also available. Memorial Day-Labor Day: daily.

MOUNTAIN LIFE MUSEUM

998 Levi Jackson Mill Road, London, 606-330-2130;
www.parks.ky.gov/findparks/recparks/lj

Split-rail fences enclose rustic cabins with household furnishings, pioneer relics, farm tools and Native American artifacts. There's also a smokehouse, blacksmith shop and barn with prairie schooner. April-October: daily.

HOTEL

★COMFORT INN

1918 W. Highway 192, London, 606-877-7848; www.choicehotels.com

62 rooms. Complimentary continental breakfast. **$**

LOUISVILLE

On the banks of the Ohio River, Louisville is sometimes called "the biggest small town in America." Its unique blend of Southern charm and urban sophistication is on display every year when the world watches the renowned Kentucky Derby, Louisville's biggest claim to fame. First run on May 17, 1875, and modeled after England's Epsom Derby, the Derby is the nation's oldest continually held race. The first Saturday in May each year, Churchill Downs hosts "the best two minutes in sports," played out against its backdrop of Edwardian towers and antique grandstands.

Louisville knows how to have a good time, and Derby festivities are the ultimate Southern party: They are a glamorous mélange of carnival, fashion show, spectacle and celebration of the horse. But if you can't make it to Louisville during these first days of May, you'll still find plenty to keep you entertained. Home to a growing art community and a hot underground music scene, the city takes its cultural life seriously. The public subscription Fund for the Arts subsidizes the Tony Award-winning Actors Theater, and the city boasts the Kentucky Center for the Arts, home of ballet, opera and music performances. For those interested in less formal entertainment, Louisville's Highlands neighborhood is a good bet. The funky district, which stretches along Bardstown Road, has nightclubs, upscale dining, art galleries and one-of-a-kind shops. Part of Louisville's charm comes from its ability to mesh its urban style with its colorful history. Founded in 1778 and named for French King Louis XVI for his help during the American Revolution, the city soon became a leader in the new nation's economic growth, thanks in part to its prime spot on the Ohio River. The city has been home to several giants of American history, too: President Zachary Taylor grew up nearby, and two Supreme Court justices—including Louis Brandeis—are from the city. F. Scott Fitzgerald was stationed at Camp Zachary Taylor during World War I and frequented the bar at the Seelbach Hotel, which was celebrated in *The Great Gatsby*.

Information: Convention and Visitors Bureau, 400 S. First St., Louisville, 502-584-2121, 800-792-5595; www.gotolouisville.com

THE RIVERWALK TOUR—ARTS, HISTORY AND OF COURSE, BASEBALL

Louisville has grown up around the falls of the Ohio River and a recent revival of the riverfront makes the city's waterfront around Main Street and Fourth Avenue a great place to begin exploring the old downtown area. From the banks, you'll catch sight of the floating Louisville Falls Fountain, which periodically shoots a geyser 375 feet into the air. At night the display is dramatically lit.

Look upriver and you'll see the *Belle of Louisville*, docked at the end of Fourth Street (502-574-2355). This 1914 steamboat continues to cruise the waters on sightseeing cruises. The *Star of Louisville* (502-589-7827) is another sightseeing boat docked a few blocks farther up on the far side of the Highway 31 bridge.

Surrounding the riverfront park is the city's historic district of old warehouses and cast-iron buildings—now restored as restaurants, galleries and shops. Start exploring around West Main Street at the southwest corner of Riverfront Park. You'll find many of the city's main attractions here, conveniently lined up in a row. Head west.

At the top of Sixth Street, the Kentucky Center for the Arts (5 Riverfront Plaza) is home to the city's resident opera, ballet, orchestra and children's theater. The dramatic glass-walled center also has an impressive collection of 20th-century sculpture. Free audiotape tours are available. The Kentucky Art and Craft Center at 609 W. Main Street displays contemporary pieces by local artists (502-589-0102). Where Seventh and Main Streets meet, you'll reach the site of Fort Nelson, where the town's original settlement was built in 1782.

The Louisville Science Center (727 W. Main St. 502-561-6100) contains five stories of hands-on exhibits in a transformed warehouse. The Egyptian mummy, space exhibits and an IMAX theater are especially popular with kids. And finally, at West Main and Eighth streets stands the landmark 120-foot-high Louisville Slugger—the world's largest baseball bat. It marks the site of the Louisville Slugger Museum (502-528-7728). Not only does the museum hold beloved baseball artifacts and memorabilia, but visitors can also watch the bats being made during the factory tour.

KENTUCKY

★
★
★
☆

WHAT TO SEE AND DO

AMERICAN PRINTING HOUSE FOR THE BLIND

1839 Frankfort Ave., Louisville, 502-895-2405; www.aph.org

This is the largest and oldest (1858) publishing house for the blind. In addition to books and music in Braille, it issues talking books, magazines, large-type textbooks and educational aids. Tours: Monday-Thursday 10 a.m.-2 p.m.

BELLARMINE UNIVERSITY

2001 Newburg Road, Louisville, 502-452-8131; www.bellarmine.edu

The university specializes in liberal arts and sciences. The 115-acre campus houses the Thomas Merton Studies Center, with his manuscripts, drawings, tapes and published works. Tuesday-Friday, by appointment. Guided campus tours are available by appointment.

CAVE HILL CEMETERY

701 Baxter Ave., Louisville, 502-451-5630; www.cavehillcemetery.com

This is the burial ground of George Rogers Clark, hero of the American Revolution and founder of the settlement that became Louisville. Col. Harland Sanders, of fried chicken fame, is also buried here. The grounds have rare trees, shrubs and plants, as well as swans, geese and ducks. Daily.

CHURCHILL DOWNS

700 Central Ave., Louisville, 502-636-4400; www.churchilldowns.com

Founded in 1875, this historic and world-famous thoroughbred racetrack is the home of the Kentucky Derby, "the most exciting two minutes in sports." Spring race meet, late April-June; fall race meet, late October-late November; Kentucky Derby, first Saturday in May.

E. P. "TOM" SAWYER STATE PARK

3000 Freys Hill Road, Louisville, 502-429-7270,
www.parks.ky.gov/findparks/recparks/ep

Named for Erbon Powers "Tom" Sawyer (father of television journalist Diane Sawyer), the park has 550 acres that make up one of Louisville's best playgrounds for outdoor enthusiasts. People come for the swimming, tennis, archery range, BMX track, ball fields, gymnasium, games area and picnicking areas.

FARMINGTON HISTORIC HOME

3033 Bardstown Road N., Louisville, 502-452-9920; www.historicfarmington.org

This Federal-style house was built from plans drawn by Thomas Jefferson. Abraham Lincoln visited here in 1841. It's furnished with pre-1820 antiques, plus it has a hidden stairway, octagonal rooms, a museum room, a blacksmith shop, a stone barn and a 19th-century garden. Tuesday-Saturday 10 a.m.-4:30 p.m., Sunday 10 a.m.-1:30 p.m.

FILSON HISTORICAL SOCIETY

1310 S. Third St., Louisville, 502-635-5083; www.filsonhistorical.org

The historical society houses a historical library (fee), a manuscript collection, photographs and a prints collection. Monday-Saturday 10 a.m.-2 p.m.

157

KENTUCKY

★
★
★
★

HISTORIC DISTRICTS

Old Louisville, between Breckinridge and Ninth streets, near Central Park

Old Louisville teems with historical districts. The West Main Street Historic District is a concentration of cast-iron buildings, many recently renovated, on Main Street between First and Eighth Streets. Butchertown is a renovated 19th-century German community between Market Street and Story Avenue. Cherokee Triangle is a well-preserved Victorian neighborhood with diverse architectural details. And Portland is an early settlement and commercial port with Irish and French heritage.

JEFFERSON COUNTY COURTHOUSE

527 W. Jefferson St., Louisville

This Greek Revival-style courthouse was designed by Gideon Shryock. A cast-iron floor in the rotunda supports a statue of Henry Clay. The 68-foot rotunda also boasts a magnificent cast-iron monumental stair and balustrade. Statues of Thomas Jefferson and Louis XVI call the courthouse home, and there's a war memorial on the grounds. Guided tours are available by appointment. Monday-Friday.

KENTUCKY CENTER FOR THE ARTS

501 W. Main St., Louisville, 502-584-7777, 800-775-7777; www.kca.org

Three stages present national and international performers showcasing a wide range of music, dance and drama. A distinctive glass-arched lobby features a collection of 20th-century sculpture and provides a panoramic view of Ohio River and Falls Fountain. There is also a restaurant and gift shop.

KENTUCKY DERBY MUSEUM

704 Central Ave., Louisville, 502-637-1111; www.derbymuseum.org

A tribute to the classic "run for the roses," the museum features exhibits on thoroughbred racing and the Kentucky Derby. Experience the excitement of Derby Day when you watch *The Greatest Day*, featured in high definition on a 360-degree screen. Check out hands-on exhibits, artifacts, educational programs, a tour and special events. There's also an outdoor paddock area with thoroughbreds. In addition, there's a shop and a café serving lunch (weekdays). Tours of Churchill Downs are available, weather permitting. Monday-Saturday 8 a.m.-5 p.m., Sunday 8 a.m.-noon.

KENTUCKY FAIR AND EXPOSITION CENTER

937 Phillips Lane, Louisville, 502-367-5000; www.kyfairexpo.org

This gigantic complex includes a coliseum, exposition halls, a stadium and an amusement park. More than 1,500 events take place throughout the year, including basketball and the Milwaukee Brewers minor league affiliate team's home games.

LOCUST GROVE

561 Blankenbaker Lane, Louisville, 502-897-9845; www.locustgrove.org

This was the home of Gen. George Rogers Clark from 1809 to 1818. The handsome Georgian mansion sits on 55 acres. It retains its original paneling, authentic furnishings and a lovely garden. There are eight restored outbuildings. The visitor center offers an audiovisual program. Monday-Saturday 10 a.m.-4:30 p.m., Sunday 1:30-4:30 p.m.

LOUISVILLE SCIENCE CENTER & IMAX THEATRE

727 W. Main St., Louisville, 502-561-6100; www.louisvillescience.org

You don't have to keep your hands to yourself in this museum. Designed to encourage exploration, the museum has exhibits that test visitors' creative-thinking skills, teach them about space travel and introduce them to natural wonders, such as a mummy, polar bears and a Gemini trainer. There's also a theater with a four-story IMAX screen (fee). Monday-Thursday 9:30 a.m.-5 p.m., Friday-Saturday 9:30 a.m.-9 p.m., Sunday noon-6 p.m.

LOUISVILLE SLUGGER MUSEUM & BAT FACTORY

800 W. Main St., Louisville, 610-524-0822; www.sluggermuseum.org

Buy me some peanuts and Cracker Jack…or just take me to this museum, a haven for baseball fans. See memorabilia and tour the factory, where Louisville Slugger baseball bats and PowerBilt golf clubs are made. No cameras are allowed. Children over 8 years only; they must be accompanied by adult. Tours are available. Monday-Saturday 9 a.m.-5 p.m., April-November: Sunday noon-5 p.m.

LOUISVILLE ZOO

1100 Trevilian Way, Louisville, 502-459-2181; www.louisvillezoo.org

More than 1,600 animals live in naturalistic settings here. Exhibits include Gorilla Forest, a four-acre display that gives visitors a look into the world of the gorillas; HerpAquarium, the home of King Louie, a rare white alligator; and Islands, which highlights endangered species and habitats. Camel and elephant rides are available (summer). September-March: daily 10 a.m.-4 p.m., rest of year: 10 a.m.-5 p.m.

OTTER CREEK PARK

850 Otter Creek Park Road, Vine Grove, 502-583-3577; www.ottercreekpark.org,

This 3,000-acre park sits on the site of Rock Haven, a town destroyed by a 1937 flood. Much of the park that fronts the Ohio River consists of steep cliffs or very wooded banks. Otter Creek is a small, deeply entrenched stream with steep banks. Artifacts found here indicate that many Native American tribes used it as hunting and fishing grounds. Visitors can use the area for its swimming pools, fishing, boating (ramp), miniature golf, tennis, basketball, picnic facilities, tent and trailer sites, cabins, lodge and restaurant. It also has a nature center and a wildlife area. Park. Daily.

★
★
★
★

RAUCH MEMORIAL PLANETARIUM

First and Brandeis streets, Louisville, 502-852-6664; www.louisville.edu/planetarium/

Planetarium shows take place on Friday and Saturday afternoons.

RIVERBOAT EXCURSION

Riverfront Plaza, Fourth Street and River Road, Louisville, 502-574-2355;
www.belleoflouisville.org

Cruise the river during a two-hour afternoon trip on sternwheeler *Belle of Louisville* or the *Spirit of Jefferson.* Memorial Day-Labor Day: Tuesday-Sunday; sunset cruise Tuesday and Thursday; dance cruise Saturday.

SIX FLAGS KENTUCKY KINGDOM

937 Phillips Lane, Louisville, 502-366-2231; www.sixflags.com

This amusement and water park is filled with more than 110 rides and attractions, including five roller coasters. Memorial Day-Labor Day: daily; early April-Memorial Day: Friday evenings, Saturday-Sunday; Labor Day-October: Saturday-Sunday.

SPALDING UNIVERSITY

845 S. Third St., Louisville, 502-585-9911; www.spalding.edu

The campus of this liberal arts college has the 1871 Whitestone Mansion, a Renaissance Revival house with period furniture (Monday-Friday), and an art gallery.

SPEED ART MUSEUM

2035 S. Third St., Louisville, 502-634-2700; www.speedmuseum.org

Kentucky's oldest and largest art museum, Speed has a collection that spans more than 6,000 years of human history. It provides traditional and modern art, an English Renaissance Room and a sculpture collection. The museum also highlights Kentucky artists. A café, shop and bookstore are on the premises; tours are available on request. Tuesday-Wednesday, Friday 10:30 a.m.-4 p.m.; Thursday 10:30 a.m.-8 p.m.; Sunday noon-5 p.m.

THOMAS EDISON HOUSE

729-731 E. Washington St., Louisville, 502-585-5247; www.edisonhouse.org

This is the restored 1850 cottage where Edison lived while working for Western Union after the Civil War. The bedroom is decorated with period furnishings. Four display rooms have Edison memorabilia and inventions, including phonographs, records and cylinders and an early light bulb collection. Tuesday-Saturday 10 a.m.-2 p.m., also by appointment.

KENTUCKY

UNIVERSITY OF LOUISVILLE

2301 S. Third St., Louisville, 502-852-5555, 800-334-8635; www.louisville.edu

This public university, home of the Cardinals, is known for its outstanding medical facilities, killer athletic programs and a recent boost in its endowment. If you tour the campus, don't miss the Ekstrom Library and the John Patterson rare book collection; the original town charter signed by Thomas Jefferson; and the Photo Archives, one of the largest photograph collections in the country. Also here is an enlarged cast of Rodin's sculpture *The Thinker*; a Foucault pendulum more than 73 feet high, which demonstrates the Earth's rotation; and one of the largest concert organs in the region. Two art galleries feature works by students and locals as well as national and international artists (Monday-Friday, Sunday). The grave of Supreme Court Justice Louis D. Brandeis is under the School of Law portico.

WATER TOWER

Zorn Avenue and River Road, Louisville, 502-896-2146; www.cem.va.gov

A restored tower and pumping station was built in the classic style in 1860. The tower houses the Louisville Visual Art Association and the Center for Contemporary Art. Exhibits vary. Daily.

ZACHARY TAYLOR NATIONAL CEMETERY

4701 Brownboro Road, Louisville, 502-893-3852

The 12th president of the United States is buried here, near the site where he lived from infancy to adulthood. Established in 1928, this national cemetery surrounds the Taylor family plot. Daily.

SPECIAL EVENTS

CORN ISLAND STORYTELLING FESTIVAL

12019 Donohue Ave., Louisville, 502-245-0643; www.cornislandstorytellingfestival.org

The festival celebrates traditions of storytelling. Events are held at various sites in the city. Programs include ghost stories at night in E.P. "Tom" Sawyer State Park and storytelling cruises. Third weekend in September.

KENTUCKY DERBY

Churchill Downs, 700 Central Ave., Louisville, 502-636-4400; www.kentuckyderby.com

This is the first jewel in the Triple Crown. First Saturday in May.

KENTUCKY DERBY FESTIVAL

1001 S. Third St., Louisville, 502-584-6383, 800-928-3378; www.kdf.org

The two-week celebration kicks off with the Pegasus Parade, the Great Steamboat Race (between *Belle of Louisville* and *Delta Queen*), the Great Balloon Race, a mini-marathon, concerts and sports tournaments. Two weeks prior to Kentucky Derby.

KENTUCKY STATE FAIR

Kentucky Fair and Exposition Center, 937 Phillips Lane, Louisville, 502-367-5002; www.kystatefair.org

America's largest air-conditioned fair, this event fills 1 million square feet of the Kentucky Exposition Center. The fair spills out into nearby fields, where fairgoers enjoy outdoor entertainment and exhibits. Livestock shows, a championship horse show, home and fine arts exhibits and a midway round out the entertainment. August.

PERFORMING ARTS

Louisville

The Louisville Orchestra (502-587-8681), the Kentucky Opera (502-584-4500), the Broadway Series (502-561-1003), the Louisville Ballet (502-583-2623) and Stage One: Louisville's Family Theatre (502-589-5964) all call the Kentucky Center for the Arts (502-584-7777) home. Other art groups include the Actors Theatre (316 W. Main Street., 502-584-1265) and the Kentucky Shakespeare Festival, which offers free plays in Central Park (Monday-Saturday, mid-June to late July).

HOTELS

★★★21C MUSEUM HOTEL

700 W. Main St., Louisville, 502-217-6300, 877-217-6400; www.21cmuseumhotel.com

This museum and hotel hybrid (with a focus on contemporary art) puts a premium on good design. Sprinkled throughout the hotel are photographs, paintings and sculptures from some of the world's top contemporary artists (one guest room even boasts

KENTUCKY

★
★
★
★

a Chuck Close portrait). Rooms are appropriately loaded with 21st-century amenities, including oversized plasma TVs and iPods (customized pre-arrival with your favorite music) as well as docking stations. The hotel includes an onsite spa and fitness center as well as the acclaimed restaurant Proof on Main. 90 rooms. Wireless Internet access. Restaurant, bar. Fitness center. Spa. **$$**

★BAYMONT INN AND SUITES LOUISVILLE
9400 Blairwood Road, Louisville, 502-339-1900; www.baymontinns.com
100 rooms. High-speed Internet access. Complimentary breakfast. Fitness center. Outdoor pool. Business center. Pets accepted. **$**

★★★THE BROWN HOTEL
335 W. Broadway, Louisville, 502-583-1234, 888-888-5252; www.brownhotel.com
The beautifully restored lobby of this hotel exudes Southern elegance, with intricate plaster moldings, polished woodwork, stained glass and crystal chandeliers. Built by philanthropist J. Graham Brown in 1923, the property's Georgian Revival-style build-ing hosts many of Louisville's swankiest parties. 293 rooms. Wireless Internet access. Restaurant, bar. Airport transportation available. **$$**

★THE CHARIOT HOTEL
1902 Embassy Square Blvd., Louisville, 502-491-2577; www.thechariothotel.com
116 rooms. High-speed Internet access. Complimentary continental breakfast. Business center. **$**

★★★EXECUTIVE INN
978 Phillips Lane, Louisville, 502-367-6161, 800-626-2706;
www.executiveinnhotel.com
This property has an interesting Tudor-style design with all the charm and warmth of a European hotel. It has richly crafted woodwork and spacious, comfortable rooms over-looking a beautiful courtyard and heated pool. It's surrounded with magnolia trees and water wheels. 472 rooms. Restaurant, bar. Fitness center. Indoor pool, outdoor pool and children's pool. Airport transportation available. Pets accepted, fee. **$**

★★EXECUTIVE WEST HOTEL
830 Phillips Lane, Louisville, 502-367-2251, 800-626-2708; www.executivewest.com
611 rooms. Restaurant, bar. Airport transportation available. Outdoor pool. **$**

★★THE GALT HOUSE HOTEL
140 N. Fourth Ave., Louisville, 502-589-5200, 800-626-1814; www.galthouse.com
1,296 rooms. Restaurant, bar. Fitness center. Outdoor pool. Business center. **$$**

★HAMPTON INN
800 Phillips Lane, Louisville, 502-366-8100; www.hamptoninn.com
130 rooms. Complimentary continental breakfast. Airport transportation available. Fitness center. Business center. **$**

★★HOLIDAY INN

1325 S. Hurstbourne Parkway, Louisville, 502-426-2600, 800-465-4329;
www.hihurstbourne.com
267 rooms. Restaurant, bar. Airport transportation available. **$**

★★HOTEL LOUISVILLE DOWNTOWN

120 W. Broadway, Louisville, 502-582-2241, 800-626-1558;
www.hotellouisvilledowntown.com
287 rooms. Wireless Internet access. Restaurant, bar. Airport transportation available. **$**

★★★HYATT REGENCY LOUISVILLE

320 W. Jefferson St., Louisville, 502-581-1234; www.hyatt.com
The hotel offers views of the Ohio River and the downtown area. It is connected
to both the Commonwealth Convention Center and the Louisville Galleria shopping
mall. 393 rooms. Restaurant, bar. **$**

★★★THE SEELBACH HILTON LOUISVILLE

500 Fourth Ave., Louisville, 502-585-3200, 800-333-3399; www.seelbachhilton.com
Elegant and historic, the Seelbach Hotel provides a luxurious home away from home.
Built in 1905 by brothers Otto and Louis Seelbach, this landmark in the heart of
downtown Louisville is immortalized in F. Scott Fitzgerald's *The Great Gatsby* as the
site of Tom and Daisy Buchanan's wedding. Magnificent belle époque architecture
and glittering interiors reflect an era long past, but the Seelbach offers all the amenities a contemporary traveler could want. The rooms and suites are charming with
period reproductions and rich fabrics. Don't miss the sensational Oakroom restaurant,
a favorite of critics and sweetheart of "best of" lists. 321 rooms. High-speed Internet
access. Complimentary continental breakfast. Restaurant, bar. Airport transportation
available. **$$**

★SIGNATURE INN LOUISVILLE SOUTH

6515 Signature Drive, Louisville, 502-968-4100, 800-822-5252; www.signatureinn.com
119 rooms. Wireless Internet access. Complimentary continental breakfast. Fitness
center. Outdoor pool. Airport transportation available. **$**

SPECIALTY LODGINGS

COLUMBINE BED AND BREAKFAST

1707 S. Third St., Louisville, 502-635-5000, 800-635-5010;
www.thecolumbine.com
The house was built in 1900 with a full-length porch. Six rooms. Children over
12 years only. Complimentary full breakfast. **$**

WOODHAVEN BED AND BREAKFAST

401 S. Hubbards Lane, Louisville, 502-895-1011; www.innatwoodhaven.com
This Gothic Revival house was built in 1853. Eight rooms. Complimentary full break-
fast. Fitness center. Business center. **$**

KENTUCKY

★
★
★
★

RESTAURANTS

★★CAFE METRO

1700 Bardstown Road, Louisville, 502-458-4830; www.cafemetrolouisville.com
American menu. Dinner. Closed Sunday. $$

★CAFE MIMOSA

1216 Bardstown Road, Louisville, 502-458-2233; www.cafemimosatogo.com
Chinese, Vietnamese menu. Lunch, dinner, Sunday brunch. $$

★★★THE ENGLISH GRILL

335 W. Broadway, Louisville, 502-583-1234; www.brownhotel.com
This ornate dining room in the Brown Hotel has a decidedly refined English feel and a menu by chef Joe Castro to match. The sophisticated service and a wine list heavy on Bordeaux complete the experience, considered by many to be the best in town. American menu. Dinner. Closed Sunday. $$$

★★EQUUS

122 Sears Ave., Louisville, 502-897-9721; www.equusrestaurant.com
American menu. Dinner. Closed Sunday. $$$

★★FIFTH QUARTER STEAKHOUSE

1241 Durrett Lane, Louisville, 502-361-2363
American menu. Lunch Sunday-Friday, dinner daily. $$

★★JACK FRY'S

1007 Bardstown Road, Louisville, 502-452-9244; www.jackfrys.com
American menu. Lunch, dinner. $$$

★JESSIE'S FAMILY RESTAURANT

9609 Dixie Highway, Louisville, 502-937-6332
American menu. Breakfast, lunch, dinner. $$

★★★LE RELAIS

2817 Taylorsville Road, Louisville, 502-451-9020; www.lerelaisrestaurant.com
This romantic French bistro is tucked away in the historic administration building in Bowman Field. The comfortable and elegant Art Deco dining room, wonderful service and creative French menu have made Le Relais one of the most beloved restaurants in Louisville. Fresh, seasonal ingredients fill the menu in dishes like herb-encrusted venison rack with braised cabbage, carrots and potatoes; certified Angus beef filet with roasted potato and root vegetables; and duck confit with sage polenta cake, flageolet beans and baby Brussels sprouts. A well-crafted wine list, which has been honored by *Wine Spectator*, beautifully complements every dish. French menu. Dinner. Closed Monday. $$$

★★★LILLY'S

1147 Bardstown Road, Louisville, 502-451-0447; www.lillyslapeche.com
A brightly colored neon sign marks the window of chef Kathy Cary's innovative dining room—a hint to the Art Deco interior that lies beyond the red-brick entrance. Her

menu changes seasonally and has an eclectic, urban edge with dishes such as seared scallops in beurre blanc served with basil couscous. International menu. Lunch, dinner. Closed Sunday-Monday. **$$$**

★★LIMESTONE
10001 Forest Green Blvd., Louisville, 502-426-7477; www.limestonerestaurant.com
American menu. Dinner. Closed Sunday. **$$**

★★★PROOF ON MAIN
702 W. Main St., Louisville, 502-217-6360; www.proofonmain.com
Art collectors and Kentucky philanthropists Steve Wilson and Laura Lee Brown (heir to a liquor fortune built by brands such as Jack Daniel's) launched this cutting-edge restaurant in 2006. Along with the adjacent 21c Museum Hotel, Proof on Main (the name is a nod to their bourbon past) is a prime spot for showcasing top-notch contemporary art and food. Executive chef Michael Paley sources local ingredients and puts them to good use in dishes such as Kentucky bison tenderloin with buttered leeks and fingerling potatoes, or smoked chicken with grain mustard and roasted string beans. Desserts include twists on Southern classics such as chocolate bread pudding with sea salt caramel gelato. American breakfast, lunch, dinner. **$$$**

★★UPTOWN CAFE
1624 Bardstown Road, Louisville, 502-458-4212; www.uptownlouisville.com
American menu. Lunch, dinner. Closed Sunday. **$$**

★★★VINCENZO'S
150 S. Fifth St., Louisville, 502-580-1350; www.vincenzositalianrestaurant.com
Italian menu. Lunch, dinner. Closed Sunday. **$$$**

★★WINSTON'S
3101 Bardstown Road, Louisville, 502-456-6505; www.sullivan.edu/winstons/index.asp
Lunch, dinner, Sunday brunch. Closed Monday-Thursday. **$$$**

★
★
★
★

MADISONVILLE
Named for President James Madison, the town is in a region of hills, rivers and creek bottoms. Recent revitalization efforts have created a charming downtown district.
Information: Madisonville-Hopkins County Chamber of Commerce,
15 E. Center St., Madisonville, 270-821-3435, 877-243-5280;
www.hopkinschamber.com

WHAT TO SEE AND DO
PENNYRILE FOREST STATE RESORT PARK
20781 Pennyrile Lodge Road, Madisonville, 270-797-3421, 800-325-1711;
www.parks.ky.gov/findparks/resortparks/pf
Head here for a slew of activities: swimming in the beach or pool, a bathhouse (seasonal), fishing, boating (no motors), hiking, riding, nine-hole and miniature golf (seasonal, rentals), tennis, picnicking, playgrounds. There's also a grocery, cottages, a lodge and tent and trailer sites (April-October, standard fees).

HOPKINS COUNTY FAIR

Hopkins County Fairgrounds, Arch St., Madisonville, 270-821-0950;
www.hopkinscounty.us/fair/default.aspx

The county fair breaks out a carnival, horse shows, agricultural exhibits, pageants and a Demolition Derby. Last week in July-first week in August.

HOTELS

★★BEST WESTERN PENNYRILE INN

Mortons Gap, 270-258-5201; www.bestwestern.com

59 rooms. High-speed Internet access. Complimentary full breakfast. Restaurant. Outdoor pool. Pets accepted. $

★★PENNYRILE FOREST STATE RESORT PARK

20781 Pennyrile Lodge Road, Madisonville, 270-797-3421, 800-325-1711;
www.parks.ky.gov

24 rooms. Restaurant. $

RESTAURANT

★★BARTHOLOMEW'S FINE FOODS

51 S. Main St., Madisonville, 270-821-1061;
www.madisonvillebedandbreakfast.com

American menu. Lunch, dinner. Closed Sunday. $$

166

KENTUCKY

★
★★★★
★★★
★★

MAMMOTH CAVE NATIONAL PARK

Mammoth Cave lives up to its name: It is the world's largest cave system, an underground complex of intertwining passages totaling more than 350 miles. Described as a "grand, gloomy and peculiar place" by early explorer Stephen Bishop, the system is home to crayfish; several species of colorless, eyeless fish; and other creatures. Visible are the remains of a crude system used to mine 400,000 pounds of nitrate to make gunpowder for the War of 1812.

Above ground, the park is 52,830 acres with sinkholes, rivers and 70 miles of hiking trails. Picnicking, lodging and camping (March-December: daily; some fees) are available. The visitor center shows an orientation movie (daily). Park interpreters conduct evening programs (summer: daily; spring and fall: weekends).

Ranger-led tours of Mammoth Cave vary greatly in distance and length. Trails are solid and fairly smooth, but require stooping or bending in places. Most tours involve steps and extensive walking; many are considered strenuous; proper footwear is recommended (no sandals). Visitors might also want to bring a sweater or extra shirt, even though it may be a hot day above ground. Tours are conducted by experienced National Park Service interpreters. For details, call the superintendent of Mammoth Cave at 270-758-2180.

Information: Highway 70, 10 miles west of Cave City or eight miles northwest of Park City on Highway 255; 270-758-2180; www.nps.gov/maca

WHAT TO SEE AND DO
CAVE TOURS
Mammoth Cave National Park, 270-758-2328, 800-967-2283;
www.mammoth.cave.national-park.com
Cave tours depart from the visitor center (schedules vary with season). Advance reservations are highly recommended. Tickets may be purchased in advance through Destinet Outlets.

MISS GREEN RIVERBOAT TRIP
511 Grinstead Mill Road, Mammoth Cave, 270-758-2243
Take an hourlong round-trip cruise through scenic and wildlife areas of the park. Advance tickets may be purchased at the visitor center. April-October: daily.

HOTEL
★MAMMOTH CAVE HOTEL
Highway 70, Mammoth Cave, 270-758-2225; www.mammothcavehotel.com
62 rooms. Restaurant. **$**

MAYSVILLE
This Ohio River town, first known as Limestone, was established by the Virginia Legislature. By 1792, it had become a leading port of entry for Kentucky settlers. Daniel Boone and his wife maintained a tavern in the town for several years. Many buildings and sites in the eight-block historic district are included on the National Register of Historic Places.
Information: Tourism Commission, 216 Bridge St., Maysville, 606-564-9419;
www.cityofmaysville.com

WHAT TO SEE AND DO
BLUE LICKS BATTLEFIELD STATE RESORT PARK
Highway 68 Maysville Road, Mount Olivet, 26 miles Southwest on High-
way 68, 859-289-5507; www.parks.ky.gov/findparks/resortparks/bl
The park preserves about 150 acres on the site of one of the Revolutionary War's bloodiest battles (August 19, 1782, a year after Cornwallis surrendered). In this final battle in Kentucky, 60 Americans died, including Daniel Boone's son, Israel. A monument in the park honors pioneers killed in an ambush. Also here is a museum with exhibits and displays depicting the history of the area from the Ice Age through the Revolution. Recreational facilities include a swimming pool, fishing, miniature golf, picnic shelters, a playground and camping (standard fees). April-October: daily.

HISTORIC WASHINGTON
2215 Old Main St., Washington, 606-759-7411; www.washingtonky.com
The original seat of Mason County, Washington was founded in 1786 and soon was the second-largest town in Kentucky, with 119 cabins. Restored buildings include the Paxton Inn (1810), Albert Sidney Johnston House (1797), Old Church Museum (1848) and Cane Brake, thought to be one of the original cabins of 1790. Guided tours are available. Mid-March to December: daily.

THE PIEDMONT ART GALLERY
115 W. Riverside Drive, Augusta, 606-756-2216
Located in one of the oldest settlements on the Ohio River, the gallery houses contemporary works by national and regional artists and craftspeople. It also spotlights antiques, paintings, sculpture, ceramics and American folk art. Thursday-Sunday.

SPECIAL EVENTS
SIMON KENTON FESTIVAL
Old Main Street Historic District, Maysville, 606-564-9411; www.cityofmaysville.com
Kin of pioneer Simon Kenton (who explored Kentucky between 1785 and 1800) congregate in Old Washington during this festival to exchange genealogy. "Living historians" reenact scenes from 18th-century life, demonstrating skills and games of early pioneers such as knife- and tomahawk-throwing contests, blacksmithing and candle making. Third weekend in September.

STERNWHEELER ANNUAL REGATTA
Riverside Drive, Augusta, 606-756-2183
Last weekend in June.

MONTICELLO
Major League baseball player Eric Reed called Monticello—and all its sprawling, natural beauty—home before hitting the big times.
Information: Monticello-Wayne County Chamber of Commerce, 157 S. Main St.,
Monticello, 270-348-3064; www.monticellokychamber.com

WHAT TO SEE AND DO
DALE HOLLOW LAKE STATE RESORT PARK
6371 State Park Road, Burkesville, 270-433-7431;
www.parks.ky.gov/findparks/resortparks/dh
The park provides a swimming pool, boat rentals, a marina (fee), a playground and camping.

HOTEL
★ ★ ★ ★ ★

★★GRIDER HILL DOCK AND INDIAN CREEK LODGE
Highway 1266, Albany, 866-387-5501; www.griderhilldock.com
34 rooms. Restaurant. Pets accepted.

MOREHEAD
In the foothills of the Appalachian Mountains, Morehead has much of the beautiful scenery that makes this part of Kentucky so appealing to travelers who seek outdoor recreation.
Information: Chamber of Commerce, 150 E. First St., Morehead, 606-784-6221,
800-654-1944; www.moreheadrowan.com

CAVE RUN LAKE
2375 Highway 801 S., Morehead, 606-784-5624; www.caverun.org

Take advantage of the beach, the bathhouse and seasonal interpretive programs at Twin Knobs and Zilpo campgrounds. Or go fishing for bass and muskie, use the 12 boat ramps, visit the two marinas with boat rentals, go hiking or camp at Twin Knobs and Zilpo campgrounds. Morehead Visitor Center, on Highway 801, provides exhibits and information. Mid-April-October: daily.

MINOR CLARK STATE FISH HATCHERY
120 Fish Hatchery Road, Morehead, 606-784-6872

Largemouth bass, smallmouth bass, walleye, muskellunge and rockfish are reared here. They are on display in an exhibition pool. May-September: Monday-Friday.

MOREHEAD STATE UNIVERSITY
150 University Blvd., Morehead, 606-783-2221; www.moreheadstate.edu

On campus, see the historic one-room schoolhouse by appointment. The Folk Art Museum, on the first floor of Claypool-Young Art Building, is open Monday to Friday. Also on campus:

MSU APPALACHIAN COLLECTION
Morehead, fifth floor of Camden Carroll Library Tower; www.morehead-st.edu

The collection includes books, periodicals, genealogical materials and government documents. Special holdings are devoted to authors James Still and Jesse Stuart and there are displays of regional art. Daily.

169

SPECIAL EVENT
BLUEGRASS 'N MORE
150 University Blvd., Morehead, 606-784-6221; www.moreheadstate.edu

This week is devoted to the history and heritage of Appalachia in Kentucky. Partake in dances, concerts, arts and crafts and exhibitions. Late June.

KENTUCKY

MOUNT VERNON

Take a step back in time when you cross the threshold of the first brick house west of the Alleghenies.
Information: 606-256-0070

★
★
★
★
★

WHAT TO SEE AND DO
WILLIAM WHITLEY HOUSE HISTORIC SITE
625 William Whitley Road, Mount Vernon, 606-355-2881;
www.parks.ky.gov/findparks/histparks/ww

The first brick house west of the Alleghenies, this building was used as a protective fort from Native Americans and as a haven for travelers on the Wilderness Road. This site is also home to the first circular racetrack built in the U.S., which earned the house the nickname "Sportsman's Hill." Unlike the tracks in England, this one ran counter-clockwise. The restored home is furnished with period pieces. Panels symbolizing each of the 13 original states are over the mantel in the parlor. Memorial Day-Labor Day: daily; rest of year: Tuesday-Sunday.

MURRAY

Here in 1892, Nathan B. Stubblefield made the first radio broadcast in history. Rainey T. Wells, attorney for the Woodmen of the World, was about one mile away when he heard Stubblefield's voice saying, "Hello Rainey! Hello Rainey!" Wells was astounded and urged Stubblefield to patent his invention. Because of delays and ill-advised deals while perfecting his invention, Stubblefield was not the first to obtain the patent. He finally received one in 1908, but died in poverty in 1928. This is the home of Murray State University (1922), of which Rainey Wells was the second president.

Information: Murray Tourism Commission, 805 N. 12th St., Murray,
270-759-2199, 800-651-1603; www.mymurray.com

SPECIAL EVENTS
CALLOWAY COUNTY FAIR
County Fairgrounds, Highway 121, Murray, 270-759-2199; www.mccfair.com
This event offers all the activities you'd expect from a great county fair: a carnival, a beauty pageant, tractor-driving contests, livestock competitions, horse shows and a demolition derby. Mid-June.

FREEDOM FEST
805 N. 12th St., Murray, 270-759-2199; www.festivalusa.com
July Fourth.

HOTEL
★DAYS INN
517 S. 12th St., Murray, 270-753-6706; www.daysinn.com
41 rooms. High-speed Internet access. Complimentary continental breakfast. Restaurant. Pets accepted. **$**

★
★★
★★★
★★★★
★★★★★

NATURAL BRIDGE STATE RESORT PARK

The sandstone arch for which this park is named is 78 feet long and 65 feet high. Visitors can hike to the natural bridge or take the Skylift, which drops riders off a mere 600 feet from the bridge. The park offers plenty of opportunities for outdoor recreation, including an open-air patio at Hoedown Island, so named for its weekly square dances. A swimming pool (seasonal), fishing, boating, nature trails and center (no pets are allowed on the trails), picnicking, a playground, a dining room, cottages, a lodge and tent and trailer sites (April-October; standard fees) will keep you busy.

Information: 2135 Natural Bridge Road, Winchester, 606-663-2214, 800-325-1710;
www.parks.ky.gov/findparks/resortparks/nb

HOTEL
★★NATURAL BRIDGE STATE PARK
2135 Natural Bridge Road, Slade, 606-663-2214, 800-325-1710
35 rooms. Restaurant. Children's activity center. **$**

OLIVE HILL

If you can't find something to do in the thousands of acres of raw outdoors just waiting to be explored here, you're just not trying.

Information: 606-286-2692

WHAT TO SEE AND DO

CARTER CAVES STATE RESORT PARK

344 Caveland Drive, Olive Hill, 606-286-4411; www.parks.ky.gov/findparks/resortparks/cc

This 1,350-acre park lies in a region of cliffs, streams and many caves, where you'll find a 30-foot underground waterfall, among other surprises. Activities abound: There's a swimming pool (seasonal), boating (rentals), fishing, canoe trips, nine-hole and miniature golf, tennis, shuffleboard, picnicking, a playground, cottages, a lodge and tent and trailer sites (fees). The park also hosts films, dances and festivals. Several guided cave tours are available. Daily.

GRAYSON LAKE STATE PARK

314 Grayson Lake Park Road, Olive Hill, 606-474-9727;
www.parks.ky.gov/findparks/recparks/gl

Nearly 75 miles of shoreline change from gentle slopes to canyons and offer a beautiful backdrop to a day on Grayson Lake. Fishing, boating (boat launch), hiking, picnicking and camping all keep park visitors busy.

HOTEL

★★CARTER CAVES STATE RESORT PARK

Olive Hill, 606-286-4411, 800-325-0059; www.parks.ky.gov/findparks/resortparks/cc/
43 rooms. $

OWENSBORO

Owensboro knows how to party: The city has crowned itself "Festival City," a nod to its many citywide celebrations. The festivals begin in February and last until mid-December, but if you arrive during an off week, the city's regular offerings promise plenty of entertainment. A progressive arts program has provided Owensboro with a symphony orchestra, fine art museum, dance theater, science museum and theater workshop. And if you're just up for a stroll, amble along tree-lined Griffith Avenue to see historic homes, a walk that's sweetened in spring by dogwood and azalea blossoms.
Information: Owensboro-Daviess County Tourist Commission, 215 E. Second St.,
Owensboro, 270-926-1100, 800-489-1131; www.visitowensboro.com

171

KENTUCKY

★
★
★
★
★

WHAT TO SEE AND DO

BEN HAWES STATE PARK

400 Boothfield Road, Owensboro, 270-687-7134;
www.parks.ky.gov/findparks/recparks/bh

The park is spread across about 300 acres with hiking, nine-hole and 18-hole golf (fee, rentals), picnicking and a playground available.

OWENSBORO AREA MUSEUM OF SCIENCE & HISTORY

122 E. Second St., Owensboro, 270-687-2732; www.owensboromuseum.com

The museum has crawly live insects and reptiles; archaeological, geological and ornithological displays; and historic items. Stop by the gift shop. Tuesday-Sunday.

OWENSBORO MUSEUM OF FINE ART

901 Frederica St., Owensboro, 270-685-3181; www.omfa.us

The permanent collection includes 16th- to 20th-century American, French and English paintings, drawings, sculpture, graphic and decorative arts. There's also a special collection of 19th- and 20th-century regional art and one of Appalachian folk art. Tuesday-Sunday.

WINDY HOLLOW RECREATION AREA
10874 Highway 81, Owensboro, 270-785-4150; www.windyhollowcampground.com
Head to these 214 acres for swimming, a 240-foot water slide (Memorial Day-Labor Day, fee), fishing, miniature golf (fee). The property includes a grocery and tent and trailer camping (fee). April-October: daily.

SPECIAL EVENTS
DAVIESS COUNTY FAIR
Highway 54 and Philpot, Owensboro, 800-489-1139; www.daviesscountyfair.com
Four days in late July-early August.

INTERNATIONAL BAR-B-Q FESTIVAL
Second St., Owensboro, 270-926-6938; www.bbqfest.com
About 80,000 people show up to inhale the smell of hickory-smoke fires and taste the glories of down-home barbecue. Cooks come with their best recipes for mutton, chicken and burgoo and battle to see who will be crowned King or Queen of the Grill. Folks who want to compete but can't cook might take part in the tobacco-spitting, pie-eating or fiddling contests. Arts and crafts, music and dancing also liven up the event. Early May.

OWENSBORO SYMPHONY ORCHESTRA
RiverPark Center, 211 E. 2nd St., Owensboro, 270-684-0661;
www.owensborosymphony.org
The orchestra has guest appearances by renowned artists and ballet companies. October-April.

KENTUCKY

★
★
★
★
★

RESTAURANT
★★COLBY'S
202 W. Third St., Owensboro, 270-685-4239
American menu. Lunch, dinner. **$$**

PADUCAH
This art-friendly city has a growing underground music scene and a thriving arts community, thanks to its Artist Relocation Program. In the historic Lowertown Arts District, artists from across the country come to live and work together, and there are gourmet restaurants and funky coffee shops.

The city doesn't play favorites: Paducah has recently begun reviving its Middletown district to serve as a haven for musicians. One major part of the renaissance is the renovation of Maggie Steed's Metropolitan Hotel, the site where musicians such as Louis Armstrong, B.B. King and Tina Turner played in the early to mid-20th century.
Information: Paducah-McCracken County Convention and Visitors Bureau,
128 Broadway, 270-443-8784, 800-723-8224; www.paducah-tourism.org

ALBEN W. BARKLEY MONUMENT
28th and Jefferson Streets, Paducah
The senator and vice president was one of Paducah's most famous citizens.

CHIEF PADUKE STATUE
19th and Jefferson Streets, Paducah
This memorial to the Chickasaw chief made by Lorado Taft.

IRVIN S. COBB MEMORIAL
Oak Grove Cemetery, 1613 Park Ave., Paducah, 270-444-5155

MARKET HOUSE
121 S. Second St., Paducah, 270-443-7759
This cultural center now houses the Market House Museum. It features early Americana, including the complete interior of a drugstore that's more than 100 years old. Other offerings include river lore, Alben Barkley and Irvin S. Cobb memorabilia, Native American artifacts and Civil War exhibits. March-December: Monday-Saturday.

MARKET HOUSE THEATRE
132 Market House Square, Paducah, 270-444-6828; www.mhtplay.com
This is a 250-seat professionally directed community playhouse. All year.

MUSEUM OF THE AMERICAN QUILTER'S SOCIETY
215 Jefferson St., Paducah, 270-442-8856; www.quiltmuseum.org
More than 200 quilts are exhibited here, with special displays scheduled regularly. Check out the gift shop. Monday-Saturday 10 a.m.-5 p.m.; Sunday 1-5 p.m. April-October.

173

WHITEHAVEN
1845 Lone Oak Road, Paducah, 270-554-2077
This antebellum mansion was remodeled in Classical Revival style in 1903; it has elaborate plasterwork, stained glass and 1860s furnishings. The state uses a portion of the house as a tourist welcome center and rest area. Tours (afternoons). Daily.

YEISER ARTS CENTER
200 Broadway, Paducah, 270-442-2453; www.theyeiser.org
The arts center has monthly changing exhibits, and its collection ranges from European masters to regional artists. There's a gift shop and tours are available. Tuesday-Sunday.

SPECIAL EVENTS

KIWANIS WEST KENTUCKY-MCCRACKEN COUNTY FAIR
301 Joe Clifton Drive, Carson Park, Paducah,
The county fair offers Society and Western horse shows, harness racing, motorcycle racing and gospel singing. Last full week in June.

KENTUCKY

★
★
★
★

PLAYERS BLUEGRASS DOWNS

150 Downs St., Paducah, 270-444-7117

See pari-mutuel horse racing here. October: Thursday-Sunday.

SUMMER FESTIVAL

Riverfront, foot of Broadway, Paducah, 270-443-8783, 800-789-8224;
www.paducahsummerfestival.com

The fest ushers in summer with hot-air balloons, a symphony, fireworks and free entertainment nightly. Events are held along the riverfront and throughout the city. Last week in July.

HOTELS

★★COURTYARD PADUCAH WEST

3835 Technology Drive, Paducah, 270-442-3600; www.marriott.com

100 rooms. **$**

★DRURY INN

3975 Hinkleville Road, Paducah, 270-443-3313; www.druryinn.com

118 rooms. High-speed Internet access. Complimentary full breakfast. Outdoor pool. **$**

★HOLIDAY INN EXPRESS

3994 Hinkleville Road, Paducah, 270-442-8874; www.hiexpress.com

76 rooms. Complimentary continental breakfast. **$**

RESTAURANTS

★C. C. COHEN

103 S. Second St., Paducah, 270-442-6391; www.cccohen.com

American menu. Lunch, dinner. Closed Sunday. **$$**

★JEREMIAH'S

225 Broadway, Paducah, 270-443-3991

Dinner. Closed Sunday. **$$**

★★WHALER'S CATCH

123 N. Second St., Paducah, 270-444-7701; www.whalerscatch.net

Southern-style seafood menu. Lunch, dinner. Closed Sunday. **$$$**

PARIS

Both Paris and Bourbon County were named in appreciation of France's aid to the colonies during the Revolution. While the French dynasty is long gone, the whiskey made in this county is a lasting tribute to the royal name.

Information: Paris-Bourbon County Tourism Commission, Courthouse-Main St.,
888-987-3205; www.parisky.com

KENTUCKY

★
★
★
★
★

WHAT TO SEE AND DO
DUNCAN TAVERN HISTORIC CENTER
323 High St., Paris, 859-987-1788

Daniel Boone joined fellow pioneers for entertainment in Duncan Tavern, constructed in 1788. Next door is the Anne Duncan House, built right next door by the innkeeper's widow, who ran the tavern for many years after his death. Both the tavern, which is made of local limestone, and the old clapboard house of log construction have been restored and furnished with period pieces. Tuesday-Saturday.

OLD CANE RIDGE MEETING HOUSE
1655 Cane Ridge Road, Paris, 859-987-5350; www.caneridge.org

This is the birthplace of the Christian Church (Disciples of Christ). The original log meetinghouse has been restored within an outer building of stone. In the early 1800s, revival meetings outside Old Cane Ridge attracted 20,000 to 30,000 people at a time. Tours are available by appointment.

SPECIAL EVENTS
BOURBON COUNTY FAIR
Bourbon County Park, Legion Road, Paris, 859-987-1895

Come for the fair's carnival and farm and craft exhibits. Late July.

CENTRAL KENTUCKY STEAM AND GAS ENGINE SHOW
Bourbon County Park, Legion Road, Paris, 859-987-3205

The show features old operating farm machinery, a flea market and country music. July.

HOTEL
★BEST WESTERN PARIS INN
2011 Alverson Drive, Paris, 859-987-0779, 800-528-1234; www.bestwestern.com

49 rooms. High-speed Internet access. Complimentary continental breakfast. Outdoor pool. $

PIKEVILLE

Surrounded by the Appalachian Mountains, Pikeville is close to Breaks Interstate Park, the "Grand Canyon of the South," and other picturesque spots in eastern Kentucky. Outdoor enthusiasts will find plenty to keep them happy year-round in this mountain retreat.

Information: Pike County Chamber of Commerce, 225 College St., Pikeville,
800-844-7453; www.tourpikecounty.com

WHAT TO SEE AND DO
FISHTRAP LAKE
2204 Fishtrap Road, Pikeville, 606-437-7496; www.parks.ky.gov/findparks/recparks/ft/

The lake offers fishing and boating (marina). In the area are opportunities for picnicking and camping, as well as a playground and ball fields. Daily.

GRAPEVINE RECREATION AREA
Fish Trap Lake Road and Highway 194, Pikeville, South via Highway 194,
606-437-7496; www.parks.ky.gov/findparks/recparks/ft/

Boating, picnicking, playground, camping are available here. May-September.

KENTUCKY

★
★
★
★
★

HILLBILLY DAYS SPRING FESTIVAL

Main St., Pikeville, 606-432-5504; www.hillbillydays.com

At this unique festival, all the fun is for a good cause: Proceeds support the Shriners Children's Hospital in Lexington. More than 100,000 hillbillies come to Pikeville for the party, which includes an antique car show, a parade, music and arts and crafts. Third weekend in April.

HOTEL

★★LANDMARK INN

190 S. Mayo Trail, Pikeville, 606-432-2545, 800-831-1469; www.the-landmark-inn.com

103 rooms. Wireless Internet access. Restaurant, bar. **$**

PINEVILLE

Picnics and playgrounds are just the tip of the iceberg in this outdoor-sport-saturated area.

Information: 502-223-8687; www.pinevillekentucky.com

WHAT TO SEE AND DO

BELL THEATRE

114 W. Kentucky Ave., Pineville, 606-337-7074; www.cinematreasures.org/theater/8676

See a film at this restored Art Deco movie house.

PINE MOUNTAIN STATE RESORT PARK

1050 State Park Road, Pineville, 606-337-3066, 800-325-1712;
www.parks.ky.gov/findparks/resortparks/pm

This 1,500-acre park, surrounded by 12,000-acre Kentucky Ridge State Forest, has a nature center, supervised recreation and Laurel Cove Amphitheater. It also has a swimming pool (seasonal), 18-hole and miniature golf, shuffleboard, picnicking, playgrounds, cottages, a lodge and camping (April-October, standard fees).

SPECIAL EVENT

MOUNTAIN LAUREL FESTIVAL

Pine Mountain State Resort Park, 1050 State Park Road, Pineville, 606-337-3066;
www.parks.ky.gov/findparks/resortparks/pm/events

At this unique pageant, college women from across Kentucky compete for the Festival Queen title. The weekend includes picnics, a parade, sporting events, concerts, a grand ball and the coronation at Pine Mountain State Resort Amphitheater. Memorial Day weekend.

HOTEL

★★PINE MOUNTAIN STATE RESORT PARK

1050 State Park Road, Pineville, 606-337-3066, 800-325-1712; www.kystateparks.com

50 rooms. Restaurant. Children's activity center. **$**

PRESTONSBURG

The Country Music Highway, known less glamorously as U.S. Route 23, runs through Prestonsburg. The highway celebrates country music history and the legends who came from this neck of the woods, including Loretta Lynn, Patty Loveless and the Judds.

Information: Floyd County Chamber of Commerce, 113 S. Central Ave., 606-886-1341; www.prestonsburgky.org

WHAT TO SEE AND DO
JENNY WILEY STATE RESORT PARK

75 Theatre Court, Prestonsburg, 606-886-1790, 800-325-0142; www.parks.ky.gov/findparks/resortparks/jw

This park has everything a guest could want: hiking trails through the mountainous terrain, water sports on 1,150-acre Dewey Lake, a disc golf course and even an outdoor amphitheater where guests can catch musical theater hits. There's also a swimming pool (seasonal), fishing, boating (rentals, ramp, dock), nine-hole golf (seasonal, fee), shuffleboard, picnicking, a playground, cottages, a lodge and tent and trailer sites (April-October, standard fees).

MOUNTAIN ARTS CENTER

1 Hal Rogers Drive, Prestonsburg, 606-886-2623; www.macarts.com

This performance theater seats 1,054. It's the home of the Kentucky Opry; a variety of entertainment is scheduled year-round.

SPECIAL EVENTS
JENNY WILEY THEATRE

Jenny Wiley State Resort Park, 75 Theatre Court, Prestonsburg, 606-886-9274; www.jwtheatre.com

Broadway musicals bring the house down at this theater. Mid-June-late August.

KENTUCKY APPLE FESTIVAL

Paintsville, 11 miles North via Highway 23/460, 606-789-4355; www.kyapplefest.org

The festival features a parade, amusement rides, an antique car show, arts and crafts, a flea market, a 5K run, square dancing, music and entertainment. First Saturday in October.

KENTUCKY

★
★
★
★

HOTELS
★★HOLIDAY INN

1887 Highway 23 North, Prestonsburg, 606-886-0001; www.holiday-inn.com

117 rooms. Restaurant, bar. **$**

★★JENNY WILEY STATE RESORT PARK

75 Theater Court, Prestonsburg, 606-886-1790

49 rooms. Restaurant. Children's activity center. **$**

RICHMOND

The scene of a major Civil War battle—the first Confederate victory in Kentucky—Richmond has one of Kentucky's finest restored 19th-century downtown districts, perfect for an afternoon stroll.

Information: Tourism & Visitor Center, 345 Lancaster Ave.,
859-626-8474, 800-866-3705

WHAT TO SEE AND DO

COURTHOUSE

Courthouse square, N. First and Main streets, Richmond

This Greek Revival courthouse in the downtown historic district was used as a hospital by Union and Confederate forces during the Civil War.

HUMMEL PLANETARIUM AND SPACE THEATER

521 Lancaster Ave., Richmond, on Eastern Kentucky University campus,
859-622-1547; www.planetarium.eku.edu

One of the largest and most sophisticated planetariums in the U.S., this place has state-of-the-art projection and audio systems and a large-format film system. Public programs are offered (Thursday-Sunday).

WHITE HALL STATE HISTORIC HOUSE

500 White Hall Shrine Road, Richmond, 859-623-9178;
www.parks.ky.gov/findparks/histparks/wh

This is the restored 44-room house of Cassius M. Clay (1810-1903), emancipationist, diplomat and publisher of *The True American*, an antislavery newspaper. The 1799 Georgian home has an Italianate addition from the 1860s. Period furnishings, some original, and personal mementos fill the space. April-Labor Day: daily; after Labor Day-October: Wednesday-Sunday.

SPECIAL EVENT

MADISON COUNTY FAIR & HORSE SHOW

Highway 52 (Irving Road), Richmond, 859-369-0005; www.themadisoncountyfair.com
Last week in July.

HOTELS

★DAYS INN

2109 Belmont Drive, Richmond, 859-624-5769, 800-329-7466; www.daysinn.com
70 rooms. High-speed Internet access. Complimentary breakfast. Outdoor pool. Pets accepted. $

★LA QUINTA INN

1751 Lexington Road, Richmond, 859-623-9121, 800-575-5339; www.laquinta.com
95 rooms. Complimentary continental breakfast. Outdoor pool. Pets accepted. $

ROUGH RIVER DAM STATE RESORT PARK

At the northeast end of Rough River Lake, this park is a prime spot for outdoor recreation. There's a beach with a bathhouse, a pool (seasonal), fishing, a boat dock (ramps, rentals), hiking, a fitness trail, nine-hole golf, a pro shop, a driving range, miniature golf, tennis, shuffleboard, picnicking, playgrounds, a lodge, a dining room, cottages and tent and trailer camping (April-October, standard fees).

Information: On Highway 79 at northeast end of Rough River Lake,
270-257-2311; www.parks.ky.gov/findparks/resortparks/rr

HOTEL
★★ROUGH RIVER DAM STATE PARK RESORT
Rough River Dam State Park, Falls of Rough, 270-257-2311, 800-325-1713;
www.parks.ky.gov/findparks/resortparks/rr
40 rooms. Restaurant. **$**

SHEPHERDSVILLE

Shepherdsville offers the granddaddy of all arboretums, clocking in at 2,000 acres.

Information: 229A Lees Valley Road, Shepherdsville,
502-543-6727; www.Shepherdsville.net

WHAT TO SEE AND DO
BERNHEIM ARBORETUM AND RESEARCH FOREST
Shepherdsville, six miles south on I-65, exit 112, then one mile east on Highway 245,
502-543-2451; www.bernheim.org
This 2,000-acre arboretum offers a nature center with trails, a nature museum, waterfowl lakes and a 12,000-acre research forest. The landscape arboretum features 1,800 species of plants. Daily 7 a.m.-sunset.

HOTEL
★★BEST WESTERN SOUTH
211 S. Lakeview Drive, Shepherdsville, 502-543-7097, 877-543-5080;
www.bestwestern.com
85 rooms. Restaurant, bar. **$**

SOMERSET

Centrally located, Somerset is only four miles from Lake Cumberland. Many of the state's most popular attractions are within an hour's drive.

Information: Somerset/Pulaski Convention & Visitors Bureau, 522 Ogden St.,
606-679-6394, 800-642-6287; www.lakecumberlandtourism.com

WHAT TO SEE AND DO
BEAVER CREEK WILDERNESS
Somerset, 15 miles south on Highway 27, 606-679-2010;
www.fs.fed.us/r8/boone/districts/stearns/beaver_creek.shtml
Towering sandstone cliffs surround this hardwood forest, where a variety of wildlife lives. Hike through the wilderness to see streams, waterfalls, flowering trees and creatures such as foxes, white-tailed deer and wild turkeys. Trails, compass hiking, backpacking and scenic overlooks will lure outdoor types. Daily.

KENTUCKY

★
★
★
★
★

GENERAL BURNSIDE STATE PARK
Burnside, 10 miles south on Highway 27, 606-561-4104;
www.parks.ky.gov/findparks/recparks/ge
On General Burnside Island in Lake Cumberland, the park offers a swimming pool, fishing, boating (ramps), 18-hole golf, picnicking, a playground and tent and trailer sites (April-October, standard fees). There's also a recreation program (June-Labor Day).

LAKE CUMBERLAND
Highway 27, Somerset, 606-679-6337; www.lakecumberlandtourism.com
This man-made lake with 1,255 miles of shoreline has five recreation areas with campsites (mid-April to October). Swimming, fishing, commercial docks, houseboats and other boats for rent are available.

SOUTH UNION
The Shakers, officially the United Society of Believers in Christ's Second Appearing, settled this town as a religious community in the 19th century. Crafters and farmers of great skill and ingenuity, the Shakers were widely known both for the quality of their products and for their religious observances. When "moved by the spirit," they performed a dance that earned them the name "Shakers." By 1922, the community had dwindled to only nine members. The property was sold at an auction, and the remaining members dispersed.
Information: Logan County Chamber of Commerce, 116 S. Main St., Russellville,
270-726-2206; www.loganchamber.com

★
★
★
★
★

WHAT TO SEE AND DO
SHAKER MUSEUM
850 Shaker Museum Road, South Union, 270-542-4167; www.shakermuseum.com
Located in the original 1824 building, the museum houses Shaker crafts, furniture, textiles and tools. March to mid-December: daily; rest of year: by appointment.

SPECIAL EVENTS
SHAKER FESTIVAL
Shaker Town Village, South Union, 800-811-8379
The fest offers a tour of historic buildings, Shaker foods, music and craft demonstrations. June.

TOBACCO FESTIVAL
116 S. Main St., Russellville, 270-726-2206;
www.loganleads.com/Chamber/tobacco_heritage/
The festival celebrates tobacco heritage with a parade, a reenactment of the Jesse James bank robbery, house tours in the historic district, tobacco displays, antiques, bicycle rides, a five-mile run and a 5K walk, along with entertainment. One week in early October.

WALTON

From Ice Age formations to prehistoric mammal life, Walton lures in folks eager to explore the past.

Information: 40 N. Main St. Walton, 859-485-4383; www.cityofwalton.org

WHAT TO SEE AND DO

BIG BONE LICK STATE PARK

3380 Beaver Road, Union, 859-384-3522; www.parks.ky.gov/sfindparks/recparks/bb

On the grounds of this 547-acre park are a museum and diorama explaining prehistoric mammal life preserved in the soft sulfur spring earth around the salt lick and displays of Ice Age formations. The swimming pool is open for campers only. Tennis and picnicking are available.

OAK CREEK CAMPGROUND

Highway 16 and Oak Creek Road, Walton, 859-485-9131, 877-604-3503;
www.oakcreekcampground.com

This highly regarded family-run campground has 99 sites with water and electric hook-ups. There are four primitive tent areas, restrooms, showers, laundry services and a pool.

WILLIAMSTOWN

From underwater (fishing) to airborne (archery), Williamstown is a go-to spot for gamers.

Information: Grant County Chamber of Commerce, 149 N. Main St.,
859-824-3322; www.grantcommerce.com

WHAT TO SEE AND DO

KINCAID LAKE STATE PARK

Williamstown, 17 miles northeast via Highway 22, then three miles north off
Highway 27, 859-654-3531; www.parks.ky.gov/findparks/recparks/kl

Kincaid Lake is stocked with bass, bluegill, crappie and channel catfish. Other than fishing it offers a swimming pool (seasonal; fee), boating (dock, rentals, maximum 16-foot and 10-HP motor), hiking, miniature golf and camping (April-October). There's also an amphitheater on the grounds.

HOTEL

★DAYS INN

211 Highway 36 W. Williamstown, 859-824-5025, 800-329-7466; www.daysinn.com

51 rooms. High-speed Internet access. Complimentary continental breakfast. Outdoor pool. Pets accepted. $

WINCHESTER

Located in Kentucky's horse country, Winchester has many of the attractions that draw visitors to the commonwealth: historical sites, natural beauty and Southern charm. This is the place where orator Henry Clay made his first and last Kentucky speeches, where the Kentucky soft drink Ale-8-One has been bottled since 1926 and where people celebrate the bluegrass culture and heritage.

Information: Winchester-Clark County Tourism Commission, 2 S. Maple St.,
859-744-0556, 800-298-9105; www.winchesterky.com

KENTUCKY

WHAT TO SEE AND DO
FORT BOONESBOROUGH STATE PARK
4375 Boonsboro Road, Winchester, 859-527-3131;
www.parks.ky.gov/findparks/recparks/fb

This is the site of the settlement where Daniel Boone defended his fort against Native American sieges. The fort houses craft shops, where costumed "pioneers" produce wares; a museum with Boone memorabilia and other historical items; and an audiovisual program (April-Labor Day: daily; after Labor Day-October: Wednesday-Sunday). Exhibits in cabins and blockhouses re-create life at the fort. A sand beach, a swimming pool, a bathhouse, fishing, boating (ramp, dock), miniature golf, picnicking, a playground, a snack bar, tent and trailer sites (standard fees) offer lots to do.

HISTORIC MAIN STREET
Main Street, Winchester

This historic block has a number of restored buildings, most from the Victorian era, and unique shops (Monday-Saturday). A walking tour is available.

OLD STONE CHURCH
Old Stone Church Road, six miles south of Highway 627, Winchester

Built in the late 1700s, this famous landmark in the Boonesboro section of Clark County is the oldest active church west of the Allegheny Mountains. Daniel Boone and his family worshipped here.

SPECIAL EVENT
DANIEL BOONE PIONEER FESTIVAL
34 S. Main St., College and Lynkins Parks, Winchester, 859-744-0556;
www.kyfestivals.com

This fest honoring Daniel Boone offers juried arts and crafts, antiques, street dance, a 5K run, a two-mile walk, concerts, music, food and fireworks. Labor Day weekend.

HOTELS
★★DAYS INN
1100 Interstate Drive, Winchester, 859-744-9111; www.daysinn.com

64 rooms. High-speed Internet access. Complimentary continental breakfast. Restaurant. Outdoor pool. Pets accepted. $

★HAMPTON INN
1025 Early Drive, Winchester, 859-745-2000; www.hamptoninn.com

60 rooms. Wireless Internet access. Complimentary continental breakfast. Swimming pool. $

RESTAURANT
★HALL'S ON THE RIVER
1225 Athens-Boonesborough Road, Winchester, 859-527-6620;
www.hallsontheriver.com

Lunch, dinner. $$

LOUISIANA

BORN OUT OF SWAMPS AND BAYOUS, CRAFTED FROM THE WORK AND TRADITION OF DOZENS
of cultures and celebrated as the home of renowned music, food and legend, Louisiana is as colorful and varied as the characters on the streets of New Orleans during Mardi Gras.

Named by the French (for Louis XIV), Louisiana was settled by both the French and the Spanish. To prevent Louisiana from falling into the hands of the English, Louis XV of France gave it to his cousin, Charles III of Spain. In 1801, Napoleon regained it for France, though no one in Louisiana knew of this until 1803, only 20 days before the Louisiana Purchase made it U.S. territory. From its earliest days, the state was home to settlers of English, Irish and German origin.

The settlers were drawn to Louisiana for any number of reasons. For some, the unique landscape is a major selling point: Louisiana is semitropical, and beautifully unusual—a land of bayous with cypress and live oak overhung with Spanish moss. Today, some Louisianans live in isolation on the bayous and riverbanks, where they still fish, trap and do a little farming.

The northern and southern parts of the state are quite different topographically. In the southern area are fine old mansions and sugarcane plantation estates, many of which are open to the public. The north is more rural, with beautiful rivers, hills, forests and cotton plantation mansions. This is the area from which the colorful politician Huey Long came; he was born in Winnfield.

Petroleum and natural gas taken from far underground, shipped abroad or processed in large plants contribute to Louisiana's thriving industrial and manufacturing economy. As these businesses expand, the service sector continually grows to meet demands.

Hurricane Katrina hit Louisiana hard in 2005, but the affected cities and towns continue the hard work of rebuilding. The storm's floodwaters washed away homes, businesses and some of the state's most beloved landmarks but failed to touch Louisiana's charm. It remains the old Deep South at its best: gracious, cultured and hospitable.

Information: www.louisianatravel.com

FUN FACTS

Louisiana is the only state that has parishes rather than counties.

Louisiana's 450-foot-tall capitol building is the tallest in the United States.

★
★
★
★
★

CAJUN COUNTRY

Among the bayous and swamps west of New Orleans lies Cajun Country, a 22-parish region with a noticeably French accent. The area's vibrant history stretches back to the 18th century, when French refugees forced out of Nova Scotia by the British sought refuge in the French colony of New Orleans.

Although Lafayette, "the Capital of French Louisiana," can be reached in two hours from New Orleans by interstate, Highway 90 offers a leisurely introduction to Cajun Country that could take a half-day or more. You can catch Highway 90 just west of the French Quarter, but you're better off bypassing suburban congestion by taking I-10 west to the I-310 spur south. Here the interstate bridge crosses a fierce bend of the Mississippi River barely contained by a high levee. West of the river, I-310 deposits you in the subtropical Cajun wetlands region onto Highway 90; follow this route west toward Gibson.

In New Iberia, a detour south on Highway 329 leads to Avery Island, home of the world-famous McIlhenny Tabasco Sauce, where you can visit the factory for free. After your detour, cross 90 and follow Bayou Teche ("Tesh") toward downtown New Iberia, settled by the Spanish in 1779. Here Shadows-on-the-Teche, built in 1834, opens a stately plantation house museum with an extensive garden of magnolias, oaks and Spanish moss on Highway 182 at 317 E. Main St. (337-369-6446).

Ten miles north of New Iberia on Highway 31, St. Martinville is famous for the live oak memorialized in Longfellow's epic poem *Evangeline*. The 1847 poem tells the story of Acadian lovers reunited under the venerable oak. Today, the Romero Brothers, a pair of local troubadours, croon Cajun standards beside the oak to re-create the romance. A statue of Evangeline stands outside the St. Martin de Tours Church in the small downtown square nearby. At the Longfellow Evangeline Commemorative Area a mile north of town, guides offer tours of the 19th-century sugar plantation house (337-394-4284).

Farther up Bayou Teche via Highway 31, Breaux Bridge proclaims itself "Crawfish Capital of the World." The town's annual Crawfish Festival on the first full weekend in May features crawfish races, a crawfish-eating contest, the crowning of the Crawfish King and Queen and continuous Cajun and zydeco music. But at any time, you can find people dancing away at Mulate's ("MOO-lots"), ¼ mile west of Highway 31, practically spitting distance south of I-10. Follow the signs.

In downtown Breaux Bridge, near the drawbridge over Bayou Teche, Cafe des Amis (337-332-5273) operates out of an old general store built in 1925, retaining the stamped tin ceiling, ceiling fans and brick walls. Stay overnight at the adjacent Maison des Amis. The visitor center at the drawbridge distributes local information (337-332-8500, 888-565-5939).

To reach Lafayette, take State Road 94 south and west. Founded as Vermilionville alongside the Bayou Vermilion in 1821, Lafayette was later renamed in honor of the Marquis de Lafayette. Today the historic attraction of Vermilionville re-creates a 19th-century village, with guides in period costume, craft demonstrations and Cajun music in the barn house. It's open daily at 1600 Surrey St. (337-233-4077). Across the bayou at Jean Lafitte National Historic Park (501 Fisher Road, 337-232-0789), a 30-minute film dramatizes the story of the British removal of the Acadians from Nova Scotia in 1755.

Two of the region's most famous restaurants are north of Lafayette off I-49. Find crawfish and blackened Cajun specialties at Prejean's ("PRAY-jhonz;" 337-896-3247) or farther north in Carenco at Enola Prudhomme's Cajun Cafe (337-896-3646), named for the sister of internationally famous chef Paul. After a visit to Cajun Country, you can easily loop back to New Orleans along I-10 East. It's approximately 350 miles.

ABITA SPRINGS

Since the late 19th century Abita Springs has been a popular resort getaway for New Orleans residents. Today it is best known for the Abita Brewing Company, which brews beer with water from the city's artesian wells.

Information: 201 Holiday Blvd., Holiday Square Plaza, Covington, 985-892-0711; www.townofabitasprings.com

WHAT TO SEE AND DO
ABITA MYSTERY HOUSE/UCM MUSEUM
22275 Highway 36, Abita Springs, 985-892-2624; www.ucmmuseum.com
Looking for something off the beaten path? Check out the comb collection, popsicle-stick marble machine or "Aliens vs. Airstream Trailer" exhibits in this museum, which bills itself as Louisiana's "most eccentric." Daily 10 a.m.-5 p.m.

RESTAURANT
★ABITA BREW PUB
72011 Holly St., Abita Springs, 985-892-5837; www.abiteabruwpub.com
Since 1986, the Abita Brewery has been gaining a following across the state with its five flagship brews and seasonal favorites. Today, the company brews more than 62,000 barrels of beer each year, including some that's sold in the brewery's pub. Stop for lunch or sample the ales and root beer at the tasting bar. American menu. Lunch, dinner. $$

ALEXANDRIA

Alexandria may be two hours from most of Louisiana's large cities and three hours from New Orleans, but locals and visitors don't need to travel far for big-city events and culture. With art museums, a zoological center and year-round live theater, the Central Louisiana city on the banks of the Red River has plenty to offer.

Information: Alexandria/Pineville Area Convention & Visitor Bureau, 707 Main St., Alexandria, 318-443-9546; www.louisianafromhere.org

WHAT TO SEE AND DO
ALEXANDRIA MUSEUM OF ART
933 Main St., Alexandria, 318-443-3458; www.themuseum.org
This art museum has national and regional exhibits. Tuesday-Saturday.

★
★
★
★
★

ALEXANDRIA NATIONAL CEMETERY

209 E. Shamrock St., Pineville, 318-449-1793;
www.cem.va.gov/CEMs/nchp/alexandriala.asp
Also in Pineville is Rapides Cemetery at David Street.

BRINGHURST PARK

3016 Masonic Drive, Alexandria, 318-473-1385
The park offers tennis, nine-hole golf, picnicking and a playground. Daily.

COTILE RECREATION AREA

75 Cotile Lake Road, Hot Wells, Boyce, 318-793-8995
Swimming, waterskiing, fishing, boating (ramp), picnicking, and tent and trailer camping (fee) are all available here. Daily. Additional fee for boat, ski rig.

KENT HOUSE

3601 Bayou Rapides Road, Alexandria, 318-487-5998; www.kenthouse.org
Built in 1796, this restored French colonial plantation house is one of Louisiana's oldest standing structures. Tour the house and outbuildings, including a millhouse, a barn, cabins, a detached kitchen, a carriage house, a sugar mill and a spinning and weaving cottage. Walk through the herb and formal gardens and check out the open-hearth cooking demonstration (October-April, Wednesday). Guided tours are available (Monday-Saturday).

KISATCHIE NATIONAL FOREST

2500 Shreveport Highway, Pineville, 318-473-7160;
www.southernregion.fs.fed.us/kisatchie
Louisiana's only national forest covers 600,000 acres. Dogwood and wild azalea bloom in the shadows of longleaf, loblolly and slash pine. Wild Azalea National Recreation Trail, the state's longest hiking trail (31 miles), is in the Evangeline District. Swimming, waterskiing, fishing, hunting, off-road vehicles, picnicking, camping (tent and trailer sites) are also some draws. Fees are charged at some recreation sites.

LOUISIANA

HOTELS

★
★
★
★
★

★BEST WESTERN OF ALEXANDRIA INN & SUITES & CONFERENCE CENTER

2720 N. Macarthur Drive, Alexandria, 318-445-5530; www.bestwestern.com
190 rooms. High-speed Internet access. Complimentary continental breakfast. Bar. Airport transportation available. Fitness center. Outdoor pool. Pets accepted. **$**

★★ HOLIDAY INN

701 Fourth St., Alexandria, 318-442-9000, 800-465-4329; www.holiday-inn.com
173 rooms. High-speed Internet access. Restaurant, bar. Airport transportation available. Business center. **$**

RESTAURANTS

★★★BISTRO ON THE BAYOU

1321 Chappie James Ave., Alexandria, 318-445-7574; www.bistroonthebayou.com
The dining room at Bistro on the Bayou, along with the adjoining lounge, occupies an expansive space in the Parc England. Low lighting and a gurgling fountain create

a serene and intimate atmosphere. A dramatic focal point is the glassed-in courtyard, filled with lush foliage and lit with fairy lights. Live jazz is offered Friday and Saturday nights. Just minutes from the airport, it is in a suburban setting on the grounds of the former England Air Force Base in Alexandria, which is now the England Air Park. American menu. Lunch, dinner. Closed Sunday. **$$$**

★★★RESTAURANT EVE
110 S. Pitt St., Alexandria, 703-706-0450; www.restauranteve.com
Chef Cathal Armstrong has earned well-deserved praise for his creative, seasonal cooking. A native of Dublin, Ireland, he cooked personal meals for Senators Kennedy and Clinton as well as President Bush who, once served, asked when he was going to open his own restaurant. The result: a place that features both a 34-seat Tasting Room and a more informal 66-seat bistro. The warm and inviting Tasting Room offers a five- or nine-course prix fixe meal and a seasonal menu featuring Creation (appetizers), Ocean (seafood), Earth and Sky (meats and game), Age (cheese) and Eden (desserts). The inviting, less-formal bistro offers favorites such as the confit of house-cured pork belly and Hawaiian king prawns with risotto. American menu. Lunch, dinner. Closed Sunday. **$$$**

BASTROP
From woodlands and bayous to 150 years of Morehouse Parish history, there's plenty to keep you busy in Bastrop.
Information: Bastrop-Morehouse Chamber of Commerce, 512 E. Jefferson Ave., 318-281-3794

WHAT TO SEE AND DO
BUSSEY BRAKE RESERVOIR
5373 Boat Dock Road, Bastrop, 318-281-4507
Go fishing, boating or camping on these 2,200 acres.

CHEMIN-A-HAUT STATE PARK
14656 State Park Road, Bastrop, 318-283-0812, 888-677-2436; www.crt.state.la.us/parks
More than 500 wooded acres are found at the intersection of bayous Chemin-a-Haut and Bartholomew. A portion of the "high road to the South" was originally a Native American trail. Visitors can swim, fish, rent a boat, hike or spend the night at one of many tent and trailer sites. All-year overnight cabins have a capacity of four people, maximum of six. Daily.

SNYDER MEMORIAL MUSEUM
1620 E. Madison Ave., Bastrop, 318-281-8760; www.museumsusa.org/museums
The museum covers 150 years of Morehouse Parish history. See antique furniture, kitchen utensils, farm equipment, clothing and Native American artifacts. The gallery features changing art and photographic exhibits. Daily.

SPECIAL EVENT
NORTH LOUISIANA COTTON FESTIVAL AND FAIR
Bastrop, 318-281-3794; www.bastroplacoc.org
September.

LOUISIANA

★
★
★
★

BATON ROUGE

Named by its French founders for a red post that marked the boundary between the lands of two Native American tribes, Baton Rouge, the busy capital of Louisiana, is also a major Mississippi River port. Clinging to its gracious past, the area has restored antebellum mansions, gardens, tree-shaded university campuses, splendid Cajun and Creole cuisine, and historic attractions that reflect the culture and struggle of living under ten flags over a period of three centuries.

When Hurricane Katrina hit the Gulf Coast in August 2005, Baton Rouge endured some minor damage, but the most pronounced effect from the storm was the influx of residents from New Orleans and other cities on the Gulf, causing a boost in population that remains today.

Baton Rouge is divided into distinct neighborhoods, each with its own flavor. One of the most popular is Spanish Town, near downtown, which attracts an eclectic crowd because of its restored historic buildings, big Mardi Gras parade and inclusive attitude. The Garden District is a good place for a casual stroll and a peek at some of the city's most beautiful historic homes, and Beauregard Town, in downtown Baton Rouge, is worth a visit; it one of the city's oldest neighborhoods.

Information: Baton Rouge Area Convention & Visitors Bureau, 730 North Blvd., 225-383-1825, 800-527-6843; www.bracvb.com

WHAT TO SEE AND DO

BREC'S BATON ROUGE ZOO

3601 Thomas Road, Baton Rouge, 225-775-3877; www.brzoo.org

Walkways overlook 140 acres of enclosed habitats for more than 1,800 animals and birds. Take in views of some of the fish, reptiles and amphibians of Louisiana at *L'aquarium de Louisiane* or take the kids to the Safari Playground or a live elephant show. $1 admission Wednesday afternoon.

BREC'S MAGNOLIA MOUND PLANTATION

2161 Nicholson Drive, Baton Rouge, 225-343-4955; www.magnoliamound.org

An early-19th-century Creole-style building was restored to emphasize the lifestyle of colonial Louisiana. See more of that lifestyle with weekly demonstrations of open-hearth Creole cooking and costumed docents. Then meander over to the visitor center and gift shop. Tuesday-Sunday.

COTTAGE PLANTATION

10528 Cottage Lane, St. Francisville, 225-635-3674; www.cottageplantation.com

The oldest part of the main house was built during Spanish control of the area. Outbuildings include a smokehouse, a school, kitchens and slave cabins. Accommodations and breakfast are available. Tours daily.

GOVERNOR'S MANSION

1001 Capitol Access Road, Baton Rouge, 225-342-5855; www.lamansionfoundation.org

On a Greek Revival/Louisiana-style plantation, the mansion was built in 1963 to replace an earlier official residence. Tours Monday-Friday, by appointment.

LOUISIANA

★
★
★
★

HERITAGE MUSEUM AND VILLAGE

1606 Main St., Baker, 225-774-1776; www.bakerheritagemuseum.org

The turn-of-the-century Victorian house showcases period rooms and exhibits. Also check out the rural village with a church, a school, a store and town hall replica buildings. Monday-Saturday.

HOUMAS HOUSE

40136 Highway 92, Burnside, 225-473-7841, 888-323-8314; www.houmashouse.com

This large restored sugar plantation (circa 1840) features a Greek Revival mansion with early Louisiana-crafted furnishings, a spiral staircase, a belvedere and hexagonal *garconnieres* in gardens. The house and grounds have been used as a set for 11 films and TV shows. Monday-Tuesday 9 a.m.-5 p.m., Wednesday-Sunday 9 a.m.-7 p.m.

LAURENS HENRY COHN, SR., MEMORIAL PLANT ARBORETUM

12056 Foster Road, Baton Rouge, 225-775-1006

This unusual 16-acre tract of rolling terrain contains more than 120 species of native and adaptable trees and shrubs; several major plant collections; an herb/fragrance garden; and a tropical collection in a greenhouse. Tours are available by appointment. Daily.

LOUISIANA ART & SCIENCE MUSEUM

100 S. River Road, Baton Rouge, 225-344-5272; www.lasm.org

Originally a railroad depot, this building houses fine art, sculpture, cultural and historical exhibits, an Egyptian exhibition, Discovery Depot (for children ages 6 months to 9 years), hands-on galleries and science exhibits for kids. The Irene W. Pennington Planetarium features large-format films and laser shows. Outside, visitors can explore a sculpture garden and a restored five-car train. Additional fees are charged for Space Theater shows. Tuesday-Saturday 10 a.m.-4 p.m., Sunday 1-4 p.m.; planetarium also open Friday-Saturday 7-10 p.m.

LOUISIANA STATE LIBRARY

401 N. Fourth St., Baton Rouge, 225-342-4913; www.state.lib.la.us

The library houses some 350,000 books, including an extensive section of Louisiana historical tomes, maps and photographs. Monday-Friday 8 a.m.-4:30 p.m.

LOUISIANA STATE UNIVERSITY

Highland Road and Dalrymple Drive, Baton Rouge, 225-388-8654; www.lsu.edu

Founded in 1860, the university is now home to some 31,000 students.

INDIAN MOUNDS

Field House and Dalrymple Drives, Baton Rouge

These mounds are believed to have served socio-religious purposes and date from 3300 to 2500 B.C.

LSU TIGERS

Nicholson and North Stadium drives, Baton Rouge, 800-960-8587;
www.lsusports.net

Louisiana State University fields 20 athletic teams and draws some of the largest crowds in college athletics. The LSU mascots are Mike the Tiger, Mike VI (a live Bengal tiger that hosts daily feedings at the Tiger Cage) and Ellis Hugh (an inflatable acrobatic tiger). LSU adopted its Fighting Tigers nickname in 1896 from a Civil War volunteer company from New Orleans called the Tiger Rifles.

MEMORIAL TOWER

Highland Road and Dalrymple Drive, Baton Rouge, 225-388-4003;
www.lsu.edu/campus/locations/MEMT.html

Built in 1923 as a monument to Louisianans who died in World War I, the tower houses the LSU Museum of Art and features original 17th- through mid-19th-century rooms from England and America. Self-guided tours are available.

MUSEUM OF NATURAL SCIENCE

119 Foster Hall, Baton Rouge, 225-578-3080; appl003.lsu.edu/natsci/lmnh.nsf/index

The museum features an extensive collection of birds from around the world; wildlife scenes include Louisiana marshlands and swamps, the Arizona desert, alpine regions and Honduran jungles. Monday-Saturday.

THE MYRTLES PLANTATION

7747 Highway 61, St. Francisville, 225-635-6277; www.myrtlesplantation.com

Known as one of America's most haunted mansions, this carefully restored house of French influence (circa 1796) boasts outstanding examples of wrought iron, ornamental plasterwork and period furniture. Visitors looking for signs of haunting can take a mystery tour, conducted Friday and Saturday evenings. Daily.

NOTTOWAY PLANTATION

30970 Highway 405, White Castle, 225-545-2730, 866-527-6884; www.nottoway.com

One of the South's most imposing houses, the 50,000-square-foot Nottoway has 64 rooms, 200 windows and 165 doors. In a near-perfect state of "originality," the house is famous for its all-white ballroom. Also on the premises are a restaurant and overnight accommodations. Tours daily.

OAKLEY HOUSE

Audubon State Historic Site, Highway 965, St. Francisville, 225-635-3739,
888-677-2838; www.nps.gov/history/nr/travel/louisiana/okl.htm

While living at Oakley and working as a tutor, John James Audubon painted 32 of his *Birds of America*. Spanish colonial Oakley is part of the Audubon State Historic Site, a 100-acre tract set aside as a wildlife sanctuary. The house and park are open daily.

OLD ARSENAL MUSEUM

State Capitol grounds, 900 Capital Lake Drive, 225-342-0401; www.sos.louisiana.gov

This one-time military garrison dates back to 1838. On the south side are formal gardens that focus on a sunken garden with a monumental statue erected over the grave of Huey P. Long, who was buried here in 1935 after being assassinated in the Capitol.

★
★
★
★
☆

OLD GOVERNOR'S MANSION

502 North Blvd., Baton Rouge, 225-387-2464; www.oldgovernorsmansion.org

The mansion is restored to the period of the 1930s, when it was built for Gov. Huey P. Long. It includes original furnishings and memorabilia of former governors. Tuesday-Friday 10 a.m.-4 p.m.

OLD STATE CAPITOL

100 North Blvd., Baton Rouge, 225-342-0500;
www.nps.gov/history/NR/travel/louisiana/ocap.htm

Completed in 1849, Louisiana's old state capitol may be the country's most extravagant example of the Gothic Revival style popularized by the British Houses of Parliament. The richly ornamented building was enlarged in 1881 and abandoned as the capitol in 1932. Self-guided tours are available. Tuesday-Sunday.

PARLANGE PLANTATION

8211 False River Road, Baton Rouge, 225-638-8410;
www.nps.gov/history/nr/travel/louisiana/par.htm

Owned by relatives of the builder, this working plantation is a National Historic Landmark. It includes a French colonial home with a rare example of *bousillage* construction. Doorways and ceiling moldings are of hand-carved cypress; two octagonal brick dovecotes flank the driveway. Daily.

PENTAGON BARRACKS MUSEUM

959 Third St., Baton Rouge, 225-342-1866;
www.nps.gov/history/nr/travel/louisiana/pen.htm

Built in 1822 as part of a U.S. military post, the columned, galleried buildings later became the first permanent home of Louisiana State University.

PLANTATIONS AND ST. FRANCISVILLE

Baton Rouge driving tour (approximately 100 miles)

Drive north from Baton Rouge on Highway 61 approximately 23 miles, then turn east on Highway 965 to:

BUTLER GREENWOOD PLANTATION

6838 Highland Road, St. Francisville, 225-655-4475; www.butlergreenwood.com

The same family has owned and lived on this plantation since it was first settled in the 1790s. Today, Greenwood is still a working plantation producing cattle, hay and pecans. Tour the house and if you like it, spend the night—it's also a bed and breakfast. Daily 9 a.m.-5 p.m.

PLAQUEMINE LOCK STATE HISTORIC SITE

57735 Main St., Plaquemine, 225-687-7158, 877-987-7158;
www.crt.state.la.us/crt/parks/plaquemine lock/plaqlock.htm

Built between 1895 and 1909 to control the water level between the Bayou Plaquemine and the Mississippi, the locks were eventually closed in 1961 following the construction of larger locks at Port Allen. Designed by George Goethals, who later designed the Panama Canal, the Plaquemine Locks once had the highest freshwater lift in the world, at 51 feet. The area features the original lockhouse and locks. There's also an interpretive center with displays. Daily.

PORT HUDSON STATE HISTORIC SITE

236 Highway 61, Jackson, 225-654-3775, 888-677-3400;
www.crt.state.la.us/crt/parks/porthud/pthudson.htm

This 650-acre area encompasses part of a Civil War battlefield, site of the longest siege in American military history. The site features viewing towers (40 feet), Civil War guns and trenches and hiking trails. Interpretive programs tell the 1863 story of how 6,800 Confederates held off a Union force of 30,000 to 40,000 men. Daily.

ROSEDOWN PLANTATION AND GARDENS

12501 Highway 10, St. Francisville, 225-635-3332, 888-376-1867;
www.crt.state.la.us/parks

This magnificently restored 1835 antebellum mansion has many original furnishings. The 28 acres of formal gardens include century-old camellias and azaleas, fountains, gazebos and an *allée* of moss-draped live oaks. Daily.

RURAL LIFE MUSEUM

4600 Essen Lane, Baton Rouge, 225-765-2437; www.rurallife.lsu.edu

The three-acre museum complex of 25 buildings is divided into plantation, folk architecture and exhibits. The plantation includes a blacksmith shop, an open-kettle sugar mill, a commissary and a church. Daily.

STATE CAPITOL

N. Third Street and State Capitol Drive, Baton Rouge, 225-342-7317, 800-527-6843;
www.nps.gov/history/NR/travel/louisiana/cap.htm

Built during Huey P. Long's administration, the 34-story, 450-foot *moderne* skyscraper capitol is decorated with 26 different varieties of marble. The Memorial Hall floor is laid with polished lava from Mount Vesuvius; the ceiling is leafed in gold. An observation tower offers views of the city. Lorado Taft sculpture groups on either side of the entrance symbolize the pioneer and patriotic spirit. Tours are available; the observation tower is open daily.

USS KIDD

305 S. River Road, Baton Rouge, 225-342-1942; www.usskidd.com

Visitors may roam the decks of the World War II Fletcher-class destroyer and explore its interior compartments. A unique dock allows the ship to be exhibited completely out of water when the Mississippi River is in its low stages. The adjacent museum houses a ship model collection, maritime artifacts and a restored P-40 Flying Tiger plane. There's a visitor center and an observation tower that overlooks the river. The Memorial Wall is dedicated to service personnel.

WEST BATON ROUGE MUSEUM

845 N. Jefferson Ave., Port Allen, 225-336-2422; www.westbatonrougemuseum.com

Exhibits include a large-scale 1904 model sugar mill, a bedroom featuring American Empire furniture and a sugar plantation slave cabin (circa 1850) and French Creole house (circa 1830). Tuesday-Saturday 10 a.m.- 4:30 p.m., Sunday 2-5 p.m.

★
★
★
★
★

SPECIAL EVENT

BLUES WEEK

730 North Blvd., Baton Rouge, 225-383-0968; www.louisianasmusic.com
The weeklong event features blues, jazz, Cajun, zydeco and gospel music. Traditional Louisiana cuisine is served. Late April-early May.

HOTELS

★BEST WESTERN RICHMOND SUITES HOTEL

5668 Hilton Ave., Baton Rouge, 225-924-6500, 800-332-2582; www.bestwestern.com
141 rooms. High-speed Internet access. Complimentary full breakfast. Fitness center. Outdoor pool, whirlpool. Pets accepted, fee. $

★★EMBASSY SUITES

4914 Constitution Ave., Baton Rouge, 225-924-6566, 800-433-4600;
www.embassybatonrouge.com
223 suites. High-speed Internet access. Complimentary full breakfast. Restaurant, bar. Airport transportation available. Fitness center. Outdoor pool. Business center. $$

★★HOLIDAY INN

9940 Airline Highway, Baton Rouge, 225-924-7021, 888-814-9602;
www.holiday-inn.com
334 rooms. Restaurant, bar. $

★★★MARRIOTT BATON ROUGE

5500 Hilton Ave., Baton Rouge, 225-924-5000; www.marriott.com
299 rooms. Restaurant, bar. Airport transportation available. Business center. $

★★★NOTTOWAY PLANTATION RESTAURANT & INN

31025 Louisiana Highway 1, White Castle, 225-545-2730, 866-527-6884;
www.nottoway.com
This Victorian-style inn was built in 1859. Today, the home retains its original hand-painted Dresden doorknobs, elaborate plaster frieze work and marble fireplaces. A lovely plantation-style restaurant serves Cajun and Southern cuisine. 15 rooms. Complimentary full breakfast. Restaurant. $

★QUALITY INN

9138 Bluebonnet Centre Blvd., Baton Rouge, 225-293-1199, 800-228-5151;
www.qualityinn.com
120 rooms. Wireless Internet access. Complimentary full breakfast. Restaurant, bar. $

★★★SHERATON BATON ROUGE CONVENTION CENTER HOTEL

102 France St., Baton Rouge, 225-242-2600; www.sheraton.com
300 rooms. High-speed Internet access. Restaurant, bar. Airport transportation available. Fitness center. Outdoor pool, whirlpool. Business center. $$

RESTAURANTS

★CABIN

Highways 22 and 44, Burnside, 225-473-3007; www.thecabinrestaurant.com
Cajun menu. Lunch, dinner. $$

193

LOUISIANA

★
★
★
★

BAYOU SAUVAGE NATIONAL WILDLIFE REFUGE

This 22,000-acre site offers ample opportunity for bird watching: Brown pelicans, peregrine falcons and bald eagles are among the species sheltered here. A variety of habitats from marshes to forests protect the park's wildlife, which includes alligators, swamp rabbits and other small mammals, reptiles and amphibians. Visitors can also hike, bike, fish and canoe. Guided tours are available on weekends, reservations required.

From New Orleans, take I-10 E to exit 246A (Chalmette I-510) to Highway 90 E exit; turn left and go approximately four miles. 985-882-2000; www.fws.gov/bayousauvage

★★DON'S SEAFOOD & STEAK HOUSE

6823 Airline Highway, Baton Rouge, 225-357-0601
Seafood. steak menu. Lunch, dinner. $$

★★★JUBAN'S

3739 Perkins Road, Baton Rouge, 225-346-8422; www.jubans.com
Diners will find fine Southern Louisiana cuisine with a Creole-American influence. For a sure thing, order the veal T-bone with shitake mushroom hash and a port wine demi-glace or the hallelujah crab topped with Creolaise sauce. Creole menu. Lunch, dinner. Closed Sunday. $$$

★★MIKE ANDERSON'S

1031 W. Lee Drive, Baton Rouge, 225-766-7823; www.mikeandersonsbr.com
Seafood menu. Lunch, dinner. $$

★★PARRAIN'S SEAFOOD RESTAURANT

3225 Perkins Road, Baton Rouge, 225-381-9922
Seafood menu. Lunch, dinner. $$

★★★RUTH'S CHRIS STEAK HOUSE

4836 Constitution Ave., Baton Rouge, 225-925-0163; www.ruthschris.com
The excellent service and atmosphere are on par with the steaks at this upscale national chain. Steak menu. Lunch, dinner. Closed Sunday. $$$

BOSSIER CITY

Located on the east bank of the Red River, Bossier City is a gambler's paradise: The city of a little more than 56,000 people has three major casinos and a thoroughbred racetrack in and around the city limits.

Information: Shreveport-Bossier Convention & Tourist Bureau, 629 Spring St., Shreveport, 318-222-9391, 800-551-8682; www.shreveport-bossier.org or www.bossiercity.org

WHAT TO SEE AND DO

EIGHTH AIR FORCE MUSEUM

Barksdale Air Force Base, 841 Fairchild Ave., Bossier City, 318-456-3067;
www.8afmuseum.net

Aircraft on display include a B-52D Stratofortress, a P-51 Mustang and an F-84F Thunderstreak. Desert Storm memorabilia is available and there's a gift shop. Daily.

ISLE OF CAPRI CASINO

711 Isle of Capri Blvd., Bossier City, 318-678-7777, 800-843-4753;
www.isleofcapricasino.com

TOUCHSTONE WILDLIFE & ART MUSEUM

3386 Highway 80, Bossier City, 318-949-2323

Various dioramas depict animals and birds in their natural habitats. Tuesday-Sunday.

SPECIAL EVENT

THOROUGHBRED RACING, LOUISIANA DOWNS

8000 E. Texas Ave., Bossier City, 800-551-7223; www.ladowns.com

Thursday-Sunday; also Memorial Day, July 4, Labor Day. Late June-mid-November.

HOTELS

★★HOLIDAY INN

2015 Old Minden Road, Bossier City, 318-742-9700, 800-465-4329;
www.holiday-inn.com

212 rooms. High-speed Internet access. Restaurant, bar. Fitness center. Business center. $

★LA QUINTA INN

309 Preston Blvd., Bossier City, 318-747-4400, 800-687-6667; www.laquinta.com

130 rooms. High-speed Internet access. Complimentary continental breakfast. Airport transportation available. Outdoor pool. Pets accepted. $

★ISLE OF CAPRI INN

711 Isle of Capri Blvd., Bossier City, 318-678-7777, 800-843-4753;
www.isleofcapricasino.com

245 rooms. Complimentary continental breakfast. Bar. Airport transportation available. $

RESTAURANT

★★RALPH & KACOO'S

1700 Old Minden Road, Bossier City, 318-747-6660; www.ralphandkacoos.com

Cajun menu. Lunch, dinner, Sunday brunch. $$

COVINGTON

Covington is in a wooded area north of Lake Pontchartrain, which is crossed via the 24-mile Lake Pontchartrain Causeway from New Orleans. With mild winters and semitropical summers, Covington is a town of vacation houses, recreational

LOUISIANA

★
★
★
★

opportunities and pecan, pine and oak woods. A number of thoroughbred horse farms are also in the area.

Information: St. Tammany Parish Tourist & Convention Commission, 68099 Highway 59, Mandeville, 985-892-0520, 800-634-9443; www.neworleansnorthshore.com

WHAT TO SEE AND DO

FONTAINEBLEAU STATE PARK
67825 Highway 190, Mandeville, 985-624-4443, 888-677-3668; www.lastateparks.com/fontaine/fontaine.htm
A live oak *allée* forms the entrance to this 2,700-acre park on the north shore of Lake Pontchartrain; on the grounds are the ruins of a plantation brickyard and sugar mill. Swimming, fishing, boating and picnicking are available. Daily.

PONTCHARTRAIN VINEYARDS & WINERY
81250 Highway 1082 (Old Military Road), Bush, 985-892-9742; www.pontchartrainvineyards.com
About an hour from New Orleans, the Pontchartrain Vineyards & Winery produces wines to complement the unique cuisine of Southern Louisiana. To sample the wines, you can drive out to the winery for a tasting, buy a case at a local spirits shop or order a bottle with your meal in any number of fine New Orleans restaurants. Wednesday-Friday 10 a.m.-5 p.m., Saturday 10 a.m.-4 p.m., Sunday noon-4 p.m.

ST. TAMMANY ART ASSOCIATION
129 N. New Hampshire St., Covington, 982-892-8650; blog.nola.com/staa

Gallery. Tuesday-Sunday.

TAMMANY TRACE
Covington, Highway 59, 800-438-7223; www.tammanytrace.org
This follows the old Illinois Central Railroad corridor for 31 miles, ending in Slidell. There's a paved hiking/biking trail and an unpaved equestrian trail. Daily.

HOTEL

★★HOLIDAY INN
501 N. Highway 190, Covington, 985-893-3580, 888-465-4329; www.holiday-inn.com
156 rooms. High-speed Internet access. Restaurant, bar. Fitness center. Indoor pool, outdoor pool. Business center. $

FRANKLIN
Reportedly named by founder Guinea Lewis for Benjamin Franklin, this town on the Bayou Teche is in the center of the Cajun Coast. It has much of the beautiful scenery outsiders imagine when they think of Louisiana's coast. Boating, fishing and hunting are popular diversions at the nearby Atchafalaya Basin.

Information: Tourism Department, City of Franklin, 300 Iberia St., 337-828-2555, 337-828-6326, 800-962-6889; www.franklin-la.org

WHAT TO SEE AND DO
CHITIMACHA CULTURAL CENTER
490 Decater St., Charenton, 504-589-3882; www.nps.gov/Jela
Museum exhibits, crafts and a ten-minute video focus on the history and culture of the Chitimacha tribe of Louisiana. Walking tours are available. This center is a unit of Jean Lafitte National Historical Park. Daily.

CYPREMORT POINT STATE PARK
306 Beach Lane, Franklin, 337-867-4510;
www.lastateparks.com/cypremor/cyprempt.htm
This 185-acre site offers access to the Gulf of Mexico. Man-made beach in the heart of a natural marsh affords fresh and saltwater fishing and other seashore recreation opportunities. Daily.

GREVEMBERG HOUSE
St. Mary Parish Museum, 407 Sterling Road, Franklin, 337-828-2092;
www.grevemberghouse.com
The Greek Revival house (circa 1850) maintains a fine collection of antique furnishings dating from the 1850s, children's toys, paintings and Civil War relics. Daily.

OAKLAWN MANOR PLANTATION
3296 E. Oaklawn Drive, Franklin, 337-828-0434; www.oaklawnmanor.com
Restored in 1927, this massive Greek Revival house has 20-inch-thick walls, is furnished with European antiques, and is surrounded by one of the largest groves of live oaks in the U.S. It's also the home of former Louisiana Gov. Mike Foster. Daily.

HOTEL
★★BEST WESTERN FOREST MOTOR INN
1909 Main St., Franklin, 337-828-1810, 800-828-1812; www.bestwestern.com
85 rooms. High-speed Internet access. Restaurant. Complimentary continental breakfast. Outdoor pool. Business center. **$**

HENDERSON
Though it's now a fishing community with a population that hovers around 1,500, Henderson originally relied heavily on agricultural production and was known as Cypremort, which means "Dead Cypress" in French.
Information: 314 E. Bridge St., Breaux Bridge, 337-332-5406

RESTAURANTS
★★PAT'S FISHERMAN'S WHARF RESTAURANT
1008 Henderson Levee, Henderson, 70517; 337-228-7512; patsfishermanswharf.com
Seafood, Steak menu. Lunch, dinner. **$$**

★★ROBIN'S
1409 Henderson Highway, Henderson, 337-228-7594
Cajun, Creole menu. Lunch, dinner. **$$**

LOUISIANA

★
★
★
★

HOUMA

Situated on Bayou Terrebonne and the Intracoastal Waterway, Houma is known as the "Venice of America," famous for its Cajun food and hospitality.

Information: Houma-Terrebonne Tourist Commission, 114 Tourist Drive, 504-868-2732, 800-688-2732; www.houmachamber.com

WHAT TO SEE AND DO

ANNIE MILLER'S SWAMP & MARSH TOURS

3718 Southdown Mandalay, Houma, 985-868-4758; www.annie-miller.com

Boat trips (two to three hours) travel through winding waterways in swamps and wild marshlands. See birds, alligators, wild game, tropical plants and flowers. March-October, two departures daily.

SOUTHDOWN PLANTATION HOUSE/TERREBONNE MUSEUM

1208 Museum Drive, Houma, 985-851-0154; www.southdownmuseum.org

The first floor, Greek Revival in style, was built in 1859; the second floor, late Victorian/Queen Anne in style, was added in 1893. The 21-room house includes stained glass, a Boehm and Doughty porcelain bird collection, a Terreboone Parish history room, a re-creation of Allen Ellender's Senate office, antique furniture and Mardi Gras costumes. Tuesday-Saturday.

SPECIAL EVENTS

BLESSING OF THE SHRIMP FLEET

Highway 56, Chauvin, 985-594-5859

April.

GRAND BOIS INTER TRIBAL

470 B Bourg Larose Highway 24, Bourg, 985-594-7410

March and September.

JACKSON

From Renaissance to Greek Revival, Jackson is a bastion of Southern architecture, with 20,000 acres of parklands to help you stretch your legs when you venture outside.

Information: Feliciana Chamber of Commerce, 3406 College St., 504-634-7155; www.felicianatourism.org

WHAT TO SEE AND DO

JACKSON HISTORIC DISTRICT

The district includes 123 structures covering approximately 65 percent of town. Architectural styles range from Renaissance and Greek Revival to Queen Anne and California stick-style bungalow.

MILBANK HISTORIC HOUSE

3045 Bank St., Jackson, 225-634-5901; www.milbankbandb.com/milbank.htm

The Revival town house, originally built as a banking house for the Clinton-Port Hudson Railroad, features first- and second-floor galleries supported by 12 30-foot columns. Overnight stays are available, as are tours. Daily.

★
★
★
★
★

JENNINGS

A small town known for its Cajun food, music and museums—including one on the history of the telephone—Jennings is also notable for its outdoor recreational opportunities, including fishing, boating and hiking. The city hosts a main street farmers market every Saturday and live country music on the last Saturday of each month.

Information: Greater Jennings Chamber of Commerce, 414 N. Cary Ave.,
337-821-5500; www.cityofjennings.com

WHAT TO SEE AND DO

W. H. TUPPER GENERAL MERCHANDISE MUSEUM

311 N. Main St., Jennings, 337-821-5532, 800-264-5521; www.tuppermuseum.com

More than 10,000 items are on display re-creating the atmosphere of early-20th-century life in rural Louisiana. You'll see a toy collection, period clothing, drugs, toiletries and Native American basketry. There is also a gift shop. Monday-Saturday 9:30 a.m.-5:30 p.m.

ZIGLER MUSEUM

411 Clara St., Jennings, 337-824-0114

The museum contains galleries of wildlife and natural history as well as European and American art. Tuesday- Sunday.

HOTEL

★★ HOLIDAY INN

603 Holiday Drive, Jennings, 337-824-5280, 800-465-4329; www.holiday-inn.com

131 rooms Restaurant, bar. $

KENNER

Slot machines, poker and black jack all vie for attention at Kenner's many casinos.
Information: 2100 Third St., Kenner, 504-464-9494; www.kennercvb.com

WHAT TO SEE AND DO

TREASURE CHEST CASINO

5050 Williams Blvd., Kenner, 504-443-8000, 800-298-0711; www.treasurechest.com

This 25,767-square-foot riverboat docked in Lake Pontchartrain holds 1,000 slot machines and table games ranging from blackjack to Caribbean stud. Food choices are an all-you-can-eat buffet or the upscale Bobby G's restaurant, while the Caribbean Showroom offers live entertainment. Daily, 24 hours.

HOTEL

★★★HILTON NEW ORLEANS AIRPORT

901 Airline Drive, Kenner, 504-469-5000, 800-872-5914; www.hilton.com

This first-class hotel caters to business travelers, but with a 21-station fitness center, outdoor pool and whirlpool, tennis courts and putting green, it is great for leisure travelers as well. 317 rooms. High-speed Internet access. Restaurant, bar. Airport transportation available. Fitness center. Tennis. Golf. Outdoor pool, whirlpool. Business center. $

LOUISIANA

★
★
★
★

LACOMBE

Nestled near the Gulf of Mexico, Lacombe is a city of 7,000 residents and plenty of sizzling Southern dishes.

Information: 27505 Highway 190, Lacombe, 985-882-7442

RESTAURANT

★★★LA PROVENCE
25020 Highway 190, E. Lacombe, 985-626-7662; www.laprovencerestaurant.com

For three decades, residents of New Orleans (and beyond) have been treated to the rustic, traditional cuisine of Southern France at La Provence, lovingly prepared by chef Randy Lewis. The restaurant was opened in 1972 by innovative chef Chris Kerageorgiou, and La Provence and has paid homage to Kerageorgiou's Mediterranean cooking ever since with steaming dishes brimming with garlic, tomatoes, olives and fresh herbs. French menu. Lunch, dinner, brunch. Closed Monday, Tuesday. **$$**

LAFAYETTE

The heart of Cajun Country lies in Lafayette, a city with French, Spanish and Caribbean traditions still present in the speech patterns, cooking and daily life of its residents. Lafayette is home to top-notch Cajun and Creole restaurants, historic homes and a backyard of outdoor activities worth exploring.

In the late 18th century, Acadians from Nova Scotia came to the Lafayette area to escape persecution by the British who took control of French Canada. Many of today's descendents of the French Acadians maintain a strong feeling of kinship with Nova Scotia and France.

Despite its urban rhythm and growing population, Lafayette has retained its small-town charm. Live oaks and azaleas bloom all around town, as do clumps of native irises. These blooms offer color to an already vibrant place.

Information: Lafayette Convention & Visitors Commission,
1400 N.W. Evangeline Thruway, 800-346-1958; www.lafayettetravel.com

WHAT TO SEE AND DO

ACADIAN VILLAGE: A MUSEUM OF ACADIAN HERITAGE AND CULTURE
200 Greenleaf Drive, Lafayette, 337-981-2364, 800-962-9133; www.acadianvillage.org

This restored 19th-century Acadian village features fine examples of unique Acadian architecture with houses, a general store and a chapel. Crafts are on display and for sale. Daily.

CHRÉTIEN POINT PLANTATION
665 Chrétien Point Road, Lafayette, 337-662-7050; www.chretienpoint.com

This restored 1831 Greek Revival mansion was the site of a Civil War battle. Daily.

LAFAYETTE MUSEUM
1122 Lafayette St., Lafayette, 337-234-2208

Once the residence of Alexandre Mouton, the first Democratic governor of the state, the house is now a museum with antique furnishings, Civil War relics and carnival costumes. Tuesday-Sunday.

LOUISIANA

LAFAYETTE NATURAL HISTORY MUSEUM AND PLANETARIUM

637 Girard Park Drive, Lafayette, 337-291-5544; www.lnhm.org

The planetarium has various programs and changing exhibits. Daily

UNIVERSITY ART MUSEUM

East Lewis and Girard Park Drives, Lafayette, 337-482-5326; www.louisiana.edu/UAM

There are two locations: The permanent collection is at 101 Girard Park Drive (Monday-Friday); changing exhibits are staged at Fletcher Hall, East Lewis and Girard Park Circle (Monday-Friday, Sunday).

UNIVERSITY OF LOUISIANA AT LAFAYETTE

200 E. University Ave., Lafayette, 337-482-1000; www.louisiana.edu

Founded in 1900, the university is now home to more than 16,000 students. The tree-shaded campus serves as an arboretum with many Southern plant species, while Cypress Lake, a miniature Louisiana cypress swamp, has fish, alligators and native irises.

SPECIAL EVENTS

AZALEA TRAIL

Lafayette, 800-346-1958

Mid-March.

FESTIVAL INTERNATIONAL DE LOUISIANE

735 Jefferson St., Lafayette, 337-232-8086; www.festivalinternational.com

The festival offers international and Louisiana performances, visual arts and cuisine. Last weekend in April.

FESTIVALS ACADIENS

Lafayette, 800-346-1958; www.festivalsacadiens.com

Cajun music and food festival. Third weekend in September.

THOROUGHBRED RACING

Evangeline Downs, 3620 N.W. Evangeline, Lafayette, 337-896-7223;
www.evangelinedowns.com

There's pari-mutuel betting here. Proper attire is required in the clubhouse. Early April-Labor Day.

HOTELS

★★BEST WESTERN HOTEL ACADIANA

1801 W. Pinhook Road, Lafayette, 337-233-8120, 800-826-8386;
www.bestwestern.com

290 rooms. Restaurant, bar. Airport transportation available. $

★★COMFORT INN

1421 S.E. Evangeline Thruway, Lafayette, 337-232-9000, 800-800-8752;
www.choicehotels.com

200 rooms. Wireless Internet access. Complimentary continental breakfast. Restaurant, bar. Airport transportation available. Fitness center. Outdoor pool. $

★
★
★
★
★

★★★HILTON LAFAYETTE AND TOWERS

800-1521 W. Pinhook Road, Lafayette, 337-235-6111; www.hilton.com

327 rooms. Restaurant, bar. Airport transportation available. Fitness center. Outdoor pool. Pets accepted. $$

★LA QUINTA INN

2100 N.E. Evangeline Thruway, Lafayette, 337-233-5610, 800-531-5900; www.laquinta.com

140 rooms. High-speed Internet access. Complimentary continental breakfast. Outdoor pool. Pets accepted. $

RESTAURANTS

★BLAIR HOUSE

1316 Surrey St., Lafayette, 337-234-0357

American, Cajun, French menu. Lunch, dinner. $$

★★BLUE DOG CAFE

1211 W. Pinhook Road, Lafayette, 337-237-0005; www.bluedogcafe.com

Cajun/Creole, seafood, steak menu. Lunch, dinner, brunch. $$

★★DON'S SEAFOOD & STEAK HOUSE

301 E. Vermilion St., Lafayette, 337-235-3551; www.donsdowntown.com

Cajun, seafood, steak menu. Lunch, dinner. $$

★★I MONELLI

4017 Johnston St., Lafayette, 337-989-9291

Italian menu. Lunch, dinner. Closed Sunday-Monday. $$

★★LA FONDA

3809 Johnston St., Lafayette, 337-984-5630

Mexican menu. Lunch, dinner. Closed Sunday-Monday. $$

★★POOR BOY'S RIVERSIDE INN

240 Tubing Road, Lafayette, 337-235-8559; www.poorboysriversideinn.com

Cajun, seafood menu. Lunch, dinner. Closed Sunday. $$

★PREJEAN'S RESTAURANT

3480 I-49N, Lafayette, 337-896-3247; www.prejeans.com

Cajun menu. Breakfast, lunch, dinner. $$

★RANDOL'S

2320 Kaliste Saloom Road, Lafayette, 337-981-7080, 800-962-2586; www.randols.com

Seafood menu. Dinner. Bar. $$

★★★RUTH'S CHRIS STEAK HOUSE

620 W. Pinhook Road, Lafayette, 337-237-6123; www.ruthschris.com

Prime steaks broiled in a custom-built oven and served sizzling in a pool of butter on a very hot plate characterize this upscale chain. À la carte vegetables include creamed

★
★
★
★
★

spinach; asparagus with hollandaise sauce; and baked, mashed, lyonnaise, or au gratin potatoes. Steak menu. Lunch, dinner. **$$$**

LAKE CHARLES

With more than 75 festivals each year, Lake Charles and the surrounding cities of Southwest Louisiana are proud to be known as the "Festival Capital" of the state. Visitors who want to bask in the tropical climate can fish or hike the Creole Nature Trail, while those looking for more temperate entertainment can take in one of the city's several museums.

Information: Southwest Louisiana Convention & Visitors Bureau,
1205 N. Lakeshore Drive, 337-436-9588, 800-456-7952; www.visitlakecharles.org

WHAT TO SEE AND DO

BRIMSTONE HISTORICAL SOCIETY MUSEUM

800 Picard Road, Sulphur, 337-527-7142; www.brimstonemuseum.org/brimstone.asp
The museum commemorates the turn-of-the-century birth of the local sulfur industry with exhibits explaining the development of the Frasch mining process; other exhibits deal with southwest Louisiana. Monday-Friday.

CREOLE NATURE TRAIL NATIONAL SCENIC BYWAY

1205 N. Lakeshore Drive, Sulphur, 800-456-7952; www.creolenaturetrail.org
The nature trail follows Highway 27 in a circular route ending back at Lake Charles. It's a unique composite of wildflowers, animals, shrimp, crab and many varieties of fish, plus one of the largest alligator populations in the world; a winter habitat of thousands of ducks and geese; views of several bayous, Intracoastal Waterway, oil platforms, beaches, four wildlife refuges and a bird sanctuary. Take the automobile nature trail (180 miles) or the walking nature trail (1 ½ miles). For a map, contact the Convention & Visitors Bureau. Daily.

HISTORIC "CHARPENTIER"

Lake Charles
The district includes 20 square blocks of downtown area; architectural styles range from Queen Anne, Eastlake and Carpenter's Gothic (known locally as "Lake Charles style") to Western stick-style bungalows. Tours (fee) and brochures describing self-guided tours may be obtained at the Convention & Visitors Bureau.

IMPERIAL CALCASIEU MUSEUM

204 W. Sallier St., Lake Charles, 337-439-3797; www.imperialcalcasieumuseum.org
Items of local historical interest, a toy collection and rare Audubon prints can be found at this museum. The Gibson-Barham Gallery houses art exhibits. On the premises is the 300-year-old Sallier oak tree. Tuesday-Saturday.

PORT OF LAKE CHARLES

150 Marine St., Lake Charles, West end of Shell Beach Drive; www.portlc.com
Docks and a turning basin are here. Ships pass down the Calcasieu ship channel and through Lake Calcasieu.

203

LOUISIANA

★
★
★
☆
☆

SAM HOUSTON JONES STATE PARK

107 Sutherland Road, Lake Charles, 888-677-7264;
www.lastateparks.com/sanhoust/Shjones.htm

The approximately 1,000 acres includes lagoons in a densely wooded area at the confluence of the west fork of the Caslcasieu and Houston Rivers and the Indian Bayou. Fishing, boating (rentals, launch), nature trails, hiking, picnicking, tent and trailer sites, cabins provide lots of recreation. Daily.

SPECIAL EVENTS

CFMA CAJUN MUSIC AND FOOD FESTIVAL

Burton Coliseum, 7001 Gulf Highway, Lake Charles, 800-456-7952;
www.cfmalakecharles.org

The festival includes entertainment, contests and arts and crafts. Late July.

CONTRABAND DAYS

Lake Charles Civic Center, 900 Lake Shore Drive, Lake Charles, 337-436-5508,
800-456-7952; www.contrabanddays.com

This event honors "gentleman pirate" Jean Lafitte. Boat races, midway, concerts and an arts and crafts display are some of the planned activities. Two weeks in early May.

HORSE RACING

2717 Deltadowns Drive, Vinton, 337-589-7441, 800-737-3358; www.deltadowns.com

Delta Downs is 30 miles west via I-10. You must be 18 to enter; a jacket is required in the Clubhouse and the Skyline. Thoroughbreds September-March, Thursday-Saturday; Sunday matinee. Quarter horse racing April-Labor Day.

HOTEL

★BEST WESTERN RICHMOND SUITES HOTEL

2600 Moeling St., Lake Charles, 337-433-5213, 800-643-2582; www.bestwestern.com

140 rooms. High-speed Internet access. Complimentary full breakfast. Airport transportation available. Fitness center. Outdoor pool. Spa. $

SPECIALTY LODGINGS

A RIVER'S EDGE BED & BREAKFAST

2035 Gus St., Westlake, 337-497-1525; www.lakecharlesbedbreakfast.com

This bed and breakfast is set between a winding bayou and its own private island. Guests are greeted with smoothies, homemade cookies, cold cuts, cheese and crackers. Three rooms. $

AUNT RUBY'S BED & BREAKFAST

504 Pujo St., Lake Charles, 318-430-0603; www.auntrubys.com

Constructed in 1911, guest rooms have private baths and there's a gourmet breakfast in the morning. Six rooms. $

C.A.'S HOUSE BED & BREAKFAST

624 Ford St., Lake Charles, 337-439-6672; www.waltersattic.com

This three-story colonial house was originally built in the early 1900s. It is in the Charpentier Historic District and was once owned by the president of the Huber Motor Oil Company and Quality Oil Company. Five rooms. $$

WALTER'S ATTIC BED & BREAKFAST
618 Ford St., Lake Charles, 337-439-6672, 866-439-6672; www.waltersattic.com
This inn is in the Charpentier Historic District and caters to couples on their honeymoons or celebrating anniversaries. It features a heated pool and fireplaces. Five rooms. Outdoor pool.

RESTAURANTS
★★PAT'S OF HENDERSON
1500 Siebarth Drive, Lake Charles, 337-439-6618; www.patsofhenderson.com
Cajun menu. Lunch, dinner. $$

★★PEKING GARDEN
2433 E. Broad St., Lake Charles, 337-436-3597
Chinese menu. Lunch, dinner. $$

★★PUJO STREET CAFE
901 Ryan St., Lake Charles, 337-439-2054; www.pujostreet.com
Creole menu. Lunch, dinner. Closed Sunday evening. $

★STEAMBOAT BILL'S
732 Martin Luther King Highway, Lake Charles, 337-494-1700;
www.steamboatbills.com
Creole menu. Lunch. $

★TONY'S PIZZA
335 E. Prien Lake Road, Lake Charles, 337-477-1611; www.tonyspizzainc.com
Italian menu. Lunch, dinner. $

MANDEVILLE
Located on the north shore of Lake Pontchartrain, across from New Orleans, Mandeville boasts a rich musical history of jazz and blues.
Information: Mandeville City Hall, 3101 E. Causeway Approach, Mandeville,
985-624-3145

RESTAURANT
★★★TREY YUEN
600 N. Causeway, Mandeville, 985-626-4476;
www.treyyuen.com/treyyuenmandeville.htm
Fresh local seafood defines the restaurant's unorthodox Chinese menu, which includes alligator dishes, soft-shell crab items and crawfish creations. Koi ponds, footbridges and custom-built carvings outside give diners a hint of Asia. Chinese menu. Lunch, dinner. $$

MANY
See 19th-century army living quarters or peer into blooming gardens.
Information: Sabine Parish Tourist Commission, 920 Fisher Road, 318-256-5880

★
★
★
★
★

WHAT TO SEE AND DO

FORT JESUP STATE HISTORIC SITE

32 Geohagan Road, Many, 318-256-4117, 888-677-5378;
www.lastateparks.com/fortjes/ftjesup.htm

This fort on 21 acres, established in 1822 by Zachary Taylor (before he took his post at the White House), features a restored 1830s army kitchen, reconstructed officers' quarters and a museum. Picnic facilities are available. Daily.

HODGES GARDENS

110 Hodges Loop, Many, 318-586-3523; www.hodgesgardens.com

Wild and cultivated flowers and plants grow year-round on 4,700 acres of gardens and greenhouses. There's also a 225-acre lake. The Terrazzo map commemorates the Louisiana Purchase. Wildlife, fishing boat rentals and picnic facilities are available. Special events include Easter service, July Fourth festival and Christmas lights festival. Daily.

SPECIAL EVENTS

BATTLE OF PLEASANT HILL RE-ENACTMENT

18 miles north on Highway 175, north of Pleasant Hill, 318-872-1310;
www.battleofpleasanthill.com

The three-day event includes a beauty pageant, Confederate ball, parade and battle reenactment. Early April.

SABINE FREE STATE FESTIVAL

237 W. Port Arthur Ave., Florien, 318-586-7286;
www.sabineparish.com/fest/freestate.asp

This festival offers a beauty pageant; syrup-making, basket-weaving and quilting demonstrations; arts and crafts exhibits; and a flea market. First weekend in November.

METAIRIE

This suburb of New Orleans lures locals and out-of-towners alike to see the Zephyrs baseball team.

Information: Jefferson Convention and Visitors Bureau,
1221 Elmwood Park Blvd., Jefferson, 504-731-7083; www.metairie.com

WHAT TO SEE AND DO

NEW ORLEANS ZEPHYRS

6000 Airline Highway (Highway 61), Metairie, 504-734-5155; www.zephyrsbaseball.com

The Zephyrs first took the field in 1993 as the AAA farm team for the Houston Astros. They play ball at the 10,000-seat Zephyr Field, cheered on by team mascots Boudreaux D. Nutria and his wife, Clotile, as well as their numerous offspring. (Nutria is a species of water-dwelling rodent, which is beneficial in Louisiana and Texas but viewed as destructive in other areas.) Early April-August.

HOTELS

★★DOUBLETREE HOTEL

3838 N. Causeway Blvd., Metairie, 504-836-5253, 800-222-8733;
www.doubletreelakeside.com

210 rooms. Restaurant, bar. Airport transportation available. $$

★★FOUR POINTS BY SHERATON NEW ORLEANS AIRPORT

6401 Veterans Memorial Blvd., Metairie, 504-885-5700; www.starwoodhotels.com
181 rooms. High-speed Internet access. Fitness center. Outdoor pool. Business center.
$$

RESTAURANTS

★★★ANDREA'S

3100 19th St., Metairie, 504-834-8583; www.andreasrestaurant.com
Italian menu. Lunch, dinner, Sunday brunch. **$$$**

★★IMPASTATO'S

3400 16th St., Metairie, 504-455-1545; www.impastatos.com
Italian menu. Dinner. Closed Sunday-Monday. **$$$**

★MORNING CALL

3325 Severn Ave., Metairie, 504-885-4068;
www.morningcallcoffeestand.com
Deli menu. Breakfast, lunch, dinner, late-night. **$**

★★MOSCA'S

4137 Highway 90 W., Avondale, 504-436-8950
Italian menu. Dinner. Closed Sunday-Monday; August. **$$$**

MINDEN

Named after a town in Germany, Minden hosted the wedding of country singer Hank
Williams Sr. in 1952.
Information: Chamber of Commerce, 110 Sibley Road, 318-377-4240, 800-264-6336;
www.minden.org

WHAT TO SEE AND DO

GERMANTOWN MUSEUM

120 Museum Road, Minden, 318-377-6061; www.mindenusa.com
The museum includes three buildings completed in 1835 by Germans seeking freedom from persecution; replicas of a communal smokehouse and a blacksmith shop;
as well as records and artifacts used by settlers. Wednesday-Sunday.

LAKE BISTINEAU STATE PARK

101 State Park Road, Minden, 318-745-3503, 888-677-2478;
www.lastateparks.com/lakebist/bistino.htm
This 750-acre park in the heart of a pine forest includes a large lake. Swimming,
waterskiing, fishing, boating (rentals, launch), tent and trailer sites and cabins are
among the offerings. Daily.

★
★
★
★

MONROE AND WEST MONROE

Located on the Ouachita River across from West Monroe, its smaller twin city,
Monroe is home to more than 50,000 residents and a University of Louisiana campus
with some 8,000 students. The city is proud of its business history; Monroe was the

first location west of the Mississippi to brew Coca-Cola and the birthplace of Delta Airlines.

Information: Monroe-West Monroe Convention & Visitors Bureau,
1333 State Farm Drive, Monroe, 318-387-5691, 800-843-1872; www.monroe.org

WHAT TO SEE AND DO
BRY HALL ART GALLERY
700 University Ave., Monroe, 318-342-1375
The gallery shows art exhibits, including photographs by American and foreign artists, students and faculty. Monday-Friday; closed mid-December-early January.

BIEDENHARN FAMILY HOUSE
2006 Riverside Drive, Monroe, 800-362-0983; www.bmuseum.org
This historic home is located at the Biedenharn Museum & Gardens. Built by Joseph Biedenharn, first bottler of Coca-Cola in 1914, the home contains antiques, fine furnishings, silver dating from the 18th century and Coca-Cola memorabilia.

BIEDENHARN MUSEUM & GARDENS
2006 Riverside Drive, Monroe, 318-387-5281; www.bmuseum.org
The property includes the Biedenharn Family House and Elsong Gardens & Conservatory. Daily.

ELSONG GARDENS & CONSERVATORY
2006 Riverside Drive, Monroe, 800-362-0983; www.bmuseum.org
Located at the Biedenharn Museum & Gardens, these formal gardens enclosed within brick walls, were originally designed to accommodate musical events. Today, visitors trigger background music when they amble through separate gardens linked by winding paths. There are four fountains, including one from the garden of Russian Empress Catherine the Great.

FISHING, WATER SPORTS
Monroe and West Monroe
To do some fishing or water sports, head to Ouachita River in the city, Chenire Lake (3,600 acres) four miles west, D'Arbonne Lake (15,000 acres) 35 miles north, Bayou DeSiard (1,200 acres) three miles northeast or Black Bayou (2,600 acres) six miles north.

LOUISIANA PURCHASE GARDENS AND ZOO
1405 Bernstien Park Drive, Monroe, 318-329-2400; www.monroezoo.org
Formal gardens, moss-laden live oaks, waterways and winding paths surround naturalistic habitats for more than 850 exotic animals in this 80-acre zoo. Boat and miniature train rides are also available, as are areas for picnics and concessions. Daily. Rides, concessions April-October only.

MASUR MUSEUM OF ART
1400 S. Grand St., Monroe and West Monroe, 318-329-2237; masurmuseum.org
The museum has permanent and changing exhibits. Tuesday-Sunday.

MUSEUM OF NATURAL HISTORY

700 University Ave., Monroe, 318-342-1868;
www.ulm.edu/~museum/Site/Welcome.html

Geological exhibits include Native American, Latin American and African artifacts. Monday-Friday; closed mid-December to early January.

MUSEUM OF ZOOLOGY

700 University Ave., Monroe, 318-342-1799

The fish collection is one of the largest and most complete in the nation. Monday-Friday; closed mid-August to early-September, mid-December to early-January.

UNIVERSITY OF LOUISIANA AT MONROE

700 University Ave., Monroe, 318-342-1000; www.ulm.edu

More than 11,000 students attend the university, founded in 1931.

HOTELS

★★HOLIDAY INN

1051 Highway, 165 Bypass, Monroe, 318-387-5100, 800-465-4329;
www.holiday-inn.com

260 rooms. High-speed Internet access. Complimentary breakfast. Restaurant, bar. Airport transportation available. Fitness center, fee. Outdoor pool. Pets accepted, fee. $

★LA QUINTA INN

1035 Highway, 165 Bypass, Monroe, 318-322-3900, 800-531-5900; www.laquinta.com

130 rooms. High-speed Internet access. Complimentary continental breakfast. Airport transportation available. Pets accepted. $

RESTAURANTS

★★CHATEAU

2007 Louisville Ave., Monroe, 318-325-0384

American, Italian menu. Lunch, dinner. Closed Sunday. $$

★★WAREHOUSE NO. 1

1 Olive St., Monroe, 318-322-1340; www.warehouseno1.com

Seafood menu. Dinner. Closed Sunday. $$$

LOUISIANA

MORGAN CITY

Morgan City is an ideal jumping-off point for almost any destination in Louisiana, located 70 miles west of New Orleans, 60 miles east of Lafayette and 60 miles south of Baton Rouge. The city is home to Louisiana's oldest harvest festival—the Shrimp and Petroleum Festival held each year over Labor Day weekend, complete with a horseshoe tournament, gospel concerts and the crowning of festival royalty.

Information: St. Mary Parish Tourist Commission, 112 Main St.,
985-395-4905, 800-256-2931; www.cityofmc.com

WHAT TO SEE AND DO

BROWNELL MEMORIAL PARK & CARILLON TOWER

3359 Highway 70, Morgan City, 985-384-2283

The park preserves swamp in its natural state; on the property is a 106-foot carillon tower with 61 bronze bells. Daily.

CAJUN JACK'S

112 Main St., Morgan City, 985-395-7420; www.cajunjack.com

See how Cajun people lived more than 200 years ago. And explore the area where the first Tarzan movie was filmed. There are two tours daily (three in summer): 9 a.m.-2.30 p.m.

FISHING AND HUNTING

A vast interlocking network of bayous, rivers and lakes with cypress, tupelo, gumwood forests and sugarcane fields makes the whole area excellent for small game and duck hunting and for fishing.

KEMPER WILLIAMS PARK

Patterson, eight miles west via Highway 90, Cotton Road exit in Patterson,
985-395-2298; www.stmaryparishdevelopment.com

This 290-acre park offers nature and jogging trails, tennis courts, a golf driving range, baseball diamonds, picnicking and camping (hookups; additional fee). Daily. 9 a.m.-6 p.m.

SCULLY'S SWAMP TOURS & RESTAURANT

3141 Highway 70, Morgan City, 985-385-2388

See local wildlife while enjoying authentic Cajun seafood on two-hour tours. Tuesday-Saturday.

SWAMP GARDENS AND WILDLIFE ZOO

In Heritage Park, 725 Myrtle St., Morgan City, 985-384-3343

Outdoor exhibits depict both the history of the human settlement of the great Atchafalaya Basin and the natural flora and fauna of the swamp. Guided walking tours are available only. Daily.

SPECIAL EVENT

LOUISIANA SHRIMP AND PETROLEUM FESTIVAL AND FAIR

715 second St., Morgan City, 985-385-0703; www.shrimp-petrofest.org

A great party with a strange name, the festival honors the men and women who work to keep the Cajun Coast afloat economically—in the fishing and petroleum industries. Labor Day weekend.

HOTEL

★★HOLIDAY INN

520 Roderick St., Morgan City, 985-385-2200; www.holiday-inn.com

224 rooms. High-speed Internet access. Restaurant, bar. Outdoor pool. Fitness center. Pets accepted, fee.

LOUISIANA

★
★
★
★
★

NATCHITOCHES

On and off the big screen (the city was the setting for the film *Steel Magnolias*), Natchitoches shines with its historic charms and outdoor attractions. Visitors can tour historic homes, working plantations and nature preserves or get in touch with their wild sides at the alligator park. The city's 33-block Historic Landmark District, home to historic houses, churches and businesses, is worth a visit.

Information: Natchitoches Parish Tourist Commission, 781 Front St., 318-352-8072, 800-259-1714; www.natchitoches.net

WHAT TO SEE AND DO

FORT ST. JEAN BAPTISTE STATE HISTORIC SITE

155 Rue Jefferson, Natchitoches, 318-357-3101; 888-677-7853; www.lastateparks.com/fortstj/ftstjean.htm

On this 5-acre site is a replica of the fort as it was when first built to halt Spanish movement into Louisiana; the restoration includes barracks, a warehouse, a chapel and a mess hall. Daily 9 a.m.-5 p.m.

MELROSE PLANTATION

3533 Highway 119, Natchitoches, 318-379-0055; www.nps.gov

The complex of eight plantation buildings includes Yucca House (circa 1795), the original cabin, the Big House and the African House. It originally was the residence of Marie Therese Coincoin, a former slave whose son developed the Spanish land grant into a thriving antebellum plantation. Melrose was restored at the turn of the 20th century by "Miss Cammie" Garrett Henry, who turned it into a repository of local arts and crafts. Tuesday-Sunday noon-4 p.m.

NATIONAL FISH HATCHERY & AQUARIUM

615 Highway 1 S., Natchitoches, 318-352-5324; www.fws.gov

The aquarium has 16 tanks of indigenous fish, turtles and alligators. Daily.

NORTHWESTERN STATE UNIVERSITY

College Avenue St., Natchitoches, 318-357-6011; www.nsula.edu

The 916-acre campus is on Chaplin's Lake. On the 9,400-student campus are the Louisiana Sports Writers Hall of Fame in Prather Coliseum, the Archives Room of Watson Memorial Library, the Folklife Center, the Williamson Archaeological Museum in Kyser Hall and the Normal Hill Historic District.

SPECIAL EVENTS

CHRISTMAS FESTIVAL OF LIGHTS

781 Front St., Natchitoches, 318-352-8072, 800-259-1714; www.christmasfestival.com

More than 140,000 lights are turned on after a full day of celebration to welcome the Christmas season. First Saturday in December.

MELROSE PLANTATION ARTS & CRAFTS FESTIVAL

3533 Highway 119, Natchitoches, 318-379-0055; www.nps.gov

The festival features juried works of more than 100 artists and craftspeople. Admission: adults $5, children $2. Second weekend in June 9 a.m.-5 p.m.

211

LOUISIANA

NATCHITOCHES-NORTHWESTERN FOLK FESTIVAL

NSU Prather Coliseum, 938 S. Jefferson St., Natchitoches, 318-357-4332; www.nsula.edu

The festival spotlights a different industry or occupation each year and works to preserve Louisiana folk art forms: music, dance, crafts, storytelling, food. Third weekend in July.

NATCHITOCHES PILGRIMAGE

781 Front St., Natchitoches, 318-352-8072; www.natchitochesfalltour.com

Take city and Cane River tours of houses and plantations, or try the candlelight tour. Second full weekend in October.

HOTEL

★COMFORT INN

5362 Highway 6, Natchitoches, 318-352-7500, 800-228-5150; www.choicehotels.com

59 rooms. High-speed Internet access. Complimentary continental breakfast. Outdoor pool. $

SPECIALTY LODGING

FLEUR DE LIS B & B

336 Second St., Natchitoches, 318-352-6621, 800-489-6621; www.fleurdelisbandb.com

This turn-of-the-century house is in the historic district of the Louisiana Purchase's oldest settlement. Five rooms. Complimentary full breakfast. $

RESTAURANT

★★LANDING

530 Front St., Natchitoches, 318-352-1579; www.thelandingrestaurantandbar.com

Cajun menu. Lunch, dinner, Sunday brunch. Closed Monday. $$

★LASYONE MEAT PIE KITCHEN

622 Second St., Natchitoches, 318-352-3353; www.lasyones.com

American, Cajun menu. Breakfast, lunch, dinner. Closed Sunday.

★★MARINERS SEAFOOD & STEAK HOUSE

5948 Highway 1 Bypass, Natchitoches, 318-357-1220; www.marinersrestaurant.com

Seafood, steak menu. Dinner, Sunday brunch. $$

NEW IBERIA

Located in the heart of Cajun country, New Iberia is home to a variety of attractions ranging from farmers markets to historic buildings (the city is home to the country's oldest rice mill) to the 200-acre Jungle Gardens. The city is known for a few Louisiana classics: swamps, bayous and alligators. Visitors looking to add some spice to their trip can watch the bottling and packing operations at the McIlhenny Company Tabasco Factory and Company Store.

Information: Iberia Parish Tourist Commission, 2704 Highway 14, 337-365-1540; www.cityofnewiberia.com

WHAT TO SEE AND DO

AVERY ISLAND

Seven miles southwest via Highway 14

Surrounded by a bayou, the island is a haven for colorful wildlife, including blue herons, white-tailed deer and small black bears. This unusual Eden is also where Tabasco sauce has been made for nearly 140 years. You have to take a toll road onto the island (fee); no bicycles or motorcycles are permitted.

BOULIGNY PLAZA

On Main Street in center of New Iberia

In the park are depictions of the history of the area as well as a gazebo, historic landmarks and a beautiful view along the bayou.

JUNGLE GARDENS

200 Center St., New Iberia Avery Island, 337-369-6243; www.junglegardens.org

Avery Island's most spectacular feature was developed by the late Edward Avery McIlhenny of Tabasco fame. Camellias, azaleas, irises and tropical plants, in season, form a beautiful display. Enormous flocks of egrets, cranes and herons, among other species, are protected here and may be seen in early spring and summer; ducks and other wild fowl can be spotted in winter. The Chinese Garden contains a fine Buddha dating from A.D. 1000. Daily.

KONRIKO RICE MILL AND COMPANY STORE

309 Ann St., New Iberia, 337-365-7242, 800-551-3245; www.conradricemill.com

Take a tour of the oldest rice mill in the U.S.; next door is a replica of the original company store, with antique fixtures and merchandise typical of Acadiana and Louisiana. Monday-Saturday.

MCILHENNY COMPANY

Highway 329, Avery Island, 337-365-8173; www.tabasco.com

Spice up your day with a tour of the Tabasco factory and Country Store. Monday-Saturday.

★
★
★
★

RIP VAN WINKLE GARDENS

5505 Rip Van Winkle Road, New Iberia, 337-359-8525; www.ripvanwinklegardens.com

Stroll through 20 acres of landscaped gardens and nature preserve. Also on the premises is the Victorian residence of 19th-century actor Joseph Jefferson (tours). Stop in the restaurant and gift shop. Admission: adults $10, children $8. Daily 9 a.m.

SHADOWS-ON-THE-TECHE

317 E. Main St., New Iberia, 337-369-6446; www.shadowsontheteche.org

The red brick and white-pillared Greek Revival house was built on the banks of the Bayou Teche in 1834 by sugar planter David Weeks. Home to four generations of his family, it served as the center of an antebellum plantation system. The house was restored and its celebrated gardens created in the 1920s by the builder's great-grandson, Weeks Hall, who used the estate to entertain such celebrities as D. W. Griffith, Anaïs Nin and Walt Disney. The house is surrounded by three acres of azaleas, camellias and massive oaks draped in Spanish moss. It's a National Trust for Historic Preservation property. Daily 9 a.m.-4:30 p.m.

ANDALUSIA MARDI GRAS PARADE

Main St., New Iberia, 337-365-1540, 888-942-3742; www.iberiatravel.com
Friday before Mardi Gras.

SUGAR CANE FESTIVAL AND FAIR

Various locations in New Iberia, 337-369-9323, 888-942-3742; www.hisugar.org
Last full weekend in September.

HOTEL
★★HOLIDAY INN

2915 Highway 14, New Iberia, 337-367-1201, 800-465-4329; www.holidayinn.com
177 rooms. Restaurant, bar. **$**

SPECIALTY LODGING
LE ROSIER

314 E. Main St., New Iberia, 337-367-5306, 888-804-7673; www.lerosier.com
The 1870 country inn is tucked behind a main house and framed by a rear deck, patio and front veranda. The gardens of antique roses, day lilies and other perennials provide an ideal setting for cocktails and wine tasting. Six rooms. Children over 12 years only. Complimentary full breakfast. **$**

RESTAURANT
★LITTLE RIVER INN

833 E. Main St., New Iberia, 337-367-7466; www.poorboysriversideinn.com
Cajun, seafood menu. Lunch, dinner. Closed Sunday. **$$**

214

LOUISIANA

★
★
★
★
★

NEW ORLEANS

New Orleans is a beguiling combination of old and new, and in the wake of Hurricane Katrina, it has become a symbol of both hardship and rebirth. Though many homes, businesses and historic landmarks were heavily damaged by the 2005 storm, Katrina failed to wash away the city's spirit, charm or storied past.

Named for the Duc d'Orleans, Regent of France, New Orleans was founded by the French, ruled by the Spanish, purchased by the United States and captured by Union forces—all in the span of about 100 years. Of course, this eclectic history has helped make New Orleans a must-see for travelers in search of great food (served with a side of music), gorgeous architecture and the colorful characters who call the "Big Easy" home.

New Orleans has a reputation for being seductive and decadent, magical and sensual. That reputation is still well deserved, even after Katrina—and subsequent broken levees—flooded the city and destroyed some of its most precious institutions. Parts of New Orleans are still recovering, but many of the city's historic districts did not flood—a hint of mercy in the midst of so much destruction. These areas, including the French Quarter and the Garden District, have been open for business for a while now, and visitors are rushing in to enjoy the famous cuisine and jazz and blues clubs that make New Orleans one of the country's most beloved destinations.

Food rules here. Locals believe they have the best cuisine in the nation, much of it influenced by Cajun and Creole cultures that flourish in Louisiana and featuring seafood from the Gulf of Mexico. Do not leave without eating a shrimp or hot sausage po' boy, gumbo, shrimp rémoulade, white-chocolate bread pudding and a few beignets.

Visitors also come for the amazing nightlife. Walking down Bourbon Street, you will hear music pouring from every doorway: Cajun, zydeco, jazz. The bottom line is that no one comes home from New Orleans disappointed.

Information: New Orleans Metropolitan Convention & Visitors Bureau, 1520 Sugar Bowl Drive, 504-566-5011, 800-672-6124; www.neworleanscvb.com

DEMYSTIFYING NEW ORLEANS-SPEAK

Cajun: Nickname for a Louisianan descended from the French-speaking people who began migrating to Louisiana from Nova Scotia (then Acadia) in 1755.

Creole: A person descended from early French or Spanish settlers of the U.S. Gulf states who preserves their speech and culture.

Creole: Highly seasoned food typically prepared with rice, okra, tomatoes and peppers.

Fais-do-do: When Cajuns partied in days gone by, they would bring their children along, bundle them in their blankets at bedtime, put them to sleep and party into the wee hours. *Fais-do-do* means "put the kids to sleep."

Faubourg: (FOE-burg) Faubourgs are neighborhoods near the French Quarter. Literally, *Faubourg* means "suburb."

French Quarter: The 90 square blocks that used to be the entire city of New Orleans and today encompasses 2,700 European- and Creole-style buildings.

Gris-gris: Means "X marks the spot." An X on a tomb indicates a voodoo spell, like that on the tomb of the mysterious Marie Laveau, New Orleans hairdresser-turned-legendary-voodoo-queen.

Gumbo ya-ya: Everybody talking at once.

Jazz: Louis Armstrong said, "If you gotta ask, you'll never know." With apologies to Armstrong, jazz mixes African and Creole rhythms with European styles. Irish, Germans and Italians added the brass.

Krewe: Wealthy 19th-century New Orleans citizens who bankrolled Mardi Gras balls and parades were members of carnival organizations with names like Rex (King of the Carnival). Members were called Krewe of Rex, a variation of the word *crew*.

Pass a good time: Live it up.

Vieux Carré: Old Square or Old Quarter, referring to the French Quarter.

Voodoo: A combination of the West African Yoruba religion and the Catholicism of French colonists in Haiti. It means "god, spirit or insight" in the Fon language of Dahomey, a former country in West Africa on the Gulf of Guinea.

Yat: A citizen. This term comes from the Ninth Ward greeting, "Where yat?"

LOUISIANA

★
★
★

WHAT TO SEE AND DO

AMPERSAND

1100 Tulane Ave., New Orleans, 504-587-3737; www.clubampersand.com

Sophisticatedly naughty, this converted bank building features two levels, two bars, a huge dance floor, an outdoor courtyard and several sitting rooms, one in the former bank vault. Appealing to serious clubbers of all stripes, Ampersand offers DJs from around the world spinning music of the techno and industrial persuasion. Friday-Saturday at 11 p.m.

AUDUBON AQUARIUM OF THE AMERICAS

1 Canal St., Riverfront Area, New Orleans, 504-861-2537, 800-774-7394; www.auduboninstitute.org

True to its name, this aquarium houses more than 10,000 aquatic creatures from all areas of the Americas. For total immersion without getting wet, walk through the aquatic tunnel in the Caribbean Reef section or catch a glimpse of a rare white alligator through the River View window in the Mississippi section. Boasting the largest collection of jellyfish in the world, the aquarium also houses penguins, sea otters and sharks—brave visitors can touch one. Combination Aquarium/Zoo, Aquarium/IMAX and Aquarium/IMAX/Zoo tickets are available. Sunday-Tuesday: 10 a.m.-5 p.m., Friday-Saturday 10 a.m.-7 p.m.

AUDUBON NATURE INSTITUTE

6500 Magazine St., New Orleans, 504-861-2537; 800-774-7394; www.auduboninstitute.org

This 400-acre park designed by the Olmsted brothers is nestled between St. Charles Avenue and the Mississippi River and is surrounded by century-old live oak trees. The park features a Par-62 18-hole golf course, bicycle and jogging paths and tennis courts. Daily.

AUDUBON ZOO

6500 Magazine St., New Orleans, 504-861-2537, 800-774-7394; www.auduboninstitute.org/zoo

More than 1,800 animals from every continent call this top-ranked zoo, part of the Audubon Nature Institute, home. Check out kangaroos from Australia, llamas from South America, white tigers from Asia and zebras from Africa, all in naturalistic habitats. Indigenous furry, feathered and scaly creatures are featured at the Louisiana Swamp Exhibit. You can get up close during the sea lion show and in the Embraceable Zoo. Discovery walks, the EarthLab and other interactive programs make the zoo an educational experience. (Just don't tell the kids.) Combination Zoo/Aquarium and Zoo/Aquarium/IMAX tickets are available. Daily from 10 a.m-4 p.m.

BAYOU BARRIERE GOLF COURSE

7427 Highway 23, Belle Chasse, 504-394-9500; www.bayoubarriere.com

This course is fairly flat but strives to offer variety from hole to hole. The fairways differ in width and water comes into play, but at different points in each hole. The prices are reasonable, and the course is open year-round. With 27 holes onsite, the facility accommodates high levels of traffic well, and you can explore various combinations of holes to find your favorite 18. The most challenging nine is the third, as the tee boxes are mostly on the course's levee.

★
★
★
★
★

BEAUREGARD-KEYES HOUSE AND GARDEN

1113 Chartres St., New Orleans, 504-523-7257; www.neworleansmuseums.com

This Greek Revival, Louisiana-raised cottage was restored by its former owner, the novelist Frances Parkinson Keyes. Confederate Army Gen. Pierre G. T. Beauregard lived here for more than a year following the Civil War. Exhibits include the main house and servant quarters, which together form a handsome shaded courtyard. (Keyes actually lived informally in the servant quarters, which are filled with her books, antiques and family heirlooms.) To the side of the main house is a formal garden (visible from both Chartres and Ursulines Streets) that is part of the guided tour conducted by costumed docents. Admission: adults $5, seniors $4, children $2. Monday-Saturday 10 a.m.-3 p.m.

BOURBON STREET

French Quarter, New Orleans, 504-525-5801; www.bourbonstreetexperience.com

No place in the world can match Bourbon Street for round-the-clock fun. With elegant hotels next door to garish strip clubs, Bourbon Street contains the ever-beating heart of the French Quarter. Visit its shops and restaurants in the daytime if you're not up for the always-rowdy nighttime crowds. But if you're visiting the Big Easy to let the good times roll, there's no better place to start a night of rambunctious partying.

BRULATOUR COURTYARD

520 Royal St., New Orleans

The Courtyard is lined with interesting shops.

THE CABILDO

217

701 Chartres St., New Orleans, 504-523-3939; www.friendsofthecabildo.org

Part of the Louisiana State Museum, the Cabildo offers exhibits on life in early New Orleans, including plantation and slave life. Construction was completed in 1799 and the building housed the city council and the Louisiana Supreme Court at various times. In 1803, the transfer of the Louisiana Purchase took place here. The museum covers diverse topics such as burial customs, women's roles in the South and immigrants' fate. Admission: adults $12, seniors $10, children free. Tuesday-Sunday 10 a.m.-1.30 p.m.

CATHEDRAL GARDEN

615 Pere Antoine Alley, New Orleans, 504-525-9585; www.stlouiscathedral.org

The monument in the center of the garden was erected in honor of French marines who died while nursing New Orleans' citizens during a yellow fever outbreak. Picturesque, narrow Pirate's Alley, bordering the garden, is a favorite spot for painters. On the Alley is the house in which William Faulkner lived when he wrote his first novel. The garden is also called St. Anthony's Square in memory of a beloved priest known as Pere Antoine.

CEMETERY & VOODOO HISTORY TOUR

334-B Royal St., New Orleans, 504-947-2120; www.tourneworleans.com

The two-hour tour features St. Louis Cemetery No. 1, the oldest and most significant burial ground in New Orleans; visits to a practicing voodoo priestess at her temple; Congo Square, the site of early slave gatherings; and a stop at the home of legendary Voodoo Queen Marie Laveau. Monday-Saturday 10 a.m. and 1 p.m.; Sunday 10 a.m.

LOUISIANA

CENTER OF BANKING

Royal Street, New Orleans

The old Louisiana State Bank was designed in 1821 by Benjamin Latrobe, one of the architects of the Capitol in Washington. The 343 Royal building was completed in the early 1800s for the old Bank of the United States. The old Bank of Louisiana, 334 Royal, was built in 1826; it is now the French Quarter Police Station.

CITY PARK

1 Palm Drive, New Orleans, 504-482-4888; www.neworleanscitypark.com

The 1,500 acres of City Park provide room for all sorts of family fun. Step into Storyland to glide down the dragon-flame slide, board Captain Hook's ship or engage with actors portraying storybook characters. Hop aboard one of two minitrains and mount a steed on one of the oldest wooden carousels in the U.S. Get some spray from Popp Fountain, get a license and catch some fish in one of the many lagoons, or bask in Marconi Meadow and catch some rays. Admire a range of architectural styles in various buildings and bridges. Appreciate the natural beauty in the Botanical Garden and see more mature oak trees than any other place in the world. Get active and rent a boat or play tennis, golf or softball in the park's facilities. Check for events at Tad Gormley Stadium.

CONTEMPORARY ARTS CENTER

900 Camp St., New Orleans, 504-528-3805; www.cacno.org

Established in 1976, the Contemporary Arts Center (CAC) is housed in an award-winning building that was renovated in 1990. Each year, CAC hosts as many as two dozen exhibitions in its 10,000 square feet of gallery space. Taking a multidisciplinary approach, the center promotes art forms as traditional as painting, photography and sculpture, and as diverse as performance art, dance, music and video. Artists Studio Days offer children and their elders a glimpse into the creative process. The Dog & Pony Theater company-in-residence presents workshops, rehearsals and dance and theater productions. CAC also hosts the annual Black Theater Festival during the first two weekends in October. Tuesday-Sunday11 a.m.-5 p.m.

CRESCENT CITY FARMERS MARKET

700 Magazine St., New Orleans, 504-861-5898; www.crescentcityfarmersmarket.org

Choose the day and location to suit your needs. At this market, regional vendors offer fresh produce, seafood, baked goods and other edibles, as well as cut flowers and bedding plants. Each location offers frequent cooking demonstrations with area chefs and a variety of food-related events. Market founders promote sound ecological and economic development in the greater New Orleans area. The Tuesday Market takes place between Levee and Broadway in the parking lot of Uptown Square, at 200 Broadway from 10 a.m. to 1 p.m. The Wednesday Market is between French Market Place and Governor Nicholls Street from 10 a.m. to 2 p.m. The Thursday Market sits on the renovated American Can Company residential development at 3700 Orleans Avenue from 3 to 7 p.m. The Saturday Market is in the downtown neighborhood known as the Warehouse District (originally known as the American Sector), at Magazine and Girod Streets, at 700 Magazine Street from 8 a.m. to noon.

THE BIG EASY

The list of nicknames for New Orleans is almost as long as a krewe parade at Mardi Gras. Most are easily understood. Because of the way the Mississippi River curves around one side of town, New Orleans is called "The Crescent City." Its lively, colorful French Quarter gave way to "The City That Care Forgot." "Parade City USA" is a tribute to Mardi Gras; "Birthplace of Jazz" is self-explanatory. And anyone who has ever set foot inside a New Orleans restaurant understands the moniker "City of the Chefs."

But what of the nickname most closely associated with the "City of Saints and Sinners" (football and revelers): The Big Easy?

Some say that the nickname is a relatively recent one. In the early 1970s, a columnist for The *Times-Picayune* compared New Orleans' relaxed style with the hurry-up pace of New York; if New York is the Big Apple, she wrote, then New Orleans is the Big Easy. In 1970, police reporter James Conaway wrote a novel of corruption and romance in New Orleans and called it *The Big Easy*. The term became firmly planted in American lexicon when the novel became a 1987 movie starring Dennis Quaid and Ellen Barkin.

But the nickname's origins are actually thought to have taken root nearly a century earlier, at the dawn of the Jazz Age. In the early 1900s, Buddy Bolden became the first of the great New Orleans jazz legends, playing his cornet in all the hot spots, including Uptown, Gretna and the new Storyville district at Rampart and Perdido Streets. He took smoky center stage at clubs like the Come Clean and the Funky Butt (which became his theme song, and where a very young Louis Armstrong listened nightly). Bolden was said to have played in a dance club called Big Easy Hall. Another early-1900s jazz legend, bass man George Pops Foster, made reference to the Big Easy club in his book *Pops Foster: The Autobiography of a New Orleans Jazz Man*. Because jazz musicians are known to give nicknames to everything and everybody, the name might refer to a dance hall, or it might have been a dance itself.

In the end, the name's relevance to the city is best summed up in the reaction a visitor is likely to get when asking about its origin. Query any two people, and the answer is likely to be the same: Just like anything else in New Orleans, they will say, it just *is*.

★
★
★
★

THE FRENCH QUARTER

New Orleans practically begs visitors to stroll her scenic streets, and the city's most prestigious addresses are all on Royal Street, which is lined with historic buildings, fine restaurants and some of the nation's most exclusive antique shops. The most refined street in the Quarter, Royal is only a block south and a world away from party-hearty Bourbon Street. Even if you cannot afford to buy the Louis XVI carved mahogany love-seat, this strip is a great place to wander and window-shop.

A good starting point for exploring this part of New Orleans is behind St. Louis Cathedral, a block up from Jackson Square, where a lush collection of tropical plants fills the compact St. Anthony's Garden. Follow the alleyway upriver to 324 Pirates Alley, where author William Faulkner lived in 1925. His fans still flock to that corner, now the home of a popular bookstore featuring the works of this bard of Southern letters. Continue down Pirates Alley and away from the river along St. Peter to return to Royal Street.

Near St. Peter and Royal Streets, the brick LaBranche buildings, with their dramatic cast-iron galleries, were built starting in 1835. Proceed upriver along Royal Street. Beyond Toulouse Street, the 1798 Court of Two Lions at 541 Royal Street features marble lions atop the entry posts. The same architect built the neighboring house (527-533 Royal Street) in 1792. Now home to the Historic New Orleans Collection (504-523-4662), the house museum displays exhibits on the city's history.

Between St. Louis and Conti Streets, the huge State Supreme Court Building dominates the block; the baroque edifice is made of white Georgia marble. Further down, between Conti and Bienville Streets, the block-long Monteleone Hotel is a posh, 600-room home-away-from-home.

Head north on Iberville to Bourbon Street, pass restaurants, night-clubs and saloons, and then drop down St. Ann Street back to Royal, where the Café des Exiles marks the historical gathering spot of French refugees from the Revolution. Further downriver, a detour down Dumaine lands you in front of Madame John's Legacy (632 Dumaine, 504-568-6968). This French cottage was one of the few structures to survive the fire that destroyed most of the city in 1794. Return to Royal and proceed downriver to the cornstalk fence at 915 Royal, a site that draws onlookers and carriage tours that stop to admire the intricate tasseled design of the ironwork.

The Gallier House at 1118-32 Royal Street (504-525-5661) was built in the 1860s by acclaimed local architect James Gallier Jr. Then head down Ursulines Avenue to the old Ursulines Convent at the corner of Chartres Street. The 1745 convent is among the oldest structures in the city. Continue down Ursulines toward the river to visit the French Market, or return upriver along Chartres Street to make it back to Jackson Square.

★
★ ★
★ ★
★

DELTA QUEEN AND MISSISSIPPI QUEEN STERNWHEELERS

1380 Port of New Orleans, Place New Orleans, 504-586-0631, 800-543-1949;
www.majesticamerica.com

The sternwheelers *Delta Queen* and *Mississippi Queen* offer three- to 12-night cruises on the Mississippi, Ohio, Cumberland and Tennessee rivers year-round.

DESTREHAN PLANTATION

13034 River Road, Destrehan, 985-764-9315, 877-453-2095;
www.destrehanplantation.org

Built in 1787, this is the oldest plantation house left intact in the lower Mississippi Valley, with ancient live oaks adorning the grounds. Guided tours are available. Daily.

ENTERGY IMAX THEATRE

1 Canal St., New Orleans, 504-581-4327, 800-774-7394;
www.auduboninstitute.org/imax

Adjacent to the Audubon Aquarium of the Americas and part of the Audubon Nature Institute, this theater showcases several films at a time in larger-than-life format and hosts a summer film festival. Combination IMAX/Aquarium and IMAX/Aquarium/Zoo tickets are available. Daily from 10 a.m.

F & F BOTANICA

801 N. Broad St., New Orleans, 504-482-9142

The oldest and largest spiritual supply store in the French Quarter, F & F Botanica offers herbs, oils, potions, candles, incense—whatever you need to enhance your spiritual practice. The store offers free spiritual consultations to help you figure out how to find what your spirit seeks. At least one staffer is sure to speak Spanish to help customers who share owner Felix Figueroa's heritage. Monday-Saturday 8 a.m.-6 p.m.

FAIR GROUNDS RACE COURSE

1751 Gentilly Blvd., New Orleans, 504-944-5515; www.fairgroundsracecourse.com

The horses have been darting out of the starting gates at this Mid-City racetrack since 1852, making it the oldest track still operating in the United States. When you're not placing bets and watching the fast-paced action, wander through the Racing Hall of Fame, which honors 110 of the sport's most revered, such as legendary jockey Bill Shoemaker and Duncan Kenner, the founding father of racing in this country. The 145-acre facility also hosts the city's annual Jazz and Heritage Festival. Thanksgiving Day-March: races start at 12:30 p.m.

FRENCH MARKET

800 Decatur St. New Orleans, 504-525-4544; www.cafedumonde.com

A farmers market for nearly two centuries, the market is home to the popular Cafe du Monde, a famous coffee stand specializing in café au lait (half coffee with chicory, half hot milk) and beignets (square-shaped doughnuts sprinkled with powdered sugar). The café never closes (except December 25), and café au lait and beignets are inexpensive. The downriver end of the French Market houses booths in which produce is sold.

LOUISIANA

★
★
★
★

FRENCH QUARTER

From Canal Street to Esplanade Avenue, and from Decatur Street on the Mississippi
River to Rampart Street, 504-636-1020; www.frenchquarter.com

Whether you are in New Orleans to party, shop till you drop, soak up Creole (or voo-doo) charms, sample Southern hospitality, delve into history or admire architecture, you can find what you want in the Vieux Carré. The oldest and only remaining French and Spanish settlement in the country, the Quarter offers sights, sounds, tastes and treasures to suit every interest.

FRENCH QUARTER WALKING TOURS

www.frenchquarter.com

Both the Friends of Cabildo (1850 House Museum Store, 523 St. Ann St. on Jackson Square, 504-523-3939) and the French Quarter Visitor Center (419 Decatur St., 504-589-2636) offer walking tours that cover the Quarter's history and architecture. The pace is not strenuous, but factor in the heat and humidity and dress accordingly. Licensed guides conduct the two-hour Friends of Cibaldo tours, while interpreters from the National Park Service lead a 90-minute free tour, which is restricted to the first 25 people who show up each day. A Cibaldo tour ticket entitles you to a discount on items at the 1850 House Museum Store. Daily.

GALLIER HOUSE

1132 Royal St., New Orleans, 504-525-5661; www.hgghh.org

For a slice of pre-Civil War life in New Orleans, check out the architect James Gal-lier Jr.'s home, which he designed for himself in 1857. Thoroughly modern for its time, the house boasts hot-and-cold running water and an indoor bathroom. Painstak-ingly restored, the house is one of New Orleans' more beautiful historic landmarks. Monday-Friday 10 a.m.-4 p.m.

THE GARDEN DISTRICT

Magazine Street and Washington Avenue, New Orleans

Once the social center of New Orleans American (as opposed to Creole) aristocracy, the district has beautiful Greek Revival and Victorian houses with palms, magnolias and enormous live oaks on the spacious grounds in this area. A walking tour of the Garden District, conducted by a national park ranger, departs from First Street and St. Charles Avenue (by appointment).

GRAY LINE BUS TOURS

1 Toulouse St., New Orleans, 504-569-1401, 800-535-7786;
www.graylineneworleans.com

View all of New Orleans' must-see sites from the comfort of an air-conditioned bus. Besides its comprehensive city tour, Gray Line offers numerous other sightseeing options, including tours of plantations, swamps and bayous, the Garden District and cemeteries. An off-the-beaten path trek takes you to such places as the childhood neighborhood of jazz great Louis Armstrong and Faubourg Marigny, one of the earliest Creole suburbs, where the striking architecture will surely grab your attention. The company now offers a Hurricane Katrina tour, highlighting the city before, during and after the storm.

★
★
★
★

GRIFFIN FISHING CHARTERS

2629 Privateer Blvd., Lafitte, 800-741-1340; www.neworleansfishintours.com

Specializing in shallow-sea fishing for speckled trout and redfish in saltwater marshes from Lafitte down to the Gulf of Mexico, owners Raymond and Belinda Griffin can also set you up for a day of deep-sea fishing. Or combine two pursuits: Play golf in the morning and then head out to the water for some fishing. Prices include an out-of-state fishing license, rods, reels, bait, tackle, ice, po' boy sandwiches, soda, water and the cleaning and packaging of caught fish. Package plans that include lodging, meals and transportation are also available.

HARRAH'S NEW ORLEANS

8 Canal St., New Orleans, 504-533-6000, 800-847-5299; www.harrahs.com

The oldest of New Orleans's land-based casinos, Harrah's is 115,000 square feet of nonstop gambling fun. More than 100 tables offer 10 different games, including poker, craps, baccarat and roulette. You can play the slots for a penny, a dollar or up to $500. Live jazz, Creole cuisine, Mardi Gras décor and an attached hotel round out the experience. Daily, 24 hours.

HERMANN-GRIMA HOUSE

820 St. Louis St., New Orleans, 504-525-5661; www.hgghh.org

The Georgian design reflects the post-Louisiana Purchase American influence on traditional French and Spanish styles in the Quarter; the furnishings typify a well-to-do lifestyle during the period of 1831-1860. The restored house has elegant interiors, two landscaped courtyards, slave quarters, a stable and a working period kitchen. Speaking of the kitchen, check out Creole cooking demonstrations on open hearth (October-May: Thursday). Tours are available as well. Monday-Friday.

223

HISTORIC NEW ORLEANS COLLECTION

533 Royal St., New Orleans, 504-523-4662; www.hnoc.org

Established in 1966 by local collectors Gen. and Mrs. Kemper Williams, the Collection comprises several historic buildings that house a museum and comprehensive research center for state and local history. The main exhibition gallery presents changing displays on Louisiana's history and culture. The 1792 Merieult House features a pictorial history of New Orleans and Louisiana; the Williams Residence shows the elegant lifestyle of the Collection's founders. Changing exhibits grace several galleries. There is also a touch tour for the visually impaired. Tuesday-Saturday 9:30 a.m.-4:30 p.m.

HOUSE OF BLUES

225 Decatur St., New Orleans, 504-310-4999; www.hob.com

Even in the eye-catching French Quarter, it is hard to miss the gaudy, neon-lit entrance to the House of Blues. Past the wildly decorated porch, you will hear live music ranging from Cajun to country and reggae to rock 'n' roll, not to mention pure, soulful blues. The Sunday Gospel brunch is justly famous and surprisingly inexpensive.

THE HOWLIN' WOLF

907 S. Peters St., New Orleans, 504-522-9653; www.howlin-wolf.com

Arguably one of New Orleans' best clubs, the Howlin' Wolf offers up live music of all sorts. Sometimes it rocks and sometimes it's got the blues, but it is always a great

LOUISIANA

★
★
★
★

place to see a show. Katrina prompted the club to move just down the street from its old digs to a venue with more space. The Howlin' Wolf is popular with college students and those looking for original music and up-and-coming acts. Check out the acoustic open-mike nights on Mondays.

JACKSON BREWERY
600 Decatur St., New Orleans, 504-566-7245; www.jacksonbrewery.com
This historic brewery was converted into a large retail, food and entertainment complex with 75 shops and restaurants, outdoor seating and a riverfront promenade. Monday-Saturday 10 a.m.-8 p.m., Sunday 10 a.m.-7 p.m.

JACKSON SQUARE
615 Pere Antoine Alley, New Orleans; www.jackson-square.com
Bordered by Chartres, St. Peter, Decatur, and St. Ann Streets, this area was established as a drill field in 1721 and was called the *Place d'Armes* until 1848, when it was renamed for Andrew Jackson, hero of the Battle of New Orleans. The statue of Jackson, the focal point of the square, was the world's first equestrian statue with more than one hoof unsupported; the American sculptor, Clark Mills, had never seen an equestrian statue and therefore did not know that the pose was thought impossible. Today, the square and surrounding plaza is one of the best places in the Quarter to catch your breath, people-watch and listen to jazz. It attracts local artists, food vendors and street performers such as mimes, magicians and musicians.

JEAN BRAGG ANTIQUES & GALLERY
600 Julia St., New Orleans, 504-895-7375; www.jeanbragg.com
The focus of this shop and gallery is on Louisianan and Southern art, especially paintings, watercolors and etchings of Louisiana and the French Quarter. Specializing in George Ohr pottery and Newcomb College pottery and craft work, the shop also offers museum-quality pieces from the late 19th and early 20th centuries. Discover vintage linens, jewelry and glassware along with Victorian furniture. Monday-Saturday 10 a.m.-5 p.m.

JOHN JAMES AUDUBON RIVERBOAT
2 Canal St., New Orleans, 504-586-8777, 800-233-2628; www.steamboatnatchez.com
The riverboat *John James Audubon* provides river transportation between the Aquarium of the Americas and the Audubon Zoo seven miles upriver, round-trip or one-way; return may be made via the St. Charles Avenue Streetcar (additional fee). The round-trip ticket price includes admission to both the Audubon Zoo and the Aquarium of the Americas.

LAFAYETTE SQUARE
6000 St. Charles Ave., New Orleans
The square features statues of Benjamin Franklin, Henry Clay and John McDonough.

LAFITTE'S BLACKSMITH SHOP
941 Bourbon St., New Orleans
This popular bar is arguably the oldest French-style building left in the French Quarter. (After two fires in the 1700s destroyed much of the city, the Spanish style dominated

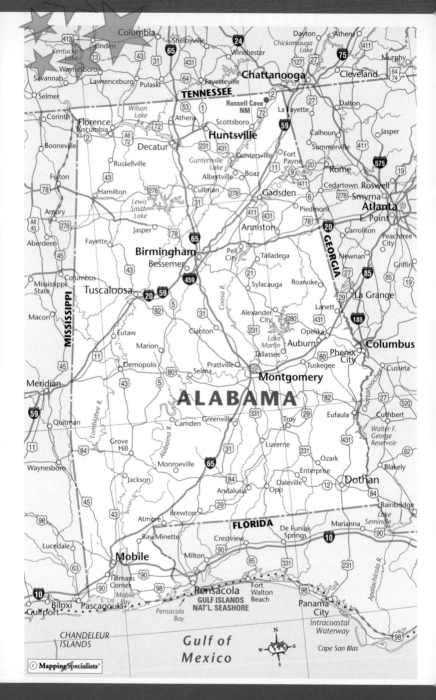

Gulf of
Mexico

CHANDELEUR
ISLANDS

© Mapping Specialists

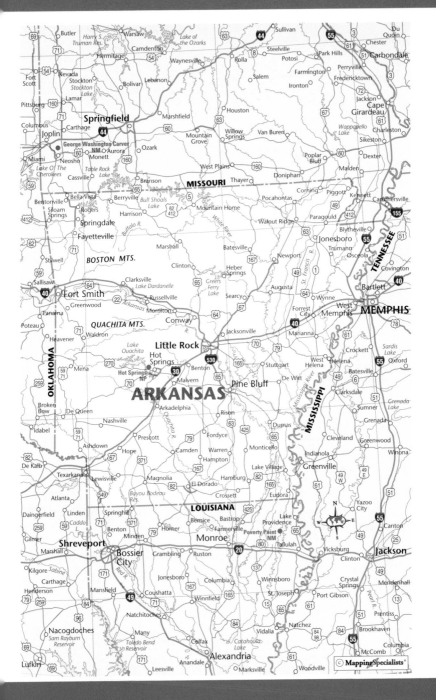

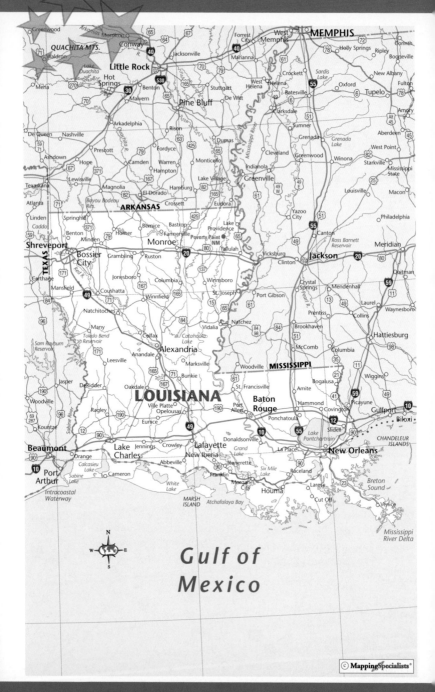

Gulf of Mexico

The Center for Hospitality Research

Hospitality Leadership Through Learning

The Cornell School of Hotel Administration's
world-class faculty explores new ways
to refine the practice of hospitality
management.

Our research drives better results.
Better strategy.
Better management.
Better operations.

See our work at:
www.chr.cornell.edu

537 Statler Hall • hosp_research@cornell.edu • 607.255.9780

Cornell University
School of Hotel Administration

rebuilding efforts.) Local lore has it that the original smithy, built sometime before 1772, served as a front for pirate Jean Lafitte's more notorious activities. The bar retains a dark, historical feel, although the local and exotic patrons lighten the atmosphere. Daily from 11 a.m.

LAKE PONTCHARTRAIN

Lakeshore Drive, New Orleans
This is a favorite spot of locals for picnicking, fishing, running, cycling, skating or simply watching sailboats pass by.

LE CHAT NOIR

715 St. Charles Ave., New Orleans, 504-581-5812; www.cabaretlechatnoir.com
Get decked out (that is, no jeans or shorts) to check out the Cat (*chat noir* means "black cat") for an ever-changing schedule of cabaret, live theater and musical performances. The Bar Noir is a cozier room, perfect for a pre-show cocktail (try the house specialty, the Black Cat) or for quiet conversation with friends.

LEE CIRCLE

Howard Avenue, New Orleans
Here you'll find a statue of Robert E. Lee by Alexander Doyle.

LONGUE VUE HOUSE & GARDENS

7 Bamboo Road, New Orleans, 504-488-5488; www.longuevue.com
A grand city estate furnished with original English and American antiques is on eight acres of formal and picturesque gardens. Plus there are changing exhibits in galleries and seasonal horticultural displays in the gardens. Tours on the hour. Admission: adults $10, students $5, children free. Monday-Saturday 10 a.m.-4.30 p.m.; Sunday 1-5 p.m.

LOUIS ARMSTRONG PARK

800 block of N. Rampart St., New Orleans
To the left of the entrance—built to resemble a Mardi Gras float—is a stand of very old live oak trees. This area was originally known as Congo Square, where slaves were permitted to congregate on Sunday afternoons; it was also the scene of voodoo rites. After the Civil War, the square was named for Gen. P. G. T. Beauregard. Louis Armstrong Park, which includes an extensive water garden that focuses upon a larger-than-life-size statue of Armstrong, was expanded from the original square and contains the municipal auditorium and the Theatre of the Performing Arts.

LOUISIANA NATURE CENTER

5601 Read Blvd., New Orleans, 504-581-4629, 800-774-7394;
www.auduboninstitute.org/lnc
You can lead yourself on an audio tour of local plant and animal life through the nature center's trails and boardwalks, or set off to explore some of the 86 acres on your own. Turtle Pond has turtles and tortoises, along with other amphibian life. The public is invited to a schedule of shows in the planetarium on Saturdays and Sundays. Tuesday-Friday 9 a.m.-5 p.m., Saturday 10 a.m.-5 p.m., Sunday noon-5 p.m.

KINGS, KREWES, BEADS AND BALLS

Mardi Gras is both a carnival and a holiday, the day before Ash Wednesday and the Lenten season of fasting and repentance. And contrary to what you might have seen on TV or read in the news, Fat Tuesday is more than the salacious frat-boy party you might imagine. It is a bash—a huge bash—but there are plenty of different ways to celebrate in New Orleans, especially when the party is as big as Mardi Gras. The Mardi Gras season begins on Twelfth Night—January 6, a time when the festive holiday season traditionally ends. In New Orleans, Twelfth Night kicks off a season of merriment. Festivities reach fever pitch 12 days before Mardi Gras and peak on the Saturday prior to Fat Tuesday, when the city celebrates with four days of nonstop jazz, food, drink and masked balls. Perhaps most closely associated with the celebrations—aside from mayhem in the French Quarter—are the colorful parades where marchers in elaborate costumes toss plastic purple, green and gold beads to onlookers. If your visit falls during Mardi Gras, be sure to hit the highlights: On Fat Tuesday, the French Quarter is alive with visitors in mysterious, beautiful masks. Accent Annex (1420 Sams Ave.), is a good place to check out costumes, beads, doubloons and other Mardi Gras items. Be sure to taste a king cake (a large cake, plain or filled with fruit or cream cheese, coated with purple, green and gold sugar and with a tiny plastic baby hidden inside). Traditionally, whoever gets the slice with the baby provides the king cake for the next party.

At 6 p.m. on Fat Monday, the King of Rex lands at the riverfront near the French Quarter. The mayor turns over the city to him for the duration of Mardi Gras. Earlier that day, the Zulu King arrives at the riverfront and the Zulus celebrate in Woldenberg Park. The meeting of the two kings is widely celebrated.

★
★★
★★
★

LOUISIANA STATE MUSEUM

751 Chartres St., New Orleans, 504-568-6968, 800-568-6968; lsm.crt.state.la.us

The museum comprises five properties in the French Quarter city and three sites outside of the city. Though only the residence is open to the public (a kitchen and servants' quarters complete the complex), Madame John's Legacy is a fine example of Creole architecture. Built in 1789 after the great fire of 1788, it is notable for surviving the subsequent 1795 fire. The 1850 House, named for the year it was built, holds an authentic collection of period furnishings. The Old U.S. Mint was the only mint in the country that printed currency for both the Confederacy and the U.S. government. The mint now holds state and local research materials and exhibits. Admission: adults $6, seniors $5, children free. Tuesday-Saturday 9 a.m.-5 p.m., Sunday noon-5 p.m.

LOUISIANA SUPERDOME

Sugar Bowl Drive, New Orleans, 504-587-3663, 800-756-7074; www.superdome.com

The Dome is home field for the New Orleans Saints (NFL football), Tulane University Green Wave (NCAA Division I football) and has hosted a variety of other sports events, including college baseball and the 2003 NCAA men's basketball Final Four. The annual Endymion Extravaganza Mardi Gras Parade and Party happens here, as well as the New Orleans Home & Garden Show, the Boat & Sport Fishing Show, the Kid's Fair & Expo and numerous concerts and other special events. In the immediate aftermath of Hurricane Katrina, the Superdome became a temporary home to thousands of people who had had to evacuate the rising floodwaters.

LOUISIANA'S CHILDREN'S MUSEUM

420 Julia St., New Orleans, 504-523-1357; www.lcm.org

Catering to toddlers and the young at heart, this museum encourages hands-on exploration. Kids can take a ride in a simulated police cruiser in the Safety First area, anchor a newscast in the Kidswatch Studio or experience bayou life in the Cajun Cottage. Other areas include Waterworks, Big City Port and Art Trek. Children under 16 must be accompanied by an adult. Tuesday-Saturday 9:30 a.m.-4:30 p.m., Sunday noon-4:30 p.m., open Monday during the summer.

LOYOLA UNIVERSITY

6363 St. Charles Ave., New Orleans, 504-865-3240, 800-465-9652; www.loyno.edu

Founded in 1912, Loyola is now home to some 3,500 students. Buildings on the 21-acre campus are Tudor Gothic in style. Tours are arranged through the Office of Admissions. Monday-Friday, twice daily.

M. S. RAU ANTIQUES

630 Royal St., New Orleans, 504-523-5660, 800-544-9440; www.rauantiques.com

Founded in 1912, this family-owned and family-run business is so confident of its merchandise that it offers a 125-percent guarantee on all in-store purchases (online purchases include a slightly modified guarantee). Internationally known names such as Paul Revere, Meissen, Faberg, Wedgwood, Tiffany and Chippendale are represented in the 25,000-square-foot showroom and extensive catalog. You can also pick up fabulous diamonds, jewelry, silver and objects d'art among the vast array of American and European antiques. Monday-Saturday 9 a.m.-5:15 p.m.

MAGAZINE STREET

Magazine St., New Orleans, 504-455-1224, 866-679-4764; www.magazinestreet.com

Fun and funky, Magazine Street offers six miles of clothing retailers, antique establishments, gift shops, eateries and more. Most of the businesses are housed in 19th-century buildings or brick-faced cottages, which help the area maintain its otherworldly charm. You can stroll from the French Quarter through Magazine Street to the Audubon Zoo, picking up some jewelry, a piece of furniture, a book or a bite to eat along the way. Make a point to stop off at the Magazine Arcade, a minimall that houses eclectic shops offering antique music boxes and musical instruments, period medical equipment, dolls and their furnishings, as well as antique household items for real people. Most shops open daily 10 a.m.-5 p.m.

MAISON LEMONNIER

640 Royal St., New Orleans

Built in 1811 and sometimes called the "Skyscraper," this was the first building in the Vieux Carré more than two stories high. This house was used as the setting of George W. Cable's novel *Sieur George*. Notice the YLR, for Yves LeMonnier, worked into the grillwork.

MARDI GRAS WORLD

233 Newton St., New Orleans, 504-361-7821, 800-362-8213;
www.mardigrasworld.com

For a fascinating look at where about 75 percent of Mardi Gras props and floats are made, visit this unique establishment—the world's largest of its kind. You can try on costumes; watch painters, sculptors and carpenters at work; and tour rooms filled with props and Mardi Gras paraphernalia. The Kern family's business also provides floats and props for parades across the country. Daily 9:30 a.m.-4:30 p.m.

MEMORIAL HALL—CONFEDERATE MUSEUM

929 Camp St., New Orleans, 504-523-4522; www.confederatemuseum.com

Louisiana veterans of the War Between the States founded the Hall as a repository for artifacts and memorabilia of the Confederate side of the Civil War. Opened in 1891, it is the nation's longest continuously operating museum. The museum houses flags, swords and uniforms from both officers and foot soldiers as well as an extensive collection of photographs. The widow of Confederate president Jefferson Davis donated many family items. Monday-Saturday 10 a.m.-4 p.m.

METAIRIE CEMETERY

5100 Pontchartrain Blvd., New Orleans, 504-486-6331; www.lakelawnmetairie.com

On the former grounds of the Metairie Race Course, the largest (150 acres) and loveliest of New Orleans' cemeteries is home to a variety of eye-catching memorials and mausoleums. Do not miss the pyramid and sphinx Brunswig mausoleum or the former gravesite of Storyville madam Josie Arlington, whose family had her body moved when tourists flocked to the crypt. But keep your eyes open: At least one of the numerous bronze statues is said to wander the grounds, a lovely setting for a quiet stroll. You can rent a taped audio tour or choose to drive around it. Daily 8:30 a.m.-5 p.m.

MOONWALK

615 Pere Antoine Alley, New Orleans, www.neworleansonline.com

Running the length of the French Quarter along the river levee, the Moonwalk is a pedestrian thoroughfare that connects many attractions along the river, including the Aquarium of the Americas and paddleboat cruises, as well as shops and restaurants. Or you can park yourself on a bench and watch the crowds and the river flow by. Locals and tourists make this a popular venue for an evening stroll, especially on a clear, moonlit night.

MUSÉE CONTI HISTORICAL WAX MUSEUM

917 Rue Conti, New Orleans, 504-581-1993, 800-233-5405; www.get-waxed.com

More than 150 wax figures illustrate the history of the city in this amazing—and sometimes eerie—museum. Catch Napoleon Bonaparte in his bath, Voodoo Queen Marie Laveau and her dancers and Duke Ellington playing some jazz. The figures are painstakingly constructed (even clean-shaven men have stubble) using a process that makes them seem nearly lifelike, and they are set in historically accurate tableaux. Monday, Friday 10 a.m.-4 p.m.

LOUISIANA

★
★
★
★
★

YOU CAN'T KEEP A GOOD MAN DOWN (BUT MAYBE YOU SHOULD)

The cemeteries of New Orleans tell a fascinating story of the city's history, geology and culture. Because the city lies below sea level, the area's earliest residents had to engineer a unique burial system. A hole dug for a six-foot grave would fill with six feet of water, causing caskets to float. Rocks placed in and on top of the coffins to weigh them down worked until a rainstorm occurred, causing the water level to rise and popping the airtight coffin right out of the ground. Eventually, large holes were drilled into the underside of the coffin so it would quickly fill with water and sink. This method, too, was abandoned, due in part to the painful sound of loved ones gurgling their way down to their final resting places.

Meanwhile, Esteban Miro, an early governor of the city, had introduced the wall vault burial system that was popular in Spain for those who wanted to be buried above ground. Economical vaults were stacked on top of one another, while wealthier families built large, ornate tombs with crypts, many of which looked like tiny mansions. Rows of tombs looked like streets, clusters of monuments looked like communities and cemeteries have thus become known as Cities of the Dead.

Several of New Orleans' 42 cemeteries offer tours. Each has its own story to tell: St. Louis Cemetery No. 1, commissioned in 1789, was the first to offer above-ground burials. Notables buried there include Homer Plessy (of Supreme Court case *Plessy* v. *Ferguson* fame) and Marie Laveau, New Orleans' mysterious voodoo queen. Lafayette Cemetery No. 1, laid out in 1833, figures prominently in Anne Rice's vampire books and was the film location for *Interview with the Vampire*. Metairie Cemetery has a broad range of architecture and is considered one of the most beautiful cemeteries in the world. It is the final resting place of nine Louisiana governors and notorious Storyville madam Josie Arlington.

Holt is the New Orleans oddity, a below-ground cemetery and perhaps the most touching of any cemetery in the city. A graveyard for indigents, the cemetery's graves are either unmarked or marked by a collection of poignant, handmade headstones. Buddy Bolden, the great early-20th-century jazz musician who spent the second half of his life in a mental institution, is buried here.

229

LOUISIANA

★
★
★
★

NATIONAL D-DAY MUSEUM
945 Magazine St., New Orleans, 504-527-6012; www.ddaymuseum.org

Opened on June 6, 2000, the 16,000 square feet of gallery space houses exhibits that trace the political and economic events leading up to the D-Day invasion in 1944. Founded by the late historian and author Stephen Ambrose, the museum offers oral histories of the men and women who participated, as well as rare film footage that helps bring World War II to life. Free lunchbox lectures on Wednesdays give insight into specific topics or personalities. Daily 9 a.m.-5 p.m.

NEW ORLEANS BOTANICAL GARDEN

1 Palm Drive, New Orleans, 504-483-9386; www.neworleanscitypark.com/ nobg.html

This beautiful public garden lost most of its collection when Hurricane Katrina landed, but it opened again to the public in March of 2006, and flowers and plants are blooming once more. Admission: adults $6, children $3. Tuesday-Sunday 10 a.m.-4:30 p.m.

NEW ORLEANS GHOST TOUR

625 St. Phillip St., New Orleans, 504-861-2727, 888-644-6787;
www.neworleansghosttour.com

New Orleans might never look the same after you've heard tales of her ghostly past on this walking tour. Hear about the mad butcher—who may have butchered more than beef—the sultan reportedly buried alive and other supernatural stories that will leave you with goose bumps.

NEW ORLEANS HISTORIC VOODOO MUSEUM

724 Dumaine, St., New Orleans, 504-680-0128; www.voodoomuseum.com

Marie Laveau reigned as voodoo queen of New Orleans throughout much of the 19th century. The Voodoo Museum displays her portrait and memorabilia. Although it sells the stereotypical voodoo supplies, the museum also offers serious exhibits on voodoo history and its artifacts. You can also purchase your own *gris-gris* bag filled with herbs, bone and charms to bring luck or love into your life. Daily 10 a.m.-dusk.

NEW ORLEANS HORNETS (NBA)

New Orleans Arena, 1501 Girod St., New Orleans, 504-301-4000;
www.nba.com/hornets

The Hornets moved from Charlotte for the 2002-2003 NBA season to give New Orleans a National Basketball Association team for the first time since the Jazz moved to Utah in 1979. They play home games at the New Orleans Arena, where the Honeybees cheer them on and mascot Hugo the Hornet is a three-time NBA Mascot Slam Dunk Champion.

NEW ORLEANS MUSEUM OF ART

City Park, 1 Collins Diboll Circle, New Orleans, 504-658-4100; www.noma.org

Established in 1911, NOMA boasts more than 40,000 objects in its permanent collection. The strengths of the permanent collection lie in its photography and glassware exhibits, as well as notable collections of American, African, Japanese and French art, including works by Edgar Degas, who visited New Orleans in the early 1870s. World-class traveling exhibits, extensive children's programs and a sculpture garden, which opened in 2002 in the adjacent City Park, round out the attractions. Wednesday noon-8 p.m., Thursday-Sunday 10 a.m.-5 p.m.

NEW ORLEANS OPERA

1010 Common St., New Orleans, 504-529-2278, 800-881-4459;
www.neworleansopera.org

Operating from the Mahalia Jackson Theatre of the Performing Arts, the New Orleans Opera Association presents four operas each season, which runs from October through March. The association was founded in 1943 and stages high-quality performances of renowned operas as well as world premieres. (The 2003-2004 season opened with the world premiere of the *Louisiana Purchase Opera*.) English translations appear in subtitles above the stage.

NEW ORLEANS PHARMACY MUSEUM (*LA PHARMACIE FRANCAISE*)

514 Chartres St., New Orleans, 504-565-8027; www.pharmacymuseum.org

Louis Dufilho, the first licensed pharmacist in the U.S., operated an apothecary shop here from 1823 to 1855. The ground floor contains pharmaceutical memorabilia of the 1800s, such as apothecary jars filled with medicinal herbs and voodoo powders, surgical instruments, pharmacy fixtures and a black-and-rose Italian marble soda fountain (circa 1855). Admission: adults $5, seniors $4. Tuesday-Sunday 10 a.m.-5 p.m.

NEW ORLEANS SAINTS (NFL)

Louisiana Superdome, Sugar Bowl Drive, New Orleans, 504-731-1700;
www.neworleanssaints.com

One of the few NFL teams that remains in its original city, the Saints joined the National Football League in 1967. The team plays home games in the Superdome, which also regularly hosts the Super Bowl, a game in which the Saints—lovingly called the "Ain'ts" by loyal but weary fans—have never played.

NEW ORLEANS SCHOOL OF COOKING & LOUISIANA GENERAL STORE

524 St. Louis St., New Orleans, 504-525-2665, 800-237-4841; www.nosoc.com

After a session at the School of Cooking, you will be a convert to Louisiana cuisine. Make a reservation for a two- or three-hour lunch class to learn the basics of Louisiana cooking and, even better, to sample the four dishes you prepare. An early 1800s-era converted molasses warehouse is home to the school and to the Louisiana General Store, where you can pick up ingredients, a cookbook and cooking utensils.

NEW ORLEANS STEAMBOAT COMPANY

2 Canal St., New Orleans, 504-586-8777, 800-233-2628; www.steamboatnatchez.com

Cruise from the heart of the French Quarter on the steamboat *Natchez*, the ninth steamer with that name. Launched in 1975, she's one of only six true steam-powered sternwheelers sailing on the Mississippi today. Cruises on the *Natchez* last two hours with an optional Creole lunch available for an additional fee. Each cruise features live narration of historical facts and highlights, jazz music in the main dining room and a calliope concert during boarding times. The Harbor/Jazz Cruises at 11:30 a.m. and 2:30 p.m. offer jazz by Duke Heitger and the Steamboat Stompers, while the 7 p.m. Dinner/Jazz Cruise features the world-renowned Dukes of Dixieland. The Dinner/Jazz Cruise offers buffet-style dining and indoor/outdoor seating. Cruises depart from the Toulouse Street Wharf.

NEW ORLEANS WALKING AND DRIVING TOUR

2020 Saint Charles Ave., New Orleans, 504-566-5011, 800-672-6124;
www.neworleanscvb.com

For a thorough tour of the many interesting points in the Vieux Carré and surrounding area, see the visitor information center.

OAK ALLEY PLANTATION

3645 Highway 18 (Great River Road), Vacherie, 225-265-2151, 800-442-5539;
www.oakalleyplantation.com

This quintessential antebellum, Greek Revival plantation house (circa 1839) has been featured in many films, including *Primary Colors* and *Interview with a Vampire*. An *allée* of 300-year-old live oaks leads to the mansion, which is surrounded by first- and second-floor galleries supported by massive columns. The interior was remodeled in the 1930s with antiques and modern furnishings of the day. You have your choice of picnicking or dining at the onsite restaurant. Admission: adult $15, students $7.50, children $4.50. Daily tours, Monday-Friday 10 a.m.-4 p.m., Saturday-Sunday 10 a.m.-5 p.m.

THE OLD U.S. MINT

400 Esplanade Ave., New Orleans, 504-568-6968; www.lsm.crt.state.la.us

Designed by William Strickland in 1835, the mint produced coins for both the U.S. and for the Confederate States. Today, the mint houses permanent exhibitions of jazz and the Louisiana State Museum's Historical Center, a research facility. Tuesday-Sunday 9 a.m.-5 p.m.; historical center also Monday, by appointment.

PADDLE WHEELER *CREOLE QUEEN* AND RIVERBOAT *CAJUN QUEEN*

2 Canal St., New Orleans, 504-524-0814; www.creolequeen.com

The *Creole Queen* offers 2½-hour sightseeing cruises to Chalmette National Historical Park, the site of the Battle of New Orleans, as well as three-hour dinner jazz cruises. The riverboat *Cajun Queen* offers harbor cruises from the Aquarium of the Americas (one-hour tour with narration).

★
★
★
★
★

PITOT HOUSE

1440 Moss St., New Orleans, 504-482-0312; www.pitothouse.org

This is one of the last remaining French colonial/West Indies-style plantation houses along Bayou St. John. Built in 1799, it was the residence of James Pitot, the first elected mayor of incorporated New Orleans. Inside the restored home you'll find antiques. Wednesday-Saturday 10 a.m.-3 p.m.

PONTALBA BUILDING

523 St. Anne St., New Orleans, 504-524-9118

Completed in 1850 and 1851 by the Baroness Pontalba to beautify the square, the building is still occupied and used as intended (with duplex apartments above ground-floor offices and shops). The buildings are now owned by the city and the Louisiana State Museum. The 1850 House is furnished in the manner of the period. Tuesday-Sunday 9 a.m.-5 p.m.

THE PRESBYTERE

751 Chartres St., New Orleans, 504-568-6968, 800-568-6968;
www.lsm.crt.la.us/presbex.htm

Built to house clergy serving the parish church, the Presbytere was never used for that purpose, thanks in part to a series of fires that kept it incomplete until 1813, when it was finished by the U.S. government. It is now a museum with a permanent exhibit on the history of Mardi Gras. The Presbytere, like the Cabildo, is part of the Louisiana State Museum complex. Tuesday-Sunday.

PRESERVATION HALL

726 St. Peter St., New Orleans, 504-522-2841; www.preservationhall.com

Since 1961, people have been warming the benches at this rustic music hall in the French Quarter for one reason: to hear traditional New Orleans jazz, which dates back to the early 1900s. The building is not much to look at, but do not let that deter you. You will sweat—no air-conditioning—and you will have a hard time finding a place to sit. But this place is worth it. The music here is enough to make you glad you came. Even if you're no jazzman, you will still want to nod your head to the beat at this swingin' joint. Bring the kids, too; the hall welcomes people of all ages. Daily 8 p.m.-midnight.

RIVER CRUISES

2 Canal St., New Orleans, 504-586-8777, 800-233-2628; www.steamboatnatchez.com

Daily excursions depart from the riverfront.

RIVERFRONT STREETCAR LINE

504-248-3900; www.norta.com

Vintage streetcars follow a 1½-mile route along the Mississippi riverfront from Esplanade past the French Quarter to the World Trade Center, Riverwalk, Convention Center and back.

RIVERWALK

1 Poydras St., New Orleans, 504-522-1555; www.riverwalkmarketplace.com

This ½-mile-long festival marketplace, converted from World's Fair pavilions, has more than 140 national and local shops, restaurants and cafés. Monday-Saturday 10 a.m.-7 p.m., Sunday noon-6 p.m.

SAN FRANCISCO PLANTATION

2646 Highway 44 (River Road), Garyville, 985-535-2341, 888-322-1756; www.sanfranciscoplantation.org

You cannot miss this colorful mansion, a far cry from what most Americans imagine when they think of plantations. The house is a remarkable example of the "Steamboat Gothic" style with its Creole structure. Authentically restored, the interior features five decorated ceilings (two are original). The house was used as the setting of Frances Parkinson Keyes' novel *Steamboat Gothic*. Daily tours 9:30 a.m.-4:40 p.m.; until 4 p.m. in winter.

LOUISIANA

★
★
★
★

SHOPS AT CANAL PLACE

333 Canal St., New Orleans, 504-522-9200; www.theshopsatcanalplace.com

More than 50 stores, many of them high-end retailers, give this shopping center a lot of cachet. Saks Fifth Avenue anchors the mall, and Gucci, Kenneth Cole and Betsey Johnson contribute to the swanky vibe. Additional amenities include a fitness club, a post office and an ATM. The Southern Repertory Theater stage is here, too. Monday-Saturday 10 a.m.-7 p.m., Sunday noon-6 p.m.

SOUTHERN REGIONAL RESEARCH CENTER

1100 Robert E. Lee Blvd., New Orleans, 504-286-4200; www.ars.usda.gov

The center is part of the U.S. Department of Agriculture, which finds and develops new and improved uses for Southern farm crops. Guided tours are available by appointment. Monday-Friday.

SOUTHERN REPERTORY THEATER

365 Canal St., New Orleans, 504-522-6545, 504-891-8332; www.southernrep.com

Permanently housed in The Shops at Canal Place mall since 1991, the Southern Repertory Theater (SRT) was founded in 1986 to promote Southern plays and playwrights. Plays by Southern luminaries such as Tennessee Williams, Pearl Cleage, Beth Henley and SRT founding member Rosary H. O'Neill form the basis of the theater's September-to-May season. Days and times vary.

ST. BERNARD STATE PARK

501 St. Bernard Parkway, Braithwaite, 504-682-2101, 888-677-7823;
www.lastateparks.com/stbernar

The park is approximately 358 acres near the Mississippi River, with many viewing points of the water and a network of artificial lagoons. Swimming, picnicking, a playground, trails and camping are all available. Daily.

ST. CHARLES AVENUE STREETCAR

6700 Plaza Drive, New Orleans, 504-827-7802; www.norta.com

The streetcars (never call them trolleys!) was added to the National Register of Historic Places in 1973. A ride is a quaint and relaxing way to view the varied architecture and exotic greenery of the aptly named Garden District. The 13.2-mile route can take you to tour Tulane University, drop you off at Audubon Park (where the zoo is located) and provide you with safe transport after imbibing in the French Quarter.

ST. LOUIS CATHEDRAL

615 Pere Antoine Alley, New Orleans, 504-525-9585; www.stlouiscathedral.org

The oldest continuously active cathedral in the United States, the St. Louis Cathedral is not much to look at. But its history is worth noting: it is the third church to stand on the site; the first was destroyed by a hurricane in 1722, and the second burned to the ground on Good Friday 1788. And in 2005, two large oaks fell during Hurricane Katrina and amputated a finger and a thumb of the statue of Jesus that stood near them. Stop inside for a chat with docents, who can tell you about the church's history, murals and windows (and about why the church is sinking). Daily.

TIPITINA'S

501 Napoleon Ave., New Orleans, 504-895-8477; www.tipitinas.com

Live music is what you find at Tip's—as the locals call it. The emphasis is on rock, but funk, Cajun and jazz all make the calendar. Tuesdays feature various local artists at the no-cover eighth-floor "Homegrown Nights," and Sundays often offer a $5 cover for the Cajun Fais-Do-Do. Shows featuring nationally and locally known talent start at 10 p.m. Thursday-Sunday.

TULANE UNIVERSITY

6823 St. Charles Ave., New Orleans, 504-865-5000; www.tulane.edu

The 110-acre main Uptown campus offers art galleries and other exhibits. The Tulane University Medical Center, located downtown, includes the School of Medicine, the School of Public Health and Tropical Medicine and a 300-bed private hospital.

UNIVERSITY OF NEW ORLEANS

2000 Lake Shore Drive, New Orleans, 504-280-6000; www.uno.edu

On the shores of Lake Pontchartrain, the 345-acre campus is the center of a residential area.

U.S. CUSTOM HOUSE

423 Canal St., New Orleans, Decatur and Canal Streets

Begun in 1848, interrupted by the Civil War and completed in 1881, the Greek Revival building with neo-Egyptian details was used in part as an office by Maj. Gen. Benjamin "Spoons" Butler during Union occupation, and in part as a prison for Confederate soldiers. A great dome was planned but the excessive weight of the existing building caused the foundation to settle and the dome was never completed. (In 1940, the building had sunk 30 inches, while the street level had been raised three feet.) Of particular interest is the famed Marble Hall, an architectural wonder. A self-guided tour is available. Monday-Friday.

WASHINGTON ARTILLERY PARK

Frenchman and Royal, New Orleans

Between the muddy Mississippi and elegant Jackson Square lies this park, named for the 141st Field Artillery, which has fought in every major conflict since the 1845 Mexican War. Broad steps serve as an amphitheater from which you can catch the escapades of the kids in the playground, the antics of the street performers, the lazy flow of the river or a great view of the French Quarter.

WHISKEY BLUE

333 Poydras St., New Orleans, 504-252-9444; www.whotels.com

Located in the nouveau-chic W Hotel, Whiskey Blue upholds the hotel's sophisticated, edgy tone with low-slung chairs, clear blue lighting and pricey (and expertly made) martinis. Smallish (it holds just 91 patrons) and intimate (there's a queen-sized bed in the middle of the place), the Blue caters to a stylish crowd taking a break from the French Quarter's free-for-all atmosphere. Monday-Saturday 4 p.m.-4 a.m.; Sunday 4 p.m.-2 a.m.

WOLDENBERG RIVERFRONT PARK

1 Canal St., New Orleans, 504-565-3033; www.auduboninstitute.org

Covering 17 acres on the riverfront, Woldenberg Park offers the city its first direct access to the river in 150 years; ships and paddle wheelers dock along the park. Visitors can choose from a variety of riverboat tours. Sunday-Thursday 6 a.m.-10 p.m., Friday-Saturday 6 a.m.-midnight.

LOUISIANA

★
★
★
★

WORLD TRADE CENTER OF NEW ORLEANS

2 Canal St., New Orleans, 504-529-1601; www.wtcno.org

This center houses the offices of many maritime companies and foreign consulates involved in international trade. Top of the Mart, a revolving restaurant and cocktail lounge on the 33rd floor, offers fine views of the city and the Mississippi River. Daily.

SPECIAL EVENTS
BRIDGE CITY GUMBO FESTIVAL

Gumbo Festival Park on Angel Square, 1701 Bridge City Ave., New Orleans,
504-436-4712; www.hgaparish.org/gumbofestival.htm

In the Gumbo Capital of the World, festival organizers cook up more than 2,000 gallons of chicken, sausage and seafood gumbos. Jambalaya, another local specialty, is also available, along with a variety of accompaniments. You can enter a cooking contest, listen to live music, enjoy carnival rides and participate in many other activities. Early November.

FRENCH QUARTER FESTIVAL

French Quarter, 100 Conti St., New Orleans, 504-522-5730, 800-673-5725;
www.fqfi.org

Fabulous and free, the French Quarter Festival showcases local musicians on 15 stages throughout the Vieux Carré. Take in the sounds of marching bands, brass bands, jazz and Dixieland bands, Cajun, country, zydeco and anything else you can imagine. Music stages are at Jackson Square, Woldenberg Riverfront Park, Bourbon Street, Royal Street, the French Market, Le Petit Theatre at St. Peter and Chartres, and Louisiana State Museum's Old U.S. Mint at Esplanade and Decatur. Don't miss the "World's Largest Jazz Brunch"—booths can be found in Jackson Square, Woldenberg Riverfront Park and Louisiana State Museum's Old U.S. Mint. April.

LOUISIANA SWAMPFEST

6500 Magazine St., New Orleans, 504-581-4629, 866-487-2966;
www.audoboninstitute.org/swampfest

Sample fried alligator tidbits while listening to local bands play Cajun and zydeco tunes. You may want to participate in the 5K run before indulging in the food and music treats, checking out the craft village or getting some hands-on experience with live creatures in the swamp exhibit. Early-mid November.

MARDI GRAS FESTIVAL

Main parade route travels down St. Charles Ave. and Bourbon St., 504-566-5011;
www.mardigras.com, www.mardigrasday.com

The biggest party of the year offers something for everyone. The party starts weeks before the actual date of Mardi Gras. Parades and parties are scheduled throughout the weeks leading up to Ash Wednesday and Lent. Though most of the balls are invitation-only, you pay nothing to watch the numerous parades sponsored by the secret societies that organize the festivities. And of course, Bourbon Street is open to all revelers who want to party. Early January-late February.

NEW ORLEANS JAZZ & HERITAGE FESTIVAL

Fair Grounds Racetrack, 1751 Gentilly Blvd., New Orleans, 504-522-4786;
www.nojazzfest.com

Each year, Jazz Fest draws 500,000 visitors from around the world for an experience that sums up the best of New Orleans—music, food and culture—in one big party. The music is eclectic: The acts on any given day can include national headliners, local zydeco musicians and regional rockabilly and country bands. The main action is at the Fair Grounds, but the fun spreads to venues throughout the city. New Orleans' own Neville Brothers are always a big draw. Late April-early May.

NOKIA SUGAR BOWL COLLEGE FOOTBALL CLASSIC

Louisiana Superdome, Sugar Bowl Drive, New Orleans, 504-525-8573;
www.nokiasugarbowl.com

Each year, two top-ranked college football teams compete in this prestigious bowl game, part of the Bowl Championship Series. From 4 p.m. to kickoff, all football lovers can party at Fan Jam, on the Gate C Bridge on the Superdome's east side. The spirited event features live music, contests, hot food and ice-cold beverages. Sugar Bowl week also includes a basketball classic and a regatta on Lake Pontchartrain. January.

SPRING FIESTA

826 St. Ann St., New Orleans, 504-581-1367; www.springfiesta.com

For two weekends every year, New Orleans celebrates its unique heritage with this springtime festival. The fun-packed festivities include a parade of horse-drawn carriages through the French Quarter, the coronation of the festival's queen at Jackson Square, and tours of private homes and courtyards and the historic Metairie Cemetery. Late March-April.

TENNESSEE WILLIAMS NEW ORLEANS LITERARY FESTIVAL

Le Petit Theatre du Vieux Carré, 616 St. Peter St., French Quarter, New Orleans,
504-581-1144, 800-965-4827; www.tennesseewilliams.net

Born in Mississippi, playwright Tennessee Williams adopted New Orleans as his spiritual home. The city honors him with an annual festival held around his March 26 birthday. The five days of the festival are filled with workshops on writing and publishing, a one-act play competition and a book fair, as well as performances of some of Williams' plays. You can join a literary walking tour or compete in a "Stanley and Stella" contest. Le Petit Theatre du Vieux Carré is the festival headquarters, but other venues also house activities. Late March.

WHITE LINEN NIGHT

900 Camp St., New Orleans, 504-528-3805; www.cacno.org

Catch some culture during this annual art walk and street party. August in the bayou is always hot and humid, so patrons and partiers don their coolest clothes and stroll through the Arts District, popping into galleries that stay open late, catching live dance and theater performances, and ending up at the Contemporary Arts Center for a party that goes on until the wee hours. First Saturday in August.

HOTELS

★★BEST WESTERN FRENCH QUARTER LANDMARK

920 N. Rampart St., New Orleans, 504-524-3333, 800-780-7234;
www.bestwestern.com

102 rooms. High-speed Internet access. Restaurant, bar. Complimentary continental breakfast. **$**

★★BIENVILLE HOUSE HOTEL

320 Decatur St., New Orleans, 800-535-9603; www.bienvillehouse.com

83 rooms. Restaurant. Complimentary continental breakfast. Outdoor pool. **$**

★★★CHATEAU SONESTA HOTEL

800 Iberville St., New Orleans, 504-586-0800; www.sonesta.com

Not only are the guest rooms at this elegant Sonesta extra large (with 12-foot ceilings), but most come with good views of well-landscaped courtyards or Bourbon Street, just steps away. As a bonus for business travelers, all the rooms come with high-speed Internet access. If you wake up hungry, La Chatelaine serves breakfast. For lunch or dinner, savor scrumptious seafood dishes at Ralph Brennan's Red Fish Grill. The unique-looking hotel dates all the way back to 1849, when Daniel Henry Holmes opened his D. H. Holmes Department Store, which did booming business on this very site until 1989. 251 rooms. High-speed Internet access. Restaurant, bar. **$$$**

★★★DAUPHINE ORLEANS HOTEL

415 Dauphine St., New Orleans, 504-586-1800, 800-521-7111;
www.dauphineorleans.com

This hotel offers guests quiet luxury and a few good stories: May Baily's Place, the hotel's bar, was once a popular 19th-century bordello in the city's red-light district. Guests and staff members claimed to have seen ghosts—perhaps the bawdy kind—lurking around here. And John James Audubon, famous naturalist and artist, painted his well-known *Birds of America* series from 1821-1822 in the hotel's main meeting room (which used to be a cottage). In addition to all the history, the charming boutique hotel serves guests a complimentary welcome cocktail, continental breakfast and afternoon tea. 111 rooms. Wireless Internet access. Complimentary continental breakfast. Bar. **$$**

★★DOUBLETREE HOTEL

300 Canal St., New Orleans, 504-581-1300; www.doubletree.com

363 rooms. Restaurant, bar. Fitness center. Outdoor pool. Business center. **$$**

★★EMBASSY SUITES

315 Julia St., New Orleans, 504-525-1993, 800-362-2779;
www.embassyneworleans.com

282 suites. Complimentary full breakfast. Restaurant, bar. **$$**

★★★HILTON NEW ORLEANS RIVERSIDE

Two Poydras St., New Orleans, 504-561-0500; www.neworleans.hilton.com

With its multiple levels, intimate sitting areas, soaring ceilings, long crosswalk and entrances in several different lobbies, the Hilton New Orleans Riverside lives up to its claim to be a city-within–a-city. This is not a quaint, cozy hotel. It's a busy place, frequented by families who are looking for activities to keep the kids happy and by travelers drawn to the amenities. Privileges to a nearby racquet and health club are available to guests for a small fee. 1,616 rooms. High-speed Internet access. Restaurant. Fitness center, fee. Outdoor pool. Business center. Pets accepted. **$**

★★★HOTEL LE CIRQUE
2 Lee Circle, New Orleans, 504-962-0900;
www.hilton.com/en_US/hi/hotel/MSYNHHH/index.do
A stylish and hip crowd checks into this chic hotel, thanks to its location in the funky Arts and Warehouse District, which is home to several cutting-edge galleries, restaurants and shops. You'll feel cosmopolitan resting in one of its smart-looking guest rooms or dining in its Lee Circle Restaurant, which dishes up tasty French Creole cuisine. The hotel has one of the best locations for enjoying Mardi Gras festivities. 137 rooms. Restaurant, bar. Airport transportation available. **$**

★★★HOTEL MONTELEONE
214 Rue Royal, New Orleans, 504-523-3341; www.hotelmonteleone.com
The French Quarter's oldest and largest hotel has been rolling out the red carpet for its guests since 1886. Katrina broke windows, so the rooms have been renovated. And though they vary in size and style, they're comfortable and well appointed. For decades, locals have favored the Monteleone's Carousel Bar, where some seats revolve around the room (hence the watering hole's name). After cocktails, take a seat inside the Hunt Room Grill for fine dining. For recreation, head up to the rooftop for a dip in the pool or a workout in the well-equipped fitness center, which offers splendid views of the French Quarter and the Mississippi River. 600 rooms. Restaurant, bar. Fitness center. Outdoor pool. **$$**

★★HOTEL PROVINCIAL
1024 Rue Chartres, New Orleans, 504-581-4995, 800-535-7922;
www.hotelprovincial.com
105 rooms. High-speed Internet. Complimentary continental breakfast. Restaurant, bar. **$**

★★★HOUSE ON BAYOU ROAD
2275 Bayou Road, New Orleans, 504-945-0992, 800-882-2968;
www.houseonbayouroad.com
Experience old New Orleans at this converted plantation home, offering two acres of gardens, ponds and patios, as well as a plantation-style breakfast. Nine rooms. Children over 12 years only. Complimentary full breakfast. Restaurant. **$**

★★IBERVILLE SUITES
910 Iberville St., New Orleans, 504-523-2400; www.ibervillesuites.com
230 suites. Wireless Internet access. Complimentary continental breakfast. Restaurant, bar. Airport transportation available. **$$**

★
★
★
★

★★★INTERCONTINENTAL NEW ORLEANS

444 St. Charles Ave., New Orleans, 504-525-5566, 800-445-6563;
www.new-orleans.interconti.com

With translation services available, a foreign currency exchange on the premises, a global newspaper service and a staff that speaks 14 languages, the InterContinental Hotel New Orleans can't help but have a European flair. The furnishings are modern and the business accoutrements are top-notch, as are the elements that bring pleasure to travel, including a terrific health club and a restaurant that serves lavish breakfast and lunch buffets, fine traditional New Orleans cuisine and a traditional jazz Sunday brunch. 479 rooms. High-speed Internet access. Restaurant, bar. Airport transportation available. Fitness center. Business center. **$$$**

★★★INTERNATIONAL HOUSE

221 Camp St., New Orleans, 504-553-9550, 800-633-5770; www.ihhotel.com

At this top-rated boutique hotel, the décor is a winning blend of New Orleans style and contemporary chic. The charming folk art and handmade furniture created by Louisiana artisans serve as a pleasant reminder of Cajun country tradition, but the stainless-steel and marble accents give the intimate hotel a cosmopolitan feel. Get in touch with the spirits at Loa (the voodoo word for "deities"), a dark bar lighted only by candles. 119 rooms. Restaurant, bar. **$$**

★★★LAFAYETTE HOTEL

600 St. Charles Ave., New Orleans, 504-524-4441, 888-856-4706;
www.thelafayettehotel.com

In 1916, this small and luxurious hotel opened in the same Beaux-Arts building in which it still pampers guests. Located on Lafayette Square in the Central Business District, it often hosts executives in town on business. Its Old World-style rooms and suites are individually decorated and come well appointed; many have French doors and wrought-iron balconies, and all have English botanical prints, overstuffed easy chairs and marble bathrooms with French-milled soaps and thick terry bathrobes. Off the small but elegant lobby, guests can dine at Mike Ditka's, a gourmet steakhouse that also serves Creole and Cajun favorites. 44 rooms. Restaurant, bar. **$**

★★★LAFITTE GUEST HOUSE

1003 Bourbon St., New Orleans, 504-581-2678, 800-331-7971;
www.lafitteguesthouse.com

Want to feel like you're visiting friends in the mid-19th century? This three-story bed and breakfast should do the trick. Each room has its own distinct Victorian flair and the Victorian ground-floor sitting room will make you want to sip a cup of afternoon tea by the crackling fireplace. Best of all, breakfast is delivered to wherever you choose: your room, your balcony or the courtyard. Most of the guest rooms have private balconies with views of Bourbon Street or the French Quarter. 14 rooms. Complimentary continental breakfast. **$**

★★★LE PAVILLON HOTEL

833 Poydras St., New Orleans, 504-581-3111; www.lepavillon.com

This historic hotel has seen it all: wars, prohibition and the birth of the horseless carriage. Through it all, it has kept its reputation as a Great Lady of New Orleans. In

★
★
★
★

1970, the Hotel Denechaud, as it was called, passed into new hands and was renamed Le Pavillon, receiving a facelift and some spectacular accoutrements: crystal chandeliers from Czechoslovakia, railings from the lobby of Paris Grand Hotel, and fine art and antiques from around the world. The Crystal Suite contains a hand-carved marble bathtub, a gift from Napoleon to a wealthy Louisiana plantation owner—just like the one in the Louvre. (But this hotel isn't too stuffy; peanut-butter-and-jelly sandwiches, milk and chocolates are offered in the lobby after hours.) 226 rooms. Restaurant, bar. Airport transportation available. $

★★★LE RICHELIEU IN THE FRENCH QUARTER

1234 Chartres St., New Orleans, 504-529-2492, 800-535-9653;
www.lerichelieuhotel.com

This family-owned hotel offers an amenity you won't find at any other hotel in the French Quarter: free self-parking. As good as that sounds, many guests keep coming back to this people-pleaser for other reasons: affordable rates; comfortable, homey rooms decorated in Creole style; a cozy bar and café; and an attractive courtyard with a pool. All these pluses got the attention of ex-Beatle Paul McCartney, who checked in here for two months in the late 1970s while he was in town doing some recording work. A suite is now named after him. 86 rooms. Wireless Internet access. Restaurant, bar. Outdoor pool. $

★★MAISON DE VILLE AND AUDUBON COTTAGES

727 Rue Toulouse, New Orleans, 504-561-5858; www.hotelmaisondeville.com

23 rooms. Children over 12 years only. Complimentary continental breakfast. Restaurant. $$

★★MAISON DUPUY

1001 Rue Toulouse, New Orleans, 504-586-8000, 800-535-9177;
www.maisondupuy.com

200 rooms. Restaurant, bar. $$

★★★MELROSE MANSION

937 Esplanade Ave., New Orleans, 504-944-2255, 800-650-3323;
www.melrosemansion.com

The Melrose Mansion, overlooking the French Quarter, was built in 1884 and purchased a few years later by a New Orleans nightclub owner as a home for the girls in his conga line. Approaching the front door of a brick welcome path, you'll walk past a wrought-iron gate and ascend the grand staircase to your suite (the suites have names like Prince Edward and Miss Kitty). Descend the next morning for fresh-baked pastries and hazelnut coffee—taken in the parlor, of course. Eight rooms. Complimentary continental breakfast. $$

★★★OMNI ROYAL CRESCENT HOTEL

535 Gravier St., New Orleans, 504-527-0006, 800-578-3200;
www.omniroyalcrescent.com

The hotel lobby is an impeccable blend of modern and traditional, with shiny brass elevators, a concierge stand and colorful fresh flowers, plus refined artwork and potted palms. Unusual in New Orleans, the Omni has a restaurant serving Thai food

LOUISIANA

★
★
★
★

(with American food for breakfast). The comfortable guest rooms feature touches of wood and brass. 97 rooms. Wireless Internet access. Restaurant. **$**

★★★OMNI ROYAL ORLEANS

621 St. Louis St., New Orleans, 504-529-5333; www.omniroyalorleans.com

For royal treatment in the French Quarter, settle into one of the many plush rooms at this luxury hotel, which has been pampering visitors to the city since 1960. In the comfort of your room, this chain property will spoil you with Irish linen sheets, marble baths and windows overlooking all the action in the Quarter. Dine on steak and seafood in the award-winning Rib Room, a local favorite for decades; or refresh yourself with a mint julep or two at the Touche Bar or the Esplanade Lounge (in the lobby). Up on the rooftop, go for a relaxing swim in the pool, work up a sweat in the fitness center or just take in the sensational views. 346 rooms. Restaurant, bar. Fitness center. Outdoor pool. **$$$**

★★★THE PONTCHARTRAIN HOTEL

2031 St. Charles Ave., New Orleans, 504-524-0581; www.pontchartrainhotel.com

For more than 75 years, this grande dame has been mixing European elegance with Southern hospitality in the city's charming Garden District. In years gone by, dignitaries and celebrities frequently registered here, explaining why some of the suites bear the names of famous folks. These days, travelers like to settle into its comfortable rooms, all of which are individually decorated with antiques and original art. At breakfast, lunch or dinner, savor classic Creole and Cajun specialties at Lafitte's Restaurant. If you start your morning there, you'll likely spot local politicos and civic leaders drinking cafe au lait and biting into beignets. After the workday, local professionals often wind down in the Bayou Bar. 104 rooms. Restaurant, bar. Airport transportation available. **$**

★★PRYTANIA PARK HOTEL

1525 Prytania St., New Orleans, 504-524-0427; www.prytaniaparkhotel.com

62 rooms .Complimentary continental breakfast. **$**

★★★RENAISSANCE PERE MARQUETTE HOTEL

817 Common St., New Orleans, 504-525-1111; www.renaissancehotels.com

Though it's housed in a historic building, this hotel has a contemporary look that appeals to those who like chic décor. Given its location in the Central Business District, the Renaissance attracts business travelers, especially because every room comes with high-speed Internet access, two-line phones with data ports and work desks with lamps. But leisure travelers book rooms here, too, for its close proximity to some of the city's best shopping, restaurants and attractions, including the French Quarter. Rene Bistrot serves award-winning French cuisine at affordable prices, so you'll be vying for a table with the locals who work downtown and know where to find the best deals. 275 rooms. High-speed Internet access. Restaurant, bar. **$$**

★★★THE RITZ-CARLTON, NEW ORLEANS

921 Canal St., New Orleans, 504-524-1331, 800-241-3333; www.ritzcarlton.com

The Ritz-Carlton brings its luxury brand to the edge of the French Quarter and offers the refined elegance travelers expect from the Ritz. The guest rooms have a timeless

★
★
★
★

elegance topped off by feather beds and deep-soaking tubs, and the spa is renowned for its unparalleled services, delivered in a gorgeous setting. If all this relaxing makes you hungry, try the casual bistro-style FQB or Victors for its dazzling backdrop and refined cuisine. The exquisite lounge offers an unrivaled afternoon tea set to the gentle strains of a harp. 527 rooms. Restaurant, bar. Airport transportation available. **$$**

★★★ROYAL SONESTA HOTEL NEW ORLEANS

300 Bourbon St., New Orleans, 504-586-0300; www.royalsonesta-neworleans.com

Gabled windows. French doors. Wrought-iron lace balconies. Gilded mirrors. Furniture reminiscent of 18th-century France. Tranquil, beautifully landscaped courtyards. This cozy but elegant property occupies a full block right on Bourbon Street, and it looks like it belongs in this historic district. If you crave a gourmet meal, sample the contemporary French and Creole cuisine served at Begues Restaurant. For something more casual, opt for the Desire Oyster Bar, where the chefs cook up both Creole and seafood dishes. Party at the Mystick Den cocktail lounge or the Can-Can Cafe and Jazz Club. If you just want to rest and relax, lounge out by the pool on an appealing third-floor terrace. 484 rooms. Restaurant, bar. Outdoor pool. **$$$**

★★★SONIAT HOUSE HOTEL

1133 Chartres St., New Orleans, 504-522-0570, 800-544-8808; www.soniathouse.com

Don't let the Soniat's location in the bustling French Quarter fool you. The quiet and intimate hotel offers an elegant respite from all the revelry outside. Its cozy rooms are housed in three Creole-style town houses dating back to the early 1800s, and are tastefully decorated with English, French and Louisiana antiques. What the property lacks in amenities—there's no pool, restaurant or fitness center—it more than makes up for with all its charm and the superior service of its friendly, attentive staff. 33 rooms. Children over 12 years only. **$$**

★★★ST. JAMES HOTEL

330 Magazine St., New Orleans, 504-304-4000, 888-856-4485;
www.saintjameshotel.com

Even though the St. James opened just a few years ago, it has the look of a distinguished older property because it occupies a renovated building from the 1850s. The hotel looks vintage New Orleans, with wrought-iron balconies and some rooms with exposed-brick walls. Business travelers like its downtown location and the two-line phones in every room. Rooftop terraces overlook a small pool in a charming courtyard. Cuvee restaurant offers contemporary Creole cuisine and more than 500 wine choices. 90 rooms. Restaurant, bar. Airport transportation available. **$$**

★★★ST. LOUIS HOTEL

730 Rue Bienville, New Orleans, 504-581-7300, 888-535-9111; www.stlouishotel.com

All guest rooms in this French Quarter boutique hotel overlook a lovely Mediterranean courtyard lush with tropical greenery, banana trees, flowering plants and a baroque fountain. Inside, the rooms are decked out in French period reproductions, and fabulous French cuisine is featured in the Louis XVI Restaurant, a New Orleans tradition. At breakfast, the hotel serves eggs Sardou and other local favorites in its courtyard. 85 rooms. Restaurant. **$**

243

LOUISIANA

★
★
★
★

★★★W NEW ORLEANS

333 Poydras St., New Orleans, 504-525-9444, 800-522-6963; www.whotels.com

This style-soaked chain is designed for savvy business travelers, but leisure guests won't mind the down comforters, Aveda products and great fitness center. Zoe Bistro offers creative French food and the lobby's Whiskey Blue bar delivers a dose of hot nightlife. 423 rooms. Restaurant, bar. Fitness center. Outdoor pool. **$$$**

★★★★WINDSOR COURT HOTEL

300 Gravier St., New Orleans, 504-523-6000, 888-596-0955;
www.windsorcourthotel.com

Located in the city's business district, the Windsor Court brings a bit of the English countryside to New Orleans. The rooms feature traditional English furnishings and artwork, while bay windows provide views of the city or the Mississippi River. This full-service hotel also includes a pool, sun deck and business and fitness centers. In a city hailed for its works of culinary genius, the Windsor Court is no exception. The Grill Room is one of the hottest tables in town, while the Polo Club Lounge is ideal for cocktails. 324 rooms. High-speed Internet access. Restaurant, bar. Fitness center. Outdoor pool. Business center. Pets accepted, some restrictions; fee. **$$$**

★★★WYNDHAM NEW ORLEANS AT CANAL PLACE

100 Rue Iberville, New Orleans, 504-566-7006; www.wyndham.com

The Wyndham's downtown location isn't the only reason business travelers give this upscale hotel a thumbs-up. They also like the oversized guest rooms and the worker-friendly amenities, including direct high-speed Internet access, ergonomic work chairs and cordless telephones. But the Wyndham's convenient location also appeals to leisure travelers. In fact, the hotel is in the Canal Place Tower, home to the Shops at Canal Place, where visitors (and locals) like to go on buying sprees in the many top-name stores, such as Saks Fifth Avenue. Everyone who beds down here appreciates the stellar views of the city from both the marble-adorned lobby (on the tower's 11th floor) and the rooms that rise above it. Hungry? The Wyndham dishes up American cuisine with a Louisiana twist in the Riverbend Grill. 438 rooms. High-speed Internet access. Restaurant, bar. Outdoor pool. **$$$**

★★★WYNDHAM WHITNEY HOTEL

610 Poydras St., New Orleans, 504-581-4222; www.wyndham.com

This building used to house a grand old bank, and the revived space is worth a stop, even if you're not a guest here. The lobby has beautiful plasterwork and distinguished pillars, and the private dining room used to be the bank's vault. The public dining room was the actual bank space and the hotel's impossibly thick doors, we assume, kept out robbers. 293 rooms. Restaurant, bar. **$**

SPECIALTY LODGINGS

CHIMES BED & BREAKFAST

1146 Constantinople St., New Orleans, 504-899-2621; www.chimesneworleans.com

Jill and Charles Abbyad were pioneers in 1987 when they opened a bed and breakfast in the servants' quarters behind their charming Victorian home near the French Quarter. The bed and breakfast craze had not yet caught on in this city of historic hotels. They remain warm, inviting hosts, offering both comfort and good cheer to their guests. Breakfast is served in the main house with a side of good advice about where to go and what to do in the city the owners know so well. Five rooms. Complimentary full breakfast. **$**

HISTORIC FRENCH MARKET INN

501 Rue Decatur, New Orleans, 504-561-5621, 888-256-9970;
www.neworleansfinehotels.com

Built in the 1800s for the fabulously wealthy Baron Joseph Xavier de Pontalba, the Historic French Market Inn was the official government house when Louisiana was still a French colony. The atmosphere has changed considerably since then; today, the original 19th-century brick walls, elegant brass beds and lush courtyard speak of romance. The grand staircase sweeps from the ground-floor rotunda to the second-floor lobby, and antique period pieces convey two centuries of New Orleans history. 108 rooms. Complimentary continental breakfast. Bar. **$**

RESTAURANTS

★★ALLEGRO BISTRO

1100 Poydras St., New Orleans, 504-582-2350
American menu. Lunch. Closed Saturday-Sunday; one week in July. **$$**

★★ANDREW JAEGER'S HOUSE OF SEAFOOD

300 Decatur St., New Orleans, 504-581-2534; www.andrewjaegers.com
Creole, seafood menu. Dinner. **$$**

★★★ANTOINE'S

713 Rue St. Louis, New Orleans, 504-581-4422; www.antoines.com
Located in the French Quarter, just a short distance from Bourbon Street, Antoine's has been a fixture since 1840. And this Creole/classic French dining spot still exudes quality. The locals know which entrees are the best—the filet and any oyster dish—Rockefeller, Bienville and Foch included. Creole menu. Lunch, dinner. Closed Sunday. **$$$**

★★★ARNAUD'S

813 Rue Bienville, New Orleans, 504-523-5433, 866-230-8891; www.arnauds.com
In the French Quarter near Bourbon Street, this exquisite restaurant heaps refined service on diners. Partake of the trout meunière and shrimp rémoulade in a wonderful, romantic atmosphere. French, Creole menu. Lunch Monday-Friday, dinner daily, Sunday brunch. **$$$**

★★★BACCO

310 Chartres St., New Orleans, 504-522-2426; www.bacco.com
A member of the Brennan family, located at the W Hotel in the French Quarter, this romantic Creole/Italian restaurant fuses local products with traditional Italian recipes. Italian menu. Lunch, dinner. **$$$**

★★★★BAYONA

430 Dauphine St., New Orleans, 504-525-4455; www.bayona.com
A little slice of the romantic Mediterranean awaits you at Bayona, a jewel of a restaurant tucked into a 200-year-old Creole cottage in the heart of the French Quarter.

LOUISIANA

★
★
★
★

The cozy room is often set with fresh flowers and is warmed by sunny lighting and bright colors. Chef Susan Spicer serves up her own interpretation of New Orleans cuisine, blending the ingredients of the Mediterranean with the flavors of Alsace, Asia, India and the Southwest. You'll find an outstanding waitstaff eager to guide you and answer questions about the menu. A great selection of beers, including several local brews, plus an extensive wine list round out the experience. International menu. Lunch, dinner. Closed Sunday-Monday. $$$

★★★BEGUE'S
300 Bourbon St., New Orleans, 504-553-2220; www.sonesta.com/begues
This French Quarter restaurant is in the Royal Sonesta Hotel. Meals are served in a relaxed atmosphere overlooking a tropical courtyard filled with orange trees. The specialty here is beautifully prepared Creole cuisine and an all-you-can-eat Sunday brunch that makes you wonder if there are crawfish or snapper left in any other part of the world. Creole menu. Breakfast, lunch, dinner, Sunday brunch. $$

★★★BELLA LUNA
914 N. Peters St., New Orleans, 504-529-1583; www.bellalunarestaurant.com
Guests get a choice of two views: the French Quarter on one side and a great romantic view of the Mississippi River on the other. The cuisine is mostly American, with a spicy Creole flavor. Local favorites are the pecan-crusted pork chops, battered soft-shell crabs and the giant stuffed Gulf shrimp. Cajun/Creole menu, Mediterranean menu. Dinner. $$$

★
★
★
★

★★BISTRO AT MAISON DE VILLE
733 Toulouse St., New Orleans, 504-528-9206, 800-634-1600; www.maisondeville.com
Creole menu. Lunch, dinner. Closed first week in August. $$$

★★BON TON CAFE
401 Magazine St., New Orleans, 504-524-3386, 888-524-5611; www.savvydiner.com
Cajun menu. Lunch, dinner. Closed Saturday-Sunday. $$

★★★BRENNAN'S
417 Royal St., New Orleans, 504-525-9711; www.brennansneworleans.com
Breakfast is king at this sister restaurant to Commander's Palace in the heart of the French Quarter, but guests will enjoy the classic upscale Creole cuisine any meal of the day. Dine in the courtyard on the decadent egg dishes. French, Creole menu. Breakfast, lunch, dinner, brunch. $$$

★★★BRIGTSEN'S
723 Dante St., New Orleans, 504-861-7610; www.brigtsens.com
Frank Brigsten is the chef/owner of this delightful Uptown spot with excellent food and service to match. It is a local favorite and offers Cajun/Creole dishes, with specialties of the house including blackened tuna and roasted duck. Creole menu. Dinner. Closed Sunday-Monday. $$

★★★BROUSSARD'S

819 Conti St., New Orleans, 504-581-3866; www.broussards.com

This award-winning restaurant has been family-owned for 75 years, albeit by different families. The current owners run things with as much care and attention to detail as the Broussards did in the early 1800s. Classically French-trained chef Gunter prepares unmatched Creole fantasies; try the house-cured salmon or grilled pompano on puff pastry accompanied by shrimp, scallops and mustard-caper sauce. Wine aficionados, prepare for the 20-page wine list. French menu. Dinner. **$$$**

★CAFE DU MONDE

800 Decatur St., New Orleans, 504-525-4544, 800-772-2927; www.cafedumonde.com

French menu. Breakfast, late-night. **$**

★★CAFE GIOVANNI

117 Rue Decatur, New Orleans, 504-529-2154; www.cafegiovanni.com

Creole, Italian menu. Dinner. Closed Sunday-Monday. **$$**

★CAFE PONTALBA

546 St. Peter St., New Orleans, 504-522-1180

Cajun, Creole menu. Lunch, dinner. **$$**

★★CAFE VOLAGE

720 Dublin St., New Orleans, 504-861-4227

French, Mediterranean menu. Lunch, dinner Monday-Saturday, Sunday brunch. **$$**

★CENTRAL GROCERY

923 Decatur St., New Orleans, 504-523-1620, 866-620-0174

Italian menu. Lunch. **$**

★★★COMMANDER'S PALACE

1403 Washington Ave., New Orleans, 504-899-8221; www.commanderspalace.com

In the center of the Garden District stands this turquoise and white Victorian monument to Creole cuisine. The famed Brennan family has presided over the dining room since 1974, but Emile Commander originally founded it in 1880 as a fine restaurant for distinguished neighborhood families. The lush garden setting hosts live Dixieland music for the lively Saturday and Sunday jazz brunches. Creole menu. Lunch, dinner, brunch. **$$$**

★★CRESCENT CITY BREWHOUSE

527 Decatur St., New Orleans, 504-522-0571, 888-819-9330; www.crescentcitybrewhouse.com

American, Cajun/Creole menu. Lunch, dinner. **$$**

★★★CUVEE

322 Magazine St., New Orleans, 504-587-9001; www.restaurantcuvee.com

Foodies love this restaurant for its innovative menu and excellent advice on wine and food pairings. Opened in 1999 and considered an upstart in this city of decades-old dining establishments, Cuvee has gained a reputation as one of New Orleans' finest gourmet restaurants. With just 85 seats, the intimate restaurant is housed in a landmark 1833 building whose age strangely complements its nouveau New Orleans cuisine (think sugarcane-smoked duck breast and crispy confit leg served with Hudson Valley foie gras and Roquefort-pecan risotto). Creole menu. Lunch, dinner. $$$

★★DESIRE OYSTER BAR
300 Bourbon St., New Orleans;
504-586-0300; www.royalsonesta.com
American, Creole, seafood menu. Lunch, dinner. $$

★★★DOMINIQUE'S
1001 Rue Toulouse St., New Orleans, 504-586-8000; www.dominiquesrestaurant.com
This French Quarter location in the beautiful Maison Dupuy Hotel features the innovative cuisine of chef Dominique Macquet. Ingredients are always the freshest available, and the breads and pastries are baked on the premises. French menu. Dinner. $$$

★★DOOKY CHASE
2301 Orleans Ave., New Orleans, 504-821-0600
Creole menu. Lunch, dinner. $$

★★★EMERIL'S RESTAURANT
800 Tchoupitoulas St., New Orleans, 504-528-9393, 800-980-8474; www.emerils.com
Emeril's is a chic and stylish hot spot in the Central Business District. With lofty ceilings, an open kitchen and a towering wooden wine wall, the restaurant is a dynamic space that suits its urban Warehouse District neighborhood. The slick food bar is a fun spot to take in the buzzing see-and-be-seen crowd. The room can get loud, but the vibe is good. The menu employs a world of herbs, spices and chilies that awaken the palate with a delicious jolt. Cajun/Creole menu. Dinner. Closed Sunday. $$$

★★FEELINGS CAFE
2600 Chartres St., New Orleans, 504-945-2222; www.feelingscafe.com
Creole menu. Lunch Friday, dinner daily, Sunday brunch. $$

★★FIVE HAPPINESS
3605 S. Carrollton Ave., New Orleans, 504-482-3935; www.fivehappiness.com
Chinese menu. Lunch, dinner. $

★FRENCH MARKET
1001 Decatur St., New Orleans, 504-525-7879; www.frenchmarket.org
Cajun/Creole, French menu. Lunch, dinner. $$

★★★GALATOIRE'S
209 Bourbon St., New Orleans, 504-525-2021; www.galatoires.com
Jean Galatoire, a Frenchman from the foothills of the Pyrenees, founded this landmark French Quarter restaurant in 1905. His descendants own and run it today. Cajun/Creole menu. Lunch, dinner. Closed Monday. $$$

★★★GAUTREAU'S

1728 Soniat St., New Orleans, 504-899-7397; www.gautreaus.net

This quintessential neighborhood bistro in Uptown is in an early 1900s-era pharmacy, with embossed tin ceilings and an antique apothecary serving as a liquor cabinet. Chef John Harris lends his classical French-trained style to a Creole-influenced menu. American, seafood menu. Dinner. Closed Sunday. **$$$**

★★GUMBO SHOP

630 St. Peter St., New Orleans, 504-525-1486; www.gumboshop.com

Creole, seafood menu. Lunch, dinner. **$$**

★★K-PAUL'S LOUISIANA KITCHEN

416 Chartres St., New Orleans, 504-524-7394; www.chefpaul.com

Cajun/Creole menu. Lunch, dinner. Closed Sunday. **$$$**

★★LA MADELEINE

547 St. Ann St., New Orleans, 504-568-0073; www.lamadeleine.com

French menu. Breakfast, lunch, dinner. **$**

★LUCY'S RETIRED SURFERS BAR & RESTAURANT

701 Tchoupitoulas St., New Orleans, 504-523-8995; www.lucysretiredsurfers.com

Mexican, California menu. Lunch, dinner, late-night, brunch. **$**

★★★MARTINIQUE

5908 Magazine St., New Orleans, 504-891-8495; www.martiniquebistro.com

French menu. Dinner. **$$**

★MICHAUL'S

840 St. Charles Ave., New Orleans, 504-522-5517, 800-563-4055; www.michauls.com

Cajun menu. Dinner. Closed Sunday; also August. **$$**

★MOTHER'S RESTAURANT

401 Poydras St., New Orleans, 504-523-9656; www.mothersrestaurant.net

Creole menu. Breakfast, lunch, dinner. **$**

★★★MR. B'S BISTRO

201 Royal St., New Orleans, 504-523-2078; www.mrbsbistro.com

This famous Brennan-family institution in the French Quarter offers Creole cuisine made with local and organically grown products. It's the power lunch spot in the French Quarter and very popular among locals and tourists alike for dinner. Creole menu. Lunch, dinner. **$$$**

★★★★THE NEW ORLEANS GRILL

300 Gravier St., New Orleans, 504-522-1994, 888-596-0955;
www.windsorcourthotel.com

Dining at The New Orleans Grill (located inside the Windsor Court Hotel) may be one of the most luxurious ways to spend an evening in the city. With a menu that changes monthly and features locally grown and organic foods whenever possible,

LOUISIANA

The New Orleans Grill is known for its fabulous contemporary American cuisine. The restaurant's lounge, the Polo Room, offers live music on Friday nights. French-influenced menu. Breakfast, lunch, dinner. $$$

★★★NOLA

534 St. Louis St., New Orleans, 504-522-6652; www.emerils.com

As the most casual and accessible of Emeril's restaurants, this French Quarter location offers innovative cuisine that will please guests with dishes such as grilled pork porterhouse with brown-sugar-glazed sweet potatoes, toasted pecans and caramelized onion reduction sauce; and spicy roasted Atlantic salmon with fennel-white bean salad, pickled cherry tomatoes and lemon-herb coulis. Creole menu. Lunch, dinner. $$$

★★★PALACE CAFÉ

605 Canal St., New Orleans, 504-523-1661; www.palacecafe.com

Crabmeat cheesecake, anyone? Both contemporary and classic Creole seafood dishes are available at this upscale, lively café on historic Canal Street. Owned by Dickie Brennan of the famous restaurant family, Palace Café is revered for signature dishes such as a creamy oyster pan roast and white chocolate bread pudding. If you can't bear to leave the bread pudding, fear not: That, plus 169 other Palace Café recipes, are available in *The Flavor of New Orleans Palace Café* cookbook, which is available for purchase. What must be experienced in person, however, is the popular Sunday brunch with live blues music. Cajun/Creole menu. Lunch, dinner, Saturday-Sunday brunch. $$

★
★
★
★
★

★★★PELICAN CLUB

312 Exchange Alley, New Orleans, 504-523-1504; www.pelicanclub.com

For fine dining in the French Quarter, look no further than this restaurant tucked away in a converted townhouse in charming Exchange Alley. Creative appetizers and sure-thing entrees, all delivered with professional service, make for an enjoyable dining experience. International menu. Dinner. $$$

★★★PERISTYLE

1041 Dumaine St., New Orleans, 504-593-9535; peristylerestaurant.com

The 19th-century French Quarter building that houses Peristyle was once a family-owned oyster house near the red-light district. Now, of course, it's home to this upscale restaurant, known for French cuisine and the large wine cellar. The menu offers dishes such as lassiette du charcutier and rosemary lamb loin chop with red onion marmalade and pine-nut-sultana red wine reduction. French menu. Dinner. Closed Sunday-Monday. $$$

★PRALINE CONNECTION

542 Frenchmen St., New Orleans, 504-943-3934; www.pralineconnection.com

Creole menu. Lunch, dinner. $$

★★RED FISH GRILL

115 Bourbon St., New Orleans, 504-598-1200; www.redfishgrill.com

Seafood menu. Lunch, dinner. $$$

★★★RESTAURANT AUGUST

301 Tchoupitoulas St., New Orleans, 504-299-9777; www.rest-august.com

Step into this converted 18th-century town house and you're sure to be greeted with a hearty welcome. August's warm, exposed-brick room features vaulted ceilings and Old World antiques. Dining at August is all about being pampered, and chef Jon Besh, a *Food & Wine* Best New Chef (1999), does a wonderful job of spreading the love from the kitchen with an innovative and delicious menu of dishes that marry robust ingredients from Spain and France with regional flavors. His menu changes season-ally, but two flawless signatures are the Moroccan-spiced duck with polenta and tem-pura dates and the BLT, made from fat, meaty fried Buster crabs, lettuce and heirloom tomatoes on a slab of brioche. French menu. Lunch, dinner. Closed Sunday. $$$$

★SNUG HARBOR JAZZ BISTRO

626 Frenchmen St., New Orleans, 504-949-0696; www.snugjazz.com

Seafood, steak menu. Dinner. $$

★★TONY MORAN'S

240 Bourbon St., New Orleans, 504-523-4640; www.tonymorans.com

Italian menu. Dinner. $$$

★★TUJAGUE'S

823 Decatur St., New Orleans, 504-525-8676; www.tujagues.com

Creole menu. Lunch, dinner. $$

★★★UPPERLINE

1413 Upperline St., New Orleans, 504-891-9822; www.upperline.com

The gracious service and excellent Creole food make this neighborhood restaurant in Uptown a local favorite. Cajun/Creole menu. Dinner. Closed Monday-Tuesday. $$

★★★VERANDA

444 St. Charles Ave., New Orleans, 504-525-5566; www.ichotelsgroup.com

On the second floor of the InterContinental Hotel New Orleans, opening onto the hotel's enormous faux-street, lamp-lined atrium, Veranda is an airy arena for a calm-ing meal. Regional fare is the ticket here; Cajun, gumbo, crawfish and other New Orleans cuisine are done up in imaginative ways, but Veranda is known primarily for its lavish breakfast and lunch buffets. And the Sunday champagne jazz brunch draws both locals and visitors. American, Creole menu. Breakfast, lunch, dinner, Sunday brunch. $$

SPA

★★★THE SPA AT THE RITZ-CARLTON, NEW ORLEANS

921 Canal St., New Orleans, 504-670-2929, 800-241-3333; www.ritzcarlton.com

Soft lighting, gleaming marble, brass chandeliers and gentle colors set a regal tone for the Spa at The Ritz-Carlton, New Orleans. This tranquil spa lets you relax and indulge like royalty—the treatment menu was inspired in part by favorite practices of French aristocrats. The Napoleon royal massage is a signature treatment that includes a heav-enly citrus-scented bath prior to a lemon-verbena-scented Swedish rubdown. The body treatments are superb, and the spa's magnolia sugar scrub gently exfoliates and

LOUISIANA

★
★
★
★

polishes skin while the scent of Louisiana's luscious magnolias blend with botanical extracts and aid relaxation.

OPELOUSAS

French is spoken as often as English in this charming old town, the third oldest in the state. Opelousas was a trading post from the early 1700s until 1774, when St. Landry's church was established.

Information: Tourist Information Center, 941 E. Vine St., 337-948-6263, 800-424-5442 or the Tourism & Activities Committee, 441 E. Grolee St., 337-948-4731; www.cityofopelousas.com

WHAT TO SEE AND DO

CHICOT STATE PARK

3469 Chicot Park Road, Opelousas, 337-363-2503, 888-677-2442; www.lastateparks.com/chicot/chicot.htm

Nearly 6,000 acres of rolling woodland surround a 2,000-acre artificial lake stocked with bream, bass and crappie. Swimming, fishing, boating (launch, rentals), hiking, picnicking, tent and trailer sites are all available. Cabins are onsite as well. Daily.

JIM BOWIE MUSEUM

Highway 90 and Academy St., Opelousas, 337-948-6263, 800-424-5442; www.cityofopelousas.com

See memorabilia from the 19th-century adventurer and his famous knife, as well as local historical items in an 18th-century colonial house built by a woman named Venus. Daily.

LOUISIANA STATE ARBORETUM

Opelousas, 337-363-6289, 888-677-6100; www.crt.state.la.us/parks

The 300-acre arboretum on Lake Chicot includes more than 150 species of plant life indigenous to Louisiana. There are also nature trails. Daily.

WASHINGTON

404 N. Main St., Washington, 337-826-3627; www.washingtonla.com

Built between 1780-1835, the antebellum buildings in this historic river port include Hinckley House (1803), House of History (1820), Camellia Cove (1825) and De la Morandiere (1830). Many houses are open for tours (fee).

SPECIAL EVENTS

LOUISIANA YAMBILEE

Fairgrounds, Highway 190 W., Opelousas, 800-210-5298; www.yambilee.com

Don't mistake the yam for a sweet potato, especially during this festival. Last full weekend in October.

ORIGINAL SOUTHWEST LOUISIANA ZYDECO MUSIC FESTIVAL

457 Zydeco Road, off Highway 167, Opelousas, 337-942-2392; www.zydeco.org

This fest celebrates the spicy culture of the Creoles. Concerts and 5K a run are among the offerings. Labor Day weekend.

HOTEL

★★AMERICAN BEST VALUE INN

4165 I-49 Service Road, Opelousas, 337-948-9500; www.choicehotels.com

67 rooms. High-speed Internet access. Restaurant, bar. Fitness center. Outdoor pool. **$**

RUSTON

Ruston rests on the eastern border of the Ark-La-Tex and is home to Louisiana Tech University (which, counting university employees, rivals the population of the city itself).

Information: Ruston/Lincoln Convention and Visitors Bureau, 900 N. Trenton St., 318-255-2031, 800-392-9032; www.rustonlincoln.com

WHAT TO SEE AND DO

LINCOLN PARISH MUSEUM

609 N. Vienna St., Ruston, 318-251-0018, lincolnparishmuseum.org/Welcome.html

This restored house from 1886 is filled with items of local history. Tuesday-Friday.

LOUISIANA TECH UNIVERSITY

152 Kenny Circle, Ruston, 318-257-3036, 800-528-3241; www.latech.edu

The wooded and hilly campus is on the west side of Ruston. The Horticulture Center—with more than 500 species of native and exotic plants and south of town, off Highway 80 W. (Monday-Friday, free)—and the Louisiana Tech Equine Center are also both part of the university (daily; free).

SPECIAL EVENTS

LOUISIANA PASSION PLAY

2111 N. Trenton St., Ruston, 318-255-2031; www.rustonlicoln.com

First weekend in September-second weekend in October.

LOUISIANA PEACH FESTIVAL

N. Trenton St., Ruston, 318-255-2031, 800-392-9032; www.louisianapeachfestival.org

Second weekend in June.

HOTELS

★BEST WESTERN KINGS INN

I-20, Highway 167 S., Ruston, 318-251-0000, 800-528-1234; www.bestwestern.com

52 rooms. Complimentary continental breakfast. **$**

★★HOWARD JOHNSON

401 N. Service Road, Ruston, 318-255-5901; www.hojo.com

228 rooms. High-speed Internet. Restaurant. Fitness center. Outdoor pool. Business center. Pets accepted. **$**

ST. MARTINVILLE

Few towns in Louisiana have a more colorful history than St. Martinville. On the winding, peaceful Bayou Teche, St. Martinville was first settled around 1760. In

LOUISIANA

the years thereafter, Acadians driven out of Nova Scotia by the British drifted into St. Martinville with the hope of finding religious tolerance. The town is the setting for part of Henry Wadsworth Longfellow's *Evangeline*, a poem about an Acadian girl who is separated from her beloved Gabriel when the British deport the Canadians from Canada during the 18th century. Evangeline eventually settles in Philadelphia, where, as an old woman, she finds her beloved in a hospital and he dies in her arms.

Today St. Martinville is a quiet, hospitable destination for visitors who want to stop by the Evangeline Oak and Commemorative Area, sample the local cuisine or spend the night in a quiet bed and breakfast.

Information: Chamber of Commerce, 337-394-7578; www.stmartinville.org

WHAT TO SEE AND DO
EVANGELINE OAK
On the bayou at end of Port St.
This ancient, moss-draped live oak is said to be the meeting place of the real Evangeline and her Gabriel.

LONGFELLOW-EVANGELINE STATE COMMEMORATIVE AREA
1200 N. Main St., St. Martinville, 337-394-3754; www.crt.state.la.us/Parks/ilongfell.aspx
This 157-acre park on the banks of the Bayou Teche is a reconstruction of a typical 19th-century plantation. Begun around 1810 by Pierre Olivier du Clozel, a French Creole, the Olivier plantation (now restored) employs wooden pegs; walls are made of Spanish moss-mixed bousillage and cypress; period furnishings fill the space; and there's a replica of an 1840s kitchen and a kitchen garden. Picnicking is permitted. Daily.

ST. MARTIN OF TOURS CATHOLIC CHURCH
133 S. Main St., St. Martinville, 337-394-7334
Established in 1765 as the mother church of the exiled Acadians, the presently restored building contains stained-glass windows; an exquisite carved baptismal font, which was a gift of Louis XVI of France; a gold and silver sanctuary light; a painting of St. Martin de Tours by Jean Francois Mouchet; and other religious artifacts. Guided tours are available by appointment only.
Behind the church's left wing is:

PETIT PARIS MUSEUM
133 S. Main St., St. Martinville, 337-394-7334
This museum contains a collection of elaborate carnival costumes, local memorabilia and a gift shop. Daily.

PRESBYTERE
133 S. Main St., St. Martinville, 337-394-7334
The priest's residence, Greek Revival in style, was constructed in 1856. By legend, it was built in such a grand manner in the hope that St. Martinville would be designated as the seat of the diocese.

LA PLACE D'EVANGELINE

220 Evangeline Blvd., St. Martinville, 337-394-4010, 800-621-3017;
www.oldcastillo.com

This historic hotel built in the early 1800s is on the banks of Bayou Teche, beneath the Evangeline Oak and near Evangeline Oak Park. Five rooms. Complimentary full breakfast. $$

SHREVEPORT

Founded in 1835 by river captain and steamboat inventor Henry Miller Shreve, Shreveport is now best known for its multiple casinos and thoroughbred racing. If you'd rather not take your chances on a slot machine, try a narrated historical tour of the Red River or tour the city's art museums, the American Rose Center or the botanical garden in RiverView Park.

Information: Shreveport-Bossier Convention & Tourist Bureau, 629 Spring St.,
318-222-9391, 800-551-8682; www.shreveport-bossier.org

WHAT TO SEE AND DO

AMERICAN ROSE CENTER

8877 Jefferson-Paige Road, Shreveport, 318-938-5402; www.ars.org

The center consists of 60 individually designed rose gardens donated by rose societies from across the U.S. April-October: Monday-Friday 9 a.m.-5 p.m., Saturday 9 a.m.-6 p.m., Sunday 1-6 p.m.

C. BICKHAM DICKSON PARK

2283 E. Bert Kouns Loop, Shreveport; 318-673-7808;
www.ci.shreveport.la.us/dept/spar/Parks/sparparks.asp

Shreveport's largest park (585 acres) contains a 200-acre oxbow lake with pier. The park offers fishing, hayrides, picnicking and a playground. Tuesday-Sunday.

LOUISIANA STATE EXHIBIT MUSEUM

3015 Greenwood Road, Shreveport; 318-632-2020; www.sos.louisiana.gov

This museum showcases remarkable dioramas and murals of the prehistory and resources of the Louisiana area. It also has exhibits of antique and modern items and a historical gallery. Tuesday-Saturday.

R. S. BARNWELL MEMORIAL GARDEN AND ART CENTER

601 Clyde Fant Parkway, Shreveport, 318-673-7703; www.nwlagardener.org

The combination art and horticulture facility has permanent and changing exhibits. Flower displays include seasonal and native plantings of the area; the sculpture garden has a walk-through bronze statue; plus, there's a fragrance garden for the visually impaired. Daily.

R. W. NORTON ART GALLERY

4747 Creswell Ave., Shreveport, 318-865-4201; www.rwnaf.org

The art gallery specializes in American and European paintings, sculpture, decorative arts and manuscripts from the 15th to 20th centuries. It also has a large collection of Western art by Frederic Remington and Charles M. Russell. Tuesday-Friday 10 a.m.-5 p.m., Saturday-Sunday 1-5 p.m.

255

LOUISIANA

★
★
★
★

THE STRAND THEATRE

619 Louisiana Ave., Shreveport, 318-226-8555; www.thestrandtheatre.com
This restored ornate theater was built in 1925.

WATER TOWN USA

7670 W. 70th St., Shreveport, 318-938-5475; www.watertownusa.com
This 20-acre water theme park features speed slides, adventure slides and a wave pool, plus two other pools. You can take a break at the restaurant and concessions. Days and times vary.

SPECIAL EVENTS

LOUISIANA STATE FAIR

Fairgrounds, 3701 Hudson Ave., Shreveport, 318-635-1361;
www.statefairoflouisiana.com
One of the largest fairs in the country, it draws more than 300,000 people annually. Entertainment includes an agriculture and livestock competition. Late October-early November.

RED RIVER REVEL ARTS FESTIVAL

Riverfront area, 101 Crockett St., Shreveport, 318-424-4000; www.redriverrevel.com
The national festival features fine arts, crafts, pottery, jewelry, music, performing arts, creative writing, poetry and ethnic foods. Late September-early October.

HOTELS

★ ★ ★ ★

★★BEST WESTERN CHATEAU SUITE HOTEL

201 Lake St., Shreveport, 318-222-7620, 800-845-9334; www.bestwestern.com
101 rooms. High-speed Internet access. Complimentary breakfast buffet. Restaurant, bar. Airport transportation available. Fitness center. Outdoor pool. Business center. $

★★★CLARION HOTEL

1419 E. 70th St., Shreveport, 318-797-9900; www.choicehotels.com
231 rooms. Wireless Internet access. Restaurant, bar. Airport transportation available. Fitness center. Business center. $

★DAYS INN

4935 W. Monkhouse Drive, Shreveport, 318-636-0080, 800-329-7466;
www.daysinn.com
148 rooms. Wireless Internet access. Complimentary continental breakfast. Outdoor pool. Pets accepted, fee. $

★FAIRFIELD INN

6245 Westport Ave., Shreveport, 318-686-0102, 800-228-2800; www.fairfieldinn.com
105 rooms. Complimentary continental breakfast. $

★★HOLIDAY INN

5555 Financial Plaza, Shreveport, 318-688-3000, 800-465-4329; www.holiday-inn.com
226 rooms. High-speed Internet access. Restaurant, bar. Airport transportation available. Pets accepted, fee. $

SPECIALTY LODGINGS

FAIRFIELD PLACE BED & BREAKFAST

2221 Fairfield Ave., Shreveport, 318-222-0048; www.fairfieldbandb.com

Six rooms. Complimentary full breakfast. $$

TWENTY-FOUR THIRTY-NINE FAIRFIELD

2439 Fairfield Ave., Shreveport, 318-424-2424; www.shreveportbedandbreakfast.com

Guests will want to explore this 1905 bed and breakfast when they see its bright turquoise, white-pillared façade. Inside, they'll find Victorian charm, lace and antiques. Downtown Shreveport, Louisiana Downs and riverboat casinos are nearby. Four rooms. Complimentary full breakfast. $$

RESTAURANTS

★★DON'S SEAFOOD

207 Milam St., Shreveport, 318-865-4291; www.ulcoleman.com

Cajun, Creole menu. Lunch, dinner. $$

★SUPERIOR GRILL

6123 Line Ave., Shreveport, 318-869-3243; www.superiorgrill.com

Mexican menu. Lunch, dinner. $$

SLIDELL

Slidell offers natural attractions and scenery in southeast Louisiana. The Honey Island Swamp encompasses the parish's eastern border. Slidell's historic district, called Olde Town, is filled with antique shops and restaurants.

Information: St. Tammany Parish Tourist & Convention Commission,

68099 Highway 59, Mandeville, 985-892-0520, 800-634-9443; www.slidell.la.us

WHAT TO SEE AND DO

FORT PIKE STATE COMMEMORATIVE AREA

Slidell, eight miles east via Highway 190, then six miles southwest on Highway 90,
504-662-5703, 888-662-5703; www.lastateparks.com/fortpike/ fortpike.htm

The fort was constructed in the 1820s to defend navigational channels leading to New Orleans. Visitors can stroll through authentic brick archways and stand overlooking the Rigolets as sentries once did. Picnicking is permitted. Daily.

OAK HARBOR GOLF COURSE

201 Oak Harbor Blvd., Slidell, 985-646-0110; www.oakharborgolf.com

Oak Harbor requires smart, often conservative play to score well, with water on 12 holes and challenging approaches to many greens. Designed in the style of Pete Dye, with railroad ties and bulkheads along the course, Oak Harbor is still only a touch more than 6,200 yards from the men's tees. A GPS system in each cart helps players estimate distances and speed play along one of New Orleans' newer courses, opened in 1992.

SLIDELL CULTURAL CENTER

444 Erlanger St., Slidell, 504-646-4375; www.slidell.la.us/arts center.htm

Art gallery. Monday-Friday 9 a.m.-4 p.m., Saturday 10 a.m.-2 p.m.

LOUISIANA

★
★
★
★

★LA QUINTA INN
794 E. I-10 Service Road, Slidel, 985-643-9770; www.lq.com/lq/properties
172 rooms. Wireless Internet access. Complimentary continental breakfast. Bar. Fitness center. Outdoor pool. Pets accepted. $

ST. FRANCISVILLE
This picturesque old town chartered under Spanish dominion has been called "two miles long and two yards wide" because it was built on a narrow ridge. St. Francisville is listed on the National Register of Historic Places and is the second-oldest incorporated town in the state.

Information: West Feliciana Historical Society, 11757 Ferdinand St., 225-635-6330; www.stfrancisville.net

WHAT TO SEE AND DO
LOUISIANA STATE PENITENTIARY MUSEUM
Highway 66, 20 miles from Highway 61, Angola, 504-655-2592; www.angolamuseum.org
An unusual find, this museum is operated inside an active prison. Exhibits include an original electric chair, original inmate record books dating from 1889 and weapons used by guards. Monday-Friday 8 a.m.-4:30 p.m., Saturday 9 a.m.-5 p.m., Sunday 1-5 p.m.

PLANTATIONS AND HISTORIC BUILDINGS
St. Francisville

258

Here are some noteworthy plantations and historic buildings: Catalpa is four miles north on Highway 61; Oakley is one mile south via Highway 61, then three miles east on Highway 965; Cottage is five miles north on Highway 61; Butler Greenwood is three miles north on Highway 61; Greenwood is three miles north on Highway 61, then 4½ miles west on Highway 66 to Highland Road; Rosedown is east of town on Highway 10. Also of interest are Grace Episcopal Church (1858), in town on Highway 10; Afton Villa Gardens, four miles north on Highway 61; and the Myrtles Plantation, one mile north on Highway 61.

SPECIAL EVENTS
ANGOLA PRISON RODEO
L. S. P. Rodeo Arena, Louisiana State Prison, Highway 66, Angola, 225-655-2592; www.angolarodeo.com
Sundays in October.

AUDUBON PILGRIMAGE
11757 Ferdinand St., St. Francisville, 225-635-6330; www.audubonpilgrimage.info
Tour the historic plantation houses, two gardens and a rural homestead. Third weekend in March.

SOUTHERN GARDEN SYMPOSIUM
9721 Charlotte Armstrong, St. Francisville, 225-635-3738; www.southerngardensymposium.org
This symposium is a tribute to Southern gardening that includes workshops and field trips. Mid-October.

LOUISIANA

SPECIALTY LODGING
BARROW HOUSE INN
9779 Royal St., St. Francisville, 225-635-4791; www.topteninn.com
Five rooms. **$**

SULPHUR
Locals rub elbows with out-of-towners in Sulphur's many restaurants that feature mouthwatering Cajun seafood.
Information: www.sulphur.org

RESTAURANT
★CAJUN CHARLIE'S SEAFOOD RESTAURANT
202 Henning Drive, Sulphur, 337-527-9044; www.cajuncharlies.com
A popular local attraction, Cajun Charlie's is known for authentic Creole seafood recipes. Lunch, dinner. **$**

THIBODAUX
Information: Chamber of Commerce, 1048 Canal Blvd., 985-446-7218; www.ci.thibodaux.la.us

WHAT TO SEE AND DO
MADEWOOD PLANTATION HOUSE
4250 Highway 308, Napoleonville, 504-369-7151; www.madewood.com
This refined example of domestic Greek Revival is furnished with period antiques and houses an extensive art collection. This house served as the setting for the movie *A Woman Called Moses*. On the grounds are the family cemetery and other historic buildings. Daily.

259

LOUISIANA

HOTEL
★★HOWARD JOHNSON
203 N. Canal Blvd., Thibodaux, 985-447-9071, 800-952-2968; www.hojo.com
118 rooms. Complimentary full breakfast. Restaurant, bar. Outdoor pool. Pets accepted, fee. **$**

WASHINGTON
Information: townofwashingtonla.org

SPECIAL EVENT
CATFISH FESTIVAL
Festival grounds, Washington, 337-826-3626; www.townofwashingtonla.org/catfish.htm
At this festival you'll find a Civil War reenactment, arts and crafts, zydeco music and, of course, plenty of catfish. Third weekend of March.

RESTAURANT
★★STEAMBOAT WAREHOUSE
525 N. Main St., Washington, 337-826-7227; www.steamboatwarehouse.com
Cajun, seafood menu. Dinner. Closed Monday. **$$**

MISSISSIPPI

MISSISSIPPI IS A LAND OF GREAT AND TRAGIC STORIES. HERE, THE BLUES WERE BORN ON A large cotton plantation in the early 20th century; many of the Civil War's bloodiest battles were fought; and some of the nation's most celebrated storytellers, including Tennessee Williams, William Faulkner and Eudora Welty, found their inspiration. It's no surprise that history is a part of the lore for the state's visitors, who will find beautifully preserved antebellum homes and tributes to the state's famous sons and daughters at almost every stop. Mississippians know how to celebrate their history: All year long, cities and towns host festivals when locals and visitors can hear the blues, honor Native American traditions or tour some of the South's most beautiful buildings.

Mississippi's recorded history begins when Hernando De Soto trekked across this land looking for gold 80 years before the Mayflower landed in Massachusetts. In 1699, French settlers established Mississippi's first permanent settlement near Biloxi. There was no gold to be found, but the Mississippi River had created something as valuable: immense valleys of rich soil on which cotton could be grown. Cotton plantations became common sights and eventually Mississippi joined other southern states in fighting against all attempts to abolish the plantations' primary source of labor: slavery.

The Civil War brought fierce battles to Mississippi. Many historians believe the 47-day Siege of Vicksburg sealed the South's fate. In the late 19th and early 20th centuries, the state had adopted Jim Crow laws that left Mississippi racially segregated. Nearly 100 years after the Civil War's end, Mississippi found itself in the midst of a set of battles during the civil-rights movement, making the state a representative of the scourge of racial oppression that has stained American history.

Today the Magnolia State is still recovering from Hurricane Katrina's destructive visit in late August of 2005. Its famous Gulf Coast, a popular destination, was ravaged by the storm, and though much of the shoreline is repaired and ready for tourists, it's still a good idea to call ahead to make sure certain attractions are open.

Sandy beaches and fresh seafood aren't all Mississippi has to offer. The John C. Stennis Space Center in Gulfport is NASA's largest rocket engine test facility and offers tours and exhibits about aerospace. In Tupelo, Elvis Presley fans can visit the small white frame house in which the King was born, and travelers who stop in Oxford, home of the University of Mississippi, will find a town that worships Ole Miss football, good food and local literary greats like Faulkner, who based his Yoknapatawpa County on surrounding Lafayette County.

In short, what Mississippi provides is a powerful character, captivating settings and stories that will amaze visitors. But it ultimately offers an opportunity to see the country from a new perspective, through the stories and characters that have shaped not just this scenic land, but the nation, too.

Information: www.visitmississippi.org

FUN FACTS

The blues were born in the Mississippi Delta, where "Father of the Delta Blues" Charley Patton first learned to play the guitar.

Elvis Presley was born in Tupelo in 1935.

THE BLUES HIGHWAY

"If I ever die before you think my time has come, I want you to bury my body out on Highway 61," said Blues icon Mississippi Fred McDowell.

One of the nation's most famous routes, the stretch of Highway 61 between Vicksburg, Miss., and the Tennessee border, travels the length of the Mississippi Delta. Blues music was born here around the turn of the 20th century, and the sound spread north to Memphis and up to Chicago along the Highway 61 corridor. Today Highway 61 is known as "The Blues Highway."

The Mississippi Delta is roughly a diamond-shaped basin, approximately 160 miles long and 50 miles wide. The land is practically treeless, and what's not a cotton field is a catfish pond. The region's main tourist attractions—beyond its rich blues history and musical landmarks—are the casinos along the Mississippi riverbank in Vicksburg, Greenville and Tunica County, just across the border from Memphis, Tennessee.

From Vicksburg, take Interstate 20 (I-20) east to Highway 61 N. to Rolling Fork, where blues marvel Muddy Waters was born in 1915. His mother died when he was three, and Muddy moved north to Clarksdale to live with his grandmother. As you head north, too, take a short detour off Highway 61 to Dockery Farms, where music historians say the blues began. At this large cotton plantation in the early 20th century, field-worker Henry Sloan showed Charley Patton how to play the guitar. Patton would eventually become known as the "Father of the Delta Blues." Continue on to Clarksdale, the ultimate destination for pilgrims on a blues tour of the Mississippi Delta. Blues legend says that bluesman Robert Johnson sold his soul to the devil here at the junction of Highways 61 and 49 in exchange for his extraordinary musical talent. Clarksdale was also home to blues icons Junior Parker, Sam Cooke and John Lee Hooker. The shack where Muddy Waters lived—the original House of Blues—was located at Stovall Farms, seven miles west of town via Oakhurst Avenue. Jazz vocalist Bessie Smith died downtown in what is now the Riverside Hotel boardinghouse at 615 Sunflower Avenue. Even the local barber is renowned as a blues artist; you can hear him busting it out at Walton's Barber Shop at 317 Issaquena Street.

For a thorough education in blues history, visit **Clarksdale's Delta Blues Museum** *(1 Blues alley 662-624-4461, 662-627-6820)*. Set in a restored 1916 freight depot, the museum chronicles the history and heritage of blues music from its African roots to its rock 'n' roll offshoots. The most notorious piece in its collection is the famous "Muddywood" guitar, constructed of wood cannibalized from Muddy Waters' cabin by ZZ Top guitarist Billy Gibbons. This is a great place to ask about what good musicians might be in town.

The next stop on the Blues Highway is Memphis, where the Delta Blues met country and gospel music—and eventually gave birth to good ol' fashioned rock 'n' roll. The fastest route back south is I-55, making the whole trip about 160 miles.

261

MISSISSIPPI

★
★
★
★

BILOXI

The oldest town in the Mississippi Valley, Biloxi has been a popular resort since the 1840s, and after Hurricane Katrina battered its shores in August 2005, the city has worked hard to regain its place as a vacation hot spot. Many of its famed casinos have reopened and at least 60 percent of the town's hotels are back in business.

Biloxi has changed, but many of its prized possessions are still here. Fresh seafood is always available, and visitors who want to catch their own can choose from freshwater, salt water and deep-sea fishing. The beaches are open for visitors who just want to relax on the sand or swim in the surf, and spas, shops and restaurants entice visitors to indulge.

Information: Visitor Center, 710 Beach Blvd., Biloxi, 228-374-3105, 800-245-6943; www.biloxi.ms.us

WHAT TO SEE AND DO
"BEAUVOIR"—JEFFERSON DAVIS HOME AND PRESIDENTIAL LIBRARY
2244 Beach Blvd., Biloxi, 228-388-4400; www.beauvoir.org

Hurricane Katrina damaged much of Beauvoir, but this historic estate was restored in mid-2008. Confederate President Jefferson Davis spent the last 12 years of his life here, writing *The Rise and Fall of the Confederate Government* and *A Short History of the Confederate States of America*. The adjoining museum holds artifacts from Davis and the Confederate states, and Beauvoir's staff has completed recovery and cataloguing of the artifacts that survived the storm. Here, too, is a cemetery with the Tomb of the Unknown Soldier of the Confederate States of America and a Presidential Library dedicated to Jefferson's tenure.

BILOXI CITY CEMETERY
1166 Irish Hill Drive, Biloxi; www.biloxi.ms.us

Across the rolling grass here are the burials ground of the French pioneer families of Biloxi and the Gulf Coast. John Cuevas, hero of Cat Island War of 1812, is buried here.

HARRISON COUNTY SAND BEACH
842 Commerce St., Biloxi, 228-896-0055; www.co.harrison.ms.us

This 300-foot-wide white sand beach stretches the entire 26-mile length of the county, with a seawall separating the beach from the highway.

SMALL CRAFT HARBOR
Main Street and Highway 90, Biloxi

Visitors can view fishing boats unloading the day's catch of Gulf game fish or chart their own deep-sea fishing boat to make the big catch themselves.

SPECIAL EVENTS
BLESSING OF THE FLEET
177 First St., Biloxi, Gulf of Mexico; www.biloxiblessing.com

Hundreds of vessels manned by descendants of settlers participate in this ritual of European origin. Last weekend in May.

GARDEN CLUB PILGRIMAGE

261 Lovers Lane, Biloxi

Visitors receive a guided tour of historic houses, sites and gardens. March and April.

MARDI GRAS

2501 Beachview Drive, Biloxi

The biggest party of the year, Mardi Gras includes a carnival and parade with colorful, festive floats. February.

SEAFOOD FESTIVAL

Point Cadet Plaza, 120 Cadet St., Biloxi

Visitors in the early fall can catch this festival, which includes an arts and crafts show, entertainment, seafood booths and contests. Mid- to late September.

HOTELS

★★★BEAU RIVAGE BY MIRAGE RESORTS

875 Beach Blvd., Biloxi, 228-386-7444, 888-567-6667; www.beaurivage.com

Las Vegas meets the French Riviera of the South at Beau Rivage. A world of its own, the resort has a 31-slip marina, a casino and other recreational and entertainment choices. The guest rooms, decorated in styles that evoke the English countryside, offer great views of the bay or ocean, and eight restaurants offer cuisine inspired by places across the globe. Sports enthusiasts charter boats for relaxing rides or sport-fishing adventures, while the spa and salon lure landlubbers with a penchant for pampering. 1,780 rooms. Restaurant, bar. Spa. **$**

★★★GRAND CASINO HOTEL BILOXI

265 Beach Blvd., Biloxi, 228-432-2500, 800-946-2946

491 rooms. Restaurant, bar. Airport transportation available. Children's activity center. **$**

RESTAURANT

★★★MARY MAHONEY'S OLD FRENCH HOUSE

Magnolia and Water streets, Biloxi, 228-374-0163; www.marymahoneys.com

Mary Mahoney, daughter of Yugoslavian immigrants, founded this Gulf Coast landmark in 1964. The menu is full of fresh seafood dishes, such as crabmeat au gratin and fried oysters. American menu. Lunch, dinner. Closed Sunday. **$$$**

CLARKSDALE

Musicians in the know point to Clarksdale as the birthplace of the blues. In the early 20th century, fieldworker Henry Sloan showed Charley Patton how to play the guitar, and Patton went on to become the "Father of the Delta Blues." Muddy Waters grew up here, as did John Lee Hooker. Actor Morgan Freeman chose Clarksdale as the site of his celebrated Ground Zero blues club and his Madidi restaurant.

Information: Coahoma County Tourism Commission, 1540 Desoto, Clarksdale, 662-627-7337, 800-626-3764; www.clarksdale.com

CARNEGIE PUBLIC LIBRARY

114 Delta Ave., Clarksdale, 662-624-4461; www.cplclarksdale.lib.ms.us

Located within the library is the Archaeology Museum, which has Native American pottery and other artifacts on exhibit. The library also contains a collection of books and reports on Lower Mississippi Valley archaeology. Monday-Saturday.

DELTA BLUES MUSEUM

1 Blues Alley, Clarksdale, 662-627-6820; www.deltabluesmuseum.org

Museum highlights include video and audio recordings as well as memorabilia about blues music. There are permanent and changing exhibits and performances as well. March-October 15: Monday-Saturday 9 a.m.-5 p.m.; rest of year: 10 a.m.-5 p.m.

NORTH DELTA MUSEUM

700 Second St., Friars Point, 662-383-2233; www.museumsusa.org/museums

Archaeological and historical exhibits of early Delta life are on display, including Native American artifacts, three original log buildings and Civil War artifacts. Tuesday-Friday, Saturday.

SPECIAL EVENTS

DELTA JUBILEE

114 Delta Ave., Clarksdale

This statewide arts and crafts festival includes the Mississippi championship pork barbecue cooking contest, a 5K run and an antique car show. First weekend in June.

264

SUNFLOWER RIVER BLUES AND GOSPEL FESTIVAL

Clarksdale, www.sunflowerfest.org

For those seeking a flavor the local music, this weekend of outdoor concerts puts on performances of the blues on Friday and Saturday, with gospel on Sunday. The food choices include local barbecue and other Southern specialties. Early August.

HOTEL

★BEST WESTERN EXECUTIVE INN

710 S. State St., Clarksdale, 662-627-9292; www.bestwestern.com

93 rooms. Complimentary continental breakfast. Restaurant. $

CLEVELAND

From music and theater to a thriving visual arts scene, Cleveland is worth exploring. A sizable state park keeps locals and out-of-towners busy with plenty of outdoor activities.

Information: Cleveland-Bolivar County Chamber of Commerce, 600 Third St., Cleveland, 662-843-2712, 800-295-7473; www.clevelandmschamber.com

WHAT TO SEE AND DO

DELTA STATE UNIVERSITY

Highway 8 W., Cleveland, 662-846-3000; www.deltastate.edu

Visitors to the campus will find more than a steady stream of students passing by. The university also hosts the Bologna Performing Arts Center and the Wright Art Center Gallery.

MISSISSIPPI

BOLOGNA PERFORMING ARTS CENTER

1003 W. Sunflower Road, Cleveland, 662-846-4626; www.bolognapac.com

The center hosts performances in music, theater and dance.

WRIGHT ART CENTER GALLERY

Highway 8, Cleveland, 662-846-4720; www.deltastate.edu

The gallery highlights the work of Southern artists.

GREAT RIVER ROAD STATE PARK

Highway 1 S., 18 miles west on Highway 8, Rosedale, 662-759-6762; www.mdwfp.com

This 800-acre park is situated on the bluffs of the Mississippi River and has the state's largest campground inside the levee. Visitors can fish on Perry Martin Lake, where one can find a boating ramp and rentals. Elsewhere at the part are nature and bicycle trails, picnicking shelters, a playground, a playing field, a snack bar, a lodge, different levels of camping facilities and a coin laundry.

HOTEL

★★HOLIDAY INN EXPRESS HOTEL & SUITES CLEVELAND

808 N. Davis Ave., Cleveland, 662-843-9300; www.hiexpress.com

119 rooms. Restaurant, bar. $

COLUMBUS

Birthplace of Pulitzer Prize-winning playwright Tennessee Williams, Columbus is a mid-sized town on the Tennessee-Tombigbee Waterway. It began as a stopover on the Military Road between New Orleans and Nashville and served as a hospital town, thereby dodging Union attacks. The Columbus Female Institute, founded in 1847, later became the first state-supported school in the United States to offer education exclusively to women, the Mississippi University for Women, established in 1884.

Information: Columbus Convention & Visitors Bureau, 662-329-1191, 800-327-2686; www.columbus-ms.org

265

MISSISSIPPI

★
★
★
★

WHAT TO SEE AND DO

BLEWETT-HARRISON-LEE MUSEUM

316 Seventh St. N., Columbus, 662-327-8888

Known also as the General Stephen D. Lee home, the museum contains articles of local history as well as Civil War exhibits.

FRIENDSHIP CEMETERY

Fourth Street S. and 13th Avenue, Columbus, 662-328-2565

The first Memorial Day—April 25, 1866—was observed here when the women of Columbus gathered to decorate graves of Union and Confederate soldiers.

HISTORIC HOUSES

Columbus

Columbus boasts more than 100 antebellum houses. Some are open for tours daily. For information, 30-minute auto tour map and narrative of houses, call the Convention & Visitors Bureau at 662-329-1191. There's a tour fee per home.

LAKE LOWNDES STATE PARK

3319 Lake Lowndes, Columbus, 662-328-2110; www.mdwfp.com

This is one of the finest recreation complexes of the state parks. The grounds are approximately 600 acres with a nature trail, tennis courts, game fields, a picnicking area, children's playground, concession stands, an indoor recreation complex, cabins, campgrounds and coin laundry. The park also has a 150-acre lake for activities such as swimming, waterskiing, fishing and boating. Ramps and rentals are available.

WAVERLY PLANTATION

1852 Waverley Mansion Road, Columbus, 662-494-1399

Here you'll find a classic Southern mansion with twin, circular, self-supporting stairways leading to a 65-foot-high observation cupola. The house contains original gold-leaf mirrors and Italian marble mantels. Daily.

SPECIAL EVENT

PILGRIMAGE

Columbus, 601-329-3533; www.historic-columbus.org

Costumed guides conduct tours through 15 historic houses. First two weeks of April.

HOTELS

★COMFORT INN

1210 Highway 45 N., Columbus, 662-329-2422, 800-228-5150; www.choicehotels.com

106 rooms. Wireless Internet access. Complimentary continental breakfast. Business center. $

★★MASTER HOST INN & SUITES

506 Highway 45 N., Columbus, 662-328-5202, 800-465-4329; www.holiday-inn.com

153 rooms. Restaurant, bar. $

RESTAURANT

★★HARVEY'S

200 Main St., Columbus, 662-327-1639; www.eatwithus.com

Southern menu. Lunch, dinner. Closed Sunday. $$

CORINTH

Corinth preserves and celebrates its Civil War history. The town's location as a major railroad junctions made it an important strategic site during the war. Between 1861 and 1865, as many as 300,000 soldiers from the north and the south occupied the town.

In a struggle for control of the area, 65,000 Union troops met 44,000 Confederate troops in the Battle of Shiloh; the Confederate soldiers lost and evacuated the city. Six months later, they attempted but failed to reclaim the city in the Battle of Corinth, the bloodiest clash of the Civil War in Mississippi.

Information: Corinth Area Tourism Promotion Council, 602 E. Waldron St., Corinth 662-287-8300, 800-748-9048; www.corinth.net

BATTERY ROBINETT

102 Linden St., Corinth, 662-287-8300

This union fort was constructed on inner defense lines during the Battle of Corinth in 1862. Monuments mark the spots where Confederate soldiers died, and headstones commemorate color-bearers who fell while trying to plant a flag during battle.

CURLEE HOUSE

705 Jackson St., Corinth, 662-287-9501; www.curleehouse.org

A restored antebellum house, this was the headquarters for Generals. Bragg, Halleck and Hood during the Civil War. Daily.

JACINTO COURTHOUSE

Jacinto, 215 N. Fillmore, 800-748-9048; www.corinth.net

This is a fine example of early federal architecture, serving first as the courthouse for old Tishomingo County. Later the site was used as both a school and a church. Tuesday-Sunday.

GREENVILLE

Greenville is in the Mississippi Delta on Lake Ferguson, an oxbow lake created by levees on the Mississippi River. Here visitors will find beautiful cypress groves, lively juke joints and the bright lights of casinos on the lake.

Information: Greenville Area Chamber of Commerce, 915 Washington Ave., 662-378-3141; Washington County Convention & Visitors Bureau, 410 Washington Ave., 662-334-2711; www.greenvilleareachamber.com

267

WHAT TO SEE AND DO

BIRTHPLACE OF THE FROG EXHIBIT

South Deer Creek Drive, East Leland, 662-686-2687; www.lelandms.org/kermit.html

It might not easy being green, but it is easy to celebrate the man who gave us Kermit the Frog. This exhibit, in the Washington County Tourist Center, houses Muppet memorabilia from collectors and the family of the late Jim Henson, the creator of Kermit, Miss Piggy and the rest of the Muppet gang. Monday-Saturday 10 a.m.-4 p.m., Sunday 2-4 p.m.; June-August: daily 10 a.m.-5 p.m.

LEROY PERCY STATE PARK

Highway 12, W., Hollandale, 662-827-5436; www.mdwfp.com

The oldest of Mississippi's state parks comprises approximately 2,400 acres of artesian springs, cypress trees and ancient oaks covered in Spanish moss. One of the four hot artesian wells provides water for an alligator pond, which can be view from the boardwalk. Nature trails lead through the Delta lowlands and a live alligator exhibit. The park also has picnicking shelters, a playground, a game field, a snack bar, a restaurant, campgrounds, cabins, a lodge and coin laundry. Fishing and hunting are also available on the grounds. Memorial Day-Labor Day: daily.

MISSISSIPPI

★
★
★
★

RIVER ROAD QUEEN

Highway 82, Greenville, 662-332-2378; www.steamboats.org

Built for 1984 World's Fair, the replica of a 19th-century paddlewheel steamboat serves as the town's welcome center. Daily.

WINTERVILLE MOUNDS STATE PARK

2415 Highway 1 N., Greenville, 662-334-4684; www.ohwy.com/ms/w/winmousp.htm

One of the largest groups of Native American mounds in the Mississippi Valley, the area was a religious site and an economic and military center for thousands of Native Americans during the Mississippian era, which ended after De Soto's exploration. The park contains the Great Temple mound, which at 55 feet high is surrounded by ten smaller mounds used for a variety of purposes. Also on the grounds are picnicking shelters, a concession stand, a children's playground and a museum that houses artifacts from the mound site and adjoining territory. Wednesday-Sunday.

SPECIAL EVENT

MISSISSIPPI DELTA BLUES AND HERITAGE FESTIVAL

Highway 1 South and Highway 454, Greenville, 601-335-3523; www.deltablues.org

The state's largest tourist attraction, this festival showcases blues musicians from across the country. More than 20,000 people arrive in Greenville to celebrate the native sounds of the Mississippi Delta, the birthplace of the blues. September.

HOTELS

★HAMPTON INN

2701 Highway 82 E., Greenville, 662-334-1818; www.hamptoninn.com

120 rooms. Complimentary continental breakfast. **$**

★★RAMADA

2700 Highway 82 E., Greenville, 662-332-4411, 800-272-6232; www.ramada.com

121 rooms. Complimentary full breakfast. Restaurant, bar. Airport transportation available. **$**

RESTAURANT

★SHERMAN'S

1400 S. Main St., Greenville, 662-332-6924

American, Italian menu. Lunch, dinner. Closed Sunday. **$$**

GREENWOOD

Lying on both banks of the Yazoo River and surrounded by rich, black delta lands, Greenwood is in the heart of the deep South. In the town's early years, cotton boosted the local economy, and Greenwood served as an important river port in the South. After the Civil War, railroads brought more resources to the flourishing town. Today Greenwood's historic downtown district is undergoing a revival. Dozens of buildings have been restored, and unique shops, restaurants and galleries are popping up in the district.

Information: Convention & Visitors Bureau, 662-453-9198, 800-748-9064; www.gcvb.com

MISSISSIPPI

★
★
★
★

COTTONLANDIA MUSEUM

1608 Highway 82 W., Greenwood, 662-453-0925; www.cottonlandia.org

Exhibits highlight the history of the Mississippi Delta, its people and its land from 10,000 B.C. to the present. There is also an exhibit focused on the work of Mississippi artists, a garden and a gift shop. Monday-Friday 9 a.m.-5 p.m., Saturday-Sunday 2-5 p.m.

FLOREWOOD RIVER PLANTATION

Highway 82, Greenwood, 662-455-3821

Here you'll find a re-creation of an 1850s plantation and outbuildings. Tours, March-November: Tuesday-Sunday; limited tours rest of year.

HOTELS

★BEST WESTERN GREENWOOD

635 Highway 82 W., Greenwood, 662-455-5777, 888-455-5770; www.bestwestern.com

100 rooms. High-speed Internet access. Complimentary continental breakfast. Outdoor pool. $

★COMFORT INN

401 W Highway 82, Greenwood, 662-453-5974, 800-228-5150; www.choicehotels.com

60 rooms. Complimentary continental breakfast. $

RESTAURANT

★★CRYSTAL GRILL

423 Carrollton Ave., Greenwood, 662-453-6530

Seafood, steak menu. Lunch, dinner. Closed Monday. $$

269

GRENADA

Home to Grenada Lake, the town in north-central Mississippi has plenty of opportunities to play outdoors. The city recently finished construction on an 18-hole golf course on the lake, and the lake attracts fishermen, boaters and campers who want to relax on its shores.

Information: Grenada Tourism Commission, 95 S.W., Frontage Road, 662-226-2571, 800-373-2571; www.grenadamississippi.com

MISSISSIPPI

★
★
★
★

WHAT TO SEE AND DO

GRENADA LAKE

2088 Scenic Loop 333, Grenada, 662-226-5911

Covering approximately 35,000 acres, with 200 miles of shoreline, the lake features swimming, water sports, fishing, hunting, boating, archery, tennis, camping and picnicking. The visitors' center is at Grenada Dam on Scenic Loop 333. Daily.

HISTORIC OLD GRENADA

Motor and walking tours are available of the historic homes and churches. Contact the Chamber of Commerce at 800-373-2571 to arrange a tour.

HUGH WHITE STATE PARK

3170 Hugh White State Park Road, Grenada, 662-226-4934; www.mdwst.com

Located on Grenada Lake, the 1,581-acre park includes a swimming beach, a pool, a boating ramp and rentals, nature and bicycle trails, campgrounds, a picnicking shelter and a lodge.

THUNDER ON WATER FESTIVAL

Grenada Lake, 800-373-2571; www.thunderonwater.com

A parade, children's fishing rodeo, antique car show, boat light parade and several speed boat races are just part of what makes up this weekend festival. Second weekend in June.

GULF ISLANDS NATIONAL SEASHORE

The nation's largest national seashore, Gulf Islands stretches 150 miles from Mississippi to Florida. The headquarters for the Mississippi district is in Ocean Springs. Sparkling beaches, coastal marshes and wildlife sanctuaries may be found on four offshore islands (Petit Bois, Horn, East Ship and West Ship) and the mainland area of Davis Bayou. The mainland areas are open year-round and are accessible from Highway 90.

In 1969, Hurricane Camille split Ship Island in two, leaving East Ship and West Ship Islands. Ship Island was once a base for French exploration and settlement 1699-1753 of the Gulf Coast from Mobile, Ala., to the mouth of the Mississippi River. What is now East Ship Island once served as the staging area for a 50-ship British armada and an unsuccessful attempt to capture New Orleans in 1815 at the end of the War of 1812.

On West Ship Island is Fort Massachusetts. Construction of this brick coastal defense began in 1859, prior to the outbreak of the Civil War. Two years later, after the state seceded from the Union, the Mississippi militia took control of the fort from the U.S. Army Corps of Engineers. The Confederates later fortified it, naming it Fort Twiggs in honor of the New Orleans Confederate general. Repeated threats by Northern forces prompted the Confederates to withdraw. The Union soldiers moved into the fort and named it Fort Massachusetts. For a time, the area east of the fort served as a prisoner-of-war camp, confining some 4,300 Confederate prisoners at one point. Tours of the fort are offered daily, March-November. Concession boats run to Fort Massachusetts and West Ship Island from Gulfport March-October, depending on weather conditions.

All four offshore islands are accessible year-round by boat only, and popular activities include wilderness camping, surf fishing, surf swimming, boating, picnicking and hiking. No motor vehicles or glass are allowed on the islands. Horn and Petit Bois are designated as wilderness areas, and special restrictions apply. Davis Bayou lures visitors to kayak through its muddy waters past alligators, turtles, frogs and other creatures.

The mainland campground has water and electric hookups at 51 sites, a public boat dock and picnic areas. The visitor center offers audiovisual programs, exhibits, boardwalks and nature trails. Pets are accepted on leash only.

Information: Park Office, 3500 Park Road, Ocean Springs, 228-875-0821; www.nps.gov/guis

270

MISSISSIPPI

★
★
★
★
★

HOTELS

★★AMERICA'S BEST VALUE INN

1750 Sunset Drive, Grenada, 662-226-7816, 800-880-8866;
www.americasbestvalueinn.com
61 rooms. Complimentary full breakfast. Restaurant. **$**

★COMFORT INN

1552 Sunset Drive, Grenada, 662-226-1683, 800-228-5150; www.choicehotels.com
64 rooms. Wireless Internet access. Complimentary continental breakfast. **$**

GULFPORT

Gulfport's greatest asset—its prime spot near the Gulf of Mexico—became a liability in August of 2005, when Hurricane Katrina damaged much of the Gulf Coast, including many of Gulfport's buildings. The city is rebuilding, and this resort town is open for business. The same beaches that attracted visitors in the 1920s await sunbathers today, and Gulfport's proximity to lakes, rivers, bays and bayous make it an angler's paradise. The city has boutique shops, colorful casinos and several 18-hole public golf courses.
Information: Chamber of Commerce, 1401 20th Ave., 228-863-2933; www.biloxi.org

WHAT TO SEE AND DO

JOHN C. STENNIS SPACE CENTER

NASA Space Center, 38 miles west via I-10, Gulfport, 228-688-2370;
www.ssc.nasa.gov
In the 1960s and 1970s, locals would quip, "If you want to go to the moon, you have to go through Hancock County, Mississippi," part of the Gulfport-Biloxi metro area and home to the Stennis Space Center. NASA's largest rocket engine test facility, the Stennis Space Center was the testing site for *Saturn V* and for the first and second stages of the Apollo manned lunar program, which landed the first men on the moon in 1969. The Stennis Space Center hosts NASA and 18 federal and state agencies involved in oceanographic, environmental and national defense programs. There is a visitor center with a 90-foot Space Tower, films, demonstrations, indoor and outdoor exhibits and guided tours. Daily.

PORT OF GULFPORT

Mississippi Technical Center, 200 E Main St., Starkville, 662-324-7776;
www.starkville.org
Extends seaward from the junction of Highway 49 and 90, located equidistant to New Orleans and Mobile, Ala., The 1,320-foot-wide harbor separates the port's two parallel piers, which includes one of the largest banana import facilities in the U.S.

SHIP ISLAND EXCURSIONS

Gulfport Yacht Harbor, Highway 90, Gulfport, 228-864-1014; www.msshipisland.com
Come here to catch a passenger ferry that leaves from the Gulfport Yacht Harbor for a one-hour trip to Ship Island, 12 miles off the coast. You can spend as much time on the island as you like, as long as you catch the last ferry of the day, at either 2:30 or 5 p.m. depending on the day and time of year. No reservations are accepted. March-October, schedule varies, one to three cruises daily.

271

MISSISSIPPI

SMALL CRAFT HARBOR
Highways 49 and 90, Gulfport
Stop here for launching ramps, charter boats and pleasure craft docking.

SPECIAL EVENT
MISSISSIPPI DEEP-SEA FISHING RODEO
Small Craft Harbor, Highways 49 and 90, Gulfport, 228-388-2271;
www.mississippideepseafishingrodeo.com
The "rodeo" attracts fishermen from the U.S., Canada and Latin America, who compete in this deep-sea and freshwater fishing classic. Children can compete, too, in the junior division. The festivities include a carnival, food and fireworks. Early July.

HOTEL
★★HOLIDAY INN
1600 E. Beach Blvd., Gulfport, 228-864-4310, 800-441-0887; www.holiday-inn.com
229 rooms. Restaurant, bar. $

RESTAURANT
★★VRAZEL'S
3206 W. Beach Blvd., Gulfport, 228-863-2229; www.vrazels.com
American menu. Lunch, dinner. Closed Sunday. $$$

HATTIESBURG

Hattiesburg's founder, William Hardy, named the town after his wife, Hattie. When railroads were routed through Hattiesburg during the late 19th century, the town began to thrive. Today, Hattiesburg boasts a booming arts scene and one of the largest historic districts in southeast Mississippi. The buildings reflect architectural styles from 1884 to 1930. Hattiesburg is also home to the University of Southern Mississippi; residents and visitors can enjoy the university's cultural and athletic events.
Information: Convention and Visitors Bureau, 1 Convention Center Plaza,
601-268-3220, 601-638-6877; www.hattiesburg.org

WHAT TO SEE AND DO
DE SOTO NATIONAL FOREST
654 W. Frontage Road, Chickasaw Ranger District, Wiggins,
601-965-4391; www.fs.fed.us/r8/mississippi
At approximately 500,000 acres, the park includes the Black Creek Float Trip, which offers 50 miles of scenic streams, and the Black Creek Trail has 41 miles of woodland paths, 10 of which go through 5,000 acres of Black Creek Wilderness. Fees may be charged at designated recreation sites. Activities include swimming, fishing, hiking, horse riding, picnicking and primitive camping. Ranger District offices are located in Laurel, Wiggins and McHenry.

PAUL B. JOHNSON STATE PARK
319 Geiger Lake Road, Hattiesburg, 601-582-7721; www.mdwfp.com
The park contains more than 805 acres of pine forest and a spring-fed lake that provides excellent facilities for water sports. Activities include swimming, waterskiing, fishing, boating, and facilities include a playground, playing fields, a snack bar,

a lodge with game room, picnicking shelters, boat ramps and rentals, campgrounds and cabins.

UNIVERSITY OF SOUTHERN MISSISSIPPI
2700 Hardy St., Hattiesburg, 601-266-4491; www.usm.edu
The University's library houses a large collection of original illustrations and manuscripts for children's books by authors and artists from here and abroad. The American Rose Society looks after a garden that blooms from spring to mid-December.

HOTELS
★★COMFORT INN
6595 Highway 49 N., Hattiesburg, 601-599-2001, 800-228-5150;
www.hattiesburginn.com
119 rooms. Complimentary full breakfast. Restaurant, bar. $

★★HOLIDAY INN
6563 Highway 49 N., Hattiesburg, 601-268-2850, 800-465-4329; www.holiday-inn.com
128 rooms. Restaurant, bar. $

RESTAURANTS
★★CHESTERFIELD'S
2507 Hardy St., Hattiesburg, 601-582-2778; www.hattiesburg.org
Seafood, steak menu. Lunch, dinner. $$

★★CRESCENT CITY GRILL
3810 Hardy St., Hattiesburg, 601-264-0657; www.nsrg.com
Creole, French menu. Lunch, dinner. $$

HOLLY SPRINGS
Holly Springs crowns the ridge along which a Native American trail once led from the Mississippi to the tribal home of the Chickasaw Nation. Holly Springs has a reputation for preserving its historical buildings, including the antebellum homes that rose during a prosperous era in the 19th century, but perhaps its most remarkable attraction is Graceland, a museum full of Elvis memorabilia, open 24 hours a day.
Information: Chamber of Commerce, 154 S. Memphis St., 662-252-2943;
www.hollyspringsnc.us

MISSISSIPPI

★
★
★
★
★

WHAT TO SEE AND DO
HOLLY SPRINGS NATIONAL FOREST
1000 Front St., Oxford, 662-965-4391; www.fs.fed.us/r8/mississippi
Intensive erosion control measures are carried out within this 152,200-acre area. Activities include fishing, large and small game hunting and boating at Puskus, Chewalla and Tillatoba lakes.

KATE MAN CLARK ART GALLERY
300 E. College Ave., Holly Springs, 662-252-4211; www.firststate.net
Endowed by the artist to house her works permanently, the gallery contains more than 1,000 paintings done while Clark studied under William Merritt Chase in New York

in the early 1900s. Clark returned to her native Holly Springs in 1923 and stored her work here until her death 40 years later. Also on site are three canvasses by Chase and one by Rockwell Kent.

MARSHALL COUNTY HISTORICAL MUSEUM

220 E. College Ave., Holly Springs, 662-252-3669;
www.marshallcountyms.org

The museum houses local historical artifacts, a Civil War room, as well as quilts, dolls, toys, antique clothing and wildlife exhibits. Library: Monday-Saturday.

RUST COLLEGE

150 Rust Ave., Holly Springs, 662-252-8000; www.rustcollege.edu

This historically black liberal arts college rests on the site of campground for General Grant's troops. On campus is Leontyne Price Library, home to the Roy Wilkins Collection on civil rights.

WALL DOXEY STATE PARK

3946 Highway 7 S., Holly Springs, 662-252-4231; www.mdwfp.com

The park covers 850 acres located on a spring-fed lake. Activities include swimming, waterskiing, fishing, boating, and facilities include a playground, playing fields, a snack bar, a lodge, picnicking shelters, boat ramps and rentals, campgrounds and cabins.

SPECIAL EVENT

PILGRIMAGE

154 S. Memphis St., Holly Springs, 662-252-2943

Here you can tour historic houses and gardens open to visitors. Mid-April.

★
★★
★★
★★
★

JACKSON

Jackson sits on the bluffs above the Pearl River, a site chosen by French Canadian pioneer Louis LeFleur for its proximity to navigable water, a necessary resource for a new settlement's economic future. Named for Maj. Gen. Andrew Jackson, the hero of the South who would become the seventh president of the United States, the growing town became the capital of Mississippi in 1821. During the Civil War, the town was burned by Union troops, and Jackson earned the unfortunate nickname "Chimneyville."

In 1868, the "Black and Tan" convention that met in Jackson was the first political organization in Mississippi with black representation. Its attendees framed a state constitution that gave black citizens the right to vote and enabled a few to attain high political office.

Not surprisingly, in the early to mid-20th century, Jackson was not immune from the increased racial tensions that plagued the nation and especially the South. During the civil-rights movement, clashes between white supremacists and black activists came to head here, when Ku Klux Klan member Byron de la Beckwith murdered civil-rights leader Medgar Evers in 1963. More than 30 years later, Beckwith was convicted of the crime.

In the second half of the 20th century, Jackson's population grew steadily and the city established itself as a main metropolis of the South. With the influx of residents came more recreational and cultural activities. Today, art galleries, museums, historic homes, theaters and blues and jazz clubs line city streets.

Jackson is Mississippi's most populated city with more than 400,000 residents, but it feels smaller because the population is relatively spread out. Most of the city's cultural offerings are downtown, but visitors trek to Jackson's different neighborhoods to get a real feel for the city. Ridgeland, a few miles from the city center, is a hotbed of restaurants, hotels and shops that range from chain stores to locally owned boutiques. Farish Street, west of downtown, was a center of African-American culture, politics and business after the Civil War. Once a vibrant community, Farish Street is now economically depressed but full of fascinating sites and stories. And Mid North, a comfortable residential area, is home to Millsaps College.

Information: Convention & Visitors Bureau, 921 N. President St., 601-960-1891, 800-354-7695; www.visitjackson.com

WHAT TO SEE AND DO

ARCHIVES AND LIBRARY DIVISION
Jackson, 601-359-6876, www.mdah.state.ms.us
Here you'll find the state archives, history collections and a research library.

BATTLEFIELD PARK
Porter Street and Langley Avenue, Jackson
The site of a Civil War battle, the park contains an original cannon and trenches.

CONFEDERATE MONUMENT
East end of Capitol Street at State Street, Jackson
This monument was built with money raised by the women of Mississippi and by legislative appropriations.

DAVIS PLANETARIUM/MCNAIR SPACE THEATER
201 E. Pascagoula St., Jackson, 601-960-1550; www.jacksonms.gov
The programs changes quarterly for the 230-seat auditorium. Daily.

GOVERNOR'S MANSION
300 E. Capitol St., Jackson, 601-359-3175; www.mdah.state.ms.us
Restored to its original Greek revival style, the mansion houses antiques and period furnishings. The grounds occupy an entire block and features gardens and gazebos. Tours: Tuesday-Friday, mornings only.

JACKSON COUNTY FAIR
Fairgrounds, 200 W. Ganson St., Jackson; www.co.jackson.ms.us
Mid-October.

JACKSON ZOOLOGICAL PARK
2918 W. Capitol St., Jackson, 601-352-2580; www.jacksonzoo.com
More than 400 mammals, birds and reptiles are housed here in naturalized habitats. Daily 9 a.m.-5 p.m.

MANSHIP HOUSE
420 E. Fortification St., Jackson, 601-961-4724; www.mdah.state.ms.us
This restored Gothic revival cottage circa 1855 was the residence of Charles Henry Manship, mayor of Jackson during the Civil War. Here you'll find period furnishings

MISSISSIPPI

★
★
★
★

as well as fine examples of wood graining and marbling. Tuesday-Friday 9 a.m.-4 p.m., Saturday 10 a.m.-4 p.m.

MISSISSIPPI AGRICULTURE & FORESTRY MUSEUM AND NATIONAL AGRICULTURAL AVIATION MUSEUM

1150 Lakeland Drive, Jackson, 601-713-3365, 800-844-8687; www.mdac.sate.ms.us
This complex, covering 39 acres, includes a museum exhibit center, forest trail, a 1920s living history town and farm. Monday-Saturday 9 a.m.-5 p.m.

MISSISSIPPI MUSEUM OF ART

201 E. Pascagoula, Jackson, 601-960-1515; www.msmuseumart.org
Exhibitions of 19th- and 20th-century works by local, regional, national and international artists are on display here. The museum's collection also includes African-American folk art, photographs, a sculpture garden, a hands-on children's gallery and a restaurant. Monday-Saturday 10 a.m.-5 p.m., Sunday noon-5 p.m.

MISSISSIPPI PETRIFIED FOREST

124 Forest Park Road, Flora, 601-879-8189; www.mspetrifiedforest.com
Surface erosion has exposed giant trees up to six feet in diameter. onsite are petrified logs that were deposited in the Mississippi area as driftwood by a prehistoric river, a self-guided nature trail and a museum at the visitor center that has a gift shops and dioramas as well as wood, gem, mineral and fossil displays. Daily.

MISSISSIPPI SPORTS HALL OF FAME AND MUSEUM

1152 Lakeland Drive, Jackson, 601-982-8264, 800-280-3263; www.msfame.com
The museum celebrates great athletes who hail from Mississippi, including Walter Payton, Archie Manning and George "Boomer" Scott. Touch-screen television kiosks play archival sports footage. Through interactive technology, visitors can play championship golf courses, kick soccer balls into "goals" and throw a baseball into a "field." Monday-Saturday 10 a.m.-4 p.m.

MUNICIPAL ART GALLERY

839 N. State St., Jackson, 601-960-1582;www.jacksonms.gov
The gallery features changing exhibits in a variety of media displayed in an antebellum house. Tuesday-Sunday.

MUSEUM OF NATURAL SCIENCE

2148 Riverside Drive, Jackson, 601-354-7303; www.mdwfp.com/museum
Collections, designed for research and education, cover Mississippi's vertebrates, invertebrates, plants and fossils. Exhibits and aquariums depict the ecological story of the region, and educational programs and workshops are offered for all ages. Monday-Friday 8 a.m.-5 p.m., Saturday 9 a.m.-5 p.m., Sunday 1-5 p.m.

MYNELLE GARDENS

4736 Clinton Blvd., Jackson, 601-960-1894
This 5-acre display garden has thousands of azaleas, camellias, daylilies, flowering trees and other perennials, reflecting pools, a statuary, an Oriental garden and an all-white garden. The turn-of-the-century Westbrook House is open for viewing. Daily.

OLD CAPITOL

100 S. State St., Jackson, 601-359-6920; www.mdah.state.ms.us/museum

The State Historical Museum here traces state history in a restored Greek revival building that was the state capitol from 1839 to 1903. Onsite is also a collection of Jefferson Davis memorabilia. Monday-Friday 8 a.m.-5 p.m., Saturday 9:30 a.m.-4:30 p.m., Sunday 12:30-4:30 p.m.

ROSS R. BARNETT RESERVOIR

115 Madison Landing Circle, Ridgeland, 601-354-3448;
www.rossbarnettreservoir.org

This reservoir is 43 miles long and was created by damming the Pearl River. Activities include swimming, fishing, boating, and facilities include a playground and picnicking shelters. Daily.

SMITH ROBERTSON MUSEUM

528 Bloom St., Jackson, 601-960-1457; www.city.jackson.ms.us

This museum highlights the history and culture of African-American Mississippians from pre-slavery times to the present. Onsite is a large collection of photos, books, documents, arts and crafts. Monday-Friday 9 a.m.-5 p.m., Saturday 10 a.m.-1 p.m., Sunday 2-5 p.m.

STATE CAPITOL

400 High St., Jackson, 601-359-3114

Impeccably restored in 1979, the lavish, Beaux-Arts-style capitol building was patterned after the national capitol in Washington. When the legislature is in session, visitors can take a seat in the chamber of the state House or Senate to watch some political wrangling. On the first floor, the Hall of Governors holds portraits of the state's governors since Mississippi Territory was created in 1798. Tours by appointment.

THE OAKS HOUSE MUSEUM

823 N Jefferson St., Jackson, 601-353-9339; www.theoakshousemuseum.org

This Greek revival cottage, built of hand-hewn timber by James H. Boyd, former mayor of Jackson, was occupied by General Sherman during the siege of 1863. The house contains period furniture. Tuesday-Saturday 10 a.m.-3 p.m.

SPECIAL EVENTS
DIXIE NATIONAL LIVESTOCK SHOW AND RODEO

Mississippi Coliseum, 1207 Mississippi St., Jackson, 601-961-4000;
www.mdac.state.ms.us

World Championship cowboys compete in a thrilling rodeo, complete with rodeo clowns, barrel racers and ropers. When you're not watching bull riders hold on for dear life, enjoy the parade, pageant and Dixie National Rodeo Dance. Late January-mid-February; rodeo second week in February.

JACKSON COUNTY FAIR

Fairgrounds, 200 W. Ganson St., Jackson; www.jacksoncountyfair.org
Mid-October.

MISSISSIPPI STATE FAIR

State Fairgrounds, Jefferson Street, Jackson, 601-961-4000; www.mdac.state.ms.us
The fair features agricultural and industrial exhibits and contests. Early-mid October.

NATIONAL CUTTING HORSE ASSOCIATION SHOW

Mississippi Coliseum, 1207 Mississippi St., Jackson, 601-961-4000;
www.dixienational.org
Challengers from across the U.S. participate in amateur and professional rider competitions. Late March.

HOTELS
★★EDISON WALTHALL HOTEL
225 E. Capitol St., Jackson, 601-948-6161, 800-932-6161;
www.edisonwalthallhotel.com
208 rooms. Restaurant, bar. Airport transportation available. Fitness center. Outdoor pool. $

★★★HILTON JACKSON
1001 E. County Line Road, Jackson, 601-957-2800, 888-263-0524; www.hilton.com
The hotel offers a full-service restaurant, a courtyard pool, a poolside fitness center, a complimentary airport shuttle and more. The property is near many of the local area attractions. 276 rooms. High-speed Internet access. Restaurant, bar. Airport transportation available. Fitness room. Outdoor pool. Business center. $

★HOLIDAY INN EXPRESS
310 Greymont Ave., Jackson, 601-948-4466, 800-465-4329; www.hiexpress.com
110 rooms. Complimentary continental breakfast. $

★LA QUINTA INN
616 Briarwood Drive, Jackson, 601-957-1741, 800-687-6667; www.laquinta.com
144 rooms. Wireless Internet access. Airport transportation available. Complimentary continental breakfast. Fitness center. Outdoor pool. Pets accepted. $

RESTAURANTS
★COCK OF THE WALK
141 Madison Ave., Jackson, 601-856-5500; www.cockofthewalk.biz
American menu. Dinner. $

★★DENNERY'S
330 Greymont Ave., Jackson, 601-354-2527
American menu. Lunch, dinner. Closed Sunday. $$

★★NICK'S
1501 Lakeland Drive, Jackson, 601-981-8017; www.nicksrestaurant.com
Seafood menu. Dinner. Closed Sunday. $$

KOSCIUSKO

Mississippi residents far and wide flock to Kosciusko for the fair. A sizable state park and art museum will keep visitors busy the rest of the year.

Information: Kosciusko-Attala Chamber of Commerce, 301 E. Jefferson, 662-289-2981; www.kosciuskotourism.com

WHAT TO SEE AND DO

HOLMES COUNTY STATE PARK

5369 State Park Road, Kosciusko, 662-653-3351; www.mdwfp.com

The 450-acre park has two lakes. Activities include fishing, boating, walking the nature trails, and archery. Facilities include picnicking shelters, a playground, skating rink, campgrounds and cabins.

KOSCIUSKO MUSEUM & INFORMATION CENTER

124 N Jackson St., Kosciusko, 662-289-2981; www.kosciuskotourism.com

The museum features information on the area. Daily.

SPECIAL EVENT

CENTRAL MISSISSIPPI FAIR

124 N Jackson St., Kosciusko, 662-289-2981; www.centralmsfair.com

The fair takes place on the Central Mississippi Fairgrounds. August.

LAUREL

Built by two sawmill men in the piney woods of southeastern Mississippi after reconstruction, Laurel is a charming southern town with oak-lined streets and historic homes.

Information: Jones County Chamber of Commerce, 601-428-0574; www.laurelms.com

WHAT TO SEE AND DO

LANDRUM'S HOMESTEAD

1356 Highway 15 S., Laurel, 601-649-2546; www.landrums.com

This recreation of a late 1800s settlement Includes a blacksmith shop, a grist mill, a display of gem mining and a general store. Monday-Saturday 9 a.m.-5 p.m.

LAUREN ROGERS MUSEUM OF ART

565 N. Fifth Ave., Laurel, 601-649-6374; www.lrma.org

The museum features 19th- and 20th-century American and European paintings, 18th-century Japanese woodblock prints, English Georgian silver and Native American baskets. Tuesday-Saturday 10 a.m.-4:45 p.m., Sunday 1-4 p.m.

HOTEL

★★RAMADA

Laurel, 601-649-9100, 800-272-6232; www.ramada.com

207 rooms. Restaurant, bar. $

LOUISVILLE

Home to two state parks and a national forest, Louisville will keep you busy outdoors.

Information: Louisville-Winston County Chamber of Commerce, 311 W. Park, 662-773-3921; www.winstoncounty.com

WHAT TO SEE AND DO

LEGION STATE PARK

635 Legion State Park Road, Louisville, 662-773-8323; www.mdwfp.com

One of the first parks developed by the Civilian Conservation Corps, the grounds contain an original stone lodge still in use. Activities include swimming, water sports, fishing, hunting, boating, camping and picnicking. Daily.

NANIH WAIYA STATE PARK

4496 Highway 393,Louisville, 662-773-7988; www.mdwfp.com/parks.asp

The legendary birthplace of the Choctaw and the site of their Sacred Mound, this area was occupied from approximately the time of Christ until Europeans arrived here. A swinging bridge leads to a cave under the mound. Daily.

TOMBIGBEE NATIONAL FOREST

North on Highway 15, Louisville, 662-965-4391; www.fs.fed.us/r8/tombigbee

This 66,000-acre forest is an outdoor enthusiast's dream. Opportunities abound for camping, hiking and picnicking. At Choctaw Lake, in the southern section, visitors can boat, fish, camp and hunt. Witchdance Horse Trail invites riders and their noble steeds to view the majestic pines and hardwoods that make up much of this huge forest. Camping is available March to November.

MCCOMB

McComb is a great stop-off for those craving water sports.

Information: Chamber of Commerce, 120 N. Railroad Blvd., 601-684-2291, 800-399-4404; www.pikeinfo.com

WHAT TO SEE AND DO

BOGUE CHITTO WATER PARK

6046 Highway 570 E., McComb, 601-684-9568; www.boguechittowaterpark.com

Activities include swimming, tubing, fishing, boating, and facilities include a playground, picnicking shelters, campgrounds and cabins. Daily.

PERCY QUIN STATE PARK

Six miles south on I-55, McComb, 601-684-3931; www.mdwfp.com

This park covers 1,700 acres on 700-acre Tangipahoa Lake with oak and pine forests. The lodge area includes an arboretum and Liberty White Railroad Museum, housed in a caboose. Activities include swimming, waterskiing, fishing, boating, and facilities include a playground, playing fields, a snack bar, a lodge, picnicking shelters, campgrounds, a miniature golf course and 27-hole golf course.

★
★
★
★
★

PIKE COUNTY AZALEA FESTIVAL

McComb, 601-291-0116

In keeping with the Japanese tradition of lighting cherry blossoms, McComb citizens have been illuminating their azaleas along different town routes since 1953. The festival also includes an arts festival and music programs. Late March or early April.

★DINNER BELL

229 Fifth Ave., McComb, 601-684-4883; www.thedinnerbell.net

American menu. Lunch, dinner. Closed Mondays. **$**

MENDENHALL

Fish, fish and more fish is one reason to visit this small city, home to lakes and 178,000 acres of forest.

Information: Chamber of Commerce, 601-847-1725

BIENVILLE NATIONAL FOREST

3473 Highway 35 S., 601-469-3811; www.fs.fed.us/r8/mississippi/bienville

Fish-filled lakes, beautiful pine woods and well-maintained campsites make Bienville an ideal place to play outdoors. The forest's 178,000 acres attract hunters, fishermen, hikers, mountain bikers and anyone who just needs to find peace, quiet and a beautiful setting. Activities include swimming, boating, hiking, horse back riding, picnicking and camping.

D'LO WATER PARK

27 miles south via Highway 49, Mendenhall, 601-847-4310; www.dlowaterpark.com

This park is spread out over 85 acres. Activities include swimming, canoeing and fishing, while facilities include a playground, playing fields, a snack bar, picnicking shelters, boat ramps and rentals, campgrounds and cabins. Daily.

MARATHON

47 miles northeast via highways 540, 18, 501, forest service roads, Mendenhall

Here you'll find a 58-acre lake for swimming, fishing and boating. Picnicking and camping are also available onsite.

SHONGELO

22 miles east and north via Highways 540 and 35, Mendenhall

Here you'll find a 5-acre lake for swimming, fishing and boating. Picnicking and camping are also available onsite.

MERIDIAN

Founded at the junction of two railroads, Meridian was Mississippi's golden city during the turn of the 20th century. Today the city has nine distinct historic districts and more downtown historic buildings than any city in the state.

Information: East Mississippi Development Corporation, 1915 Front St., Union Station, 601-693-1306, 800-748-9970; www.meridianms.org

281

MISSISSIPPI

★
★
★
★

WHAT TO SEE AND DO

BIENVILLE NATIONAL FOREST
3473 Highway 35, 601-469-3811; www.fs.fed.us/r8/mississippi/bienville
Fish-filled lakes, beautiful pine woods and well-maintained campsites make Bienville an ideal place to play outdoors. The forest's 178,000 acres attract hunters, fishermen, hikers, mountain bikers and anyone who just needs to find peace, quiet and a beautiful setting. Activities include swimming, boating, hiking, bridle trails, picnicking and camping.

CLARKCO STATE PARK
Highway 45 N., Quitman, 601-776-6651; www.mdwfp.com
This park covers 815 acres situated on a 65-acre lake. Activities include swimming, waterskiing, fishing, boating and tennis and facilities include a playground, a snack bar, picnicking shelters and campgrounds.

FRANK W. WILLIAMS HOUSE
905 Martin Luther King, Jr. Memorial Drive, Meridian, 601-483-8439
This Victorian home, circa 1886, features stained glass, oak paneling, parquet floors and detailed gingerbread. There are special Christmas tours. Monday-Saturday.

JIMMIE RODGERS MUSEUM
1725 Jimmie Rodgers Drive, Meridian, 601-485-1808; www.jimmierodgers.com
Fashioned after an old train depot, the museum houses souvenirs and memorabilia of the "Father of Country Music," including a rare Martin 00045 guitar. Daily.

MERIDIAN MUSEUM OF ART
628 25th Ave., Meridian, 601-693-1501; www.meridianmuseum.org
Permanent and changing exhibits include paintings, graphics, photographs, sculpture and crafts by regional artists. Tuesday-Sunday.

MERREHOPE
905 Martin Luther King Jr. Memorial Drive, Meridian, 601-483-8439;
www.merrehope.com
The stately 20-room mansion, first built in 1859, features unusual woodwork, handsome columns, mantels and stairway. There are special Christmas tours. Monday-Saturday.

OKATIBBEE DAM AND RESERVOIR
Okatibbee Dam Road, Meridian, 601-626-8431; www.sam.usace.army.mil
A 3,800-acre lake with swimming seasonal, waterskiing, water slides, fishing, boating (ramps, marina). Picnicking and lodging are available.

SPECIAL EVENTS

ARTS IN THE PARK
Meridian, 601-693-2787; www.meridianms.org/artcalendar.htm
Check the calendar for this set of concerts, plays, art shows and children's programs. First weekend in April.

★
★
★
★
★

JIMMIE RODGERS MEMORIAL FESTIVAL
Meridian, 601-693-2686; www.jimmierodgers.com/festival.html
Boot-scoot to Meridian for this festival, which celebrates country and western music with performances by big-name headliners and local talent, a barbecue cook-off and car show. May.

QUEEN CITY STATE FAIR
Meridian, 601-693-5465; www.queencityfair.net
The fair features agricultural exhibits and a carnival. October.

HOTEL
★BEST WESTERN OF MERIDIAN
2219 S. Frontage Road, Meridian, 601-693-3210, 800-528-1234;
www.bestwestern.com
122 rooms. High-speed Internet access available. Outdoor pool. $

NATCHEZ
Natchez delivers the enchantment of the Old South, with a plantation atmosphere where everything seems beautiful and romantic. Greek revival mansions, manicured gardens and lawns, tree-shaded streets and southern hospitality abound in this museum of the antebellum South.

Named for a Native American tribe, Natchez has seen French, Spanish, English, Confederate and U.S. flags fly over the city, one of the oldest in the Mississippi Valley. Vestiges of the Spanish influence can still be seen along South Wall Street, near Washington Street, a charming neighborhood once restricted to the Spanish dons.

Information: Convention and Visitors Bureau; 640 S. Canal, 601-446-6345,
800-647-6724; www.natchez.ms.us

WHAT TO SEE AND DO
CANAL STREET DEPOT
Canal and State streets, Natchez
Located one block from the Mississippi River, the Depot houses the Natchez Pilgrimage Tour and Tourist Headquarters, a children's factory outlet and old-fashioned shops. Also available is information on historic Natchez and the surrounding area as well as carriage tours through the Natchez Historic District, presented with a 35-minute overview of the town's antebellum history along with tours of Victorian townhouses and churches. Daily.

EMERALD MOUND
2680 Natchez Trace Parkway, Natchez, 601-442-2658; www.cr.nps.gov
One of the largest mounds in North America, Emerald Mound was a ceremonial center for ancestors of the Natchez Indians between A.D. 1250 and 1600.

GRAND VILLAGE OF THE NATCHEZ
400 Jefferson Davis Blvd., Natchez, 601-446-6502; www.mdah.state.ms.us
Here you'll find a museum, an archaeological site, nature trails, a picnic area and a gift shop. Daily.

SIGHTSEEING IN THE HISTORIC DISTRICT

Visit Natchez for a glimpse of the antebellum South. Built on a high bluff overlooking the Mississippi River, the town has a compact downtown area that history buffs will want to explore. Many of the historic buildings now house museums, where visitors can learn more about the town's fascinating history, and there are plenty of restaurants, cafés and shops to break up a day of sightseeing. Start upriver and work your way back down. The oldest house in town, built in 1799, is the small two-story **House on Ellicott Hill** *(North Canal at Jefferson, 601-442-2011)*. Settler Andrew Elliott raised the American flag here in defiance of Spain, which claimed the broad plain along the Gulf to the Mississippi River as Spanish West Florida.

Walk away from the river down Jefferson, then up Pearl Street a block to **Stanton Hall** *(601-442-6282)*. A stately mansion built in 1857, Stanton Hall fits the classic image of opulent antebellum architecture. Find fine dining and theater in the cottage house. Keeping strolling down Pearl Street toward the commercial district.

Two blocks down, carriage tours depart from the entranceway of the Natchez Eola Hotel. Around the corner on Main Street, in the old Post Office building, the **Museum of Afro-American History and Culture** *(601-445-0728)*, provides an important reminder of the other side of the town's antebellum history.

Two blocks farther south along Pearl, **Magnolia Hall** *(215 S. Pearl St., 601-442-6672)*, a Greek revival mansion, built in 1858, is now a house museum. A block west toward the river is the **Governor Holmes House** *(207 S. Wall St., 601-442-2366)*. Home of the last governor of the Mississippi Territory, Holmes became the first state governor when Mississippi joined the Union in 1817. Like many of the historic houses in town, it also operates as an inn.

At Wall Street and Washington, get a bite to eat at one of the cafés or a great area bookshop. Cross Canal Street and skip down a block to visit **Rosalie**, on the bluff at South Broadway *(601-445-4555)*, a lovely brick mansion that served as Union Army headquarters during the Civil War.

Walk upriver a couple of blocks until you see the steep road leading down the bluff. This leads to Natchez Under-the-Hill, once the neighborhood that catered to the seedier side of the steamboat trade. Today it is harmless, though it retains the look and spirit of the Old West frontier. There are several family restaurants and a tavern called the Saloon, all with great river views. Down at the water, the Lady Luck riverboat casino operates around the clock. If you've parked at the visitor center, your car is right up the hill from here.

HISTORIC JEFFERSON COLLEGE

16 Old North St., Washington, 601-442-2901; www.mdah.state.ms.us

The Jefferson College campus was the site, in 1817, of the first state Constitutional Convention. Jefferson Davis was among the famous Mississippians who attended the school. No longer used as a college, it is now listed on the National Register of Historic places. A museum interprets the early history of the territory. The site includes nature trails and an area for picnicking. Monday-Saturday 9 a.m.-5 p.m., Sunday 1-5 p.m.

HISTORIC SPRINGFIELD PLANTATION

Natchez, Highway 553 Fayette Mississippi, 601-786-3802

Believed to be the first mansion erected in Mississippi, the main house remains nearly intact with little remodeling over the years. Built for Thomas Marston Green Jr. a wealthy planter from Virginia, and the site of Andrew Jackson's wedding, the mansion displays original hand-carved woodwork, Civil War equipment, railroad memorabilia and a narrow-gauge locomotive. Daily.

HOMOCHITTO NATIONAL FOREST

Natchez, northeast and southeast via Highway 84, 98, 33, 601-965-4391;
www.fs.fed.us/r8/mississippi/homochitto

This 189,000-acre forest was the first of Mississippi's six national forests, established in 1936. Camp in any of the three recreation areas, and hike through the eastern half of the park, renowned among hikers for its irregular terrain and excellent trail system. Activities include swimming, fishing, hunting, picnicking and camping.

THE HOUSE ON ELLICOTT HILL

211 N. Canal St., Natchez, 601-442-2011

This is the site where, in 1797, Andrew Ellicott raised the first American flag in the lower Mississippi Valley. Built in 1798, the house overlooks both the Mississippi and the terminus of the Natchez Trace. The house is fully restored and authentically furnished. Daily.

ISLE CAPRI CASINO

21 Silver St., Natchez, 601-445-0605, 800-722-5825; www.isleofcapricasinos.com

LONGWOOD

140 Lower Woodville Road, Natchez, 601-442-5193

This enormous, Italianate-detailed "octagon house" is crowned with an onion dome. Because the house was under construction at the start of the Civil War, its interiors were never completed above first floor. Containing 1840 furnishings, Longwood is owned and operated by the Pilgrimage Garden Club. Daily; days vary during Pilgrimages.

MAGNOLIA HALL

South Pearl and Washington, Natchez, 601-442-6672;
www.natchezgardenclub.com

The last great mansion to be erected in the city before the outbreak of the Civil War, Magnolia Hall is an outstanding example of Greek revival architecture. The mansion contains period antiques and a costume museum. Daily.

MELROSE ESTATE HOME

1 Melrose Ave., off Highway 61, Natchez, 601-446-5790;
www.nps.gov/natc

The National Park Service oversees this historic mansion and grounds and tells the plantation story from a national perspective. The house is open for guided tours only, with self-guided tours available for the slave quarters. Daily.

MISSISSIPPI

★
★
★
★

MONMOUTH

36 Melrose Ave., Natchez, 601-442-5852; www.monmouthplantation.com

Registered as a National Historic Landmark, the monumental Greek revival house and auxiliary buildings, once owned by Mexican War hero General John Anthony Quitman, have been completely restored, with antique furnishings and extensive gardens. Monmouth also has guest rooms and tours available. Daily.

MOUNT LOCUST

2680 Natchez Trace Parkway, Natchez, 601-445-4211

One of Mississippi's oldest structures, Mount Locust was built in the 1780s and used as an inn on the Natchez Trail.

NATCHEZ STATE PARK

230B Wickliff Road, Natchez, 601-442-2658

The park's horse trails are believed to be abandoned plantation roads that lead to Brandon Hall, home of the first native Mississippi governor, Gerard Brandon, who served 1826-1831. Activities here include fishing, boating, picnicking and camping.

NATCHEZ VISITOR CENTER

640 S. Canal, Natchez, 800-647-6742; www.cityofnatchez.com

This spacious visitor center on the bluff above the Mississippi River offers tourist services, including a film on the city's history and heritage. Daily.

ROSALIE

100 Orleans St., Natchez, 601-445-4555; www.rosalie.net

This red brick Georgian mansion with a Greek revival portico served as the headquarters for the Union Army during occupation of Natchez. The original furnishings date from 1857, and the grounds contain gardens overlooking the Mississippi River. Daily 9:30 a.m.-4:30 p.m.

MISSISSIPPI

★
★ ★
★ ★
★

NATCHEZ TRACE PARKWAY

One of the earliest "interstates," the Natchez Trace stretched from Natchez, Miss., to Nashville, Tenn., and was the most heavily traveled road in the Old Southwest from approximately 1785 to 1820. Boatmen floated their products downriver to Natchez or New Orleans, sold them and walked or rode home over the Natchez Trace. It was still in use, to some extent, as late as the 1830s, though its importance diminished after the invention of the steam engine.

Today the 444-mile-long parkway closely follows the original trace, often crossing over it and passing many points of historic interest, including Emerald Mound. The parkway headquarters and visitor center are five miles north of Tupelo, at junction Highway 45 Business sign reads Highway 145 and the parkway. Interpretive facilities include a visitor center with exhibits depicting the history of the area. Park Service personnel can provide information about self-guided trails, wayside exhibits, interpretive programs, camping and picnicking facilities along the parkway. 2680 Natchez Trace Parkway, Tupelo, 662-680-4025, 800-305-7417.

STANTON HALL

401 High St., Natchez, 601-446-6631;
www.natchezmansions.com

This elaborate antebellum mansion is surrounded by giant oaks and contains original chandeliers, marble mantels, Sheffield hardware and French mirrors. Owned and operated by the Pilgrimage Garden Club, it offers tours every half-hour. Daily 9 a.m.-4:30 p.m.; closed during pilgrimages.

SPECIAL EVENTS

GREAT MISSISSIPPI RIVER BALLOON RACE WEEKEND

640 S. Canal St., Natchez; www.natchezballoonrace.com

As many as 100 hot-air balloons fly at once during this fall festival, which also offers musical entertainment and food. Third weekend in October.

NATCHEZ OPERA FESTIVAL

64 Homochitto St., Natchez; www.alcorn.edu/opera

At the Margaret Martin Performing Arts Center on the Mississippi River, the festival draws performers from different parts of the country to Natchez's fine stage in the spring. April-May.

NATCHEZ PILGRIMAGE TOURS

200 State St., Natchez; 800-647-6742; www.natchezpilgrimage.com

Three times a year, the Natchez Pilgrimage Association leads tours of antebellum houses. The spring event happens in March and early April; the fall, in October. In December, the tours have a holiday theme.

HOTELS

★★★DUNLEITH PLANTATION

84 Homochitto St., Natchez, 601-446-8500, 800-433-2445;
www.dunleithplantation.com

This luxurious home has recently been restored to its pre-Civil War style. Nine rooms. Children over 14 years only. Complimentary full breakfast. $$

★★ISLE OF CAPRI CASINO & HOTEL

645 S. Canal St., Natchez, 601-445-0605, 800-722-5825; www.isleofcapricasino.com
147 rooms. Restaurant. $

★★★MONMOUTH PLANTATION

36 Melrose Ave., Natchez, 601-442-5852, 800-828-4531;
www.monmouthplantation.com

Visitors might expect to see Scarlet O'Hara herself gliding through the vast courtyards of this beautiful plantation home. During the day, stroll or take a carriage ride through the historic site; in the evening, enjoy a five-course dinner served in the elegant dining room. 30 rooms. Children over 14 years only. Complimentary full breakfast. $$

★★NATCHEZ EOLA HOTEL

110 Pearl St., Natchez, 601-445-6000; www.natchezeola.com
131 rooms. Restaurant, bar. Fitness center. Business center. $

MISSISSIPPI

BRIARS BED AND BREAKFAST

31 Irving Lane, Natchez, 601-446-9654, 800-634-1818; www.thebriarsinn.com

Listed on the National Register of Historic Places, this 19-acre property is covered with manicured gardens, brick walkways and pecan and magnolia trees. The owners, both interior designers, have restored and renovated all guest rooms. Jefferson Davis was married here in 1845. 14 rooms. Children over 12 years only. Complimentary full breakfast. **$$**

THE BURN ANTEBELLUM BED AND BREAKFAST INN

712 N. Union St., Natchez, 601-442-1344, 800-654-8859; www.theburnbnb.com

This early Greek revival house was built in 1834 with a semi-spiral staircase in central hall, and was used as a headquarters and hospital by Union troops during Civil War. Seven rooms. Children over 12 years only. Complimentary full breakfast. **$**

RESTAURANT

★★CARRIAGE HOUSE

401 High St., Natchez, 601-445-5151; www.stantonhall.com

American menu. Lunch. **$$**

OCEAN SPRINGS

Across the bay from Biloxi, Ocean Springs was severely damaged by Hurricane Katrina in August 2005. The popular Ocean Springs Yacht Club is gone, as are several of the area's historic buildings. The bridge that connected Ocean Springs and Biloxi was destroyed, but a new bridge was completed in 2008. Despite Katrina's wallop, Ocean Springs is still a beautiful destination. It has a thriving arts community and a secluded downtown area with galleries, unique restaurants and diverse architecture.

Information: Chamber of Commerce, 1000 Washington Ave., 228-875-4424; www.oceanspringschamber.com

★COCK OF THE WALK

200 N. Broadway, Natchez, 601-446-8920; www.cockofthewalk.biz

American menu. Dinner. **$$**

WHAT TO SEE AND DO

GULF COAST RESEARCH LAB/J. L. SCOTT MARINE EDUCATION CENTER & AQUARIUM

703 E. Beach Drive, Ocean Springs, 228-374-5550; www.usm.edu/gcrl

The J.L. Scott Marine Education Center in Biloxi was destroyed by Hurricane Katrina in August 2005. Employees of the aquarium recovered many of the animals, and facilities in the Southeast have adopted the animals until the aquarium is rebuilt. The research lab still hosts professional events and programs for locals, such as a children's sea camp.

288

MISSISSIPPI

★
★
★
★
★

GARDEN AND HOME PILGRIMAGE

Ocean Springs, 228-875-4424

Late March or early April.

★★JOCELYN'S

Highway 90 E., Ocean Springs, 228-875-1925

French, Creole menu. Dinner. Closed Sunday-Monday. **$$**

OXFORD

Oxford was named for the English university city in an effort to lure the University of Mississippi to the site. It worked. In 1848 the university opened. Today, "Ole Miss," with its forested, hilly campus, dominates the area, and Oxford relishes its role as a college town.

Locals also relish Oxford's reputation as a jewel of the South, complete with an historic town square, eclectic restaurants, stylish boutiques and tree-lined neighborhoods. Stick around long enough and you'll hear a local mantra: "We may never win every game, but we aren't never lost a party."

The city knows how to have a good time, but it also has a certain appeal for writers. William Faulkner, Nobel Prize-winning author, lived near the university at "Rowan Oak," and many landmarks of his fictional Yoknapatawpha County can be found in surrounding Lafayette County. John Grisham keeps a house here, too.

Information: Oxford Tourism Council, 662-234-4680, 800-758-9177;
www.oxfordms.com

UNIVERSITY ARCHIVES

University Library, Oxford, 662-232-7408

Here you'll find the historical and literary works by and about Mississippians. The Faulkner collection includes translations of his writings in 35 languages; exhibit of his awards, including the Nobel Prize; manuscripts and first editions. Monday-Friday 8 a.m.-5 p.m.

UNIVERSITY MUSEUMS

University Avenue and Fifth Street, Oxford, 662-232-7073

Housed in two adjoining buildings, the collections include Greek and Roman antiquities, antique scientific instruments as well as African-American, Caribbean and Southern folk art. Tuesday-Saturday 9:30 a.m.-4:30 p.m., Sunday 1-4 p.m.

UNIVERSITY OF MISSISSIPPI

University Avenue, Oxford, 662-915-5993; www.olemiss.edu

Football is religion here, and the Rebels' fans take it very seriously. If you're here on game day, you'd better root for the right team. If you miss the game, Ole Miss still has plenty of offerings for visitors.

SPECIAL EVENT

FAULKNER CONFERENCE

Center for Study of Southern Culture, University of Mississippi,
Grove Loop at Sorority Row, Oxford, 662-232-7282; www.olemiss.edu
Various programs celebrate the author's accomplishments. Last week in July.

HOTELS

★BEST WESTERN DOWNTOWN OXFORD INN & SUITES

400 N. Lamar Blvd., Oxford, 662-234-3031, 800-780-7234; www.bestwestern.com
123 rooms. Airport transportation available. $

★DAYS INN

1101 Frontage Road, Oxford, 662-234-9500; www.daysinn.com
100 rooms. Wireless Internet access. Restaurant. Outdoor pool. Pets accepted. $

★SUPER 8

2201 Jackson Ave. W., Oxford, 662-234-7013; www.super8.com
116 rooms. High-speed Internet access. Complimentary continental breakfast. Outdoor pool. Pets accepted. $

SPECIALITY LODGING

OLIVER-BRITT HOUSE INN & TEAROOM

512 Van Buren Ave., Oxford, 662-234-8043; www.oliverbritthouse.com
This is a restored manor house built in 1905, with period furnishings. Five rooms. Complimentary full breakfast. $

RESTAURANT

★★DOWNTOWN GRILL

110 Courthouse Square, Oxford, 662-234-2659; www.downtowngrill.net
American menu. Breakfast, lunch, dinner. Closed Sunday. $$

PASCAGOULA

Hurricane Katrina heavily damaged Pascagoula during her rampage of the Gulf Coast in August 2005. Still, this resort town, which is also Mississippi's busiest port, is rebuilding and welcomes visitors who want to smell the salt air, play a little golf or try their luck with a fishing pole.

The town gets its name from the Pascagoula Native Americans, who lived here before European settlers arrived. Local legend says that a young chieftain wooed and won the heart of a princess in the neighboring Biloxi tribe, even though she was betrothed. The Biloxi chief, enraged, attacked the Pascagoula tribe. Realizing they would not win, the Pascagoula joined hands and walked, singing, into the river that bears their name. To this day, the legend says, you'll hear their singing from the Pascagoula River.

Information: Jackson County Chamber of Commerce, 720 Krebs Ave., 228-762-3391;
www.jcchamber.com

WHAT TO SEE AND DO
MISSISSIPPI SANDHILL CRANE NATIONAL WILDLIFE REFUGE
7200 Gautier Vancleave Road, Pascagoula, 228-497-6322;
www.mississippisandhillcrane.fws.gov

Established to protect endangered cranes, the refuge has three units that total 18,000 acres. Also here is a three-quarter-mile wildlife trail mile with interpretive panels, an outdoor exhibit and areas for bird-watching. The visitor center has slide programs by request, a wildlife exhibit, paintings and maps. Tours: January-February, by appointment. Visitor center: Monday-Friday 8 a.m.-4 p.m.

OLD SPANISH FORT AND MUSEUM
4602 Fort St., Pascagoula, 228-769-1505

Built by the French, later captured by the Spanish, the fort has walls of massive cypress timbers cemented with oyster shells, mud and moss that are 18 inches thick. Said to be the oldest structure in the Mississippi Valley, the site contains a museum with Native American relics as part of its collection. Daily.

SCRANTON NATURE CENTER
IG Levy Park at Pascagoula River, Pascagoula, 228-762-6017;
www.cityofpascagoula.com

The Center has marine and wetlands exhibits housed in a restored shrimping boat. Tuesday-Sunday.

SINGING RIVER
Pascagoula River, Pascagoula

There is indeed a singing sound from the river, which is best heard on late summer and autumn nights. The sound seems to get louder, coming nearer until it seems to be underfoot. Scientists have made several guesses about the sound's source: It could be made by fish, sand scraping the hard slate bottom, natural gas escaping from the sand bed or a current sucked past a hidden cave. But no one has ever confirmed the exact source.

SPECIAL EVENTS
GARDEN CLUB PILGRIMAGE
Pascagoula

This tour takes you past historic houses and gardens in town. For route and exact date information, call the Jackson County Chamber of Commerce at 228-762-3391. Late March-early April.

MARDI GRAS
Pascagoula; www.gogulfcoast.biz/mardigras/parades.html

This takes place in the month leading up to Ash Wednesday.

RIVER JAMBOREE

North on Highway 63, Moss Point, 228-474-6103

The event features arts and crafts and games. First Saturday in May.

★★LA FONT INN

2703 Denny Ave., Pascagoula, 228-762-7111, 800-647-6077; www.lafontinn.com

192 rooms. Restaurant, bar. Fitness center. **$**

PASS CHRISTIAN

Hurricane Katrina almost completely destroyed this little town in August 2005, but Pass Christian is rebuilding, hoping to regain its status as a scenic resort town, a reputation it first earned before the Civil War. Pass Christian was the site of the South's first yacht club, and it has hosted six vacationing U.S. presidents: Jackson, Taylor, Grant, Theodore Roosevelt, Wilson and Truman. And as if that's not enough, the world's largest oyster reef is offshore.

Information: Chamber of Commerce, 228-452-2252; www.pass-christian.ms.us

WHAT TO SEE AND DO

THE FRIENDSHIP OAK

University of Southern Mississippi's Gulf Park campus, Pass Christian, 228-865-4500; www.usm.edu

The Oak has become a symbol of the Gulf Coast's strength in the wake of Hurricane Katrina. It has been standing since 1487, five years before Columbus arrived in the new world. The oak has a 16-foot trunk, limbs larger than 5 feet in diameter and a root system that held fast enough to keep the tree standing through the storm. Legend says that people who stand together in the tree's shadow will remain friends forever.

SPECIAL EVENTS

BLESSING OF THE FLEET

Pass Christian, 228-865-4500

This festival includes a boat decorations competition, music and other forms of entertainment. Last Sunday in May.

GARDEN CLUB PILGRIMAGE

Pass Christian, 228-865-4500

This takes place at the Small Craft Harbor and includes visits to several historic houses and gardens in town. Late March.

MARDI GRAS

Pass Christian, 228-865-4500

The festivities include a carnival ball and parade. Saturday, Sunday before Ash Wednesday.

SEAFOOD FESTIVAL

104 Hurshey Ave., Pass Christian, 228-868-5421; www.seafood.passchristian.net

Mid-July.

★★CASINO MAGIC BAY TOWER HOTEL

711 Hollywood Blvd., Bay St. Louis, 228-467-9257, 800-562-4425;
www.casinomagic.com

201 rooms. Four restaurants, bars. **$**

PORT GIBSON

Port Gibson is where the Blues Highway and the Natchez Trace meet, which makes it a good place to begin an adventure in western Mississippi. Many antebellum houses and buildings remain in Port Gibson, lending support to the story that during the Civil War, Union General Grant spared the town on his march to Vicksburg with the words, "It's too beautiful to burn."

Information: Port Gibson-Claiborne County Chamber of Commerce,
601-437-4351; www.portgibson.org

WHAT TO SEE AND DO

ENERGY CENTRAL

Grand Gulf Road, Port Gibson, 601-437-6393

Here you'll find exhibits and hands-on displays about nuclear energy and electricity. Monday-Friday.

FIRST PRESBYTERIAN CHURCH

Church and Walnut streets, Port Gibson, www.fpcportgibson.org

The church features a gold-leaf hand with a finger pointing skyward that tops its steeple. The interior includes an old slave gallery and chandeliers taken from the steamboat *Robert E. Lee.*

GRAND GULF MILITARY PARK

Grand Gulf Road, Port Gibson, 601-437-5911; www.grandgulfpark.state.ms.us

This site marks the former town of Grand Gulf, which lost 55 of 75 city blocks to Mississippi floods between 1855 and 1860. During the Civil War, the town's population was waning when Confederate troops and Union forces clashed here, first in the spring of 1862 and again in the spring of 1863. The park today includes fortifications, an observation tower, a cemetery, sawmill, dog-trot house, memorial chapel, water wheel and grist mill, a carriage house with vehicles used by the Confederates, a four-room cottage reconstructed from the early days of Grand Gulf and several other pre-Civil War buildings. A museum in the visitor center displays Civil War, Native American and prehistoric artifacts. Daily 8 a.m.-5 p.m.

OAK SQUARE

1207 Church St., Port Gibson, 601-437-4350

This restored 30-room mansion has six fluted, Corinthian columns, each standing 22 feet tall, as well as antique furnishings from the 18th and 19th centuries. There are extensive grounds, a courtyard and a gazebo. Guest rooms are available. Tours can be made by appointment.

293

MISSISSIPPI

★
★
★
★

ROSSWOOD PLANTATION

Highway 552, Lorman, 800-533-5889; www.rosswood.net

This classic Greek revival mansion designed by David Shroder, architect of Windsor, features columned galleries, 10 fireplaces, 15-foot ceilings, a winding stairway and slave quarters in the basement. The first owner's diary has survived and offers details of antebellum life on a cotton plantation. The 14 rooms are furnished with antiques. Guest rooms are available. Tours March-December.

THE RUINS OF WINDSOR

Old Rodney Road, Port Gibson, 601-437-4351; home.olemiss.edu

These 23 stately columns are all that is left of a four-story mansion built in 1860 at a cost of $175,000 and destroyed by fire in 1890. Its proximity to the river and size made it a natural marker for Mississippi River pilots, including Samuel Clemens (better known as Mark Twain).

SPECIAL EVENT

SPRING PILGRIMAGE

1601 Church St., Port Gibson, 601-437-4351

This includes tours of historic houses. Early spring.

SPECIALITY LODGINGS

OAK SQUARE COUNTRY INN

1207 Church St., Port Gibson, 601-437-4350, 800-729-0240

This is a restored antebellum mansion, circa 1850. 12 rooms. Complimentary full breakfast. $

ROSSWOOD PLANTATION

Highway 552 E., Lorman, 601-437-4215, 800-533-5889; www.rosswood.net

This landmark 1857 Greek Revival mansion is on a working Christmas tree plantation. Four rooms. Complimentary full breakfast. $$

SARDIS

From antebellum architecture to thousands of acres of parks, Sardis is a bit of the South that's just waiting to be explored.

Information: Chamber of Commerce, 114 W. Lee St., 662-487-3451

WHAT TO SEE AND DO

ENID LAKE AND DAM

21 miles south on I-55, then one mile east, Sardis, 662-563-4571; www.mvk.usace.army.mil

Activities here include swimming, boating, picnicking, camping. Facilities include an amphitheater.

GEORGE PAYNE COSSAR STATE PARK

165 County Road 170, Oakland, 662-623-7356

The park, covering 900 acres, is situated on a peninsula jutting into Enid Lake. Activities include swimming, camping, waterskiing and fishing, and facilities include a boating ramp, nature and bicycle trails, a miniature golf area, picnicking shelters, a playground, a concession stand, a restaurant (year-round, Wednesday-Sunday), a lodge, cabins and coin laundry.

HEFLIN HOUSE MUSEUM

304 S. Main, Sardis, 662-487-3451

One of the few remaining antebellum structures in Sardis and Panola County, this house features exhibits on the history of Panola County from the pre-Columbus period to 1900. Monday-Friday by appointment.

JOHN W. KYLE STATE PARK

4235 State Park Road, Sardis, 662-487-1345

Activities include swimming, canoeing, and fishing and facilities include a playground, playing fields, a snack bar, picnicking shelters, boat ramps and rentals, campgrounds and cabins.

SARDIS LAKE AND DAM

Nine miles east off I-55, Sardis, 662-563-4531; www.sardislake.com

This lake, with a 260-mile shoreline formed by damming the Little Tallahatchie River, is part of the Yazoo Basin flood control project, and is noted for its natural white sand beaches. Activities include swimming, and facilities include a playground, playing fields, a snack bar, picnicking shelters, boat ramps and rentals, campgrounds and cabins.

STARKVILLE

Mississippi State University makes its home here and drives the local economy. Starkville got a piece of the country music spotlight when Johnny Cash sang about the town in a song called "Starkville County Jail."

Information: Convention and Visitors Bureau, 322 University Drive, 662-323-3322, 800-649-8687; www.starkville.org

WHAT TO SEE AND DO

MISSISSIPPI STATE UNIVERSITY

One mile east on University Drive, Starkville, 662-325-2323; www.msstate.edu

Originally Mississippi Agricultural and Mechanical College, the college became a state university in 1958. The Bulldogs' campus is approximately 750 acres, and visitors are welcome to tour many of the university's buildings and collections. A few to consider: the Arboretum; the Charles H. Templeton, Sr. Music Museum, with more than 200 self-playing instruments; Dunn Seiler Museum, home to geological pieces including a triceratops skull and saber-toothed tiger head; University Art Gallery; and the Chapel of Memories.

NATIONAL WILDLIFE REFUGE

Starkville, 662-323-5548; www.fws.gov/noxubee

This 48,000-acre refuge, which includes a 1,200-acre Bluff Lake, offers space for more than 200 species of birds, including waterfowl, wild turkey, the endangered bald eagle and red-cockaded woodpecker, as well as alligators and deer. Fishing: March-October. Daily.

MISSISSIPPI

OKTIBBEHA COUNTY HERITAGE MUSEUM

206 Fellowship St., Starkville, Fellowship and Russell Streets, 662-323-0211;
www.cityofstarkville.org

Artifacts from the county's past are housed in the former GM&O railroad station.
Tuesday-Thursday or by appointment.

HOTEL

★RAMADA

403 Highway 12 E., Starkville, 662-323-6161; www.ramada.com

173 rooms. Bar. $

RESTAURANT

★★HARVEY'S

406 Highway 12 E., Starkville, 662-323-1639; www.eatwithus.com

Seafood, steak menu. Lunch, dinner. Closed Sunday. $$

TUPELO

Tupelo was once home to "rock 'n' roll" royalty: Elvis Presley was born in a two-
room house here in 1935. Not surprisingly, tourism gives a big economic boost to this
mid-sized town in northeast Mississippi. Visitors are also drawn by the Natchez Trace
Parkway, a scenic route from Natchez, Miss., to Nashville, Tenn., which commemo-
rates a route taken by Native Americans and early pioneers.

Information: Convention & Visitors Bureau, 399 E Main St., 662-841-6521,
800-533-0611; www.tupelo.net

WHAT TO SEE AND DO

ELVIS PRESLEY PARK AND MUSEUM

306 Elvis Presley Drive, Tupelo, 662-841-1245; www.elvispresleybirthplace.com

More than 50,000 die-hard Elvis fans make a pilgrimage to the small white frame
house where the King lived for the first three years of his life. The museum houses a
collection of Elvis memorabilia as well as a chapel. May-September: Monday-Saturday
9 a.m.-5:30 p.m.; rest of year 9 a.m-5 p.m.; also Sunday 1-5 p.m., year-round.

NATCHEZ TRACE PARKWAY VISITOR CENTER

300 W. Main St., Tupelo; www.nps.gov/natr

The 444-mile parkway commemorates the route, used by Native Americans and early
settlers, that connected the Mississippi River to central Tennessee.

OREN DUNN MUSEUM OF TUPELO

689 Rutherford Drive, Tupelo, 662-841-6438; www.orendunnmuseum.org

Displays include NASA space equipment used in Apollo missions; Elvis Presley
room; reproductions of Western Union office, general store, train station, log cabin;
as well as Civil War and Chickasaw items. Daily.

★
★
★
★
★

TOMBIGBEE NATIONAL FOREST

Tupelo, 20 miles south, off Natchez Trace Parkway, 601-965-4391;
www.fs.fed.us/r8/tombigbee

This section of the forest, along with a tract to the south on Highway 15 near Louisville, totals 66,341 acres. Davis Lake provides swimming, fishing, picnicking, and camping, with electric hookups and a dump station available. Recreation area: March to mid-November.

TOMBIGBEE STATE PARK

264 Cabin Drive, Tupelo, 662-842-7669; www.mdwfp.com

This is a 702-acre park with a spring-fed lake. Activities include swimming, archery and fishing. Facilities include a playground, playing fields, a snack bar, picnicking shelters, boat ramps and rentals, campgrounds and cabins.

TRACE STATE PARK

2139 Faulkner Road, Belden, 662-489-2958;
www.roadcamping.com/rv/Mississippi/Belden

On 2,500 acres with a 600-acre lake, you can find activities that include swimming, canoeing, and fishing and facilities include a playground, a boat ramp, a horse riding trail, a golf course, a snack bar, picnicking shelters, boat ramps and rentals, campgrounds and cabins.

TUPELO NATIONAL BATTLEFIELD

2680 Natchez Trace Parkway, Tupelo, 601-680-4025; www.nps.gov/tupe

This is a one-acre tract near the area where the Confederate line was formed to attack the Union position. You'll find a marker with texts and maps that explain the battle. Daily.

HOTELS

★HOLIDAY INN EXPRESS

1612 McClure Cove, Tupelo, 662-620-8184, 800-465-4329; www.hiexpress.com

124 rooms. Complimentary continental breakfast. $

★RAMADA

854 N. Gloster St., Tupelo, 662-844-4111, 800-272-6232; www.ramada.com

230 rooms. Restaurant, bar. Airport transportation available. $

SPECIALITY LODGING

MOCKINGBIRD INN BED AND BREAKFAST

305 N. Gloster St., Tupelo, 662-841-0286; www.bbonline.com/ms/mockingbird

Seven rooms. Children over 10 years only. Complimentary full breakfast. $

RESTAURANTS

★JEFFERSON PLACE

823 Jefferson St., Tupelo, 662-844-8696; www.jeffersonplacetupelo.com

American menu. Lunch, dinner. Closed Sunday. $$

★
★
★
★
★

★MALONE'S FISH & STEAK HOUSE
1349 Highway 41, Tupelo, 662-842-2747
Steak menu. Dinner. Closed Sunday-Monday. $

★★PAPA VANELLI'S
1302 N. Gloster, Tupelo, 662-844-4410; www.vanellis.com/papavanelli.html
Greek, Italian menu. Lunch, dinner. $$

VICKSBURG
Originally an important river port, Vicksburg has a fascinating riverfront along the Mississippi River and the Yazoo Canal. Part of the town sits on a high bluff overlooking the river, a location that led to what is perhaps Vicksburg's biggest role in America history: the Civil War's Siege of Vicksburg.

By June 1862, the Union controlled the Mississippi River with the exception of Vicksburg, which was in Confederate hands. The town's location made it impossible for Union leaders to move traffic up or down the river without subjecting the boats to withering fire from strong Confederate batteries. This position made it possible to maintain communication lines with Louisiana, which were vital to the Confederacy.

The soldiers in Vicksburg fought off Union advances several times before General Grant's army surrounded the city and laid siege. For 47 days, Grant's army pounded Vicksburg with mortar and cannon fire, and the local citizens, hiding in caves, nearly starved. Eventually, on July 4, 1863, the Confederates agreed to surrender the city, a move that gave the North strategic power and led to its victory. Because the city fell on July 4, the citizens of Vicksburg did not celebrate Independence Day until World War II.

Modern Vicksburg is nearly surrounded by the Vicksburg National Military Park, which is as much a part of the town as the streets and antebellum houses. The downtown district has art galleries, shops, restaurants, museums and antique stores, and Vicksburg's natural beauty makes it a haven for visitors who want to spend time outdoors.
Information: Convention & Visitors Bureau, 1221 Washington St., 601-636-9421,
800-221-3536; www.vicksburgcvb.org

WHAT TO SEE AND DO
ANCHUCA HISTORIC MANSION AND INN
1010 First East St., Vicksburg, 601-661-0111; www.anchucamansion.com
This restored Greek revival mansion is furnished with period antiques and gas-burning lanterns. The site also includes guest rooms, landscaped gardens and a brick courtyard. Daily.

BIEDENHARN MUSEUM OF COCA-COLA MEMORABILIA
1107 Washington St., Vicksburg, 601-638-6514;
www.biedenharncoca-colamuseum.com
This is the building in which Coca-Cola was first bottled in 1894. The museum includes a restored candy store, an old-fashioned soda fountain and a collection of Coca-Cola advertising and memorabilia. Daily.

CEDAR GROVE

2200 Oak St., Vicksburg, 601-636-1000, 800-862-1300; www.cedargroveinn.com

This mansion was shelled by Union gunboats during the Civil War. Though it's restored, a cannonball is still lodged in the parlor wall. The site includes a roof garden with view of the Mississippi and Yazoo rivers, a tea room, many original furnishing, more than 4 acres of formal gardens, courtyards, fountains, guest rooms and gazebos. Daily.

DUFF GREEN

1114 First East St., Vicksburg, 601-636-6968, 800-992-0037;
www.duffgreenmansion.com

This mansion features Palladian architecture. Shelled by Union forces during the Civil War, the site was then used as a hospital for Confederate and Union troops. The house is now restored with antique furnishings. Guided tours, guest rooms and high tea are available by reservation. Daily.

MARTHA VICK HOUSE

1300 Grove St., Vicksburg, 601-638-7036; www.marthavickhouse.com

Built by the daughter of the founder of Vicksburg, Newit Vick, the house features a Greek revival façade, a restored interior furnished with 18th- and 19th-century antiques and an outstanding art collection. Daily.

MCRAVEN HOME

1445 Harrison St., Vicksburg, 601-636-1663; www.mcraventourhome.com

This home was the heaviest-shelled house during the Siege of Vicksburg. Visitors can take a view of the architectural record of Vicksburg history, from frontier cottage 1797 to Empire 1836 and finally to elegant Greek revival townhouse 1849, as well as many original furnishings. Original brick walks surround the house, and outside is a garden of live oaks, boxwood, magnolia and many plants. Guided tours are available daily March-November.

OLD COURT HOUSE MUSEUM

1008 Cherry St., Vicksburg, 601-636-0741; www.oldcourthouse.org

Built with slave labor, this building offers a view of the Yazoo Canal from its hilltop position. Here, Grant raised the U.S. flag on July 4, 1863, signifying the end of fighting after 47 days. The courthouse now houses an extensive display of Americana. The Confederate room contains weapons and documents on the siege of Vicksburg. There is also a pioneer room, a furniture room as well as Native American displays and objets d'art. Monday-Saturday 8:30 a.m.-4:30 p.m., Sunday 1:30-4:30 p.m.

TOURIST INFORMATION CENTER

3300 Clay St., Vicksburg, 601-636-9421, 800-221-3536; www.vicksburgcvb.org

Here you'll find information, maps and brochures on points of interest and historic houses. Guide services are free. Daily.

VICKSBURG NATIONAL MILITARY PARK & CEMETERY

3201 Clay St., Vicksburg, 601-636-0583; www.nps.gov/vick

This historic park, the site of Union siege lines and a hardened Confederate defense, borders the eastern and northern sections of the city. A visitor center is at the park entrance, on Clay Street at I-20. The site also contains a museum with exhibits and audiovisual aids. Take a self-guided 16-minute tour. Daily 8 a.m.-5 p.m.

SPECIAL EVENT
VICKSBURG PILGRIMAGE
Vicksburg, www.vicksburgpilgrimage.com
Fifteen antebellum houses are open for viewing. Two tours are held daily. Since tour dates vary, check the Web site for upcoming tours.

HOTELS
★★★ANCHUCA
1010 First E. St., Vicksburg, 601-661-0111, 800-469-2597; www.anchucamansion.com
Climb the narrow, greenery-lined steps to this pre-Civil-War mansion offering guest rooms with private baths, a full breakfast and afternoon tea. Built around 1830 in Greek revival style, the common rooms are furnished with period antiques and romantic, gas-burning chandeliers. Seven rooms. Complimentary full breakfast. **$**

★★BATTLEFIELD INN
4137 I-20 N Frontage Road, Vicksburg, 601-638-5811, 800-359-9363;
www.battlefieldinn.org
117 rooms. Complimentary continental breakfast. Restaurant, bar. **$**

★BEST INN
2390 S. Frontage Road, Vicksburg, 601-634-8607, 800-237-8466; www.bestinn.com
70 rooms. High-speed Internet access. Pets accepted. **$**

★★★CEDAR GROVE MANSION INN
2300 Washington St., Vicksburg, 601-636-1000, 800-862-1300;
www.cedargroveinn.com
This 5-acre, garden-like property includes guest rooms, cottages and suites. All accommodations include a full breakfast, afternoon tea and evening sherry and chocolates. The inn's chef, Andre Flowers, turns out New Orleans cuisine at Andre's Restaurant. 34 rooms. Complimentary full breakfast. Restaurant. **$**

★★★DUFF GREEN MANSION
1114 First East St., Vicksburg, 601-638-6662, 800-992-0037;
www.duffgreenmansion.com
This large 1856 Palladian mansion was used as a hospital for both Confederate and Union soldiers during the Siege of Vicksburg. Each of the bedrooms has a fireplace and porch and are furnished in period antiques and reproductions. Seven rooms. Complimentary full breakfast. Business center. **$**

★MOTEL 6
4127 N. Frontage Road, Vicksburg, 601-638-5077, 800-466-8356; www.motel6.com
62 rooms. Pets accepted. **$**

★
★
★
★
★

ANNABELLE BED AND BREAKFAST

501 Speed St., Vicksburg, 601-638-2000, 800-791-2000; www.annabellebnb.com
Perched along the Mississippi River Valley and shaded by magnolia trees, this Victorian-Italianate home and guesthouse were built in 1868 and 1881, respectively. Eight rooms. Complimentary full breakfast. **$**

CORNERS BED AND BREAKFAST INN

601 Klein St., Vicksburg, 601-636-7421, 800-444-7421; www.thecorners.com
15 rooms. Complimentary full breakfast. **$**

RESTAURANTS
★★CEDAR GROVE

2200 Oak St., Vicksburg, 601-636-1000; www.cedargroveinn.com
American menu. Dinner. Closed Monday. **$$**

★★EDDIE MONSOUR'S

127 Country Club Drive, Vicksburg, 601-638-1571
American menu. Lunch, dinner. Closed Sunday. **$$**

★WALNUT HILLS ROUND TABLES

1214 Adams St., Vicksburg, 601-638-4910; www.walnuthillsms.com
American menu. Lunch, dinner. Closed Saturday. **$$**

WOODVILLE

301

First settled in the 18th century, Woodville is the home of *The Woodville Republican*, the oldest newspaper and the oldest business institution in Mississippi. The town still has many beautiful 19th-century houses and some of the state's first churches. These include Woodville Baptist, 1809; Woodville Methodist, 1824; and St. Paul's Episcopal 1823, which has an Erben organ from 1837.
Information: Woodville Civic Club, 601-888-3998

MISSISSIPPI

WHAT TO SEE AND DO
ROSEMONT PLANTATION

Main Street, Woodville, 601-888-6809; www.rosemontplantation1810.com
This was home of Jefferson Davis and his family. His parents, Samuel and Jane Davis, moved to Woodville and built the house when the boy was 2 years old. The Confederate president grew up here and returned to visit his family throughout his life. Many family furnishings remain, including a spinning wheel that belonged to Jane. Five generations of the Davis family are buried on this 300-acre plantation. Tuesday-Saturday 10 a.m.-5 p.m.

WILKINSON COUNTY MUSEUM

Bank Street, Woodville, 601-888-3998; www.historicwoodville.org
Housed in a Greek revival-style building, the museum features changing exhibits and period room settings. Monday-Saturday.

YAZOO CITY

Railroad aficionados, you're in for a treat. Yazoo City is home to the Casey Jones Railroad Museum, site of the 1900 train wreck.

Information: Convention and Visitors Bureau, 323 N. Main St., 662-746-1815, 800-381-0662; www.yazoo.org

WHAT TO SEE AND DO

CASEY JONES RAILROAD MUSEUM

10901 Vaughan Road, Vaughan, 662-673-9864; www.trainweb.org

Site of the famous 1900 Casey Jones train wreck, the state-owned museum covers the story of the crash, local railroad history and folklore. Artifacts, including a 1923 steam locomotive, are on display. Monday-Saturday.

DELTA NATIONAL FOREST

Ranger's Office, Rolling Fork, 601-873-6256; www.fs.fed.us/r8/mississippi/delta

Here you'll find numerous small lakes, streams and green tree reservoirs contained on 59,500 acres. Activities include primitive camping, fishing and hunting for squirrel, raccoon, turkey, waterfowl, rabbit, woodcock and deer. There is also the Blue Lake picnic area and walking trail as well as the Sweetgum, Overcup Oak and Green Ash natural areas.

YAZOO HISTORICAL MUSEUM

Triangle Cultural Center, 332 N. Main St., Yazoo City, 662-746-2273

302

Exhibits cover the history of Yazoo County from prehistoric times to the present, with Civil War artifacts and fossils. Tours: Monday-Friday.

MISSISSIPPI

★
★
★
★
★

TENNESSEE

TENNESSEE IS A PLACE OF CONTRASTS. IT'S HEARING THE BLUES ON MEMPHIS' FAMOUS Beale Street and paying homage to the King of Rock 'n' Roll at Graceland. It's hiking through the Great Smoky Mountains and cruising along the Mississippi River. It's strolling through historic Civil War battlefields and learning about the power of the atomic bomb at Oak Ridge National Laboratory.

Tennessee's landscape is no less diverse. The eastern part of the state is characterized by mountains, including the picturesque Great Smokies. West of the mountains, the land stretches into valleys surrounded by wooded ridges. Here visitors find Knoxville, a short drive from Great Smoky Mountains National Park. Knoxville is home of the University of Tennessee—which inspires great devotion among locals—and a blossoming music scene. Further west and south, Chattanooga is an outdoor enthusiast's dream, thanks to its spot in the Appalachian Mountains near the Cumberland Plateau. On a clear day, visitors can see Tennessee, Georgia, North and South Carolina and Alabama from the top of Lookout Mountain.

The center of the state is dominated by the Cumberland Plateau's flat-topped mountains and further west, the Highland Rim, an elevated plain surrounding the Nashville Basin. Here, the center of the country music universe doubles as the state's capital. Nashville is home to the *Grand Ole Opry*, the country's longest continuously running live radio show, and The District, a lively downtown neighborhood where visitors will find music stars and starry-eyed hopefuls singing their hearts out after hours. Beyond its country music mayhem, the state capital is also a sophisticated city of museums, universities, historical sites and first-class dining.

West Tennessee flattens out into the Gulf Coastal Plain. Most of the region has rolling hills, but near the Mississippi River on the western edge of the state, the land flattens out. Memphis is the urban hub here, and a recent renaissance in the downtown core has given Memphis a new vibe. No longer second fiddle to Nashville's music scene, Memphis celebrates its reputation as the home of the blues and the birthplace of rock 'n' roll.

Of course, these cities are separated by Tennessee's many small and mid-sized towns, each of which has a unique story to tell. Tennessee has been inspired and molded by some of America's greatest legends—Davy Crockett, Daniel Boone, W.C. Handy, B.B. King, Elvis Presley, Alex Haley and three American presidents among them—and numerous historic landmarks chronicle the state's movers and shakers.

Tennessee's tourism bureau has a motto: "the stage is set for you." It's true. So pick your scene and your role, and grab your share of Tennessee's limelight.

Information: www.tnvacation.com

FUN FACTS

The Ocoee River is among the nation's wildest white-water rivers, attracting some of the world's best paddlers.

Tennessee is home to more caves than anywhere else in the country, with 3,800 documented caves.

CARYVILLE

WHAT TO SEE AND DO

COVE LAKE STATE PARK

110 Cove Lake Lane, Caryville, 423-566-9701; state.tn.us

The park's approximately 700 acres include 300-acre Cove Lake, where hundreds of Canada geese stay for the winter. There's plenty to keep humans here, too: a pool, a wading pool, fishing, boat rentals, nature trails, picnicking, a restaurant, a playground, game courts, camping and tent and trailer sites.

HOTELS

★DAYS INN

221 Colonial Lane, Lake City, 865-426-2816, 800-329-7466; www.daysinn.com

60 rooms. High-speed Internet access. Complimentary continental breakfast. Outdoor pool. Pets accepted. $

★HAMPTON INN

4459 Veterans Memorial Highway, Caryville, 423-562-9888, 800-426-7866; www.hamptoninn.com

62 rooms. Complimentary full breakfast. $

CELINA

Located in the scenic Upper Cumberland section of Tennessee, Celina is the location of the first law office of Cordell Hull, who wrote the blueprint for the United Nations. Locals and visitors enjoy outdoor recreation on the area's Dale Hollow Lake.

Information: Dale Hollow-Clay County Chamber of Commerce, 931-243-3338; www.dalehollowlake.org

WHAT TO SEE AND DO

DALE HOLLOW LAKE

Celina, 931-243-3136

This lake stretches 61 miles and provides plenty of space for visitors to play in its crystal-clear water and its wooded shores. There's swimming, a bathhouse, fishing, boating (14 commercial docks), hunting, primitive and improved camping (May-October). Daily.

STANDING STONE STATE PARK

Celina, 10 miles south on Highway 52, 931-823-6347; www.state.tn.us

Nearly 11,000 acres of park attract visitors who can hike near the area's colorful spring wildflowers, catch sight of wildlife and fish in the park's lake. There's also a swimming pool, a bathhouse, boating (rentals), tennis, picnicking, a playground and concessions. In addition, tent and trailer sites as well as cabins are available.

HOTEL

★★CEDAR HILL RESORT

705 Cedar Hill Road, Celina, 931-243-3201, 800-872-8393; www.cedarhillresort.com

47 rooms. Restaurant. $

CHATTANOOGA

Walled in on three sides by the Appalachian Mountains and the Cumberland Plateau, Chattanooga has one of the South's most beautiful natural settings, which makes it a popular destination with outdoor enthusiasts. But its urban cultural offerings are also a draw: Here visitors find one of the world's largest freshwater aquariums, several noted art museums and theaters and even a museum dedicated to car towing. Chattanooga is the birthplace of miniature golf, the site of the first Coca-Cola bottling plant and has the steepest passenger incline railway in the country.

It's a city celebrated in song and heralded in history. The Cherokees called it "Tsatanugi" ("rock coming to a point"), describing Lookout Mountain, which stands like a sentinel over the city. They called the creek here "Chickamauga" ("river of blood").

Cherokee Chief John Ross founded the city. It was a starting point for the "Trail of Tears," when Native Americans from three states were herded by federal troops and forced to march to Oklahoma in the winter of 1838. Chattanooga also had a front-row seat to one of the Civil War's fateful battles: the Battle of Chickamauga in the fall of 1863 was one of the turning points of the Civil War. It ended when Union forces overpowered entrenched Confederate forces on Missionary Ridge; more than 34,500 men died. General. Sherman's march to the sea began immediately thereafter.

Chattanooga emerged as an important industrial city at the end of the Civil War, when soldiers from both sides returned to stake their futures in this commercially strategic city. In 1878, Adolph S. Ochs moved to Chattanooga from Knoxville, purchased the *Chattanooga Times* and made it one of the state's most influential newspapers. Although he later went on to publish the *New York Times*, Ochs retained control of the Chattanooga journal until his death in 1935.

Sparked by the Tennessee Valley Authority, the city's greatest period of growth began in the 1930s. In the past few years, millions of dollars have been spent along Chattanooga's riverfront, making it a popular visitor destination.

Information: Chattanooga Area Convention and Visitors Bureau, 2 Broad St., Chattanooga, 423-756-8687, 800-964-8600; www.chattanoogacvb.com

WHAT TO SEE AND DO

BATTLES FOR CHATTANOOGA MUSEUM

1110 E. Brow Road, Lookout Mountain, 423-821-2812; www.battlesforchattanooga.com

An automated, 3-D display re-creates the Civil War Battles of Chattanooga using 5,000 miniature soldiers, flashing lights, smoking cannons and crackling rifles. Also here are dioramas of area history prior to the Civil War. Summer: 9 a.m.-5 p.m.; rest of year: 10 a.m.-5 p.m.

BOOKER T. WASHINGTON STATE PARK

5801 Champion Road, Chattanooga, 423-894-4955; state.tn.us

Chickamauga Lake is spread across more than 350 acres. It has swimming pools, fishing, boating (rentals, launch), a nature trail, picnicking, a playground and a lodge. Some facilities are seasonal.

TENNESSEE

THE COPPER BASIN

For a look at some of Tennessee's most beautiful landscapes, take a drive along Highway 64 east of Chattanooga. You'll cruise through the scenic Cherokee National Forest, alongside the churning Ocoee River and through the badlands of the Copper Basin.

From Chattanooga, take I-75 north toward Cleveland and then take Highway 64 east to the Georgia border (take the bypass around Cleveland). From outside the town of Ocoee, Highway 64 runs east through 24 miles of the Cherokee National Forest alongside the Ocoee River.

The river, which hosted the 1996 Olympic Whitewater Competition, lures daring paddlers to one of the premier white-water runs in the country. A series of Class III and IV rapids with nicknames like "Broken Nose," "Diamond Splitter," "Tablesaw" and "Hell Hole" hints at the river's reputation as one of the Southeast's greatest white-water runs (overall rating: Class IV). The acclaimed white water lies between two dams built and managed by the Tennessee Valley Authority (TVA) for hydroelectric power. The TVA can dry up or "turn on" the white water as easily as turning a spigot. Two dozen outfitters around Ocoee lead guided rafting expeditions downriver for half-day or full-day excursions; try **Nantahala Outdoor Center** *(800-232-7238)*, **Ocoee Outdoors** *(800-533-7767)* or **Southeastern Expeditions** *(800-868-7238)*.

Connect with the outdoors in a more laid-back fashion at the Parksville Lake Recreation Area, 11 miles from Ocoee off Highway 64. The park offers a nice spot for picnics, boating or camping in stands of pine and dogwood trees. Enjoy a few leisurely hours here before continuing on to the Copper Basin.

Between Ducktown and Copperhill at the Georgia border, the Copper Basin gets its name from the copper mines that flourished here in the 1800s. Unfortunately, the industry clear-cut the forest and generated copper sulfide fumes that devastated what was then left of the local environment, creating a stark desert out of the once-lush forested terrain. In the 1930s, the Civilian Conservation Corps was sent in to restore the area, and after five forgiving decades and active land reclamation, the Copper Basin is beginning to recover. **The Ducktown Basin Museum**, 1/4 mile north of Highway 64 on Highway 68 *(423-496-5778)*, tells the story of the copper industry. The remains of the town's first copper mine are nearby, as are the towns of Copperhill, Tennessee, and McCaysville, Georgia, both of which have historic districts worth a visit. From downtown Copperhill, the **Blue Ridge Scenic Railway** *(800-934-1898)*, an antique locomotive with a red caboose, takes passengers to Blue Ridge, Georgia. There are several restaurants and cafés right across the street from the depot. Self-guided walking- and driving-tour maps are available at the **visitor center in downtown Copperhill** *(615-496-1012)*; *Approximately 75 miles.*

★
★
★
★

CHATTANOOGA AFRICAN-AMERICAN MUSEUM

200 E. Martin Luther King Blvd., Chattanooga, 423-266-8658; www.caamhistory.com
This educational institution highlights African-American contributions to the growth of Chattanooga and the nation. Monday-Friday 10 a.m.-5 p.m., Saturday noon-4 p.m.

CHATTANOOGA CHOO-CHOO

Terminal Station, 1400 Market St., Chattanooga, 423-266-5000, 800-872-2529;
www.choochoo.com
The song made it famous, but the Chattanooga Choo-Choo began chugging through the South and Midwest in the 1880s. The converted 1909 train station contains a hotel and restaurants. It also boasts formal gardens, fountains, pools, turn-of-the-century shops, gaslights, a trolley ride and a model railroad museum. Daily 8 a.m.-10 p.m.

CHATTANOOGA NATURE CENTER AT REFLECTION RIDING

400 Garden Road, Chattanooga, 423-821-1160; www.reflectionriding.org
This park meant for leisurely driving offers winding three-mile trips with vistas: historic sites, trees, wildflowers, shrubs, reflecting pools. It's also a wetland walkway, with a nature center, hiking trails and outdoorsy programs. Monday-Saturday.

CHESTER FROST PARK

2318 Gold Point Circle, Hixson, 423-824-3306; www.hamittontn.gov
Activities abound at the park: swimming, a sand beach, a bathhouse, fishing, boating (ramps), hiking, picnicking, concessions, camping (fee; electricity, water). Islands in the park are accessible by causeways.

CRAVENS HOUSE

Chattanooga, 423-821-7786
The house is the oldest-surviving structure on the mountain, restored with period furnishings. The original house, which was the center of the "Battle Above the Clouds," was destroyed; the present structure was erected on the original foundations in 1866. Mid-June to mid-August: daily.

CREATIVE DISCOVERY MUSEUM

321 Chestnut St., Chattanooga, 423-756-2738; www.cdmfun.org
The museum encourages children to learn about the world by playing instruments, climbing through a replica of a riverboat and creating art, among other hands-on activities. Exhibit areas include the Artist's Studio, Inventor's Clubhouse, Musician's Studio and Excavation Station. 10 a.m.-5 p.m.; closed Wednesday from September-May.

INTERNATIONAL TOWING & RECOVERY HALL OF FAME & MUSEUM

3315 Broad St., Chattanooga, 423-267-3132; www.internationaltowingmuseum.org
The museum spotlights the people and vehicles that are reliable as soon as your car decides that it isn't. Dedicated in the autumn of 1995, this museum is just a block away from where the Ernest Holmes Company made the very first automobile wrecker. The museum has a large collection of antique toy trucks and towing and wrecking equipment, as well as a hall of fame. Monday-Saturday 10 a.m.-4:30 p.m., Sunday 11 a.m.-5 p.m.

HARRISON BAY STATE PARK

8411 Harrison Bay Road, Harrison, 423-344-6214; www.state.tn.us

The park is spread across more than 1,200 acres on Chickamauga Lake. There's a swimming pool, fishing, boating (ramp, marina), picnicking, a playground, a snack bar, a restaurant, a camp store and camping, all of which are seasonal. Daily 8 a.m.-10 p.m.

HOUSTON MUSEUM OF DECORATIVE ARTS

201 High St., Chattanooga, 423-267-7176; www.thehoustonmuseum.com

The museum features glass, porcelain, pottery, music boxes, dolls, a collection of pitchers and country-style furniture. Monday-Friday 9:30 a.m.-4 p.m., open seasonally on Saturday and Sunday.

HUNTER MUSEUM OF AMERICAN ART

10 Bluff View, Chattanooga, 423-267-0968; www.huntermuseum.org

Built on a bluff overlooking the Tennessee River, the museum has an outdoor beauty that's rivaled only by its art collection. The offerings include paintings, sculpture, glass, drawings, a permanent collection of major American artists and changing exhibits. Tuesday-Saturday 9:30 a.m.-5 p.m., Sunday noon-5 p.m.

IMAX 3D THEATER

201 Chestnut St., Chattanooga, 800-262-0695; www.tnaqua.org

See a flick on the IMAX's six-story movie screen. The Tennessee Aquarium, which is near by, offers discounted combination tickets. Daily.

★
★ ★
★ ★
★ ★
★

LOOKOUT MOUNTAIN

Chattanooga, south of town via Ochs Highway and Scenic Highway;
www.lookoutmountain.com

The mountain towers more than 2,120 feet above the city, offering clear-day views of Tennessee, Georgia, North Carolina, South Carolina and Alabama. During the Civil War, the "Battle Above the Clouds" was fought on the slope.

LOOKOUT MOUNTAIN INCLINE RAILWAY

3917 St. Elmo Ave., Chattanooga, Lower Station, 423-821-4224;
www.lookoutmountain.com

The world's steepest passenger incline railway climbs Lookout Mountain to 2,100-feet altitude. Near the top, the grade reaches a 72.7 degree angle; passengers ride glass-roofed cars to witness the steepness. The Smoky Mountains (200 miles away) can be seen from Upper Station observation deck. Round trip, it takes approximately 30 minutes. Daily.

NATIONAL KNIFE MUSEUM

7201 Shallowford Road, Chattanooga, 423-892-5007;

The permanent display shows knives of every age and description. There are also changing exhibits. Monday-Friday 10 a.m.-4 p.m.

NICKAJACK DAM AND LAKE

3490 TVA Road, Jasper

The Tennessee Valley Authority dam impounds the lake with 192 miles of shoreline and 10,370 acres of water surface. Fishing and a boat launch are available.

POINT PARK

110 Point Park Road., Lookout Mountain, 423-821-7786

Get a view of Chattanooga and Moccasin Bend from the observatory. Monuments, plaques and a museum tell the story of battle. There's also a visitor center for the park, which is part of Chickamauga and Chattanooga National Military Park. Daily.

RACCOON MOUNTAIN CAVERNS AND CAMPGROUND

319 W. Hills Drive, Chattanooga, 800-823-2267; www.raccoonmountain.com

More than 5½ miles of underground passageways offer views of beautiful rock formations. Opt for the Crystal Palace Tour for an overview of the cave's history and geology, or get a little dirty on one of the "wild" cave expeditions that give visitors a chance to examine undeveloped parts of the caverns. Several of these expeditions offer overnight stays in the cave. It's also a full-facility campground. Daily.

ROCK CITY GARDENS

1400 Pattern Road, Lookout Mountain, 706-820-2531; www.seerockcity.com

Among these 14 acres of mountaintop trails and vistas, visitors will find unique rock formations (including one called Fat Man's Squeeze), a 180-foot "swing-a-long" bridge and a critter classroom, where visitors learn about the creatures that live on or near Lookout Mountain. A restaurant and shops are on the premises. Daily from 8:30 a.m.; closing times vary.

RUBY FALLS-LOOKOUT MOUNTAIN CAVERNS

1720 S. Scenic Highway, Chattanooga, 423-821-2544; www.rubyfalls.com

Under the battlefield are twin caves with onyx formations, giant stalactites and stalagmites of various hues; at 1,120 feet below the surface, Ruby Falls is a 145-foot waterfall inside Lookout Mountain Caverns. Get a view of the city from the tower above the entrance building. Guided tours are available. Daily.

SIGNAL POINT ON SIGNAL MOUNTAIN

Chattanooga, nine miles north on Ridgeway Avenue; www.sigmtn.com

The mountain was used for signaling by Cherokees and later by Confederates. By looking almost straight down to the Tennessee River from Signal Point Military Park (off St. James Boulevard), visitors get a glimpse of the "Grand Canyon of Tennessee."

TENNESSEE

SOUTHERN BELLE RIVERBOAT

201 Riverfront Parkway, Chattanooga, 423-266-4488, 800-766-2784;
www.chattanoogariverboat.com

Sightseeing, breakfast, lunch and dinner cruises take place on a 500-passenger river-boat. April-December: daily.

TENNESSEE AQUARIUM

1 Broad St., Chattanooga, 423-265-0695, 800-262-0695; www.tnaqua.org

The aquarium was the first major freshwater life center in the country, focusing primarily on the natural habitats and wildlife of the Tennessee River and related ecosystems. Within this 130,000-square-foot complex are more than 9,000 animals in their natural habitats. The aquarium recreates riverine habitats in seven major freshwater tanks and two terrestrial environments and is organized into five major galleries: Appalachian Cove Forest; Tennessee River Gallery; Discovery Falls; Mississippi Delta; and Rivers of the World. The highlight of the aquarium is the 60-foot-high central canyon, designed to give visitors a sense of immersion into the river. Daily 9:30 a.m.-6 p.m.

TENNESSEE VALLEY RAILROAD

4119 Cromwell Road, Chattanooga, 423-894-8028; www.tvrail.com

The South's largest operating historic railroad has steam locomotives, diesels and passenger coaches of various types. Trains take passengers on a six-mile ride, including through a tunnel. There's an audiovisual show and displays. June-Labor Day: daily; April-May and September to mid-November: Monday-Friday.

UNIVERSITY OF TENNESSEE AT CHATTANOOGA

615 McCallie Ave., Chattanooga, 423-425-4111, 800-882-6627; www.utc.edu

The Fine Arts Center has McKenzie Arena to host entertainment and special events. Tours of the campus are by appointment.

SPECIAL EVENTS
RIVERBEND FESTIVAL

180 Hamm Road, Chattanooga, 423-265-4112; www.riverbendfestival.com

More than 100 musicians perform during the nine-day festival along the Tennessee River. The fest also offers sporting events, children's activities and a fireworks display. Mid-June.

CHATTANOOGA ON STAGE

Chattanooga; www.chattanooga.gov

The city has several venues that stage live theater. Tivoli Theater (box office 423-757-5042) shows a variety of events, including plays, concerts and opera. Chattanooga Theatre Centre (400 River St., box office 423-267-8534) and Memorial Auditorium (399 McCallie Ave., box office 423-757-5042) also stage productions. The Chattanooga Symphony and Opera Association (423-267-8583) hosts 25 concerts and two opera productions yearly. Backstage Playhouse (3264 Brainerd Road, 423-629-1565) offers dinner theater.

CHEROKEE NATIONAL FOREST

This 630,000-acre forest, cut by river gorges and creased by rugged mountains, lies in two separate strips along the Tennessee-North Carolina boundary, northeast and southwest of Great Smoky Mountains National Park. A region of thick forests, streams and waterfalls, the forest takes its name from the Native American tribe. There are more than 700 miles of hiking trails, including part of the Appalachian Trail. The forest's 30 campgrounds, 30 picnic areas, eight swimming sites, 13 boating sites and seven white-water rivers practically guarantee that visitors will find outdoor adventure and scenic beauty on this expanse of land. Hunting for game, including wild boar, deer and turkey, is permitted under Tennessee game regulations. Fees may be charged at recreation sites.

Information: Cleveland, northeast, southeast and southwest of Johnson City via Highway. 23, 321, Highway. 91, east of Cleveland on Highway. 64, 423-476-9700; www.southernregion.fs.fed.us/cherokee

HOTELS

★★★CHATTANOOGA MARRIOTT AT THE CONVENTION CENTER

2 Carter Plaza, Chattanooga, 423-756-0002, 800-228-9290; www.marriott.com

This high-rise hotel is in the heart of downtown, next to the convention center and near shopping, restaurants and great nightlife. Guest rooms feature contemporary furnishings and décor. Great downtown views can be seen from the third-floor outdoor pool area. 342 rooms. High-speed Internet access. Two restaurants, bar. Outdoor pool. $

★★CLARION HOTEL

407 Chestnut St., Chattanooga, 423-756-5150; chattanooga.doubletree.com

186 rooms. High-speed Internet access. Restaurant, bar. Business center. Pets accepted. $

★HAMPTON INN CHATTANOOGA

7013 Shallowford Road, Chattanooga, 423-855-0095, 800-426-7866;
www.hamptoninn.com

167 rooms. Wireless Internet access. Complimentary full breakfast. Airport transportation available. $

★★HOLIDAY INN CHATTANOOGA-CHOO CHOO

1400 Market St., Chattanooga, 423-266-5000, 800-872-2529; www.choochoo.com

363 rooms. Wireless Internet access. Three restaurants, bar. Children's activity center. Airport transportation available. Fitness center. Outdoor pool. $

★LA QUINTA INN & SUITES CHATTANOOGA

7015 Shallowford Road, Chattanooga, 423-855-0011, 800-531-5900;
www.laquinta.com

136 rooms. Wireless Internet access. Complimentary continental breakfast. Outdoor pool, children's pool. $

TENNESSEE

★
★
★
★

★QUALITY SUITES CHATTANOOGA

7324 Shallowford Road, Chattanooga, 423-892-1500; www.qschattanooga.com

62 rooms. Wireless Internet access. Complimentary full breakfast. Fitness center. **$**

SPECIALTY LODGINGS
BLUFF VIEW INN BED AND BREAKFAST

411 E. Second St., Chattanooga, 423-265-5033; www.bluffviewinn.com

Located in the historic Bluff View art district, this property includes three turn-of-the-century homes: an English Tudor, a Colonial and a Victorian. Some rooms feature bluff views overlooking the Tennessee River. 16 rooms. Complimentary full breakfast. **$**

RESTAURANTS
★★★212 MARKET

212 Market St., Chattanooga, 423-265-1212; www.212market.com

Local produce and meats are used in the frequently changing menu at 212 Market, a family-owned and -operated restaurant in the heart of downtown Chattanooga. The brick exterior is set off with striped awnings and flower boxes, and the interior features contemporary/Southwest décor, set off by colorful dinnerware, oak tables and chairs, local artwork and live plants. Guests can dine upstairs on the outdoor balcony, where there is seating at wrought-iron umbrella tables. A pianist performs every Friday evening, and a jazz band performs every third Sunday of the month. Contemporary American menu. Lunch, dinner. **$$**

★COUNTRY PLACE

7320 Shallowford Road, Chattanooga, 423-855-1392;
www.countryplacerestaurant.com

Southern menu. Breakfast, lunch, dinner, brunch. **$**

★★MOUNT VERNON RESTAURANT

3535 Broad St., Chattanooga, 423-266-6591; www.mymtvernon.com

American, Southern menu. Lunch, dinner. Closed Sunday. **$$**

CLARKSVILLE

Many of Clarksville's first settlers were American Revolutionary War veterans who received land here when the government couldn't afford to pay them for their services. Today it is one of Tennessee's fastest-growing areas. The town's attractions are diverse. The Downtown Artists' Co-op supports the city's visual arts community, while the performing arts center attracts national headliners and international legends to its stage. Nearby parks preserve the natural beauty and historic significance of Clarksville and its surroundings.

Information: Clarksville/Montgomery County Tourist Commission, 312 Madison St.,
931-647-2331, 800-530-2487; www.clarksvillechamber.com

WHAT TO SEE AND DO
BEACHHAVEN VINEYARD & WINERY

1100 Dunlap Lane, Clarksville, 931-645-8867; www.beachavenwinery.com

Tour the vineyard and winery and then hit the tasting room. There is also a picnic area on the grounds. Daily.

CUSTOMS HOUSE MUSEUM

200 S. Second St., Clarksville, 931-648-5780; www.customshousemuseum.org
Built in 1898 as a U.S. Post Office and Customs House, the museum houses changing history, science and art exhibits. Tuesday-Saturday 10 a.m.-5 p.m., Sunday 1-5 p.m.

DUNBAR CAVE STATE NATURAL AREA

Clarksville, five miles southeast via Highway 79, 931-648-5526; www.tennessee.gov
This 110-acre park with a small scenic lake was once a fashionable resort; the cave itself housed big-band dances. The old bathhouse has been refurbished to serve as a museum and visitor center. Park daily; cave June-August, weekends, by reservation only.

PORT ROYAL STATE HISTORIC AREA

Five miles east via Highway 76, near Adams, 931-358-9696;
www.state.tn.us
At the confluence of Sulphur Fork Creek and the Red River, Port Royal was one of the state's earliest communities and trading centers. A 300-foot covered bridge spans the river. Daily 8 a.m.-sundown.

SPECIAL EVENT
OLD-TIME FIDDLERS CHAMPIONSHIP

Clarksville; www.tnfiddlers.com
Late March.

HOTELS

★COUNTRY INN & SUITES BY CARLSON CLARKSVILLE

3075 Wilma Rudolph Blvd., Clarksville, 931-645-1400, 800-531-1900;
www.countryinns.com
125 rooms. High-speed Internet access. Complimentary full breakfast. Fitness center. Indoor pool. **$**

★HAMPTON INN

190 Holiday Road, Clarksville, 931-552-2255; www.hamptoninn.com
77 rooms. High-speed Internet access. Complimentary continental breakfast. **$**

★QUALITY INN

803 N. Second St., Clarksville, 931-645-9084; www.qualityinn.com
130 rooms. High-speed Internet access. Complimentary continental breakfast. Bar. **$**

★★RIVERVIEW INN

50 College St., Clarksville, 931-552-3331, 877-487-4837; www.theriverviewinn.com
154 rooms. Restaurant, bar. Outdoor pool. **$**

CLEVELAND

The superintendent's office of the Cherokee National Forest is here.
Information: Cleveland/Bradley Chamber of Commerce, 225 Keith St.,
423-472-6587; www.clevelandchamber.com

TENNESSEE

★
★
★
★
★

HOTELS

★BAYMONT INN

107 Interstate Drive N.W., Cleveland, 423-339-1000; www.baymontinns.com

100 rooms. Complimentary continental breakfast. **$**

★QUALITY INN

2595 Georgetown Road. N.W., Cleveland, 423-476-8511, 800-228-5151;
www.qualityinn.com

97 rooms. High-speed Internet access. Complimentary continental breakfast. Restaurant, bar. Outdoor pool. **$**

COLUMBIA

James K. Polk, 11th president of the United States, spent his boyhood in Columbia and returned here to open his first law office. The town attracts visitors who want to see Polk's ancestral home, tour the town's many antebellum houses or celebrate mules, which Columbia does with great fanfare one week each April.

Information: Maury County Convention & Visitors Bureau, Public Square,
931-381-7176, 888-852-1860; www.columbiatn.com

WHAT TO SEE AND DO

ANCESTRAL HOME OF JAMES K. POLK

301 W. Seventh St., Columbia, 931-388-2354; www.jameskpolk.com

Built by Samuel Polk, father of the president, the federal-style house is furnished with family possessions, including furniture and portraits used at the White House. Gardens link the house to an adjacent 1818 building owned by the president's sisters. There's also a visitor center. April-October: Monday-Saturday 9 a.m.-5 p.m., Sunday 1-5 p.m.; rest of year: Monday-Saturday 9 a.m.-4 p.m., Sunday 1-5 p.m.

THE ATHENAEUM

808 Athenaeum St., Columbia, 931-381-4822; www.athenaeumrectory.com

These Moorish buildings were used as a girls' school after 1852. During the Civil War, the rectory became headquarters of Union Generals. Negeley and Schofield. February-December: Tuesday-Sunday; fall tour September.

SPECIAL EVENTS

MAURY COUNTY FAIR

Maury County Park Fairgrounds, 1018 Maury County Park Drive, Columbia,
931-381-2900; www.maurycountyfair.com

Late August-early September.

MULE DAY

Mule Day Office, 1018 Maury County Park Drive, Columbia, 931-381-9557;
www.muleday.com

To honor the role mules played in the town's history—providing important labor for farms—Columbia celebrates with activities including a liar's contest, an auction, a parade, a mule pull, a square dance, bluegrass night, a pioneer craft festival and a knife and coin show. First weekend in April.

NATIONAL TENNESSEE WALKINGHORSE JUBILEE

Maury County Park, 1018 Maury County Park Drive, Columbia, 931-388-0303

Late May-early June.

PLANTATION CHRISTMAS TOUR OF HOMES

Columbia

First weekend in December.

HOTEL

★DAYS INN

1504 Nashville Highway, Columbia, 931-381-3297; www.daysinn.com

54 rooms. High-speed Internet access. Complimentary continental breakfast. Outdoor pool. Pets accepted. **$**

RESTAURANT

★★THE OLE LAMPLIGHTER

1000 Riverside Drive, Columbia, 931-381-3837

Seafood, steak menu. Dinner. **$$$**

COOKEVILLE

Cookeville is part of the state's upper Cumberland region, an area rich with public lands and waterways. Visitors trek to this region for outdoor recreation, including hiking, white-water rafting, golf, fishing and camping. For folks who don't want to be quite so close to Mother Nature, there are several historic museums, a couple of wineries and plenty of shops that sell antiques, arts and crafts in this part of Tennessee.

Information: Cookeville Area-Putnam County Chamber of Commerce,

302 S. Jefferson Ave., 931-526-2211, 800-264-5541; www.cookevillechamber.com

WHAT TO SEE AND DO

APPALACHIAN CENTER FOR CRAFTS

1560 Craft Center Drive, Smithville, 615-597-6801; www.tntech.edu/craftcenter

The center is on 600 acres overlooking Center Hill Lake. Operated by Tennessee Technological University, it has teaching programs in fiber, metal, wood, glass and clay. There are also exhibition galleries. Daily 9 a.m.-5 p.m.

BURGESS FALLS STATE NATURAL AREA

4000 Burgess Falls Drive, Sparta; www.state.tn.us/environment/parks/BurgessFalls

The scenic riverside trail (¾ mile) leads to an overlook of a 130-foot waterfall, considered one of the most beautiful in the state, in a gorge on the Falling Water River. Fishing (Burgess Falls Lake and River below dam), hiking trails and picnicking (below dam) are also available. Daily 8 a.m. until 30 minutes before sundown.

CENTER HILL DAM AND LAKE

158 Resource Lane, Lancaster, 931-858-3125; www.smithvilletn.com

This 250-foot-tall dam controls the flood waters of the Caney Fork River and provides electric power. The lake has a 415-mile shoreline. It provides ample opportunities for swimming, waterskiing, fishing, boating, hunting, picnicking at six recreation areas around the reservoir and camping. Some facilities are closed October-mid-April.

EDGAR EVINS STATE PARK

1630 Edgar Evins State Park Road, Silver Point, 931-858-2446, 800-250-8619;
www.tennessee.gov

This 6,000-acre park has boat launch facilities, camping sites and cabins. Daily 6
a.m.-10:30 p.m.

HOTELS
★BEST WESTERN THUNDERBIRD MOTEL

900 S. Jefferson Ave., Cookeville, 931-526-7115, 800-528-1234;
www.bestwestern.com

76 rooms. Wireless Internet access. Complimentary continental breakfast. Fitness center.
Outdoor pool. Pets accepted. $

★★HOLIDAY INN COOKEVILLE

970 S. Jefferson Ave., Cookeville, 931-526-7125, 800-465-4329; www.clarionhotel.com
198 rooms. Wireless Internet access. Complimentary continental breakfast. Restaurant. Bar. Children's activity center. $

RESTAURANT
★★NICK'S

895 S. Jefferson Ave., Cookeville, 931-528-1434
Seafood, steak menu. Lunch, dinner, brunch. Closed Monday. $$

CROSSVILLE

More than 36,000 tons of multicolored quartzite are quarried in the Crossville area
each year and sold for construction projects throughout the country. But visitors come
here for something else: golf. The self-titled "Golf Capital of Tennessee," Crossville
has a dozen courses, including Tennessee's highest elevation course at Renegade
Mountain. The area offers more than 200 holes, enough to keep even the most avid
golfer busy for a while.

Information: Greater Cumberland County Chamber of Commerce, 34 S. Main St.,
931-484-8444; www.crossville-chamber.com

WHAT TO SEE AND DO
CUMBERLAND COUNTY PLAYHOUSE

221 Tennessee Ave., Crossville, 931-484-5000; www.ccplayhouse.com
The playhouse offers indoor stage presentations by both professional and community
actors. There are also picnic facilities.

CUMBERLAND MOUNTAIN STATE PARK

24 Office Drive, Crossville, 931-484-6138; www.state.tn.us
This park, along the Cumberland Plateau, is 1,820 feet above sea level. It stands on
the largest remaining timberland plateau in America and has a 35-acre lake. The park
also provides a pool, a bathhouse, fishing, boating (rentals), nature trails and pro-
grams, tennis, picnicking, a playground, a snack bar, a dining room, camping, tent and
trailer sites and cabins. Daily 7 a.m.-10 p.m.

HOMESTEADS TOWER MUSEUM
96 Highway 68, Crossville, 931-456-9663
The tower was built in 1937-1938 to house administrative offices of the Cumberland Homesteads, a New Deal-era project. A winding stairway leads to a lookout platform at the top of the octagonal stone tower. At the base of the tower is a museum with photos, documents and artifacts from the 1930s and 1940s. March-December: daily.

SPECIAL EVENT
CUMBERLAND COUNTY FAIR
4000 Burgess Falls Road, Sparta, 931-484-9454; www.ncagr.gov
The county fair hosts exhibits; horse, cattle and other animal shows; mule pulls; and a fiddlers' contest. Late August.

HOTEL
★LA QUINTA INN CROSSVILLE
4038 Highway 127 N., Crossville, 931-456-9338, 800-531-5900; www.laquinta.com
60 rooms. Wireless Internet access. Complimentary continental breakfast. Outdoor pool. Business center. Pets accepted. $

ELIZABETHTON
A monument on the lawn of the Carter County Courthouse marks the spot where pioneers established the Watauga Association, the first independent regional government outside the 13 colonies, in 1772. Perhaps it is the area's natural beauty that inspired their ambition: Elizabethton is near the edge of Cherokee National Forest in a river basin surrounded by mountain ridges.

Information: Elizabethton/Carter County Chamber of Commerce, 500 Veterans Memorial Parkway, Elizabethton, 423-547-3850; www.tourelizabethton.com

317

WHAT TO SEE AND DO
ROAN MOUNTAIN STATE PARK
1015 Highway 143, Roan Mountain, 423-772-3303, 800-250-8620; www.state.tn.us
The park is home to 6,285-foot Roan Mountain, one of the highest peaks in the eastern U.S. Atop the mountain is a 600-acre garden of rhododendron, which blooms in late June. The grounds also have a pool, fishing, a nature trail, cross-country skiing, picnicking, a playground, a snack bar, camping and cabins. Daily 8 a.m.-4:30 p.m.

SYCAMORE SHOALS STATE HISTORIC AREA
1651 W. Elk Ave., Elizabethton 423-543-5808; www.state.tn.us
The first colonial settlement west of the Blue Ridge Mountains, the area has a reconstructed fort consisting of five buildings and palisade walls. There's also a visitor center with a museum and theater (daily). Tours of nearby Carter Mansion are available by appointment. Monday-Saturday 8 a.m.-4:30 p.m., Sunday 1-4:30 p.m.

TENNESSEE

★
★
★
★

FORT DONELSON NATIONAL BATTLEFIELD AND CEMETERY

The site of the Union's first major victory during the Civil War, Fort Donelson is famous for General Ulysses S. Grant's demand for "unconditional and immediate surrender" when Confederate General Simon B. Bucker proposed a truce. Nothing helped Grant so much during this four-day battle as weak generalship on the part of Confederate commanders John B. Floyd and Gideon J. Pillow. Although the Confederates repelled an attack by federal ironclad gunboats, bad decisions by the Confederate leaders left them with no choice but to surrender. Thanks to Grant's victory at Fort Donelson, coupled with the fall of Fort Henry 10 days earlier, the Union had passageways to the heart of the South: the Tennessee and Cumberland rivers. In Grant, northerners had a new hero. His terse surrender message stirred their imaginations, and he was quickly dubbed "Unconditional Surrender" Grant.

Today the fort walls, outer defenses and river batteries still remain and are well-marked to give the story of the battle. A visitor center features a 10-minute slide program, a museum and touch exhibits (daily). A six-mile, self-guided auto tour includes a visit to the fort, the cemetery and the Dover Hotel, where Buckner surrendered. The park is open year-round, dawn to dusk.

Information: One mile west of Dover on Highway 79, 931-232-5348; www.nps.gov/fodo

TENNESSEE

★
★
★
★
☆

SPECIAL EVENTS

COVERED BRIDGE CELEBRATION

Elizabethton, Elk Avenue, downtown; www.elizabethtonchamber.com/specialevents.html
The celebration includes an arts and crafts festival and an antiques show. Area country music stars and local talent perform. Four nights in early June.

OUTDOOR DRAMA

Sycamore Shoals State Historic Area, 1651 W. Elk Ave., Elizabethton, 423-543-5808; www.tennessee.org
This drama depicts the muster of Overmountain Men, who marched to King's Mountain, South Carolina, and defeated the British during the American Revolution. Historians identify the victory as a turning point for the American colonists during the war. Mid-July.

OVERMOUNTAIN VICTORY TRAIL CELEBRATION

Elizabethton, 815-543-5808
People don period costume for this reenactment of the original 200-mile march to King's Mountain, South Carolina. Late September.

RHODODENDRON FESTIVAL

Roan Mountain State Park, 1015 Highway 143, Elizabethton; www.state.tn.us
Mid- to late June.

ROAN MOUNTAIN WILD FLOWER TOURS AND BIRD WALKS

Roan Mountain State Park, 1015 Highway 143, Elizabethton

May.

FRANKLIN

Franklin is a favorite of Civil War buffs, who come to retrace the Battle of Franklin, a decisive clash that took place November 30, 1864. General John B. Hood, attempting to prevent two Union armies from uniting, outflanked the troops of General John Schofield. Late that afternoon, Hood discovered the Union troops, dug-in around the Carter House. For five hours the battle raged. In the morning Hood found that the Schofield troops had escaped across the river to join forces with the Union army at Nashville. The Confederates suffered 6,252 casualties, including the loss of five generals at Carnton Plantation and a sixth general 10 days after the battle. The North suffered 2,326 casualties.

Information: Williamson County Convention and Visitors Bureau, 615-794-1225, 800-356-3445; www.williamsoncvb.org

WHAT TO SEE AND DO

CARTER HOUSE

1140 Columbia Ave., Franklin, 615-791-1861; www.carterhouse1864.com

The house served as the command post for the Union forces during the Battle of Franklin. It now houses a Confederate museum with documents, uniforms, flags, guns, maps and Civil War prints. Go on a guided tour of house and grounds and see a video presentation. Monday-Saturday 9 a.m.-5 p.m., Sunday 9 a.m.-1 p.m.

319

HERITAGE TRAIL

Franklin, north and south on Highway 31

The trail provides a scenic drive along the highway from Brentwood through Franklin to Spring Hill, an area that was plantation country in the mid-1800s. Southern culture is reflected in the drive's many antebellum and Victorian houses; Williamson County was one of the richest areas in Tennessee when the Civil War broke out.

HISTORIC CARNTON AND MCGAVOCK CONFEDERATE CEMETERY

1345 Carnton Lane, Franklin, 615-794-0903; www.carnton.org

This federal-type house was modified in the 1840s to reflect Greek Revival style. Built by an early mayor of Nashville, the house was a social and political center. At the end of the Battle of Franklin, which was fought nearby, four Confederate generals lay dead on the back porch. The nation's largest private Confederate cemetery is adjacent. Daily.

HISTORIC DISTRICT

First Avenue and North Margin Street surrounding the Town Square and the Confederate Monument, Franklin

See the earliest buildings of Franklin, dating back to 1800; those along Main Street are exceptional in their architectural designs and are part of a historic preservation project.

TENNESSEE

CARTER HOUSE CHRISTMAS CANDLELIGHT TOUR
1140 Columbia Ave., Franklin, 615-791-1861; www.carter-house.org
Early December.

HERITAGE FOUNDATION TOWN & COUNTRY TOUR
Franklin, 615-591-8500; www.historicfranklin.com
Tour the interiors of nine Franklin and Williamson County historic homes. First weekend in May.

HOTEL
★BEST WESTERN FRANKLIN INN
1308 Murfreesboro Road, Franklin, 615-790-0570
142 rooms. Complimentary continental breakfast. Outdoor pool. $

SPECIALTY LODGINGS
A HOMEPLACE BED AND BREAKFAST
7826 Nolensville Road, Nolensville, 615-776-5181
This pre-Civil War era home is hidden in dense forests. Each room has a canopy bed and fireplace. Three rooms. $

THE INN AT WALKING HORSE FARM
1490 Lewisburg Pike, Franklin, 615-790-2076
The inn and horse farm is set on 40 acres of rolling pastureland with eight walking horses. Guests are welcome to bring their own horses as well. Boarding, meals and grooming are available. Four rooms. $$

320

TENNESSEE

★
★
★
★
★

GALLATIN
About 25 miles from Nashville, Gallatin still has an air of the antebellum South, thanks to its historic town square. Visitors come to this area for outdoor recreation, a dose of American history and an opportunity to find antiques.
Information: Chamber of Commerce, 118 W. Main St., Gallatin, 615-452-4000; www.gallatintn.org

WHAT TO SEE AND DO
BLEDSOE CREEK STATE PARK
400 Zieglers Fort Road, Gallatin, 615-452-3706; www.tennessee.gov
The park offers waterskiing, fishing, boating (launch), nature trails, a playground and camping. Daily 7 a.m.-sunset.

CRAGFONT
200 Cragfont Road, Castalian Springs, 615-452-7070;
www.tennesseeanytime.org
This late Georgian-style house was built for General. James Winchester, Revolutionary War hero, by masons and carpenters brought from Maryland. It is named for the rocky bluff (with spring below) on which it stands. It has a galleried ballroom, weaving room, wine cellar and federal-period furnishings. There are also restored gardens. Mid-April-November: Tuesday-Saturday 10 a.m.-5 p.m.; Sunday 10 a.m.-1 p.m.; rest of year: by appointment.

TROUSDALE PLACE

183 W. Main St., Gallatin, 615-452-5648; www.trousdaleplace.com

The two-story brick house built in the early 1800s was the residence of Governor William Trousdale. Inside is period furniture and a military history library.

WYNNEWOOD

210 Old Highway 25, Castalian Springs, 615-452-5463;
www.sumnercountytourism.com

Considered the oldest and largest log structure ever built in Tennessee, this log inn was originally constructed as a stagecoach stop and mineral springs resort. President Andrew Jackson visited here many times. April-October: daily; rest of year: Monday-Saturday.

SPECIAL EVENT
SUMNER COUNTY PILGRIMAGE

200 Cragfont Road, Castalian Springs, 615-452-7070

Take a tour of historic houses. Last Saturday in April.

HOTELS
★GUESTHOUSE INN GALLATIN

221 W. Main St., Gallatin, 615-452-5433; www.guesthouseintl.com

86 rooms. High-speed Internet access. $

★HOLIDAY INN EXPRESS

615 E. Main St., Hendersonville, 615-824-0022; www.holiday-inn.com

93 rooms. Complimentary breakfast. Outdoor pool. $

GATLINBURG

Gatlinburg has retained most of its mountain charm while tapping into the stream of tourists that flows through the town en route to Great Smoky Mountains National Park, the country's most visited national park. Home to only about 3,500 people, the city has accommodations for 40,000 guests, who stop here to experience the town's mountain heritage. Visitors can wander through local shops, many of which sell mountain handicrafts. For folks looking for a quieter stroll, visitors might choose the river walk along Little Pigeon River. The area offers outdoor activities year-round, including downhill skiing, horseback riding, golf and hiking.

Information: Chamber of Commerce, 811 E. Parkway, 865-430-4148, 800-900-4148;
www.gatlinburg.com

TENNESSEE

★
★
★
★

WHAT TO SEE AND DO
AERIAL TRAMWAY-OBER GATLINBURG SKI RESORT

1001 Parkway, Gatlinburg, 865-436-5423; www.obergatlinburg.com

A 10-minute, two-mile tram ride goes to the top of Mount Harrison. Daily.

GATLINBURG SPACE NEEDLE

115 Historic Nature Trail, Gatlinburg, 865-436-4629; www.gatlinburgspaceneedle.com

A glass-enclosed elevator takes you to a 342-foot-high observation deck for a view of the Smoky Mountains. Daily.

OBER GATLINBURG SKI RESORT

1001 Parkway, Gatlinburg, 865-436-5423, 800-251-9202; www.obergatlinburg.com

This ski resort touts double, two-quad chairlifts; a patrol; a school; rentals; snowmaking; a concession area; and a restaurant and bar. The longest run measures 5,000 feet; the vertical drop is 600 feet. Night skiing is available, and there's also an alpine slide and indoor ice skating arena. Monday-Saturday 9:30 a.m.-9:20 p.m., Sunday 9:30 a.m.-6:20 p.m.

SIGHTSEEING CHAIRLIFT-OBER GATLINBURG SKI RESORT

Ski Mountain Road, Gatlinburg

A double chairlift operates to the top of Mount Harrison. March-Memorial Day: daily.

SKY LIFT

765 Parkway, Gatlinburg, 865-436-4307; www.gatlinburgskylift.com

The double-chairlift ride up to Crockett Mountain is 2,300 feet. Get a view of the Smoky Mountains en route and from observation deck at the summit. A snack bar and gift shop are available. Daily, weather permitting.

SPECIAL EVENTS

CRAFTSMEN'S FAIRS

121 Silverbell Lane, Gatlinburg, 865-436-7479; www.craftsmenfair.com

See craft demonstrations and hear folk music at this event. Late July-early August; also mid-October.

★
★
★
★

SCOTTISH FESTIVAL AND GAMES

Gatlinburg; www.gsfg.org

Sample Scottish heritage with bagpipe marching bands, highland dancing and sheep dog demonstrations. Third weekend in May.

SMOKY MOUNTAIN LIGHTS & WINTERFEST

107 Park Headquarters Road, Gatlinburg, 865-453-6411;
www.smokymountainwinterfest.com

The citywide winter celebration includes Yule log burnings, more than 2 million lights and other special events. Late November-February.

SPRING WILDFLOWER PILGRIMAGE

Gatlinburg Chamber of Commerce, 888-898-9102;
www.springwildflowerpilgrimage.org

This event offers numerous wildflower, fauna and natural history walks, seminars, art classes and a variety of other programs. It is held outdoors at the Great Smoky Mountains National Park, as well as in a variety of indoor venues around Gatlinburg. Seven days in late April.

SWEET FANNY ADAMS THEATER

461 Parkway, Gatlinburg, 877-388-5784; www.sweetfannyadams.com

The professional theater presents musical comedies and old-time singalong. Reservations are recommended. Nightly except Sunday. Late April-November.

HOTELS

★★BUCKHORN INN

2140 Tudor Mountain Road, Gatlinburg, 865-436-4668, 866-941-0460;
www.buckhorninn.com
16 rooms. Complimentary full breakfast. Restaurant. Whirlpool. **$$**

★★★CHRISTOPHER PLACE, AN INTIMATE RESORT

1500 Pinnacles Way, Newport, 423-623-6555, 800-595-9441;
www.christopherplace.com
Tucked away in the scenic Smoky Mountains of Tennessee, this antebellum inn is restored to its original splendor. Enjoy the romantic ambience of the Mountain View dining room while savoring four courses selected daily by the chef. Eight rooms. Children over 13 years only. Complimentary full breakfast. **$$**

★★EDGEWATER HOTEL-GATLINBURG

402 River Road, Gatlinburg, 865-436-4151, 800-423-9582; www.edgewater-hotel.com
205 rooms. Wireless Internet access. Complimentary continental breakfast. Bar. Children's activity center. Fitness center. Outdoor pool. Business center. **$**

★★★EIGHT GABLES INN

219 N. Mountain Trail, Gatlinburg, 865-430-3344, 800-279-5716; www.eightgables.com
In a wooded setting that inspires tranquility, this country inn is perfect for a romantic getaway. Explore nearby attractions such as fly fishing, golf and white-water rafting, or opt to spend the afternoon on the porch, admiring the grounds. Guest rooms are furnished with feather-top beds; suites have fireplaces and two-person whirlpool tubs. In addition to a five-course breakfast, the room rate includes nightly dessert and access to the inn's pantry. The Magnolia Tea Room serves lunch (open to the public). The inn serves candlelight dinners of regional Southern cuisine three days a week. 19 rooms. Wireless Internet access. Children over 10 years only. Complimentary full breakfast. Restaurant. Spa. **$$**

★GREYSTONE LODGE AT THE AQUARIUM

559 Parkway, Gatlinburg, 865-436-5621, 800-451-9202; www.greystonelodgetn.com
257 rooms. Complimentary continental breakfast. **$**

★HAMPTON INN GATLINBURG

967 Parkway, Gatlinburg, 865-436-4878, 888-476-6597;
www.hamptoninngatlinburg.com
97 rooms. Wireless Internet access. Complimentary continental breakfast. Outdoor pool. **$**

★★HOLIDAY INN SUNSPREE RESORT GATLINBURG

520 Historic Nature Trail, Gatlinburg, 865-436-9201, 800-435-9201; www.4lodging.com
400 rooms. Wireless Internet access. Two restaurants, bar. Children's activity center. Fitness center, Outdoor pool. **$**

★JOHNSON'S INN

242 Bishop Lane, Gatlinburg, 865-436-4881, 800-842-1930; www.johnsonsinn.com
32 rooms. Complimentary continental breakfast. **$**

GREAT SMOKY MOUNTAINS NATIONAL PARK

The park straddles the Tennessee-North Carolina border amid the lofty peaks of the Appalachian Mountains. The most visited of the national parks, it attracts more than 9 million visitors a year, who come to play in one of the East's best destinations for outdoor recreation. The park's reputation as a haven for wildlife and a variety of plant life—including fields of colorful wildflowers—does not hurt, either.

More than 900 miles of trails snake through the park, giving hikers intimate views of the mountain ridges wrapped in "smoky" fog. Seventy miles of the Appalachian Trail follow the state line along the high ridge of the park. For a less traveled trek, head toward Buckhorn Gap or Ramsey Cascade to wander through the quiet old-growth forests, home to a variety of giant trees. If you are in search of good photo ops, hike to any one of the park's many waterfalls, fueled by the area's 85 inches of annual rainfall. Among the most popular are Abrams, Grotto, Hen Wallow, Juney Whank, Laurel and Rainbow falls, though most of the rivers and streams in the park have waterfalls.

The park is not just for outdoor enthusiasts. History buffs too will find adventures, thanks to nearly 80 preserved historic structures, including houses, barns, churches and grist mills. Cades Cove is an outdoor museum reflecting the life of the original mountain settlers. Visitors will also see remnants of the Cherokee Indian Nation throughout the park. The Cherokee occupied these mountains before European settlers arrived, but in the winter of 1838-1839, the Cherokee were forced to travel the "Trail of Tears" to Oklahoma.

At the start of your visit to Great Smoky Mountains National Park, stop at one of the three visitor centers: Oconaluftee (daily) in North Carolina, two miles north of Cherokee on Highway 441; Sugarlands (daily) in Tennessee, two miles south of Gatlinburg; and Cades Cove (daily) in Tennessee, 10 miles southwest of Townsend. All have exhibits and information about the park. Camping reservations may be made up to three months in advance by calling 800-365-2267 from mid-May to October for Elkmont, Cades Cove and Smokemont; reservations are not taken for other sites.

Park naturalists conduct campfire programs and hikes during summer. There are also self-guided nature trails. LeConte Lodge, accessible only on foot or horseback, is a concession within the park (late March to mid-November). Fishing is permitted with a Tennessee or North Carolina state fishing license. Obtain regulations at visitor centers and campgrounds. Information: Townsend, 44 miles southeast of Knoxville via Highway 441; www.recreation.gov

★MIDTOWN LODGE

805 Parkway, Gatlinburg, 865-436-5691, 800-633-2446; www.midtownlodge.com
135 rooms. Complimentary continental breakfast. Outdoor pool, children's pool. $

★ROCKY WATERS MOTOR INN & SUITES

333 Parkway, Gatlinburg, 865-436-7861, 800-824-1111;www.rockywatersmotorinn.com
105 rooms. Wireless Internet access. Complimentary continental breakfast. Outdoor pool. $

★★PARK VISTA HOTEL & CONVENTION CENTER

705 Cherokee Orchard Road, Gatlinburg, 865-436-9211, 800-421-7275;
www.parkvista.com

312 rooms. Wireless Internet access. Restaurant, bar. Children's activity center. Outdoor pool. Fitness center. Business center. $

RESTAURANTS
★BRASS LANTERN

710 Parkway, Gatlinburg, 865-436-4345; www.brasslantern-gatlinburg.com
American menu. Lunch, dinner. $$

★★MAXWELL'S STEAK AND SEAFOOD

1103 Parkway, Gatlinburg, 865-436-3738; www.maxwells-inc.com
American menu. Dinner. $$

★★PARK GRILL

110 Parkway, Gatlinburg, 865-436-2300; www.parkgrillgatlinburg.com
American menu. Dinner. $$

★★THE PEDDLER RESTAURANT

820 River Road, Gatlinburg, 865-436-5794; www.peddlerparkgrill.com
Steak menu. Dinner. $$

GREENEVILLE

Some of Tennessee's most rugged heroes come from Greeneville: Davy Crockett was born a few miles outside of town in 1786, and President Andrew Johnson lived here and became the town's alderman. Eventually, he climbed the political ladder to the White House, where he served as Lincoln's vice president and then, after Lincoln's assassination, the president of the United States.

Information: Greene County Partnership, 115 Academy St., 423-638-4111;
www.greenecountypartnership.com

TENNESSEE

★
★
★
★
★

WHAT TO SEE AND DO
DAVY CROCKETT BIRTHPLACE STATE PARK

1245 Davy Crockett Park Road, Limestone, 423-257-2167;
www.state.tn.us

The 100-acre site overlooking the Nolichuckey River serves as a memorial to Crockett—humorist, bear hunter, congressman and hero of the Alamo. A small monument marks Crockett's birthplace; nearby is a replica of the log cabin in which he was born in 1786. The park also has a swimming pool, picnicking, camping, a museum and visitors center. Park: daily 8 a.m.-dusk.

KINSER PARK

650 Kinser Park Lane, Greeneville, 423-639-5912

The 285-acre park surrounded by woodland overlooks the Nolichuckey River. Activities abound with a swimming pool (bathhouses, waterslide), boating (ramp), nature trails, tennis courts, a golf course, miniature golf, playing fields, a go-cart track, picnic facilities, playgrounds and camping. Mid-March-October: daily.

ANDREW JOHNSON NATIONAL HISTORIC SITE

See the tailor shop, two houses and the burial place of the 17th president of the United States. Apprenticed to a tailor during his youth, Andrew Johnson came to Greeneville, Tenn., from his native Raleigh, N. C. in 1826. After years of service in local, state and federal governments, Sen. Johnson remained loyal to the Union when Tennessee seceded. After serving as military governor of Tennessee, Johnson was elected vice president in 1864. On April 15, 1865, he became president following the assassination of Abraham Lincoln. Continued opposition to the radical program of Reconstruction led to his impeachment in 1868. Acquitted by the Senate, he continued to serve as president until 1869. In 1875, Johnson became the only former president to be elected to the U.S. Senate.
Information: Monument Avenue, Greeneville, College and Depot Streets; www.nps.gov/anjo

HOTELS

★★CHARRAY INN
121 Serral Drive, Greeneville, 423-638-1331, 800-852-4682; www.charrayinn.com
36 rooms. High-speed Internet access. Complimentary full breakfast. Restaurant. Airport transportation available. $

★COMFORT INN
1790 E. Andrew Johnson Highway, Greeneville, 423-639-4185, 888-557-5007; www.choicehotels.com
90 rooms. Wireless Internet access. Complimentary continental breakfast. Restaurant, bar. Pets accepted. $

HURRICANE MILLS

This Tennessee town is best known for being the site of country singer Loretta Lynn's ranch.
Information: Humphreys County Chamber of Commerce, 124 E. Main St., Waverly, 931-296-4865; www.waverly.net/hcchamber

WHAT TO SEE AND DO

LORETTA LYNN'S RANCH
44 Hurricane Mills Road, Hurricane Mills, 931-296-7700; www.lorettalynn.com
Tours take guests through the country music star's house, a museum, Mooney's Ranch Office, the Butcher Holler Home and a simulated coal mine. Plus, they'll get a peek at Western and general stores and Loretta Lynn's Record Shop. The ranch also offers swimming, fishing, hiking, tennis and camping. Special events are also held there, including concerts, trail rides and campfires. April-October: daily.

NOLAN HOUSE
375 Highway 13 N., Waverly, 931-296-2511
This restored 12-room Victorian house (circa 1870) offers period furnishings, a redoubt trail, a dog-trot and a family graveyard. Overnight stays are available. Tours Monday-Saturday.

HOTELS
★★BEST WESTERN OF HURRICANE MILLS
15542 Highway 13 S., Hurricane Mills, 931-296-4251; www.bestwestern.com
89 rooms. High-speed Internet access. Restaurant. Complimentary breakfast. Outdoor pool. Pets accepted. **$**

★DAYS INN
15415 Highway 13 S., Hurricane Mills, 931-296-7647; www.daysinn.com
78 rooms. High-speed Internet access. Restaurant. Outdoor pool. Pets accepted. **$**

JACKSON
Located between Memphis and Nashville in western Tennessee, Jackson is named for President Andrew Jackson; many of the president's soldiers and his wife's relatives settled here. The city's other famous son, John Luther "Casey" Jones, a railroad engineer, died in 1900 trying to stop his train from hitting a stopped freight train in Mississippi. Jones was the only one to die in the crash, making him a hero immortalized in ballads and legends.
Information: Jackson County Convention and Visitors Bureau, 197 Auditorium St., 731-425-8333, 800-498-4748; www.jacksontncvb.com

WHAT TO SEE AND DO
BROOKS SHAW & SON OLD COUNTRY STORE
56 Casey Jones Lane, Jackson, 731-668-1223; www.caseyjonesvillage.com
This turn-of-the-century general store, located in Casey Jones Village, keeps more than 15,000 antiques on display. If you get hungry, there's also a restaurant, an ice-cream parlor and a confectionery shop. Daily.

CASEY JONES HOME AND RAILROAD MUSEUM
30 Casey Jones Lane, Jackson, 731-668-1222; www.caseyjones.com
See the original house of the high-rolling engineer who, on April 30, 1900, climbed into the cab of "Old 382" on the Illinois Central Railroad and took his "farewell trip to that promised land"—and a place in American folklore. On display are Jones' personal and railroad memorabilia, including railroad passes, timetables, bells and steam whistles; also check out the type of steam locomotive that was driven by Jones and restored 1890s coach cars. Daily.

CASEY JONES VILLAGE
56 Casey Jones Lane, Jackson, 731-668-1223; www.caseyjones.com
This complex of turn-of-the-century shops and buildings focuses on the life of one of America's most famous railroad heroes. Daily 6.30 a.m.-9 p.m.

CHICKASAW STATE RUSTIC PARK
20 Cabin Lake, Henderson, 731-989-5141, 800-458-1752; www.state.tn.us
The park covers 11,215 acres features two lakes. Swimming, fishing, boating (rentals), horseback riding, picnicking, a playground, a recreation lodge, tent and trailer sites and cabins are all available. Daily 6 a.m.-10 p.m.

327

TENNESSEE

★
★
★
★

CYPRESS GROVE NATURE PARK

866 Highway 70 W., Jackson, 731-425-8316; www.jacksonrecandparks.com

A boardwalk winds through a 165-acre cypress forest. There's also an observation tower, a nature center and a picnic shelter. Daily.

PINSON MOUNDS STATE ARCHAEOLOGICAL AREA

460 Ozier Road, Pinson, 731-425-8316; www.state.tn.us

The area contains the remains of ancient mounds of the Middle Woodland Mound period and more than 10 ceremonial and burial mounds of various sizes, including Sauls (72 feet high). There's also a nature trail, picnicking and a museum. Museum: March-November: daily; rest of year: Monday-Saturday, 8 a.m.-4:30 p.m., Sunday 1-5 p.m.

HOTELS

★AMERICA'S BEST VALUE INN

21045 Highway 22 N., Wildersville, 731-968-2532; www.bestvalueinn.com

40 rooms. High-speed Internet access. Complimentary continental breakfast. Outdoor pool. Pets accepted. $

★ECONO LODGE

1963 Highway 45 Bypass, Jackson, 731-668-4100, 800-850-1131; www.econolodge.com

203 rooms. Complimentary continental breakfast. $

★★HOLIDAY INN

541 Carriage House Drive, Jackson, 731-668-6000, 800-222-3297; www.holiday-inn.com

136 rooms. High-speed Internet access. Restaurant, bar. Fitness center. Outdoor pool. Business center. $

★★THE OLD ENGLISH INN

2267 N. Highland Ave., Jackson, 731-668-1571

80 rooms. High-speed Internet access. Complimentary continental breakfast. $

RESTAURANT

★OLD COUNTRY STORE

56 Casey Jones Lane, Jackson, 731-668-1223; www.caseyjonesvillage.com

American menu. Breakfast, lunch, dinner. $

JAMESTOWN

Once a hunting ground for Davy Crockett and later Sergeant Alvin C. York, Jamestown was also the home of Cordell Hull, FDR's secretary of state.

Information: Fentress County Chamber of Commerce, 114 Central Ave. W., 931-879-9948, 800-327-3945; www.jamestowntn.org

BIG SOUTH FORK NATIONAL RIVER/RECREATION AREA

4564 Leatherwood Road, Oneida, 423-569-2404; www.nps.gov/biso

This place is spread over approximately 105,000 acres on the Cumberland Plateau. Go there for the swimming pool, fishing, white-water canoeing, rafting, kayaking, nature trails, hiking, backpacking, bridle trails and hunting. If you want to stay a while, check out the primitive and improved camping (year-round). Brandy Creek Visitor Center: daily 8 a.m.-4:30 p.m. Stearns Visitor Center: April-late October: daily 9:30 a.m.-5 p.m.

HISTORIC RUGBY

Highway 5517, Rugby, 423-628-2441, 888-214-3400; www.historicrugby.org

Social reformer Thomas Hughes founded this English colony in the 1880s in hopes of creating a utopian society founded on cooperative enterprise and Christian values. Residents enjoyed natural parks, recreation and cultural activities such as literary societies. Financial problems, a typhoid epidemic and unusually severe winters contributed to the community's demise, but much as been preserved for visitors' pleasure today. Of 17 original Victorian buildings remaining, four are open to the public. Hughes Public Library, unchanged since opening in 1882, contains a unique 7,000-volume collection from the Victorian era. A visitor center is in Rugby Schoolhouse; guided walking tours are available. There is also picnicking and hiking in surrounding river gorges on trails built by original colonists. Monday-Saturday 9:30 a.m.-5:30 p.m., Sunday noon-5:30 p.m.

PICKETT STATE RUSTIC PARK

329

4605 Pickett Park Highway, Jamestown, 931-879-5821; www.state.tn.us

The park covers 14,000 acres in Cumberland Mountains. It offers unusual rock formations, caves and natural bridges. There's much to do there: a sand beach, swimming, fishing, boating (rentals), nature trails, backpacking, picnicking, concessions, a recreation lodge, camping and cabins. Daily 7:30 a.m.-dark.

JOHNSON CITY

TENNESSEE

A favorite of lists ranking the nation's best small cities, Johnson City mixes a metropolitan style with mountain air, affordable living and some of Tennessee's wildest history. (Legend has it that the city was one of Al Capone's alcohol distribution points during Prohibition.)

Information: Convention and Visitors Bureau, 601 E. Main St., Johnson City, 423-434-6000, 800-852-3392; www.johnsoncitytn.com

WHAT TO SEE AND DO
APPALACHIAN CAVERNS

420 Cave Hill Road, Blountville, 423-323-2337; www.appalachiancaverns.com

When it is hot, caving will cool you off. These giant underground chambers—made colorful by deposits of manganese, copper, calcium and other elements—served Native Americans in need of shelter, hid soldiers during the Civil War and protected moon shiners during Prohibition. Guided tours are available. Monday-Saturday 9 a.m.-6 p.m., Sunday 1-6 p.m.

EAST TENNESSEE STATE UNIVERSITY

807 University Parkway, Johnson City, 423-439-1000; www.etsu.edu

The campus has 63 buildings on 366 acres, including Slocumb Galleries, Memorial Center (where sports are held) and the James H. Quillen College of Medicine. Tours of campus are available.

HANDS ON! REGIONAL MUSEUM

315 E. Main St., Johnson City, 423-434-4263; www.handsonmuseum.org

The museum showcases more than 20 hands-on exhibits designed for children of all ages. Traveling shows also stop by. June-August: Monday-Friday 9 a.m.-5 p.m., Saturday 10 a.m. -5 p.m., Sunday 1-5 p.m.

HISTORIC DISTRICT

Visitors Center, 117 Boone St., Jonesborough, 423-753-5961

This four-by-six-block area through the heart of town reflects 200 years of history. See private residences; commercial and public buildings of federal, Greek Revival and Victorian styles; brick sidewalks; and old-style lampposts. Obtain walking-tour brochures at the Visitors Center.

JONESBOROUGH

Jonesborough, six miles west off Highway 11 E., 423-753-1030;
www.jonesboroughtn.org

It's the oldest town in Tennessee and the first capital of the state of Franklin (prior to Tennessee obtaining statehood).

JONESBOROUGH HISTORY MUSEUM

117 Boone St., Johnson City, 423-753-1015; www.jonesboroughtn.org

Exhibits highlight the history of Jonesborough from pioneer days to the early 20th century. Daily.

ROCKY MOUNT HISTORIC SITE & OVERMOUNTAIN MUSEUM

200 Hyder Hill Road, Piney Flats, 423-538-7396

The log house (circa 1770), territorial capitol under Governor William Blount from 1790 to 1792, is restored to original simplicity with 18th-century furniture, a log kitchen, a slave cabin, a barn, a blacksmith shop and a smokehouse. Costumed interpreters reenact a day in the life of a typical pioneer family; the 1½-hour tour includes Cobb-Massengill house, the kitchen and slave cabin, as well as a self-guided tour through the adjacent Museum of Overmountain History. Monday-Saturday.

TIPTON-HAYNES HISTORIC SITE

2620 S. Roan St., Johnson City, 423-926-3631; www.tipton-haynes.org

This was the site of the 1788 Battle of the Lost State of Franklin. Six original buildings and four reconstructions span American history from pre-colonial days through the Civil War. The visitor center has a museum display. April-October: daily; rest of year: Monday-Friday.

WATAUGA DAM AND LAKE

Hampton, about 20 miles east of Johnson City off Highway 321

Surrounded by the Cherokee National Forest and flanked by the Appalachian Mountains, Watauga Reservoir is arguably one of the most beautiful in the world and boasts excellent fishing. Below Watauga Dam is a wildlife observation area, where visitors can view waterfowl. The Appalachian Trail passes nearby.

WHITEWATER RAFTING

Cherokee Adventures, 2000 Jonesborough Road, Erwin, 423-743-7733, 800-445-7238; www.cherokeeadventures.com

A variety of guided white-water rafting trips blast through the Nolichucky Canyon and some of the deepest gorges east of the Mississippi River and along the Watauga and Russell Fork rivers. March-November.

SPECIAL EVENTS
APPALACHIAN FAIR

100 Lakeview St., Gray, 423-477-3211; www.appalachianfair.com

The regional fair features livestock, agriculture and youth exhibits, an antiques display and entertainment. Nine days in late August.

CHRISTMAS IN JONESBOROUGH

Jonesborough

Take a tour of historic houses, see a tree decoration, join workshops and partake of old-time holiday events. December.

JONESBOROUGH DAYS

Jonesborough; www.jonesboroughtn.org

The celebration includes a parade, an art show, crafts, old-time games, traditional music, square dancing and clogging, and food. July 4 weekend.

NATIONAL STORYTELLING FESTIVAL

116 W. Main St., Jonesborough, Johnson City, 423-753-2171; www.storytellingcenter.com

Johnson City calls itself the storytelling capital of the world, and this festival is lauded as one of the finest sources of entertainment in the country. During this three-day gathering, story lovers come to hear tales told by some of the country's best storytellers. First weekend in October.

HOTELS
★★BEST WESTERN JOHNSON CITY HOTEL & CONFERENCE CENTER

2406 N. Roan St., Johnson City, 423-282-2161, 877-504-1007; www.bwjohnsoncity.com

180 rooms. High-speed Internet access. Complimentary full breakfast. Restaurant, bar. Airport transportation available. $

★★DOUBLETREE HOTEL JOHNSON CITY

211 Mockingbird Lane, Johnson City, 423-929-2000, 800-222-8733; www.doubletreejohnsoncity.com

184 rooms. Wireless Internet access. Restaurant, bar. Airport transportation available. Fitness center. Outdoor pool. $

331

TENNESSEE

★
★
★
★

★HAMPTON INN

508 N. State of Franklin Road, Johnson City, 423-929-8000, 800-426-7866;
www.hamptoninn.com
77 rooms. Wireless Internet access. Complimentary full breakfast. Outdoor pool. $

★★HOLIDAY INN

101 W. Springbrook Drive, Johnson City, 423-282-4611, 866-400-0541;
www.holiday-inn.com
204 rooms. Wireless Internet access. Restaurant, bar. Outdoor pool. $

RESTAURANTS
★FIREHOUSE

627 W. Walnut St., Johnson City, 423-929-7377; www.thefirehouse.com
American menu. Lunch, dinner. Closed Sunday. $

★★PEERLESS

2531 N. Roan St., Johnson City, 423-282-2351; www.thepeerlessinc.com
American menu. Dinner. Closed Sunday. $$

KINGSPORT

In the northeast corner of the state, Kingsport was one of the first stops for 18th-century pioneers heading west. The Great Indian Warrior & Trader Path cut through this area, as did Island Road, the first road built in Tennessee. Kingsport has come a long way from its days as a pioneer outpost. Today it is a popular destination for golfers and outdoor enthusiasts.

Information: Convention and Visitors Bureau, 151 E. Main St., 423-392-8820,
800-743-5282; www.kcvb.org

WHAT TO SEE AND DO
BAYS MOUNTAIN PLANETARIUM

853 Bays Mountain Park Road, Kingsport, 423-229-9447; www.baysmountain.com
The plant and animal sanctuary covers 3,000 acres, offers 25 miles of trails. On the grounds you'll also find a nature interpretive center; an aviary; a deer pen; otter, bobcat and wolf habitats; nature programs (summer, daily; rest of year, weekends); an ocean pool; a planetarium (shows daily in summer; rest of year, weekends); an exhibition gallery and library. Stop by the observation tower and the 19th-century farmstead museum and take a barge ride on the 44-acre lake. Daily.

BOATYARD PARK

151 E. Main St., Kingsport, 423-246-2010; www.kingsportparksandrecreation.org
On the banks of the north and south forks of the Holston River, the park offers the Netherland Inn museum, picnic areas, playgrounds, boating, fishing and footpaths along the river (two miles).

BOONE DAM AND LAKE

Kingsport, 12 miles southeast via Highways 36 and 75, 423-279-3500
The dam creates a 33-mile-long lake with 130 miles of shoreline, which provide ample opportunity for swimming, fishing and boating (marina). Daily.

★
★★
★★★
★★★★

EXCHANGE PLACE

4812 Orebank Road, Kingsport, 423-288-6071; www.exchangeplace.info

The restored 19th-century farm once served as a facility for exchanging horses and Virginia currency for Tennessee currency. There's also a crafts center onsite. May-October, weekends or by appointment.

FORT PATRICK HENRY DAM AND LAKE

490 Hemlock Park, Kingsport, 423-247-7891

Companion to Boone Dam, this Tennessee Valley Authority dam impounds a 10-mile-long lake. Go there for swimming, fishing and boating. Daily.

NETHERLAND INN

2144 Netherland Inn Road, Kingsport, 423-335-5552; www.netherlandinn.com

The large frame and stone structure on the site of King's Boat Yard was a celebrated stop on the Great Stage Road and was operated for more than 150 years as an inn and the town's entertainment center. U.S. presidents Andrew Jackson, Andrew Johnson and James K. Polk visited the inn during its heyday, between 1818 and 1841. Now a museum with 18th- and 19th-century furnishings, the complex includes a well house, flatboat, garden, log cabin, children's museum and museum shop. May-September: Saturday-Monday; April, October: Saturday-Sunday.

WARRIORS' PATH STATE PARK

490 Hemlock Road, Kingsport, 423-239-8531;
www.state.tn.us

A swimming pool, a water slide, a bathhouse, fishing and boating (marina, ramp, rentals), nature bridle trails, 18-hole golf, a driving range, disc golf, a playground and concessions keep this park busy. The campground is on the shores of Patrick Henry Reservoir on the Holston River. The first-come, first-served wooded sites have picnic tables and grills. But plan ahead—the sites are usually full by Tuesday of race week. There are 135 sites, 94 full hook-ups, water stations, restrooms and showers.

SPECIAL EVENT
KINGSPORT FUN FEST

151 E. Main St., Kingsport, 423-392-8800; www.funfest.net

The citywide fest has more than 100 events, including hot-air balloon races, sports and entertainment. Nine days in late July.

HOTELS
★★DAYS INN

805 Lynn Garden Drive, Kingsport, 423-246-7126, 800-329-7466; www.daysinn.com

65 rooms. High-speed Internet access. Complimentary continental breakfast. Outdoor pool. $

★★★MARRIOTT MEADOWVIEW RESORT

1901 Meadowview Parkway, Kingsport, 423-578-6600, 800-228-9290;
www.meadowviewresort.com

Whether you decide to stick around the beautiful grounds of this vast resort or catch the excitement of a race at Bristol, the amenities and atmosphere here will not

333

TENNESSEE

★
★
★
★

disappoint. For sporty types, the resort offers tennis, basketball, golf, mountain biking, freshwater fishing and volleyball; for those looking to relax, a dip in the outdoor pool or a nap in one of the resort's guest rooms is a surefire way to recharge. 195 rooms. High-speed Internet access. Restaurant, bar. Airport transportation available. Tennis. Golf. Outdoor pool. $

KNOXVILLE

The first capital of Tennessee, Knoxville began as a frontier outpost on the edge of the Cherokee nation, the last stop for 18th-century pioneers on their way west. It was known for whiskey and wild times, but as it grew up, Knoxville became a commercial leader, leveraging its prime spot on the Tennessee River to boost its economy. During the Civil War, east Tennessee had many Union sympathizers, and though Confederate troops seized the city initially, it eventually fell to Union forces.

The 20th century brought growth and prosperity to Knoxville, and this growth has continued into the 21st century. This is the land of bluegrass and country music, but Knoxville also knows how to rock. Visitors will find a booming music scene and several citywide festivals that highlight the region's talent and celebrate its culture and history. Old City, the restored warehouse district near the river, was Knoxville's black eye at the turn of the 20th century, but today, it's the lively geographic heart of the city, full of coffee shops, art galleries, jazz clubs and boutiques.

Part of the city's culture is its allegiance to the University of Tennessee, located in Knoxville. Football fans, wearing (and sometimes painted) orange flood the stadium in the fall to cheer on the Volunteers, and in the off-season, the town enjoys the cultural benefits of the local university.

Information: Convention and Visitors Bureau, 601 W Summitt Hill Drive, 865-523-7263, 800-727-8045; www.knoxville.org

WHAT TO SEE AND DO

BECK CULTURAL EXCHANGE CENTER-MUSEUM OF BLACK HISTORY AND CULTURE

1927 Dandridge Ave., Knoxville, 865-524-8461; www.discoveret.org/beckcec/

The center preserves the achievements of Knoxville's African-American citizens from the early 1800s. The gallery features changing exhibits of local and regional artists. Tuesday-Saturday.

CONFEDERATE MEMORIAL HALL

3148 Kingston Pike S.W., Knoxville, 865-522-2371; www.knoxvillecmh.org

The antebellum mansion with Mediterranean-style gardens served as headquarters of Confederate General. James Longstreet during the siege of Knoxville. Maintained as a Confederate memorial, the 15-room house is furnished with museum pieces, a collection of Southern and Civil War relics and a library of Southern literature. Tuesday, Thursday, Friday.

CRESCENT BEND (ARMSTRONG-LOCKETT HOUSE) AND W. PERRY TOMS MEMORIAL GARDENS

2728 Kingston Pike, Knoxville, 865-637-3163

Here you'll find collections of American and English furniture, English silver and extensive terraced gardens. March-December: Tuesday-Sunday.

EAST TENNESSEE DISCOVERY CENTER & AKIMA PLANETARIUM

516 N. Beaman St., Knoxville, Chilhowee Park, 865-594-1494; www.etdiscovery.org

Much more fun than high school biology, this museum has interactive exhibits that kids and adults will find fascinating. Exhibits include a live honey bee colony, an arthropod exhibit with giant Madagascar missing cockroaches, a series of exhibits that teach about energy and a space shuttle with interactive control panels. Monday-Saturday.

GOV. WILLIAM BLOUNT MANSION

200 W. Hill Ave., Knoxville, 865-525-2375; www.blountmansion.org

The house of William Blount, governor of the Southwest Territory and signer of the U.S. Constitution, was the center of political and social activity in the territory. It's been restored to its condition of late 1700s with period furnishings, Blount memorabilia and an 18th-century garden. Tennessee's first state constitution was drafted in the governor's office behind the mansion. April to mid-December: Monday-Saturday 9:30 a.m.-5 p.m.; early January-late March: Monday-Friday 9:30 a.m.-5 p.m.

JAMES WHITE'S FORT

205 E. Hill Ave., Knoxville, 865-525-6514; www.discoveret.org

The original pioneer house was built by the founder and first settler of Knoxville. Restored buildings include the smokehouse, blacksmith shop and museum. March to mid-December: Monday-Saturday; January-February: Monday-Friday.

KNOXVILLE MUSEUM OF ART

1050 World's Fair Park, Knoxville, 865-525-6101; www.knoxart.org

The museum holds four galleries, gardens, a great hall and the ARTcade. See the collection of graphics. Tuesday-Wednesday noon-8 p.m., Thursday-Friday noon-9 p.m., Saturday-Sunday 11 a.m.-5 p.m.

KNOXVILLE ZOO

3500 Knoxville Zoo Drive, Knoxville, 865-637-5331; www.knoxville-zoo.org

The zoo is home to more than 1,000 animals, including red pandas (which the zoo has had much success breeding), snow leopards, gorillas, elephants and about 100 species of reptiles. The African elephants Mamie, Jana, Edie and Tonka paint with their trunks, and their artwork has sold for as much as $1,350. Kiddies will enjoy the petting zoo. Daily.

MARBLE SPRINGS

1220 W. Gov. John Sevier Highway, 865-573-5508; www.discoveret.org/jsma

This is the restored house of John Sevier, the state's first governor. The original cabin and other restored buildings rest on 36 acres. Tuesday-Sunday.

MCCLUNG HISTORICAL COLLECTION

East Tennessee Historical Center, 500 W. Church Ave., 865-544-5744

More than 38,000 volumes of history and genealogy covering Tennessee and Southeastern U.S. are housed in the center. Daily.

335

TENNESSEE

★
★
★
★

RAMSEY HOUSE (SWAN POND)

2614 Thorngrove Pike, Knoxville, 865-546-0745; www.ramseyhouse.org

The first stone house in Knox County, built for Col. Francis A. Ramsey, was a social, religious and political center of early Tennessee. The restored gabled house with an attached kitchen features ornamental cornices, keystone arches and period furnishings. Picnicking is available. April-October: Tuesday-Saturday, Sunday; rest of year: by appointment.

TENNESSEE VALLEY AUTHORITY

400 W. Summit Hill Drive, Knoxville, 865-632-2101; www.tva.gov

One of the South's largest projects is the Tennessee Valley Authority, an independent corporate agency owned by the federal government created by an Act of Congress on May 18, 1933. Designed to lift the South out of a long-term economic slump, the TVA was the brainchild of President Franklin D. Roosevelt. The TVA produces power, controls navigation and prevents floods and erosion for most of Tennessee; areas of Alabama, Mississippi and Kentucky; and small sections of Virginia, Georgia and North Carolina. A lot of the TVA's work goes on behind the scenes, but the most visible benefit for visitors (aside from electricity, of course) is the 600,000 surface acres of water and 11,000 miles of shoreline created by the TVA dams. The lakes provide excellent fishing for bass, walleye, crappie and other fish, with no closed season, and public parks line the lakes. In the 1960s, the TVA developed a 40-mile-long recreational and environmental education area in western Kentucky and Tennessee called Land Between the Lakes.

UNIVERSITY OF TENNESSEE, KNOXVILLE

Knoxville, W. Cumberland Ave.; www.utk.edu

On campus, check out the Frank H. McClung Museum (daily; 865-974-2144) and the Clarence Brown Theater (206 McClung Tower, 865-974-5161). Campus tours are offered.

SPECIAL EVENTS

DOGWOOD ARTS FESTIVAL

106 W. Summit Hill Drive, Knoxville, 865-637-4561; www.dogwoodarts.com

The fest offers more than 150 events and activities throughout the community, including arts and crafts exhibits and shows; more than 80 public and private gardens on display; musical entertainment; parades; sporting events; more than 60 miles of marked dogwood trails for auto or free bus tours; special children's and senior citizen activities. Mid-late April.

TENNESSEE VALLEY FAIR

Chilhowee Park, 3301 E. Magnolia Ave., Knoxville, 865-637-5840, 865-215-1471; www.tnvalleyfair.org

At the fair, get some entertainment, take a spin on the carnival rides, see livestock and agricultural shows, enter contests and view exhibits and fireworks. Ten days in early to mid-September.

HOTELS

★★COURTYARD KNOVILLE CEDAR BLUFF
216 Langley Place, Knoxville, 865-539-0600; www.courtyard.com
78 rooms. High-speed Internet access. Restaurant. $

★★★CROWNE PLAZA KNOXVILLE
401 Summit Hill Drive, Knoxville, 865-522-2600; www.crowneplaza.com
Located in the heart of downtown Knoxville, this hotel is convenient to many attractions, including the historic shopping district and the Old City. 197 rooms. Wireless Internet access. Restaurant, bar. Fitness center. $

★HAMPTON INN
117 Cedar Lane, Knoxville, 865-689-1011; www.hamptoninn.com
130 rooms. Complimentary continental breakfast. $

★★HOLIDAY INN
1315 Kirby Road, Knoxville, 865-584-3911, 800-854-8315; www.holiday-inn.com
240 rooms. Wireless Internet access. Restaurant, bar. Airport transportation available. Outdoor pool. Pets accepted. $

★★HOLIDAY INN SELECT-KNOXVILLE
525 Henley St., Knoxville, 865-522-2800; www.holiday-inn.com
293 rooms. Wireless Internet access. Restaurant, bar. Outdoor pool. $

★★★HILTON KNOXVILLE
501 W. Church Ave., Knoxville, 865-523-2300; www.hilton.com
Located in downtown Knoxville and near the Tennessee River, this hotel offers great views from the upper floors. The University of Tennessee Conference Center is across the street, and many attractions and restaurants are nearby. The décor and furnishings are contemporary, and the lobby features a large granite fireplace with bookshelves on either side. 317 rooms. Wireless Internet access. Restaurant, bar. Fitness center. Outdoor pool. $

RESTAURANTS

★APPLE CAKE TEA ROOM
11312 Station W. Drive, Knoxville, 865-966-7848; knoxville.org
American menu. Lunch. Closed Sunday.

★BUTCHER SHOP
806 World Fair Park Drive, Knoxville, 865-637-0204; www.thebutchershop.com
Steak menu. Dinner. $$

★★CALHOUN'S
10020 Kingston Pike, Knoxville, 865-673-3444; www.calhouns.com
American menu. Lunch, dinner. $$

★★CHESAPEAKE'S
500 N. Henley St., Knoxville, 865-673-3433; www.chesapeakes.com
Seafood menu. Lunch, dinner. $$

337

TENNESSEE

★
★
★
★

★★COPPER CELLAR
1807 Cumberland Ave., Knoxville, 865-673-3411; www.coppercellar.com
American menu. Dinner. Closed Sunday. $$

★★LITTON'S
2803 Essary Road, Knoxville, 865-688-0429; littonburgers.com
American menu. Lunch, dinner. Closed Sunday. $

★★NAPLES
5500 Kingston Pike, Knoxville, 865-584-5033; naplesitalianrestaurant.net
Italian menu. Lunch, dinner. $$

★★★THE ORANGERY
5412 Kingston Pike, Knoxville, 865-588-2964; www.theorangeryrestaurant.com
A beautiful winding staircase is the first thing diners notice when they enter this elegant restaurant. Its interior is decorated with French provincial furnishings, chandeliers and antiques. A piano player entertains diners in the lounge, and large windows provide natural light and wonderful views of the beautiful gardens in the courtyard. The continental menu features specialties such as veal porterhouse, prime New York strip steak, buffalo with caramelized shallots, and elk chop with vegetable puree. Diners are sure to find perfect pairings for their meals on the restaurant's extensive wine list. Continental menu. Lunch, dinner. Closed Sunday. $$$

★★★REGAS
318 N. Gay St., Knoxville, 865-637-3427; www.connorconcepts.com
First opened as a stool-and-counter joint in 1919, Regas has since become one of Knoxville's most popular restaurants. The décor has a rich, Old World elegance with a cozy fireplace, beamed ceilings and brick-and-wood walls. The hearty lunch and dinner menus feature classic American cuisine, including steaks, chops, seafood and chicken. Save room for Regas' famous red velvet cake. American menu. Lunch, dinner. Closed Sunday. $$

LEBANON
Because tall red cedars thrive in this area as they did in the biblical lands of Lebanon, the town's founders named it Lebanon. Since 1842, Lebanon has been the home of Cumberland University.
Information: Convention and Visitors Bureau, 149 Public Square, 615-453-9655, 800-789-1327; www.wilsoncounty.com

WHAT TO SEE AND DO
CEDARS OF LEBANON STATE PARK
328 Cedar Forest Road, Lebanon, 615-443-2769, 800-713-5180; www.state.tn.us
The park takes up about 831 acres within this 9,000-acre state forest. The limestone cavern and sinks were reforested in the 1930s with juniper. There are also swimming and wading pools, hiking, game courts, picnicking, a playground, a recreation lodge, tent and trailer sites, cabins and a nature center.

HOTEL

★HAMPTON INN

704 S. Cumberland St., Lebanon, 615-444-7400, 800-426-7866;
www.hamptoninn.com

87 rooms. High-speed Internet access. Complimentary continental breakfast. Fitness center. Pets accepted. **$**

LENOIR CITY

Information: Loudon County Chamber of Commerce, 318 Angel Row, 865-458-2067;
www.loudoncountychamber.org

WHAT TO SEE AND DO

FORT LOUDOUN DAM AND LAKE

U.S. Highway 321, Lenoir City, 865-986-3737; www.tva.gov

This Tennessee Valley Authority dam, with a lock chamber to permit navigation of the river, transforms a 61-mile stretch of once unruly river into a placid lake extending to Knoxville. Go fishing and boating on the 14,600-acre lake.

HOTELS

★DAYS INN

1110 Highway 321 N. Lenoir City, 865-986-2011, 800-289-0822; www.daysinn.com

80 rooms. High-speed Internet access. Complimentary continental breakfast. Restaurant. Outdoor pool. Pets accepted. **$**

★★★WHITESTONE COUNTRY INN

1200 Paint Rock Road, Kingston, 865-376-0113; www.whitestoneinn.com

Find countryside leisure at this peaceful, 360-acre property bordering Watts Bar Lake, just 40 minutes west of Knoxville. The farmhouse and barn (two of the property's five buildings) hold eight bedrooms and five suites, each with a private bath, whirlpool tub and fireplace. 21 rooms. Complimentary full breakfast. Restaurant. Children's activity center. Airport transportation available. **$$**

LEWISBURG

Named for Meriwether Lewis, of the Lewis and Clark expeditions, Lewisburg is in south central Tennessee.

Information: Marshall County Chamber of Commerce, 227 Second Ave. N.,
931-359-3863; www.lewisburgtn.com

WHAT TO SEE AND DO

HENRY HORTON STATE RESORT PARK

4358 Nashville Highway, Chapel Hill, 931-364-2319, 800-250-8612;
www.state.tn.us

The park sits on the estate of a former Tennessee governor and is bordered by the scenic Duck River, a popular canoeing and fishing river. Facilities include swimming and wading pools, a clubhouse, a golf course, lighted tennis courts, a skeet and trap range, a restaurant, tent and trailer sites, cabins and a resort inn.

TENNESSEE

★
★
★
★

**TENNESSEE WALKING HORSE BREEDERS' AND EXHIBITORS'
ASSOCIATION**

250 N. Ellington Parkway, Lewisburg, 931-359-1574; www.twhbea.com

All registrations, transfers and decisions concerning the walking horse breed are
made at this world headquarters. Open to visitors, the building contains a gallery of
world champions. Monday-Friday.

MANCHESTER

*Information: Chamber of Commerce, 110 E. Main St., 931-728-7635;
www.cityofmanchestertn.com*

WHAT TO SEE AND DO

JACK DANIEL'S DISTILLERY

280 Lynchburg Highway, Lynchburg, 931-759-4221; www.jackdaniels.com

This is the nation's oldest registered distillery. Eighty-minute guided tours include
a look at the rustic grounds, limestone spring cave and old office. Daily 9 a.m.-
4:30 p.m.

NORMANDY LAKE

*Manchester, eight miles west, two miles upstream from Normandy;
www.tva.gov*

Completed in 1976, the dam that impounds the lake is 2,734 feet high. Controlled
releases provide a scenic float way (28 miles) below the dam with public access points
along the way. During the summer, the pool is open; in the spring and fall, there's
excellent fishing. Picnicking and camping are available as well.

★
★
★
★
★

OLD STONE FORT STATE ARCHAEOLOGICAL PARK

*732 Stone Fort Drive, Manchester, 931-723-5073;
www.state.tn.us.environment*

The 600-acre park surrounds the earthen remains of a more than 2,000-year-old
walled structure built along the bluffs of the Duck River. Fishing, picnicking, a playground and camping are available. In addition, there's a museum (daily 8 a.m.-4:30
p.m.). Park daily 8 a.m.-sunset.

SPECIAL EVENT

OLD TIMER'S DAY

City Square, Manchester; www.cityofmanchestertn.com

The special day gets festive with a parade, a pet contest, entertainment, games and
food. Late September-early October.

HOTEL

★★AMBASSADOR INN AND LUXURY SUITES

*925 Interstate Drive, Manchester, 931-728-2200, 800-237-9228;
www.ambassadorinn.com*

105 rooms. Complimentary continental breakfast. Fitness center. $

★OAK

947 Interstate Drive, Manchester, 931-728-5777
American menu. Lunch, dinner, brunch. Closed Monday. $

MARYVILLE

Maryville and its twin city, Alcoa, provide a scenic gateway to the Great Smoky Mountains National Park. Maryville was once the home of Sam Houston, the only man in U.S. history to serve as governor of two states. In 1807 he moved to this area from Virginia with his widowed mother and eight brothers.

Information: Blount County Chamber of Commerce, 201 S. Washington St.,
865-983-2241; www.blountchamber.com

WHAT TO SEE AND DO

MARYVILLE COLLEGE

502 E. Lamar Alexander Parkway, Maryville, 865-981-8000; www.maryvillecollege.edu
This liberal arts college has 20 buildings that represent architectural trends from 1869-1922. The Fine Arts Center has plays, concerts and exhibits. Tours of the campus leave Fayerweather Hall from the admissions office twice daily Monday through Friday.

SAM HOUSTON SCHOOLHOUSE

3650 Old Sam Houston School Road, Maryville, 865-983-1550;
www.geocities.com/samhoustonschoolhouse
The restored log building was where Sam Houston taught in 1812 at a tuition rate of $8 per term. There's a museum of Houston memorabilia in the nearby visitor center. Tuesday-Saturday 10 a.m.-5 p.m., Sunday 1-5 p.m.

HOTEL

★★★★BLACKBERRY FARM

1471 W. Millers Cove Road, Walland, 37886, 865-984-8166; www.blackberryfarm.com
On a 4,200-acre estate in the foothills of Tennessee's Smoky Mountains, Blackberry is one of the South's most celebrated country inns. Those in the know commend its exquisite location, first-rate service and delicious food (The inn produces its own cheese, eggs, honey, vegetables and fruit for its guests). The property's two ponds and stream beckon anglers who travel here solely for the Orvis-endorsed fly fishing; other diversions include horseback riding, swimming, hiking and tennis. Epicureans savor the regionally inspired haute cuisine. Housed in a charming 1870s farmhouse, the Aveda Concept Spa offers signature treatments using local blackberries to soothe and rejuvenate the body. 44 rooms. Children over 10 years only, excluding holidays. Restaurant. Airport transportation available. $$$

RESTAURANT

★★★★THE BARN AT BLACKBERRY FARM

1471 W. Millers Cove Road, Walland, 800-648-4252; www.blackberryfarm.com
Designed in the same country-meets-luxury style that Blackberry Farm exhibits in its rooms, the visually stunning Barn restaurant allows guests to sample regionally inspired dishes on a nightly basis. Executive chef John Fleer uses the freshest

341

TENNESSEE

★
★
★
★

ingredients from Blackberry Farm's onsite heirloom garden and its housemade cheese, eggs and honey, and incorporates these ingredients into his unique Smoky Mountain "Foothills Cuisine." Diners choose from three menus: A chef's tasting menu, an à la carte menu or a garden tasting, featuring items such as seared foie gras with blackberries, frisee and toast. American menu. Dinner. Casual attire. $$$

MCMINNVILLE

Information: McMinnville-Warren County Chamber of Commerce, 110 S. Court Square, 931-473-6611; www.warrentn.com

WHAT TO SEE AND DO

CUMBERLAND CAVERNS PARK

1437 Cumberland Caverns Road, McMinnville, 931-668-4396; www.cumberlandcaverns.com

Mined for saltpeter as long ago as the Civil War but not yet fully explored, the Cumberland Caverns offer a variety of underground formations and sights: old saltpeter mines, "Hall of the Mountain King" (600 feet wide, 140 feet tall) and an underground dining room. It's at a constant 56 degrees. There's a picnic area above ground. The days and times of tours vary.

FALL CREEK FALLS STATE RESORT PARK

2009 Village Camp Road Highway 3, Pikeville, 423-881-5241, 800-250-8611; www.state.tn.us

Come to the park for the mountain scenery, 256-foot Fall Creek Falls and great fishing. A swimming pool, boating (rentals), nature trails, backpacking, riding, 18-hole golf, sports facilities, a restaurant, an inn, tent and trailer sites and cabins are also draws. Daily.

ROCK ISLAND STATE RUSTIC PARK

82 Beach Road, Rock Island, 931-686-2471; www.state.tn.us/environment/parks/RockIsland

The 850-acre park is on Center Hill Reservoir. Daily 7:30 a.m.-10 p.m.

SPECIALTY LODGING

FALCON MANOR

2645 Faulkner Springs Road, McMinnville, 931-668-4444; www.falconmanor.com

The Falcon Manor is an authentically restored Victorian mansion built in 1896. Four rooms. Children over 11 years only. Complimentary full breakfast. $

MEMPHIS

Old South meets modern metropolis in Memphis, thanks in part to a recent revival of the downtown area. This rebirth has given Memphis a shiny new face to go with its epic musical legacy and prime location on the banks of the Mississippi River.

Named after the Egyptian city, Memphis means "place of good abode," a translation that rings true for Elvis fans, who make Graceland the second most-visited home in the U.S. (Only the White House attracts more visitors each year.) But if you have no interest in searching for the King's ghost, Memphis is still a hot destination, especially for music lovers.

Don't let Nashville fool you: American music owes a lot of its success to Memphis. "Father of the Blues" W.C. Handy scribbled the first written blues music here, Elvis made his first recording here and on Beale Street, legends such as B.B. King and Muddy Waters gave life to the blues. Rock 'n' roll grew up here, too, when Sam Phillips of Sun Studio recorded musicians who fused country music and blues into rockabilly, the precursor to rock 'n' roll.

Memphis offers more than music history (though that's the prime attraction). It is home to more than a dozen institutions of higher learning, including the University of Memphis and Rhodes College. A civic ballet, a symphony orchestra, an opera company, a repertory theater and art galleries help create the city's rich cultural life.

Information: Convention and Visitors Bureau, 47 Union Ave., Memphis, 901-543-5300; www.memphistravel.com

WHAT TO SEE AND DO
BEALE STREET
203 Beale St., Memphis, 901-526-0110; www.bealestreet.com
This is part of a seven-block entertainment district stretching east from the Mississippi River bluffs with restaurants, shops, parks and theaters. There's a statue of W. C. Handy in Handy Park (Third and Beale streets).

CIRCUIT PLAYHOUSE
1705 Poplar Ave., Memphis, 901-726-5523; www.playhouseonthesquare.org
Comedies, musicals and dramas all take the stage here.

THE CHILDREN'S MUSEUM OF MEMPHIS
2525 Central Ave., Memphis, 901-458-2678; www.cmom.com
This hands-on discovery museum has created an interactive "kid-sized city," including a bank, grocery store and skyscraper, among others. Other exhibits include Art Smart, where kids sculpt, paint and draw; Going Places, where children "fly" a real airplane and watch a hot-air balloon ride. Save time to explore other special workshops and exhibits. Monday-Saturday 9 a.m.-5 p.m., Sunday noon-5 p.m.

CHUCALISSA ARCHAEOLOGICAL MUSEUM
1987 Indian Village Drive, Memphis, 901-785-3160; www.cas.memphis.edu
The archaeological project of the University of Memphis sits at the site of a Native American village founded about A.D. 900 and abandoned circa 1500. Native houses and temple have been reconstructed; archaeological exhibits are on display. The museum showcases artifacts and dioramas and there's a 15-minute slide program. Tuesday-Sunday.

CRYSTAL SHRINE GROTTO
5668 Poplar Ave., Memphis, 901-767-8930
This crystal cave made of natural rock, quartz, crystal and semiprecious stones was carved out of a hillside by naturalistic artist Dionicio Rodriguez in the late 1930s. There are also scenes by the artist depicting the life of Jesus and biblical characters. Daily.

TENNESSEE

BEALE STREET

Ever since W. C. Handy set up shop in the early 1900s, Beale Street has been known around the world as the home of the blues and the inspiration for rock 'n' roll. Blues legends such as B. B. King, Furry Lewis and Rufus Thomas got their starts here, and the street still attracts budding musicians to its nightclubs. Beale Street was a thriving commercial center for Memphis's African-American community for much of the 20th century and today, it is the city's prime entertainment district. Some say the strip lost its character in the transition from a gritty no-man's-land, but the folks dancing on the sidewalks to street musicians' tunes don't seem to mind a bit.

From the top of the hill at Second Street you can look down on all the action. Here you'll find B. B. King's club and Elvis Presley's, both upscale supper clubs with name entertainment—sometimes even the King of the Blues himself. Stay on the lookout for the ghost of Elvis.

At Third Street and Beale, a statue of W. C. Handy stands in front of an amphitheater that is the venue for many local music festivals, concerts and other events. Down the street, the Orpheum Theatre hosts Broadway shows, and the New Daisy Theatre welcomes up-and-comers (and occasionally, artists who are their way back down).
Information: www.bealestreet.com

W. C. HANDY'S HOME

352 Beale St., Memphis, 901-522-1556
W. C. Handy wrote "Memphis Blues," "St. Louis Blues" and other classic tunes here. It also houses a collection of Handy memorabilia. Tuesday-Saturday 11 a.m.-4 p.m.

DELTA QUEEN, MISSISSIPPI QUEEN, AMERICAN QUEEN

Memphis, 800-543-1949
These paddle wheelers offer three- to 12-night cruises on the Mississippi, Ohio, Cumberland and Tennessee rivers.

DIXON GALLERY AND GARDENS

4339 Park Ave., Memphis, 901-761-5250; www.dixon.org
Hugo Norton Dixon and Margaret Oates Dixon, philanthropists and community leaders, left their home, grounds and a large portion of their estate to fund this museum and garden complex for the enjoyment and education of Memphis residents and visitors. The museum is surrounded by 17 acres of formal gardens with a camellia house and garden statuary. The exhibition galleries display American and French Impressionist and post-Impressionist art, British portraits and landscapes, English antique furnishings and 18th-century German porcelain. Tuesday-Friday 10 a.m.-4 p.m., Saturday 10 a.m.-5 p.m.

GRACELAND

3734 Elvis Presley Blvd., Memphis, 901-332-3322, 800-238-2000; www.elvis.com
No visit to Memphis is complete without a stop at Graceland to pay homage to the King of Rock 'n' Roll. The main attraction is the 60- to 90-minute tour of the

home, where visitors swoon over the King's living room, dining room, music room, jungle room and kitchen, among other spaces. You'll also see the trophy room, where Elvis' gold records and awards are kept, and the Meditation Garden, where Elvis' own eternal flame blazes. Here, too, see Elvis' gravesite, likely covered in flowers and mementos from devoted fans. You can take separate tours of the Automobile Museum, which features Elvis' collection of Cadillacs—including the famous 1955 pink Cadillac—and other cars and motorcycles; his custom jets, the *Lisa Marie* and the *Hound Dog II*; and Sincerely Elvis, a small museum of fan-related items. Don't miss the nearby gift shops for an amazing assortment of Elvis-related kitsch. March-October: Monday-Saturday 9 a.m.-5 p.m., Sunday 10 a.m.-4 p.m.; November-February: Monday, Wednesday-Sunday 10 a.m.-4 p.m.

HUNT-PHELAN HOME

533 Beale St., Memphis, 901-344-3166, 800-350-9009; www.huntphelan.co

This restored antebellum house retains its original furniture, some dating back to early 1608. April-August: daily; rest of year: Thursday-Monday.

LICHTERMAN NATURE CENTER

5992 Quince Road, Memphis, 901-767-7322; www.memphismuseums.org

The 65-acre wildlife sanctuary includes a 12-acre lake, greenhouse and hospital for wild animals. There are also three miles of hiking trails and places for picnicking. Tuesday-Sunday.

MAGEVNEY HOUSE

198 Adams Ave., Memphis, 901-320-6370; www.memphismuseums.org

The restored house belonged to pioneer schoolmaster Eugene Magevney. It's the oldest middle-class dwelling in the city, furnished with artifacts of the period. Friday-Saturday noon-4 p.m. Venue closed temporarily.

MALLORY-NEELY HOUSE

652 Adams Ave., Memphis, 901-320-6370; www.memphismuseum.org/mallory.htm

The preserved 25-room Italianate mansion retains its original furnishings. Tuesday-Saturday 10 a.m.-4 p.m., Sunday 1-4 p.m. Venue closed temporarily.

MEEMAN-SHELBY FOREST STATE PARK

910 Riddick Road, Millington, 901-876-5215, 800-471-5293; www.state.tn.us

This 13,467-acre pristine state park features two lakes, a campground, fishing, boating and a swimming pool and is a beautiful setting for a leisurely hike or walk. Meeman-Shelby Forest State Park has more than 20 miles of hiking trails. However, since some of the trails are in the Mississippi River bottom, they are off limits during managed hunts. Daily 7 a.m.-10 p.m.

MEMPHIS BOTANIC GARDEN

750 Cherry Road, Memphis, 901-576-4100; www.memphisbotanicgarden.com

The garden encompasses 96 acres; 20 formal gardens here include the Japanese Garden of Tranquility, the Rose Garden and the Wildflower Garden. A special Sensory Garden stimulates all five senses. Days and times vary.

TENNESSEE

MEMPHIS BELLE

Jim Webb Restoration Center, 8101 Hornet Ave., Millington, 901-412-8071, 800-507-6507

Named for the pilot's wartime sweetheart, this B-17 bomber and her crew were the first to complete 25 missions over Nazi targets and return to the U.S. during WWII without losing any crew members or incurring any major injuries. The *Memphis Belle* shot down eight enemy fighters, most likely destroyed five others and damaged at least a dozen more. The famous plane is undergoing restoration at Millington Municipal Airport, after which she will be moved to a new museum. The public may visit the "Belle" at hangar N7 while she is under restoration. Tuesday-Friday 10 a.m.-3 p.m.; Monday, Saturday by appointment.

MEMPHIS BROOKS MUSEUM OF ART

1934 Poplar Ave., Memphis, 901-544-6200; www.brooksmuseum.org

The largest art museum in Tennessee has more than 7,000 pieces in its permanent collection, including drawings, paintings, sculpture, prints, photographs and decorative arts such as glass and textiles. Its collections contain three centuries' worth of works from Africa, Asia, Europe and North and South America, with an emphasis on European and American art of the 18th through 20th centuries. Highlights include paintings by Andrew Wyeth, Winslow Homer and Georgia O'Keeffe; sculptures by Auguste Rodin; and prints by Thomas Hart Benton. The museum's Brushmark Restaurant, with terrific views of Overton Park through the floor-to-ceiling windows or on the outdoor terrace, serves lunch. Tuesday-Friday 10 a.m.-4 p.m., Thursday 10 a.m.-8 p.m., Saturday 10 a.m.-5 p.m., Sunday 11:30 a.m.-5 p.m.

★
★
★
★
★

MEMPHIS PINK PALACE MUSEUM AND PLANETARIUM

3050 Central Ave., Memphis, 901-320-6320; www.memphismuseums.org

Exhibits at this recently expanded and remodeled museum focus on the natural and cultural history of the Mid-South. Visitors might enjoy the full-scale reproduction of an original Piggly Wiggly grocery store and a replica of an old-fashioned pharmacy with a soda fountain. The themes of the exhibits reflect the area's diversity: insects, birds, mammals, geology, pioneer life, medical history and the Civil War. The museum also has a planetarium and an IMAX Theater. Monday-Thursday 9 a.m.-4 p.m., Friday-Saturday 9 a.m.-9 p.m., Sunday noon-6 p.m.

MEMPHIS QUEEN LINE RIVERBOATS

45 Riverside Drive, Memphis, 901-527-5694; www.memphisqueen.com

Troll the river on one of the sightseeing or Evening Music Cruises aboard a Mississippi riverboat. Sightseeing: March-November: daily; evening cruises: April-October: Friday-Saturday.

MEMPHIS ROCK 'N' SOUL MUSEUM

FedExForum, 191 Beale St., Memphis, 901-205-2533; www.memphisrocknsoul.org

Showcasing Memphis as the crossroads of blues, rock 'n' roll and country music, this museum features exhibits such as B. B. King's first "Lucille" guitar and Dick Clark's podium from *American Bandstand*. Daily 10 a.m.-7 p.m.

MEMPHIS ZOO

2000 Prentiss Place, Memphis, 901-333-6500, 800-290-6041; www.memphiszoo.org

The Memphis Zoo houses more than 3,500 animals in naturalistic habitats with names such as Cat Country, Primate Canyon, Animals of the Night, China and Once Upon a Farm. Two of the most popular animals at the zoo are Ya Ya and Le Le, the giant pandas from China—do not miss them. The zoo is large, but it's easy to get around, especially if you board the tram and cruise around the park. Take a break from viewing the animals to go for a ride on the carousel or get a bite to eat at the café. March-October: daily 9 a.m.-6 p.m.; November-February: daily 9 a.m.-5 p.m.

MUD ISLAND RIVER PARK

125 N. Front St., Memphis, 901-576-7241, 800-507-6507; www.mudisland.com

This 52-acre island, accessible by monorail or pedestrian walkway, is a unique park designed to showcase the character of the river. The River Walk is a five-block-long scale model of the lower Mississippi River from Cairo, Ill., to the Gulf of Mexico (guided tours are available). The River Museum features 18 galleries that chronicle the development of river music, art, lore and history. Also here are films, a playground, riverboat excursions, shops, restaurants and a 5,400-seat amphitheater. Late May-September: daily 10 a.m.-6 p.m.; early September-late October, mid-April-late May: Tuesday-Sunday 10 a.m.-5 p.m.

NATIONAL CIVIL RIGHTS MUSEUM

450 Mulberry St., Memphis, 901-521-9699; www.civilrightsmuseum.org

Opened in 1991, this is the nation's first civil-rights museum. It honors the American civil-rights movement and the people behind it, from colonial to present times. The museum is at the former Lorraine Motel, where Dr. Martin Luther King Jr. was assassinated in 1968. Exhibits include sound and light displays, audiovisual presentations and visitor participation programs. There is also an auditorium, a gift shop and a courtyard. June-August: Monday, Wednesday-Saturday 9 a.m.-6 p.m., Sunday 1-6 p.m.; rest of year: Monday, Wednesday-Saturday 9 a.m.-5 p.m., Sunday 1-5 p.m.

NATIONAL ORNAMENTAL METAL MUSEUM

374 Metal Museum Drive, Memphis, 901-774-6380; www.metalmuseum.org

The museum features architectural and decorative metalwork. Tuesday-Saturday 10 a.m.-5 p.m., Sunday noon-5 p.m.

PLAYHOUSE ON THE SQUARE

51 S. Cooper St., Memphis, 901-725-0776; www.playhouseonthesquare.org

Professional theater.

PYRAMID ARENA

1 Auction Ave., Memphis, 901-521-9675

This 32-story, 22,500-seat stainless-steel and concrete pyramid, which overlooks the Mississippi River, is fashioned after the ancient Egyptian Great Pyramid of Cheops. It's used as a multi-sports and entertainment arena. The NBA's Memphis Grizzlies left the Pyramid for the FedEx Forum in the 2006-2007 season, and tours are not available.

347

TENNESSEE

RACE-ON DRIVING EXPERIENCE

3638 Fite Road Millington, Memphis, 901-527-6174, 866-472-2366; www.4raceon.com
If you are jealous of watching the pros have all the fun, test your skills behind the wheel of a NASCAR vehicle around the 3/4-mile paved tri-oval track at Memphis Motorsports Park (on nonrace days, of course). The season runs from March to November, but times and dates vary, so call for a schedule.

RHODES COLLEGE

2000 N. Parkway, Memphis, 901-843-3000, 800-844-5969; www.rhodes.edu
On campus is the 140-foot-high Richard Halliburton Memorial Tower, with first editions of Halliburton's books and memorabilia. The Clough-Hanson Gallery has changing art exhibits (Tuesday-Saturday 10 a.m.-7 p.m.). Tours of campus operate daily during the school year and Monday to Friday in the summer.

STAX MUSEUM OF AMERICAN SOUL MUSIC

926 E. McLemore Ave., Memphis, 901-946-2535; www.soulsvilleusa.com
This museum is built on the original site of Stax Records, the Memphis-based record label that launched the careers of Otis Redding, Isaac Hayes, Sam and Dave and other stars of the 1960s and 1970s. Featured here are more than 2,000 exhibits, including Hayes' gold-trimmed, peacock-blue "Superfly" Cadillac. March-October: Monday-Saturday 9 a.m.-4 p.m., Sunday 1-4 p.m.; November-February: Monday-Saturday 10 a.m.-4 p.m., Sunday 1-4 p.m.

SUN STUDIO

706 Union Ave., Memphis, 901-521-0664, 800-441-6249; www.sunstudio.com
Music legends such as Elvis Presley, Jerry Lee Lewis, Johnny Cash, B. B. King, Roy Orbison and Carl Perkins made their first recordings in this small studio. The 45-minute tour (last tour begins 30 minutes before closing) is worth the stop, and you can even make your own custom recording. Daily 10 a.m.-6 p.m.

T. O. FULLER STATE PARK

1500 Mitchell Road, Memphis, 901-543-7581; www.tennessee.gov
This 384-acre park is where Spanish explorer Hernando De Soto is believed to have crossed the Mississippi. It has a swimming pool, a bathhouse, golf, picnicking and campsites. Daily 8 a.m.-sunset.

VICTORIAN VILLAGE

600 Adams Ave., Memphis
These 18 landmark buildings, either preserved or restored, range in style from Gothic Revival to neo-classical.

WOODRUFF-FONTAINE HOUSE

680 Adams Ave., Memphis, 901-526-1469
The restored and furnished Second Empire/Victorian mansion has an antique textile/costume collection. Wednesday-Sunday noon-4 p.m.

BEALE STREET MUSIC FESTIVAL

Memphis; www.memphisinmay.org

One of the country's best blues events, the festival happens in what blues buffs consider the center of the universe. Musicians from around the world come to Memphis for this musical family reunion, part of the "Memphis in May" festivities. Early May.

CARNIVAL MEMPHIS

2693 Union Ave., Memphis, 901-458-2500; www.carnivalmemphis.org

The carnival features a parade, exhibits and the Cottonmaker's Jubilee. Ten days in early June.

ELVIS PRESLEY INTERNATIONAL TRIBUTE WEEK

3734 Elvis Presley Blvd., Memphis, 901-332-3322, 800-238-2000;
www.elvis.com

Thousands of people come to Memphis from all around the world for this event-packed week to celebrate and remember the King of Rock 'n' Roll. More than 30 events—including concerts, tours, street parties, fan forums and even an Elvis fashion show—take place. Mid-August.

MEMPHIS IN MAY INTERNATIONAL FESTIVAL

88 Union Ave., Memphis, 901-525-4611; www.memphisinmay.org

The month-long community-wide celebration focuses on the cultural and artistic heritage of Memphis while featuring a different nation each year. Major events occur weekends, but activities are held daily. It includes the Beale Street Music Festival, World Championship Barbecue Cooking Contest and Sunset Symphony. May.

349

MID-SOUTH FAIR AND EXPOSITION

Mid-South Fairgrounds, 940 Early Maxwell Boulevard, Memphis, 901-274-8800;
www.midsouthfair.org

This festival includes the largest rodeo east of the Mississippi, midway rides, concerts and agricultural and industrial exhibits. Late September-early October.

TENNESSEE

THEATRE MEMPHIS

630 Perkins Extended, Memphis, 901-682-8323; www.theatrememphis.org

The internationally acclaimed community theater offers a six-play season September-June on the main stage; the Little Theatre features a four-play season from July to May.

★
★
★
★
★

ZYDECO FESTIVAL

Beale Street, Memphis

Cajun-Creole and zydeco blues bands entertain in Beale Street clubs. Early February.

HOTELS

★★COURTYARD MEMPHIS EAST
6015 Park Ave., Memphis, 901-761-0330, 800-321-2211;
www.memphisparkavecourtyard.com
146 rooms. High-speed Internet access. Restaurant. $

★★DOUBLETREE HOTEL
5069 Sanderlin Ave., Memphis, 901-767-6666; www.doubletree.com
265 rooms. Wireless Internet access. Restaurant, bar. Airport transportation available.
Fitness center. Outdoor pool. $

★★DOUBLETREE HOTEL MEMPHIS DOWNTOWN
185 Union Ave., Memphis, 901-528-1800, 800-222-8733
280 rooms. Wireless Internet access. Restaurant, bar. Fitness center. Outdoor pool. $

★★EMBASSY SUITES
1022 S. Shady Grove Road, Memphis, 901-684-1777, 800-362-2779;
www.embassysuites.com
125 suites. Wireless Internet access. Complimentary full breakfast. Restaurant, bar.
Children's activity center. Airport transportation available. Fitness center. Outdoor
pool. $

★★HOLIDAY INN
160 Union Ave., Memphis, 901-525-5491, 888-300-5491;
www.hisdowntownmemphis.com
192 rooms. Wireless Internet access. Two restaurants, bar. $$

★★★HILTON MEMPHIS
939 Ridge Lake Blvd., Memphis, 901-684-6664, 800-445-8667; www.hilton.com
Towering 27 stories above the Memphis area, this hotel looks ultramodern on the
outside but is bright and roomy on the inside. The hotel is in the entertainment and
business district, just minutes from downtown Memphis. 405 rooms. Wireless Inter-
net access. Restaurant, bar. Airport transportation available. Fitness center. Outdoor
pool. $$

★★★MADISON HOTEL
79 Madison Ave., Memphis, 901-333-1200; www.madisonhotelmemphis.com
The jazzy spirit of Memphis is brought to life at the Madison Hotel. This boutique
hotel dazzles the senses with its striking interiors, which employs bold colors, geo-
metric patterns and modern furnishings. The Madison is located in the heart of the
city's business and entertainment districts and is within walking distance to the famed
Beale Street and Orpheum Theatre. Guest rooms are fitted with state-of-the-art technology for those traveling on business, while luxurious Italian bed linens, duvets and
whirlpool baths appeal to all visitors. 110 rooms, 15 story. Complimentary continental breakfast. High-speed Internet access. Restaurant, bar. Fitness room. Indoor pool.
Business center. $$$

★
★
★
★

★★★MARRIOTT MEMPHIS

2625 Thousand Oaks Blvd., Memphis, 901-362-6200, 800-627-3587;
www.marriott.com

Near this property are attractions such as Graceland and the Mall of Memphis. 320 rooms. Wireless Internet access. Restaurant, bar. Airport transportation available. **$**

★★★MARRIOTT MEMPHIS DOWNTOWN

250 N. Main St., Memphis, 901-527-7300, 888-557-8740;
www.memphismarriottdowntown.com

This hotel, offering spacious guest rooms, is 20 minutes from the Memphis International Airport and near shopping, museums, the world-famous Beale Street and Mud Island. 600 rooms. Wireless Internet access. Restaurant, bar. Children's activity center. Airport transportation available. **$$**

★★★★THE PEABODY MEMPHIS

149 Union Ave., Memphis, 901-529-4000, 800-732-2639; www.peabodymemphis.com

The Peabody is a Memphis landmark. Perhaps best known for its signature ducks that march twice daily to splash in the hotel's fountain, this grand hotel is also a shopping destination (it's the home of Lansky's, Elvis' favorite clothing store). The hotel's impressive array of amenities include a comprehensive health club, an indoor pool and Gould's Day Spa and Salon. The hotel's popular Capriccio Restaurant, Bar and Café serves delicious Italian dishes, while Chez Philippe adds a little twist to traditional French cuisine. 464 rooms. Wireless Internet access. Two restaurants, two bars. Airport transportation available. Fitness center. Indoor pool. Spa.

★★★SHERATON CASINO AND HOTEL

1107 Casino Center Drive, Robinsonville, 662-363-4900; www.harrahs.com

Try your luck at blackjack, roulette, craps, Caribbean stud poker or slots at this 92,000-square-foot casino. The Tudor-style mansion houses 40 table games and 1,300 slot and video poker machines, an adjoining hotel, a restaurant, a spa and live entertainment seven days a week. 134 rooms. Restaurant, bar. Airport transportation available. Spa. **$$**

TENNESSEE

RESTAURANTS

★ALFRED'S

197 Beale St., Memphis, 901-525-3711, 888-433-3711; www.alfreds-on-beale.com

American menu. Lunch, dinner, late-night. **$$**

★BUCKLEY'S FINE FILET GRILL

5355 Poplar Ave., Memphis, 901-683-4538; www.buckleysgrill.com

Italian, steak menu. Dinner. **$$**

★CHARLIE VERGOS RENDEZVOUS

52 S. Second St., Memphis, 901-523-2746, 888-464-7359; www.hogsfly.com

Barbecue menu. Lunch, dinner. Closed Sunday-Monday. **$**

★★AUTOMATIC SLIM'S TONGA CLUB

83 S. Second St., Memphis, 901-525-7948

Caribbean menu. Lunch, dinner, late-night. Closed Sunday. **$$**

★★CAFÉ 61

85 S. Second St., Memphis, 901-523-9351; www.cafe61memphis.com
Cajun, Southern, Asian menu. Lunch, dinner, late-night, brunch. $$

★★★★CHEZ PHILIPPE

149 Union Ave., Memphis, 901-529-4188, 800-732-2639; www.peabodymemphis.com
For more than a decade, this sexy, sophisticated restaurant in the historic Peabody Hotel
has been a favorite of foodies, movie stars, celebrity chefs and well-heeled locals. Like
clockwork, the crowds show up every evening, filling Chez Philippe's stunning dining
room for the opportunity to feast on the culinary artwork on display. The service is effi-
cient and unobtrusive, and the atmosphere is hushed, elegant and refined. Chef Rein-
aldo Alfonso applies simple, seasonal ingredients to the delicate dishes of French and
Asian origin, occasionally accented with regional flair. Leave room for dessert: Chez
Philippe is known for its soufflés. French menu. Dinner. Closed Sunday-Monday. $$$

★THE CUPBOARD

1400 Union Ave., Memphis, 901-276-8015
American menu. Lunch, dinner. $

★★★ERLING JENSEN

1044 S. Yates Road, Memphis, 901-763-3700; www.ejensen.com
This cutting-edge restaurant is one of the most popular in Memphis. Savor the shrimp
and lobster terrine trimmed with mesclun greens and champagne vinaigrette, the
quail and red cabbage, or the rich creamy bisques and foie gras preparations. Interna-
tional menu. Dinner. $$$

★
★
★
★
★

★★★GRILL 83

83 Madison Ave., Memphis, 901-333-1224; www.grill83.com
Uniquely decorated, this chic restaurant is a good choice for a romantic evening or a
special occasion. All the mouthwatering steak selections are accompanied with cab-
ernet reduction, maitre d' butter and tobacco onions. Enticing nonsteak options, such
as pan-seared Tasmanian salmon and pan-roasted breast of Ashley Farms chicken,
are also offered. Conveniently located in the heart of downtown Memphis, Grill 83 is
close to historic Beale Street, entertainment and the Mississippi River. Steak menu.
Breakfast, lunch, dinner. $$$

★INDIA PALACE

1720 Poplar Ave., Memphis, 38104, 901-278-1199
Indian menu. Lunch, dinner. $$

★★PAULETTE'S

2110 Madison Ave., Memphis, 901-726-5128; www.paulettes.net
French menu. Lunch, dinner, brunch. $$

★★★RONALDO GRISANTI AND SONS

2855 Poplar Ave., Memphis, 901-323-0007
Everything is freshly prepared at this restaurant, which is in a small strip mall east of
downtown. Specialties of the northern Italian menu include gorgonzola-stuffed filets,

fresh sea bass and pasta la elfo with shrimp, garlic and mushrooms. Italian menu. Dinner. Closed Sunday. $$$

MONTEAGLE

A popular summer resort for more than a century, Monteagle is also famous for its Chautauqua Assembly, which has been held every summer since 1882.

Information: Monteagle Mountain Chamber of Commerce, 931-924-5353;
www.monteaglemtnchamber.com

WHAT TO SEE AND DO

CARTER STATE NATURAL AREA

Sewanee, five miles south of on Highway 56, 615-532-0436;
www.state.tn.us

The 140-acre that includes the Lost Cove Caves.

FOSTER FALLS SMALL WILD AREA

498 Foster Road, Sequatchie; www.tva.gov

Foster Falls has the largest volume of water of any falls in the South Cumberland Recreation Area. It provides for scenic hiking, picnicking and camping (mid-April to mid-October).

GREAT STONE DOOR

South Cumberland State Park, 11745 Highway 41, Monteagle, 931-692-3887

This 150-foot-high crevice at the crest of the Cumberland Plateau marks an area popular with hikers. It offers a panoramic view of the area.

GRUNDY FOREST STATE NATURAL AREA

11745 Highway 41, Monteagle, 931-924-2980; www.state.tn.us

Highlights of this recreational area include Sycamore Falls, a 12-foot-high waterfall in the bottom of the Fiery Gizzard Gorge, and Chimney Rocks, a unique geological formation. The Fiery Gizzard Hiking Trail winds around moss-laden cliffs and mountain laurel to connect the forest with the Foster Falls Small Wild Area.

TENNESSEE

★
★
★
★
★

GRUNDY LAKES STATE PARK

South Cumberland State Park, 11745 Highway 41, Monteagle;
www.tennessee.gov

An 81-acre site features the Lone Rock Coke Ovens. These ovens, operated in the late 1800s with convict labor, were used in making coke for the smelting of iron ore. The park also offers swimming, hiking and picnicking.

NATURAL BRIDGE

11745 Highway 41, Monteagle; www.state.tn.us

The 2-acre area features a 25-foot sandstone arch overlooking Lost Cove.

SAVAGE GULF STATE NATURAL AREA
Palmer, 27 miles northeast on County 399 E.;
www.state.tn.us
Covering 11,500 acres, the area offers backcountry camping, rock climbing and 70 miles of wilderness hiking trails. The Savage Gulf cuts deep into the Cumberland Plateau and shelters virgin timber, rock cliffs, caves and many waterfalls.

SOUTH CUMBERLAND STATE PARK
Highway 41, Monteagle, 931-924-2980;
www.state.tn.us
The extensive park system in southeastern Tennessee is composed of 10 separate areas. The visitor center is east of Monteagle on Highway 41. Daily 7 a.m.-sunset.

UNIVERSITY OF THE SOUTH
735 University Ave., Sewanee, 931-598-1000; www.sewanee.edu
Covering 10,000 acres at an elevation of 2,000 feet, the campus features scenic mountain overlooks, hiking trails, waterfalls and caves as well as Gothic Revival architecture. On campus are the DuPont Library Collection of rare books and manuscripts (Monday-Saturday), All Saints' Chapel and the Leonidas Polk Carillon (concerts Sunday). Guided tours are available.

SPECIAL EVENTS
MONTEAGLE CHAUTAUQUA ASSEMBLY
850 W. Main St., Monteagle, 931-924-2268; www.thesmokehouse.com
Concerts, lectures, academic courses and art classes are all offered. Early July-late August.

SEWANEE SUMMER MUSIC CENTER CONCERTS
Guerry Hall, University of the South, 735 University Ave., Sewanee, 931-598-1225;
www.sewanee.edu
The four-day festival concludes the performance season. Weekends, late June-early August.

HOTEL
★★BEST WESTERN SMOKEHOUSE LODGE
850 W. Main St., Monteagle, 931-924-2268
85 rooms. Restaurant. $

SPECIALTY LODGING
ADAMS HISTORIC EDGEWORTH INN
Monteagle Assembly Grounds, Monteagle, 931-924-4000, 877-352-9466;
www.relaxinn.com
11 rooms. Complimentary full breakfast. $

MORRISTOWN
Bounded by Clinch Mountain and the Great Smoky Mountains, Morristown seems a fitting place for Davy Crockett to grow up, which he did here from 1794 to 1809.
Information: Chamber of Commerce, 825 W. First North St., 423-586-6382;
www.morristownchamber.com

PANTHER CREEK STATE PARK

210 Panther Creek Road, Morristown, 423-587-7046;
www.state.tn.us

The park sits on more than 1,400 acres on Cherokee Lake. It also has a swimming pool, fishing, hiking trails, picnic sites, a playground, a campground and a visitor center. Daily 6 a.m.-dark.

ROSE CENTER

442 W. Second North St., Morristown, 423-581-4330; www.rosecenter.org

The historic building serves as a cultural center and includes a hands-on children's museum, a historical classroom art gallery and a historical museum. Monday-Friday.

HOTELS
★DAYS INN

2512 E. Andrew Johnson Highway, Morristown, 423-587-2200, 800-329-7466;
www.morristowndaysinn.com

64 rooms. High-speed Internet access. Complimentary continental breakfast. Outdoor pool. $

★★HOLIDAY INN

5435 S. Davy Crockett Parkway, Morristown, 423-587-2400, 800-465-4329;
www.holiday-inn.com

111 rooms. High-speed Internet access. Complimentary breakfast. Restaurant. Fitness center. Outdoor pool. Pets accepted. $

355

MURFREESBORO

Thanks to Murfreesboro's location in the center of Tennessee, it was almost named the state capital. The legislature met here from 1819 to 1826, but it never returned after convening in Nashville. The area is rich in Civil War history and is known for its antique shops.

Information: Rutherford County Chamber of Commerce, 501 Memorial Blvd.,
615-893-6565, 800-716-7560; www.rutherfordchamber.org

WHAT TO SEE AND DO
OAKLANDS

900 N. Maney Ave., Murfreesboro, 615-893-0022; www.oaklandsmuseum.org

This 19th-century mansion, an architectural blend of four different periods, was a social center before the Civil War and was the command headquarters for Union Col. W. W. Duffield, who surrendered Murfreesboro to Confederate General. Nathan Bedford Forrest at the house. Rooms are restored and furnished with items appropriate to the Civil War period. Grounds are landscaped in period style. Tuesday-Saturday 10 a.m.- 4 p.m., Sunday 1-4 p.m.

TENNESSEE

★
★
★
★
★

SPECIAL EVENTS

INTERNATIONAL GRAND CHAMPIONSHIP WALKING HORSE SHOW

Tennessee Miller Coliseum, 304 W. Thompson Lane, Murfreesboro, 615-890-9120;
www.walkinghorseowners.com
Early August and October.

STREET FESTIVAL

Murfreesboro
Arts and crafts. Early May.

UNCLE DAVE MACON DAYS

Cannonsburgh Village, 105 S. Church St., Murfreesboro, 615-893-2369;
www.uncledavemacondays.com
The event offers old-time music, dance, arts and crafts. Second weekend in July.

HOTELS

★★DOUBLETREE HOTEL MURFREESBORO

1850 Old Fort Parkway, Murfreesboro, 615-895-5555, 800-222-8733;
www.doubletree.com
168 rooms. Wireless Internet access. Complimentary continental breakfast. Restaurant, bar. Fitness center. Outdoor pool. Pets accepted. $

★GUESTHOUSE MURFREESBORO

1954 S. Church St., Murfreesboro, 615-896-6030
125 rooms. $

★ BAYMONT INN AND SUITES MURFREESBORO

2230 Armory Drive, Murfreesboro, 615-896-1172, 800-426-7866;
www.baymontinns.com
114 rooms. Wireless Internet access. Complimentary full breakfast. Fitness center. Outdoor pool. Business center. Pets accepted. $

★★CLARION INN & SUITES

2227 Old Fort Parkway, Murfreesboro, 615-896-2420, 800-465-4329;
www.clarionhotel.com
179 rooms. Two restaurants, bar. Airport transportation available. $

★SUPER 8

1414 Princeton Place, Hermitage, 615-871-4545; www.super8.com
65 rooms. Complimentary continental breakfast. $

RESTAURANTS

★★PARTHENON MEDITERRANEAN

1935 S. Church St., Murfreesboro, 615-895-2665; www.parthenondinning.com
Mediterranean menu. Lunch Sunday, dinner, late-night Saturday-Sunday. $$

★SANTA FE STEAK CO

1824 Old Fort Parkway, Murfreesboro, 615-890-3030; www.santafecattle.com
American menu. Lunch, dinner, late-night Saturday-Sunday. $$

356

TENNESSEE

★
★
★
★
★

NASHVILLE

Nashville's role as the capital of Tennessee gets overshadowed by its reputation as Music City, center of the country music universe. But Nashville is more than a town crawling with country music stars and starry-eyed hopefuls. It's a sophisticated city with impressive museums, eclectic restaurants, more than one major-league sports team and a lively downtown district.

Of course, for most visitors, great restaurants and world-class museums are just icing on the country music cake: They come here to feel the rhythm of a city where unknowns sing their hearts out in hopes of a shot at stardom and where country music gods and goddesses record albums, cut deals and sometimes even perform in some of the city's most intimate clubs.

One of the best places to feel this rhythm is downtown, a historic neighborhood that was recently revitalized. The offerings here vary from big-name nightclubs, including B. B. King Blues Club & Grill and the famous Wildhorse Saloon, to dive bars where musicians play day and night in hopes of a big break. In between the clubs and bars are restaurants, shops and historic landmarks.

No visit to Nashville would be complete without a stop by the *Grand Old Opry* in the Music Valley area. The *Opry* began as a weekly radio show in 1925, and crowds flocked to the studio to see performers as they sang on air, prompting the show to move several times into larger and larger facilities. The show airs every weekend from its updated digs at the Grand Ole Opry House and draws some of country music's hottest stars and living legends.

Often called the "Athens of the South" for its rich cultural and intellectual life, Nashville is home to 16 colleges and universities, several major religious publishing firms and about 750 churches. And to top it all off, the city's Parthenon is the world's only full-size replica of the Athenian architectural masterpiece.

If you don't know George Straight from George Jones, you'll have fun in Nashville, but if you're a true fan of country music, a visit to Nashville will be pure heaven.
Information: Convention and Visitors Bureau, 211 Commerce St., 615-743-3000, 800-657-6910; www.nashvillecvb.com

WHAT TO SEE AND DO
ADVENTURE SCIENCE MUSEUM
800 Fort Negley Blvd., Nashville, 615-862-5160; www.adventuresci.com
Kids will love this hands-on science museum. There are six main areas to explore here: Earth Science, Creativity and Invention, Sound and Light, Air and Space, Health and Energy. You can find all of these concepts represented on the Adventure Tower, a 75-foot-tall structure with seven levels of activities. Other exhibits include Construction Junction, Mission Impossible and Dino Rumble. Tuesday-Sunday.

BELLE MEADE PLANTATION
5025 Harding Road, Nashville, 615-356-0501, 800-270-3991; www.bellemeadeplantation.com
The antebellum mansion and outbuildings were once part of a 5,300-acre working plantation. At the turn of the 20th century, John Harding's Belle Meade was considered the greatest thoroughbred breeding farm in the country. Visitors will get a glimpse of the elegance of late-19th-century Southern aristocrats in this 14-room Greek Revival mansion, which contains Empire and Victorian furnishings and an heirloom showcase

TENNESSEE

with racing trophies and mementos. Also on the grounds are the Dunham Station log cabin and the Carriage House, containing one of the South's largest carriage collections. Monday-Saturday 9 a.m.-5 p.m., Sunday 11 a.m.-5 p.m.

BELMONT MANSION

1900 Belmont Blvd., Nashville, 615-460-5459; www.belmontmansion.com

Built in the 1850s in the style of an Italian villa, this mansion, once considered one of the finest private residences in the U.S., has original marble statues, Venetian glass, gasoliers, mirrors and paintings in the 15 rooms open to the public; gardens feature a large collection of 19th-century ornaments and cast-iron gazebos. Monthly garden tours are also available. Monday-Saturday 10 a.m.-4 p.m., Sunday 1-4 p.m.

CENTENNIAL SPORTSPLEX

222 25th Ave. N., Nashville, 615-862-8480; www.nashville.org/sportsplex

This 17-acre fitness and recreation facility is mainly for middle Tennessee residents, but visitors can purchase passes in blocks of ten visits. The complex includes an aquatic center, a fitness center, a tennis center and two ice rinks (fee) that are open to the public. Its also home to the Nashville Predators, the area's NHL team.

CHEEKWOOD BOTANICAL GARDEN AND MUSEUM OF ART

1200 Forrest Park Drive, Nashville, 615-356-8000; www.cheekwood.org

This one is for art lovers and garden fanatics. Cheekwood, once the private home and estate of the Cheek family, is now a cultural center set on 55 acres. The site, which was opened to the public in 1960, includes a museum with a permanent collection of 19th- and 20th-century American art; a Botanic Hall with an atrium of tropical flora and changing plant exhibits; public greenhouses featuring orchids, camellias and plants from Central American cloud forests; and five major gardens specializing in dogwood, wildflowers, herbs, daffodils, roses and tulips. Tuesday-Saturday 9:30 a.m.-4:30 p.m., Sunday 11 a.m.-4:30 p.m.

COUNTRY MUSIC HALL OF FAME AND MUSEUM

222 Fifth Ave. S. Nashville, 615-416-2001, 800-852-6437;
www.countrymusichalloffame.com

A tribute to all things country music, this museum will give fans goose bumps, and even folks who aren't interested in the tunes will appreciate the history and American pop culture on display here. Elvis's gold-leafed Cadillac is parked here, and visitors can gawk at a lyric sheet scribbled with Bob Dylan's signature. This $37 million complex includes displays with costumes and instruments donated by country music legends from Minnie Pearl to George Jones. You can also check out the restored Historic RCA Studio B, where more than 1,000 top 10 hits from Elvis Presley, Willie Nelson and other stars were recorded. Daily 9 a.m.-5 p.m.

ELLINGTON AGRICULTURAL CENTER

440 Hogan Road, Nashville, 615-837-5197;
www.state.tn.us

This former horse barn sits on a historic estate. It's the oldest Agricultural Hall of Fame in the U.S. In it, you'll find farm tools, equipment and household items of the 19th century. Monday-Friday.

ERNEST TUBB RECORD SHOP

417 Broadway, Nashville, 615-255-7503; www.etrecordshop.com

When Ernest Tubb and the Texas Troubadours weren't out touring in a big silver bus, the country music star was tending to his other love, the Ernest Tubb Record Shop. The original E.T. died in 1984, but the store continues to sell nothing but country music releases. Offerings range from hard-to-find treasures to the newest smash hits. The store on Music Valley Drive (2416 Music Valley Drive, 615-889-2474) also features the Texas Troubadour Theatre, home of the Midnight Jamboree every Saturday.

FISK UNIVERSITY

1000 17th Ave. N., Nashville, 615-329-8500; www.fisk.edu

The university is a National Historic District with Jubilee Hall deemed a historic landmark. The Carl Van Vechten Art Gallery houses the Stieglitz Collection of modern art. The Aaron Douglas Gallery holds a collection of African art.

FORT NASHBOROUGH

170 First Ave. N., Nashville, 615-862-8400; www.nitinol.info

Patterned after the pioneer fort established several blocks from this site in 1779, the replica is smaller and has fewer cabins. There are stockaded walls and exhibits of pioneer implements. Tuesday-Sunday, weather permitting.

GENERAL JACKSON SHOWBOAT

Opry Mills, Opry Mills Drive, Nashville, 615-458-3900; www.generaljackson.com

Named after the first steamboat working the Cumberland River as far back as 1817, this 300-foot paddlewheel riverboat—the world's largest showboat these days—offers lunch cruises (a buffet plus a country music show) and elegant dinner cruises (includes a Broadway-style show).

GRAND OLE OPRY

2802 Opryland Drive, Nashville, 615-871-5043; www.opry.com

You haven't made it in Music City USA as a country star until you've graced the stage of the world's longest-running radio show. Every weekend, the *Opry* showcases the best of bluegrass, country, gospel, swing and Cajun. Part of the thrill for the audience is never knowing which stars will make surprise appearances. Friday 7:30 p.m., Saturday 6:30 p.m. and 9:30 p.m.; also Tuesday in summer, 7 p.m.

GRAND OLE OPRY TOURS

2800 Opryland Drive, Nashville, 615-883-2211; www.gaylordhotels.com

One-hour, three-hour and all-day bus tours take visitors to houses of country music stars, Music Row, recording studios and on a backstage visit to the Grand Ole Opry House.

THE HERMITAGE

4580 Rachel's Lane, Nashville, 615-889-2941; www.thehermitage.com

Rebuilt after a fire in 1834, this Greek Revival residence of President Andrew Jackson is furnished almost entirely with original family pieces, many of which were associated with Jackson's military career and years in the White House. The mansion has been completely restored to its appearance from 1837 to 1845, Jackson's retirement years. Tours of the 660-acre estate are narrated by historically costumed interpreters.

The tour includes a museum; the Tulip Grove Mansion; the Hermitage Church; a garden with graves of Jackson and his wife, Rachel; two log cabins; a visitor center; and a biographical film on Jackson. Daily 9 a.m.-5 p.m.

J. PERCY PRIEST LAKE

3737 Bell Road, Nashville, 615-889-1975; www.lrn.usace.army.mil

The lake is a prime spot for waterskiing, fishing, boating (ramps, commercial boat docks), picnicking and tent and trailer sites (fee). There's a visitor center near the dam (Monday-Friday). Some areas are closed November-March.

NASHVILLE ZOO

3777 Nolensville Road, Nashville, 615-833-1534; www.nashvillezoo.org

At the Nashville Zoo, designers have gone to great lengths to make it seem as if you're simply walking through the woods and stumbling upon otters, cheetahs, apes, macaws and other animals. The zoo recently added an African elephant savannah exhibit. April-October: daily 9 a.m.-6 p.m.; November-March: daily 9 a.m.-4 p.m.

OLD HICKORY LAKE

Nashville, six miles northeast of Nashville on the Cumberland River, 615-822-4846; www.lrn.usace.army.mil

This 22,000-acre lake has 440 miles of shoreline, eight marinas and an abundance of water fowl and wading birds—a perfect place to spend a lazy day on the water. The lake is shared by pleasure boats, sailboats, personal watercraft, fishing boats and commercial barges. Daily; some areas closed October-April.

OPRY MILLS

433 Opry Mills Drive, Nashville, 615-514-1000, 800-746-7386; www.oprymills.com

There's something for just about everyone at this 1.2 million-square-foot shopping, dining and entertainment complex. The mall's unique combination of manufacturers' outlets and specialty stores provides shoppers with everything from clothing bargains to high-end sporting and outdoor goods. Noteworthy stores include Banana Republic Factory Store; Off 5th (the Saks Fifth Ave. outlet); and Barnes & Noble. Keep in mind the whopping 9.25 percent sales tax when making your purchasing decisions. When you're ready for a break from shopping, have a bite at Rainforest Café, enjoy a sundae at Ghirardelli Chocolate Shop, or take in a movie on one of 20 screens or at the IMAX theater. Monday-Saturday10 a.m.-9:30 p.m., Sunday 11 a.m.-7 p.m.

THE PARTHENON

2600 W. End Ave., Nashville, 615-862-8431; www.nashville.gov/parthenon

The replica of the Parthenon of Pericles' time was built in plaster for the Tennessee Centennial of 1897 and later reconstructed in concrete aggregate. As in the original, there is not a straight horizontal or vertical line, and no two columns are placed the same distance apart. A 42-foot-tall statue of the goddess Athena stands inside; she is the tallest indoor statue in the country. It also houses 19th- and 20th-century artworks, changing art exhibits and replicas of Elgin Marbles. Tuesday-Saturday 9 a.m.-4:30 p.m.; also Sunday 12:30-4:30 p.m. from April-September.

RADNOR LAKE STATE NATURAL AREA

1160 Otter Creek Road, Nashville, 615-373-3467; www.state.tn.us

Located just south of Nashville, this 1,100-acre environmental preserve features an 85-acre lake and some of the highest hills in the Nashville Basin. The area provides scenic, biological and geological areas for hiking, observation, photography and nature study. Daily.

RYMAN AUDITORIUM & MUSEUM

116 Fifth Ave. N., Nashville, 615-458-8700; www.ryman.com

The Mother Church of Country Music underwent an $8.5 million facelift in the 1990s. Now this National Historic Landmark hosts concerts and a museum that tells its story. (Don't leave without buying a box of GooGoos in the museum gift shop.) A tour of the auditorium is available. Daily 9 a.m.-4 p.m.; evening show times vary.

SAM DAVIS HOME

1399 Sam Davis Road, Nashville, 615-459-2341; www.samdavishome.org

Described as "the most beautiful shrine to a private soldier in the U.S.," this stately house and 168-acre working farm have been preserved as a memorial to Sam Davis, a Confederate scout caught behind Union lines and tried as a spy. Offered his life if he revealed the name of his informer, Davis chose to die on the gallows. His boyhood home is restored and furnished with many original pieces; the grounds include a kitchen, a smokehouse, slave cabins and a family cemetery where Davis is buried. Monday-Saturday 10 a.m.-4 p.m., Sunday 1-4 p.m.

STATE CAPITOL

600 Charlotte Ave., Nashville, 615-741-1886; www.state.tn.us

The capitol building is a distinguished reminder that Nashville is not just the capital of the country music world. Construction of the capitol began in 1845 and lasted until 1859, and it is built of local Tennessee limestone and marble quarried and cut by slaves and convicts. The architect, William Strickland, died before the building was completed, and his body was entombed within the building's northeast wall. The Greek Revival structure has an 80-foot tower that rises above the city, and columns grace the ends and sides. The building houses the governor's offices, the chambers of the state Senate and the House of Representatives. During Union occupation of Nashville from 1862 to 1865, the capitol was used as Fortress Andrew Johnson. Monday-Friday.

TENNESSEE

TENNESSEE STATE MUSEUM

Polk Cultural Center, 505 Deaderick St., Nashville, 615-741-2692, 800-407-4324; www.tnmuseum.org

This museum is one of the largest in the nation, with 60,000 square feet of exhibition space. It houses an awesome Civil War collection. The permanent exhibits illustrating life in Tennessee focus on the prehistoric, Frontier, Age of Jackson, Antebellum, Civil War and Reconstruction periods. Artifacts on display include Andrew Jackson's 1829 inaugural hat, an 1850s-style parlor, a steatite shaman's medicine tube and a hand-drawn map of the Shiloh battlefield prepared for Confederate General. Beauregard. After visiting the main museum, walk across the street to check out the Military Museum in the War Memorial Building. Tuesday-Saturday 10 a.m.-5 p.m., Sunday 1-5 p.m.

TENNESSEE TITANS (NFL)

The Coliseum, 1 Titans Way, Nashville, 615-565-4200; www.titansonline.com

Tennesseans have enthusiastically embraced their NFL team, the Titans (formerly the Houston Oilers). The 68,000-seat Coliseum, an outdoor stadium set on the Cumberland River with a great view of downtown Nashville, regularly fills with rabid fans. If you stay downtown, the stadium is just a short walk across the river. Tickets can be tough to come by, so make sure to call well in advance.

TRAVELLERS REST PLANTATION AND MUSEUM

636 Farrell Parkway, Nashville, 615-832-8197; www.travellersrestplantation.org

This restored federal-style house belonged to Judge John Overton. Maintained as a historical museum with period furniture, records and letters, the building reflects the history and development of early Tennessee. The 11-acre grounds have formal gardens, a weaving house and a smokehouse. Allow at least 45 minutes for your visit. Monday-Saturday 10 a.m.-4 p.m., Sunday 1-4 p.m.

THE UPPER ROOM CHAPEL AND MUSEUM

1908 Grand Ave., Nashville, 615-340-7200; www.upperroom.org

The chapel has a polychrome wood carving of Leonardo da Vinci's *The Last Supper*, said to be the largest of its kind in the world. The museum contains various religious artifacts, including seasonal displays of 100 Nativity scenes and Ukrainian Easter eggs. Monday-Friday.

VANDERBILT UNIVERSITY

W. End Avenue and 21st Avenue S., Nashville, 615-322-7311; www.vanderbilt.edu

The 330-acre campus features 19th- and 20th-century architectural styles. The Fine Arts Gallery has a permanent collection supplemented by traveling exhibits. The Blair School of Music offers regular concerts. Campus tours are available all year long.

WILDHORSE SALOON

120 Second Ave. N., Nashville, 615-902-8200; www.wildhorsesaloon.com

Welcome to boot-scootin' paradise. The Wildhorse Saloon is the place to go line dancing in Nashville, and even if you have two left feet, you should go for the live music and celebrity sightings. Set in a three-level historic warehouse on Nashville's Music Row, the club features live country acts Tuesday through Saturday nights. A DJ supplements the acts, and the saloon offers free dance lessons for folks who aren't too shy to shake their hips with the experts. If all that dancing makes you hungry, the restaurant serves award-winning Southern barbecue from 11 a.m. to midnight. Children younger than 18 are allowed with parents. Restaurant: daily 11 a.m.-midnight; club: until 2 a.m.

SPECIAL EVENTS
A COUNTRY CHRISTMAS

Gaylord Opryland Resort and Convention Center, 2800 Opryland Drive, Nashville, 615-871-7637; www.gaylordhotel.com

This holiday event features the Rockettes, Fantasy on Ice, Treasures for the Holidays, the Enchanted Forest dinner and a tour of the Country Music Hall of Fame.

MUSIC FESTIVALS

Nashville is host to many festivals: the International Country Music Fan Fair with its Grand Master Old-Time Fiddling Championship (early June), Gospel Music Week (April) and the Franklin Jazz Festival (August).

RUNNING OF THE IROQUOIS MEMORIAL STEEPLECHASE

Percy Warner Park, 2500 Old Hickory Blvd., Nashville, 615-352-6299; www.iroquoissteeplechase.org

The event begins at the entrance to Percy Warner Park. The amphitheater seats 100,000. Second Saturday in May.

TENNESSEE STATE FAIR

Tennessee State Fairgrounds, 626 Smith Ave., Nashville, 615-862-8980; www.tennesseestatefair.org

The state fair offers music, art, baking contests, agricultural exhibits and livestock competitions. Ten days starting on the first Friday after Labor Day.

HOTELS

★AMERISUITES

202 Summit View Drive, Brentwood, 615-661-9477; www.amerisuites.com

126 suites. High-speed Internet access. Complimentary continental breakfast. Fitness center. Outdoor pool. $

★★COURTYARD VANDERBILT/WEST END

1901 W. End Ave., Nashville, 615-327-9900, 800-245-1959; www.courtyard.com

223 rooms. High-speed Internet access. Restaurant. Fitness center. Outdoor pool, whirlpool. $

★★DOUBLETREE HOTEL

315 Fourth Ave. N., Nashville 615-244-8200, 800-222-8733; www.nashville.doubletree.com

337 rooms. High-speed Internet access. Restaurant, bar. Airport transportation available. Fitness center. Outdoor pool. Business center. $$

★★EMBASSY SUITES HOTEL NASHVILLE-AIRPORT

10 Century Blvd., Nashville, 615-871-0033, 800-362-2779; www.nashvilleairport.embassysuites.com

296 suites. Wireless Internet access. Complimentary full breakfast. Restaurant, bar. Children's activity center. Airport transportation available. Fitness center. Outdoor pool. Business center. $

★FAIRFIELD INN BY MARRIOTT NASHVILLE OPRYLAND

211 Music City Circle, Nashville, 615-872-8939; www.marriott.com

109 rooms. Wireless Internet access. Complimentary continental breakfast. Airport transportation available. Fitness center. Business center. $

★★HOLIDAY INN

2613 W. End Ave., Nashville, 615-327-4707, 800-465-4329; www.holiday-inn.com
300 rooms. Wireless Internet access. Restaurant, bar. Airport transportation available. Outdoor pool. $

★★★GAYLORD OPRYLAND RESORT AND CONVENTION CENTER

2800 Opryland Drive, Nashville, 615-889-1000, 888-777-6779; www.gaylordhotels.com
Adjacent to the Grand Ole Opry, this resort is a natural choice for music fans, but with championship golf, outlet mall shopping, riverboat cruises and plenty of other activities nearby, this resort has something for everyone. Nine acres of tropical gardens and flowing rivers are tucked inside climate-controlled glass atriums, allowing guests to enjoy the "outdoors" year-round. Guests can even take a ride aboard the hotel's Delta Flatboats without ever going outside. For those who do want to venture out, two outdoor pools beckon sunbathers and swimmers. Variety is the spice of life here, with an endless supply of dining and recreational choices. 2,881 rooms. High-speed Internet access. Nine restaurants, seven bars. Children's activity center. Airport transportation available. Two outdoor pools. Spa. $$$

★★★★★THE HERMITAGE HOTEL

231 Sixth Ave. N., Nashville, 615-244-3121, 888-888-9414;
www.thehermitagehotel.com
The Hermitage Hotel is the Grand Dame of Nashville's hotels. Opened in 1910 and renovated in 2003, this glorious downtown hotel offers white-glove service and plenty of opportunities to indulge. Its lobby is magnificent, with vaulted ceilings of stained glass, arches decorated with frescoes and intricate stonework. The spacious guest rooms are filled with elegant traditional furnishings, creating a warm and welcoming atmosphere. On the lower level, you will find the Capitol Grille, one of Nashville's best restaurants. The adjacent Oak Bar, with its emerald-green club chairs and dark wood paneling, is a top spot for relaxing before or after dinner. 122 rooms. Wireless Internet access. Restaurant, bar. Fitness center. Spa. Business center. Pets accepted. $$$

★★★HOTEL PRESTON

733 Briley Parkway, Nashville, 615-361-5900, 877-361-5500; www.hotelpreston.com
This stylish spot is more city chic than cowboy country, though Opryland and all of the city's famous places are within easy reach. The guestrooms and suites blend sophistication with a bit of whimsy—you can get everything from a lava lamp to a pet fish, an art kit and even a rubber ducky upon check-in. Café Isabella whips up Italian favorites with a dash of Southern spirit (think baked ziti and chicken pot pie), while the trendy Pink Slip bar provides libations and live, local music. 190 rooms. Wireless Internet. Restaurant, bar. $$$

★★★LOEWS VANDERBILT HOTEL NASHVILLE

2100 W. End Ave., Nashville, 615-320-1700, 800-336-3335; www.loewshotels.com
This upscale property is conveniently in the heart of the Vanderbilt district, between Vanderbilt University and downtown. The exterior is nicely landscaped, featuring a fountain in the front and patio seating. Comfortable guest rooms, which offer views of either the campus or city, feature quality bedding, minibars, plush robes and Bloom toiletries. The works of Harold Kraus, a renowned Nashville artist, are featured onsite

★
★
★
★
★

at the Kraus Gallery. 340 rooms. High-speed Internet access. Two restaurants, two bars. Airport transportation available. Children's activity center. Fitness center. Spa. Business center. **$$**

★★★MARRIOTT NASHVILLE AIRPORT

600 Marriott Drive, Nashville, 615-889-9300, 800-228-9290; www.marriott.com/bnatn
This resort-like property is situated on a beautiful 17-acre setting. 392 rooms. Restaurant, bar. Fitness center. Tennis. Indoor pool. Spa. Business center. **$$**

★★★MILLENNIUM MAXWELL HOUSE NASHVILLE

2025 Metro Center Blvd., Nashville, 615-259-4343, 866-866-8086; www.millenniumhotels.com
This modern hotel offers personalized service and excellent accommodations. Just five minutes north of downtown Nashville and 15 minutes from the Grand Ole Opry, the hotel is a perfect base for all travelers. Guests can enjoy views of the city from the upper floors. 287 rooms. Wireless Internet access. Restaurant, bar. Airport transportation available. **$$**

★★★RENAISSANCE NASHVILLE HOTEL

611 Commerce St., Nashville, 615-255-8400, 800-327-6618; www.renaissancehotels.com/bnash
Located between the business district and the city's tourist area, this hotel is near fine dining, great shopping and plenty of attractions. 673 rooms. Restaurant, bar. Fitness center. Indoor pool. Business center. **$$**

★★★SHERATON MUSIC CITY

777 McGavok Pike, Nashville, 615-885-2200, 800-325-3535; www.sheratonmusiccity.com
This property resembles a mansion in the Deep South. It is convenient to Nashville proper—three miles from the airport, five miles from Opry Mills and seven miles from downtown. 410 rooms. High-speed Internet access. Complimentary continental breakfast. Restaurant, bar. Airport transportation available. Indoor, outdoor pool, whirlpool. Spa. Business center. **$$**

★★★SHERATON NASHVILLE DOWNTOWN HOTEL

623 Union St., Nashville, 615-259-2000, 800-447-9825; www.sheraton-nashville.com
This contemporary hotel is in the heart of downtown Nashville near the capitol building, a location that makes it popular with business travelers and legislators. Guests are offered a host of amenities and services, including room service, turndown service, plush robes and Sheraton's signature beds. The concierge provides carefree planning regardless of whether you are in Nashville for business, pleasure or a little of both. 474 rooms. Wireless Internet access. Restaurant, bar. Fitness center. **$$**

★★★WYNDHAM UNION STATION HOTEL

1001 Broadway, Nashville, 615-726-1001; www.unionstationhotelnashville.com
Housed in a historic 1897 train station, the Wyndham Union Station is a National Historic Landmark. The lobby has marble floors, a vaulted ceiling of Tiffany stained glass

TENNESSEE

★
★
★
★

and ornate carved woodwork. Business services and concierge service help make each guest's stay pleasant and carefree, and complimentary wine and cheese is offered to guests in the evening. With its downtown location only a few blocks from Second Avenue and Music Row, the Wyndham is close to much of the entertainment, dining and nightlife that Nashville has to offer, with complimentary shuttle service to nearby attractions. 137 rooms. Wireless Internet access. Restaurant, bar. Business center. **$$**

RESTAURANTS

★BOSCOS PIZZA KITCHEN AND BREWERY

1805 21st Ave. S., Nashville, 615-385-0050; www.boscosbeer.com
Italian, pizza menu. Lunch, dinner, late-night, Sunday brunch. **$$**

★★BOUND'RY

911 20th Ave. S., Nashville, 615-321-3043; www.pansouth.net
International menu. Dinner, late-night. **$$$**

★★★★CAPITOL GRILLE

231 Sixth Ave. N., Nashville, 615-345-7116; www.thehermitagehotel.com
Located in the elegant Hermitage Hotel, the Capitol Grille offers an equally posh dining experience. Near the state capitol, the Grille hosts many a power lunch, but it's also a popular spot for theatergoers who want to enjoy a fine meal before a show at the nearby Tennessee Performing Arts Center. Executive Chef Tyler Brown oversees creative Southern cuisine; the menu is full of such dishes as Niman Ranch pork with sweet potato juice and veal loin with root vegetables. Truffle mac and cheese and spicy fried green tomato with spicy pepper relish are just a few of the restaurant's irresistible side dishes, and desserts like flourless chocolate ganache torte end the evening on a perfect note. Located downstairs in the historic Hermitage Hotel, this Southern-influenced restaurant offers a different menu each week. American, Southern menu. Breakfast, lunch, dinner, late-night, Sunday brunch. **$$$**

★★DARFONS RESTAURANT & LOUNGE

2810 Elm Hill Pike, Nashville, 615-889-3032; www.darfonsrestaurant.com
American menu. Lunch, dinner. Closed Sunday. **$$**

★★★F. SCOTT'S

2210 Crestmoor Road, Nashville, 615-269-5861; www.fscotts.com
This large restaurant gives off a friendly, elegant vibe, thanks to several small dining rooms. Popular jazz musicians play nightly, and chef Will Uhlhorn's menu features contemporary American dishes such as seared New York strop with spicy pecan sweet potato hash, squash casserole and thyme chive Barnaise, and spicy cornmeal-dusted pan-fried trout. American menu. Dinner. Bar. **$$$**

★★GERMANTOWN CAFÉ

1200 Fifth Ave. N., Nashville, 615-242-3226; www.germantowncafe.com
American menu. Lunch, dinner, Sunday brunch. **$$**

★
★★
★★
★

★★LOVELESS CAFÉ

8400 Highway 100, Nashville, 615-646-9700; www.lovelesscafe.com

American, Southern menu. Breakfast, lunch, dinner. $

★★MAD PLATTER

1239 Sixth Ave. North, Nashville, 615-242-2563; www.themadplatterrestaurant.com

American, International menu. Lunch, dinner. $$

★★MARGOT CAFÉ

1017 Woodland St., Nashville, 615-227-4668; www.margotcafe.com

Mediterranean menu. Dinner, Sunday brunch. Closed Monday. $$

★★MERCHANTS

401 Broadway, Nashville, 615-254-1892; www.merchantsrestaurant.com

American menu. Lunch, dinner. $$$

★★MIDTOWN CAFÉ

102 19th Ave. S., Nashville, 615-320-7176; www.midtowncafe.com

Southern eclectic menu. Lunch, dinner. $$$

★MONELL'S

1235 Sixth Ave. N., Nashville, 615-248-4747; www.monellsdining.ypguides.net

Southern menu. Breakfast, lunch, dinner. $

★★★THE OLD HICKORY STEAKHOUSE

2800 Opryland Drive, Nashville, 615-871-6848; www.gaylordopryland.com

Located in the Opryland Hotel, this special-occasion steakhouse offers refined dining in an atmosphere of dark wooden furniture and dimly lit rooms. Designed as an elegant plantation-style house, the restaurant offers wraparound porch seating. Elegant table settings and beautiful gardens complete the setting. The restaurant also offers a cigar lounge and special-event wine tastings. In addition, there is an artisanal cheese cart with 25 varieties of cheeses and a large wine selection. Steak menu. Dinner. $$$$

★★★THE PALM

140 Fifth Ave. S., Nashville, 615-742-7256; www.thepalm.com

A great spot for star-gazing—not the celestial kind—and beef-eating, The Palm is one of Nashville's most popular scenes. Serious-sized steaks, chops and seafood dishes grace the menu at this legendary steakhouse. Also found among the meaty menu selections are Italian-tinged dishes like linguine and clams, spaghetti marinara and tomato capri salad. Going strong since 1926, The Palm has expanded its empire to 25 cities across the country, including Philadelphia, Las Vegas and Dallas. Steak menu. Lunch, dinner. $$$

★★★RUTH'S CHRIS STEAK HOUSE

2100 W. End Ave., Nashville, 615-320-0163; www.ruthschris.com

Born from a single New Orleans restaurant that Ruth Fertel bought in 1965 for $22,000, the Ruth's Chris Steak House chain has made it to the top of every steak lover's list. Aged prime Midwestern beef is broiled to your liking and served on a heated

TENNESSEE

★
★★
★
★

plate, sizzling in butter, a staple ingredient used generously in most entrees. Sides like creamed spinach and fresh asparagus with hollandaise are not to be missed, and seven different potato preparations, from a one-pound baked potato with everything to au gratin potatoes with cream sauce and cheese are offered. The rich, dark wood walls, bar, tables and chairs and dim lighting give the dining room a cozy feel, making it perfect for special dinners. Steak menu. Dinner. $$$

★SITAR INDIAN RESTAURANT
116 21st Ave. N., Nashville, 615-321-8889; www.sitarnashville.com
Indian menu. Lunch, dinner. $

★★SPERRY'S
5109 Harding Road, Nashville, 615-353-0809; www.sperrys.com
Seafood, steak menu. Dinner. $$$

★★STOCK-YARD
901 Second Ave. N., Nashville, 615-255-6464; www.stock-yardrestaurant.com
Steak menu. Dinner. $$$

★★SUNSET GRILL
2001 Belcourt Ave., Nashville, 615-386-3663, 866-496-3663; www.sunsetgrill.com
International menu. Lunch, dinner, late-night. $$

★★TAYST
2100 21st Ave. S., Nashville, 615-383-1953; www.tayst.info
American, Mediterranean menu. Dinner. Closed Sunday-Monday. $$

★★TIN ANGEL
3201 W. End Ave., Nashville, 615-298-3444; www.tinangel.net
International menu. Lunch, dinner, Sunday brunch. $$

★★★VALENTINO'S
1907 W. End Ave., Nashville, 615-327-0148; www.valentinosnashville.com
A popular spot for romantic dinners, Valentino's is set in a charming old house with several dining areas that feature beautiful Old World décor. The menu features rustic Italian fare such as vegetable ravioli, farfalle with salmon and chicken Marsala. Italian menu. Lunch, dinner. Closed Sunday. $$$

★★ZOLA
3001 W. End Ave., Nashville, 615-320-7778; www.restaurantzola.com
Mediterranean menu. Dinner. $$$

NATCHEZ TRACE STATE RESORT PARK

Named for the pioneer trail that connected Nashville and Natchez, Miss., this 48,000-acre park is the largest recreation area in western Tennessee. If the near limitless outdoor recreation is not enough to attract you, the park is also home to a pecan tree that is said to be the world's third largest. Four lakes provide swimming, fishing, boating (launch, rentals), nature trails, backpacking, picnicking, a playground and a recreation lodge. Tent and trailer sites, cabins and an inn are also at the park.

Information: Lexington, 40 miles northeast of Jackson off Interstate-40, 731-968-3742; www.tennessee.gov

HOTELS
★COUNTRY HEARTH INN & SUITES
21045 Highway 22 N., Wildersville, 731-968-2532, 800-780-7234; www.countryhearth.com
40 rooms. High-speed Internet access. Complimentary continental breakfast. $

★PIN OAK LODGE
567 Pin Oak Lodge Lane, Wildersville, 731-968-8176, 800-250-8616; www.tnstateparks.com
47 rooms. Complimentary continental breakfast. Restaurant. Outdoor pools. $

OAK RIDGE
Oak Ridge was built during World War II to house Manhattan Project workers involved in the production of uranium 235 (the first atomic bomb's explosive element). Once one of the most secret places in the United States, Oak Ridge is now host to thousands who come each year, drawn by the mysteries of nuclear energy. Built by the U.S. government, Oak Ridge is known for scientific research and development. Although many of the installations are still classified, the city has not been restricted since March 1949.

Information: Convention & Visitors Bureau, 302 S. Tulane Ave., 865-482-7821, 800-887-3429; www.visit-or.org

WHAT TO SEE AND DO
AMERICAN MUSEUM OF SCIENCE AND ENERGY
300 S. Tulane Ave., Oak Ridge, 865-576-3200; www.amse.org
Much cooler than physics class, this museum is one of the world's largest energy exhibitions. Here you'll learn about fossil fuels, energy alternatives, resources and research through hands-on exhibits, displays, models, films, games and live demonstrations. Monday-Saturday 9 a.m.-5 p.m., Sunday 1-5 p.m.

CHILDREN'S MUSEUM OF OAK RIDGE
461 W. Outer Drive, Oak Ridge, 865-482-1074; www.childrensmuseumofoakridge.org
Hands-on exhibits and displays include the International Gallery, Discovery Lab, Playscape, Nature Walk, Pioneer Living and Oak Ridge history. Performances, exhibits, seminars, workshops are also on offer. September-May: Tuesday-Friday 9 a.m.-5 p.m., Saturday 10 a.m.-4 p.m., Sunday 1-4 p.m. June-August: Monday-Friday 9 a.m.-5 p.m., Saturday 10 a.m.-4 p.m., Sunday 1-4 p.m.

FROZEN HEAD STATE PARK
964 Flat Fork Road, Wartburg, 37887, 423-346-3318; www.state.tn.us
The park takes up more than 12,000 acres in Cumberland Mountains. It offers trout fishing, hiking trails (50 miles), picnicking, a playground, primitive camping and a visitor center. Daily 8 a.m.-sunset.

INTERNATIONAL FRIENDSHIP BELL

Badger Avenue, Oak Ridge

A symbol of everlasting peace, the bell was designed to celebrate the dedication of Manhattan Project workers. Daily.

MELTON HILL DAM AND LAKE

Oak Ridge, 15 miles southwest; www.tva.gov

This Tennessee Valley Authority dam extends barge travel up the Clinch River to Clinton and provides electric power. The dam (103 feet high, 1,020 feet long) impounds a 44-mile-long lake. Fishing, boating, camping (fee) and a visitor overlook are all available. Daily.

OAK RIDGE ART CENTER

201 Badger Ave., Oak Ridge, 865-482-1441; www.oakridgeartcenter.org

The center holds a permanent collection of original paintings, drawings and prints. Tuesday-Friday 9 a.m.-5 p.m., Saturday-Monday 1-4 p.m.

UNIVERSITY OF TENNESSEE ARBORETUM

901 S. Illinois Ave., Oak Ridge, 865-483-3571;
www.forestry.tennessee.edu

This arboretum is part of the University of Tennessee Forestry Experimental Station. More than 1,000 species of trees, shrubs and flowering plants thrive on 250 acres. Self-guided tours and a visitor center are available. Monday-Friday 8 a.m.-noon, 1-5 p.m.

SPECIAL EVENTS

APPALACHIAN FEST

Children's Museum of Oak Ridge, 61 Outer Drive, Oak Ridge

Traditional crafts and music. Late November.

HOTELS

★DAYS INN

206 S. Illinois Ave., Oak Ridge, 865-483-5615, 800-329-7466; www.daysinn.com

80 rooms. High-speed Internet access. Complimentary continental breakfast. Outdoor pool. Pets accepted. $

★★DOUBLETREE HOTEL

215 S. Illinois Ave., Oak Ridge, 865-481-2468; www.doubletree.com

167 rooms. Restaurant, bar. Fitness center. Outdoor pool. Business center. Pets accepted, some restrictions; fee. $

★HAMPTON INN

208 S. Illinois Ave., Oak Ridge, 865-482-7889, 800-426-7866; www.hamptoninn.com

60 rooms. High-speed Internet access. Complimentary continental breakfast. Outdoor pool. Business center. $

PARIS

Do not let the 60-foot replica of the Eiffel Tower fool you: Paris, Tenn., is a long way from its namesake. But this small town near Kentucky Lake is a great place for outdoor recreation and a quiet stroll down the downtown streets, which are lined with many buildings that date back to 1900. If you are in town in late April, you will enjoy the self-titled "World's Biggest Fish Fry," when revelers consume about 12,500 pounds of catfish.

Information: Paris-Henry County Chamber of Commerce, 2508 E. Wood St., 731-642-3431, 800-345-1103; www.paristnchamber.com

WHAT TO SEE AND DO
NATHAN BEDFORD FORREST STATE PARK
1825 Pilot Knob Road, Eva, 731-584-6356; www.state.tn.us

On the west bank of Kentucky Lake, a monument marks the spot where, in 1864, Confederate General. Forrest set up artillery. Undetected by Union forces, the hidden batteries destroyed both the Union base on the opposite shore and its protective warships on the Tennessee River. The area is now an 800-acre park offering fishing and canoe access to the lake. Nature trails and programs, backpacking, picnicking, a playground, camping and a group lodge are available. There's also a museum (Wednesday-Sunday). Trace Creek Annex, located across Kentucky Lake, interprets a portion of the military history of the area. Daily 7 a.m.-10 p.m.

PARIS LANDING STATE PARK
16055 Highway 79 N., Buchanan, 731-641-4465, 800-250-8614; www.state.tn.us

The 840-acre park on Kentucky Lake boasts a swimming beach, pools, waterskiing, boating (launch, rentals, marina), golf, tennis courts, picnicking, a playground, lodging, a restaurant and camping. Daily, 24 hours.

SPECIAL EVENTS
EIFFEL TOWER DAY & HOT-AIR BALLOON FESTIVAL
Memorial Park, Paris
Second weekend in September.

WORLD'S BIGGEST FISH FRY
Henry County Fairgrounds, Paris; www.paristnchamber.com
Yes, partygoers consume about 12,500 pounds of catfish at this festival. When they are not eating, they enjoy a rodeo, a square dance and contests (including a catfish race). Last full week in April.

HOTEL
★ECONO LODGE PARIS
1297 E. Wood St., Paris, 731-642-8881; www.choicehotels.com
98 rooms. Complimentary continental breakfast. Outdoor pool. $

TENNESSEE

★
★
★
★

PIGEON FORGE
Located in the shadow of the Smokies, this resort town is a popular destination for vacationing families. The town has everything from outlet malls and the Dollywood theme park to theaters and go-cart tracks.

Information: Department of Tourism, 2450 Parkway, 865-453-8574, 800-251-9100; www.mypigeonforge.com

WHAT TO SEE AND DO

THE COMEDY BARN

2775 Parkway, Pigeon Forge, 865-428-5222; www.comedybarn.com

This family comedy variety show has magicians, jugglers, comedians and live music. March-December: daily.

COUNTRY TONITE THEATRE

129 Showplace Blvd., Pigeon Forge, 865-453-2003, 800-792-4308; www.countrytonitepf.com

This two-hour show features singing, dancing and comedy. March-December: Tuesday-Sunday.

DOLLYWOOD

1020 Dollywood Lane, Pigeon Forge, 865-428-9488; www.dollywood.com

Dolly Parton's entertainment park provides more than 40 musical shows daily. It also has more than 30 rides and attractions and 70 shops and restaurants.

FLYAWAY INDOOR SKYDIVING

3106 Parkway, Pigeon Forge, 877-293-0639; www.flyawayindoorskydiving.com

A vertical wind tunnel simulates skydiving. The instructor assists participants in the flight chamber and explains how to maneuver the body to soar, turn and descend. There's also an observation gallery. March-November: daily; winter schedule varies.

MEMORIES THEATRE

2141 Parkway, Pigeon Forge, 865-428-7852, 800-325-3078; www.memoriestheatre.com

Each show is a tribute to musical legends of the past and present, such as Tom Jones, Cher, Elvis Presley, Kenny Rogers and Buddy Holly. Monday-Saturday 8 p.m.

OGLE'S WATER PARK

2530 Parkway, Pigeon Forge, 865-453-8741; www.mypigeonforge.com/

An 8-acre water amusement park features a Lazy River ride, giant wave pools, water slides and a children's play area. Tube and locker rentals, dressing rooms and restaurants are on the premises as well. June-August: daily; May and September: weekends.

THE OLD MILL

2944 Middle Creek Road, Pigeon Forge, 865-453-4628; www.old-mill.com

This water-powered mill has been in continuous operation since 1830, grinding cornmeal, grits, whole wheat, rye and buckwheat flours. The dam falls are illuminated at night. Guided tours are available. April-November: Monday-Saturday.

SMOKY MOUNTAIN CAR MUSEUM

2970 Parkway, Pigeon Forge, 865-453-3433

Cloud nine for car lovers, this museum houses more than 30 gas, electric and steam autos, including Hank Williams Jr.'s "Silver Dollar" car, James Bond's "007" Aston Martin, Al Capone's bulletproof Cadillac, the patrol car of Sheriff Buford Pusser from the movie *Walking Tall* and Elvis Presley's Mercedes. May-October: daily.

SMOKY MOUNTAIN JUBILEE

2115 Parkway, Pigeon Forge, 865-428-1836; www.smokymtnjubilee.com

Clogging, singing, dancing and comedy for the whole family are available at this event. Shows at 8 p.m.

HOTELS

★BEST WESTERN PLAZA INN

3755 Parkway, Pigeon Forge, 865-453-5538, 800-232-5656; www.bwplazainn.com

201 rooms. Complimentary continental breakfast. **$**

★BRIARSTONE INN

3626 Parkway, Pigeon Forge, 865-453-4225, 866-883-4225; www.briarstoneinn.net

57 rooms. High-speed Internet access. Outdoor pool. Pets accepted. **$**

★COLONIAL HOUSE

3545 Parkway, Pigeon Forge, 865-453-0717, 800-662-5444;
www.colonialhousemotel.com

63 rooms. Complimentary continental breakfast. Indoor pool, outdoor pool. **$**

★CREEKSTONE INN

4034 S. River Road, Pigeon Forge, 865-453-3557; www.smokymountainresorts.com

112 rooms. High-speed Internet access. Complimentary continental breakfast. Outdoor pool. **$**

★★HOLIDAY INN

3230 Parkway, Pigeon Forge, 865-428-2700, 800-782-3119; www.4lodging.com

210 rooms. High-speed Internet access. Restaurant. Children's activity center. Fitness center. Indoor pool, whirlpool. Pets accepted, fee. **$**

★HOTEL PIGEON FORGE INN & SUITES

2179 Parkway, Pigeon Forge, 865-428-7305, 866-896-2950;
www.hotel-pigeonforge.com

123 rooms. Wireless Internet access. Complimentary continental breakfast. **$**

★QUALITY INN

3756 Parkway, Pigeon Forge, 865-453-3490, 800-925-4443;
www.qualityinnpigeonforge.com

127 rooms. High-speed Internet access. Complimentary continental breakfast. Restaurant. Indoor pool, outdoor pool. **$**

SPECIALTY LODGING

HILTON'S BLUFF B&B INN

2654 Valley Heights Drive, Pigeon Forge, 865-428-9765, 800-441-4188;
www.hiltonsbluff.com

10 rooms. High-speed Internet access. Children over 9 years only. Complimentary full breakfast. **$**

★
★
★
★

RESTAURANT
★OLD MILL
164 Old Mill Ave., Pigeon Forge, 865-429-3463; www.old-mill.com
American menu. Breakfast, lunch, dinner. $$

SAVANNAH
Information: Visitors Bureau, 507 Main St., 731-925-2364, 800-552-3866;
www.cityofsavannah.org

WHAT TO SEE AND DO
PICKWICK LANDING DAM, LOCK AND LAKE
Savannah, 14 miles south on Highway 128, 901-925-4346;
www.tva.com/sites/pickwick.htm
This Tennessee Valley Authority dam impounds a 53-mile-long lake with 496 miles of
shoreline. There's a Navigation Museum at the lock. Daily.

HOTEL
★★PICKWICK INN
Highway 57, Pickwick Dam, 800-250-8615, 731-689-3135; www.tnstateparks.com
119 rooms. Restaurant. $

SEVIERVILLE
Founded as part of the independent state of Franklin, the town and surrounding
county were named for John Sevier, who later became the first governor of Tennessee.
Minutes from the Great Smoky Mountain National Park, the town is a good base for
people who want to enjoy some of Tennessee's most scenic land.
Information: Chamber of Commerce, 110 Gary Wade Blvd., 865-453-6411,
888-766-5948; www.seviervillechamber.org

WHAT TO SEE AND DO
DOUGLAS DAM AND LAKE
Sevierville, 11 miles northeast off Highway 66, 865-453-3889; www.tva.gov/
This Tennessee Valley Authority dam on the French Broad River was built on a
24-hour work schedule during World War II to furnish power for national defense. It
impounds a lake that's 43 miles long with 555 miles of shoreline. At Douglas, you can
go swimming, fishing, boating and camping. Daily.

FORBIDDEN CAVERNS
455 Blowing Cave Road, Sevierville, 865-453-5972; www.forbiddencavern.com
Tennessee has more caves than any other state, and the tour through the Forbidden
Caverns is a spectacular show, even if it does get a little help from manmade addi-
tions, like lights and stereophonic sound presentation. The caves, which have natural
chimneys and underground streams, are 58F. April-November: daily 10 a.m.-6 p.m.

NASCAR SPEEDPARK
1545 Parkway, Sevierville, 865-908-5500; www.nascarspeedpark.com
Raring for some time on the racetrack? You can get into the action—and into the
cars—at NASCAR SpeedPark. Eight tracks offer levels ranging from the quarter-mile

Smoky Mountain Speedway for drivers 16 and older, down to the Baby Bristol, a 200-foot starter track for kids. Or climb into a mock stock car and experience centrifugal forces, turns and crash impacts as you "drive" a full-motion NASCAR Silicon Motor Speedway simulator. Other attractions include a state-of-the-art arcade, kiddie rides, an indoor climbing wall, miniature golf and bumper boats.

SMOKY MOUNTAIN DEER FARM

478 Happy Hollow Lane, Sevierville, 865-428-3337; www.deerfarmzoo.com
The petting zoo includes deer, zebra, pygmy goats and llamas. There are also pony rides and horseback riding (fee). Daily 10 a.m.-5:30 p.m.

HOTELS
★COMFORT INN MOUNTAIN RIVER SUITES

860 Winfield Dunn Parkway, Sevierville, 865-428-5519, 800-441-0311; www.comfortinn.com
97 rooms. High-speed Internet access. Complimentary continental breakfast. Indoor, outdoor pool. Pets accepted, fee. $

★RAMADA

4010 Parkway, Sevierville, 865-453-1823, 800-272-6232; www.ramada.com
134 rooms. High-speed Internet access. Pets accepted. Outdoor pool. Free parking. Complimentary continental breakfast. Children's activity center. $

SPECIALTY LODGING
LITTLE GREENBRIER LODGE

3685 Lyon Springs Road, Sevierville, 865-429-2500; www.littlegreenbrierlodge.com
This lodge, filled with antiques and Victorian décor, was built in 1939. Nine rooms. Children over 12 years only. Complimentary full breakfast. $

RESTAURANT
★APPLEWOOD FARM HOUSE

240 Apple Valley Road, Sevierville, 865-428-1222
American menu. Breakfast, lunch, dinner. $

SHELBYVILLE

The Tennessee walking horse, celebrated for high-stepping dignity and high-level intelligence, is king here. There are 50 walking-horse farms and training stables within a 14-mile radius of town; obtain maps at the Chamber of Commerce.
Information: Shelbyville & Bedford County Chamber of Commerce,
100 N Cannon Blvd., 931-684-3482, 888-662-2525; www.shelbyvilletn.com

SPECIAL EVENTS
SPRING FUN SHOW

Celebration Grounds, 1110 Evans St., Shelbyville, 931-684-5915; www.twhnc.com/springfunshow.htm
Amateur and professional-class walking horses compete. Three days in late May.

TENNESSEE

TENNESSEE WALKING HORSE NATIONAL CELEBRATION

Celebration Grounds, 1110 Evans St., Shelbyville, 931-684-5915;
www.twhnc.com/celebration.htm

More than 2,100 horses participate in this celebration. Events conclude with crowning ceremonies for the world grand champion walking horse. Late August.

HOTEL

★★BEST WESTERN CELEBRATION INN AND SUITES

724 Madison St., Shelbyville, 931-684-2378, 800-528-1234; www.bestwestern.com

58 rooms. High-speed Internet access. Complimentary continental breakfast. Indoor pool. Pets accepted, fee. $

SHILOH NATIONAL MILITARY PARK

Bitter, bloody Shiloh was the first major Civil War battle in the West and one of the fiercest in history. In two days, April 6 and 7, 1862, nearly 24,000 men were killed, wounded or missing. The South's failure to destroy General Grant's army opened the way for the attack on and siege of Vicksburg, Miss., but it was also a costly battle for the North.

Grant's Army of the Tennessee, numbering almost 40,000, was camped near Pittsburg Landing and Shiloh Church, waiting for the Army of the Ohio under General Don Carlos Buell to attack the Confederates who, they thought, were near Corinth, Mississippi, 20 miles south. But the brilliant Southern General Albert Sidney Johnston surprised Grant with an attack at dawn on April 6.

Although Johnston was mortally wounded on the first day, the Southerners successfully pushed the Union Army back and nearly captured their supply base at Pittsburg Landing. On the second day, however, the Northerners, reinforced by the 17,918-man Army of the Ohio, counterattacked and forced the Confederates to retreat toward Corinth.

At Shiloh, one of the first tent field hospitals ever established helped save the lives of many Union and Confederate soldiers. Among the men who fought this dreadful battle were John Wesley Powell, who lost an arm but later went down the Colorado River by boat and became head of the U.S. Geological Survey; James A. Garfield, 20th president of the United States; Ambrose Bierce, famous satirist and short-story writer; and Henry Morton Stanley, who later uttered the famous phrase, "Dr. Livingstone, I presume."

Information: Savannah, 901-689-5696; www.nps.gov/shil

WHAT TO SEE AND DO

NATIONAL CEMETERY

Savannah

The cemetery sits on 10 acres on a bluff overlooking Pittsburg Landing and the Tennessee River. Buried here are about 3,800 soldiers, two-thirds of whom are unidentified.

VISITOR CENTER

Savannah, one mile from park entrance, east off Highway 22, near Pittsburg Landing

Museum exhibits and 23-minute historical film; bookstore opposite. Daily.

SWEETWATER

Information: Monroe County Chamber of Commerce Visitor Center, 4765 Highway 68,
Madisonville, 423-442-9147, 800-245-5428; www.monroecounty.com

WHAT TO SEE AND DO
LOST SEA

140 Lost Sea Road, Sweetwater, 423-337-6616; www.thelostsea.com

Glass-bottom boats explore the nation's largest underground lake (4½ acres) in the
Lost Sea Caverns. Guided tours last one hour. The temperature is constant at 58F.
November-February: daily 9 a.m.-5 p.m.; September-October, March-April: daily
9 a.m.-6 p.m.; May-June, August: daily 9 a.m.-7 p.m.; July: daily 9 a.m.-8 p.m.

HOTEL
★COMFORT INN

731 S. Main St., Sweetwater, 423-337-6646, 800-638-7949; www.comfortinn.com

59 rooms. High-speed Internet access. Complimentary full breakfast. Pets accepted,
fee. $

RESTAURANT
★DINNER BELL

576 Oakland Road, Sweetwater, 423-337-5825

Breakfast, lunch, dinner. $

TIPTONVILLE

Information: Reelfoot Area Chamber of Commerce, 130 S. Court St.,
731-253-8144; www.reelfootareachamber.com

WHAT TO SEE AND DO
MCMINN COUNTY LIVING HERITAGE MUSEUM

522 W. Madison Ave., Athens, 423-745-0329; www.livingheritagemuseum.com

The museum contains 26 exhibit areas with more than 6,000 items that reflect life
in this region from the days of Cherokees to the Great Depression. Monday-Friday
10 a.m.-5 p.m., Saturday 10 a.m.-4 p.m.

REELFOOT LAKE

3120 State Route 213, Tiptonville; www.state.tn.us

This 13,000-acre lake, 18 miles long and more than two miles wide, was created
by the New Madrid earthquakes of 1811-1812. A bird and game refuge of unusual
beauty, the lake has an untamed quality with vast expanses of lily pads and giant
cypress trees growing from the water. More than 56 species of fish inhabit these
waters, and 260 species of water and land fowl populate the area. Resorts around the
lake provide boat rentals and guide services.

HOTEL
★★REELFOOT LAKE STATE PARK

Highways 78 and 213, Tiptonville, 731-253-7756, 800-250-8617;
www.state.tn.us

25 rooms. Complimentary continental breakfast. Restaurant. Pets accepted. $

TENNESSEE

★
★
★
★
★

RESTAURANT
★BOYETTE'S DINING ROOM
Highway 21, Tiptonville, 731-253-7307; www.reelfoot.com
American menu. Lunch, dinner. $

TOWNSEND
Information: Chamber of Commerce, 125 Townsend Park Road;
www.townsendchamber.org

WHAT TO SEE AND DO
TUCKALEECHEE CAVERNS
825 Caverns Road, Townsend, 865-448-2274; www.tuckaleecheecaverns.com
This cathedral-like main chamber is the largest cavern room in the eastern U.S. There are drapery formations, a walkway over subterranean streams and flowstone falls. The temperature is 58F, in the caverns. Go on the waterfalls tour. Daily 9 a.m.-6 p.m.

HOTEL
★COMFORT INN
7824 E. Lamar Alexander Parkway, Townsend, 865-448-9000,
800-348-7090; www.choicehotels.com
54 rooms. High-speed Internet access. Complimentary continental breakfast. Pets accepted, fee. $

SPECIALTY LODGINGS
★★★RICHMONT INN B&B
220 Winterberry Lane, Townsend, 865-448-6751, 866-267-7086; www.richmontinn.com
Just 10 minutes from the entrance to Great Smoky Mountains National Park, this charming inn affords an elegant escape. The comfort and coziness of the rustic accents, such as wide-planked and slate floors, high exposed-beam ceilings and country furniture, are enhanced by the formal, attentive service. 14 rooms. Children over 12 years only. Complimentary full breakfast. Restaurant. $

★TALLEY HO INN
8314 Highway 73, Townsend, 865-448-2463, 800-448-2465; www.talleyhoinn.com
46 rooms. High-speed Internet access. $

★VALLEY VIEW LODGE
Highway 321, Townsend, 865-448-2237, 800-292-4844; www.valleyviewlodge.com
138 rooms. Complimentary continental breakfast. Children's activity center. Outdoor pool, indoor pool. Pets accepted, fee. $

378

TENNESSEE

★
★
★
★
★

INDEX

379

INDEX

★
★ ★
★ ★
★

383

INDEX

★
★
★
★

INDEX

★
★
★
★

INDEX

★
★
★
★

389

INDEX

★
★
★
★

INDEX

★
★
★
★

394

INDEX

★
★
★
★
★

395

INDEX

★
★
★
★

I

INDEX

398

INDEX

★
★★
★★
★

Melrose Plantation Arts & Crafts Festival (Natchitoches, LA), *211*

Melton Hill Dam and Lake, *370*

Memorial Hall—Confederate Museum (New Orleans, LA), *228*

Memorial Tower (Baton Rouge, LA), *190*

Memories Theatre (Pigeon Forge, TN), *372*

Memphis Belle (Millington, TN), *346*

Memphis Botanic Garden (Memphis, TN), *345*

Memphis Brooks Museum of Art (Memphis, TN), *346*

Memphis in May International Festival (Memphis, TN), *349*

Memphis Pink Palace Museum and Planetarium (Memphis, TN), *346*

Memphis Queen Line Riverboats (Memphis, TN), *346*

Memphis Rock 'n' Soul Museum (Memphis, TN), *346*

Memphis Zoo (Memphis, TN), *347*

Merchants (Nashville, TN), *367*

Meridian Museum of Art (Meridian, MS), *282*

Merrehope (Meridian, MS), *282*

Merrick Inn (Lexington, KY), *154*

Metairie Cemetery (New Orleans, LA), *228*

Michaul's (New Orleans, LA), *249*

Mid-America Science Museum (Hot Springs, AR), *89*

Mid-South Fair and Exposition (Memphis, TN), *349*

Midtown Café (Nashville, TN), *367*

Midtown Lodge (Gatlinburg, TN), *324*

Mike Anderson's (Baton Rouge, LA), *194*

Mike Fink (Covington, KY), *128*

Mikee's Seafood (Gulf Shores, AL), *37*

Milbank Historic House (Jackson, LA), *198*

Miles College (Fairfield, AL), *18*

Millennium Maxwell House Nashville (Nashville, TN), *365*

Millwood State Park (Ashdown, AR), *66*

Minor Clark State Fish Hatchery (Morehead, KY), *169*

The Miracle Worker (Ivy Green, AL), *55*

Miss Green Riverboat Trip (Mammoth Cave, KY), *167*

Mississippi Agriculture & Forestry Museum and National Agricultural Aviation Museum (Jackson, MS), *276*

Mississippi Deep-Sea Fishing Rodeo (Gulfport, MS), *272*

Mississippi Delta Blues and Heritage Festival (Greenville, MS), *268*

Mississippi Museum of Art (Jackson, MS), *276*

Mississippi Petrified Forest (Flora, MS), *276*

Mississippi Sandhill Crane National Wildlife Refuge (Pascagoula, MS), *291*

Mississippi Sports Hall of Fame and Museum (Jackson, MS), *276*

Mississippi State Fair (Jackson, MS), *278*

Mississippi State University (Starkville, MS), *295*

Mobile Medical Museum (Mobile, AL), *43*

Mobile Museum of Art (Mobile, AL), *44*

Mockingbird Inn Bed and Breakfast (Tupelo, MS), *297*

Mollie's (Hot Springs, AR), *91*

Monell's (Nashville, TN), *367*

Monmouth (Natchez, MS), *286*

Monmouth Plantation (Natchez, MS), *287*

Monte Sano State Park (Huntsville, AL), *40*

Monteagle Chautauqua Assembly (Monteagle, TN), *354*

Montgomery Inn (Versailles, KY), *153*

Montgomery Museum of Fine Arts (Montgomery, AL), *48*

Montgomery Zoo (Montgomery, AL), *48*

Moonwalk (New Orleans, LA), *228*

Mooresville (Mooresville, AL), *25*

Morehead State University (Morehead, KY), *169*

Morgan Row (Harrodsburg, KY), *140*

Morning Call (Metairie, LA), *207*

Moro Bay State Park (Jersey, AR), *74*

Mosca's (Avondale, LA), *207*

★
★
★
★

INDEX

★
★
★
★

★
★
★
★

INDEX

★
★
★
★

409

INDEX

★
★
★
★

411

INDEX

★
★
★
★

412

INDEX

★
★
★
★
★

413

INDEX

★
★
★
★

NOTES

INDEX

NOTES

★
★★
★★
★

NOTES

INDEX